The 101 Best Jazz Albums

The 101 Best

Jazz Albums

A HISTORY OF JAZZ ON RECORDS

by Len Lyons

WILLIAM MORROW AND COMPANY, INC.
New York   1980

Library of Congress Cataloging in Publication Data

Lyons, Len.
    The 101 best jazz albums.

    "Morrow quill paperbacks."

    Bibliography: p.
    Includes discographies and index.
    1. Jazz music—United States. 2. Jazz music—
United States—Discography. I. Title.
[ML3508.L93 1980b]   785.42'0973   80-20735
ISBN 0-688-03720-8
ISBN 0-688-08720-5 (pbk.)

Printed in the United States of America

First Morrow Quill Paperback Edition

1 2 3 4 5 6 7 8 9 10

BOOK DESIGN BY BERNARD SCHLEIFER

*This book is dedicated
to the memory of my mother,*
GERTRUDE SIAGEL LYONS,
*who encouraged me to love music and books
and to cherish many of the values
which have become permanent in my life.*

PREFACE

THIS IS THE BOOK I wish had been around when I began collecting jazz albums. It tells the stories of jazz's most important creators, what their contributions have been to the music's development, and where their essential music can be found on commercially available albums. In addition to the 101 "best" albums, intended as a historically comprehensive collection, the book discusses and recommends hundreds more of the best available records by major musicians of all styles and eras. In other words, this book is an informative consumers' guide to the enormous amount of jazz on records, explaining, so far as possible, just what is so great about the great jazz albums.

Jazz has no better friend than records. As the music is characterized by spontaneous, emotional improvising, a jazz performance can never be repeated with exactly the same feeling, even by the same players. The music's foremost heroes have peak periods of creativity, freshness of imagination, and technical skill which they themselves cannot recapture once the delicate web of circumstances is altered. Nor can the best jazz, which always involves an element personal to the musicians involved, be written down in all its nuances for "duplication" by others. Thus sound recording is the only means of documenting jazz's development and its artistic triumphs.

The history of jazz on records could not have been written when I began collecting albums in about 1960, nor at any time for the next fifteen to eighteen years. Most jazz albums were then ephemeral entities, thrown casually into the marketplace with little concern for their staying power. While the recording process has served jazz well, the same cannot be said of the record companies. In their hands, jazz discs became as elusive as a magician's props, disappearing suddenly and later reappearing without explanation (or publicity) between different covers, only to drop out of sight again unannounced. Partly because rock and roll dominated the music industry, few companies, if any, marketed their historic jazz with competence or enthusiasm. Compiling a first-rate historical collection of jazz on available LP's during these years would have entailed looking for frequently invisible needles in ever-changing haystacks.

While the jazz record business still has its vagaries and indiscretions, the trend since the mid-1970's has been in precisely the opposite direction: Never before has there been such an abundance of crucial music available from every era and style of jazz's history. The age of plenty was inaugurated in 1972, when Fantasy Records acquired the Riverside and Prestige catalogs, which included classic sessions from the New Orleans and modern periods. Fantasy set the industry's tone by "reissuing" out-of-print LP's on low-priced, well-annotated, apparently permanent two-record sets.

Fantasy was soon joined in the reissue field by Savoy, Blue Note, Bluebird, MCA, Commodore, Verve, and Columbia, as well as several lesser-known labels, which drew upon rich vaults of recordings dating, in some cases, from the 1970's back to the early 1920's. The reissue business was simultaneously stimulated by jazz's top-selling fusion style, a synthesis of modern jazz with rock, soul, and pop (see Chapter 7), and by the gold and platinum albums of Herbie Hancock, George Benson, The Crusaders, and Chuck Mangione who put jazz into a kind of commercial limelight. While the companies knew that Louis Armstrong, Count Basie, Duke Ellington, and Miles Davis could never sell millions of records, they also realized that without studio costs, classic jazz could be repackaged inexpensively. Fusion generated enough publicity and spin-off interest in all jazz to make every reissue a good bet.

By 1978, according to an estimate in *Rolling Stone,* one out of every three albums released in the jazz field was a reissue of historic material. By 1980, Fantasy, still the numerical leader of the reissue race, had close to 200 reissue packages available. Meanwhile, the dozens of companies listed in Appendix B have driven the total number of available jazz albums into the thousands. To a great extent, every decade of jazz has come to life again, offering fans, students of the music, and collectors an unprecedented opportunity. The historic recording sessions now available greatly outnumber those yet to be reissued.

Of course, not all the gaps have been filled in, as many collectors will mournfully confirm. For example, the best sides of Duke Ellington's "Jungle Band," recorded for RCA and Columbia, are available only from the French divisions of those labels. The same is true for the RCA sessions of Jelly Roll Morton and His Red Hot Peppers. The best sessions of Clifford Brown and Sarah Vaughan dropped out of circulation—temporarily one hopes—when Trip Records went out of business in 1978. Thus the present abundance of jazz on record still leaves us much to look forward to if the reissue trend continues.

The concept of availability needs further clarification. The criterion I have adopted is that for an album to be "available," it must appear in the 1979 in-house catalog of its label. This means that the album, even if it is not stocked in a particular store, can be ordered by that store with a good chance of delivery. Although this is the most dependable way to confirm availability, the system is not infallible. Occasionally some albums may in fact be out-of-print (and not scheduled for re-pressing) without being deleted from the catalog. On the brighter side, many albums are in fact obtainable through well-stocked stores or special-order houses, even though they have been deleted from the catalog and are thus theoretically out-of-print. For this reason, important out-of-print albums are identified in the discussions ahead, although they are not recommended in the General Discographies, due to the absence of a currently valid catalog number.

The title of this volume will perhaps be thought presumptuous, audacious, or even absurd by jazz's long-standing *aficionados*, who are likely to believe 101 albums a ridiculously small number in which to represent the history and glories of this music. In truth, there were many painful choices to be made among competing "best" albums. I have been consoled in making these hard decisions by the thought that no matter which album was finally selected, the choice would draw deserved attention to other albums discussed in the text and recommended in the General Discographies at the end of each chapter. Many of these other recommended albums are every bit as exciting as the 101 "best," even though space and historical considerations argued against their ultimate selection.

A list of the 101 selected albums can be found in Appendix A. Musical quality, historic significance, comprehensiveness, and balanced representation of a style and era were chief among the selection criteria. The major figures of jazz are represented heavily, because I believe it is far better to immerse oneself deeply in the masters than to cover more ground more superficially. (For the same reason, I have avoided multistylistic anthologies, except for the superbly annotated *Smithsonian Collection of Classic Jazz*, which is recommended in the General Discography to Chapter 3.) There are a large number of albums devoted to the music of Louis Armstrong, Duke Ellington, Thelonious Monk, Charlie Parker, Dizzy Gillespie, Miles Davis, and John Coltrane—twenty-six in all, yet that number seemed pitifully small when trying to share with the reader the hours of beautiful recorded music they have given us. The other historic figures are represented by one, two, or three albums each from the remaining seventy-five. Again I must stress that the 101 "best" are focal points for discussions in which hundreds of additional albums receive equally deserved attention.

The formats for identifying the albums in this book are basically consistent. Album titles appear in italics and song titles in quotation marks. Except for out-of-print titles, catalog numbers have been provided to facilitate identification and ordering. However, the reader should be aware of a few unavoidable irregularities. In the Selected Discographies, the composer's name is included parenthetically in the list of song titles only when that information is germane to the discussion. In the General Discographies, some albums are indicated as "Of historical interest," implying that they are not peak performances but are especially valuable to collectors and fans of the musicians in question. In both the Selected and General Discographies, the year in which an album was recorded follows the title parenthetically when the date is significant but not obvious from the context. The number of discs contained in each album has been noted in the text where convenient. But in the General Discographies, the number of discs per album can only be gleaned from its catalog number when a single digit appears separated from the main numeric component: LA472-H2 is a Blue Note two-disc set; ANL*1*-2811 is an RCA single LP; and AT-*3*-600 is an Atlantic three-disc set. The two-disc sets on Columbia, Prestige, Milestone, and several other labels are not so easily determined by catalog number. Albums recommended in the discussions, except for the selected albums themselves, are also listed in the General Discographies with catalog number and label.

The subject of record labels and the companies which own and distribute them can be a confusing one. The list in Appendix B includes all the important domestic labels. (ECM is actually based in West Germany but it is dependably available in the United States and too important historically to omit.) Imported albums—with a few well-noted, compelling exceptions—have been excluded, because they are extremely expensive, difficult to find and order, and irreplaceable in cases of manufacturing defects. I have also barred bootlegs and outright piracies as not deserving recommendation on moral grounds. Besides, there is no real need for these records any longer since the reissue boom. Some of the labels appearing in this book—the Smithsonian Collection, Time-Life Records, and Book-of-the-Month Club Records are the most prominent examples—are distributed only by mail, while a few more are distributed both by mail and through retail stores. The list in Appendix B indicates mail-order and partly mail-order companies.

Inevitably there will be albums I have overlooked or not had the time to consider. For these omissions, I can only apologize and hope that the reader will be led to them ultimately through informed and selective record buying.

Above all, I hope none of my record discussions have—as Duke Ellington once put it—reduced a flower to a handful of petals. My goal has always been to enhance enjoyment of the music by bringing facts, anecdotes, and concepts to bear upon it. But by far the best way to appreciate jazz is expressed in the following brief jazz poem by Jon Hendricks: "Listen!"

LEN LYONS

Berkeley, California
March 1980

ACKNOWLEDGMENTS

MY DEEPEST GRATITUDE, for their sustained and sustaining assistance, to: My wife, Maxine, and our daughter, Gila Rachel, for providing a source of continuous joy and sense of purpose. They transformed the fifteen difficult, often frustrating months of work on this book into a happy, fulfilling period of personal growth.

Mike Larsen, for tireless assistance in getting this project off the ground.

Michael Evans, for exceptional insight, advice, and caring.

My editors, Meredith C. Davis and Jim Landis, for their continued patience and support.

Thanks, too, to the following record companies and their personnel for providing review copies of albums, up-to-date in-house catalogs, and countless varieties of crucial information. Without their cooperation, this project would hardly have been feasible:

ABC/Impulse/MCA (Elaine Cooper, John Young); A & M (Rick Galliani); 1750 Arch (Phil Sawyer); Arista (Kathy Wagner, Patti Wright); Artists House (Jim Gicking); Atlantic (Kathy Aquaviva, Paul Cooper); Audiofidelity (Mary Welch); Biograph (Arnold Caplin); Blue Note (Jack Shields); CBS/Columbia/Columbia Special Products (John Franks, Judy Shaw, Marcia Smith, Carol Van Brunt, George Wannamaker); Concord Jazz (Carl Jefferson); Contemporary Records (John Koenig, Vicky Koenig); CTI (Arnold Jay Smith); Delmark (Steve Tomashofsky); ECM (see Warner Brothers); Elektra/Asylum/Nonesuch (Sue Satriano); Everest (Bernard C. Solomon); Fantasy/Prestige/Milestone/Galaxy (Orrin Keepnews, Terri Hinte, Gretchen Horton); Folkways (Moe Asch); GNP Crescendo (Gene Norman); Halcyon (Marian McPartland); Inner City (Andrew Sussman); Improvising Artists, Inc. (Paul Bley, David Goode, Carol Goss); Jazz Archives (Marvin

Goldsmith); New Music Distribution Service (Dave Hunt); New World Records (Patty Dann); Pablo (Mauri Blumenfeld; Monique Wilmes); Polygram (Eileen Schneider); Polydor (Len Epand); RCA (Elliot Horne, Grelun Landon); Roulette (Mel Fuhrman); Savoy (Bob Porter); Smithsonian Institution (Sally Rothman, Martin Williams); Time-Life Records (Jim Coakley); Vanguard (Laurel Dann; John Boulos); Verve (see Polydor); Warner Brothers (Bob Merlis, Les Schwartz); Watt (Carla Bley, Dave Hunt); Xanadu (Don Schlitten).

Special thanks for their generous assistance in obtaining rare historic photographs to: Phil Bray; the office of Dave Brubeck; Fran Carroll; Chick Corea Productions; Lester Glassner; Don Hunstein; Orrin Keepnews; Beth Miller; and Duncan Schiedt.

A long-deserved thank-you to Tod Barkan and the staff at the Keystone Korner in San Francisco, and Tom and Jeanie Bradshaw and the staff at the Great American Music Hall in San Francisco, for their cooperation with the author over the years, and for their genuine commitment to jazz.

The following sources have been helpful to the author to an extent which cannot be acknowledged adequately in a footnote:

Leonard Feather's and Ira Gitler's *The Encyclopedia of Jazz in the Seventies* and Feather's *The New Edition of the Encyclopedia of Jazz* (1960), the standard biographical reference works in the field.

Down Beat magazine, whose perennial coverage of jazz through interviews with its important musicians has been a crucial source of insight.

Gunther Schuller's *Early Jazz*, a scholarly examination of jazz prior to 1935.

Ekkehard Jost's *Free Jazz*, a bold, provocative look at some of jazz's most adventurous improvisers since 1965.

Scott Yanow's *Record Review* magazine articles on Duke Ellington, Benny Goodman, Lester Young, and Billie Holiday, which were an asset to the author's research into those musicians' discographies.

CONTENTS

PART TWO: MODERN JAZZ

PART THREE: CONTEMPORARY JAZZ

The 101 Best Jazz Albums

WHAT IS THIS THING CALLED JAZZ?

1

BLACK AMERICAN MUSIC is virtually omnipresent in the western world. Spirituals, soul, rhythm-and-blues, rock, and jazz are all directly traceable to an Afro-American presence as old as our country itself. Jazz, however, is unique among these forms in its longevity, continuity of development, and internal variety. Only jazz can be played with equal authenticity by a soloist, a small combo, or a small orchestra, each capable of conveying emotional tones ranging from tenderness to fierce intensity. There is such diversity within jazz that it is hard to believe that its disparate styles are all part of a single tradition.

Fixing the music's date of birth is of course impossible, although its earliest forms—ragtime piano and brass bands—had matured to some extent by 1900. The chronological history of jazz, however, will be told in the chapter introductions which follow. The present task is to identify and uncover the origins of jazz's fundamental elements.

Some principal ingredients can be identified at the outset: a special rhythmic momentum, often described as "swinging"; a tonal orientation toward "the blues"; improvisational playing; speechlike intonation in the wind instruments; and a harmonic structure derived primarily from European music. The diffused and overlapping sources of these elements are the rhythmic, instrumental, and tonal characteristics of some West African music; European classical, folk, and band music; and indigenous black American forms such as the blues, work songs, shouts, and spirituals.

But there is not a single characteristic among those listed above that is absolutely essential to jazz. Indeed, jazz cannot be defined adequately because it is not just a conceptual entity—it needs to be experienced.

According to a famous anecdote, when Louis Armstrong was asked by an admiring socialite to tell her what jazz is, he replied, "Lady, if you got to ask what it is, you'll never know." To Armstrong's remark one must add a rather crucial qualifier—"until you start listening." The only way to know what jazz is—and, even more important, to enjoy and appreciate it—is to listen to it, preferably to the best examples of each style. It is also crucial to hear how interconnected these styles are. At the heart of the matter, jazz comes down to a certain *feeling* in the music, one which eludes precise verbal formulation. (Keeping the limitations of definitions in mind, it may be interesting to read several which have been formulated through the decades. The reader who wishes to do so should refer to footnote 1 at the end of this chapter.) The remainder of the present chapter is devoted to a closer look at the music's vital parts, for even if jazz cannot be defined, a good deal can be said about what has gone into it and where it came from.

Strangers in a Strange Land—The African Connection

The extent to which African musical practices have left their imprint upon jazz is much debated, but it can not be denied that black Americans arrived from Africa with a history and customs that affected every aspect of their lives. In music the influence of this background was subtle but pervasive.

Most of the blacks who were brought to America as slaves were living on what was known as the Gold Coast or the Ivory Coast in western Africa. Of course, when the first slave ships put into port in Jamestown, Virginia, in the early 1600's, there was little evidence of the music that was to come from the descendants of those blacks three centuries later. As LeRoi Jones states sardonically in *Blues People*: "Undoubtedly, none of the African prisoners broke out into 'St. James Infirmary' the minute the first of them was herded off the ship." But they did bring with them a repertoire of social and linguistic customs which set them even farther apart musically from their European masters.

First, music had an entirely functional role in the West African society of that time. There were work songs, battle songs, courtship songs, lullabies, religious music, and chants for healing, fertility, and almost every human endeavor. The idea of making music for listening only was unknown: Music was participatory. (The modern jazz musicians' practice of concertizing is thus conspicuously European, although handclapping in rhythm and other signs of audience involvement in jazz concerts are encouraged, as they most certainly are not at a concert of European music.) The word "art," referring to a creative process set apart from the normal activities of life, did not exist in the African language. Music, however, was inescapable. In describing his native Guinea, Olaudah Equiano, one of the first Africans to publish in English, wrote in 1789:

> We are almost a nation of dancers, musicians, and poets. Thus every great event . . . is celebrated in public dances which are accompanied with songs and music suited to the occasion.[2]

In America the Africans continued to work, socialize, and worship to music, but the new environment, strange and oppressive, altered the content of their songs forever.

Language itself in many West African tribes was tonal in nature. The meanings of words were determined by pitch and inflection, not solely by vowel and consonant sounds. To speak and understand was thus a quasi-musical experience. The English expression "Hey!" provides a rough notion of how tonal languages work. "Hey" can be an expression of pleasant surprise, a means of attracting someone's attention, or a stern threat to proceed no farther—depending upon the voice's pitch and inflection. The African talking drums communicate in this way. They do not tap out some sort of Morse code but actually simulate the sounds of African words and the rhythmic speech patterns of sentences. (Animal horns and the *balaphon*, a forerunner of the xylophone and the jazz player's vibraharp, were used to the same effect.) Thus it was not without rationale that prior to the Civil War, many of the slave states prohibited the manufacture and playing of African drums—perhaps the most subtle abridgment of free speech ever perpetrated in America.

In Africa, then, a musical instrument was a vehicle of personal expression, which is a function it retained for the Afro-American. It was once thought that jazz musicians were somehow unable to achieve the uniform concert tones common to symphonic players of the European tradition, but of course they were striving for just the opposite: a more individualized sound, one far more difficult to obtain on the highly mechanized western instruments. During the final five minutes of "What Love" (*Charles Mingus Presents*, Chapter 6), Mingus's string bass and Eric Dolphy's bass clarinet engage in what could be nothing other than a conversation. One can even understand the literal meaning of parts of their dialogue. In the album's liner notes, Dolphy is quoted as stating: "I want to say more on my horn than I ever could in ordinary speech." However, the speech metaphor should not be carried too far, for it is pure emotions that jazz expresses most readily —not only the musicians' feelings at the moment of playing but their relationship to society as well.

Improvising, too, has its precedent in the African heritage. On the simplest level, work songs were led by one person who adapted rhythms, words, and tempos to the task at hand. The leader was answered by his crew in a uniform response so that the rhythms of song and work coincided, making the task more tolerable. Thomas Bowdich, who was sent to Africa by the British government in 1817, reported that many of the leader's melodies were improvised on the spot while others had been passed down from one generation to the next. Moreover, he noticed, "melodic embellishment of, or improvisation on, the basic melody was quite extensive, often to the point that the original tune was no longer identifiable." [3] In river songs a more rapid tempo might signal the oarsmen to quicken their pace. In America, where the work-song tradition survived nearly intact for two centuries, the leader might pause at the end of a verse to give the picks and shovels an extra moment's rest. Through his song it was possible to communicate clandestinely with the workers, beyond the comprehension of the white overseers.

In jazz, too, the major improviser leads and coordinates his group, determining repertoire, tempo, and musical nuances in performance. By contrast, all the instruments in a European chamber group are "equals"; leading with one's instrument has no function, for ideally all the details are planned (rehearsed) prior to the performance. Like the African model, jazz has a strong element of call-and-response, or antiphonal, interchange between the leader and the band or even two sections of the band. On the title track to Count Basie's *Sixteen Men Swinging* (Chapter 4), for example, the trumpet section is clearly affirming the saxophone section's melodic statement in the second eight-measure chorus. A similar dynamic occurs between the horns and the rhythm section in the Cannonball Adderley Quintet's "This Here" (*Coast to Coast*, Chapter 5). The device known as "trading fours" also derives from the antiphonal model. The alternating four-bar solos among the players are related to one another in that each comments upon or continues the expression of the preceding soloist. For example, the Modern Jazz Quartet accomplishes this beautifully on "I'll Remember April" from their *European Concert* album (Chapter 5).

Anthropologist Ernest Borneman, in his essay "The Roots of Jazz," identifies another Africanism within the improvisational concept. "In language," he writes,

> the African tradition aims at circumlocution rather than an exact definition. The direct statement is considered crude and unimaginative; the veiling of all contents in ever-changing paraphrases is considered the criterion of intelligence and personality.[4]

As in literature, the message is to be communicated through intimation and nuances, not by bald, mundane statements of fact. Charlie Parker, a founding father of bebop and modern jazz, is a model of circumlocutionary eloquence in *The Very Best of Bird* (Chapter 5), in which he virtually weaves epic tales around a simple, blues-based story line. Miles Davis, on the other hand, demonstrates (Chapters 5 and 6) the art of understatement, conveying his "meaning" with subtlety. If imaginative indirectness is "the criterion of intelligence and personality," these men have earned their reputations as geniuses of the jazz idiom.

"The Sound of Surprise"

No characteristic of jazz receives more attention than improvisation, or extemporaneous playing by one or more performers. In fact, improvisation is often mistakenly thought to be an essential ingredient of jazz, although numerous examples—most notably the music of Duke Ellington—prove that jazz is not incompatible with note-for-note composition. Neither is improvisation unique to jazz, for it existed, as mentioned earlier, in African music and to a modest extent in the European tradition. Bach, Beethoven, and Chopin were, as a matter of fact, celebrated in their day for extemporaneously created themes and variations.

Nevertheless, improvising injects jazz with an unpredictable excitement, aptly dubbed by critic Whitney Balliett "the sound of surprise." [5] There is also a deeper source of surprise in high-quality improvisation—the creative juxtaposition of ideas. This involves more than simply not knowing what comes next. It is the element which keeps an improvisation fresh, witty, and revealing, even when heard several times in succession. To use an example from far afield, surrealist paintings illustrate this expanded idea of surprise in the extreme. In his work "The Persistence of Memory," for example, Salvador Dali depicts soft pocket watches draped over a rocky terrain, thus combining familiar elements in a fresh, meaningful way. The sensuous improvisations of Eric Dolphy (Chapter 6) are analogous in their dexterous leaps and swerves, keeping his music alive with surprise (in the broad sense of the term) no matter how frequently it is heard.

Improvisation is not a monolithic or one-dimensional practice, but an approach to playing which can take strikingly different forms. In turn-of-the-century New Orleans, the brass bands improvised collectively, an unprecedented development in western music and a highly practical one, since most of those musicians could not read music. Their style was to embellish upon the melody in a theme-and-variations pattern. About 1925 Louis Armstrong inaugurated the era of the soloist when, using the rest of the band as a backdrop, he composed essentially new melodies based upon the song's original harmonic structure. (Radically distinctive soloing approaches were discovered and developed by Lester Young (Chapter 4), Charlie Parker, Dizzy Gillespie, Miles Davis (Chapter 5), and John Coltrane (Chapter 6); all of these approaches will be discussed in detail later on.)

By 1960 a more adventurous mode of improvising was being explored by some musicians, who put to a radically new use the collective style of New Orleans. In Ornette Coleman's *Free Jazz* (Chapter 8), an eight-piece ensemble plays with no prior agreements on rhythm, harmony, melody, nor even a "key" as such—with virtually no structure to hold on to. Both Coleman and pianist Cecil Taylor (Chapter 8) began to improvise structures as well as "content." By the 1970's there were minimally "planned" improvisations, like those of the Art Ensemble of Chicago, in which each player has a role but no specific lines to deliver, and intentionally *un*planned performances, like Keith Jarrett's lengthy piano solos, before which he attempts to "erase all musical memory."

Improvisation is as personal as a fingerprint, a direct expression of an individual's (or a group's) ideas, emotions, and experiences. In extemporaneous playing, there is no time for editing or censoring; spontaneity and imagination are crucial. The listener is taken on an excursion to an unknown destination through which the player's character is often revealed profoundly. In *A Love Supreme* (Chapter 6), John Coltrane's journey is intensely spiritual, while in *Young Louis Armstrong* (Chapter 3), a much earthier jaunt is in progress.

Oddly in *Negro Folk Music: U.S.A.*, a generally brilliant musicological study, Harold Courlander bemoans the lack of what he calls "objective analyses" in jazz criticism. "Indeed," he writes, "if some jazz commentators were deprived of the use of names of performers and performing groups, they would have great difficulty in talking about jazz at all." [6] As a matter of fact, Courlander understates the difficulty: It would be impossible! Because of improvisation it is virtually pointless to write about jazz without reference to specific musicians, bands, and their stylistic differences: *what* is being played is always a consequence of *who* is playing. Thus improvising leads to a unique sense of intimacy between player and listener.

The Color of Jazz

Despite the individual differences emphasized by improvisation, there is one melodic/harmonic element common to most jazz: a preference for the tonality, or feeling, of a black American folk music known as "the blues." The sound of the blues is probably familiar to anyone within range of commercial radio: Rock, rhythm-and-blues (R & B), soul music, and the new "disco" genre are its descendants. To a certain extent, jazz is too: Blues made up most of the early New Orleans repertoire and much of the raw material of bebop. Naturally it became a prominent element in the jazz/R & B fusion style, exemplified by Herbie Hancock in most of his albums after 1972 (Chapter 7), and the moan of a blues cadence can still be heard in the nearly atonal chord "clusters" of Cecil Taylor. While jazz involves much more than the blues, nothing could be more fundamental to it.

According to some historians, the blues was sung by lone performers accompanying themselves on guitar or banjo (an African word) even before the Civil War. While spirituals expressed the religious attitudes of blacks as a group, the blues tended to recount their personal and secular lives. It was, and remains at the core, a folk music of American blacks. Like the other Afro-American musics, the blues is extemporized to some extent. As singer Big Bill Broonzy says, ". . . the real blues is played and sung the way you feel and no man or woman feels the same way every day . . ." [7]

The belief that there is only one standard blues form, consisting of twelve measures and a special harmonic pattern derived from church music, is a myth. In the early blues styles a singer would often strum along until he recalled, or thought up, the next verse. The number of measures might vary from eight to sixteen, including odd numbers. There were two practical reasons for the standardizing of blues forms. First, musicians, especially jazz musicians in New Orleans, began to play blues songs in groups, which required coming to some agreement on exactly what the song was to be. Second, W. C. Handy, and others a bit later, began to publish existing songs and compose new ones in the blues style. "St. Louis Blues," dated 1914, is the most famous of these early-vintage songs. The mere fact that the blues was written down suggested there was a "correct" form for the idiom, but this uniformity was illusory. Even Handy's compositions are different from each other in musical structure.

The blues is characterized less by a harmonic pattern than by a special tonality conveyed by a scale, known, not surprisingly, as the blues scale. This scale's distinctive feature is the presence of "blue" notes, loosely and inaccurately represented in western notation as the flatted third, flatted seventh, and sometimes, flatted fifth tones of the tempered diatonic scale. A prevailing opinion has been that these notes are a consequence of the African pentatonic, or five-note, scale, thought to be missing the third and seventh tones: that is, *do, re, fa, sol, la, do*, instead of *do, re, MI, fa, sol, la, TI, do*. As West Africans gradually came under the influence of European music in America, the story goes, they supplied their own slurred, bent, or "blued" versions of the unfamiliar tones. Marshall W. Stearns upholds this theory in *The Story of Jazz*, adding that blue notes are not, precisely speaking, flatted thirds or sevenths after all. They are only rough approximations which, upon electronic measurement, are discovered to fall somewhere between a major (natural) and a minor (flatted) tone, leading to what Stearns calls "neutral" thirds and sevenths.[8]

While Stearns correctly maintains that blue notes are only "roughly" flatted thirds and sevenths, the theory that these notes filled in the gaps of African scales is debatable. The research of Dr. A. M. Jones in his *Studies in African Music* (1954) proved that Africa's music is not at all uniform. In fact, diatonic scales are indigenous to certain regions of the west coast of Africa; and, moreover, some pentatonic patterns do include the third tone. Although the role played by the third and seventh scale positions probably has something to do with African scale patterns, the spontaneous and gradual evolution of the blues makes a definitive account highly unlikely.[9]

The slurred or bent quality of blue notes is a more profitable matter to consider because these microtonal variations of sound are widely present in jazz, regardless of scale position. John Storm Roberts, who cites numerous examples of slurred or bent notes in African instrumental and vocal music, writes in his *Black Music of Two Worlds* (1974): "The possibility of a connection between speech tone and blues scales has not yet received enough attention."[10] Traditional African singing techniques do make use of variable scale tones, achieved by altering intonation and inflection. Again, the influence of tonal languages cannot be ignored, for they may have led not only to jazz's speech-inflected instrumental approach but to the techniques for "blueing" notes. The emotional impact of slurred notes, or variable scale tones, is investigated more closely in the discussion of Billie Holiday's singing (Chapter 4) because she incorporated a blues feeling into her music without relying (as Bessie Smith did, for example) on the blues form.

There is no doubt that the blues feeling, its tonality, and even its various folk forms occur more often than not in jazz. However, like improvisation, the blues is not an essential ingredient of jazz. Neither the compositions of Scott Joplin (Chapter 2) nor the collective improvisations of Oregon (Chapter 8) communicate a blues sensibility, but to sever them from the jazz tradition for that reason alone would be to elevate some sort of theory above the reality of the music's broad-based evolution. LeRoi Jones correctly observes that "blues means a Negro experience," while "ragtime, dixieland, and jazz are all American terms." [11] The blues, then, is close to the core of jazz, but is only one of the elements it has synthesized.

"It Don't Mean a Thing, If It Ain't Got That Swing"

An African proverb says: "Without a song, the bush knife is dull." Because African music was tied intimately to various activities, nothing could be more central to it than an appropriate rhythm. Jazz, too, abides for the most part by a similar credo, summarized in Duke Ellington's 1932 song title "It Don't Mean a Thing, If It Ain't Got That Swing." There are many ways to swing, however, and jazz rhythmic feeling, which evolved at an even faster rate than improvisation, soon became a barometer of stylistic change.

A common element in nearly all jazz (excepting only the tempo-less excursions of free jazz) is a peculiar momentum established by the co-existence of contrasting rhythmic patterns, often called cross-rhythms. Not surprisingly, a precedent for this has been found in the polyrhythmic music of West Africa by Dr. A. M. Jones, who diagrammed indigenous poly-phonic, or multivoiced, music, with electronic "phonophotography." The results were astounding. In African ensembles as many as seven players pursued distinct rhythmic patterns, all hovering around one implied, unifying pulse, but in such a way that their downbeats never coincided. Despite overwhelming (to the western ear) diversity, the music coalesced. Jazz is seldom so complex and usually maintains the European convention (again, except for certain styles of free jazz) of measures, or bar lines, which divide time into metric patterns ($\frac{2}{4}$, $\frac{3}{4}$, and so on). Although jazz is not polyrhythmic in the African sense, it is based upon a similar principle: simultaneous conflicting rhythmic patterns.

The momentum of jazz, its sense of swing, is generated by the rhythmic pattern of the melody set against the background rhythm of the accompaniment, or if there is no accompaniment, against the implied background rhythm. The simplest example is found in ragtime's "syncopation," in which the pianist's right hand emphasizes the weak beats of the measure while the left hand hits the strong beats (Chapter 2). A similar cross-rhythm was heard in the early New Orleans brass bands and black marching bands elsewhere at the turn of the century. The popularity of marching bands, comprised of either blacks or whites, playing frequent outdoor concerts or leading parades, was partly responsible for the ²⁄₄ meter of early jazz. Two (quarter-note) beats per measure corresponded to the marchers' feet.

Jazz accelerated its pace during the 1920's with Louis Armstrong and others, who made ⁴⁄₄ time—four quarter notes to the measure—more common. With Charlie Parker's dexterity and melodic complexity, measures seemed more frequently divided into eighth-note units. John Coltrane, creating what were called for a variety of reasons "sheets of sound," proved that improvising could presuppose a division of the melody into sixteenth or even thirty-second notes. Finally, free jazz, beginning with experimentation during the 1950's by Charles Mingus (Chapter 6), showed that metric patterns could vary within a given piece or could be disregarded altogether in favor of the somewhat looser notion of "pulse." At the same time, polyrhythmic complexity in jazz was increasing, growing closer to the African model from which it was derived.

Jazz: A Four-letter Word

Despite its historical connections with Africa and Europe, jazz is a distinctively American music form to which a uniquely American term has been applied. "Jazz" is, of course, untranslatable and, in that sense, is an international word, one that actually carries laudatory connotations abroad. Yet many American musicians resent its being used to label their work, fearing that the word conjures up the image of an "esoteric," "inaccessible" art of limited commercial appeal. Their point of view will be examined more closely in the introduction to Chapter 7, although their argument seems a bit obsolete in light of jazz record sales during the 1970's.

A more long-standing objection to the term, one often voiced by Duke Ellington, is based upon its origins in brothels and "sporting houses," where the music was played in its early years. Jazz, it seems, has a secret meaning. An itinerant composer and performer, Clay Smith, warned in a 1924 *Étude* magazine: "If the truth were known about the origin of that word, it would never be mentioned in polite society." As a matter of fact, Smith might have said the same for "jelly roll," "cat," "boogie-woogie," and several more covertly sexual terms in musicians' argot. It is commonly accepted among scholars that jazz in the early 1900's referred to sexual intercourse, although no concrete documentation of its use in this sense has been turned up. The word appeared in print for the first time in 1913, when it was mentioned rather innocently by an editor of the *San Francisco Call*, a black-owned newspaper. It caught on as a musical label when the Original Dixieland Jass Band, a white group (Chapter 3), used it on the first "jass" record in 1917.

Sources remote from the world of musical entertainment developed sim-

ilar associations to jazz. The title of a 1923 *Ladies' Home Journal* article
boldly asked: "Does Jazz Put the Sin in Syncopation?" F. Scott Fitzgerald,
in his celebrated essay "Echoes of the Jazz Age," a work only peripherally
concerned with the music itself, wrote: "The word jazz in its progress toward
respectability has meant first sex, then dancing, then music." Herman Hesse
expressed his reaction to the music's sound through the hero of his great
Freudian novel *Steppenwolf*: ". . . its raw and savage gaiety reached an
underworld of instinct and breathed a simple, honest sensuality."

There are still more competing derivations of the word. One of the most
*un*likely attributes it to the names of black performers, like the dancing
slave Jasper, known as Jass, or the Chicago musician Jasbo (Jass) Brown.
"Jass" has also been identified as an Elizabethan slang term meaning "to
do things with gusto and enthusiasm," which may well be the precursor to
the contemporary expression "to jazz it up." A more likely candidate is the
Creole verb *jaser*, meaning "to speed up, chatter, or make fun." But the
American Dictionary of Words and Phrases considers *jaser* to be imported
from the northwest coast of Africa, where its African predecessor *jaiza* is
used to refer to "the rumbling of distant drums." [12] Perhaps jazz is not such
an inappropriate word after all if its ultimate origins relate not to sex but
to African drums. A conclusive etymology, however, is certainly lost to history by now.

The Unity of Jazz

The historical continuity of jazz is part of every musician's experience.
Ideas and techniques are passed down aurally through personal instruction
and by witnessing performances and listening to records. Duke Ellington
readily attributed the development of his piano style to hearing James P.
Johnson and Willie "The Lion" Smith attempting to outdo, or "cut" each
other at the Harlem rent parties of the early 1920's. Lester Young, whose
tone on tenor saxophone was the earliest expression of "cool" jazz, openly
credited Frankie Trumbauer's C-melody sax solo on Bix Beiderbecke's
recording of "Singin' the Blues" (Chapter 3) with providing his initial spark
of inspiration. Similarly, in the 1930's Charlie Parker's first great strides as a
saxophonist were made by memorizing Lester Young's solos from records of
Count Basie's band.

Even Cecil Taylor, despite his reputation as a musical revolutionary and
iconoclast, has expressed his reverence for continuity and tradition:

> Right now we have Louis Armstrong playing at the same time as
> John Coltrane and Duke Ellington. . . . I can react emotionally to
> the things Louis plays, as well as know what they signify technically.
> You cannot deny the validity of all the beautiful things that have hap-

pened in the past. And you cannot claim that the energies of the past have no relationship to whatever you're engaged in now.[13]

There is no more convenient illustration of continuity in jazz than the albums selected in this volume, the last of which, recorded in 1979 by the free jazz collective Air, returns to the turn-of-the-century compositions "Maple Leaf Rag" and "King Porter Stomp" by Scott Joplin (Chapter 2) and Jelly Roll Morton (Chapter 3).

The seven stylistic categories used in this book are one way of presenting the whole of jazz without ignoring its complexity. This method is not without its problems. Admittedly, stylistic divisions cannot be drawn precisely. Moreover, to "label" musicians with a style by discussing them within its context may erroneously be taken to suggest that they are limited to that style. Thus it must be stated clearly that styles are not historical cells to which individuals are confined. As a reflection of that fact, several musicians in this volume are represented in more than one chapter. Furthermore, to deny that styles exist is as foolish as pretending they have clearly defined boundaries. Just like members of a family, musicians can remain quite different from one another and yet share certain characteristics, basic goals, and a common heritage. The style-based organization of the following chapters does not ignore the multistylistic potential of many musicians, which is taken up in the individual discographies. Its purpose is to elucidate the continuity and unity of this vast and varied musical form.

References and Notes

1. **The forties:** Paul Eduard Miller, "An Analysis of the Art of Jazz," *Esquire's 1946 Jazz Book* (New York: A. S. Barnes & Co., 1946), pp. 139–140:

> . . . Jazz differs from classic in the following characteristics: (1) *Rhythm.* A rigid 4/4 beat (occasionally 2/4 or 8/8) combined with polyrhythms, or cross-rhythms more commonly known as syncopation, and the use of free rubato (variations in tempo). (2) *Harmony.* The blues triad . . . which has been intermixed with harmonies stemming from European traditions, including polyphony and polytonality. (3) *Figurations.* Refers chiefly to suspensions, afterbeats, passing tones and melodic intervals . . . the disregard of the so-called pure tone and subsequent utilization of what has come to be known as jazz intonation.

The fifties: Barry Ulanov, *A History of Jazz in America* (New York: Viking Press, Inc., 1952), p. 7:

> (A music) that constantly involves improvisation. . . . In the course of creating jazz, a melody or its underlying chords may be altered. The rhythmic valuations of notes may be lengthened or shortened according to a regular scheme, syncopated or not, or there may be no consistent pattern

of rhythmic variations so long as a steady beat remains implicit or explicit. The beat is usually four quarter-notes to the bar, serving as a solid rhythmic base for the soloists or groups playing eight or twelve measures or some multiple or dividend thereof.

Marshall Stearns, *The Story of Jazz* (London: Oxford University Press, 1956), p. 282:

> . . . we may define jazz tentatively as a semi-improvisational American music distinguished by an immediacy of communication, an expressiveness characteristic of the free use of the human voice, and a complex flowing rhythm; it is the result of three hundred years' blending in the United States of the European and West African musical traditions; and its predominant components are European harmony, Euro-African melody, and African rhythm.

The sixties: Andre Hodier, *Jazz: Its Evolution and Essence* (New York: Grove Press, Inc., 1961), p. 240:

> By our definition, jazz consists essentially of an inseparable but extremely variable mixture of relaxation and tension (that is, of swing and the hot manner of playing).

Hodier explains earlier, on page 197, the "five optimal conditions for the production of swing":

> 1. the right infrastructure (basically, rhythm—Author);
> 2. the right superstructure (basically, phrasing—Author);
> 3. getting the notes and accents in the right place;
> 4. relaxation;
> 5. vital drive.
>
> The first three are technical in nature and can be understood rationally; the last two, which are psycho-physical, must be grasped intuitively.

Nat Hentoff, as quoted in Harold Courlander, *Negro Folk Music, U.S.A.* (New York: Columbia University Press, 1963), p. 31 (it is never stated that Hentoff considers himself to be offering a definition of jazz, but this passage is similar to other explicit attempts):

> Its essentials are a pulsating (but not necessarily regular) rhythm; a feeling of improvisation (it is possible to write jazz so idiomatically that written notes sound improvised); vocalized instrumental technique and, conversely, instrumentalized phrasing in jazz singing; timbres and polyrhythmic usages that are rooted in the Afro-American folk music of three centuries.

The seventies: Leroy Ostransky, *Understanding Jazz* (Englewood Cliffs, N.J.: Prentice-Hall, Inc., 1977), p. 40:

> Here, then, is the working definition: Jazz is the comprehensive name for a variety of specific musical styles generally characterized by attempts at creative improvisation on a given theme (melodic or harmonic), over a foundation of complex, steadily flowing rhythm (melodic or percussive)

and European harmonies; although the various styles of jazz may on occasion overlap, a style is distinguished from other styles by a preponderance of those specific qualities peculiar to each style.

2. Eileen Southern, *The Music of Black Americans: A History* (New York: W. W. Norton, Inc., 1971), p. 5.

3. *Ibid.*, p. 18. (Southern quotes Bowdich's *Mission from Cape Coast Castle to Ashantee*, London, 1819; third edition, 1966.)

4. Ernest Borneman, "The Roots of Jazz," in Nat Hentoff and Albert J. McCarthy, *Jazz: New Perspectives* (New York: Da Capo Press, Inc., 1975), p. 17. (First printing, Holt, Rinehart & Winston, Inc., New York, 1959.)

5. Whitney Balliett, *The Sound of Surprise* (New York: E. P. Dutton & Co., Inc., 1959).

6. Harold Courlander, *op. cit.*, p. 31.

7. Marshall Stearns, *op. cit.*, p. 103.

8. *Ibid.*, p. 277.

9. A less common but plausible theory can be found in Schuller's *Early Jazz* (New York & London: Oxford University Press, 1968), Chapter 1.

10. John Storm Roberts, *Black Music of Two Worlds* (New York: William Morrow & Company, Inc., 1974), p. 189 and pp. 212–213.

11. LeRoi Jones, *Blues People* (New York: William Morrow & Company, Inc., 1963), pp. 94–95.

12. *American Dictionary of Words and Phrases* (New York: Harper & Row, 1962), p. 188; and *The American Language: Supplement II* (New York: Alfred Knopf, 1948), pp. 708–710.

13. As told to Nat Hentoff, reprinted in the liner notes to *Nefertiti: The Beautiful One Has Come* (General Discography, Chapter 8).

part one
TRADITIONAL JAZZ

RAGTIME: CLASSIC AND HARLEM

Ragtime Revisited

RAGTIME, the first popular music craze in America, was nearly an overnight sensation; it was spread across the country with amazing rapidity by vaudeville, the player piano, and countless dance-hall and amateur pianists. The composers who created the style were from the Midwest, where popular march music stamped its two-beat feeling and four thematic divisions upon their work: They were Scott Joplin, the most gifted of them, a somber, determined son of an ex-slave, born in Texarkana, Texas, in 1868; Tom Turpin, a three-hundred-pound pianist and barroom owner; Louis Chauvin, who could neither read nor write music; and a few others who wrote memorable rags, like James Scott, Arthur Marshall, and the only white member of the group, Joseph Lamb. These men were composers of "art" music for the piano, which, as they saw it, belonged on the concert stage along with the works of Beethoven or Chopin. Technology did not allow them to record their own work, except indirectly through piano rolls, because neither Edison's cylinders nor Berliner's new discs were able to capture the range and dynamics of the piano.

The roots of ragtime are numerous and impossible to disentangle completely. Although ragtime was primarily piano music, the marching bands of the late 1800's left their imprint in the "two-step" regularity of its $\frac{2}{4}$ meter. Like march music, ragtime was written in four themes, or strains, of approximately equal importance, and the changes of key through the progression of themes often reflected well-known marches. It is no surprise to find allusions to this inheritance in ragtime titles like Joplin's "Combination March." But there is a world of difference between march music and ragtime, a difference largely accounted for by syncopation, a lilting rhythm that can be traced to this country's antebellum period.

Probably the earliest precursor of syncopated rhythm evolved from a plantation slave dance known as the "cakewalk." This dance was done at Sunday afternoon social gatherings of the type described by Shephard N. Edmonds, the son of freed slaves: ". . . the slaves both young and old would dress up in hand-me-down finery and do a high-kicking, prancing walk-around. They did a take off on the high manners of the white folks in the 'big house,' but their masters, who gathered around to watch the fun, missed the point." [1] The dance derived its name from the custom of awarding a cake to "the couple that did the proudest movements."

Banjos generally supplied the music for the cakewalk. The cross-rhythm generated by the bass string working against the higher-melody strings later found its way onto the piano keyboard, where the left hand kept up an oompah, duple-meter bass against a tendency toward $\frac{3}{4}$ or $\frac{6}{8}$ groupings of three in the treble. The banjo, in fact, was the first instrument on which ragtime music was recorded. Due to the banjo's narrow range and the quick "decay" of its notes, its sound was more easily captured on primitive recording equipment.

The "coon song," another quasi-syncopated form, was a feature of the minstrel show, a racially derisive species of entertainment which had begun as early as 1799, when Johann Graupner, a German singer, appeared with cork-blackened skin on a stage in Boston.[2] Although the coon songs were a demeaning caricature of the black man as "carefree, inept, and mischievous," they were the mainstay of both black and white entertainers. The melody as a whole was not syncopated as in ragtime, but certain phrases were, and again banjo-derived rhythms played a significant role. In fact, a coon song published later as the piano piece "New Coon in Town" is subtitled "Banjo Imitation." [3]

In various ways these songs remain part of Americana. "Ole Zip Coon," popular in New York in 1834, made its mark with an energetic refrain whose rhythmic pattern was found in several ragtime pieces. The lyrics went, "Possum up a gum tree, coony on a stump . . . ;" and the music (without its lyrics) was popularized later under the new title "Turkey in the Straw." Another of the lingering pieces was composed in 1830 by the actor Thomas Rice, who stole the lyric from a black street performer: "Wheel about an' turn about an' do jes' so / An ebry time I wheel about I *Jump Jim Crow*." [4]

The cakewalk, too, outlived the plantations where it was born, becoming another staple of minstrelsy, in which the "interlocutor" grandiloquently referred to it as "peregrinatin' for the pastry." The cakewalk was a vehicle for the popularization of ragtime around the turn of the century, when it became fashionable as "the ragtime dance" in white American and European society (which, of course, failed to recognize its exaggerated strutting as a parody of itself). Vestiges of the cakewalk remain in the familiar refrain of a popular song from 1914 "Darktown Strutters Ball," and in Debussy's piano chestnut of 1909, "Golliwogg's Cakewalk." (The golliwogg was a black doll in a children's story.)

The genius of the ragtime synthesis is that a unique, integral style sprang from these diverse elements. Along with the marches, coon songs, and dance music for the cakewalk and two-step, elements of French quadrilles, schottisches, polkas, and even the blues have been identified. The word *rag*, then, correctly suggests that the new music was created from bits and scraps of disparate origin.

The origin of the word, however, is less easy to discern. In *Shining Trumpets*, Rudi Blesh cites black parlance in the Georgia Sea Islands, where Africanisms lingered long after they had disappeared elsewhere: ". . . *rags* have always meant sinful, i.e., secular, songs." Yet Rupert Hughes, a novelist and music critic, noted in the *Boston Musical Record* of 1899: "Negroes call their clog dancing 'ragging' and the dance 'a rag,' a dance largely shuffling." [5] Another view states that the term referred to the beat, which, due to its cross-rhythmic feeling, was heard as "torn" or "ragged." Although the word's etymology is not likely to be revealed conclusively at this point, it is safe to assume that it had something to do with ragtime's key element, its beat.

There were many midwestern cities where ragtime was played, but none was more a center of creative output than Sedalia, Missouri, where Scott Joplin settled in 1896. Joplin was one of many itinerant pianists who worked in saloons and sporting houses, where frequent "cutting contests" showed off the players' dexterity and newest compositions. The Maple Leaf Club was one of the popular social halls on Main Street in Sedalia; its name was destined for posterity. Joplin's "Maple Leaf Rag" of 1899 helped to ignite the wildfire-like spread of ragtime; one hundred thousand copies of the sheet music were sold within six months, an astonishing volume considering that its publisher, a local music-store owner, did nothing at all to promote or advertise the piece.

Joplin was not the first composer to publish ragtime piano music, but he was the first to elevate it well above the barroom genre to the level of deeply affecting art. On the heels of the "Maple Leaf," Joplin and the several composers mentioned earlier in this introduction produced dozens of lovely syncopated rags, many of which were studied as classics by pianists of the next three decades. In fact, the music later became known as "classic" ragtime because it was written down rather than improvised, and also because it emulated the purity and status of European art music. The music has endured due to its emotional tone of bittersweet gaiety, deadly rigid underneath with its martial oompah bass but fun loving and capricious in its treble melodies. Ragtime is neither happy nor sad, fast nor slow, playful nor entirely serious. Its mood is poignant and unresolved.

From Rags to Riches

The classic ragtime composers were dismayed by what happened to their music between 1900 and 1917, the year of Joplin's death. The rag, which they had envisioned as America's answer to the sonata, the étude, and the polonaise, became hopelessly confused with the ephemeral drivel of Tin Pan Alley. First of all, piano rolls were cut by the hundreds for the Pianola, which served as the record player of its day. Sheet music was sold at twenty-five cents a copy for those who could play the piano and for the thousands more who suddenly wanted to learn. Such fads are what fortunes are made of, as illustrated by the case of Axel Christiansen, a young, struggling Danish piano teacher. In 1903 Christiansen and his wife opened a small studio in Chicago, advertising, rather implausibly, "Ragtime Taught in Ten Easy Lessons." A decade later he owned thirty-five schools across the nation.[6] The slightly "off," slightly up, and famously "intoxicating" beat of good ragtime can not be written down upon or read from a piece of composition paper, of course, for it is primarily an emanation of the pianist's genuine feeling for the cross-rhythm. But ragtime had become too popular too quickly for its own good.

Most commonly, the rag was transformed into popular vocal music. Vaudeville troupes dubbed their material ragtime whether it was or not. John Philip Sousa's band, famous for its marches, incorporated ragtime into its repertoire, taking the music on several tours of Europe. From high society to the *hoi polloi*, in America and abroad, they all danced the cakewalk, the two-step, the buck-and-wing, and the slow drag to ragtime and facsimiles of it. Meanwhile, the hacks of Tin Pan Alley, New York's music factory, cranked out countless imitative ditties to cash in on the music's appeal.

Since the name ragtime was tacked on to whatever anyone wanted to sell, there was a great deal of confusion over what it was. For example, the musicologist Maude Cuney-Hare was clearly misled in 1936 when she decried the music she believed had "poisoned" the youth of the day: "Not only were the popular ballads in Ragtime destroying an appreciation for the classics; they also prevented an acquirement of good taste for poetry. The verses lacked literary value, the words were vulgar, and the sentiments execrable." [7] Of course, ragtime was never intended by its creators as a vehicle for popular verse. That was the work of Tin Pan Alley tunesmiths. Yet the misunderstanding here was prevalent until 1950, when Rudi Blesh and Harriet Janis clarified this misconception in a work which has since become the Bible of the field, *They All Played Ragtime.*

The Ragtime Revival

The general public did not catch up with genuine classic ragtime until the 1970's, when a series of developments made it more available on records. The first breakthrough came with Joshua Rifkin's 1970 album *Piano Rags by Scott Joplin*, which surprisingly topped the classical music charts for months. Rifkin's rather sober approach was to render each piece with the scrupulous accuracy the composer desired. Max Morath, an entertainer and ragtime enthusiast of long standing, took a looser approach, presenting a one-man revue of the era in concert and on educational television. After Rifkin's success on the classical Nonesuch label, Vanguard recorded several albums by Morath, one of which is discussed in the Selected Discography.

In 1972 Joplin's scores were at last made generally available to pianists in *The Collected Works of Scott Joplin*, compiled by Vera Brodsky Lawrence and issued by the New York Public Library. Ragtime's ascent reached its peak in 1974, when Joplin's "The Entertainer," published in 1902, could barely be dislodged from the top of the pop charts, where it was known as the theme from the movie *The Sting*. Joplin's music was suddenly more popular than it had been even in the heyday of the "Maple Leaf Rag."

Absurdly enough, many people were led to believe that *The Sting*'s theme had been written by Marvin Hamlisch, a popular Hollywood arranger hired to score the film. The confusion suggests that ragtime's popularity still seems to breed misunderstandings. "The Entertainer" was selected for the film's theme on the strength of Gunther Schuller's orchestrated rag album *The Red Back Book* (see General Discography), which had caught the attention of the producer, George Roy Hill. Schuller, whose previous commitments prevented him from writing the score, was listed as arranger on the award-winning sound track, while Joplin, of course, received the composer's credit. Naturally Hamlisch, who contributed least of all, received the most public acclaim, along with the Oscar.

But ragtime has encountered more serious challenges than Hollywood. Many musicologists do not see ragtime as part of jazz at all. For example, in *Blues People*, LeRoi Jones calls it "a premature attempt at the socio-cultural merger that later produced jazz." [8] In the rag, Jones believes, the black has abandoned too much of his African inheritance in favor of a "more formalized, less spontaneous music." [9] Ragtime's development, however, was less clear-cut than Jones implies and certainly was not inconsistent with the character of the jazz tradition. S. Brun Campbell, a student of Joplin's who witnessed many of the masters perform, recalled that "None of the original pianists played ragtime the way it was written. They played their own style . . . if you knew the player and heard him a block away, you could name him by his ragtime style." [10] Even though most ragtime is played note for note as written, that does not disqualify it from the jazz tradition, for the reasons discussed in Chapter 1.[11]

Max Morath, writing on the ragtime revival for *Contemporary Keyboard* magazine (January 1979), helps to bring the emphasis on accuracy into focus: "The early ragtime composer's admonition to play the notes as written was a request for clean delivery without sloppiness. . . ." Morath claims too much has been made of their classical pretensions, and he believes Joplin would have been delighted with Dick Hyman's improvising on the tenth side of his five-record set *Scott Joplin, The Complete Works for Piano* (General Discography). Moreover, the ragtime tradition of the East Coast, as we shall see later, is both connected to the classic style and highly improvisational. For a variety of reasons, then, severing ragtime from jazz on the grounds of its formalism cannot be justified.

Perhaps the most compelling reason for listening to ragtime as an integral part of jazz is that the musicians themselves hear it that way. It is well known that Jelly Roll Morton (Chapter 3) solicited Joplin's advice on his own work, that both Fats Waller and Duke Ellington (Chapter 4) studied and used the ragtime repertoire, and that jazz's most contemporary improvisers return to it for inspiration. One need only turn to the last album discussed in this volume, recorded in 1979 by the free-jazz collective Air, to find Joplin reexamined and incorporated into the music's cutting edge.

Ragtime Strides into Harlem

Black pianists along the eastern seaboard found themselves faced with the same dilemma that plagued their midwestern brothers: Their music was irresistible to many but seldom taken seriously. The best of the "ticklers"— Luckey Roberts, Willie "The Lion" Smith, James P. Johnson, Fats Waller, and Eubie Blake—were thought of in their prime as entertainers, an opinion they seemed to confirm by writing some of the nation's most popular music. Blake, for example, wrote "I'm Just Wild About Harry"; Johnson, "The Charleston"; and Waller, "Ain't Misbehavin'." Yet, from a musical point of view, the innovative, enduring contribution of these men is found in their jazz piano playing, which evolved into a style known as "stride."

East Coast ragtime was even more a player's medium than the classic style. It was more improvisational and demanded a precise, tireless technique. If the goal of the midwesterners was to inspire rapture and "appreciation," the stride pianists wished to dazzle and excite. The albums in the Selected Discography demonstrate why pianists from Art Tatum to Thelonious Monk looked to the stride pianists as the old masters.

Stride clearly departed from classic ragtime in its tempo and rhythm. While Joplin held to a slow march tempo, insisting "it is never correct to play ragtime fast," the more urbane pianists of the eastern cities would tear along at breakneck speed, as fast as a pair of hands could clap to the beat. The left hand leaps (strides) from a single note in the bass register to a chord in the middle register, as in classic ragtime, with the melody spun out in the right hand. Prior to the days when pianists were aided with bass and drum accompaniment, the ragtime players handled rhythm, harmony, and melody alone. The martial regularity of the classic school gave way in the East to constantly shifting accents: one-TWO-three-FOUR/ONE-TWO-THREE-four/ONE-two-THREE-four. At other times, four beats per measure could be felt in a "walking" bass line of single notes, octaves, or tenths. This does not mean the Harlem players ignored the classic rag style or felt they were above it. They were avid students of the midwestern composers. James P. Johnson believed Joplin was "fifty years ahead of his time," and both Johnson and Blake play Joplin's compositions in the selected albums listed later in this chapter, though not as the composer would have played them.

Another influence was also active—the dances and "ring shouts" of African origin. The ring shout was a religious chant inclined to bring on a sense of possession and frenzy. In Africa it assumed a call-and-response form in which the worshippers did a circle dance around a deity. (It was in fact more of a shuffle than a dance, for the feet were not allowed to cross.) The ceremony was preserved nearly intact on the Georgia Sea Islands, but it also evolved into closely related dances performed in Congo Square in New Orleans and even in New York. Willie "The Lion" Smith testifies to the connection between the religious ceremony and the rhythm of stride:

> Shouts are stride piano—when James P. and Fats and I would get a romp-down shout going, that was playing rocky, just like the Baptist people sing. You don't just play a chord to that (on the keyboard)— you got to move it. . . . Want to see a ring-shout? Go out to the Convent Avenue Baptist Church (in New York) any Sunday." [12]

James P. Johnson remembers hearing them as a child in his own living room: "They danced around in a shuffle and then they would shove a man or a woman into the center and clap hands. This would go on all night and I would fall asleep sitting at the top of the stairs in the dark." [13]

The shout survived outside of its religious domain in the rhythm of the black folk-style dances at the turn of the century. Johnson's earliest ragtime was composed for—and probably *on*—the dance floor in about 1913:

> The Charleston, which became a popular dance step on its own, was just a regulation cotillion step without a name. . . It was while playing for these southern dancers that I composed a number of Charlestons—eight in all—all with the same rhythm. One of these later became my famous *Charleston* when it hit Broadway.
>
> My *Carolina Shout* was another type of ragtime arrangement of a set dance of this period.[14]

Johnson noted that among the southern blacks who had moved north for longshoremen's work "there were even some Gullahs," residents of the Georgia Sea Islands where the ring shout was preserved more authentically than elsewhere.

The best stride piano of all was often heard in a low-income Harlem apartment on a beat-up, out-of-tune upright piano. There, the famous rent parties began as informal gatherings where a local "tickler" could be heard for a small admission charge and bring-your-own refreshments. During the Depression, the parties began in earnest with printed tickets and bathtub gin for sale until the family had made enough to get by for another month.

The Harlem pianists, who were generally very supportive of each other, competed on these homespun proving grounds as if their reputations depended upon it—which in many minds they did. Johnson told an interviewer for the *Jazz Review*: "I did double glissandos straight and backhand, glissandos in sixths and double tremolos. These would run other ticklers out of the place at cutting sessions (usually taking place at the rent parties). They wouldn't play after me." [15] The young Duke Ellington, having just arrived from Washington, often attended these parties with Johnson, The Lion, or Fats, picking up a few tricks for his own use.

Much of this dexterity and outright flamboyance of technique was made possible by studying the European classics. Waller said that many of his bass configurations came from a study of Bach inventions and toccatas, while his harmonic transitions between choruses were occasionally rescued by a deft plagiarism of Chopin or Liszt. Johnson, too, studied, practiced, and composed in the European classical style throughout most of his life.

What the Harlem ragtimers possessed above all was a sense of fun, an awareness of the uplifting moment, and a joy of playing. Perhaps that is why James P. and Fats, the epitome of Harlem stride, are more closely identified with jazz than are the composers of classic rags. Their stride style can be heard to varying degrees in nearly all of jazz piano to follow. Jazz *is* serious music, but not in the European sense which Joplin and his colleagues strove to achieve. It is a people's music as well, one that excites and entertains. The fact that jazz can be serious and popular simultaneously is one of its unique and vital qualities.

SCOTT JOPLIN

Scott Joplin—1916

Biograph, BLP-1006
one disc, good liner notes
1916

Musicians: Scott Joplin, six piano rolls on side one. W. Arlington and W. Axtmann, piano rolls on side two.
Compositions (all by Scott Joplin except "Ole Miss Rag"): *Side one:* Maple Leaf Rag; Something Doing; Weeping Willow; Maple Leaf Rag (take 2); Ole Miss Rag (W. C. Handy); Magnetic Rag. *Side two:* Ragtime Oriole (James Scott); Quality Rag

(Scott); Agitation Rag (R. Hampton); Tickled to Death (C. Hunter); Grace and Beauty (Scott); Twelfth Street Rag (Euday Bowman); Anoma (Ford Dabney); Cannon Ball (J. Northrup). All compositions were published between 1899 and 1916.

SCOTT JOPLIN'S RAGS are the supreme examples of the form, and, although his status did not bring him prosperity, Joplin was the composer most respected by his peers and colleagues. Solidly built, neatly dressed, and always the gentleman, Joplin was a remote man, poised and ambitious. There are disputes about his abilities as a pianist, for some witnesses describe his style as stiff and wooden. In any case, he was a reluctant performer, preferring to make his living as a composer.

Scott Joplin—1916, a collection of several piano rolls recorded by him in New York, is the only available example of the master's playing. For the most part, the style reflects the straight, unadorned manner for which he was known. Only occasionally is there evidence that the piano-roll company tampered with the roll to suit their marketing needs. For example, the "walking" boogie-woogie bass line that appears magically in the third theme of "Magnetic Rag" is a stylistic device that Joplin shunned as being beneath the rag, a form he considered comparable to the classic sonata in stature. On two tracks there are note combinations which would be impossible for one pianist to play. These indiscretions, however, do not detract from the thrill of knowing this music came from the hands of Joplin himself. Moreover, the prim, understated tone and irrepressible motion of the player piano convey a charm evocative of the era.

Joplin, born in 1868 to a musical family in Texarkana, Texas, taught himself to play the piano with such proficiency that he was offered scholarship lessons at the age of eleven by a teacher in the nearby white community. He set out in his teens to play in the honky-tonks of St. Louis, moving to Sedalia, Missouri, in 1895, where he played cornet in a band whose repertoire included marches, popular songs, and symphonic works. After traveling briefly with a vocal group he had formed, Joplin returned to Sedalia, attending George Smith College, where he learned to transcribe his compositions into conventional notation. At the same time, he became a major attraction at the Maple Leaf Club, although the environment of promiscuity made him ill at ease. Joplin had one published composition by 1899, "Original Rags," and he had been attempting to sell another which, atypically for him, emphasized a heady percussive rhythm rather than a flowing melody. He may have named the piece after the club or perhaps after the "Maple Leaf Waltz," which was popular in Sedalia at the time. In any case, he told his student Arthur Marshall, "Arthur, the 'Maple Leaf' will make me King of Ragtime Composers." The first two publishers rejected the piece, but Joplin's confidence was not misplaced. John Stillwell Stark, a local music-store owner who became Joplin's publisher and confidant for many years, brought the piece out. Within six months Joplin retired as a pianist and bought a large house in St. Louis. Stark, who could barely keep up with the demand for sheet music to the "Maple Leaf Rag," soon moved to New York, where he became one of the country's top ragtime publishers until his death in 1922.

The third theme of the "Maple Leaf," which may be diagrammed thematically as AA BB A CC DD, is the climax of its rhythmic drama. The cross-rhythm of the C theme has not lost a bit of its power over the years, nor its ability to catch the listener off guard as accents are suddenly thrown to a new part of the measure. In fact, the C theme contrasts sharply with the others, pointing to another talent unique to Joplin: while most ragtime composers displayed thematic similarity within a piece, Joplin could embrace a diversity of moods without sacrificing the unity of the rag.

"Something Doing" illustrates the common practice of collaboration, a natural consequence of the close-knit black musical society of the Midwest. Composers and players often sought out one another to learn, try out new ideas, and even share living quarters. Joplin wrote this piece in 1903 with Scott Hayden, who had been his student. They first collaborated on "Sunflower Slow Drag" (the "slow drag" was a dance), which rivaled the "Maple Leaf's" popularity during 1901. Soon after, Joplin married Hayden's widowed sister, and the two couples lived together in Joplin's new St. Louis home. "Something Doing," like their earlier rag, excels—especially in the second theme—in its flowing melodic quality. (Hayden and Joplin were to collaborate on only three more rags, for Hayden moved to Chicago where he died of tuberculosis at thirty-three, having spent the last dozen years of his life as an elevator operator.)

The piano rolls on side two were not cut by Joplin but are attributed to two individuals who the album's producers suspect are really one man. Except for famous names like Joplin's, it was considered bad form for a company to have all its material played by one pianist. Here the music's major attraction is that it includes three compositions by James Scott, another Joplin protégé, who was every bit as prolific and occasionally more brilliant than his mentor. Scott was more inclined to explore pianistic possibilities, while Joplin pursued emotions and moods. "Grace and Beauty" is said to be Scott's best rag.

Joplin's composing reveals an increasing harmonic complexity and emotional subtlety. After 1909 he tried to liberate ragtime from its oompah bass with the more implied rhythmic figurations heard in "Magnetic Rag." At the same time, he was a crusader for the purity of the style. Nothing infuriated or discouraged him more than the imitation rags of Tin Pan Alley which he inadvertently helped to popularize. He was finally moved to write an instruction book showing how to play ragtime rhythm properly and insisting that ragtime is not to be played fast. Of course, he could no more slow the tempos of trickster barroom pianists than he could counter the distortions of Tin Pan Alley.

Joplin's financial success was sporadic. Worse still, he became bitterly dissatisfied with the scope of his work—a feeling intensified by the onset of his illness. He tried to expand his scope by composing two ill-fated folk operas. The manuscript to *A Guest of Honor* (1903) has vanished. *Treemonisha*, which runs 230 pages in the piano score, played once in Harlem in 1915 but it left the audience cold, faring little better upon its resurrection on Broadway in 1972. Joplin's efforts left him exhausted and destitute.

Joplin's past as a performer in brothels and sporting houses soon overtook him. His later years were wracked with nervous disorder, searing pain, and bouts of insanity brought on by tertiary syphilis. His performance of "Maple Leaf" during this period was described as "pitiful to hear"; [16] yet he continued to compose in moments of lucidity. Joplin died at forty-nine in 1917, the year of the first New Orleans-style recording by the Original Dixieland Jass Band.

Historical considerations aside, there are acoustically preferable albums on which to hear Joplin's rags as he intended them to sound. Joshua Rifkin's *Piano Rags by Scott Joplin*, which topped the classical music charts in 1970, must be the first choice. Rifkin, a professor of music at Brandeis University and, for a time, the music director of Nonesuch, has performed in a variety of genres, from jug bands to classics. He is a faithful interpreter, observing Joplin's wishes for restraint and precision, yet sensitive to the melancholy, wistful mood which underlies even the brightest of the composer's works. The choice of repertoire is excellent: "Maple Leaf Rag," a symbol of the era; "The Entertainer" popularized in the sound track to *The Sting*; and two selections from Joplin's harmonically advanced period—"Magnetic Rag" and "Euphonic Sounds." *Volumes II* and *III* by Rifkin (General Discography) complete the set of important Joplin rags.

Dick Hyman's *Scott Joplin: The Complete Works for Piano* is an equally good choice, available in single discs or in a boxed set on RCA (General Discography). *The Red Back Book* on Angel (1973), containing the eleven-piece orchestrations of Joplin's most popular work originally commissioned by his publisher John Stillwell Stark, is the album which inspired the sound track to *The Sting*. Gunther Schuller conducts the New England Conservatory Ragtime Ensemble in a period piece persuasively recalling an era of band concerts and bittersweet gaiety.

MAX MORATH

The World of Scott Joplin

Vanguard, SRV-310 SD
one disc, liner notes
1973

Musicians: Max Morath, piano.
Compositions: Side one: Reflection Rag—Syncopated Musings (Joplin, 1917); Frog Legs Rag (James Scott, 1906); Palm Leaf Rag—A Slow Drag (Joplin, 1903); Kinklets—Two Step (Arthur Marshall, 1906); A Breeze from Alabama (Joplin, 1902); Golden Hours (Morath, 1966); The Ragtime Oriole (Scott, 1911). *Side two:* Searchlight Rag (Joplin, 1907); The Pippin Rag (Marshall, 1908); Top Liner Rag (Joseph Lamb, 1916); One for Amelia (Morath, 1964); Broadway Rag—A Classic (Scott, 1922); The Chrysanthemum—An Afro-American Intermezzo (Joplin, 1904); Maple Leaf Rag (Joplin, 1899).

WHAT MAKES MAX MORATH a vibrant interpreter of ragtime is that he is in love with the entire era, not just its music. He had been a mainstream pianist and an all-around entertainer until 1950, when he first used ragtime to accompany a dramatic performance. Gradually he added rags to his normal repertoire, which was no easy task in those years because the music, so long neglected, was out of print. Even photocopies were difficult to track down. By 1959 Morath was one of the few rag aficionados and found himself invited by National Educational Television to write and host *The Ragtime Era*, a project which provided the opportunity for even more research.

Still, recording ragtime was a labor of love if not folly. His first two albums were on Gold Camp Recordings, a now-defunct label he owned with his engineer. He also recorded on the Epic label in the mid-1960's; but Epic's parent company, Columbia, because of the first album's sales, never even pressed the last one. Morath finally found a home on Vanguard at a propitious time, for Joshua Rifkin's *Piano Rags by Scott Joplin* (General Discography), to the astonishment of the industry, hit the top of the classical music sales charts. Morath's album *The World of Scott Joplin* came out as the "ragtime revival" was gathering steam.

One of Morath's assumptions is that the *world* of Joplin's music deserves to be revived along with the master's work, so he draws half of his repertoire on this album from Joplin's contemporaries. The album is thus broadened into an ode to an entire style rather than to one individual.

James Scott, born in 1886 to freed slaves, was one of the major figures of Joplin's world. Scott arrived in St. Louis at nineteen with several compositions in his suitcase. They had been written in Carthage, Missouri, where he worked in a music store washing windows until the owner realized he could read music. He was quickly promoted to plugging popular songs at the piano. Scott idolized the composer of the "Maple Leaf" and wasted no time trying to locate Joplin at Tom Turpin's Rosebud Café. Eventually he was directed to Joplin's home where he was invited to play for the master. Joplin saw his own influence in the younger man's work and a blossoming originality as well. He introduced Scott to John Stillwell Stark, highly recommending one of his pieces, which Stark published the following year (1906) as "Frog Legs Rag." Until he retired in 1922, Stark remained Scott's publisher.

As Morath plays the rag, it has vivacity above all. In fact, that is generally true of Morath's style. This is a young rag, bursting with playfulness, and it warrants an energetic treatment. Joplin must have had no difficulty recognizing his own influence when Scott played it for him, for the second theme is a variation upon the second theme of the "Maple Leaf." The A and C themes are very closely related to each other. David Jasen and Trebor Tichenor observe in *Rags and Ragtime* that Scott tended to write in one sustained mood rather than in a variety of them. Thus he moves "one step away from the oldest concept of ragtime, that of a patchwork of various different musical ideas." [17] In effect, he is approaching the later jazz tradition of establishing one dominant theme upon which variations are improvised. The final strain is even more clearly approachable in a jazz context with its call-and-response melody, the echo occurring one octave above the rest of the melodic line. The section continues in a long, sinuous line which takes some surprising curves and bends.

The classic ragtime triumvirate is completed by Joseph Lamb, the only superlative white composer of the era. His "Top Liner Rag" (1916) may be the best of his thirty-four published pieces. Like Scott, his career also began with Joplin's help. The two met in New York, where the Stark offices had moved temporarily. Lamb had come there to buy at a discount everything Joplin had written, and the composer, whom Lamb had never seen, was standing beside him as he made the purchase. They returned to the boardinghouse where Joplin was staying, and Lamb performed his "Sensation—A Rag" for an impromptu black audience. It must have required some courage on Lamb's part to play *their* music and in their midst. But Joplin liked what he heard. "That's a good rag," he reportedly told Lamb, "a regular Negro rag." [18] Again, Stark published the piece on Joplin's advice, initiating Lamb's fifteen-year songwriting career. (Lamb lived until 1960, but could no longer make a living through ragtime after 1922. He would have fared better in the 1970's.)

Lamb's "Top Liner" has the gentlest lilt of any track on the record. Its melody is pure fun and joy, but not the bittersweet variety which Joplin evoked. Morath's instinct is to give the rag even more lift and buoyancy, enhancing its mood. The piece bears several listenings because it has a subtle force, not the explosive brilliance of someone like James Scott, who snaps the listener to attention. Morath then plays his own "One for Amelia," named for Lamb's widow. It is also gentle in feeling and rhythm but tricky. Morath once said, in an interview with *Contemporary Keyboard* magazine, that the next step for ragtime must be taken by modern players composing inventively in the accepted format. He has done that here, for the cyclical rhythmic feeling is ingenious. Just before the end of each phrase, the rag shifts into two measures of ¾ (waltz) time while continuing the duple meter of the melody itself, leaving the listener to wonder how Morath reached the end of the phrase on time.

"Reflections" is Joplin's only posthumously published work. It has five themes which Morath believes were pieced together by John Stillwell Stark. The B theme has an unusual minor melody, a type Joplin used only after he went to New York. It resembles an Eastern European or a Yiddish folk tune. One might guess he had heard some of these, as there were many immigrants from Eastern Europe in New York at the time of Joplin's move there. "The Golden Hours" is another Morath original in which once again the melody fits cleverly into the rag's even structure. A striking dissonance occurs near the end of the first strain (which is repeated). To use dissonance in such well-ordered music provides an excellent contrast. The B theme builds to a powerful, orchestral climax. Morath's version of "Maple Leaf Rag" is the only disappointment on the album. He rushes it by giving the left hand a kind of "hop," creating a momentum that is too fast for the rag's sensitive, Mona Lisa mood. But it is the only track in which Morath's inclination leads to a less-than-superb treatment.

Morath's *The World of Scott Joplin, Volume 2* contains a similar balance of traditional and contemporary rag compositions, emphasizing, in Joplin's case, the harmonically rich material of his later period, with the exception of the 1901 two-step "Easy Winners." However, William Bolcom's *Heliotrope Bouquet: Piano Rags 1900–1970* (General Discography) is a more interesting second choice for the sensuous title track, a collaboration by Joplin and the Creole genius Louis Chauvin. Bolcom, a professor of music and composer of rags, treats the gentle "Heliotrope" with appropriate delicacy.

EUBIE BLAKE

The 86 Years of Eubie Blake

Columbia, C2S-847
two discs, good liner notes
1969

Musicians: Eubie Blake, piano. (Sides three and four with Noble Sissle, vocals.)
Compositions: Side one: Dream Rag; Charleston Rag; Maple Leaf Rag; Semper Fidelis; Eubie's Boogie; Poor Jimmy Green; Tricky Fingers. *Side two:* Stars and Stripes Forever; Baltimore Toldolo; Poor Katie Red; Kitchen Tom; Troublesome Ivories; Chevy Chase; Brittwood Rag. *Sides three and four—Theater and Ragtime:* Bleeding Moon; Under the Bamboo Tree; It's All Your Fault; Shuffle Along—medley; I'm Just Wild About Harry; Spanish Venus; As Long As You Live; Charleston; Old Fashioned Love; If I Could Be with You; You Were Meant for Me; Blues, Why Don't You Let Me Alone?; Dixie Moon; Blue Rag in Twelve Keys; Memories of You.

EUBIE BLAKE, who was eighty-six at the time of this vibrant, energetic performance, personifies traditional ragtime. He combines classic ragtime sources with the rough-hewn East Coast style of playing and, as sides three and four demonstrate, a flair for popular composition. Blake helped to create the black musicals which became the preoccupation of facile songwriters like Fats Waller.

Blake was such a proficient pianist in the early 1900's that he had to simplify his music drastically to get it into print. When he took his earliest work, "Charleston Rag," to publisher Joseph Stern, Stern told him, "Sure it's good—it's wonderful—but who could play it but you and Luckey Roberts?" [19] Stern finally did publish Blake's famous "Chevy Chase" in 1914 but in simplified form. Blake was forced to write "for the girls in the five-and-ten-cent stores" who had to demonstrate his music. Naturally Blake himself improvised; it was the only way to make his mark as a performer. He could even play a song in all twelve keys, a rare capacity, which he demonstrates here on "Blue Rag."

Blake was born in 1883 in Baltimore to former slaves, the only one of their eleven children who lived to adulthood. An aggressive music-store owner placed a seventy-five-dollar organ in the Blake home at the cost of twenty-five cents per week, and young Hubert taught himself to play. At fifteen he was working at Agnes Shelton's sporting house in Baltimore's tenderloin, over the objections of his mother, a religious woman who was opposed to any form of secular music.

Blake set his sights higher than the brothel. By 1905 he established himself in Atlantic City, where his reputation as a dynamic and dazzling showman attracted admirers from New York like James P. Johnson, who considered him "one of the foremost pianists of all time." Blake's masterpiece "Troublesome Ivories," revived with undiminished abandon on *86 Years*, and "Chevy Chase" became standards in the repertoire of Johnson, Willie "The Lion" Smith, and Fats Waller.

In 1915, the year after "Chevy Chase" came out, Blake met the lyricist Noble Sissle, and together they decided to crash the gates of Tin Pan Alley. Their break came when Sophie Tucker sang their first collaboration, "It's All Your Fault" (on side three with Sissle and Blake singing), a short ballad with an easy lilt. In a *Contemporary Keyboard* magazine interview (August 1977), Blake described how their first sale was made. Sissle had suggested they go see the singer while she played a theater in town. "You can't look at a white woman. We're colored," Blake reminded him. "Are you going with me or not?" Sissle asked him. "Yes, I'll stand outside when they kick you out the door." But Sophie Tucker not only bought the song, she paid to have it orchestrated.

Their most powerful imprint upon the American theater was made with the 1921 black musical *Shuffle Along*, which ran for a year and a half on Broadway. The songs "I'm Just Wild About Harry" and "Love Will Find a Way" became national hits, the former used as Harry Truman's anthem in the 1948 presidential campaign. Side four here also contains his "Memories of You," a ballad of lasting merit. Eubie Blake initiated the heyday of the black musicals, and his work was in demand through the 1920's.

Eubie's mother, however, was not won over by her son's success. *They All Played Ragtime* tells of a gala performance of *Shuffle Along* in Baltimore at which blacks by special permission were allowed to sit in the boxes. When the elderly Mrs. Blake was congratulated at a backstage party on Eubie's great achievements, she replied, "Some may see it that way but he might have done it all for Jesus instead."

Blake toured for the USO during World War II, returned to earn a degree in music from New York University, and gradually began to perform again. His success at the Newport Jazz Festival of 1969 led to the *86 Years* retrospective, a testimony to his continued vitality and dual achievements as a composer and powerful player. (Unfortunately, Biograph's two volumes of piano rolls, *Blues and Ragtime, 1917–1921*, are the only representations of the early years.)

Side one's "Dream Rag," one of the earliest pieces in the East Coast ragtime repertoire, has known a variety of titles, most of which are sexual in import. Its composer, Jesse Pickett who died in the 1920's, was a pimp and gambler well known in Baltimore during the Gay Nineties. Pickett called the piece "The Bull Dyke's Dream" because of the effect he believed it to have on the prostitutes who worked for him. Blake says he plays it here as Pickett taught it to him before the turn of the century. It opens with a tango rhythm, for which it was known at the time as a "Spanish piece." (Having traced the influx of West Africans into the West Indies and into South America, we know that the *habanera* is actually of African origin.) Like strictly composed ragtime, which Blake's version is not, there is a succession of themes but only three instead of four. Before the concluding two chords, the bass register of the piano is transformed into a virtual marching drum corps. On "Charleston Rag," Blake demonstrates the boogie-woogie bass of the blues and barrelhouse players. The piece then assumes a more typical rag feeling with three independent themes and a striding, oompah left hand. The melody, unlike the previous rag, is essentially a rhythmic figure, swinging the rag more percussively. Recalling the fluid lines of the midwestern composers, we can hear how the right hand alone accounts for much of the difference between classic and East Coast ragtime.

Eubie's version of "Maple Leaf" is not Joplinesque, but a more developed improvisation on the piece. It is rougher, faster, and lustier than the sedate composer's intentions. He seems to hurl his fingers at the keyboard, but gets away with it by emphasizing his interpretive playing rather than the composition itself. "Eubie's Boogie" probably bears the stamp of William Turk, a ragtime pianist in Baltimore who died in 1911. Turk supposedly developed a boogie bass because he was too obese to stride his left hand from the bass to the middle register of the keyboard. Musically it did him no harm, for Blake has said Turk "had a left hand like God." (Harlem ragtime, because its rhythm digs in harder, is often preoccupied with the left hand: It is the master drum in the essential cross-rhythm. James P. Johnson said of the obscure Abba Labba, according to Blesh and Janis, that "he had a left hand like a walking beam.") "Eubie's Boogie" also uses a typical blues chord progression, one quite out of character with the midwestern tradition.

The music of Eubie Blake makes it clear that on the East Coast, rags and blues merged readily, a synthesis of great consequence for jazz, for it enabled these folk and art forms to transcend their points of origin. Still performing at ninety-seven, Blake himself has become a figure of consequence to jazz, a symbol of its vitality and longevity. Eubie Blake Music, his own mail-order label (see Appendix), distributes recordings of the 1970's by both Eubie and his protégés (General Discography).

**LUCKEY ROBERTS and
WILLIE "THE LION" SMITH**

Luckey and the Lion: Harlem Piano

Good Time Jazz, S10035
one disc, liner notes
1958

Musicians: Luckey Roberts, piano. Willie "The Lion" Smith, piano.
Compositions: Side one (compositions by Luckey Roberts): Nothin'; Spanish Fandango;
Railroad Blues; Complainin'; Inner Space; Outer Space. *Side two* (compositions by
Willie "The Lion" Smith, except "Between the Devil"): Between the Devil and
the Deep Blue Sea (Arlen-Koehler); Morning Air; Relaxin'; Rippling Water; Tango
La Caprice; Concentratin'.

CHARLES LUCKEYETH ROBERTS and Willie "The Lion" Smith are major
creators of the Harlem ragtime style, exemplifying its rhythmic power, compositional form, inventiveness, and—in Luckey's case—emphasis on technical mastery of the keyboard. They were not sufficiently recorded in their
prime, due in part to the popularity of New Orleans and swing bands during
the 1920's and 1930's. Nevertheless, their legendary performances at rent
parties and cutting contests (although Roberts spent most of his time as a
society bandleader) earned them a retinue of admirers, most of whom
eventually surpassed them: James P. Johnson, Fats Waller, Art Tatum, Erroll
Garner, and even the young Duke Ellington. Thus it is especially fortunate
to find their best-recorded work on a single album.

Roberts, born in 1891, traveled as a child acrobat and was making a
living as a bandleader by his teens. His astounding technique, even more
fluid than James P.'s in the right hand, caught the ear of New York's upper
crust, and he became "house" pianist in the mansions of the Vanderbilts and
the Astors. His orchestra performed regularly at their eighty-room, ocean-
view summer homes in Newport, Rhode Island, where the garish bashes
F. Scott Fitzgerald dreamed of attending were held. It is interesting to spec-
ulate how much more fitting a recording legacy Roberts might have left had
he not been paid thousands of dollars weekly to play at these extravagant
parties.

Roberts's dexterity never seemed to diminish. Because he was a Quaker,
alcohol, tobacco, and probably any sort of personal indulgence were alien
to him. It is clear from the piece "Nothin'," composed at the turn of the
century, that he remained sharp and robust in his later years. The right
hand unleashes a cascade of notes that flow over a contrasting, rocking left-

hand bass, one which still bears the stamp of march music. "Spanish Fandango" is the smooth, romantic sort of ballad which must have endeared Roberts to his wealthy patrons. His blues roots, which do not show through quite as readily, are best heard on "Railroad Blues," a boogie-woogie exercise elevated above the barrelhouse genre by the integrity of Roberts's syncopation. While these half-dozen tracks cannot be assumed to measure up to Luckey's more youthful performances, they are all we have left (an excellent Herwin album is out of print) and deserve to be cherished accordingly.

The Lion, whose epithet came from bravery in action during World War I, was born William Henry Joseph Berthol Bonaparte Bertholoff, the son of black and Jewish parents. The mythic proportions of his character seemed to match his name. The Lion dressed, danced, and dined to the hilt, usually with a cigar burning between his teeth. He, James P., and Fats eventually became the reigning triumvirate at the rent-party contests, and Smith was the scene-stealer. James P. used to say, "When Willie Smith walked into a place, his every move was a picture." Duke Ellington learned his ragtime—and possibly a bit of his conspicuous poise and grace—from Smith, honoring him with "Portrait of the Lion" (*Duke Ellington—1939*; General Discography, Chapter 4). Willie must have absorbed the music of both black and Jewish traditions, for he served briefly as a cantor in a Harlem synagogue. He carried a calling card which identified him as *Der Yiddishe Chazan*, perhaps attempting to give a little *naches* to both parents.

Smith's weakness was that he succumbed to popular taste in the form of vocal performances, which invariably proved detrimental to his playing. (The General Discography lists these albums because they are all we have.) Thus the piano-only collection here is a welcome treat. The simplicity of "Relaxin' " makes the track a good introduction to his style, which depends upon rhythmic control and subtlety. Notice, for example, the gradual harmonic movement obtained in the left hand by varying only one note of the pattern at a time. "Morning Air," on the other hand, shows his capacity for bolder harmony where he desires it. As Ellington observed in his foreword to Smith's autobiography (*Music on My Mind*), "Even the great Art Tatum . . . showed strong patterns of Willie Smithisms after being exposed to The Lion."

Luckey and The Lion exhibit beauty through balance, form, and the joy they seem to take in their own creativity. Hearing the music they were capable of producing, one can only regret they did not leave us more of their influential piano music.

JAMES P. JOHNSON

The Original James P. Johnson

Folkways, FJ 2850
one disc, liner notes
1943–1945

Musicians: James P. Johnson, piano.
Compositions (all by James P. Johnson): *Side one:* Daintiness Rag; Blues for Jimmy; Jersey Sweet (two takes); Keep Movin'; Jungle Drums; Snowy Morning Blues; Twilight Rag. *Side two:* Liza; Aunt Hagar's Blues; Sweet Lorraine (two takes); The Dream; Memphis Blues; Euphonic Sounds (Joplin); St. Louis Blues.

JAMES P. JOHNSON was the father of stride piano. His highly rhythmic solos, buoyant in spirit, constantly rolling in motion, established a new integrity in the East Coast piano style. His right hand weaves in and out of the syncopated beats, wrapping them in tightly conceived, imaginative melodies, while his left hand propels the music like a piston, pumping furiously from an octave or a tenth in the bass register to a solidly hit middle-register chord. He is a facile inventor of catchy phrases, as on "Snowy Morning Blues" here, but his music has a meaning beyond entertainment, reflecting his serious nature. Johnson's solo-piano concept was carried on in the best work of his celebrated pupil Fats Waller, and his influence is also recognizable in the styles of Ellington and Thelonious Monk.

Johnson was born in New Brunswick, New Jersey, in either 1891 or 1894 —biographical sources disagree—and learned piano from his mother, who was active in the local Methodist choir. In his early teens, after the family had moved to New York, Johnson began playing ragtime and an early version of stride (influenced by Luckey Roberts and the legendary Abba Labba) at summer resorts on Long Island. Later on he studied with a classical music instructor, Bruno Giannini, from whom he learned harmony, counterpoint, and correct piano fingering at a dollar a lesson. Johnson developed a flawless, even athletic, technique, and his "glissandos in sixths and double tremolos . . . would run other ticklers out of the place at cutting sessions." Johnson admitted to adapting passages from Liszt as an introduction to a stomp, and dropping abruptly from loud to soft, imitating the dynamics of a Beethoven sonata.

In 1917 Johnson began to record piano rolls for Q.R.S., most of which are available on two Biograph LP's (General Discography). *James P. John-*

son, 1917–1921 contains two versions of his "Carolina Shout," which became a test piece for the pianists who followed him. Duke Ellington, who called it his "party piece," learned Johnson's version note for note by slowing down his player piano and watching how the keys went down. *James P. Johnson: Ragtime* is less interesting, save for a live track from 1939, which also appears on an excellent Columbia LP, *The Father of Stride Piano. The Father*, however, was regrettably deleted by Columbia in 1979.

Johnson's piano playing was seldom recorded during the 1920's because he was in great demand as a composer of black musical comedies. His hit tune "The Charleston" (1923) and revues like *Running Wild* led to his scoring short films, including the classic *St. Louis Blues* starring Bessie Smith. [Johnson can also be heard accompanying Bessie on *Nobody's Blues but Mine* (Chapter 3).] The bubble burst with the Depression, which forced Johnson into semiretirement. He began to work on several symphonic works ("Harlem Symphony," "Symphony in Brown"), which were performed but never recorded, and a long choral work, "Yamekraw" (General Discography), which made use of spirituals and some of his earlier show music.

The Original James P. Johnson is a small legacy of his piano style but a crucial one, especially now that the 1939 Columbia session and possibly a superior one made for Blue Note in 1943 are unavailable. Although Johnson had suffered a minor stroke in 1940, there is little evidence of diminished technical prowess. He was in fact working regularly in Greenwich Village at this time. The repertoire is a varied and thus an enlightening one. His melodies are of two basic types: the short, repetitive (ostinato) figures ("Twilight Rag") commonly used in blues piano; and the fast, flowing lines which proceed scalelike to an unexpected twist of direction or a sudden break. Seldom does one hear the sweeping, romantic intervals between notes one expects from the popular ballad. ("Blues for Jimmy" is the one exception here.) This does not mean there is minimal melodic content in Johnson's music, as some critics have maintained, but only that the melodic style is of a different sort.

The variety of influences which Johnson synthesized are detected on these cuts but are invariably transformed by his personal touch. The classic ragtime form dominates "Daintiness Rag," except for passages like the descending parallel chords in the third theme, a violation of counterpoint the midwestern composers would have scorned. But Johnson's harmonic imagination is assertive, as the virtuoso performance of Gershwin's "Liza" demonstrates. "Liza" also displays an excursion into contrary motion of the hands, a facility he acquired in playing Bach. Meanwhile, "St. Louis Blues" and "Keep Movin' " reveal his affinity for the drumlike left-hand style of the boogie-woogie pianists Jimmy Yancey, Meade Lux Lewis, and Albert Ammons. James P.'s inventiveness surfaces in the two versions of "Sweet Lorraine" and of "Jersey Sweet," in which his improvisation varies with each performance.

There is one more available Johnson session from this period—two sides of MCA's *Art Tatum Masterpieces, Volume II, and James P. Johnson Plays Fats Waller* (1944; see General Discography).

In the late 1940's Johnson turned to composing again, producing the show *Sugar Hill*, which ran for three months on Broadway. Orchestral writing continued to lure him, but a severe stroke in 1951 left him bedridden, unable to work or speak. He died in 1955, denied the recognition he sought as a symphonic composer. Among jazz musicians, however, the memory of him sitting at an upright piano in Harlem inspires nothing short of reverence.

FATS WALLER

Fats Waller Piano Solos, 1929–1941

Bluebird, AXM2-5518
two discs, liner notes

Musicians: Thomas "Fats" Waller, piano, accompanied by Benny Payne, piano, on "St. Louis Blues" and "After You've Gone" only.

Compositions (music by Waller unless otherwise indicated): *Side one:* Handful of Keys; Numb Fumblin'; Ain't Misbehavin'; Sweet Savannah Sue; I've Got a Feeling I'm Falling; Love Me or Leave Me (Donaldson-Gus); Gladyse; Valentine Stomp. *Side two:* Waitin' At the End of the Road (Berlin); Baby, Oh Where Can You Be? (Magine-Koehler); Goin' About; My Feelings Are Hurt; Smashing Thirds; My Fate Is in Your Hands; Turn on the Heat (DeSylva-Brown-Henderson); St. Louis Blues (Handy). *Side three:* After You've Gone (Creamer-Layton); African Ripples; Clothes Line Ballet; Alligator Crawl; Viper's Drag; Russian Fantasy; E-Flat Blues; Keepin' Out of Mischief Now; Stardust (Carmichael). *Side four:* Tea for Two (Youmans); Basin Street Blues (Williams); I Ain't Got Nobody (Williams-Graham); Georgia on My Mind (Carmichael); Rockin' Chair (Carmichael); Carolina Shout (James P. Johnson); Honeysuckle Rose; Ring Dem Bells (Ellington-Mills).

IF JAMES P. JOHNSON was the father of stride piano, Thomas "Fats" Waller, Johnson's protégé, was its favorite son. In fact, he was too popular for his own good. With song royalties, Broadway shows, his own radio show, and, eventually, film roles being cast in his path like garlands, it should not be surprising that he strayed from his real musical identity. RCA Victor did not help by recording him with the most desultory inconsistency. Fats became an accompanist, a bandleader, and the tongue-in-cheek purveyor of original

show tunes which he could literally whip up in minutes. Somewhere in the wax morgue of RCA there lies a disc of Fats performing Bach fugues too, though that session never saw the light of day. Waller's talent bubbled over in everything he touched. He also had an indefatigable appetite for food, drink, fun, and high living. As an entertainer, he was an unbeatable combination.

But Fats Waller the pianist, a major influence upon Earl Hines, Count Basie, and Art Tatum, nearly disappeared. Not counting his early piano rolls (the Biograph albums, General Discography) cut under the aegis of Johnson, there are no more than a few dozen piano solos in nearly fifteen years of recording. Of course, these are priceless gems and reveal in profusion the joyous moments Waller was capable of. Thus *Piano Solos* is the essential Waller album, for which some credit is due producer Frank Driggs, who chose to package all the solo tracks together. Consequently, all the sessions of Fats Waller and His Rhythm—the quintet he maintained throughout his career—are on *The Complete Fats Waller, Volume 1, 1934–1935,* a decidedly commercial anthology. The remaining RCA reissue, *A Legendary Performer* (one disc), contains three solos already on *Piano Solos,* a few later Rhythm tracks, and the only available Waller cut of "Jitterbug Waltz" (1942), probably the first jazz composition written in $\frac{3}{4}$ time.

Fats may have been a *bon vivant,* but he was extremely conscientious about his music. Born in 1904 in New York, Waller studied piano with his mother, who started him on the European classics. As he began to learn pieces like James P. Johnson's "Carolina Shout" on his own by ear, his father, a clergyman, tried to wean him from ragtime, which he considered "the Devil's music." As an antidote, his father took him to hear Paderewski perform at Carnegie Hall in 1915. But Fats never lost interest in either ragtime or European music, and he would later study privately with the classical master Leopold Godowsky.

Fats also played at his father's Abyssinian Baptist Church, where he learned to perform impressively on the Hammond organ and pipe organ. At sixteen he played regularly for the silent movies on a $10,000 Wurlitzer grand at the Lincoln Theater in Harlem. One of his fans was the young William "Count" Basie, who learned to play the organ from Fats during that year. Waller was the first pianist to adapt the organ to jazz, turning in his best recorded performance in 1939, accompanying his own vocals, on Deluxe's *Fine Arabian Stuff.*

Waller's proficiency introduced him to the inner circle of Harlem rent-party and cutting-contest champions like James P., with whom he began to study quite seriously. Johnson's wife frequently had to ask young Thomas to leave their home because he liked to practice on his teacher's piano until well past midnight. By the time *Piano Solos* was recorded, Waller had made dozens of piano rolls, proving himself as awesome a stride artist as Johnson himself, and noticeably less bound by the roots of the style.

The brilliant "Handful of Keys" and "Numb Fumblin' " provide an excellent introduction to Waller's playing. They were waxed "after a long night of serious drinking and a morning of hasty mental sketching of material for the date." [20] Nevertheless, the results are stupendous. The first is a "shout"— glib, spontaneous, and joyous; the second, a blues of thick, meaty chords and liquid lines. Waller told *Metronome* magazine in 1935 that the left hand held the key to the style:

> Formerly, the right hand was given all the work and the other hand left to shift for itself, thumping out a plain octave or chord foundation. There was no attempt at figuration. But that is all in the past. Now it's more evenly divided and the left hand has to know its stuff, its chords and its figuration . . . I consider the thorough bass foundation I got in the study of Bach the best part of my training.[21]

The stride left hand is the underpinning for one of the most magnificent cross-rhythms obtainable on the piano, and the most contemporary pianists will still revert to its original form. The rousing fireworks of "Smashing Thirds" is another high point of the stride style, and was spontaneously conceived minutes before it was recorded. Fats was a fountain of melodies, copyrighting some four hundred songs in his nineteen years as a composer.

Like James P., Fats liked to borrow from the classics, as we hear in the lush, romantic harmonies of "Ain't Misbehavin'," probably his best show tune. In the first improvised chorus we hear some of the chord transitions Art Tatum (Chapter 4) was to develop to a florid degree. Waller reveals his structural awareness in "Valentine Stomp," essentially a rag of five distinct themes that holds together miraculously. Yet the delicate, open-textured "Clothes Line Ballet," a beautifully whimsical piece, seems to have no origin other than Waller's fertile imagination.

Waller commands an entire spectrum of moods in the kaleidoscopic version of "Honeysuckle Rose," one of his most memorable compositions. Its melody is exquisitely raggy, and the arrangement here, like Waller himself, seems to be heading in several directions simultaneously. That is the source of its excitement and its weakness. Like the album cover, the track is a collage of his many faces, all of them radiant, lovable, and perhaps a shade too insouciant.

Fats, a nickname which had stuck with him since high school, was prodigious in more than technique and compositional facility. For most of his life, his five-foot eleven-inch frame endured 285 pounds. He was, however, blessed with a pianist's large hands, capable of spanning thirteen keys to the average man's ten. The blind pianist George Shearing once remarked that shaking Waller's hands felt like grabbing a bunch of bananas. Waller's size became a liability in another sense, for it gave him more of himself to abuse. At his best he was nonchalant about his health, but normally his eating, drinking, and capacity to entertain knew no limits. In 1943 shortly after the opening of *Stormy Weather*—in which, according to some critics, he stole the show by simply raising an eyebrow—Waller died on a train trip from Hollywood to New York, a victim of influenza and a history of binges. His piano solos attest to the gaiety and genius he held in his great hands for thirty-nine short years.

References and Notes

1. Rudi Blesh and Harriet Janis, *They All Played Ragtime* (New York: Oak Publications, Inc., 1971), p. 96. This volume, originally published by Alfred A. Knopf, Inc., New York, in 1950, was the first major work of research on the ragtime era, its data compiled while many first-hand witnesses were still living.

2. Rex Harris, *Jazz* (Baltimore: Penguin Books, Inc., 1952), p. 60.

3. *Ibid.*

4. Sigmund Spaeth, *A History of Popular Music in America* (New York: Random House, Inc., 1948), p. 71.

5. As quoted in John Storm Roberts, *Black Music of Two Worlds* (New York: William Morrow & Co., Inc., 1974), p. 199.

6. Blesh and Janis, *op. cit.*, p. 130ff.

7. Maude Cuney-Hare, *Negro Musicians and Their Music* (Washington, D.C.: Associated Publishers, 1936), pp. 133–134. This book is a delightful compendium of common fallacies about jazz and other forms of black American music. For example, on page 140 the author refers to W. C. Handy as "the originator of the blues."

8. LeRoi Jones, *Blues People* (New York: William Morrow & Co., Inc., 1963), p. 148.

9. *Ibid.*, p. 90.

10. David Jasen and Trebor Tichenor, *Rags and Ragtime* (New York: The Seabury Press, Inc., 1978), p. 6n.

11. Jones's assessment of ragtime as being more formalized and less spontaneous than later jazz is correct. It is maintained here, however, that ragtime must be heard as part of jazz in spite of these characteristics.

12. Blesh and Janis, *op. cit.*, p. 188.

13. *Ibid.*, p. 190.

14. Richard Hadlock, *Jazz Masters of the Twenties* (New York: Macmillan, Inc., 1974), p. 146.

15. *Ibid.*, p. 147.

16. Blesh and Janis, *op. cit.*, p. 243.

17. Jasen and Tichenor, *op. cit.*, p. 112.

18. James Haskins, *Scott Joplin: The Man Who Made Ragtime* (New York: Doubleday & Co., 1978), pp. 153–154.

19. Blesh and Janis, *op. cit.*, p. 197.

20. Hadlock, *op. cit.*, p. 157.

21. *Ibid.*, p. 153.

General Discography of Available, Recommended Albums

Classic Ragtime

WILLIAM BOLCOM
> *Heliotrope Bouquet*, H-71257, Nonesuch. *Bolcom Plays His Own Rags*, JCE-72, Jazzology.

JOE "FINGERS" CARR
> *Plays the Classics*, T-649, Capitol.

ANN CHARTERS
> *A Joplin Bouquet*, 9021, GNP Crescendo. *Essay in Ragtime*, FG-3453, Folkways. *The Genius of Scott Joplin*, 9032, GNP Crescendo.

BOB DARCH
> *Ragtime Piano*, UAL-3120, United Artists.

DICK HYMAN
> *Scott Joplin: The Complete Works for Piano*, CRL5-1106, RCA.

SCOTT JOPLIN (as composer, not pianist)
> *Scott Joplin: The Entertainer*, BLP-1013Q, Biograph. *Elite Syncopations*, BLP-1014Q, Biograph. *Classic Rags Composed by the King of Ragtime Writers*, BLP-1008Q, Biograph. *Rare Piano Roll Recordings*, BLP-1010Q, Biograph.

JOSEPH LAMB
> *A Study in Classic Ragtime*, FG 3562, Folkways.

MAX MORATH
> *The World of Scott Joplin, Vol. 3*, SRV-351SD, Vanguard. *The Best of Scott Joplin and Others*, VSD 39/40, Vanguard. *Irving Berlin: The Ragtime Years* (vocals), VSD-79346, Vanguard. *Max Morath Plays Ragtime*, VSD 83/84, Vanguard.

ITZHAK PERLMAN and ANDRÉ PREVIN
> *The Easy Winners* (violin/piano), 5-37113, Angel.

JOSHUA RIFKIN
> *Piano Rags by Scott Joplin, Vols. I, II,* and *III*, H-71248, H-71264, H-71305, Nonesuch.

GUNTHER SCHULLER
> *The Red Back Book* (orchestrated rags), 5-36060, Angel.

JAMES SCOTT
> *James Scott: Classic Ragtime*, BLP-1016Q, Biograph.

DICK WELLSTOOD
> (See Harlem Ragtime.)

MISCELLANEOUS
> *They All Played Ragtime* (Trebor Tichenor), JCE-73, Jazzology. *The New*

Orleans Ragtime Orchestra: Grace and Beauty, DS-214, Delmark. *Classic Rags and Ragtime Songs* (arranged by T. J. Anderson), N-001, Smithsonian Collection (mail). *Scott Joplin: Magnetic Rag, The Southland Stingers* (orchestrated), S-36078, Angel. *The Sting: Original Ragtime Piano Originals*, RF-23; *Ragtime Piano Interpretations*, RF-24; *Early Piano Ragtime, 1913–1930*, RF-33; *Late Piano Ragtime* (compiled by David Jasen), RF-35; Folkways. *Fiedler in Rags* (Boston Pops), PD-6033, Polydor. *The Entertainer*, 2115, MCA. *Palm Leaf Rag* (Stingers; orchestrated), S-37113, Angel.

Harlem Ragtime/Stride Piano

EUBIE BLAKE
Eubie Blake, EBM-1; *Rags to Classics*, EBM-2; *Live Concert*, EBM-5; Eubie Blake Music (Address: 284-A Stuyvesant Avenue, Brooklyn, N.Y. 11211). *Blues and Ragtime* (rolls), BLP-1011Q; *Blues and Spirituals* (rolls), BLP-1012Q; Biograph. *The Wizard of the Ragtime Piano*, 3003, 20th Century-Fox. Eubie Blake Music catalog numbers EBM-3, -4, -6, -7, -8, and -9 (write for catalog). *Wild About Eubie* (Joan Morris, vocals), 34504, Columbia. *Eubie!* (a revue), HS-3267, Warner Brothers.

JAMES P. JOHNSON
Father of Stride Piano (deleted, 1979). *Parlor Piano Solos from Rare Rolls, 1917–1921*; *Earliest Ragtime Piano Rolls, 1917—Vol. 2*; Biograph. *Yamekra*, FS-2842, Folkways. *Art Tatum Masterpieces, Volume II, and James P. Johnson Plays Fats Waller*, MCA2-4112, MCA.

WILLIE "THE LION" SMITH
Live at Blues Alley (club date, informal), CR-104, Chiaroscuro. *Willie "The Lion" Smith*, GNPS-9011, GNP Crescendo.

RALPH SUTTON
Ragtime, U.S.A., R-25232, Roulette.

FATS WALLER
The Complete Fats Waller, Vol. 1, 1934–1935 (with Rhythm), SXM 2-551, RCA. *A Legendary Performer* (photo-liner booklet), CPL-1-2904e, RCA. *Piano Rolls, Vol. 1, 1923–1924*, BLP-1002Q; *Piano Rolls, Vol. 2, 1924–1931*, BLP-1005Q; *Piano Rolls, Vol. 3*, BPL-1015Q; Biograph. *Fine Arabian Stuff* (piano/organ/vocals), DE-601, Muse. *Ain't Misbehavin'* (Broadway musical, 1978, original cast), CBL-2-2965, RCA.

DICK WELLSTOOD
Alone, JCE-73, Jazzology. *Live at the Cookery*, CR-139, Chiaroscuro.

MISCELLANEOUS
Parlor Piano (rolls), BLP-1001Q, Biograph. *Black & White Piano Ragtime* (various artists, 1921–1939), BLP-12047, Biograph. *Early Piano Ragtime, 1913–1930*, RF-33, Folkways.

NEW ORLEANS, DIXIELAND, AND THE JAZZ SOLO

New Orleans and "The Jazz Age"

F. SCOTT FITZGERALD dubbed the 1920's "the jazz age" for America's frantic buying spree, sexual awakening, and reckless optimism after World War I. Of course, every decade of the century has been a jazz age of some sort so far as the music is concerned, but Fitzgerald understood little of jazz as music. For him, it was all mood. Nevertheless, he was correct to assume an inevitable connection between the mood of the country and the way its music would evolve.

In addition to fueling its emotional verve, the 1920's affected jazz in practical ways. Prohibition caused drinking to be concentrated in dives, private clubs, and "speaks," where a band was always in demand—the hotter the better. The buying fervor encouraged new companies like Okeh, Gennett, Victor, Paramount, Vocalion, Decca, and Columbia Gramophone to market records in volume. In 1921 alone, record sales totaled $100 million. The figure is dwarfed by the $3.8 billion total for American sales in 1978, but it was a bumper year for an industry just getting started. Records were not marketed en masse as they are today. Individual stores were, in effect, franchised by the companies, of which there were fewer than a dozen, and thus the retailer never carried competing labels. Music from the Afro-American tradition was classified as "race music" and was not available outside the ghetto. It is a testimony to the power of jazz that in spite of these limitations its records sold in the millions and had an impact more far-reaching than anything else being cut in wax.[1]

In 1925 electronic sound reproduction by means of a condenser microphone brought a greater variety of instruments into the recording studio (in jazz, notably the drummer's kit) and captured them with improved fidelity. For the first time bands were formed—like Louis Armstrong's Hot

Five and Jelly Roll Morton's Red Hot Peppers—not to play for people but for the electronic "ear" of American technology. With the coming of jazz records, musical innovations were circulated more quickly and stylistic development accelerated accordingly.

The New Orleans style had begun around 1900 with brass ensembles which, like ragtime, took the marching military bands as their models. In addition to cornets, trombones, and an occasional tuba, these groups included clarinets, banjos or guitars, and fiddles. The bass and the piano were excluded because of their size, although the piano was a popular solo instrument in the dives, honky-tonks, and "sporting houses." The marching bands were famous for accompanying funeral processions back from the cemetery with a spirited version of "Didn't He Ramble (Before the Butcher Cut Him Down)?"; however, they played at all sorts of functions from picnics to "breakdowns" (community dances). There was a virtual academy of music in the streets of New Orleans, dominated by legendary aggregations of black and Creole musicians, most of whom worked simultaneously as laborers and artisans. Buddy Bolden's band with Bunk Johnson was playing in honky-tonks as early as 1895, and the Olympia Brass Band existed on and off from 1900 to 1915 led by cornetist Freddie Keppard, with Joe Oliver playing second cornet and Alphonse Picou, Sidney Bechet, and Lorenzo Tio on clarinets. Oscar "Papa" Celestin formed the Original Tuxedo Orchestra in 1910. Keppard later led the Original Creole Band, while Joe Oliver worked for trombonist Kid Ory in his Brownskin Band. When Oliver left for Chicago, as Keppard had done, Louis Armstrong replaced him on cornet. There were probably a hundred of these seminal groups, and their players seemed infinitely interchangeable. All of them understood the basic premise of the music: collective improvisation.

The improvisation of multiple melodic voices simultaneously, known as "polyphony," was the major characteristic of early New Orleans music and an innovation in western music as well. The musicians improvised collectively in a way that complemented each other without duplication of musical parts. Like an indigenous African ensemble, the various instrumental voices coalesced while their melodic statements diverged. The sound was rougher and more swinging than ragtime. The feeling of four beats to a measure, instead of the stiff oompah of $\frac{2}{4}$ marches, was common in later New Orleans music and may have cropped up here and there in pre-recording days. The influence of the Caribbean and the Crescent City's cultural background was heard in what Jelly Roll Morton referred to as "the Spanish tinge," the Latin beats which are still a part of jazz. Lastly, the blues, which had saturated New Orleans, colored the music in a way that transformed even the ragtime repertoire into a markedly new sound.

The ragtimers, incidentally, were by no means unanimously in favor of these innovations. The roughness of New Orleans playing irked their classic sense of form, and the $\frac{4}{4}$ beat seemed rushed to them. For these reasons John Stillwell Stark, publisher of the great Scotts (Scott Joplin, Scott Hayden, and James Scott), insisted that a later rag by James Scott be entitled "Don't Jazz Me—Rag (I'm Music)."

But there were even greater transitions under way within five years of the first black jazz group's recording in the early 1920's. (The recording of white New Orleans jazz, known as Dixieland, had begun in 1917.) The unprecedented abilities of Louis Armstrong—his technical mastery, sense of form, and imagination—fashioned the role of the improvising soloist. He was the first player who did not, perhaps *could* not, submerge himself in the band but used it instead as a backdrop for his own personal expression. Improvisation soon came to mean extemporaneous composition within the harmonies of the original theme, rather than simple embellishment of the melodic line. In *Music: Black, White & Blue*, Ortiz M. Walton suggests that soloing marks a major departure of jazz from its African origins, in which music remained more collective and democratically participatory. The emergence of the soloist, he speculates, was motivated by the black American's need to prove and distinguish himself as an individual, for to white society he had no identity other than his blackness. Of course, this sort of theory, while worth keeping in mind, evades any conclusive proof or refutation. But regardless of its psychosocial motivation, soloing—after Armstrong—became the high point of jazz performance for thirty-five years. (After 1960 collective improvisation was again adopted in the strikingly new idiom of free jazz, to be discussed in Chapter 8.)

New Orleans musicians also mastered the blues tonality, absorbing it so thoroughly that there is occasionally no demarcation possible between the blues and early jazz. As late as the mid-1920's, for example, Bessie Smith (Selected Discography) could be described with equal justification as the first jazz singer and the Empress of the Blues. At the same time, jazz began to adopt uniquely structured compositional forms, transcending the march, ragtime, and blues formulas. Jelly Roll Morton (Selected Discography) was the first to arrange and compose for a band in a jazz idiom, making brilliant use of contrasting instrumental colors and the crucial stop-time device known as the "break." Breaks in ensemble playing open up space for a single instrumental statement. They were probably the forerunners of solo improvisations.

Although New Orleans techniques sound traditional decades later, there is a freshness and energy in this music that has not aged at all. The music is full of color and life; it is effervescent, even lusty. Above all, its style is very much a product of the multicultural city—and the wild night life—in which it matured.

Music, Hot as Sin!

In 1900 the city of New Orleans was opulent, erotic, bawdy, and daring in spirit. Jazz was its music. It took the U.S. Department of the Navy to close down its tenderloin once and for all in 1917. Yet New Orleans was also fertile ground for the blossoming of jazz for historical reasons. Governed first by the Spanish and then by the French prior to the purchase of the Louisiana Territory in 1803, La Nouvelle Orléans (now a section of the city known as the French Quarter, or the Vieux Carré) was the paragon of cultural pluralism. One heard the strains of quadrilles, waltzes, mazurkas, polkas, marches, blues, and European and Afro-American church music during most of the nineteenth century. The opera was thriving, and the *bamboula*, a dance to an African drum of the same name, was enjoyed by both races in Congo Square. The rhythm of the dance, which involved the stamping of bare feet, was probably the predecessor of the "stomps" heard on many of the New Orleans albums.

The city was predominantly Catholic. Since the Church held that all men were equal before God, black and white frequently worshipped together even before the Civil War. There was, in fact, much more segregation after 1900 than before 1800. French and Spanish masters were inclined to free their slaves after years of service. Racially mixed family lines became increasingly common, and a large group of light-skinned blacks known as Creoles soon traced their lineage back to this Euro-African ancestry. According to the 1860 census, there were 400,000 Creoles in Louisiana. They were freed long before their black "cousins," and their French and Spanish surnames appeared on church registries followed by the letters F.M.C., for "Free Man of Color."

The chasm between Creoles living downtown as artisans and shopkeepers, and uptown blacks laboring in the fields or on the levees was in its own way as broad as that separating blacks from whites. Their musical environments reflected the disparity. Creoles read music and studied it formally. They patronized the opera and concert hall. Blacks, however, were self-taught improvisers for whom the blues was a primary folk music; European classics meant little to them. The spirit of competition was occasionally nasty. Jelly Roll Morton, a Creole whose name at birth was Ferdinand La-Menthe, Jr., spoke disparagingly of "black Negroes" because they couldn't stick to "those little black dots" on his scores. Blacks were known to the Creoles as "fakers" for their extemporaneous playing. In *Mister Jelly Roll*, the guitarist Johnny St. Cyr told Alan Lomax: "The mulattoes were actually more prejudiced than the white people of that time." [2] There was also animosity on the other side of town: the blacks accused the "high yaller" Creoles of practicing *passé blanc* and trying to deny their own origins.

Symbolically enough, the tenderloin, the hotbed of New Orleans jazz, lay precisely along Canal Street, the downtown and uptown dividing line. It was bisected by Basin Street, running past the French Opera House on the Creole side and the honky-tonks on the Negro side. The district took the name Storyville to the chagrin of the crusading politician, Sidney Story, who initiated the ordinance in 1896 confining prostitution to its thirty-eight blocks.

Storyville enjoyed most of the vices known to western civilization and may have invented a few of its own. According to Jelly Roll's vivid depiction of the neighborhood as it was in 1902 when he was working there as a seventeen-year-old "professor" (piano player) in the "mansions" (brothels), music poured into the streets all night long; the "chippies in their little girl dresses were standing in the crib doors singing the blues"; diamonds, "coke," and "hop" were common sights; and the mansions themselves had ornate mirrors at the feet and heads of all the beds.[3] Morton began to work in this orgiastic environment at the age of thirteen, receiving up to a hundred dollars a day in pay.[4] Although Morton had a well-known compulsion to exaggerate, his account is consistent with other tales of the district. To the musicians of New Orleans, the tenderloin was both a spawning ground and a gold mine.

If there was anything that could bring the prideful Creole and robust black together in New Orleans, it was the growing white population which viewed colored citizens of any shade or hue as inferior and threatening. In 1894 the enactment of Code No. 111 invoked "white supremacy" and effectively evicted Creoles from the white downtown area. As they gradually and reluctantly emigrated uptown, Creoles and blacks found their musical traditions beginning to mingle. The Creoles learned to their dismay that they had to play "rowdy" like Buddy Bolden to get any of the Storyville jobs. "See, us Downtown people, we didn't think so much of this Uptown Jazz until we couldn't make a living otherwise," old Paul Dominguez bitterly complained to Alan Lomax. The district transformed him from a violinist into a fiddler. Yet his anger was tinged with admiration: "Bolden cause all that . . . He cause these younger Creoles, men like Bechet and Keppard, to have a different style altogether from the old heads like Tio and Perez. I don't know how they do it . . . But Goddam, they'll do it. Can't tell you what's there on paper, but just play the hell out of it. . . ."[5]

The most touching stories are of the younger Creole students learning to improvise in the rough, spirited style under the tutelage of the black band-leaders. Alphonse Picou, who had studied clarinet formally, recounted his initiation to Nat Hentoff and Nat Shapiro for their compendium of interviews *Hear Me Talkin' to Ya*. Boo Fortunea, a trombonist (and a barber by trade) had invited Alphonse to a band rehearsal, after hearing the sixteen-year-old practicing in his room:

> "Is there any music?" He said "Music? You don't need none." I said, "How am I going to play?" He said, "You're going to come in on the choruses." . . . He said that when I couldn't come in, to stay out and listen until I could come in. I did just what he told me and we got into it, and through with it, and the whole band shook my hand and told me I was great.[6]

If blacks liberated Creoles from the tyranny of the printed score, Creoles offered something of nearly equal value in return—a disciplined technique, a familiarity with European harmony, and the ability to arrange and structure music. Both groups shared a common African heritage, an approach to music as an integral part of life. The sophistication of Sidney Bechet, Jelly Roll Morton (LaMenthe), Alphonse Picou, and Papa Celestin was crucial in making full use of the power and guts of Buddy Bolden, Bunk Johnson, King Oliver, and Louis Armstrong. It was an explosive, fecund combination, summed up well by Alan Lomax: "This is the master formula of jazz—mulatto (Creole) knowingness ripened by black sorrow." [7]

The opportunities presented by Storyville were only a part of the environment so hospitable to jazz. Dozens of social clubs and fraternal orders supported the music by hiring bands at the slightest provocation—from picnics to funerals. According to the banjo player Danny Barker,

> It was not rare to see funerals which had three or four brass bands in the procession, because a member probably was active in eight to twelve organizations . . . It was more than likely his request to be buried as he lived, among a crowd and lots of music.[8]

In *Music: Black, White & Blue*, Ortiz M. Walton interprets the abundance of these clubs in New Orleans as a means of relieving black "status anxiety." Marshall Stearns interprets the funeral bands as an "appeasement" of the deceased, a vestige of African ancestor worship. These are interesting hypotheses, but there is a more practical level of explanation. The clubs were in fact self-help groups, not only ensuring a proper burial but caring for the sick, providing emergency funds, planning annual social events and dances. Although it was not their *raison d'être*, one of the club's principal activities became the engaging of bands.

Aside from the music New Orleans pumped into the American mainstream, its related traditions donated several expressions to our vernacular. For example, a dance was advertised by pulling the band through town playing on a horse-drawn wagon. A painted sign told everyone when and where the dance would be held, while the band gave them a taste of the hot music they could expect. Sometimes the bands for competing dances would pull alongside each other and try to play their rivals down. In any case, the musicians not working usually drank together to pass the time. Thus if a musician was not drinking, he was said to be "on the wagon." Not surprisingly, the trombonist in the group had to stand in the back so that he could let his slide out over the tailgate, which is why the instrument was called "tailgate trombone." The brothels which employed pianists were also known as juke joints, or juke houses. Morton refers to them this way in recalling his earliest haunts. Lorenzo Turner, an authority on African loan words, says that *juke* is a corruption of a term from a language of Senegal, *dzug*, which means to lead a disorderly life or misconduct oneself.[9] As late as 1945 a Georgia grand jury charged that houses of ill repute "generally referred to as *jouk-joints*

have become a menace to society and the welfare of the people." [10] The word
has since dropped its whorehouse connotation, but it retains its connection
to the music played at roadside houses in the "juke box."

Chicago, Chicago!

In the paranoia of a world war and with prohibitionist fervor goading
America's puritanical conscience, Storyville's red lights seemed to wink too
seductively at the sailors protecting the Gulf of Mexico and the mouth of the
Mississippi River. Josephus Daniels, Secretary of the Navy, issued an order
prohibiting open prostitution within five miles of any naval base. New
Orleans was the prime target of the order. What Sidney Story had set in
motion in 1896 as a local movement had to be finished by the federal government from Washington, D.C. On November 14, 1917, the lights were
snuffed out.

The mansions and tonks closed down, although it was jazz, not prostitution, that fell victim. It was easy to move sex to more clandestine quarters,
but music was deprived of the night life which had been its lifeblood. Jazz,
however, was already on its feet and on the move. By one year after Storyville's demise, most of the best musicians had left town: Jelly Roll Morton;
Freddie Keppard; Jimmy Noone; Sidney Bechet; Johnny Dodds and his
brother, "Baby" Dodds; Johnny St. Cyr; and Joe "King" Oliver. Louis
Armstrong, who was in his early twenties, remained. He had inherited the
lead cornet spot in Kid Ory's Brownskin Band when Joe Oliver left to work
in Chicago with Freddie Keppard.

Chicago was not the only destination of the new itinerant musicians.
They traveled from New York to Los Angeles, disseminating what they believed was an indigenous New Orleans sound only to find it identified as
somehow "typically American." Occasionally provincialism got the better
of them. While Jelly Roll Morton was in Los Angeles in 1918, he sent for
three New Orleans musicians (Buddy Petit, Frankie Dusen, and Wade
Waley) to play with him at a popular restaurant in Watts. They arrived in
boxback coats and skintight pants, considered stylish in old Storyville.
Buddy's trumpet was in his suitcase, Dusen's trombone was wrapped in
newspaper, and Waley's clarinet was in sections in his pockets. On the job
the three visitors insisted upon cooking a bucket of red beans and rice they
had brought along, as they had always done in the tonks of Perdido Street.
Morton tried to shame them into abandoning their custom, and in retaliation
Petit and Dusen threatened to kill him, but instead left California the next
day without notice. Fortunately, most musicians were assimilated into the
American mainstream with less difficulty.

Chicago, though, was the new secular mecca. The showboats of the Mississippi had long been regular employers of New Orleans entertainment, and
the waterway was a cheap and familiar route north. Blacks had begun to see

sharecropping as a disappointment and a dead end. Chicago's wings were spreading; there were stories then that cash flowed like booze in the speakeasies, and blacks were called "Mister" and "Missus" like everyone else. Between 1917 and 1922, 400,000 blacks moved from the South to Chicago. Jazz had its natural-born audience there. What the musicians never suspected was that the white fans would soon greatly outnumber them, and that white musicians would absorb, or at worst imitate, the New Orleans style and record it themselves under the lucrative banner of Dixieland.

In 1922 Joe "King" Oliver's group became the first of the black bands to record. Louis Armstrong, whom Oliver had sent for, joined him for the recording and moved in with Oliver's family when he arrived in Chicago. He felt intimidated by the size and fast pace of Chicago and, equally, by the reputation of Oliver's band. Armstrong was also homesick for the New Orleans bands, as a personal letter, printed in the liner notes to *King Oliver's Jazz Band, 1923*, reveals:

> I heard all about you all having all those funerals down there. I'm sorry I ain't down there to make some of them with you all. The boys give me h . . . all the time because (I'm) forever talking about the Brass band and how I youster like to make these parades. . . .

The transition from the Oliver-Armstrong collective improvisational style to Louis's innovative soloing is the subject of the album discussions in the Selected Discography.

Way Up North, in Dixie

Dixieland jazz, a white musicians' derivative of New Orleans-style playing, has suffered in recent years from a kind of reverse racism. The stigma of being white has led to the style's dismissal by some critics as a movement of charlatans, or, at best, uniformly incompetent imitators. There is some truth in this point of view, but also much exaggeration. While black musicians are—not surprisingly—the major innovators in an Afro-American idiom, it does not follow that players of any other extraction are necessarily inept or of no consequence. In fact, white and Oriental players are using the jazz language with increasing fluency and authenticity in the modern and contemporary periods. Even in the music's early years, a distinction must be made between the collectively improvisational New Orleans Rhythm Kings (NORK) and the stiff, commercial Original Dixieland Jass Band (ODJB); and, similarly, between cornetists Bix Beiderbecke (Selected Discography), Jimmy McPartland, and Bobby Hackett; trombonist Jack Teagarden; clarinetist Pee Wee Russell (these last four the so-called Chicago stylists) and lightweight entertainers whose albums will not be listed in this book.

Nevertheless, Dixieland's success in the early years far outstripped its contribution to the music. Didactic jazz historians find it ironic that the ODJB was the first New Orleans group to record ("Dixie Jass Band One-Step," for Victor in 1917). Understandably so! For there was nothing original about the Original Dixieland Jass Band save for their overnight commercial success. Their million-seller "Livery Stable Blues," also known as "Barnyard Blues," featured instrumental imitations of a crowing rooster, braying donkey, and whinnying horse—novelty effects which Buddy Bolden's band had indulged in at the turn of the century. Furthermore, their rhythm was jerky, and improvisation occurred, if at all, only on occasion in live performance. It has also been argued speculatively that Dixieland retarded the progress of jazz by pressuring the early black recording bands—King Oliver's Creole Jazz Band, for example—into imitating their imitators. In any case the ODJB produced nothing worth preserving except for historical reasons. In that regard RCA's *The Best of Dixieland* (General Discography), a good anthology of twelve Dixieland groups, includes an electronically salvaged reissue of the ODJB's "Livery Stable Blues."

Interestingly, a black band could have garnered the distinction of being the first to record jazz. Cornetist Freddie Keppard's Original Creole Band was the first to be offered a contract by Victor, but Keppard, fearing his material and style would be copied, rejected the idea.[11]

The New Orleans Rhythm Kings (General Discography) were a more auspicious exponent of the Crescent City style, playing with a smoother rhythm and more improvisation, and with an acknowledged respect for the blacks they emulated. The band, which varied its personnel, was built around three New Orleanians: Paul Mares on cornet, Leon Rappolo on clarinet, and George Brunis on trombone. Their lasting contribution to jazz, however, is in their influence upon Bix Beiderbecke, an intense and contemplative stylist whose originality of tone and phrasing on cornet attracted even the black instrumentalists of the day. In Chicago Bix had a cult following, or nearly so, known as the Austin High School Gang, including cornetist Jimmy Mc-Partland, clarinetist Frank Teschemacher, and tenor saxophonist Bud Freeman. In New York a "modernist" Dixieland clique, which worked from the Beiderbecke repertoire, included Eddie Condon on guitar, Max Kaminsky on trumpet, and Pee Wee Russell on clarinet. Bix's descendants could be extended to encompass the Dorsey brothers, drummer Gene Krupa (with Benny Goodman, Chapter 4), and several other prominent white players who eventually became entrenched in other styles. The significance of this lineage is that it attests to the spread of jazz among white musicians, most of whom had never been to the dynamic, fertile city where the soul of their music had been conceived.

The most flagrant misrepresentation of early jazz was probably committed by Paul Whiteman (born, coincidentally, with the perfect surname), whose twenty- to thirty-piece orchestra dressed in formal attire to play a kind of sweet, quasi-symphonic "jumbo" jazz. Although Whiteman's bands included at various times soloists like Beiderbecke, saxophonist Frankie Trumbauer, the Dorsey brothers, violinist Joe Venuti, guitarist Eddie Lang, and vibraharpist Red Norvo, improvising was virtually eliminated in favor of popularized orchestration. To that extent the Paul Whiteman Orchestra can be construed as a precursor to the worst of jazz/pop in the 1970's. Unfortunately, Whiteman, who starred in a 1930 film called *The King of Jazz*, persuaded many Americans of his generation (like F. Scott Fitzgerald) that his extravaganza was the real thing.

The swan song of the Dixieland style began in 1942, when Bunk Johnson, discovered picking vegetables on a farm in the South, was resurrected as the figurehead of a New Orleans revival. Johnson, who had played with Buddy Bolden's band (thought to be the first to play jazz) recorded the sound of his cornet for the first time at the age of sixty. However, his embouchure was gone, and his embittered personality prevented him from working regularly with anyone. Bunk was briefly hosted by the West Coast Yerba Buena Jazz Band of Turk Murphy and Lu Watters, (General Discography), which managed to stimulate on its own a renewed interest in early New Orleans music. They rejected the *nouveau* Dixieland of Eddie Condon, Pee Wee Russell, and other "modernists," dedicating themselves to the authentic styles and compositions of Kid Ory, King Oliver, and Jelly Roll Morton. At least one dormant career was revived successfully, that of clarinetist George Lewis (General Discography), whose musicianship remained undiminished from his pre-1920 days with Buddy Petit's Black and Tan Band.

By the 1970's Dixieland had become ossified, with a provincial following here and there, from Earthquake McGoon's in San Francisco—the home of Turk Murphy's ensemble—to Preservation Hall in New Orleans, where the Preservation Hall Jazz Band (General Discography) is a major tourist attraction. The New Orleans style of Armstrong and King Oliver, however, has undergone a fascinating transformation in contemporary jazz, which has revived the technique of collective improvisation. The collectivism of early New Orleans, which will be examined once again in Chapter 8, has become the backbone of the most advanced free jazz.

**KING OLIVER and HIS
CREOLE JAZZ BAND**

King Oliver's Jazz Band, 1923

Smithsonian Collection, R-001
two discs, excellent liner notes
(mail order, see Appendix)

Musicians: Joe "King" Oliver's Creole Jazz Band. Oliver, cornet; Louis Armstrong, cornet; Jimmy Noone, clarinet; Johnny St. Cyr, banjo; Warren "Baby" Dodds, drums and probably slide whistle; Ed Atkins or Honoré Dutrey, trombone; Lil Hardin (Armstrong), piano. On several tracks there are a few replacements in the ensembles and two vaudeville vocalists.

Compositions: Side one: Snake Rag; Sweet Lovin' Man; High Society Rag; Sobbin' Blues; Where Did You Stay Last Night?; Dippermouth Blues; Jazzin' Babies Blues. *Side two:* Chattanooga Stomp; London (Café) Blues; Camp Meeting Blues; New Orleans Stomp; Buddy's Habit; Tears; I Ain't Gonna Tell Nobody. *Side three:* Room Rent Blues; Riverside Blues; Sweet Baby Doll; Working Man Blues; Mabel's Dream; Kiss Me Sweet; Construction Gang; Morning Dove Blues. *Side four:* Devil Dance Blues; Every Dog Has His Day; Red River Blues; Mountain City Blues; Empty Bed Blues; West End Blues; Get up off Your Knees.

KING OLIVER'S Creole Jazz Band with Louis Armstrong was an exuberant ode to an era that would soon flicker and dim as collective improvisation bowed to the reign of the soloist. Polyphonic playing, however, was natural to this band, for they grew up playing music no other way. Even Louis Armstrong, whom Oliver summoned to Chicago for the session (Armstrong's debut on records), submits his superior blowing power and imagination to the leader's stringent notion of how a band should play: "I never did try to overblow Joe at any time . . . I always played pretty under him. Until I left Joe I never did tear out." [12] In fact, it took Lil Hardin, the band's pianist (whom Louis married in 1924), to persuade him to leave an environment which had begun to restrict him. Louis's sense of obligation ran deep.

Oliver's group achieved harmonious arrangements with such spontaneity that musicians without a New Orleans background were incredulous. Louis explained to Ralph J. Gleason how these "arrangements" were created:

> I put notes to his (Oliver's) lead, whatever he made . . . we didn't write it, he'd tell me while the band was playing what he gonna play on top wa wa wa wa and I'd pick out my notes. . . . Bix and Louis Pancio and Paul Whiteman and all the boys used to come around, and they thought that was sumpin'. Whatever he was gonna do he'd let me

know about four, five bars ahead while the band was jumpin' heh heh heh.[13]

The double-cornet passage in "Mabel's Dream" (the third strain of the rag), which is recorded with exceptional clarity, is a testimony to their joyful togetherness.

The Oliver-Armstrong collaboration is also historic because Oliver was the major influence upon Louis's style; and each was the best cornetist in his own generation. (The trumpet was not commonly used until the late 1920's.) Oliver, born in 1885 on a plantation where his mother worked as a cook, dominated the local music scene shortly after 1900, the year of Louis's birth. The legendary Buddy Bolden was by this time losing his mind, and if Bunk Johnson (who did not record until he was sixty) or Freddie Keppard were any better than Oliver, there is no proof of it.

Joe "King" Oliver began to learn trombone and cornet during his teens, mostly by following the marching brass bands and listening carefully in the tonks and clubs of the tenderloin. Within five years he was working with the famous Olympia Brass Band, playing dances at the Tulane University gymnasium, and finally leading his own band with the clarinetist Sidney Bechet at The 25s, a popular Storyville cabaret. Oliver is credited with inventing the plunger mute, though he did not use it on records, by placing the fat end of a bottle in the bell of his cornet to soften its sound. In 1918 he was offered a job in Chicago which he accepted with trepidation, for the cold, urban North was foreign to everything he knew. Nevertheless, he succeeded admirably, pioneering the territory for others. The Creole Jazz Band was organized within two years, and by 1922 became the first black group with a recording contract.

There is much to be learned about the New Orleans style from these sessions. They demonstrate the crucial distinction between leading—a lead voice being compatible with collective playing—and soloing, through which the music's identity is dominated by a single instrument. A comparison of Louis Armstrong's lead cornet on "Tears" with his "West End Blues" solo on *The Genius of Louis Armstrong* (see discussion ahead) will demonstrate the difference. The excellent series of clarinet and trombone *breaks* on "Riverside Blues" illustrates another vital New Orleans convention. The break, in which a single instrument is sprung loose from the group, may well have provided the space and freedom in which the solo developed. Breaks were used brilliantly by Jelly Roll Morton, as we shall hear, in his elegant big-band arrangements. The improvised cornet breaks were certainly the most dependable high points of the Creole Jazz Band performances.

Oliver must have understood that the momentum of a band comes from the beat, not the tempo, for he never allowed his musicians to play faster than their technical skills permitted. The exceptional drive on "Chattanooga Stomp" and "I Ain't Gonna Tell Nobody," which practically defines the word "hot," shows the excitement that can be generated even at a relaxed pace. Many of the Dixieland groups should have noted that principle. They often attempted to accomplish in speed what they could not achieve in syncopation, so that we are left with the uncomfortable feeling that the horns are working too hard to keep up the pace. Oliver avoids this excess; in fact, he avoids every excess. The major criticism of his music may be just that it is too steady and predictable. A welcome exception, though, is heard on "Dipper Mouth Blues," in which the cornets blasting on top of the four regular banjo beats offer a rare climactic moment. "Dipper Mouth," recorded frequently in subsequent years as "Sugar Foot Stomp," also contains three choruses of Oliver playing alone (though not soloing in the fullest improvisational sense). Armstrong plays the lead-in, offering a good opportunity to compare their tones and articulations.

New Orleans music was often peppered with colorful, unusual instrumental sounds, even more so in live performance than on record. There is one such example here in the slide whistle's wistful call on "Sobbin' Blues." It is probably played by Warren "Baby" Dodds, whose function as drummer was reduced to the playing of wood blocks and little else—a victim of the acoustic recording process.

Oliver's group with Armstrong was the high-water mark of his career, which began to deteriorate when Louis went to New York one year later to work for Fletcher Henderson's Orchestra. Before that occurred, however, the band cut several other sessions for Gennett (the Smithsonian albums are culled from the Columbia and Okeh companies), which are reissued on Milestone's *Louis Armstrong and King Oliver* (General Discography), an album of good music with disturbingly poor sound reproduction. But even the flawed fidelity cannot dim the brilliance of the trumpet/piano duets by Oliver and Jelly Roll Morton on Morton's "King Porter Stomp" and "Tom Cat Blues." These tracks, which inspired the awesome trumpet/piano triumph of Armstrong and Hines on "Weather Bird" (see discussion ahead), should lay to rest disputes over Morton's pianistic abilities. Compared with Lil Hardin, Hersal Thomas, and Clarence Williams, he shines like a diamond amid cut glass. The Milestone, two-disc set also has one side devoted to the Red Onion Jazz Babies, Louis's group between his years with Oliver and the formation of the Hot Five, a historically important transitional period. The Smithsonian and Milestone albums complete Oliver's available discography. The few remaining cuts, of the thirty-seven-track total, are out of print on the defunct Herwin label.

Oliver's star sank inexorably once his best musicians, following Armstrong, headed for New York. Worse still, a gum disease diminished his capacity to perform over the years. When he died in 1938, he was working in Savannah, Georgia, as a custodian in a pool parlor. Nevertheless, Oliver never lost the respect of his colleagues; Armstrong, for example, frequently alluded to Joe Oliver as his teacher and inspiration.

**LOUIS ARMSTRONG and
EARL HINES**

*The Genius of Louis Armstrong, Volume I,
1923–1933*

Columbia, CG 30416
two discs, liner notes

Musicians: Louis Armstrong and His Hot Five, Hot Seven, and assorted ensembles. Louis Armstrong, cornet, trumpet, and vocals; Earl "Fatha" Hines or Lil Hardin (Armstrong), piano; Kid Ory or Fred Robinson, trombone; Johnny Dodds or Jimmy Strong, clarinet; Zutty Singleton or Warren "Baby" Dodds, drums; Johnny St. Cyr or Mancy Cara, banjo or guitar; Sidney Bechet (one cut only), soprano sax and sarrusophone.

Compositions: Side one: Mandy, Make up Your Mind; Lonesome, All Alone, and Blue; The Birdwell Blues; Cornet Chop Suey; Oriental Strut; Willie the Weeper; Wild Man Blues; Chicago Breakdown. *Side two:* A Monday Date; West End Blues; Sugar Foot Strut; Squeeze Me; Savoyagers' Stomp; Beau Koo Jack; Save It, Pretty Mama. *Side three:* Alligator Crawl; Potato Head Blues; Weary Blues; S.O.L. Blues; That's When I'll Come Back to You; Once in a While; Fireworks. *Side four:* Mahogany Hall Stomp; St. Louis Blues; I'm a Ding Dong Daddy; I'll Be Glad When You're Dead, You Rascal, You; The Lonesome Road; Kickin' the Gong Around; Lawd, You Made the Night Too Long.

Louis Armstrong and Earl Hines, 1928

Smithsonian Collection, R-002
two discs, liner notes
(mail order; see Appendix)

Musicians: Louis Armstrong, trumpet, cornet, and vocals; Earl "Fatha" Hines, piano. The Hot Five, Hot Seven, and various ensembles, including many of the same musicians on the preceding album.

Compositions: Side one: Chicago Breakdown; You're a Real Sweetheart; Too Busy; Last Night I Dreamed You Kissed Me; Fireworks; Skip the Gutter; A Monday Date; Don't Jive Me. *Side two:* West End Blues; Sugar Foot Strut; Two Deuces; Squeeze Me; Knee Drops; Symphonic Touches; Savoyagers' Stomp; No (No, Papa, No). *Side three:* Basin Street Blues; No One Else but You; Beau Koo Jack; Save It, Pretty Mama; Weather Bird; Muggles; Caution Blues; A Monday Date. *Side four:* Baby; Sweethearts on Parade; I Must Have That Man; I Ain't Got Nobody; Fifty-Seven Varieties; Heah Me Talkin' to Ya?; St. James Infirmary; Tight Like This.

THE HOT FIVE and Hot Seven recordings on these two albums are among the most influential in jazz, introducing the newly blossomed art of soloing through the work of Louis Armstrong and Earl "Fatha" Hines, the best musical minds of their day. Both albums, despite the duplication on nine out of thirty-two tracks, are essential because of invaluable cuts like "Potato Head Blues" (on *The Genius*) and the transcendent duet on King Oliver's "Weather Bird" (on *1928*). These are nearly microcosms of Armstrong's and Hines's innovations. On "Potato Head," for example, Armstrong divides the beat ingeniously, holding notes, cutting them off, varying their patterns, making use of the whole band to produce a maximum feeling of swing. "Weather Bird" reveals Hines's brilliance of rhythm and tone, intricacy, and mystical rapport with Armstrong. His right hand "trumpets" the melody, while his left is harmonically expressive, creating an orchestral keyboard approach reflected in later pianists like Teddy Wilson, Art Tatum, and Oscar Peterson. (Also see Hines, Selected Discography, Chapter 4.) The spontaneity of arrangements like "Skip the Gutter" (on *1928*) with its breaks, double-timed passages, call-and-response interaction, and imaginative improvising, set a standard that was not surpassed until the bebop quintets of the 1940's. Armstrong and Hines seem to boost each other to heights they might not have achieved separately, which is what made these records an inspiration to their successors. (Some of these tracks can be heard on Time-Life's *Giants of Jazz* package, released too late for discussion here. The three-disc set surveys Armstrong's career from 1923 to 1950 and includes an excellent liner booklet. See General Discography.)

Louis Armstrong was born on July 4, 1900, in a district of New Orleans, Louisiana, known as The Battleground. Knifings, shootings, whoring, gambling, and drunkenness were common. His parents separated when he was still an infant, and he was left in the care of his grandmother. When he returned home a few years later, his mother was living off Perdido Street, where sex was sold at even cheaper rates than in Storyville. In his fascinating autobiography, *Satchmo*, Louis claims he cannot say whether his mother did any "hustling," but he clearly remembers a succession of "stepfathers" in and out of the house. One of them left a .38 caliber pistol in his mother's footlocker which Louis "borrowed" and fired into the air on New Year's Eve of 1913. He was arrested immediately, taken to jail, and then sent to the Colored Waifs' Home for Boys. It may have seemed like the end of the road to him then, but the Home turned out to be more of a health club and boarding school than a jail. He learned to play the cornet there, eventually leading the marching band.

When he was finally released to his mother, who was ill, he supported both of them by delivering coal. Slowly he became one of the most sought-after musicians in New Orleans, one of the few who was good enough to earn a living by playing. Thus when Oliver went to Chicago, Louis was hired to replace him in Kid Ory's Brownskin Band. His reputation soon spread, and Fletcher Henderson, a rising bandleader in New York, offered him a job. However, Armstrong was timid and agreed to come only if his friend, drummer Zutty Singleton, was hired too. Since Henderson already had a drummer, Armstrong remained in New Orleans until Oliver summoned him to Chicago. (Singleton is reunited with Louis on these albums.)

Louis's first year in Chicago was spent recording with King Oliver (see previous album). A year later he was in New York, dominating the Fletcher Henderson Orchestra and accompanying Bessie Smith on her best sessions (see next album). He returned to Chicago in 1925, a more accomplished musician for his big-band schooling and bursting with energy and inventiveness.

Armstrong and Hines first met over a game of pool, an omnipresent means of recreation for early jazz players and a source of income for some of them. The way Hines tells it, the music in this hall was far from satisfactory, so Louis put down his cue stick and announced he was going up to the bandstand to take over the trumpet. Hines agreed to follow on piano, although neither knew the other to be a musician. "When I met Louis he was playing the same style that I [had] wanted to play on cornet [Hines's first instrument, which his father had also played]. And when I was playing on piano we'd sit there and play and we used each other's ideas and say 'thank you' for it." [14]

Hines's clarion right hand, using octaves in the upper register to etch the melody into the harmonic backdrop, enabled him to project his sound through the larger ensembles. He developed this "trumpet-style" piano with the Lois Deppe band of Ohio years before meeting Armstrong. The style also involved a tremolo of two notes within the octave that was imitative of the trumpet's vibrato, an effect heard conspicuously on "I Ain't Got Nobody." Relative to Armstrong's vocally inflected style, Hines is a sophisticated instrumentalist, obtaining a full, orchestral keyboard sound ("Knee Drops" and "A Monday Date") and generating melodic lines of uncommon length ("Muggles").

Hines and Armstrong teamed up in Carroll Dickerson's orchestra at the Sunset Cabaret, an establishment owned by Joe Glaser, who was to become Louis's lifelong manager. Louis, who was being billed as "The World's Greatest Trumpet Player," was invited by Okeh to form a group solely for the studio, providing the impetus for the Hot Five and Hot Seven bands.

The artistic significance of the music cannot be overstated. Gunther Schuller, for example, is willing to hear the cascading introduction to "West End Blues" (on both *1928* and *The Genius*) as definitive of jazz sensibility:

> The first phrase startles us with the powerful thrust and punch of its first four notes. We are immediately aware of their terrific swing, despite the fact that these first four notes occur *on* the beat. . . . These four notes should be heard by all people who do not understand the difference between jazz and other music. . . . The way Louis attacks each note, the quality and duration of each pitch, the manner in which he releases the note, and the split-second silence before the next note . . . present in capsule form all the essential characteristics of jazz inflection.[15]

These sessions did not have to wait long for recognition. In fact, they were such instant hits for Okeh that other companies began to cultivate their own trumpet or cornet sensations to rival Armstrong. Victor engaged Henry "Red" Allen, who became an important figure in the New Orleans revival two decades later. Brunswick hired the technically flashy "Jabbo" Smith. However, Armstrong remained matchless for musical content, for soul, and for wit. He touched jazz in the mid-1920's with a magic wand—in the form of a cornet—and the music was transformed forever.

The gutsy "Satchmo"—an abbreviation of "satchel mouth"—had a powerful embouchure and a pair of strong lips he would continue to play on even while they bled. His lungs were tireless. His technique surpassed anything imagined for his instrument at the time.

Trumpeter Roy Eldridge's description of an early performance, cited in the liner notes to *The Genius*, conveys the stunning nature of Louis's originality: "He started out like a new book, building and building, chorus after chorus, and finally reaching a full climax. . . . The rhythm was rocking. . . . Everybody was standing up, including me. He was building the thing all the time instead of just playing in a straight line."

Soloing, lifting the music to personal moments of intensity, is fundamental to Louis's dramatic style. On the historic cuts like "Potato Head Blues," "Skip the Gutter," and "Squeeze Me," it is obvious that, except for Hines, his colleagues do not understand the solo concept and thus recede into the background, providing a generally lackluster accompaniment. Because Armstrong's ideas are interesting and varied enough, his improvisations can stretch out for several choruses of a melody. These extemporaneous passages were newly composed melodies which seemed, as on the celebrated last chorus of "West End Blues," to float above the harmonic structure of the song, disengaged from the song as written. No longer were simple embellishments of the melody creative enough.

Armstrong uses long-held notes, interspersed with punched-out staccato attacks, to control the tension and relaxation of the rhythm. The unaccompanied "Potato Head" solo (on *The Genius*) illustrates fluid held notes alternating with triplet patterns, as well as double- and triple-tongued notes, for rhythmic effect. On "Mahogany Hall," in which the first appearance of the string bass illustrates its capacity to swing, he holds a muted tone after the banjo solo for ten measures. In the last chorus of "Muggles" (on *1928*), he revives the song's flagging momentum by doubling the time. These rhythmic innovations quickly became a part of the jazz language once Armstrong introduced them.

In terms of instrumental technique, he extended the trumpet's domain to include the higher register, where his characteristic sound (also noticeable on the "Potato Head" solo) was a "rip" up to the high notes. Consistent with the African tradition, his goal was not the pure and precise realization of the written tone, but rather an opportunity for personal expression. Louis tears up to a high note, giving it a dynamic thrust. The intensity of his vibrato is another pervasive quality which adds momentum to every note he plays, whether syncopated or on the beat.

His singing, an essential part of his style once he left Oliver's band, is inimitable. He sings like he plays, or vice-versa, which is not surprising in view of the profound connection between music and speech in the African heritage. His scat singing on "That's When I'll Come Back to You" (on *The Genius*) and at the end of his trumpet solo on "A Monday Date" (also on *The Genius*) is clearly a vocalization of his instrumental phrasing and inflection. (Scatting is vocalizing in nonsense syllables, usually in imitation of an instrument. Armstrong once said he invented scatting—an unlikely claim —but he was the first to use it on records.) Many of the Hot Five tunes were made up in the studio and, if anything went wrong, scatting often came to the rescue, just as it had in the early New Orleans bands. Louis's voice had a warmth, buoyancy, and roughness that immediately became legend. Earl Hines once said that Satchmo's singing was so popular "musicians were sticking their heads out windows trying to catch a cold so they could sound like him."

In 1929 Armstrong and Hines parted company, Hines to lead a big band for two decades (Chapter 4) and Louis to embark upon an all-too-thorough commercialization of his talent under the guidance of Joe Glaser. Armstrong's pop hits began with Fats Waller's "Ain't Misbehavin'," which he debuted in the *Hot Chocolates of 1930*, and culminated in the hit song from the show *Hello, Dolly!* in the 1960's. Bluebird has reissued the earliest orchestra dates on *Young Louis Armstrong: 1932–1933*, and MCA has two poorly packaged (no dates, credits, or personnel listed) sets of the All-Stars (Jack Teagarden, Sid Catlett, Barney Bigard, and others) on *At the Crescendo* and *At Symphony Hall*. Columbia Special Products has the best available All-Stars LPs from the mid-'50s (with Bigard and Trummy Young): *Louis Armstrong Plays W. C. Handy*, which includes one of the definitive versions of "St. Louis Blues"; and *Satch Plays Fats*, a tribute to Waller. (A Jazz Archives album of the All-Stars from 1948 with Earl Hines has been deleted.) But the only important retrospective is RCA's two-disc *Louis Armstrong: July 4, 1900/July 6, 1971*, with representative tracks from 1932 to 1956.

Armstrong's radiant optimism and indefatigable sense of fun played a great role in promoting jazz. It endeared him to his fans, but he weathered much criticism for his "just keep smilin' " image. Those who knew him took pains to point out that he was more serious than was acknowledged. It infuriated and disgusted Armstrong that he could lunch with the President of Brazil, receive an audience with the Pope, and play for the Queen of England; but in the South of his own country he could not rent a room in a top hotel or eat at a restaurant. In the 1950's Louis, exasperated, canceled his State Department tour of Russia to protest President Eisenhower's do-nothing policy toward black civil rights in the South. But this was not the Louis who came across on stage or on record. Listen to the way he teases Hines in the opening to "A Monday Date," or the tone in which he lambastes his adversary in "I'll Be Glad When You're Dead, You Rascal, You." The latter's lyrics are unsavory at best, but Louis's delivery can only be described as lovable. Louis always came across as a wellspring of goodness, which—irrespective of his social activism—was highly advantageous to jazz's image in America and abroad.

By the time of his death in 1971, he had acquired two more nicknames which help indicate the stature he had achieved. One was "Ambassador Satch," a title earned by virtue of his State Department tours, through which he came to symbolize jazz to the world. The other derives from his profound influence upon musicians—like the great trumpeters Roy Eldridge, Dizzy Gillespie, and Miles Davis—to whom Armstrong is "Pops," the patriarch of their own stylistic development.

BESSIE SMITH

Nobody's Blues but Mine

Columbia, CG 31093
two discs, liner notes
1925–1927

Musicians: Bessie Smith, vocals, with Clara Smith, vocals, on two songs. Louis Armstrong, cornet; Charlie Green, trombone; Fred Longshaw, piano. Also accompanied on solo piano by James P. Johnson, Fletcher Henderson, or Clarence Williams. On various cuts: Joe Smith, trumpet; Don Redman, clarinet and alto sax; Coleman Hawkins, clarinet.

Compositions: Side one: Careless Love Blues (Handy); J. C. Holmes Blues (Horsley); I Ain't Going to Play No Second Fiddle (Bradford); He's Gone Blues (B. Smith); Nobody's Blues but Mine (Williams); I Ain't Got Nobody (Graham-S. Williams); My Man Blues (B. Smith); New Gulf Coast Blues (Williams). *Side two:* Florida Bound (Williams); At the Christmas Ball (Longshaw); I've Been Mistreated (Longshaw); Red Mountain Blues (Troy); Golden Rule Blues (B. Smith); Lonesome Desert Blues (B. Smith); Them 'Has Been' Blues (Skidmore-Walker); Squeeze Me (Williams-Waller). *Side three:* What's the Matter Now? (Williams-S. Williams); I Want Every Bit of It (Williams-S. Williams); Jazzbo Brown from Memphis Town (Brooks); The Gin House Blues (Troy-F. Henderson); Money Blues (Kapp-Coleman-Eller); Baby Doll (B. Smith); Hard Driving Papa (Brooks); Lost Your Head Blues (B. Smith). *Side four:* Hard Time Blues (B. Smith); Honey Man Blues (Brooks); One and Two Blues (Brooks); Young Woman's Blues, Preachin' the Blues, and Back Water Blues (all by B. Smith); After You've Gone (Layton-Creamer); Alexander's Ragtime Band (I. Berlin).

BESSIE SMITH, a singer of great dramatic strength and intensity, cut a total of 159 sides for Columbia from 1923 to 1933, all of which are reissued on a series of two-disc sets compiled by her biographer Chris Albertson (General Discography). She was known as the Empress of the Blues, but in fact she transcended the rigid form of the blues as a folk music, becoming the first major jazz singer. Bessie was born in a poor section of Chattanooga, Tennessee, sometime before 1900; the exact date is unknown because in the South black people's birth records were not commonly maintained. As a tall, broad-shouldered teenager, she traveled with Gertrude "Ma" Rainey's Rabbit Foot Minstrels, an itinerant tent-show troupe. It was from Rainey that Bessie learned her blues, but a comparison with Rainey (General Discography) will clearly show the distinction between singing the blues as a folk form and *using* the blues in jazz.

Nobody's Blues but Mine is the high point of her career. In 1925 Bessie was the highest paid black musician in history, and her records probably rescued Columbia from bankruptcy. The company's "race" catalog was inaugurated in 1923 with Smith's vocals, which sold in the millions. In 1925 Bessie was still happily married, a state of affairs which did not last long. She was also past her initial stiffness in the recording studio; and the 1927 sessions here preceded her bouts with excessive drinking and the mismanagement of her affairs by her husband. Furthermore, Louis Armstrong was in New York working for Fletcher Henderson that year; their collaboration on the first three tracks of side one are possibly Bessie's best work.

On "Careless Love Blues," "J. C. Holmes Blues," and "I Ain't Gonna Play No Second Fiddle," she is comfortably buoyed by the band's New Orleans ensemble feeling, especially the interplay between Armstrong's cornet and the trombone of Charlie Green, one of Basie's favorite accompanists. Armstrong supplies some wonderful obbligato melodies on "Second Fiddle." Fred Longshaw is the pianist, not Fletcher Henderson as the liner notes indicate. Longshaw and Porter Grainger (not on this album) were Bessie's favorite pianists, although the two duets with James P. Johnson here suggest a deep rapport; Henderson, in any case, did not have the blues tonality Bessie needed.

The instrumental inflection in Bessie Smith's phrasing (which served as the foundation for Billie Holiday's development) is crucial in elevating Bessie above the predominance of blues in her repertoire. She appears confined to the limitations of the folk genre only on a song like "I Want Every Bit of It," which is saddled with the undisguised sexual lyric reminiscent of jazz's honky-tonk and bordello origins.

Bessie's inflection derives from the natural diction of everyday speech and could not be more remote from the aesthetic "distance" and formality of the conservatory-trained voice. The effect of natural diction is to make each piece a vehicle for personal expression, one which radiates spontaneity (even though Bessie planned most of her melodic interpretations in advance of the recording session).

Each note she sings is individualized further by her variations in pitch, a part of the African legacy (Chapter 1). She slides about on the word "love" ("Careless Love Blues") and sings an entire chorus of "No, Lord!" ("Lonesome Desert Blues") in which every *no* is different from the last, due to her swoops and glides around the note. Gunther Schuller has looked more closely into her pronunciation, dividing its function into pitch and rhythm: ". . . vowels carry the pitch, while opening and closing consonants (if any), or glottal attacks, specify the attack and decay pattern of a note." [16] Rhythm is associated with attack-and-decay patterns. Like Armstrong, Bessie knows how to swing a phrase against the band by her intuitive sense of when to hold on to a note and when to cut it off.

Bessie's voice quality possessed a depth and a drama that remained unsurpassed even by her great successor, Billie Holiday. She transforms a commercial ballad, like "After You've Gone" on side four, into a "shout" of rich blues tonality and expressive power. Her voice is womanly and weighty, in proportion to her near-200-pound frame, never girlish or sweet. Interestingly, the Okeh company turned her down after a 1921 audition, on the grounds that she sounded "too rough." Her accompanist later recommended Bessie to the Columbia executive Frank Walker, the producer of the sessions heard on *Nobody's Blues but Mine* and Bessie's astute personal manager until 1928.

Bessie Smith's voice reflects the pain and sorrow of the life she lived and knew. Her black audience understood this all too well. Bessie also became her own worst enemy in two respects. Her drinking increased along with her fame, bringing her weight to over 200 pounds and destroying, as evident in the early 1930 sessions, her powerful voice. Second, she dismissed Frank Walker, her far-sighted manager, leaving her affairs to her husband, a former night watchman, who encouraged her to record more commercial material while doing nothing to curb her lavish spending. By 1933 her greatest achievements seemed well beyond her abilities.

A Bessie Smith comeback was the hope of John Hammond, jazz's first great talent scout and producer, who had already guided Benny Goodman from New York studio sessions into national prominence. In 1937 Hammond left for Mississippi to escort Bessie personally back to New York with a new contract. En route he learned she had died after an automobile accident. According to initial reports, the nearest hospital had denied her admission as a black, and she bled to death on the way to another hospital. Subsequent reports, which received far less publicity, contradicted this version, and the eventual blurring of the truth became the subject of an Edward Albee play, *The Death of Bessie Smith*.

As her biographer Chris Albertson points out, it would be a shame to remember Bessie better for the way she died than for what she achieved during her life. The deeply moving music on her albums is only part of the legacy. She also began a tradition of jazz singing which can be heard in the music of Billie Holiday, Sarah Vaughan, and—to a lesser extent—in the styles of Ella Fitzgerald and Betty Carter.

JELLY ROLL MORTON

Jelly Roll Morton and His Red Hot Peppers (1926–1927), Volume 3

RCA (France) 731 059
one disc, liner notes in French

Musicians: Jelly Roll Morton, piano; Kid Ory, trombone; George Mitchell, cornet; Omer Simeon, clarinet; Johnny St. Cyr, banjo; John Lindsay, bass; Andrew Hilaire, drums. Also Barney Bigard and Darnell Howard, clarinets. Also Johnny Dodds, clarinet; Warren "Baby" Dodds, drums; Stump Evans, alto sax; Bud Scott, guitar; Lew LeMar, vocals.

Compositions: Side one: Black Bottom Stomp (Morton); The Chant (Stitzel) (two takes); Sidewalk Blues (Morton); Dead Man Blues (Morton); Steamboat Stomp (Morton); Someday Sweetheart (Morton-Spikes). *Side two:* Someday Sweetheart (take two); Grandpa's Spells (Morton, attributed incorrectly to "Ch. Luke" on jacket); Original Jelly Roll Blues (Morton) (two takes); Doctor Jazz (Oliver); Cannonball Blues (Morton); Hyena Stomp (Morton): Billy Goat Stomp (Morton).

Jelly Roll Morton, 1923–1924

Milestone, M-47018
two discs, good liner notes

Musicians: Jelly Roll Morton, piano (sides one and two and first three selections on side
   three). Also Morton with both large and small ensembles, including kazoo and
   comb players (whether alto, tenor, or baritone comb is not specified).
Compositions (all compositions by Jelly Roll Morton): *Side one:* King Porter Stomp;
   New Orleans Joys; Grandpa's Spells; Kansas City Stomp; Wolverine Blues; The
   Pearls; Tia Juana; Shreveport Stomp. *Side two:* Frog-i-More Rag; Mamanita; Jelly
   Roll Blues; Big Foot Ham; Tom Cat Blues; Stratford Hunch; Perfect Rag. *Side
   three:* Mamanita (another take); Thirty-Fifth Street Blues; London Blues; Muddy
   Water Blues; Big Fat Ham; Mr. Jelly Lord (three takes). *Side four:* Steady Roll;
   Wolverine Blues (band take); My Gal; Fish Tail Blues; High Society; Weary
   Blues; Tiger Rag.

THE STATE OF jazz reissues is nowhere more disgraceful than in the case
of Jelly Roll Morton. Morton was a pompous, egotistical pool hustler,
gambler, nightclub owner, and pianist, who insisted that he "invented jazz
about 1905." He did cut some of the best New Orleans-style music on
records in 1926 and 1927 with his Red Hot Peppers. These recordings
achieved astonishing fidelity for the day, and the way instruments weave in
and out of Morton's bright, solid texture is a joy to hear. His artful use of
the break, which made room for a featured instrument, contributed to the
development of the extended jazz solo. The flashy, intelligent strength behind
cuts like "Black Bottom Stomp" and "The Chant" (two takes) is exhilarating,
timeless music and crucial jazz history.

Unfortunately, the dozens of sides cut during this period, owned by RCA
Victor and previously available on their Vintage series, have been out of
print for years. Considering some of the far less worthy material reissued
by RCA on its Bluebird label, it is surprising that nothing has been done to
reactivate the Morton titles. RCA Victor in France deserves credit for the
Red Hot Peppers album shown above, obtainable by special order or, with
luck, at outlets specializing in jazz. Listeners will be repaid for their trouble.

The high praise for the Peppers' sides is not meant to detract from the
Oliver and Armstrong albums discussed earlier. Their goals were different.
King Oliver was much closer to the traditional New Orleans brass bands,
perhaps because he remained in their midst a dozen years after Morton had

left town seeking broader horizons. Louis Armstrong was setting precedents for the small-combo soloist.

Although Jelly Roll's boast that he invented jazz is absurd, there is good reason to see him as a transitional figure from the relative stiffness of ragtime to the flexibility of later jazz. In fact, Morton always maintained that any music could be "jazzed," while he recognized both ragtime and the blues as more strictly defined forms. His piano playing exemplifies the transition in its increased swing and feeling of freedom. The rag's rigid, occasionally martial bass is smoothed out by Morton. While the ragtimer's left hand almost never syncopates, Morton's left frequently hits slightly (about a sixteenth note) before the beat, introducing another dimension to the cross-rhythm. His right hand is more expansive and extemporaneous. Morton's abundant thematic improvisations were his pride. "Grandpa's Spells" (the solo on the Milestone set) demonstrates the range of his dynamics, from the smooth-as-glass opening to the bass-register bombs he drops during the later theme.

Morton's facility as a pianist probably developed greatly during his long, titillating nights as a professor in the Storyville mansions. There he would play for singers, for dancers, and for listening. Like every great soloist, he could juggle rhythm, harmony, and melody confidently. It is somewhat astonishing to find Duke Ellington disparaging Morton's abilities (some say this is due to his personal dislike for the man) and the circumspect critic Leonard Feather calling him "overrated." Listening to these sessions, or to the duet on *Louis Armstrong and King Oliver* noted in the King Oliver discussion, one certainly hears the equal of Eubie Blake or James P. Johnson, even if not of Earl Hines. As a New Orleans-style pianist, Morton could not possibly be overrated.

For Morton the relationship between his piano playing and his bands was a rare and impressive one. While his use of the keyboard was orchestral, aspiring to the ideal of the pianist as one-man-band, he was able to wear the arranger's hat with a completely fresh perspective, hearing valid combinations and sonorities which did not derive from the keyboard. "Jelly Roll Blues" and "Grandpa's Spells," played both solo and by the Peppers on these albums, are excellent examples of how he worked. Notice, to begin with, how the guitar is assigned the piano's melodic voice in the opening for a completely different effect. But there are similarities too, such as the parallel between the role of the "tailgate" trombone and the melodic movement of Morton's left hand. His affinity for the trombone is attributed to the fact that his father (Ed LaMenthe) played it.

Morton relied heavily on the ragtime form and always wrote in its multithematic structure. However, what he did within that structure was unique. The different strains were orchestrated for high contrast, while most rags (except Joplin's) adhered to a single mood. He used both the break and the riff, a short melodic phrase used cumulatively for effect ("Grandpa's Spells") or as a response to a higher-order melodic statement ("The Chant"). Melodically, he incorporated blues tonality ("London Blues," on the Milestone recording) without bowing to its folk forms. Even if Morton did not "invent" jazz, he was certainly the first composer to carry the written score beyond its basic building blocks.

His brilliance and scope as a composer can be appreciated by examining several of the cuts on *Red Hot Peppers*, isolating the key features of his arranging. The first track, "Black Bottom Stomp," is a rocking rag, but the variations on each theme are so radical that each could pass for a different theme altogether. Morton's use of the string bass is superb, even more admirable in that his awareness of its potential predated its general use by nearly three years. New Orleans musicians shunned the unwieldy bass for marching, using a tuba instead. How tightly and precisely Morton's arrangements are executed! He went over the written parts with everyone before recording, paying them for rehearsal time, a rare practice. Opinions differ on how much freedom he allowed his musicians on their solo breaks. It seems there were some players he never interfered with and others for whom he wrote out parts.

"Grandpa's Spells" (also in piano solo on side one of the Milestone recording) is one of Morton's best compositions, swinging perfectly from start to finish, exemplifying his capacity to hear great contrasts of texture. We hear another example on "Steamboat Stomp," where Jelly Roll's lyrical right-hand improvising over the horns sets off the thick ensemble underneath him. "Spells" warrants comparison with the piano solo on other grounds. Morton's arranging, like his playing, maintains density without becoming cluttered. The pianistic "bombs" mentioned earlier are taken over in the Hot Peppers' version by the drums and cymbal. On "Doctor Jazz Stomp," the sense of motion is accentuated when the clarinet holds its note on top and the rhythm section stomps on underneath—a contrast of rhythm rather than texture. The final choruses, incidentally, contain excellent examples of Morton's dramatic use of the two-bar break (The last two cuts, "Hyena Stomp" and "Billy Goat Stomp," are probably motivated by the commercial success of imitating the animal effects in the ODJB's top-selling "Barnyard Blues.")

On *Jelly Roll Morton, 1923–1924*, the piano solos of sides one and two display the same kind of energy and wit Morton possessed as an arranger. They are considerably sharper and closer to his creative core than the acoustically superior recordings from the late 1930's—several issued by the Library of Congress (no longer available, by order of Morton's estate), and Commodore's reissue of a dozen 1939 solos on *New Orleans Memories Plus Two* (General Discography). Sides three and four of this album contain band tracks which in general, after comparison with the Red Hot Peppers' sessions two years later, are a disappointment.

Morton's soloing, however, reveals in delightful imaginative pieces his musical inheritance and his goals. His indebtedness to ragtime is obvious in the "Frog-i-More Rag," written in 1918 to accompany a minstrel show contortionist who dressed up as a frog, and "King Porter Stomp," named after the ragtime and blues pianist Porter King. "King Porter," Morton's most enduring composition, was a mainstay of the swing-era repertoire, one of Benny Goodman's biggest hits, and was revived as recently as 1979 by the free jazz collective Air (Selected Discography, Chapter 8). Morton is said to have enlisted Scott Joplin's help in working out one of its themes.[17]

Morton's theme-and-variations style of improvising—while prolific on a piece like "Frog-i-More," the product of a fertile imagination—ultimately limited him to the style of playing which preceded Armstrong and Hines. Yet even within that context, he was often ahead of his time. For example, in the third chorus break to "Kansas City Stomp," Jelly Roll ingeniously implies the rhythm over two measures by using only three right-hand notes. Then in "Wolverine Blues," he introduces a passage entirely of chords in an uncommon voicing so as to contrast with the independent motion of his hands elsewhere. Finally, Morton believed strongly that the "Spanish tinge" is an important element of jazz, a view confirmed by the music of Dizzy Gillespie, Horace Silver, Chick Corea, and others who have explored these Latin rhythms.

Morton was a brilliant exponent of the New Orleans synthesis, though his adherence to its style prevented him from keeping up with the music's progress. Yet Morton suffered as well from difficulties of a more personal nature. He was a compulsive braggart and insisted upon having the last word on everything. Thus he worked only infrequently in Chicago during the 1920's, because the mobsters who controlled the night life could not tolerate his defiant nature. He was unpopular with musicians for the same reasons, as one may gather from the recollections of bandleader George Morrison, who had once hired Morton: "Of course, he didn't last too long because he was too eccentric and too temperamental, and he was a one-man-band himself; he wanted to be everything. . . ."[18]

Sadly, some of the younger musicians in the 1930's began to taunt Morton just to hear him brag, laughing over it behind his back. His dislike for the rougher playing of "black Negroes" only alienated him further. Morton cast himself as a proud and stubborn Creole, and it ruined him

Before he died in 1941, he left a document equal in value to his music. Sitting at the piano in the Coolidge Chamber Music Auditorium of the Library of Congress, he taped a month of interviews with Alan Lomax, displaying an apparently total recall of the spirit and detail of early New Orleans life. He illustrated the city's musical history on the keyboard, generating the out-of-print Library of Congress records alluded to earlier. These interviews became the foundation of Lomax's superb biography, *Mister Jelly Roll*, the most enjoyable and informative book available on the New Orleans period.

BIX BEIDERBECKE

*The Bix Beiderbecke Story: Bix and Tram,
Volume 2*

Columbia, CL 845
one disc, liner notes

Musicians: Bix Beiderbecke, cornet; Jimmy Dorsey, clarinet; Miff Mole, trombone; Doc
Ryker, alto sax; Frank Trumbauer, C-melody sax; Itzy Riskin, piano; Eddie Lang,
guitar; Chauncey Morehouse, drums. Other ensembles with a few replacements,
including Joe Venuti, violin; Bing Crosby, vocals.
Compositions: Side one: Singin' the Blues (Robinson-Conrad); Clarinet Marmalade
(Shields-Ragas); Way Down Yonder in New Orleans (Creamer-Layton); Missis-
sippi Mud (Barris); For No Reason at All in C (Beiderbecke-Trumbauer); There'll
Come a Time (Mannone-Mole). *Side two:* I'm Coming, Virginia (Heywood);
Ostrich Walk (ODJB); A Good Man Is Hard to Find (Green); Wringin' and
Twistin' (Trumbauer-Walter-Trent); Crying All Day (Trumbauer-Morehouse);
Riverboat Shuffle (Voynow-Carmichael-Mills).

The cornet playing of Leon "Bix" Beiderbecke, born in 1903 in Davenport, Iowa, is the earliest proof that it is possible to play in a sensitive, contemplative, "pretty" style—instead of hot and hard—without a loss of jazz
feeling. In Bix's music one hears the roots of inner intensity, a contrast to
the outgoing, aggressive excitement generated by Armstrong.

Bix was an individualist to a greater extent than any other white, jazz-
influenced musician of his time. His impact upon other musicians bordered
on cultism, and he has been the perennially cited exception to the rule that
all the innovators in jazz are blacks. Louis Armstrong, King Oliver, and the
black New Orleans bands were at most an indirect influence upon his style.
He may have heard them when they played in Davenport on the Mississippi
riverboat circuit, but there is no confirmation that he did. Bix, who was
self-taught on both cornet and piano, spent his formative years listening to
Dixieland groups, from the commercially oriented Original Dixieland Jass
Band to the more improvisational New Orleans Rhythm Kings. By 1924 he
was leading his own group in a similar style—the Wolverines, the first significant (white) band composed of non-New Orleans musicians. The
Wolverines, whose entire recorded legacy is heard (with surprising clarity)
on the 1924 *Bix Beiderbecke and the Chicago Cornets* (General Discography), is a bench-mark band, attesting to the jazz language's permeation of
white society in the North.

The Wolverines attracted the attention of the Gennett Company through their performances at Indiana University, where they had been hired for ten successive weeks by an admiring student and talented composer, Hoagy Carmichael. Bix is able to swing the band on these cuts, but the poignant tone for which he became known later does not yet shine through. The two-disc set, however, contains some historical foundations of Dixieland, including tracks with Jimmy McPartland on cornet; George Brunis, the ex-NORK trombonist; Tommy Dorsey (with a different Bix band); and the Armstrong disciple Muggsy Spanier with his Bucktown Five. *Chicago Cornets* is also enhanced by an informative set of liners by the British jazz historian Max Harrison.

Bix outgrew the Wolverines rather quickly and moved to New York. His playing improved enormously there under the wing of Frankie Trumbauer, or Tram, who was the musical director of one of Jean Goldkette's jazz and dance bands. Bix was in need of a guardian angel. His personal habits, from excessive drinking down to "forgetting" to change and clean his clothes, were early intimations of self-destruction. He was also a poor sight reader, a distinct liability in the Goldkette organization. Tram's paternal interest in him had a salubrious effect. Bix further developed his pure, poetic tone, along with an advanced harmonic conception enriched by his interest in Stravinsky, Debussy, and the American composer Edward MacDowell. His best playing was done shortly afterward, from 1927 to 1929, when Okeh recorded him with alumni from the Goldkette band (*Bix and His Gang: The Bix Beiderbecke Story, Volume 1*), with Tram and other close associates (*Bix and Tram, Volume 2*), and finally with the Paul Whiteman Orchestra, which absorbed Bix and Tram after the Goldkette band had broken up (*Whiteman Days, Volume 3*).

Tram's dependable lightness served as an excellent foil for the dead-serious, bittersweet mood which Bix characteristically exuded. Bix and Tram worked frequently on their own, creating the impromptu "head" arrangements heard on this album, although Bill Challis, who cared a great deal for Bix's playing, is responsible for the arrangements to "Clarinet Marmalade" and "Ostrich Walk." The album contains Bix's best solos, the relaxed, lyrical "I'm Coming, Virginia" and "Singin' the Blues," the most imitated solo of the 1920's, save for Armstrong's "West End Blues." All of the men who were to help Dixieland evolve into something more subtle and swinging —Jimmy McPartland, Bobby Hackett, the guitarist Eddie Condon, clarinetist Pee Wee Russell, and Red Nichols, leader of the Five Pennies—learned and recorded Bix's material, and even the Ellingtonian trumpeter Rex Stewart fell under his spell for a time. Tram had his own, more clandestine influence on the great Lester Young (Chapter 4) with his airy C-melody sax. Young said that Trumbauer showed him the virtues of a softer approach to tenor sax, citing Tram's performance on "Singin' the Blues" as the decisive recording.

Nearly everything Bix felt is contained in the sound of his horn, which, thanks to the advent of electronic recording, survives well on the three-volume Columbia series. Yet musicians who heard him in person claim that no recording could have done him justice. They describe his sound as "sharp as a rifle crack" and as clear and ringing as "shooting bullets at a bell." The guitarist and entrepreneur Eddie Condon, master of the bon mot, said Bix's horn sounded to him "like a girl saying *yes.*" It comes through with especial clarity in the slow tempo of "Way Down Yonder in New Orleans" and at full strength in "Singin' the Blues," in which an atypical "rip" up to a high note bursts through an otherwise introverted improvisation. Bix's phrasing conveys his natural, if pained, originality. He anticipates modern jazz in lagging slightly behind the beat. Using highly unorthodox technique, he moves around his horn with confidence and ease. He never rushes, never quite conforms to a strict beat, and rarely displays a cheerful emotion.

Bix and Tram also contains a sadly revealing period piece in Bing Crosby's recording debut on "Mississippi Mud," in which, the lyric tells us, the "happy darkies" beat their feet contentedly. This throwback to minstrelsy is the album's sole concession to commercial (lack of) taste. Crosby makes several more appearances, however, on *Whiteman Days, Volume 3*, which suffers instead from its limited improvising space for Bix, a summation of his fate in the thirty-man Whiteman behemoth. The high point of *Volume 3* is Bix's piano solo on his most famous composition "In a Mist," which, by its use of ninth, eleventh, and thirteenth intervals of the scale, serves as a telescope through which jazz harmony of the future can be glimpsed. "In a Mist" is an eternally fresh and historically astonishing piece of music.

Beiderbecke's impact on jazz is also astonishing, considering the brevity of his career. He lost the battle with alcoholism, and when the stock market collapsed in 1929, he lost all his money, too. Thus it was a broke and broken man who played the sad sessions in 1930 with Benny Goodman and a few other swing-era newcomers; some of these sessions are available on the Archives of Folk and Jazz recording *Bix Beiderbecke*. The next year at the age of twenty-eight, Bix died of pneumonia, or perhaps as the writer Frank Norris said, "he died of everything."

Bix's legend grew quickly, abetted by his dissolute life-style, his allegedly close friendship with Babe Ruth (although musicians generally held that *nobody* was close to Bix), and Dorothy Baker's novel (later a film) *Young Man with a Horn*, which was inspired by his life. In 1974 two major biographies were published (Bibliography), separating fact from fantasy, adding to numerous critical, interpretive essays which began to appear in jazz anthologies by the 1960's. Bix was even linked—not unreasonably so—with Miles Davis's contemplative balladic style and the quiet intensity of Davis's tone in the albums arranged by Gil Evans (Chapter 5). While a direct influence is out of the question in Miles's case, Bix certainly set out upon a lonely path which became quite crowded long after his death. The best tribute to Bix on records is on MCA's *Shades of Bix: Jimmy McPartland and Bobby Hackett*, a collection of Beiderbecke repertoire recorded from 1936 to 1956 by two trumpeters who remain respectful but not imitative. The belated interest in Bix is perhaps the final irony of his story, for while he was alive, his name appeared in print only three times.

References and Notes

1. Ortiz M. Walton, *Music: Black, White & Blue* (New York: William Morrow & Co., Inc., 1972), p. 66. Additional statistics come from the Bulletin of the Recording Industry Association of America, 1977, based on a survey by *Billboard* magazine.

2. Alan Lomax, *Mister Jelly Roll* (Berkeley: University of California Press, 1973), p. 80 (first published, 1950).

3. *Ibid.*, pp. 49–50; and Nat Shapiro and Nat Hentoff, eds., *Hear Me Talkin' to Ya* (New York: Dover Publications, Inc., 1966), p. 6.

4. Rudi Blesh, *Shining Trumpets: A History of Jazz* (New York: Da Capo Press, Inc., 1976), p. 199 (originally published, 1946).

5. Lomax, *op. cit.*, p. 86.

6. Shapiro and Hentoff, *op. cit.*, p. 19.

7. Lomax, *op. cit.*, p. 93.

8. Shapiro and Hentoff, *op. cit.*, p. 16.

9. *The American Language: Supplement II* (New York: Alfred Knopf, 1948), p. 710.

10. *Ibid.*, footnote 3.

11. Gunther Schuller, *Early Jazz* (London: Oxford University Press, 1968), pp. 138–139f; and Blesh, *op. cit.*, p. 221.

12. Richard Hadlock, *Jazz Masters of the Twenties* (New York: Macmillan, 1974), p. 15 (originally published, 1965).

13. Ralph J. Gleason, *Celebrating the Duke & . . . Other Heroes* (Boston: Little, Brown & Co., Inc., 1975), p. 44.

14. Liner notes to the Smithsonian Collection's *Louis Armstrong and Earl Hines*, 1928.

15. Schuller, *op. cit.*, p. 116.

16. *Ibid.*, pp. 229–230.

17. Rudi Blesh and Harriet Janis, *They All Played Ragtime* (New York: Oak Publications, 1971), p. 181.

18. Lomax, *op. cit.*, pp. 175–176.

General Discography of Available, Recommended Albums

LOUIS ARMSTRONG

 The Louis Armstrong Story, Vols. 1–4: and His Hot Five, CL-851; *and His Hot Seven*, CL-852; *and Earl Hines*, CL-853; *Favorites*, CL854; Columbia [most tracks reissued on *The Genius of Louis Armstrong* (Selected Discography)]. *Satchmo at Symphony Hall*, MCA 2-24057, MCA. *Louis Armstrong's Greatest Hits*, CS-9438, Columbia. *The Best of Louis Armstrong*, MCA 2-4035, MCA. *Louis Armstrong, July 4, 1900/July 6, 1971*, VPM-6044, RCA. *Louis Armstrong: A Legendary Performer* (photo-liner booklet), CPL1-2659(e), RCA. *Giants of Jazz: Louis Armstrong* (3 discs, liner booklet), Time-Life Records (mail only). *Louis Armstrong and King Oliver*, M-47017, Milestone. *Young Louis Armstrong*, AXM2-5519, Bluebird (RCA). *Louis Armstrong at the Crescendo*, MCA2-4013, MCA. *Satchmo–Autobiography* (4 discs), MCA-10006, MCA. *America's Musical Ambassador* (live, previously unreleased—1978, 5 discs), MF-208/5, M.F. *Plays W. C. Handy*, JCL-591; *Satch Plays Fats*, JCL-708; *Ambassador Satch*, JCL-840; Collectors' Series.

BIX BEIDERBECKE

 The Bix Beiderbecke Story, Vols. 1 and *3: Bix and His Gang*, CL-844; *Whiteman Days*, CO-846; Columbia. *Bix Beiderbecke and the Chicago Cornets*, M-47019, Milestone. Derivative: *Shades of Bix: Jimmy McPartland and Bobby Hackett*, MCA2-4110, MCA. *Bix Beiderbecke* (with Goodman, Dorsey brothers, Krupa), FS-317 (Everest).

SIDNEY BECHET

 Sidney Bechet: Master Musician, 1938–1941, AXM2-5516, Bluebird (RCA). *Sidney Bechet, Vols. I, II*, FS-228, FS-323, Everest. *Bechet*, GNP-9012; GNP Crescendo. *Bechet in Philadelphia*, Vol. 2, JA-37, Jazz Archives. *The Legendary Sidney Bechet*, GNP-9037, BNP Crescendo. *Sidney Bechet: Jazz Classics, Vols. I* and *II*, BST-81201; BST-81202; Blue Note.

EDDIE CONDON

 Windy City Seven and Jam Sessions at Commodore, XFL-14427, Commodore. *The Best of Eddie Condon*, MCA2-4071, MCA. *Town Hall Concerts, Vols. I* and *II*, 108; 112; Chiaroscuro.

EARL "FATHA" HINES

 A Monday Date: 1928 (see Hines, Selected and General Discographies, Chapter 4).

BUNK JOHNSON

 Bunk Johnson (last recording, 1947), JCL-829, Collectors' Series.

GEORGE LEWIS

And His Mustache Stompers, CEN-1, Biograph. *New Orleans Jazz Band: Doctor Jazz*, DL-201; *On Parade*, DL-202; *Memorial Album*, DL-203; Delmark. *George Lewis Ragtime Jazz Band*, GHB-108; *At Congo Square*, JCE-27; Jazzology. *George Lewis, Vols. I* and *II*, BST-81205, BST-81206; *In Concert*, BST-81208; Blue Note.

JIMMY McPARTLAND

Shades of Bix (with Buddy Hackett), MCA2-4110, MCA. *Swingin'* (with Buddy Tate and Vic Dickenson), H-114, Halcyon.

FERDINAND "JELLY ROLL" MORTON

New Orleans Memories Plus Two (recorded 1939), XSF-14942, Commodore. *Jelly Roll Morton: Played by Turk Murphy and Wally Rose*, JCL-559, Columbia Special Products. Morton Library of Congress series—out-of-print. *With the New Orleans Rhythm Kings*, M-47020, Milestone. *Music of Jelly Roll Morton* (Dick Hyman on piano and ensemble), N-006, Smithsonian Collection. *Jelly Roll Morton* (rolls, 1924), FS-267 (Everest). *Blues and Stomp: Rare Piano Rolls, 1924–1926*, BLP-1004Q, Biograph. *Jelly Roll Morton, Composer* (arranged for orchestra by Dick Hyman), M-32587, Columbia.

JOE "KING" OLIVER

Louis Armstrong and King Oliver (1923–1924), M-47017, Milestone.

ORIGINAL TUXEDO JAZZ BAND

(See *New Orleans Jazz: The Twenties*, Miscellaneous.)

GERTRUDE "MA" RAINEY

Ma Rainey, M-47021, Milestone (the fidelity on all Ma Rainey albums is less than desirable). *Queen of the Blues* (1923–1924), BLP-12032; *With Her Georgia Jazz Band: Oh My Babe Blues* (1924–1928), BLP-12011; Biograph.

PEE WEE RUSSELL

Salute to Newport: Dedication Series, Vol. XV, IA-9359/2, ABC. *The Individualism of Pee Wee Russell*, SSL-2228, Savoy.

BESSIE SMITH

World's Greatest Blues Singer, CG-33; *Any Woman's Blues*, CG-30126; *Empty Bed Blues*, CG-30450; *The Empress*, CG-30818; Columbia.
Singers: Bessie Smith (1 track), *Louis Armstrong* (2 tracks), *Cab Calloway* (5 tracks), BLP-M-3, Biograph. *Jazz Singers, Vol. 4* (Smith, Armstrong, Morton, Rainey, et al.), FJ-2804, Folkways.

MUGGSY SPANIER

Dixieland Jazz in the Forties (Side B: Frank Signorelli Group), FJ-2853, Folkways. *Muggsy Spanier*, FS-226, Archives. *With Earl Hines All Stars*, GNPS-9042, GNP Crescendo.

JACK TEAGARDEN

Meet Me Where They Play the Blues, BCP-6040, Bethlehem. *The Great Soloists*, 1929–1936, BLP-C2, Biograph. *Original Dixieland*, FS-335, Archives. *King of Blues Trombone*, JSN-6044, Collectors' Series. *Jack Teagarden/Max Kaminsky*, XFL-14940, Commodore.

MISCELLANEOUS

The Smithsonian Collection of Classic Jazz (6 discs: 18 tracks—New Orleans), P-11891, Smithsonian Collection (mail). *Jazz Odyssey, Vol. 1. The*

Sound of New Orleans (3 discs: Armstrong, Oliver, Manone), JC-3L30, CSP (Columbia). *The Roots of Dixieland Jazz, Vols. I* and *II*, FS-274; FS-320; Archives. *Dixieland: The Commodore Jazz Classics* (3 discs: Bechet, Spanier, Condon, Russell), Book-of-the-Month Club Records (mail). *Pete Fountain: New Orleans All Stars*, FS-229, Archives. *Turk Murphy's San Francisco Jazz, Vol. 2*, 12027; *Bob Scobey's Frisco Band, Vol. 1*, 12032. *Lu Watters, Stomps and the Blues*, 12003; Good Time Jazz (GTJ plans to repress other masters in their catalog). *Johnny Dodds & Kid Ory*, 1926–1928, JLA 16004, Collectors' Series. *Jabbo Smith, Vols. 1* and *2*, MLP-7326; MLP-7327; Biograph. *Johnny Dodds & Tommy Ladnier, 1923–1928*, BLP-12024, Biograph. *Ethel Waters, Vols. 1 and 2* (1921–1924) BLP-12022; (1921–1927), BLP-12026; Biograph. *Recorded in New Orleans, Vols. 1* and *2*, L-12019; L-12020; Good Time Jazz. *Little Brother Montgomery: Crescent City Blues*, AXM2-5522, Bluebird (RCA). (Jazzology distributes over one hundred New Orleans and Dixieland albums—write for catalog.) *Take It, Bunny* (Bunny Berigan), JLN-3109; *The Hackett Horn* (Bobby Hackett), JEE-22003; CSP. *Barney Bigard & Orchestra: Clarinet Gumbo* (1973), APLI-1744, RCA. *Sweet Emma and Her Preservation Hall Jazz Band*, VPH-VPS-2, Preservation Hall Records (mail) (Address: 726 St. Peter Street, New Orleans, La. 70116). *Jazz, Vol. 3, New Orleans*, F-2803; *Vols. 5* and *6, Chicago (1)* and *Chicago (2)*, F-2805; F-2806; Folkways. *New Orleans Jazz: The Twenties* (liner booklet), RBF-203; *Jazz: Some Cities and Towns*, RF-32; Folkways. *Preservation Hall* (Jazz Band), M-34549, Columbia. *New Orleans* (anthology, Oliver, Armstrong, Morton, Dodds, etc.), FJ-2803, Folkways.

SWING
AND THE
BIG BANDS

4

THE WORD *swing* has probably been used with more frequency in this book than any other term in the jazz jargon. It is indispensable for describing what the music does rhythmically. Barry Ulanov asked several musicians to define it for his *History of Jazz in America* and received this classic response from Ella Fitzgerald: "Why, er—swing is—well, you sort of feel—uh—uh— I don't know—you just swing." According to Count Basie, quoted in Stanley Dance's *The World of Swing*, swing is "something to pat your foot by." These answers (*non*-answers perhaps) are appropriate and, in their way, accurate. The more basic a musical quality, the less definable it is.

Nevertheless, scholars rush in where angels fear to tread. In *Early Jazz*, Gunther Schuller attempts an analytical definition of swing in terms of "(1) a specific type of accentuation and inflection with which notes are played or sung, and (2) the continuity, the forward-propelling directionality, with which individual notes are linked together." [1] This is reminiscent of Hodier's five preconditions for swing enumerated in footnote 1 of Chapter 1. A more common, all-around conception focuses on the conflict between the rhythm of the melody and the music's fundamental rhythm (a steady beat).

Linguistically the word *swing* went through a curious evolution from a verb form to a noun. The music did not simply swing—it *was* swing. The transformation occurred during the mid-1930's, when "hot jazz," as it was first called, spread overseas. The music was played frequently on the radio in England. However, the BBC believed the phrase "hot jazz" to have sexual connotations not in keeping with its image. Announcers were instructed to use the phrase "swing music" instead, alluding perhaps to Duke Ellington's song title of 1932 "It Don't Mean a Thing, If It Ain't Got That Swing." Thus the music was labeled almost a full decade after it had begun stylistically.

Swing has been used, due to its belated coinage, to refer primarily to the white bands of Goodman, Glenn Miller, the Dorsey brothers, and other popular leaders of the late 1930's. However, here the word is broadened to include all big-band music of the era, and certainly the black bands led by Fletcher Henderson, Count Basie, Duke Ellington, Jimmie Lunceford, Chick Webb, and others, whose innovative practices were responsible for the style.

The BBC may have been overly cautious in banning "hot jazz" for its suspected sexual innuendos, but recalling Herman Hesse's similar allusions to its "raw and savage gaiety" in *Steppenwolf* (Chapter 1) makes their reaction seem a bit less prissy. Ironically the BBC's substitute word acquired its own risqué overtones during the 1960's, when "swinging" became a euphemism for sexual freedom. According to C. Major's *Dictionary of Afro-American Slang* (International Publishers, 1970), a swinger originally meant "a thrilling musician" and later "a professional pleasure seeker."

Interestingly, another jazz-related idiom of the era—to get off—also found its way into the slang of the 1960's, as a reference to sexual orgasm or a drug-induced high. In discussing dance bands in the jargon of their day, the historian Marshall W. Stearns writes: "The formula consisted of importing one or two 'hot' soloists, or 'get-off' men, letting them take a chorus once in a while surrounded by acres of uninspired fellow musicians." [2] Benny Goodman, in his autobiography *The Kingdom of Swing* (1939), says: "But the art of making an arrangement a band can play with swing . . . one that really helps a solo player to *get off*, and gives him the right background to work with—that's something very few musicians can do." [3] (Of course, these etymologies are speculative but plausible.)

The music's evolution was under way as early as the mid-1920's. The Fletcher Henderson Orchestra, playing at the Club Alabam and the Roseland Ballroom in New York, foreshadowed many of the changes ahead in the arrangements of the brilliant, nearly forgotten Don Redman. The conspicuous and immediate change was in the size of the bands. New Orleans polyphony was generally created with a trumpet, clarinet, and trombone deftly crisscrossing melody lines above a foundation of piano or guitar, drums, and tuba. However, it was a homophonic, or single-voiced, music which grew out of the big bands. Once a dominant melody was supported harmonically by the other instruments, it became possible to expand, without musical chaos, into *sections* of several trumpets, trombones, and reeds. The piano, guitar, drums, and string bass (which had replaced the tuba in most bands by the 1930's) were also welded into a rhythm section. The sections worked as tightly knit units, answering each other in the call-and-response pattern (Chapter 1) with shorter, bluesy melodic fragments, or "riffs," played repetitively. The riff became hypnotic in effect, involving the listener, focusing concentration, and stoking the band's fire with each repetition.

The big band grew to a sixteen-piece unit by the mid-1930's with seven brass, five reeds, and four rhythm instruments. Stearns speculated that this development began as a result of America's penchant for bigness. However, the motivation for growth for Fletcher Henderson, Count Basie, Duke Ellington, and their ilk was surely the additional harmonic and textural possibilities. Moreover, on a practical level, a small combo simply could not satisfy the tremendous crowds who wanted to dance.

The big bands confronted serious commercial obstacles during their formative years. First of all, after 1929 records could no longer be counted on to promote them. The record business had been expanding at full tilt throughout the 1920's. The Radio Corporation of America (RCA) must have seen the future through rose-colored glasses when it merged with the Victor Talking Machine Company in the spring of 1929. But in October the Roaring Twenties ended with the ominous crash of the stock market, and RCA Victor was soon struggling along with its competitors for mere survival. Records, although they sold for less than a dollar, were simply crossed off the shopping list of a nation which had legitimate fears of starvation. Record sales dropped from $75 million in 1929 to $18 million by 1931, and to an all-time low of $5.5 million in 1933.

The bands, which had been growing like summer wildflowers in the late 1920's, were thinned out drastically, although America wanted to dance its way through poverty. Itinerant groups played for marathon dance contests, drumming up a false gaiety nobody felt. A few—like Duke Ellington's band —played in private clubs for the wealthy or fled to Europe for as long as possible. Musicians were reduced to meaningless labor or worse. Clarinetist Sidney Bechet opened a shoeshine stand. Charlie Green, a trombonist with Fletcher Henderson and one of Bessie Smith's favorite accompanists, was found frozen on a Harlem stoop.

The demise of the disc was being predicted. As if low sales were not enough of a threat, the radio, previously a hobby for those with a high tolerance for static, was made suitable for general marketing and for music. A new electronic volume control improved the sound of the old crystal sets enormously. More than 600 licensed stations spread across the country, and radio became the handmaiden to music—hour after hour of it absolutely free. But a more profound diversion still had captivated the public eyes and ears. The first "talkie," *The Jazz Singer* starring Al Jolson, had opened in 1927. Of course, the film had no more to do with jazz than F. Scott Fitzgerald's "Echoes of the Jazz Age," but it did make several million dollars for Warner Brothers, spurring the young industry on to redouble its efforts. The public had discovered in movies a form of escapism that would be unrivaled until the mass production of television sets two decades later.

A Tale of Two Cities

Despite the threat to its livelihood from the Depression, radio, and motion pictures, jazz managed to make major artistic advances in the entertainment caldrons of the Southwest and the East. During the Prohibition years in the Southwest, Kansas City was jazz's focal point. The city was not just permissive, it was gloriously corrupt. The political machinery of Boss Tom Pendergast seldom broke down. The city manager, one Henry McElroy, conveniently adjusted the books to whitewash all of Pendergast's kickbacks, payoffs, and graft. (When McElroy died in 1937, shortly after Pendergast's conviction on charges of income tax evasion, it was discovered he had left the city $20 million in debt.[4]) Another Pendergast associate was the racketeer Tom Lazia, who had been serving time for armed robbery when he was paroled to become the Boss's aide. He was not one to forget the friends he had left behind. Lazia arranged for the release of sixty convicts and thoughtfully provided them with jobs as police officers. By 1934 it was estimated that 10 percent of the Kansas City police force had criminal records.[5] Bootleg booze was building fortunes, and jazz, the hottest music around, could draw the biggest crowds.

The jazz district in Kansas City ran from Twelfth to Eighteenth Streets, where there were allegedly fifty clubs within six square blocks. Euday L. Bowman's "Twelfth Street Rag" alludes to one of this district's boundaries. Kansas City was developing its own style of hard-driving band music based largely on the blues and forged during hot jam sessions into spontaneous "head" arrangements (or—simply—"heads"). These players generally had less formal training than those in the East, but their instincts ran deep into the roots of the jazz language. Walter Page's Blue Devils and a group led by Bennie Moten merged into one unit under the guidance of William "Count" Basie, the young pianist. When he played with Basie's band, Lester Young brought a revolutionary approach to the tenor sax which would eclipse the influence of Coleman Hawkins by the next decade.

New York celebrities like Louis Armstrong, Duke Ellington, and Fletcher Henderson visited occasionally. The local players came out in force to listen, but so committed were they to their own hard-driving, bluesy riffs that they were little impressed by these "schooled" musicians. Jam sessions and cutting sessions were common, however, and ideas were gradually traded even if they were not immediately absorbed. In fact, Kansas City jam sessions were ubiquitous, visitors or not. Endurance grew to be legendary, as pianist Sam Price recalled:

> Jam sessions in Kansas City? I remember once at the Subway Club, on Eighteenth Street, I came by a session at about ten o'clock and then went home to clean up and change my clothes. I came back a little after one o'clock and they were still playing the same song.[6]

Out of this constant interchange came a unique rapport and the ability to swing *as a group*. The precision and power achieved by the Kansas City bands exceeded anything the East Coast players could read from composition paper.

The rhythmic premise of jazz was changing dramatically in a manner stated bluntly by Count Basie in the liner notes to an out-of-print Decca album: "I don't dig that two-beat jive the New Orleans cats play, 'cause my boys and I got to have four heavy beats to the bar and no cheating." Of course, much of the New Orleans music did have four beats to the measure, but in swing the beat is smoother and more evenly accented. As Joachim Berendt noted in *The Jazz Book*, "syncopation" no longer characterizes swing as it did ragtime, for there is no strong sense of irregularity in the beat.[7] For example, Jo Jones, a drummer with Basie's band, "discovered he could play the *flow* of the rhythm and not its demarcation." [8] He accomplished this by pedaling the bass drum only occasionally (instead of on one and three, or on two and four as in the New Orleans style). Time was kept on the high-hat cymbal. Like Jo Jones, Chick Webb increased the legato flow by streamlining the drum set and using the cymbal, not the snare, to create momentum with a continually pulsating, ringing "sizzle." In his liner notes to *The Drums* (an anthology of styles, Impulse-9272) Robert Palmer illustrates the distinction by noting that "Sid Catlett (with Louis Armstrong's band) was a drummer who was seen and heard, while Jo Jones was often simply felt."

The string bass became indispensable to the new rhythmic sense, for the tuba was no longer playable as a rhythm instrument—no one had the wind to blow it on all four beats. More significantly, the pizzicato (plucked) bass conveys, in Schuller's phrase, a natural "forward-propelling directionality," a sound whose rise and decay is ideally suited to the music's rhythmic needs.[9] [The earliest uses of the bass were heard on cuts made by Jelly Roll Morton (1926) and Louis Armstrong (1929)—see Selected Discography, Chapter 2.]

What the big band learned to do during the 1930's was to play as hot and as driving as a smaller combo. Basie stressed this goal:

> I wanted my fifteen piece band to work together just like those nine pieces did. . . . I wanted those four trumpets and three trombones to bite with real guts. But I wanted that bite to be just as tasty and subtle as if it were the three brass I used to use. In fact, the only reason I enlarged the brass was to get a richer harmonic structure.[10]

And from Benny Goodman: "The whole idea is that the ensemble passages where the whole band is playing together or one section has the lead have to be written in more or less the same style that a soloist would use if he were improvising." [11]

New York's assets at this time were equally spectacular but quite different. The most influential and innovative music was being created by Duke Ellington, a pianist and self-taught composer and arranger who had moved there from Washington, D.C., in 1924. Jazz life was centered in Harlem, a place of special fascination for the white intelligentsia, who in the late 1920's began to think they had "discovered" the black man. Black life was romanticized *ad absurdum* in novels such as Carl Van Vechten's *Nigger Heaven*, which purported to be an inside look at Harlem. In fact, whites seldom saw the inside of the great black dance halls like the Savoy Ballroom, "the home of happy feet." But they did flock to what was called "jungle alley" to visit the Club Alabam or the Cotton Club on a mission which fell somewhere between "slumming" and attending a travelogue of the Dark Continent via black American music.

The interest in black roots was mostly superficial, motivated by a desire to be entertained not informed. Of course, the clubs catered to this level of curiosity with appropriately absurd pageantry, musically illustrated at the Cotton Club by Ellington's group. Marshall Stearns described one such show:

> . . . a light-skinned and magnificently muscled Negro burst through a papier-mâché jungle onto the dance floor, clad in an aviator's helmet, goggles, and shorts. He had obviously been "forced down in darkest Africa," and in the center of the floor he came upon a "white" goddess clad in long golden tresses and being worshipped by a circle of cringing "blacks." Producing a bull-whip from heaven knows where, the aviator rescued the blonde and they did an erotic dance. In the background, Bubber Miley, Tricky Sam Nanton and other members of the Ellington band growled, wheezed, and snorted obscenely.[12]

Although Ellington's program music was often tongue in cheek, the quasi-African motif gave him the opportunity to experiment with exotic and even bizarre effects which were put to serious purpose in a style that came to be called "jungle music."

Ellington soon acquired his own retinue of soloists—Bubber Miley, Cootie Williams, Joe "Tricky Sam" Nanton, Barney Bigard, and Johnny Hodges—who were capable of playing their instruments with a highly vocalized intonation. The Duke's use of tonal color, texture, and even harmonies and voicings were as distinctive and inimitable as Basie's brand of swing. Ellington was at times far ahead of the general public. Rudy Vallee, the pop song idol, typified the mystified listener, claiming in his autobiography that "the weird orchestral efforts of various bands up in Harlem" have "no distinguishable melody . . . it is absolutely impossible for even a musical ear to tell the name of a piece." [13] Ellington was pioneering new territory by writing longer compositions and ignoring the customary eight- or twelve-bar forms, and every piece was tailored to the individual sounds of his own players.

Thus in the East and the Southwest, a new and beautiful American entity, the big band, had burst from its cocoon. All it required now was an audience. Rescue was on the way, for the country returned to its senses about Prohibition. The "noble experiment" had not inspired abstinence, but rather the most ignoble binge of gangsterism America had ever encountered. In 1933 Congress acted upon this return to reason, and the economic clouds began to lift. Cabarets opened their doors wide and enlarged their dance floors. Bars which could not afford live music installed the new juke boxes; these machines were an elixir to the record business, for they were simultaneously consumers and promoters of every new release.

By the mid-1930's the swing craze was swinging madly. Teenagers invented "The Shag," though even the pre-Depression fads remained in fashion. Adults were still dancing "The Lindy Hop," which in fact commemorated Charles Lindbergh's hop across the Atlantic in 1927. Countless white bands were organized on the Henderson, Basie, and Ellington models. Their leaders became household names: the Dorsey brothers, Glenn Miller, Harry James, Woody Herman, and the so-called "King of Swing," Benny Goodman. His popularity—not his musical innovations—justified the title. In March 1937, twenty-one thousand people attended an all-day Goodman performance at the Paramount Theater in New York. The black bands enjoyed a stupendous turnout one year later when Basie, Jimmie Lunceford, and a few other bands at the Randall's Island (New York City) Carnival of Swing drew twenty-three thousand.

The bands and their vast audiences spawned a generation of singers. Even those whose reputations were made in the pop field fell under the influence of jazz sensibility. Frank Sinatra writes in George T. Simon's *The Big Bands*: "My greatest teacher was not a vocal coach, nor the work of other singers, but the way Tommy Dorsey breathed and phrased on the trombone." [14] Most of these singers—Peggy Lee, Doris Day, Sinatra, Perry Como, and Rosemary Clooney, to name a few—were quick to part company with jazz once the bands fell out of favor. A few were to have novel destinies. Dale Evans teamed up with Roy Rogers to become the nation's first modern cowgirl. Harriet Hilliard married her bandleader, Ozzie Nelson; together they brought the whole family into American homes weekly with the "Ozzie and Harriet" TV series. Of course, there were jazz singers to the core who can be heard on the selected albums in the chapters following. Jimmy Rushing, who was steeped in the blues, recorded with the early Basie band; and Billie Holiday, with Lester Young and Teddy Wilson. Ella Fitzgerald and Sarah Vaughan started out with Chick Webb and Earl Hines, respectively, but their best albums come from a later vintage.

New York and Kansas City did not remain distinguishable as local styles for long. Once Prohibition was repealed, the bands traveled to dance halls all over the country on grueling strings of one-nighters. Players from the different regions soon began working together; and after Benny Goodman broke through the color line by hiring black pianist Teddy Wilson and vibraharpist Lionel Hampton, racially mixed bands became more common. Record companies and promoters, just beginning to discover the arcane science of publicity, attempted to market these bands to the masses. This was not difficult to do because dancing was still the country's favorite pastime. Radio, too, was a decentralizing force. By 1936 or so, each band was known for its own sound, regardless of its point of origin, and jazz had gone national in a bigger way than ever.

**FLETCHER HENDERSON and
DON REDMAN**

*Developing an American Orchestra,
1923–1937*

Smithsonian Collection, R006 (mail order;
see Appendix)
two discs, excellent liner notes

Musicians: Fletcher Henderson, piano; with various bands such as Louis Armstrong's. Elmer Chambers, Howard Scott, trumpets; Coleman Hawkins, tenor sax and clarinet; Don Redman, Buster Bailey, alto sax and clarinet; Charlie Dixon, banjo; Ralph Escudero, tuba; Kaiser Marshall, drums. Also with Rex Stewart, Russell Smith, Bobby Stark, trumpets; J. C. Higgenbotham, trombone; Russell Procope, Hilton Jefferson, alto sax and clarinet; Coleman Hawkins, tenor sax; Freddie White, guitar; John Kirby, bass; and Walter Johnson, drums. Other personnel of note include Fats Waller, piano; Benny Morton, trombone; Benny Carter, alto sax; and Roy Eldridge, trumpet.

Compositions (most arrangements on sides one and two by Don Redman): *Side one:* Dicty Blues; The Gouge of Armour Avenue; Go 'long Mule; Shanghai Shuffle; Copenhagen; Naughty Man; TNT; The Stampede. *Side two:* The Henderson Stomp; Snag It; Rocky Mountain Blues; Tozo; Wabash Blues; Whiteman Stomp; I'm Coming, Virginia; Hop Off. *Side three:* King Porter Stomp; Blazin'; Somebody Loves Me; Keep a Song in Your Soul; Sugar Foot Stomp; Hot and Anxious; Honeysuckle Rose; New King Porter Stomp. *Side four:* Yeah Man!; King Porter Stomp; Queer Notions; Can You Take It?; Christopher Columbus; Blue Lou; Stealin' Apples; Sing You Sinners.

FLETCHER HENDERSON'S Orchestra was the first of the influential big bands, developing the foundations of the swing style as early as the mid-1920's. Under the inspired direction of Don Redman, the group introduced blues-tinged riffs, voiced for multiple brass and reeds or for sections, a call-and-response dialogue between these sections, and alternating ensemble and solo passages. Jazz's first soloist, Louis Armstrong, and the father of the tenor sax, Coleman Hawkins, were launched by Henderson's orchestra, and at a time when the Paul Whiteman organization was proclaiming the "death of improvising" and the supremacy of the arrangement. Henderson's music proved jazz could have the best of both worlds—arrangement and improvisation.

Musicians considered it an honor to work with "Smack" (an epithet deriving from Henderson's college baseball batting average), because his book (of arrangements) was the most difficult of its day, demanding sight-reading skills beyond those of most New Orleans players. Smack had a marvelous ear for talent too. His manner was relaxed and unimposing, encouraging the soloists to express themselves freely.

Henderson came to New York in 1920 from his native Georgia with a college degree in chemistry and every intention of doing further research. As a black man, he could find no acceptable employment in the field, so he went to work as a pianist for W. C. Handy's fledgling record company, Black Swan; its claim to distinction read: "The only genuinely colored record . . . the rest are only passing." Henderson received a good musical education, mostly from his mother, but he had been quite rigorously sheltered from the "unwholesome" influence of ragtime and blues. In fact, Ethel Waters, the singer Henderson first accompanied in New York, insisted he listen to James P. Johnson records (Chapter 2) because his feeling for the blues was so inadequate. Henderson was also reticent, refined, and accommodating to a fault. He had little appetite for the music business and none of the ambition or relentless perfectionism which served Duke Ellington and Benny Goodman so well. At first, Henderson's success was due primarily to his association with Don Redman and the most exciting soloists of the 1920's.

Don Redman, whose contribution to jazz arranging has often been overlooked, was the brilliant mind behind the group's early achievements. Redman, a child prodigy born in Virginia in 1900, played practically every instrument in the band and received a thorough training in composition at the Boston Conservatory of Music. Even Redman's alto sax playing was ahead of its time, as demonstrated in his accompaniment of Bessie Smith (see Chapter 2). Henderson himself was more of a catalyst than an arranger in his own band, not acquiring Redman's sophistication until the mid-1930's, when he also wrote some of Benny Goodman's most exciting charts (see Goodman discussion ahead).

This Smithsonian album, culled primarily from Columbia's out-of-print four-disc set, is a documentation of the band's historic development from a rough-running prototype to a tight, well-oiled machine. The only comparable collection is RCA's two-disc Bluebird set, *The Complete Fletcher Henderson,* which aside from the advanced soloing of Coleman Hawkins and Roy Eldridge, contains many weak concessions to commercialism in the form of insipid vocals. (See also General Discography.)

On the Smithsonian, "Dicty Blues" (1923) reveals the influence of New Orleans polyphony and the collective style of King Oliver's Creole Jazz Band, which had also recorded for the first time during that year in Chicago. When Louis Armstrong left Oliver to join Henderson in 1924, changes became obvious immediately, as on "Go 'long Mule" (1924) and "TNT" (1925); Redman suddenly had a soloist around whom he could build thicker instrumental textures. The "TNT" track previews an exciting dynamic of the swing-era band, when the horn sections "answer" the soloist in harmonized variations upon the theme. Coleman Hawkins learned quickly from Louis Armstrong, as we hear on "The Stampede" (1926), on which he has given up the jerky "slap tongue" articulation of the preceding year and seems to float above the band.

Redman has found his stride by "Rocky Mountain Blues" (1927), in which the "seamless" arrangement flows smoothly between the dense, powerful band sound and brief solo breaks by trumpeters Joe Smith and Tommy Ladnier, Coleman Hawkins on tenor sax, and Benny Morton on trombone. (The album liner notes, which offer a thorough historical study of Henderson by J. R. Taylor, indicate the order of the soloists.) The band has become flexible in Redman's hands, varying its texture with apparent ease. Such is the precedent followed by Benny Carter on "Blazin' " (1929) after Redman had left the group to work with McKinney's Cotton Pickers. Carter sets off Rex Stewart's trumpet solo beautifully by varying the background and using the sax section in a call-and-response pattern.

"Somebody Loves Me" (1930) ushers in an important rhythmic advance in the substitution of John Kirby's bass for the tuba and, for that matter, the guitar of Clarence Holiday (Billie's father) for the anachronistic banjo. The bass creates momentum from the bottom, allowing Hawkins to solo more expressively without causing the orchestra to sound top-heavy. Henderson's own first arrangement on Oliver's "Sugar Foot Stomp" (1931), is actually a reworking of a Redman chart, not at all an auspicious debut save for the invigorating "shout" in the last chorus, in which the brass punctuates the saxophones' riff. However, the new version of Jelly Roll's "King Porter Stomp" (1933) on side four, on which the sections' trading of riffs builds to an explosive level, is the album's peak performance for sheer excitement. The orchestra was not known for its precise technique but for its capacity to swing, a talent Henderson was finally able to tap with his own writing, as side four demonstrates.

The Henderson organization finally fell victim to the Depression years, but, as we shall see ahead, Henderson himself acquired even more widespread recognition for his arrangements of "King Porter," "Blue Skies," and "Sometimes I'm Happy" for the Benny Goodman orchestra. Henderson worked sporadically as an accompanist, arranger, and bandleader until a stroke forced his retirement in 1950 at the age of forty-seven. He died two years later.

DUKE ELLINGTON

"Rockin' in Rhythm"/Duke Ellington and the Jungle Band, Volume 3, 1929–1931

MCA-2077, MCA
one disc, liner notes

Musicians: Duke Ellington, piano; Arthur Whetsol, Freddie Jenkins, Cootie Williams, trumpets; Joe "Tricky Sam" Nanton, Juan Tizol, trombones; Johnny Hodges, alto and soprano saxes; Barney Bigard, clarinet; Harry Carney, baritone sax; Fred Guy, banjo; Wellman Braud, bass; Sonny Greer, drums. Occasional vocals by Irving Mills or Benny Payne.

Compositions (by Ellington where indicated; all arrangements by Ellington): *Side one:* Sweet Mama (Ellington); Wall Street Wail (Ellington); Cincinnati Daddy (Ellington); When You're Smiling; Admiration; Double Check Stomp; Cotton Club Stomp (Ellington *et al.*); Runnin' Wild. *Side two:* Mood Indigo (Ellington); Home Again Blues; Wang Wang Blues; Rockin' in Rhythm (Ellington); Twelfth Street Rag; Creole Rhapsody (Ellington); Is That Religion?

Duke Ellington—1940

Smithsonian Collection, R-013
two discs, excellent liner notes
(mail order; see Appendix)

Musicians: Duke Ellington, piano; Cootie Williams, Wallace Jones, trumpets; Rex Stewart, cornet; Joe "Tricky Sam" Nanton, Lawrence Brown, trombones; Juan Tizol, valve trombone; Barney Bigard, clarinet and tenor sax; Johnny Hodges, alto sax and soprano sax; Otto Hardwick, Ben Webster, tenor sax; Harry Carney, baritone sax, alto sax, and clarinet; Fred Guy, guitar; Jimmy Blanton, bass; Sonny Green, drums; Ivie Anderson and Herb Jeffries, vocals. Also Ellington-Blanton duets (on tracks marked *).

Compositions (all compositions by Ellington except "Body and Soul," "Chloe," and "Sidewalks of New York"; all arrangements by Ellington except "Chloe"): *Side* *one:* Jack the Bear; Ko-Ko (alternate master); Ko-Ko; Morning Glory; Conga Brava; Concerto For Cootie; Me and You; Cotton Tail. *Side two:* Never No Lament; Dusk; Bojangles; A Portrait of Bert Williams; Blue Goose; Harlem Airshaft; At a Dixie Roadside Diner; All Too Soon. *Side three:* Rumpus In Richmond; Sepia Panorama; Sepia Panorama (alternate master); In a Mellotone; Warm Valley; Pitter, Panther, Patter*; Body and Soul.* *Side four:* Sophisticated Lady*; Mr. J. B. Blues*; Mr. J. B. Blues* (alternate master); The Flaming Sword; Across the Track Blues; Chloe; I Never Felt This Way Before; Sidewalks of New York.

The Duke Ellington Carnegie Hall Concerts—January, 1943

Prestige, P-34004
three discs, good liner notes

Musicians: Duke Ellington, piano; Rex Stewart, Harold Baker, Wallace Jones, Ray Nance, trumpets; Ray Nance, violin; Joe "Tricky Sam" Nanton, Juan Tizol, Lawrence Brown, trombones; Johnny Hodges, alto sax; Ben Webster, Otto Hardwicke, Chauncey Haughton, tenor saxes and reeds; Harry Carney, baritone sax; Fred Guy, guitar; Junior Raglin, bass; Sonny Greer, drums; Betty Roche, vocal on "Brown" in "Black, Brown and Beige."

Compositions (all compositions by Ellington, except as indicated; all arrangements by Ellington and assistant arranger Billy Strayhorn): *Side one:* The Star-Spangled Banner (Francis Scott Key); Black and Tan Fantasy; Rockin' in Rhythm; Moon Mist; Jumpin' Punkins (Mercer-Ellington). *Side two:* Portrait of Bert Williams; Portrait of Bojangles; Portrait of Florence Mills; Ko-Ko; Dirge (Strayhorn); Stomp (Strayhorn); Are You Stickin'? *Side three:* Black, Brown and Beige; Bakiff (Tizol); Jack the Bear; Blue Bells of Harlem; Cotton Tail; Day Dream (Strayhorn). *Side four:* Boy Meets Horn; Rose of the Rio Grande (Leslie-Warren-Gorman); Don't Get Around Much Anymore; Goin' Up; Mood Indigo.

The Golden Duke

Prestige, P-24029
two discs, liner notes
1946, 1950

Musicians: Duke Ellington, piano; with Cootie Williams, Taft Jordan, Harold Baker, Shelton Hemphill, trumpets; Ray Nance, trumpet and violin; Cat Anderson, trumpet (five tracks only); Lawrence Brown, Claude Jones, Wilbur DeParis, trombones; Jimmy Hamilton, clarinet and tenor sax; Johnny Hodges, alto sax; Russell Procope, alto sax and clarinet; Al Sears, tenor sax; Harry Carney, baritone sax and clarinet; Fred Guy, guitar; Oscar Pettiford, bass; Sonny Greer, drums. Also Ellington and Billy Strayhorn in piano duets, also along with Wendell Marshall on bass—all of side three plus two tracks of side four; and with Oscar Pettiford, cello; Lloyd Trotman, bass; and Jo Jones, drums—on four tracks of side four.

Compositions (by Ellington unless otherwise indicated): *Side one:* Jam-a-Ditty; Diminuendo in Blue; Magenta Haze; Blue Skies (I. Berlin); The Beautiful Indians—Hiawatha; The Beautiful Indians—Minnehaha; Overture to a Jam Session (Strayhorn). *Side two:* Flippant Flurry (Strayhorn); Golden Feather; Tulip or Turnip; It Shouldn't Happen to a Dream; Sultry Sunset; Happy-Go-Lucky Local. *Side three:* Cottontail; C-Jam Blues; Flamingo (Grouya-Anderson); Bang-Up Blues; Tonk; Johnny Come Lately (Strayhorn). *Side four:* In a Blue Summer Garden; Great Times; Perdido (Tizol); Take the "A" Train (Strayhorn); Oscalypso (Pettiford-Trotman); Blues for Blanton (Duke and Mercer Ellington).

Pure Gold

RCA, ANL1-2811
one disc, no liner notes
1966

Musicians: Duke Ellington, piano; Cootie Williams, Cat Anderson, Mercer Ellington, Herbie Jones, trumpets; Harry Carney, baritone sax; Russell Procope, alto sax and clarinet; Johnny Hodges, alto sax; Jimmy Hamilton, Paul Gonsalves, tenor saxes; Lawrence Brown, Buster Cooper, Chuck Connors, trombones; John Lamb, bass; Sam Woodyard, drums.

Compositions: Side one: Take the "A" Train; I Got It Bad (and That Ain't Good); Perdido; Mood Indigo; Black and Tan Fantasy. *Side two:* The Twitch; Solitude; Do Nothin' Til You Hear from Me; The Mooche; Sophisticated Lady; Creole Love Call. (All compositions by Ellington except " 'A' Train" by Strayhorn and "Perdido" by Tizol. Arrangements are not credited but are probably Ellington's, except for " 'A' Train.")

"ELLINGTON PLAYS the piano, but his real instrument is his band," his close collaborator Billy Strayhorn once remarked. Duke Ellington is jazz's greatest composer and arranger, credited with approximately five thousand original works, ranging from the rich, intensely compacted "miniatures" designed for the three-minute limit of early recording equipment to the forty-eight-minute suite of "Black, Brown and Beige," introduced at his first Carnegie Hall concert in 1943. The forms he mastered encompass the popular and the symphonic, dirty blues and sacred music, tender, sensuous ballads and swinging romps. Looking back upon Ellington's forty-seven-year recording career (from 1926 to 1973), the listener is overwhelmed by the feeling that the man could do everything. Although a familiar refrain, it cannot be said too often that Duke Ellington's work is the towering monument in the field of jazz and, consequently, in American music, too.

In an unprecedented manner, Ellington created a musical world which is reflected by the critical language surrounding it. Facts about his life, work habits, and the loyal musicians who traveled with him for decades are *Ellingtonia;* music which resembles the unique coloration and vocalized inflection of "Harlem Airshaft" and "Sepia Panorama" are described as *Ellingtonian;* and his legacy of albums is called a *Ducal* discography. Ellington's autobiography, *Music Is My Mistress,* Barry Ulanov's *Duke Ellington,* and Stanley Dance's *The World of Duke Ellington* are the best sources for further investigation of that world.

Naturally the full Ducal discography cannot be examined in a comprehensive volume such as this one. Thus the albums that have been selected present, at memorable peaks, the crucial aspects of Ellington's contribution: the innovative composer and arranger, the pianist, and the popular songwriter. The reader must be warned that there is a dearth of material from the important period from 1927 to 1937 due to Columbia's recent deletion of *The Ellington Era, Volume 1, 1927–1940.* RCA has also neglected to keep its excellent early Ellington in print. These boxed sets are available, however, through French RCA and CBS for listeners with the time and budget to obtain them. Thus the MCA (then known as Decca) sides on *Rockin' in Rhythm* (1929–1931) have been selected here as a second-best, but by no means unsatisfying, substitute. (Note: Too late for discussion in this volume, Time-Life Records has released *Duke Ellington: Giants of Jazz*—three discs of tracks from 1926 to 1956, including eight tracks from before 1933.)

Ellington's childhood was not at all characterized by a passion for music. Born Edward Kennedy Ellington in Washington, D.C., in 1899, Duke was brought up in a well-to-do family; his father served as chief butler to a prominent doctor and, later, was a blueprint designer. Young Edward, who was nicknamed Duke in high school for his sartorial elegance, showed an early talent for drawing too, winning a poster contest sponsored by the NAACP. He had begun piano lessons with a teacher named, oddly enough, Mrs. Clinkscales, but he was more interested in baseball, girls, and art. As a teenager, however, his interest in the piano grew under the influence of the Harlem ragtime style. Duke learned James P. Johnson's "Carolina Shout" by putting the roll on a player piano and watching how the keys went down. Duke called it his "party piece," for he quickly became aware of the social advantages of playing the piano. Soon he formed a band to cater to Washington night life during the war years, and this group included his friend, drummer Sonny Greer, who remained with him until 1953. Duke had not abandoned art; he worked regularly as a commercial sign painter. In fact, Ellington was offered a scholarship to the Pratt Institute in Brooklyn, but the money he was making in Washington appealed to him more.

In 1922 Duke brought his band to New York as The Washingtonians, but the group, which included Greer, Arthur Whetsol on trumpet, Elmer Snowden on banjo, and Toby Hardwick on bass and alto sax, failed to find work and eventually joined a larger band led by Wilbur Sweatman. Although Duke failed commercially, the year he spent in New York was of great educational benefit due to the Harlem rent parties and cutting contests dominated by Johnson, Willie "The Lion" Smith, and Fats Waller. The Harlem stride pianists were the only identifiable influences upon his style, conspicuous as late as 1943 in his piano interlude on "Portrait of Florence Mills." Having run out of funds, The Washingtonians returned home, until, at the urging of Fats Waller, they tried New York once more in 1923.

Ellington's musical education had been scant. He learned to arrange and compose on the job by trial and error when his band started at the Kentucky

Club, where it would remain for almost five years. Ellington never regretted that he was self-taught, noting later that formal education might have stifled his originality and encouraged him to employ the methods of the past rather than a personalized style. The Ellington style, however, was very much a function of the musicians in his band. He always tailored each part to the strengths of his players, whom he knew, according to trumpeter Rex Stewart, "down to the way they played poker." Strayhorn later commented, "I have often seen him exchange parts in the middle of a piece because the man and the part weren't (of) the same character." [15]

The musicians who most affected Duke's early writing were cornetist Bubber Miley and trombonist Joe "Tricky Sam" Nanton, both of whom were in the Kentucky Club group by 1926 and were capable of playing with a very highly vocalized inflection. If King Oliver invented the plunger mute, Ellington brought it to a point of sophistication not yet surpassed. He got Miley and Nanton to sound like a zoo full of animals, crying babies, and panting lovers. Duke had new tunes, like "Black and Tan Fantasy," which was written in a taxi cab on the way to a recording session (a stunning version appears on *Carnegie Hall Concerts—1943*); in them the modest horn section nearly "spoke" to the audience. Radio broadcasts of the band made the Kentucky Club a hot spot, and one night Irving Mills, Duke's manager for many years afterward, stopped in for a drink. Hearing Miley "growling away obscenely" on the cornet, he knew this was no ordinary dance band. He had them booked into the more impressive Cotton Club by the end of 1927.

Ellington remained at the Cotton Club for five years, during which his band established itself as the most innovative orchestra in jazz. (Actually the field was rather empty at the time; Fletcher Henderson's group waned when Don Redman left it for McKinney's Cotton Pickers, and Count Basie and Benny Goodman—who were no match for Ellington orchestrally—had not yet formed their hard-swinging groups.) The band expanded to eleven members, including new and important instrumentalists: Wellman Braud on bass had replaced the tuba by 1926, increasing the group's swing; Juan Tizol (later the composer of "Perdido" and "Caravan," two of the band's classics) on the rare valve trombone, and Harry Carney on baritone sax gave Ellington unique tonal colors in the bass register; Johnny Hodges, the major alto sax stylist before Charlie Parker, provided a sexy, sultry sonority in the higher register; Cootie Williams replaced Bubber Miley on cornet, but with an equally vocalized style and more accomplished technique; and Barney Bigard filled in the middle register with the clarinet.

Ellington's "jungle music" band was in full bloom, accompanying nightly the bizarre floor shows with the quasi-African motifs alluded to in the introduction to this chapter. Ellington was now a musical illustrator of sorts, rotating tonal effects with kaleidoscopic variety, a quality heard in abundance on all the albums selected here. Similarly his increasingly vocalized brass and reed sections began to speak with an enlarged vocabulary. Dense, mysterious ensemble sections were juxtaposed with an isolated, "talking" horn. Ellington's group recorded plentifully in these years, often under pseudonyms to escape contractual obligations. While *Rockin' in Rhythm*, as explained earlier, is not the best of the group's music from 1929 to 1931, it does contain three individually excellent and historically significant tracks. "Mood Indigo" was Duke's first popular hit, written in fifteen minutes while he was waiting for his mother to cook dinner. As its title implies, it creates a unique mood made possible by the muted, vocal use of the horns. "Rockin' " itself, written as a dance number, is simply a masterpiece of swing. The most auspicious track of all, "Creole Rhapsody," originally released on two sides of a shellac disc, is unprecedented in its six-minute length, revealing the composer's immediate need to expand the boundaries of jazz composition. Duke's wonderfully dissonant piano interludes here show his indebtedness to the Harlem stride style as well as his harmonic advances beyond it.

In short, the Ellington band was not a showcase for a string of solos or simply a riffing machine; it was, as Strayhorn might have put it, a powerful, variegated new instrument in Duke's hands. Another innovation of this period was the use of the human voice not to sing lyrics but as an instrument itself on "Creole Love Call" (1927), "The Mooche" (1928), and "Hot and Bothered" (1928). Ellington was also expanding his jazz compositional form by using melodic ideas that did not conform to the four- or eight-bar mode. "Reminiscing in Tempo" (1935), written upon the death of his mother, was another composition which crossed the three-minute recording boundary.

The Ellington band suffered less than most during the Depression years because of the international reputation it had acquired while at the Cotton Club. Still when the band returned home from its first European tour in 1933, it recorded relatively little due to the economic crisis. During the 1930's, however, Duke wrote many of his most popular songs (to be discussed ahead) and acquired the cornetist Rex Stewart, who went even farther than Cootie Williams in creating naturalistic (some say weird) tonal ("half-valve") effects. The Smithsonian's *Duke Ellington—1938* and *Duke Ellington—1939*, two well-annotated two-disc sets containing some excellent tracks—like "Skrontch" (*1938*) and "Portrait of the Lion" (*1939*)—are nevertheless not representative of the 1930's. The band had been weakened due to illness and the atypical fluctuations of personnel. These years proved to be the darkness before a new dawn.

Duke Ellington—1940 is an album of consistency and brilliance which inaugurates a lustrous golden period lasting through 1943. Several changes coincided to bring this about. Duke was writing better and more original music than at any time since the Cotton Club days. The most impressive roster of soloists yet assembled were in the band. Ben Webster, Duke's first great tenor sax soloist, had been flirting with the group and finally made a commitment. Cootie Williams, who would soon depart, was still there with Rex Stewart behind him. The young genius Jimmy Blanton, the first solo artist of the string bass, added another melodic voice to the rhythm section, one that Duke used copiously on pieces like "Sepia Panorama," "Jack the Bear," and in the fascinating piano duets on side four of this album. Blanton, who was only nineteen years old, had been discovered by Webster at a jam session in a St. Louis restaurant and was hired within days. Ellington, who avoided firing a man at all costs, carried two bassists for a while until Billy Taylor bowed out gracefully, telling Duke, "I'm not going to stand up next to that young boy playing all that bass and be embarrassed." Just listening to Blanton's bowed solo on "Body and Soul" or "Sophisticated Lady" adequately demonstrates his awesome maturity.

Most important of all, Ellington met and hired Billy Strayhorn, who had auditioned some of his own compositions for Ellington on the band's tour through Pennsylvania the preceding year. "Strays" relieved Duke of some of the arranging chores and also contributed major works to the band's book, like "Take the 'A' Train" (1941), which became their theme song. The artistic compatibility of these men was singular, leading to the incomparable two-piano collaborations of *The Golden Duke*. Strayhorn continued to serve as Duke's second pair of hands until his death in 1967.

At full strength Ellington and the band could produce masterpieces like "Ko-Ko," "Sepia Panorama," "Cotton Tail," and "Harlem Airshaft." "Ko-Ko," part of a projected opera with an African motif, epitomizes several of the Ellington achievements: the naturalistic ("jungle music") feeling of the first theme; the plumbing of the bass-register sonorities in Harry Carney's opening baritone sax lead followed by Juan Tizol's valve trombone; the climactic dissonance of Ellington's piano juxtaposed with the horns, as his chords crash and splash behind them; and finally, the vocal, individualized sound of all the instruments, a quality which profoundly influenced later jazz composers like Charles Mingus (Chapter 6).

"Sepia Panorama," basically a blues surrounded by disparate yet interconnected ideas, illustrates Duke's ability to make melodies emerge magically from a richly colored environment. He did not simply set the melody on top of the background. In the midst of the ensemble, Duke's dissonant solo, with its large silent spaces, reveals one source of his impact on the style of Thelonious Monk (Chapter 5). "Concerto for Cootie," which later became "Do Nothin' Til You Hear From Me," is the classic case of spontaneity without improvisation. Although Williams does not ad lib a note of his solo, the music seems to come directly from him, a tribute to the personalized quality of Duke's writing.

The liner notes to this album, written by Larry Gushee, a music professor, provide pages of detailed commentary on the tracks, making *1940* an aesthetic and educational treasure. Yet another album of the band's peak year, *Duke Ellington at Fargo, 1940: Live!*, captures a brilliant performance, perhaps richer in soloing than the Smithsonian album. The three-disc set is available through Book-of-the-Month Club Records by mail order (see Appendix).

The Carnegie Hall Concerts: January, 1943 contains the first jazz concert presented in this prestigious hall since Benny Goodman's swing festival of 1938 (see the Goodman discography ahead). Duke premiered the forty-eight-minute "Black, Brown and Beige" suite, which he introduces as a "parallel to the history of the American Negro." The ambitious work is a *tour de force* containing the memorable spiritual "Come Sunday," which follows the work song of the first movement. The alto sax solo by Johnny Hodges is, according to Leonard Feather, "arguably the most exquisite moments of music ever heard on a concert stage." This album contains the only complete version of the suite on record. There is much else of singular value on these three discs: a new "Black and Tan Fantasy" with Ray Nance (also a violinist) on the "talking" trumpet part; the early hit "Rockin' in Rhythm"; the series of portraits of black entertainers, especially "Portrait of Florence Mills," with Duke's stride-piano solo and more of that compressed orchestral variety; and new versions of "Ko-Ko," "Cotton Tail," and "Mood Indigo." [Prestige has released three more two-disc sets (General Discography) of Duke's seven Carnegie Hall concerts, the best of these being *1947* for the percussive "Liberian Suite" and the nearly atonal "Clothed Woman."]

Thus, Duke Ellington's classic period (from 1940 to 1943) is characterized by overwhelming variety in structure, individualized instrumental sounds, a broad spectrum of tonal colors, and unique, memorable melodies. The pianist and conductor André Previn paid tribute to the inimitability of it all in a famous comment made to the critic Ralph J. Gleason:

> You know Stan Kenton can stand in front of a thousand fiddles and a thousand brass and make a dramatic gesture and every studio arranger can nod his head and say, "Oh yes, that's done like this." But Duke merely lifts his little finger, three horns make a sound, and I don't know what it is.[16]

The years from 1946 to 1950, which are represented on *The Golden Duke*, brought more fluctuation into the band's ranks, resulting in the loss of Rex Stewart and Joe "Tricky Sam" Nanton. On the plus side, Oscar Pettiford, the artistic heir to Blanton (who had died at twenty-one of tuberculosis), took over the melodic bass style, and Cat Anderson boosted the brassiness of the trumpets. On sides one and two the swinging "Jam-a-Ditty," the trumpet *tours de force* of "Blue Skies," and the band's superb "Happy-Go-Lucky Local" are the often-praised legacy of the 1946 band. Nevertheless, the importance of this album is found on sides three and four in the sensational piano duets of Ellington and Strayhorn. With the uncertain availability of the album *Money Jungle* (with Charles Mingus and Max Roach), these tracks—originally recorded for Duke's label Mercer Records, named after his son—become the most revealing examples of his playing apart from the orchestra.

Ellington's piano style establishes a dividing line between those who use the instrument percussively (Duke Ellington, Thelonious Monk, McCoy Tyner, Cecil Taylor) and those who emphasize its harmonic-melodic flow

(Earl Hines, Art Tatum, Oscar Peterson, Bill Evans). Naturally these styles are not mutually exclusive, and they share a common bond in their Harlem ragtime roots. Nevertheless, Ellington's strong use of the bass register—perhaps a reflection of his orchestral thinking—his sharp striking of the keys, and his dissonant chords comprise a distinctive pianistic concept. Especially in contrast with Strayhorn's lush background harmonies, Duke is authoritative, virile, and stirring. Fantasy's *The Pianist* is a later, less characteristic session of Ellington with a trio.

The popular Duke Ellington—which in fact had been the original title of *Pure Gold*—began in 1930 with his first hit, "Mood Indigo." "Sophisticated Lady" and "In a Sentimental Mood" followed soon after. By the 1950's the Ellington "songbook" included "Don't Get Around Much Anymore," "I Got It Bad (and That Ain't Good)," "I'm Beginning to See the Light," and "Satin Doll." Ellington's romantic sentiments on *Pure Gold* never compromise the band's dignity or strength, and his weighty, rhythmic piano playing adds a prominent tonal color, especially on " 'A' Train" and "Black and Tan Fantasy," in which he punctuates the band's statements forcefully.

Perhaps the world of Ellington albums is best left for the reader to explore with the General Discography as a supplementary guide. However, two more albums must be singled out. Columbia's *Ellington at Newport (1956)* captures a live performance that is legendary because of the rousing twenty-seven-chorus solo on "Diminuendo and Crescendo in Blue" by Paul Gonsalves, the tenor saxophonist who inherited Ben Webster's chair. Another wonderfully alive date from 1966 is found on Verve's *Duke Ellington & Ella Fitzgerald at the Côte d'Azur*. Ella sings less frequently here than one would like, but there are some thrilling moments which are recorded with vibrant fidelity.

Ellington's band continued to tour year-round until his last recorded session (*Eastbourne Performance*, 1973), a year before his death of lung cancer on May 24, 1974. Keeping his orchestra on the road was one of the keys to his success, for he was able to hear, revise, and improve upon his compositions almost before the ink was dry, an asset not even the great European composers enjoyed. Hearing his new music immediately, played by instrumentalists whose styles he knew intimately, was his biggest thrill. He paid some of them up to $600 per week, and there were many who had been with him a total of twenty years: Johnny Hodges, Cootie Williams, Ray Nance, Lawrence Brown, Jimmy Hamilton, and Russell Procope. Asked why he did not simply retire and live off his abundant royalties, Duke replied, "I let them have all the money, and I have all the fun." Ellington, however, was ultimately serious, and his contribution to jazz, profound. Even his speaking voice, recorded while introducing "Black, Brown and Beige," communicates *savoir-faire*, intelligence, and dignity. The Duke's epithet was a fitting one. He not only created elegant music that commanded respect—he was a regal human being.

**COUNT BASIE
and HIS ORCHESTRA**

The Best of Count Basie

MCA, MCA2-4050
two discs, brief liner notes, no credits or
dates
1937–1939

Musicians: Count Basie, piano; Lester Young, Herschel Evans, tenor saxes; Joe Keyes,
Carl Smith, Buck Clayton, trumpets; George Hunt, Dan Minor, trombones; Jack
Washington, alto and baritone saxes; Caughey Roberts, alto sax; Claude Williams,
guitar; Walter Page, bass; Jo Jones, drums. Most tracks with Freddie Green or
Eddie Durham replacing Williams on guitar; and Dickie Wells or Eddie Durham,
trombone; replacing Hunt and Minor. Other soloists include Harry "Sweets"
Edison, trumpet; Chu Berry, tenor sax; and Jimmy Rushing, vocals on four tracks,
and Helen Humes, vocals on one track.
Compositions: Side one: One O'Clock Jump; Swinging at the Daisy Chain; Texas Shuffle;
Time Out; You Can Depend on Me; Panassié Stomp. *Side two:* Swinging the Blues;
Blue and Sentimental; John's Idea; Sent for You Yesterday; Blame It on My Last
Affair; Cherokee. *Side three:* Jumpin' at the Woodside; Honeysuckle Rose; Boogie
Woogie; Oh, Lady Be Good; Shorty George; Out the Window. *Side four:* Doggin'
Around; Topsy; Every Tub; Blues in the Dark; Roseland Shuffle; Jive at Five.

Sixteen Men Swinging

Verve, V-2-2517
two discs, liner notes
1953–1954

Musicians: Count Basie, piano; Thad Jones, Joe Newman, Reunald Jones, Wendell
Culley, trumpets; Frank Wess, Bill Graham, Marshall Royal, Frank Foster, Charlie
Fowlkes, tenor saxes; Ernie Wilkins, alto sax; Henry Coker, Bill Hughes, Ben
Powell, trombones; Eddie Jones, bass; Freddie Green, guitar; Gus Johnson,
drums.
Compositions: Side one: Straight Life; Basie Goes Wess; Softly with Feeling; Cherry

Point; Bubbles; Right On; Blues Done Come Back. *Side two:* Peace Pipe; Stereo-phonic; Mambo Mist; Sixteen Men Swinging; She's Just My Size; I Feel Like a New Man. *Side three:* You for Me; Soft Drink; Two for the Blues; Slow but Sure; Blues Backstage; Down for the Count. *Side four:* Perdido; Ska-Di-Dle-Dee-Bee-Doo; Two Franks; Rails; Even Tide; Ain't Misbehavin'.

WITH ITS DRIVE, spontaneity, and blues riffs, the early Count Basie Orchestra evokes the jumping, nonstop night life of Prohibition-era Kansas City. Years of jamming together had produced in these soloists, among the best of the 1930's, a telepathic rapport, unsurpassed in any other large ensemble. The cuts on MCA's *The Best of Count Basie*, the records which made Basie's reputation, are "head" arrangements, not written down until years after they had been played and perfected. As drummer Jo Jones recalled, nobody had to be told what or when to play—"spiritually, they knew when to come in." Two decades later in the 1950's, the Count Basie Orchestra became an "arranger's band," which nevertheless managed to preserve its pristine qual-ities under the superbly crafted scores of Ernie Wilkins, Chico O'Farrill, Quincy Jones, Oliver Nelson, and Neal Hefti. Basie remained steadfastly at the helm throughout the 1970's, keeping his light, powerful rhythm section on course with "four heavy [that is, strong] beats to the bar and no cheating."

The Count, born William Basie in 1904 in Red Bank, New Jersey, learned to play piano from his mother. He soon became a fan of the Harlem stride pianists, especially Fats Waller with whom he studied the organ on an informal basis. Basie began to accompany traveling vaudeville groups until he found himself stranded and broke in Kansas City. After playing back-ground piano in silent-movie theaters and with little-known groups, Basie was invited to join the best of the local bands in 1928—Walter Page's Blue Devils—which then included the powerful blues shouter Jimmy Rushing. Thus Basie had already met the key personnel in his own big band, for it was Page's bass which gave his piano playing its rhythmic punch. This group also included Oran "Hot Lips" Page on trumpet and Eddie Durham, who would play both trombone and electric guitar (the first on record) for Basie.

By 1929 Basie and Durham had been lured with higher salaries away from the Blue Devils by Page's rival, Bennie Moten, a talented pianist and bandleader. Although Lester Young worked briefly for Page subsequently, Moten's group had the most powerful lineup of soloists, dominating Kansas City and the Southwest until Moten died suddenly in 1935 during a tonsil-lectomy. Basie then formed a seven- to nine-piece band, drawing from the best of the Moten and Page organizations.

The original Basie band, which had acquired a subtle, flowing drummer in Jo Jones and an innovative, melodic tenor soloist in Lester Young, settled in at the Reno Club from which they broadcast nightly. Basie was dubbed the Count on one of these shows by an announcer who thought he needed the title to keep up with an Earl Hines and a Duke Ellington. John Ham-mond and Benny Goodman heard one of these broadcasts on short-wave radio, and flew to Kansas City to hear them in person. On their advice Willard Alexander, president of the Music Corporation of America (MCA), booked Basie in Chicago and New York, and arranged to have him record his first twenty-four sides for Decca (later bought by MCA); these sessions are available on *The Best of Count Basie*. (The earliest Basie cuts, which he negotiated by himself much to his disadvantage, are available on Columbia's *Super Chief*.)

The Basie classics on the MCA set—"One O'Clock Jump," "Jumpin' at the Woodside," "Panassié Stomp," and "Every Tub"—are credited to the leader, but they are cooperative efforts, reflecting the band's unanimity of spirit. Buster Smith recalls the origin of "One O'Clock Jump," first called "Blue Balls" until a radio announcer retitled it on a 1:00 A.M. broadcast:

> We were fooling around at the [Reno] Club and Basie was playing along in F. That was his favorite key. He hollered at me that he was going to switch to D-flat and for me to "set something." I started play-ing that opening reed riff [from Don Redman's arrangement to "Six or Seven Times"] on alto. Lips Page jumped in with the trumpet part without any trouble and Dan Minor thought up the trombone part. That was it—a head.[17]

"One O'Clock Jump" turned out in the Decca studio to be less an ex-ample of the Basie full-band style than of its stunning array of soloists. Herschel Evans's full-bodied, Hawkins-style tenor, shimmering with vibrato, followed by Lester Young's high-pitched, airy, and ingeniously phrased tenor, already provide more spark and colorful contrast than most groups have in a whole lineup. These solos are framed by Basie's muscular, Waller-inspired stride and the smooth melodic trumpet playing of Buck Clayton. Harry "Sweets" Edison replaces Clayton on "Sent for You Yesterday," a blues featuring Jimmy Rushing, whose high-pitched shout resembles Lester's tenor in its quality. In this number Edison's sensitive obbligato behind Jimmy shifts into a higher gear on his trumpet break, a serpentine line that would have been modern in the 1950's.

These are soloists with a broad palette of ideas. Basie's uniquely light touch incorporates highly charged silences within a solo and gives the piano a new voice on "Texas Shuffle." On "Every Tub" and "Oh, Lady Be Good," Lester breaks loose like a racehorse given its head, slicing through chord changes and across bar lines. In short, Basie's band was a caldron of inven-tion, and that was only half of its power.

The early Basie band expanded the emotional resonance of the blues, transforming it into an expression less of sorrow than of joy. This was accom-plished with the rhythmic, powerful riff and the hard, clean bite of the brass and reeds as in "Jumpin' at the Woodside," "Every Tub," and Waller's "Honeysuckle Rose." The sections are in constant call-and-response, driving the level of intensity higher with every repetition. Basie wanted his band to have the agility of a small group. In fact, he increased the personnel from nine to fifteen only at the urging of Hammond and Goodman, who recognized that greater harmonic texture was necessary to compete with the slicker sounds of Duke Ellington, Jimmie Lunceford, and Goodman's Fletcher Henderson charts. In any case Basie kept the band sounding small, an achievement made possible by its members' intuitive rapport. This band "pops" and "kicks"—Basie's description—all the way through the blues.

Although this MCA set is the definitive Basie album of the period, there are other good anthologies available. The aforementioned *Super Chief* covers sessions from 1936 to 1942 with vocalists Jimmy Rushing, Helen Humes, Mildred Bailey, and Billie Holiday. Outtakes from the classic Decca sessions of 1936–1939 are available on *Good Morning Blues: Count Basie and His Orchestra* with plenty of soloing and vocals by Rushing and Humes. Columbia's *The Lester Young Story, Volume 3: Enter the Count* is discussed in the Lester Young discography.

In 1940, Lester Young was dropped from the Basie band, reportedly because he refused to record on Friday the thirteenth. For a variety of reasons, other key soloists began to leave, initiating the first of many turnovers the band has survived. Some of the important new soloists were saxophonists Don Byas, Illinois Jacquet, Paul Gonsalves, and trumpeter Joe Newman. The recordings for RCA during these years have not been reissued. Basie's reputation and his managerial skills kept the band afloat during the postwar years, when the closing of the large dance halls forced most of the bigger groups to sink into oblivion. By 1950, however, even Basie had to cut back to seven pieces for a year, the only time since 1936 that he had been without a full band.

The new Basie band of 1952 derived its identity in part from the spirited, sophisticated arranging of Neal Hefti, who in the 1940's had been the pen behind the Woody Herman band. Moreover, Joe Newman's trumpet and the saxes of Marshall Royal, Ernie Wilkins, Frank Foster, and Frank Wess added a more modern, if less distinctive, feeling to the horn sections. The elements of continuity were maintained by the rhythm section—Basie and guitarist Freddie Green keeping up a light, steady beat—the constant call-and-response riffing, and the impeccable togetherness which has been and is the band's trademark. *Sixteen Men Swinging* is an excellent example of the third-generation Basie group, revealing moods from the blistering brass blasts of the title track (arranged by Wilkins), and "Perdido" and "Ska-Di-Dle-Dee-Bee-Doo" (by Hefti) to Hefti's quiet, wee-small-hours ballad "Softly with Feeling"—a colorful tapestry of reeds and Basie's tinkling, high-contrast piano. Trumpeter Thad Jones, who later co-led his own big band (Chapter 6), was a consistently exciting soloist for Basie during the 1950's.

Basie's best Verve album, *Count Basie Swings and Joe Williams Sings*, grew out of a successful Birdland engagement. Williams has a strong, full voice, and their collaboration on "Every Day I Have the Blues" renewed the band's popularity. Another Birdland band date from 1959 has been re-issued on Roulette's *The Best of Basie*, containing the brilliant Neal Hefti arrangement of "Li'l Darlin'," a piece which swings mightily at a tempo in which other bands would simply plod. A few more sessions from the 1960's and 1970's are recommended in the General Discography, although 1960 marks the end—thus far—of inspired Basie performances. The band is still alive, however, and records for Granz's Pablo label. Basie and guitarist Freddie Green continue after forty-five years together to power the rhythm section with four heavy beats to the bar "and no cheating."

EARL "FATHA" HINES

Another Monday Date

Prestige, P-24043
two discs, liner notes
1956

Musicians: Earl "Fatha" Hines, solo piano. Also with Eddie Duran, guitar; Dean Reilly, bass; and Earl Watkins, drums on sides one and two.
Compositions: Side one: Jitterbug Waltz; Darktown Strutters Ball; Black and Blue; Blue Turning Gray over You; Honeysuckle Rose; Squeeze Me. *Side two:* Ain't Misbehavin'; Keepin' out of Mischief Now; I Can't Give You Anything but Love; I'm Gonna Sit Right Down and Write Myself a Letter; Lulu's Back in Town; Two Sleepy People. *Side three:* Deep Forest; Everything Depends on You; Am I Too Late?; Blues for Tatum; In San Francisco; Ann. *Side four:* You Can Depend on Me; When I Dream of You; R. R. Blues; Straight to Love; Piano Man; My Monday Date.

EARL HINES is the originator of modern jazz piano in the sense that he was the first to offer an alternative to the regimentation of ragtime and stride. As we heard on the Louis Armstrong albums (Selected Discography, Chapter 3), Hines's trumpet-style right hand allowed the piano to project itself above the band, making more complex melodic lines feasible; at the same time, he was able to explore more sophisticated harmonic ideas and a subtle rhythmic feeling. Hines is a pianist who combines imagination and technical brilliance with confidence and charm, qualities that emerge strongly on sides three and four of *Another Monday Date*. The first two sides, which reissue a Hines-plays-Waller date, accompanied by the trio, are pleasant but ultimately restrictive, stultifying Hines's natural warmth and inventiveness.

The album's title is meant as a sequel to Hines's preceding solo appearance, also his debut album, *A Monday Date: 1928* (General Discography), recorded for QRS in New York shortly after Hines left Armstrong's Hot Seven band. Apart from six virtually inaudible tracks with the Lois Deppe band, *1928* is an astonishing display of Hines's ability to toss off passing tones, left-hand melodies, and abrupt changes of tempo and rhythm.

Born in 1905 near Pittsburgh, Pennsylvania, he studied classical European music with several teachers and with the encouragement and guidance of his mother. Exposed to the local night life as a teenager, he began experimenting with what was then called "rhythm music." An aunt introduced him to Eubie Blake, who was impressed by the boy's playing and urged him strongly to go to New York. Hines dragged his heels, and Blake found him still at home, an even better pianist, on his next trip to Pittsburgh. Blake allegedly told him, "If you're here when I come back, I'll wrap my cane around your head." [18] Hines, however, made an even better choice by moving to Chicago in 1923 because it was then the center of recording activity. His historic sessions with Armstrong in 1927 and 1928 (Chapter 3) were recorded there.

Hines's big band also originated in Chicago at the Grand Terrace's Ballroom, which enjoyed a status similar to New York's Cotton Club. The band hit the peak of its popularity with Billy Eckstine's vocals on "Jelly, Jelly" and "Stormy Monday Blues," available on RCA's Bluebird reissue *The Father Jumps*, the best of the Hines big-band sets. "Rosetta," his most popular composition for the band, is not available on records. The most historic of the Hines groups included Charlie Parker, Dizzy Gillespie, and Sarah Vaughan, but this supergroup coincided with the union's recording ban; thus there is no documentation of its sound. Hines is often credited with discovering Sarah Vaughan, but it was Eckstine who heard her at the Apollo Theater and recognized her talent first.

Hines was forced to disband at the end of the big-band era, and he reunited with Armstrong from 1948 to 1951 but no record of that band is currently available. Hines and Barney Bigard recorded well in 1950 with a quintet (*Earl Hines*, see General Discography). Hines then moved to Oakland, California, where occasional recordings, such as *Another Monday Date*, revealed undiminished technique and imagination. After Art Tatum's death in 1956, Hines was probably the only pianist capable of sustaining an entire solo LP until the format was revived once again in the 1970's by Keith Jarrett.

Although Hines was known as a bandleader from 1928 to 1948, his artistry is best expressed—and certainly better represented on records—at the piano. "My Monday Date" is itself exemplary and typical of Hines's pianistic advances. If stride is marked by a leaping left hand establishing the rhythm, Hines's piano is one of metric suggestion. By the placement of accents and his facility for creating cross-rhythms, he is able to imply four strong beats while playing only one or two notes per measure with his left hand. Once the song's momentum becomes firmly established, he is free to pursue even greater harmonic variety, much of which is expressed in chord inversions and chromatic movement. Hines was also capable of wild rhythmic breaks or harmonic exploration in the midst of a steadily moving left hand (in "Ann," "Everything Depends on You," and "Am I Too Late?," respectively).

Art Tatum, as we shall hear, carried the Hines breakthrough to its ultimate conclusion, but other pianists, like Teddy Wilson and Nat "King" Cole (before he discovered the commercial worth of his voice), were quick to apply the Hines techniques to their own purposes. The long-range significance of Hines was well stated in an essay by Richard Hadlock:

> Morton and other early pianists attempted to emulate the sound of an orchestra; Earl wanted to achieve the sound of a horn soloist over supporting rhythmic and harmonic figures. The older view followed logically from ragtime and New Orleans preferences for ensemble playing. . . . Earl's attitude made perfect sense in the light of new trends towards solo exposition ushered in largely by Louis Armstrong.[19]

Hines's career was rejuvenated in 1964 with a New York piano concert preserved on *The Legendary Little Theater Concert*, two spirited volumes of a Hines trio. Two later solo albums—Biograph's *Solo Walk in Tokyo* (1972) and Delmark's *Earl Hines at Home* (1974)—which he recorded on a $15,000 antique Steinway in his living room, are looser and quieter, and perhaps a sign that the "Fatha" would not be jumping quite as high or as hard as he once did. Still, they are warm, sensitive improvisations which the Hines collector will enjoy. The rave reviews that followed the Little Theater Concert led to an engagement at Birdland and a Hines sextet featuring singer Marva Josie, which continues to tour worldwide. Several good Hines albums, both solo and small combo, are recommended in the General Discography.

BENNY GOODMAN

Carnegie Hall Jazz Concert—1938

Columbia, CSL-160
two discs, liner notes

Musicians: Benny Goodman (clarinet) and His Orchestra: Hymie Schertzer, alto sax; George Koenig, Babe Russin, Art Rollini, tenor saxes; Harry James, Ziggy Elman, Gordon Griffin, trumpets; Vernon Brown, Red Ballard, trombones; Allan Reuss, guitar; Jess Stacy, piano; Harry Goodman, bass; Gene Krupa, drums. Also with the trio: Goodman; Teddy Wilson, piano; and Gene Krupa, drums. And with the quartet, add Lionel Hampton, vibes (seven tracks). Also with the Count Basie Orchestra, plus members of the Duke Ellington Orchestra, in a jam session (on "Honeysuckle Rose").

Compositions: Side one: Don't Be That Way; One O'Clock Jump; Twenty Years of Jazz (retrospective): Sensation Rag; I'm Coming, Virginia; When My Baby Smiles at Me; Shine; Blue Reverie; Life Goes to a Party. *Side two:* JAM SESSION: Honeysuckle Rose. TRIO: Body and Soul. QUARTET: Avalon, The Man I Love; I Got Rhythm. *Side three:* BAND: Blue Skies; Loch Lomond; Blue Room; Swingtime in the Rockies; Bei Mir Bist Du Schön. *Side four:* TRIO: China Boy. QUARTET: Stompin' at the Savoy; Dizzy Spells; Sing, Sing, Sing; Big John Special.

CHARLIE CHRISTIAN

Solo Flight: The Genius of Charlie Christian

Columbia, CG 30779
two discs, liner notes
1939–1941

Musicians: Charlie Christian (amplified guitar) with Benny Goodman, clarinet; Lionel Hampton, vibes; Fletcher Henderson, piano; Artie Bernstein, bass; Nick Fatool, drums. Also with the Benny Goodman All-Star Nine: Goodman; Harry James, trumpet; Jack Teagarden, trombone; Benny Carter, alto sax; Eddie Miller, tenor

sax; Jess Stacy, piano; Bob Haggart, bass; Gene Krupa, drums. Also with Goodman,
Hampton, and Count Basie, piano; Bernstein; Fatool. Also with Cootie Williams,
trumpet; Georgie Auld, tenor sax; Johnny Guarnieri, piano; Bernstein; Dave
Tough, drums.
Compositions: Side one: Rose Room; Memories of You; Seven Come Eleven; Honey-
suckle Rose; All-Star Strut; Till Tom Special; Gone with What Wind. *Side two:* I
Got Rhythm; Stardust; Tea for Two; Boy Meets Goy; Six Appeal; Good Enough
to Keep (Air Mail Special); Wholly Cats. *Side three:* Wholly Cats (alternate
master); As Long As I Live; Benny Bugle; Royal Garden Blues; Breakfast Feud;
I Can't Give You Anything but Love; Gilly. *Side four:* Breakfast Feud (new ses-
sion); On the Alamo; I've Found a New Baby; Solo Flight; Blues in B; Waitin' for
Benny; Good Enough to Keep (Air Mail Special) (new session).

THE "KING OF SWING" was first served to the public on a Ritz cracker. The
debut occurred in December 1934, when the National Biscuit Company was
bravely promoting its newest product with a weekly radio show called "Let's
Dance." Three dissimilar bands were being broadcast over fifty-five stations
to a dance-crazed audience: Ken Murray's sweet society orchestra; Xavier
Cugat's rhumba band; and a hot group led by Benny Goodman. Fortunately
for Goodman, the show had a budget for arrangements, and, at the suggestion of producer John Hammond, Goodman contacted Fletcher Henderson,
who wrote the band's most exciting material. The radio show generated
enough interest for a cross-country tour, which raised few temperatures until,
going for broke, Goodman pulled out the hottest Fletcher Henderson charts
in the group's repertoire. The crowd stopped dancing, mobbed the bandstand, and Goodman was held over for a month. On the way back to New
York, the band was held over in Chicago for eight months. Goodman became the most popular bandleader in music—not just in jazz. In 1937 when
the King of Swing played the Paramount Theater in New York, he drew an
audience of twenty-one thousand, and the group was getting even better. The
twenty-year-old trumpeter Harry James, who had been with the band of
Ben Pollack, Goodman's first employer, joined to become one of the star
soloists along with Gene Krupa and Goodman himself.

Goodman's earliest recordings are still available on MCA's *A Jazz Holiday*, which captures him at seventeen while he was a member of Ben
Pollack's Californians. The historic two-disc set also includes his recordings
with Red Nichols and the Five Pennies (1930), with Joe Venuti and Eddie
Lang, and with various members of the Chicago-Beiderbecke school—like
Jimmy McPartland, Tommy Dorsey, and Benny's friend Jack Teagarden
on trombone. The early work of Venuti and Teagarden is the high point of
these tracks.

Goodman's style up to this point had been derived to a certain extent
from Jimmy Noone and Leon Rappolo of the New Orleans Rhythm Kings,
but his style was also a result of applying uncommonly good classical technique to jazz concepts. Born in 1909, he grew up in a poor immigrant section of Chicago, the eighth of twelve children in a Jewish family which
had recently fled the anti-Semitic pogroms of Russia. Benny and two of his
brothers were provided with free music lessons at a nearby synagogue until

the funds ran out. The three boys were then enrolled in a social service project known as Hull House, where Benny continued to study until he outgrew the instruction. The lasting influence of his training came from Franz Schoeppe, a Chicago Musical College instructor, who had also coached Noone and Buster Bailey. Schoeppe had little respect for jazz, however, and instilled in his students a habit of accuracy, a facility for sight reading, and a "legitimate" technique. Goodman left him after two years, more competent in the European tradition than in improvisation.

After leaving Pollack in 1929, Goodman, whose technique, sight reading, and versatility were unparalleled, was one of the busiest free-lancers in New York, even during the Depression years. In fact, he played in Bessie Smith's first session and Billie Holiday's last, hired by the man who engineered his career, John Hammond. Although Hammond was with Columbia, the developing Goodman band's best sides were recorded on RCA, which has reissued five volumes of two-disc sets on its Bluebird series (General Discography) entitled *The Complete Benny Goodman*. The most memorable are *Volume I* (1935) with Goodman's best vocalist, Helen Ward, trumpeter Bunny Berigan, and the Henderson-arranged hits "King Porter Stomp" and "Sometimes I'm Happy" and *Volume IV* (1936–1937) with eight small-group tracks including Lionel Hampton, whom Goodman had discovered in 1937 playing vibes in a small Los Angeles nightclub. *Volume V* (1937–1938) contains another half-dozen quartet sides as well as the band's last stand just before Krupa departed.

Goodman's *Jazz Concert—1938* catches the band at its peak, with its best personnel, and in front of the volatile kind of audience on which it thrived. This concert was also jazz's debut in Carnegie Hall. The album, recorded with surprising success from a single overhead microphone, is virtually a festival of swing because of its "Honeysuckle Rose" jam, which includes solos by outstanding members of the Basie and Ellington bands. Lester Young's three-chorus opener steals this show, displaying the relaxed swing and light tone which made him the most innovative improviser of his time.

"Body and Soul" and "Avalon" introduce the seven "chamber group" tracks of Benny Goodman, Teddy Wilson, Lionel Hampton, and Gene Krupa, the first racially mixed performing group. Their instruments merge in a single, swift voice, a good contrast with the dense section playing and tension-raising dynamics of standards like "Stompin' at the Savoy" and "Sing, Sing, Sing." Teddy Wilson's glistening right-hand runs and left-hand countermelodies on piano were major steps toward modernization, as was Lionel Hampton's constant feeling of motion on vibes. The kind of soloing this band elicited from its showmen is evident on "Savoy" (James), "Sing" (Krupa), and Basie's "One O'Clock Jump" (Goodman). On "Sing" also, the call-and-response between clarinet, trumpets, and Krupa's tom-toms illustrates how quickly the level of excitement can be raised by the precision for which Goodman was known.

In addition to Columbia's *Carnegie Hall*, a two-disc collection, *The King of Swing*, contains various air checks and performances of the same big band, trio, and quartet from the banner years 1937–1938. By 1939, when Harry James and Gene Krupa left to form their own groups, Goodman's big band had seen its best days.

Nineteen thirty-nine was the end of one Goodman era but the beginning of a more profound one musically speaking, when he crossed paths with Charlie Christian, the originator of modern jazz guitar and one of the innovative minds responsible for bebop. Modernizing the guitar was a major milestone in jazz's development. Since 1917, the guitar has been a poor cousin of the banjo because its relatively delicate music could not be picked up by the sound-gathering horns of the early recording studios. On stage both instruments were confined to a rhythmic role. Django Reinhardt, a contemporary of Charlie's, pioneered the single-note melodic line in Europe, but his virtuosity bordered on rococo embellishment. Christian gave the guitar its genuine jazz voice, and electronic amplification was the technology that made his sound possible. It made notes louder and, equally important, sustained them longer, permitting a smooth, legato feeling in the flow of the melodic lines.

Goodman and Christian were an odd couple of comic proportions. Goodman was suave, polished, and a perfectionist; Christian was a country boy from Oklahoma, an inveterate partygoer and playboy. Goodman was the richest musician in jazz (perhaps in popular music too), while the nineteen-year-old Christian worked three nights per week for $7.50 at a café called the Ritz, coincidentally an important name in Goodman's biography as well. Ralph Ellison, whose younger brother was a grammar school classmate of Charlie's, writes in *Shadow and Act* that he does not recall a time the boy was not known for his adeptness on the guitar. Charlie's experience was broadened by his blind father who brought his two sons into the nicer neighborhoods to serenade the white middle-class families with a repertoire ranging from blues to light classics. Later Charlie heard the Kansas City swing bands which were touring the Southwest, and became intrigued with the relaxed, even phrasing of Lester Young.

The first meeting of these men was not auspicious for Christian. In 1939 Hammond, who had auditioned Charlie in Oklahoma, wired funds for Charlie's transportation to a Columbia recording session in New York. It was the King of Swing's date, and the distinguished Fletcher Henderson was at the piano. The band had been working on his arrangement of a light classical piece by Mendelssohn. The dapper Goodman, who was too conscientious to hire anyone on hearsay, had been talked into giving Christian a tryout by Hammond. Two hours late, Charlie breezed in toting his guitar and amplifier, "resplendent in a ten-gallon hat, pointed yellow shoes, a bright green suit over a purple shirt and, for the final elegant touch—a string bowtie." [20] Goodman wanted no part of him. He left the studio for dinner without giving Charlie a chance to plug in his amplifier.

Fate gave him a second chance. At the band's evening engagement, bassist Artie Bernstein and Lionel Hampton, feeling sorry for Charlie, covertly installed him on the stand for the quartet segment. When Goodman realized what was going on, it was too late to do anything but play. The first tune was "Rose Room" (also the first track on *Solo Flight*), and it lasted over three-quarters of an hour. Charlie kept feeding Benny new riffs, rhythms, and chords to play on. Then he soloed, and Hammond said he had never seen Benny so "knocked out" by anyone.

Solo Flight is like a breath of fresh air in the occasionally heavy atmosphere of the big band's megasound. The sextet tracks depend on spontaneous "head" arrangements of exciting, speech-like riffs, many of which derive from Christian's improvisational style. "Seven Come Eleven" makes use of scale patterns and intervals which would soon become part of bebop. Christian's solos are long, sinuous, and unpredictable, as exemplified by the shifting rhythmic emphasis on "Seven." Even Goodman's tone is looser, warmer, and more vocal under Christian's influence. Yet Goodman's lines are still short phrases compared with Charlie's "complete sentences."

Christian expands his concept daringly on the first three tracks of side two, which were cut privately with Goodman absent. His soloing sings in graceful phrasing, as at the end of his "Stardust" improvisation. "Tea for Two" is another solo of dramatic heights, dips, and swerves. "Breakfast Feud" is an example of his ability to build intensity, elevating the piece emotionally before turning it over to the next soloist.

The title track and "Honeysuckle Rose" arranged by Henderson with Christian's warm, amplified tones sailing above the full band and swinging it with ease, indicate the kind of group that might have been born of this unlikely marriage of styles. But the honeymoon did not last long, nor did Charlie Christian.

(One more album of this group is available, however, on Jazz Archives' *Charlie Christian Live!*—a collection of air checks from 1939 to 1941 with many of the same songs and remarkably different solos. Another Jazz Archives album with Christian and Lester Young has sadly been deleted from the catalog.)

By 1940 Charlie Christian's salary had jumped from $7.50 to $150 per week, and he lived to its limit, jamming nights on end at Minton's Playhouse, where his elongated phrasing markedly accelerated the development of bebop. Many of these sessions included Thelonious Monk, who can be heard with Christian on Everest's *Charlie Christian* (General Discography). Christian threw himself into New York's night life, and kept on going even with a diagnosed case of tuberculosis. Finally Hammond and Goodman had him committed to a sanitarium. During the snowy winter of 1942, at the age of twenty-three Christian contracted pneumonia, the final blow to his ravaged lungs.

The sensible Goodman, by contrast, continued sporadic performing and recording, even up to the present time, with virtually no evolution in his own style.

LIONEL HAMPTON

The Complete Lionel Hampton, 1937–1941

RCA, AXM6-5536
six discs, liner booklet

Musicians: Lionel Hampton (vibes, piano, drums, and vocals) in bands of four to ten pieces, including nearly every major swing musician (see discussion below). A partial list of personnel: Cootie Williams, Ziggy Elman, Harry James, Henry "Red" Allen, Jonah Jones, Dizzy Gillespie, trumpets; Johnny Hodges, Benny Carter, Russell Procope, Hymie Shertzer, alto saxes; Ben Webster, Coleman Hawkins, Chu Berry, Herschel Evans, tenor saxes; Harry Carney, baritone sax; Lawrence Brown, J. C. Higgenbotham, trombones; Omer Simeon, Buster Bailey, Marshall Royal, clarinets; Gene Krupa, Cozy Cole, Zutty Singleton, drums; Jess Stavey, Clyde Hart, Nat "King" Cole, pianos; Charlie Christian, guitar; Milt Hinton, bass.
Compositions: Side A: My Last Affair; Jivin' the Vibes; The Mood That I'm in; Hampton Stomp; Buzzin' Around with the Bee; Whoa Babe; Stompology. *Side B:* On the Sunny Side of the Street; Rhythm, Rhythm; China Stomp; I Know That You Know; I'm Confessin'; Drum Stomp (Crazy Rhythm); Piano Stomp (Shine); I Surrender, Dear. *Side C:* The Object of My Affection; Judy; Baby, Won't You Please Come Home?; I Just Couldn't Take It, Baby; You're My Ideal; The Sun Will Shine Tonight. *Side D:* Ring Dem Bells; Don't Be That Way; I'm in the Mood for Swing; Shoe Shiner's Drag; Any Time at All; Muskrat Ramble; Down Home Jump; Rock Hill Special. *Side E:* Fiddle Diddle; I Can Give You Love; High Society; It Don't Mean a Thing, If It Ain't Got That Swing; Johnny Get Your Horn and Blow It; Sweethearts on Parade; Shufflin' at the Hollywood (two takes). *Side F:* Denison Swings; Wizzin' the Wiz; If It's Good (Then I Want It); Stand By; Ain'tcha Comin' Home?; Big Wig in the Wigwam; Memories of You; The Jumpin' Jive. *Side G:* Twelfth Street Rag; When Lights Are Low (two takes); One Sweet Letter from You; Hot Mallets; Early Session Hop; I'm on My Way from You; Haven't Named It Yet. *Side H:* Heebie Jeebies (two takes); The Munson Street Breakdown; I've Found a New Baby; Can't Get Started; Four or Five Times; Gin for Christmas; Dinah. *Side I:* Dinah; My Buddy; Singin' the Blues Til My Daddy Comes Home; Shades of Jade; Till Tom Special; Flying Home; Save It, Pretty Mama; Tempo and Swing. *Side J:* House of Morgan; I'd Be Lost Without You; Central Avenue Breakdown; Jack the Bellboy; Dough-Rey-Mi; Jivin' with Jarvis; Blue (Because of You); I Don't Stand a Ghost of a Chance with You. *Side K:* Just for Laffs; Martin on Every Block; Pig Foot Sonata; Charlie Was a Sailor; Lost Love; I Nearly Lost My Mind; Attitude; Fiddle Dee Doo. *Side L:* Bogo Jo; Open House; Smart Aleck; Bouncing at the Beacon; Give Me Some Skin; Now That You're Mine; Chasin' with Chase; Three-Quarter Boogie.

LIONEL HAMPTON WAS the first jazz vibraphonist (or "vibraharpist") and was the master of a rhythmic vitality that enlivened every band he played in. During the 1920's, Hamp's only predecessor, Red Norvo, began using the xylophone and marimba, similar to vibes except for their wooden keys.

Vibes have the advantages of a sustain pedal and resonating tubes under metal keys, creating a fuller, more flexible sound. No one came close to Hampton's swing and fluidity on the instrument until the late 1940's, when Milt Jackson began playing vibes with Dizzy Gillespie's band.

Hampton was born in Louisville, Kentucky, in 1913, the son of a pianist and singer who was killed in action in World War I. Raised by his mother and her parents in a religious environment, Hamp was eventually sent to Holy Rosary Academy, where he was taught to play drums by a Franciscan nun. When he was fourteen, his grandparents made him a present of a drum set, which soon made him popular with numerous bands in the Midwest. In 1927 Hampton went to California to join the Quality Serenaders with his friend, saxophonist Les Hite. In 1930 Hite and Hampton eventually took their own band into the Cotton Club in Culver City, where they backed Louis Armstrong who was on a West Coast tour.

Armstrong was a sensation in Los Angeles and remained at the club for nine months, influencing Hampton profoundly. "Hamp" also listened to the records of Louis's former colleagues, Earl Hines and Coleman Hawkins. When Louis recorded that summer with the Cotton Club band backing him, Hamp played vibes for the first time backing Armstrong on "Memories of You" at Louis's suggestion.

In 1930 Hamp also met Gladys Riddle, who became his wife and manager. Realizing that Armstrong liked her fiancé's sound on this new instrument, she bought him a set of vibes, which he began to practice regularly at home. Under Gladys's influence Hamp attended the University of Southern California for eighteen months, studying harmony and learning to play the piano. His interest in the vibraphone, however, forced him to resign from the Hite band, where he was needed only on drums. Thus Hampton formed his own group, including future Count Basie soloists Herschel Evans and Buck Clayton, which played up and down the West Coast until it found a semipermanent home at the Paradise Club in Los Angeles.

The turning point in Hampton's career came in 1936, when Benny Goodman walked into the Paradise Club with his clarinet, eager to sit in with Hamp's popular local group. The next night Benny brought Teddy Wilson and Gene Krupa with him, and the historic quartet (previously discussed) had come together, recording "Moonglow" that August. A short time later, Hampton joined Goodman in New York, where his flowing improvised lines and rhythmic drive made him the most consistently satisfying soloist in the group.

By 1937 Hampton had an open invitation to record for RCA Victor whenever he was in New York. This resulted in the ensembles of swing superstars that are collected in *The Complete Lionel Hampton*, whose last sessions in 1941 preceded the formation of Lionel's own big band. The unusual agreement between Hamp and RCA was modeled after Brunswick's open-format offer to the other Goodman soloist, Teddy Wilson (see Billie Holiday discussion ahead). The Wilson sessions have endured primarily because Billie

Holiday, then a new voice in the recording studio, brought them depth and originality. The Hampton sessions, however, excel in sheer musicianship. As the list of personnel indicates, Hamp drew wisely from the bands of Ellington, Basie, Goodman, and Hines. Every major player of the era is represented here except for Lester Young, Buck Clayton, and the band-leaders who would have been considered Hamp's competition. The illustrated booklet of explanatory notes by Stanley Dance identifies the musicians on each cut and discusses Hamp's background and influences in detail.

The six discs in this boxed set, which were collector's items prior to reissue, present a wonderfully broad picture of the era's soloists: Disc one begins with the Goodman sidemen, but by disc three we have heard the Ellingtonians and the Basie-ites; disc four unites a young Dizzy Gillespie with Coleman Hawkins in his peak year, supported by Ben Webster, Benny Carter, Chu Berry, and Charlie Christian; disc five has some of the best Coleman Hawkins available, followed by tracks of Hamp with the original Nat "King" Cole trio. Small combo tracks with plenty of room for the soloists to stretch out frequently alternate with riffed heads played by up to ten pieces.

Hamp's many talents are marked by a rhythmic sense which allows him to play around the beat, lagging or anticipating with complete confidence, as a surfer rides a wave. His speed is fluid and effortless, never interfering with his lyricism. As a drummer he has flawless control of the mallets, which flutter like a bee's wings on the up-tempo numbers. His drum solo on "Drum Stomp" is an impressive burst of fireworks, executed with the same precision and quickness he displays on vibes. Oddly he developed a similar piano technique by playing with two fingers as if they were sticks. Hamp's occasional vocals are homespun, but also delivered with warmth and ease.

Even alongside Hamp's fleet lines, Johnny Hodges is a commanding solo voice on sides A and B (especially on "Sunny Side of the Street" and "I Know That You Know"). Cootie Williams and Lawrence Brown (on "Stompology" in particular) also reveal free and expressive natures outside of the Ellington environment. Coleman Hawkins, who had recently recorded his 1939 masterpiece "Body and Soul," dominates Side I with newly acquired spiraling melodies and a breathier tone. "Dinah" and "My Buddy" do not rival "Body and Soul" for originality, but neither do they lack any of its lyric qualities. Side I also contains two of Hamps best riff tunes—"Till Tom Special," worked out with Benny Goodman and Charlie Christian, and "Flying Home," a hit from Hampton's big band in 1942.

Side J's high point is the piano playing of Nat "King" Cole. Had Cole not found fame and fortune with his velvety voice, he might have made the perfect pianist for Hampton. Both had a tremendous gift for linear improvisation, a matching technical dexterity, and a tendency to liquefy a beat. "House of Morgan" displays a phrasing and a rhythmic fluidity which seem to belie the 1940 recording date. "I'd Be Lost Without You" demonstrates how agile and versatile Cole could be. The hot, raggy, boogie-woogie feeling contrasts sharply with the previous cut, yet maintains its mood with equal authority.

Hamp's showmanship and effervescence made him a successful band-leader through the 1940's, during which he recorded periodically for Decca. Those sessions and others of the 1950's—a mixture of swing, early "bop" improvising, and unabashed entertainment—are available on MCA's *The Best of Lionel Hampton* and Audiofidelity's *Hamp's Big Band*. During the 1950's, Hampton played frequently in Europe, recording at home for Norman Granz's Clef label. Some sessions with Stan Getz are no longer in print, but two 1955 LP's with Art Tatum—a very compatible partner who usually upstaged Hamp—can be heard on Pablo's *Tatum/Hampton/Rich*.

Hampton led his band through the mid 1960's, performing more like an entertainer than a creative improviser. However, he was still showing up at festivals in the 1970's, frequently proving that he could swing as hard as his many descendants on the vibraphone, notably Milt Jackson, Gary Burton, and Bobby Hutcherson. After all, it was Hamp who gave the instrument its voice in jazz.

LESTER YOUNG

The Lester Young Story, Volume I

Columbia, JG 33502
two discs, liner notes
1936–1937

Musicians: Lester Young, tenor sax; with Carl Smith, trumpet; Count Basie, piano; Walter Page, bass; Jo Jones, drums; and Jimmy Rushing, vocal (one track). Also with Teddy Wilson, piano; Buck Clayton, trumpet; Benny Goodman, clarinet; Freddie Green, guitar; Walter Page, Jo Jones, and Billie Holiday, vocals (most tracks). Also with previous band plus Johnny Hodges, alto sax; and Cozy Cole, drums (four tracks).
Compositions: Side one: Shoe Shine Boy (plus alternate master); Evenin'; Boogie-Woogie; Oh, Lady Be Good. *Side two:* He Ain't Got Rhythm; This Year's Kisses; Why Was I Born?; I Must Have That Man; Sun Showers; Yours and Mine. *Side three:* Mean to Me (plus alternate master); Fooling Myself; Easy Living; I'll Never Be the Same; I've Found a New Baby (plus alternate master). *Side four:* Me, Myself, and I Are All in Love with You (plus alternate master); A Sailboat in the Moonlight; Born to Love; Without Your Love (plus alternate master).

LESTER YOUNG WAS the most innovative instrumentalist in jazz between Louis Armstrong and Charlie Parker, the originator of the relaxed, airy style of playing known as "cool" jazz (Chapter 5), and a unique personality, a sad caricature of "the alienated jazz musician." Young's importance to the tenor sax ranks with that of Coleman Hawkins and John Coltrane. It was Hawkins who, as a member of Fletcher Henderson's Orchestra, dominated the tenor first, much as Armstrong had dominated the trumpet. Before the age of electronic microphones the saxes of the 1920's had been hard put to compete with the mighty trumpet for a prominent role in the band. Hawkins discovered that a stiff reed and a customized mouthpiece increased his blowing power, as did his heavy vibrato and virile articulation of each note. Hawkins and his disciples, notably Chu Berry, Don Byas, and Ben Webster, relied on patterns of dotted eighth notes and sixteenth notes to produce an abrupt, stop-start kind of swing. Hawkins also adopted a "vertical" improvisational concept that emphasized the harmonic steps of the chord rather than linear melodic development. The elegance of his approach is epitomized by his famous "Body and Soul" solo of 1939, available on *The Smithsonian Collection of Classic Jazz*. By that time, however, Lester Young had established an equally viable alternative to the Hawkins sound, one which may fairly be described as its antithesis.

Young was born in 1909 in Mississippi into a family of musicians. The family soon moved to New Orleans, where Lester studied drums, violin, trumpet, and alto sax primarily with his father, who had been a student at Tuskegee Institute and had traveled with minstrel shows. Ten years later the family moved again—to Minneapolis, Minnesota, where they formed a family band with Lester's brother Lee on drums. The Young troupe traveled frequently in the Midwest and Southwest until Lester ran away at the age of eighteen, reportedly unable to bear the racism he encountered on the road.

From 1927 to 1934 he worked for the aging King Oliver, Art Bronson's Bostonians, and the Basie band's rivals—Walter Page's Blue Devils. A radio broadcast of the Count Basie-Bennie Moten band persuaded Lester that they needed a good tenor, and he wrote Bill Basie requesting an audition. He joined Basie's band in 1934 but not for long, for he was invited to replace Coleman Hawkins who had left for his five-year residence in Europe in the more famous Fletcher Henderson Orchestra. Yet Lester's tenure with Henderson was to be cut short.

During these years, Lester had been listening intently to the records of Frankie Trumbauer and Jimmy Dorsey. Trumbauer's C-melody sax, pitched between alto and tenor, was the only influence upon his tone Young acknowledged:

> I had a decision to make between Frankie Trumbauer and Jimmy Dorsey, you dig, and I wasn't sure which way I wanted to go. I'd buy me all those records and I'd play one by Jimmy and one by Trumbauer,

you dig? I didn't know nothing about Hawk then, and they were the only ones telling a story I liked to hear. I had both of them made . . . Did you ever hear him [Trumbauer] play "Singin' the Blues"? [*Bix and Tram*, Selected Discography, Chapter 3.] That tricked me right there and that's where I went.[21]

This remains one of the few cases in which a major black innovator was significantly influenced by a white instrumentalist.

Fletcher Henderson, however, was not impressed by Lester, who he imagined would play like Hawkins. Mrs. Henderson used to play Hawk's records for Young in the hopes that he would desert his light, linear, breathy style. Lester listened only out of politeness and soon requested leave of Henderson along with a letter indicating that he had not been fired. Six months later he rejoined Count Basie's band (Bennie Moten had died) which had attracted the attention of Benny Goodman and John Hammond.

Lester Young's Columbia sessions, from 1936 to 1939, are collected on *The Lester Young Story, Volumes I–IV*, two-disc sets that reveal him at the peak of his creative powers with the orchestras of Count Basie, Teddy Wilson, and Billie Holiday. On *Volume I* his classic "Shoe Shine Boy" (two takes) and his "Oh, Lady Be Good" solos of sixty-four bars each constitute a microcosm of Lester's contribution to jazz. His light, buoyant tone was the most obvious departure from the conventions of the day. Herschel Evans, Young's partner in the Basie sax section, was fond of ridiculing Lester's upper-register playing for sounding "like an alto"; but Lester, undaunted, insisted that the tenor need not be "all belly."

"Shoe Shine Boy," Lester's debut on records, finds him smoothing out the more jagged Hawkins swing with evenly played, flowing eighth notes. The clean, clear, yet casual quality of his lines profoundly affected the modern tenor saxophonists of the next two decades, players like Stan Getz, Zoot Sims, Lee Konitz, and, to a less-predominant extent, Dexter Gordon and Gene Ammons. These were also the records that were memorized by the young, developing Charlie Parker, justifying the historical view of Young as a crucial bridge between swing and bebop.

Lester's solos were also daring in their willingness to ignore the accepted notes within a chord. His strong melodic sense allowed him to venture outside of the chord, as on "Oh, Lady Be Good." He shows little regard for Gershwin's melody and uses it only as a springboard for his own ideas. The last eight bars are brilliant; accents fall where we least expect them, the line soars and plunges repeatedly, but the logic, symmetry, and grace of this statement absorb its novelty.

Jimmy Rushing, the best of the Kansas City blues shouters, had recently joined the band; he appears on two cuts with a hornlike inflection. Basie's Waller-influenced solos on side one, especially the opening to "Shoe Shine Boy," are a rare treat. He seldom played such full-bodied piano on the band's sessions for Decca (now on MCA).

Billie Holiday played a major role in Lester's life, beginning with their first session together—"He Ain't Got Rhythm" in 1937. (Their personal relationship is touched upon in the Holiday discussion ahead.) It was Billie who coined Lester's enduring nickname Prez, for "president of the tenors," just as he had dubbed her Lady Day. Their musical rapport was exquisite, since Billie was strongly influenced by Prez's understated, vibrato-less tone. Lester, unlike other soloists of the 1930's, did not always play the same way but varied his mood with the context. Thus he is more pensive in Billie's company than elsewhere, as we hear on the beautiful obbligato to "I'll Never Be the Same."

The remaining three volumes of the Columbia series are equally fine collections of his work. Young played with a consistency, energy, and innocence which were greatly impaired by his disastrous Army experience later on. *Volume II* includes the "Honeysuckle Rose" jam session from the Benny Goodman Carnegie Hall concert of 1938, in which Lester's opening solo eclipses everything that follows it. *Volume III, Enter the Count* contains predominantly Basie band sides, including "Taxi War Dance" (two takes), which inspired Lester's imagination, and historic tracks with vocalist Helen Humes. *Volume IV, Lester Leaps In* is named for Young's composition (two takes), on which he plays stunning sixty-four-bar solos. These solos are part of the fourteen cuts of the Kansas City Seven, a Basie unit smaller than the orchestra and therefore more generous with its solo allotments. Four cuts of "Dickie's Dream" by trombonist Dickie Wells reveal Lester's inventiveness, for three of them are quite dissimilar.

Another album of this fertile period, Commodore's *Lester Young* recorded in 1938, contains excellent sessions of the Kansas City Five and the Kansas City Six—with Young, trumpeter Buck Clayton, guitarists Eddie Durham and Freddie Green, bassist Walter Page, and drummer Jo Jones. This is essentially the Basie group but without the Count, who was signed to Decca. Young's clarinet playing is soft and fluid, a startling alternative to the outgoing, popular, post-Dixieland feeling of Benny Goodman. Eddie Durham's electric guitar here marks that instrument's debut on records.

Young was dropped from the Basie band suddenly and rather absurdly in 1940, allegedly because he refused to record with them on Friday the thirteenth. For a brief time he led a group with his brother Lee on drums, but lacked the business acumen and pragmatism necessary to succeed as a leader. He rejoined Basie in 1943, a reunion that was not preserved due to the wartime recording ban. He was inducted into the Army in 1944, and in a little over a year, his experiences there proved to be a catastrophe from which he never quite recovered.

A born nonconformist, Lester could not begin to cope with army life, and was in line for a discharge after three months. While filling out routine medical papers, he naïvely admitted to smoking marijuana. An officer found the drug among his belongings and—motivated, according to some witnesses, by the fact that Lester's wife was white—brought charges against him. The five-year sentence was reduced to one year, but then was increased after an escape attempt and further drug use. Incarcerated at a detention center in Georgia, Lester spent fifteen months there terrified for his life.

When Lester finally returned to the recording studio in late 1945, the bebop innovators had overturned much of the thinking which Lester and Basie had helped to formulate. Thus it was a bitter, isolated, and confused man who tried to begin life over again during the 1940's, himself nearing the age of forty. Blue Note's *The Aladdin Sessions* (1945–1948) show Lester matched with good bebop pianists—Dodo Marmarosa and Joe Albany—but not able to capture the carefree confidence of his Basie days. The most interesting cuts are his own "Jumpin' with Symphony Sid," named for a New York City deejay, a new "Lester Leaps In," and the early traces of bebop influence on tracks like "Movin' with Lester." A more interesting album still is Verve's *Bird and Pres: The '46 Concerts*, culled from Norman Granz's "Jazz at the Philharmonic" dates. Lester is generally ineffective here except for his rousing solo on "I Got Rhythm," but the lineup (including Charlie Parker, Dizzy Gillespie, Coleman Hawkins, and Buck Clayton) is a glimpse at the emergence of a new musical era. Due to Bird's ill health and the "older" style of Hawk, Buck, and Prez, Dizzy steals the show.

Lester's eccentricities were getting out of hand in the early 1950's. Eventually he made a fetish out of being different, wearing his hair at collar length, affecting effeminacy at times, holding his horn at an impossible angle, and speaking in ludicrous profanity or imaginative slang. Lester has been credited with coining the expressions "cool," "I got eyes for that," and "I got it made." For the most part, his behavior was not constructive; it reflected his intense alienation and perpetuated it. Three more Verve studio albums were made during this period of decline, all two-disc sets: *Lester Swings*, which actually includes eight tracks from the antedated 1945 sessions with Nat "King" Cole at the piano; *Pres and Teddy and Oscar,* its best tracks due to the Peterson trio of Ray Brown and Barney Kessel; and *The Jazz Giants: '56,* a last, occasionally successful, reunion with Teddy Wilson. Young uses the lower register of his horn with greater frequency in this period and clearly makes no attempt to emulate his former self. These are albums for the collector of Young's work, not for hearing the essence of his contribution to a cooler, more subtle style of jazz.

Lester's last years were marked by hospitalizations for alcoholism and nervous disorders. He moved into a dismal hotel on Fifty-second Street in Manhattan, where he spent hours listening to records, drinking, and staring out at Birdland across the street. In early 1959 he left for Paris, where he worked until he became too ill. He returned home in March and resumed his routine in his hotel room, where he died two days later.

BILLIE HOLIDAY

The Billie Holiday Story, Volume II

Columbia, KG 32124
two discs, liner notes
1935–1941

Musicians: Billie Holiday (vocals) and Her Orchestra: Lester Young, Earl Warren, tenor saxes; Jack Washington, alto sax; Buck Clayton, Harry Edison, trumpets; Joe Sullivan, piano; Freddie Green, guitar; Walter Page, bass; and Jo Jones, drums. Also with Teddy Wilson and His Orchestra: Wilson, piano; Roy Eldridge, trumpet; Ben Webster, tenor sax; Cecil Scott, clarinet; Hilton Jefferson, alto sax; Lawrence Lucie, guitar; John Kirby, bass; Cozy Cole, drums. Other personnel of note include Johnny Hodges, alto sax; Grachan Moncur, bass; Jonah Jones, Henry "Red" Allen, trumpets; Buster Bailey, clarinet; Cootie Williams, trumpet; and Harry Carney, baritone sax.

Compositions: Side one: Some Other Spring; The Man I Love; Ghost of Yesterday; Body and Soul; I'm Pulling Through; Tell Me More; Laughing at Life; Time on My Hands. *Side two:* Georgia on My Mind; Romance in the Dark; All of Me; God Bless the Child; Am I Blue?; I Cover the Waterfront; Love Me or Leave Me; Gloomy Sunday. *Side three:* A Sunbonnet Blue; I'm Painting the Town Red; What a Night, What a Moon, What a Girl; You Let Me Down; It's Too Hot for Words; It's Like Reaching for the Moon; One Never Knows, Does One?; I've Got My Love to Keep Me Warm. *Side four:* My Last Affair; You Showed Me the Way; Sentimental and Melancholy; Let's Call the Whole Thing Off; Moanin' Low; Carelessly; Where Is the Sun?; How Could You?

BILLIE HOLIDAY COULD TRANSFORM the most banal pop ballad into a painfully intense, subtle work of art. She was the ultimate jazz singer, relying on a deeply honest delivery and an exquisite control of her rather small range. Her tone was strongly influenced by the instrumentalists she knew, especially the light, understated sound of Lester Young, with whom she was close during her most creative years. When Young was staying with the Holidays in Harlem, Billie's mother claimed that from an adjoining room she could barely distinguish between her daughter's humming and Lester's playing. Louis Armstrong's personalized rephrasing of a song also contributed to her style; and his 1928 "West End Blues," recorded the year she moved from Baltimore to New York, was one of her favorite records.[22] Although Billie's own repertoire was virtually devoid of the blues form, she inherited an omnipresent feeling for the blues from Bessie Smith. Bessie, whose enormous voice Billie could not hope to match, communicated with drama; Billie, with subtle variations of pitch contained in the nuances of her pronunciation.

To Billie the blues was not just music but her life story. Born to un-
married teenagers in 1915, her father, Clarence Holiday, soon left the
family to play banjo and guitar with Fletcher Henderson's Orchestra. He
nicknamed her Bill for her tomboyish nature, but she changed it to Billie
after Billie Dove, a popular movie actress of the day. At ten she was raped
by a tenant in her mother's rooming house and was briefly confined to a
Catholic home for girls on the grounds that she had been provocative.

Two years later she moved to New York with her mother, who became
ill during the Depression years. Billie turned to prostitution for an income
and, for escape, to drugs, leading to the heroin addiction which ruined her
personal life. In the winter of 1932 she walked down Seventh Avenue, door
to door, looking for work, eventually auditioning as a dancer. After Billie's
pitiful performance, the piano player, feeling sorry for her, asked her if she
could sing, something she had always done for her own enjoyment but never
considered as a career. She sang "Travelin' All Alone," and when she had
finished, there were thirty-eight dollars in tips on the floor and a steady job
for eighteen dollars per week.

John Hammond discovered her at a supper club the following year, and,
impressed by her dignity and sensitive phrasing, persuaded Benny Goodman
to use her on his 1933 recordings of "Your Mother's Son-in-Law" and
"Riffin' the Scotch," which are available on *The Billie Holiday Story, Volume I*. Neither Benny nor Billie had reached their full capacity; thus these
tracks are primarily of historical interest. Two years later, however, Hammond paired up Billie with Teddy Wilson, whose orchestra was recording
on the company's seventy-five-cent Brunswick label; Billie was to be marketed to the urban black public on the cheaper Vocalion discs, which sold
for thirty-five cents.[23]

The Wilson-Holiday sessions, which were recorded casually and on a low
budget, did not seem destined for history, although they changed jazz singing
forever. Their spontaneity was no doubt in their favor. For the most part,
Billie was provided with a stack of forty second-rate Tin Pan Alley tunes,
while the hits went to the established popular singers on Brunswick. Wilson,
who tried to line up the best jazz talent in town for accompaniment (the
Basie band members whenever possible) selected four of these songs along
with Billie. While Billie learned the words and worked out her phrasing,
the band experimented with "head" arrangements, sometimes writing out an
eight-bar ending. Two takes were standard procedure in case one of the wax-
ings was damaged. Within two hours it was all over.

For listeners it was only the beginning of Billie's golden years on records,
which were to last until 1942. Before examining Billie's style more closely
on the selected album, it is worth pausing for an overview of the sessions
available from this period, which fortunately include nearly everything she
recorded. The single LP *Lady Day* contains the first session with Wilson,
Billie's first tracks as the featured performer, and several cuts made with
Lester Young, who invariably provided the most sensitive obbligatos to Billie's

melodies. Lester dubbed Billie "Lady," although it was an epithet he conferred upon every musician, male or female. Lester and Billie were also lovers for a time, a period marked by spats, quarrels, and frequent moments of musical bliss.

The Billie Holiday Story, Volumes I–III is the most complete set from this period, containing nearly two hundred tracks, many with Teddy Wilson, Lester Young, and the Ellington or Basie band members. Billie could not record with the Basie band itself for contractual reasons, although three excellent air checks—"I Can't Get Started," "Swing, Brother, Swing," and "They Can't Take That Away from Me"—have been included in *Volume I*. *Volume II*, which was selected simply on the grounds of personal taste, will be discussed later. *Volume III*, covering the years from 1937 to 1942, includes the superb "Mean to Me," "I'm in a Lowdown Groove," and "It's a Sin to Tell a Lie." The best soloists of the era appear on these three two-disc sets: Teddy Wilson, Lester Young, Roy Eldridge, Buck Clayton, Ben Webster, Johnny Hodges, and Cootie Williams, every one of whom can be heard on *Volume II*.

Interestingly Billie's most sensational recording in these years, "Strange Fruit," was not made for Columbia, which preferred to avoid its profoundly disturbing subject matter. She had received the lyrics in 1939 from the poet Lewis Allen as a protest against the lynching of blacks in the South. Obtaining a release from Columbia, she recorded it for Milt Gabler's Commodore label in a chilling performance backed up by the small band that was then accompanying her at club Café Society. Two takes, along with other cuts from 1939 and 1944, were reissued on Commodore's *Billie Holiday: Fine and Mellow*, an ironically inappropriate title considering the repertoire. Alternative takes from the same session can be heard on Atlantic's *Strange Fruit*. This is the essential Billie Holiday period, although there is much good music on the MCA and Verve reissues which document the period from 1944 to 1956.

The Billie Holiday Story: Volume II includes her own most lasting composition, "God Bless the Child," and ten cuts each with Teddy Wilson and Lester Young, demonstrating the natural, sympathetic rapport she had with both. Their respective solos on "Laughing at Life," for example, are sensitive to Billie while maintaining the personal identity each man had as an improviser. Billie's treatment of a song, however, is deeply moving even with more commonplace accompaniment. She was uncanny at invention and simplification, even revising good melodies—like the bridge to "Body and Soul" (the second time around)—for the better. She never succumbs to the superfluous frill or flourish, improvising with ingenuous brilliance to rescue stiff, jerky lines like those of "Love Me or Leave Me." Billie did not sing only the song but also its emotional core, often one she had given it herself.

Billie's intensity derives from her subtly effective use of language. Like Bessie Smith, or virtually any singer of black American music, Billie bends notes, varying the scale tones enormously and with consummate skill. Examples of her gliding up to or down from a pitch need not be singled out because they are everywhere. Moreover, Glenn Coulter has astutely observed that unlike other singers she used these distortions of pitch to manipulate the beat.[24] The sustaining of a syllable or the anticipation of a harmonic change create an irregularity and tension which keep the music moving. They also cause the listener to pay attention to Billie's words in a way the spongy lyrics alone could never do.

Billie's pitch-bending explains another anomaly in her recorded work which bears on its emotional message. Of the hundreds of sessions cut between 1933 and 1959, there were no more than a dozen genuine blues. Yet the blues is very much a part of her style. Two consequences of her pitch distortions resolve this apparent paradox. First, the speech-related import of a protracted syllable is usually an intense feeling. When one says "Oh, no!" the length of the "No-o-o-o!" is usually an indication of how serious the matter is; and in the deepest grief the voice will undoubtedly slide through numerous pitches. Thus Billie invokes this unconscious association to intensity with her "tonal" use of language (Chapter 1). Further, she frequently hits so-called blue notes during these swoops and glides about the pitch. Three tracks exemplify this quite clearly: on "Laughing at Life," the words "today" and "away"; in the third verse of "Tell Me More," the word "tell"; and in the bridge to "I'm Pulling Through," the word "wrong." In sum, intensity and actual blues tonality are often present in Billie's singing though they are rarely part of the original material.

Recording technology is part of the story. As Gene Lees points out in the liner notes to *God Bless the Child*, a two-disc reshuffling of the Columbia material, "the microphone made possible for the singer what the motion picture (camera) made possible for the actor." Just as a slight grimace or raised eyebrow magnified on the screen could communicate powerfully, so could the singer's slightest nuance of inflection when amplified. This fine shading became one of Billie's trademarks.

Billie's next recording period, from 1944 to 1950, was on Decca Records (now owned by MCA), where, at her request, she was generally backed up by strings or a vocal choir. On the available two-disc anthology of these sessions, *The Billie Holiday Story*, we hear her rise above the inflated format, remaining sensitive without sentimentalizing, her voice at full strength and, of course, recorded with a greater fidelity than was possible in the 1930's. "Lover Man," one of her biggest commercial hits, is on this album.

Billie's heroin habit was now dominating her life, absorbing hundreds of dollars a week of her substantial earnings and resulting in hospitalizations, arrests, and a short prison term. From 1952 to 1956, Norman Granz recorded her for Verve with excellent small jazz groups, conducive to the kind of singing she had excelled at but could no longer do. Her voice had coarsened from excessive drinking, her health was failing, and her self-confidence, which had never been secure, was irreparably shaken. Despite a sensitive accompaniment by pianist Jimmy Rowles, Harry "Sweets" Edison on trumpet, and Ben Webster and Benny Carter on saxophones, *The First Verve Sessions*, *Stormy Blues*, and *All or Nothing at All* are a progressive testimony to her decline.

Billie continued to tour and even recorded again for Columbia (*Lady in Satin*) in 1958, accompanied by strings, but the next year she was hospitalized with a liver ailment which proved fatal. As if symbolic of her lifelong agony, she was arrested on her deathbed for a small quantity of heroin found in her room. Whether she was responsible for its presence was never established, for she died a few days later, just four months after her soul mate Lester Young. *Lady Sings the Blues*, an autobiography published in 1956, is the most thorough examination of the close relationship between her personal life and her music, a subject treated quite irreverently by the film of the same name.

ART TATUM

The Tatum Solo Masterpieces, Volume 3

Pablo, 2310-730
one disc, liner notes
1953–1955

Musicians: Art Tatum, solo piano.
Compositions: Side one: Yesterdays; Tenderly; Jitterbug Waltz; Love Me or Leave Me; Deep Purple. *Side two:* Begin the Beguine; Dixieland Band; All the Things You Are; Crazy Rhythm; Prisoner of Love.

ART TATUM, born nearly blind in Toledo, Ohio, in 1910, was one of the great interpretive artists of the piano. Improvising melodies was not his forte, but he could transform pop songs, blues, and even light classics into elegant, imaginative tapestries. His extraordinary technique was a source of intimidation to many other pianists: The classical virtuosos Leopold Godowsky, Vladimir Horowitz, and Walter Gieseking reportedly sat in awe at the Onyx Club on Fifty-second Street. Art Tatum was the last of the great cutting-contest champions (since the custom seemed to pass out of style by the end of the 1940's), though no other pianists were seriously willing to challenge him. Allegedly, Bud Powell—with the fastest right hand in bebop—*did* challenge Art when he was in an inebriated condition. Tatum told him to sober up and then come back, promising that "anything you play with your right hand I'll play with my left." [25] The outcome varies with the two versions of the story. Tatum practiced away from the piano by running filbert nuts across his fingers like a magician. He could play any song in his vast repertoire in any key, allowing him to cushion his speed in the luxuriant softness of D♭, A♭, and G♭, keys rarely used because of their numerous flatted notes.

Tatum's youth was spent in Toledo, where a local piano teacher, Overton G. Rainey, tried to steer him toward a career in the classics. However, Fats Waller, whom he heard frequently on the air, exerted a stronger pull. At eighteen Tatum began performing on radio station WSPD in Toledo, and moved to New York in 1932 to accompany the singer Adelaide Hall. He recorded his first solos the next year in a highly energetic, harmonically rich stride derived from Waller, Hines, and Teddy Wilson. His earliest sessions (four cuts from 1933) are available on Columbia's *The Piano Starts Here*, which contains classic early Tatum on eight cuts from a 1949 Los Angeles concert arranged by deejay Gene Norman. Much of his perennial repertoire —"Yesterdays," "Someone to Watch Over Me," "Willow Weep For Me"— was in full bloom. The album is a monumental collection of constantly shifting rhythmic patterns and thick substitution chords laced together by blistering, tortuous runs.

Tatum's next important recordings were made in trio with bassist Slam Stewart and guitarist Tiny Grimes, with whom Tatum could exchange melodic and rhythmic ideas at breakneck pace. The trio had a lasting impact on Tatum's most capable disciple, Oscar Peterson (Chapter 5), who duplicated its instrumentation in his own peak performances of the 1950's with Ray Brown on bass and Barney Kessel or Herb Ellis on guitar. The trio is best heard on MCA's *Art Tatum: Masterpieces* (1941–1944), which devotes one of its two discs to solo Tatum. The solo cuts show a marked improvement over the frantic speed of the 1930's. His "Tiger Rag" is still at the "impossible" tempo level, but it moves effortlessly; an eight-measure chorus of his standby crowd-pleaser "Yesterdays" is spun out in a glistening waterfall of notes, each one retaining its individuality. The trio cuts are no less precise and articulate, their timbres merging as one jubilant voice on "I Got Rhythm." Side four contains a wonderful set with Joe Turner, perhaps the best of the Kansas City shouters, singing blues like "Corrine, Corrina," "Wee Baby Blues," and "Lonesome Graveyard Blues." His phrasing is relaxed, the "jump" feeling is omnipresent, and those who believe Art Tatum cannot play the blues are in for a shock.

Yet Tatum's highest achievements were still several years ahead, when he was willing to sacrifice a bit of speed in favor of his rich harmonic imagination. He was at his best as an after-hours pianist or in a friend's living room, where he was given carte blanche on repertoire and where he had an intimate audience to excite him with its ooh's and aah's. (One of the best Tatum albums was taped at just such a house party in early 1955, but it disappeared with the Twentieth Fox label.) In these settings Tatum defies the critical opinion that considers him an ornate musical illustrator but lacking in substance. While there is some validity to this evaluation from a melodic viewpoint, Tatum's artistry is expressed in harmonic terms.

Norman Granz, owner of the Verve label, abundantly taped the mature Art Tatum of the 1950's as his health was gradually failing. Tatum played whatever came to mind on these sessions, achieving a semblance of the after-hours looseness he preferred. The results are uniformly excellent, and are available on Pablo's *The Tatum Solo Masterpieces, Volumes 1–9* (either separately or in a boxed set). Granz simultaneously recorded Tatum in a variety of small bands (*The Art Tatum Group Masterpieces, Volumes 1–8*), the most exciting of which is with Ben Webster (Volume 6). The others are listed in the General Discography.

Solo Masterpieces, Volume 3 reveals the stunning harmonic and rhythmic variety Tatum displayed. Yet his rhapsodic tendencies are held in check by an acute sense of the beat, as evident in the incessant, rolling swing of "Love Me or Leave Me," in which Tatum's left hand is an independent and powerful rhythmic lever. At the romantic end of the spectrum, Tatum played with tempo-less rubato phrasing, as on "Tenderly," one of his favorite vehicles for kaleidoscopic invention. "Yesterdays," harmonically richer than the MCA version of ten years earlier, goes well beyond the "decorative" revision of the melody of which Tatum was occasionally guilty. His thematic variations only imply the original song, expanding its chord progressions beyond recognition, at the same time holding together numerous rhythmic changes of pace in the first thirty-two bars.

Tatum did not add any new idioms to the jazz language, but he used more of the piano within that language than anyone had before him. Tatum thus elevated the standards of achievement on his instrument, and continued to do so until his death of uremia in 1956.

WOODY HERMAN ORCHESTRA

The Three Herds

Columbia Special Products, JCL-592
one disc, good liner notes (by Herman)
1945–1954

Musicians: Woody Herman, clarinet and vocals. The members of the three Herds include Stan Getz, Flip Phillips, Zoot Sims, Herbie Steward, Jerry Coker, tenor saxes; Serge Chaloff, baritone sax; Kai Winding, Urbie Green, Bill Harris, Vern Friley, trombones; Shorty Rogers, Neal Hefti, Peter Condoli, Sonny Berman, Dick Collins, Al Porcino, trumpets; Cy Touff, bass trumpet; Billy Bauer, Chuck Wayne, guitars; Nat Pierce, Ralph Burns, pianos; Chubby Jackson, bass; Dave Tough, Don Lamond, drums.

Compositions: Side one: Non-Alcoholic; Caldonia; Sidewalks of Cuba; The Good Earth; Four Brothers; The Goof and I. *Side two:* Keen and Peachy; Early Autumn; Four Others; Blame Boehm; Mulligan Tawny; The Third Herd.

WOODY HERMAN IS one of the three bandleaders of institutional status. The various Herman "Herds"—a label coined in 1944 by George T. Simon of of the now-defunct *Metronome* magazine—survived along with the Basie and Ellington groups, from the swing era into the 1970's. Basie had rhythmic drive, exciting soloists, and, eventually, sophisticated arrangers; Ellington was simply profound. Woody Herman's talent, above all, was finding talent and organizing it. Budding soloists like young Stan Getz, the brilliant trombonist Flip Phillips, Bill Harris, Pete Condoli, Zoot Sims (and others not represented on this album) seemed dependably to "find themselves" in the Herds' ranks; and the arrangers, Neal Hefti (also on trumpet), Jimmy Guiffre, and Ralph Burns (on piano), pioneered new ideas in section writing, creating classics like "Four Brothers," "Early Autumn," and "The Good Earth." Although Herman played clarinet and alto sax competently and sang the blues passably, the band's identity was more a function of its members than its leader. Woody's crucial role was to focus and merge the musical potential he attracted and to mix it in just the right proportions.

Herman's band was also the first to absorb the innovations of bebop phrasing, making the band's early style a transitional one between the swing and modern eras (see Chapter 5).

Woodrow Charles Herman was born in Milwaukee, Wisconsin, in 1913, and at the age of six began to sing and dance in local theaters. He also worked with his parents in vaudeville, billed at the age of nine as "The Boy Wonder of the Clarinet." In his teens Herman went out on the road, joining the Isham Jones band in 1934 as a vocalist and saxophonist. When the Jones band broke up two years later, Woody organized its key members into a group known as "The Band That Plays the Blues." Their first hit in 1939 was a riffed blues by Joe Bishop, "Woodchopper's Ball," which eventually sold a million copies in the Decca version. MCA's *The Best of Woody Herman* contains the original cut along with the band's first theme, "Blue Flame" (1941), and eighteen other commercially motivated sides up to 1943. This album is of historical interest but is barely listenable today.

"The Band That Plays the Blues" evolved into the first Herd over the next year with fortuitous changes in personnel: Billy Bauer on guitar, Chubby Jackson on bass, and Dave Tough on drums added precision and power to the rhythm section; pianist Ralph Burns and vocalist Frances Wayne defected from the Charlie Barnet Band; and the fiery brass soloists Flip Phillips, Bill Harris, and Pete Condoli also joined. *The Three Herds*, the best survey of the essential Herman groups, presents two crucial cuts from the first Herd. "Caldonia," a blues which was adapted by Burns from a Louis Jordan vocal, became a Herman standard, featuring one of Woody's most effective vocals. "The Good Earth," the first arrangement for the band by Neal Hefti, elevated its reputation considerably, and it is easy to hear why. The band is not a showcase for soloists but a dynamic unit, pitting brass against reeds in sharply punctuated dialogue. There is a nice, sailing clarinet lead by Herman and a good tenor solo probably by Phillips. Over the next decade, the band's ability to swing was second to none.

Strangely enough, the first Herd was a commercial success, while Count Basie, Duke Ellington, and Earl Hines had fallen upon hard times. In fact, Herman claims that his band grossed a million dollars in one year. Nevertheless, he broke up the group in 1947 so that he could spend more time with his family, playing a farewell concert in Carnegie Hall at which the band premiered Igor Stravinsky's "Ebony Concerto."

The second Herd reflected the important changes ushered in by the innovators of bebop. The arrangement of "Four Brothers" (1947) by Jimmy Guiffre, a brilliantly serpentine melodic line, characterized the new Herman sound with its unusually reedy voicing of three tenors and a baritone, a stylistic device which became permanent. The light, "cool" solos by (in order) Zoot Sims, Herbie Steward, Serge Chaloff (baritone), and Stan Getz reveal the profound influence of Lester Young on the white saxophonists of the 1940's. The band is buoyant and packs a somewhat harder punch due to the drumming of Don Lamond, the replacement for Davey Tough who had fallen ill. The next two tracks emphasize the trumpets, especially that of Shorty Rogers (twenty-one years old at the time) who takes the lead on the "head" arrangement to "Keen and Peachy." "The Goof and I" by Al Cohn is a good vehicle for Lamond but not a particularly successful chart. Herman claims the record helped introduce the word "goof," musicians' slang for a mistake, into the vernacular.

The most memorable product of the second Herd was "Early Autumn," part four of a Ralph Burns suite entitled "Summer Sequence." Again, the sensuous reed section dominates the band; this beautiful piece launched the career of Stan Getz. Although Bill Perkins from the third Herd plays the tenor sax solo here, Getz's original cut is available on Capitol's *Early Autumn* (General Discography). The second Herd came to an end at about the same time as the Earl Hines Orchestra—in 1948, when the closing of dance halls due to the tax on dancing made big bands economically unfeasible.

The remainder of side two is representative of the third Herd, which was organized in 1952 with Bill Perkins, Jerry Coker, and Chuck Flores, and arrangements were added to the already impressive book by Jimmy Guiffre, Al Cohn, and Bill Holman. Bebop had now taken over the soloists' styles, but the band's texture, precise sense of swing, and upbeat mood remained constants. The memorable track here is Guiffre's "Four Others," featuring an abundantly talented trombone section with solos by (in order) Kai Winding, Frank Rehak, Vern Friley, and Urbie Green. The third Herd's tenure was three years, and subsequent incarnations of the Herman orchestra were too numerous to warrant labeling them.

Conspicuously absent from *The Three Herds* are two tunes which helped to establish the band during the 1940's—the famous "Woodchopper's Ball" and a rousing "head" of potent riffs called "Apple Honey." Both are included on Columbia's *The Beat of the Big Bands*, an anthology of vintage Herman repertoire shamefully packaged without listing either the personnel or the recording dates. The music, however, is excellent.

Almost all the material discussed above was played at the band's fortieth anniversary Carnegie Hall concert recorded in 1974. This was conceived as a Herman reunion by critic Leonard Feather, and Woody and his manager Hermie Dressel succeeded in gathering an all-star group for a brilliant re-creation of the band's past. The personnel included Stan Getz, Ralph Burns, Pete Condoli, Don Lamond, Chubby Jackson, Flip Phillips, Zoot Sims, Nat Pierce, and Jimmy Rowles. The results are available on RCA's two-disc *Woody Herman: The 40th Anniversary Carnegie Hall Concert* (General Discography).

A key to Herman's success in the 1970's was his openness to material of various idioms. During this decade he distinguished himself on two Fantasy albums: *Giant Steps* (1973), a tribute to the music of John Coltrane (Chapter 6); and *Children of Lima* (1975) with two long compositions by New Zealander pianist Alan Broadbent (Herman's arranging discovery of the 1970's), performed by the Thundering Herd and the Houston Symphony Orchestra.

Notes

1. Gunther Schuller, *Early Jazz* (New York and London: Oxford University Press, 1968), p. 7.

2. Marshall W. Stearns, *The Story of Jazz* (New York and London: Oxford University Press, 1956), p. 180

3. *Ibid.*, p. 240n.

4. Leroy Ostransky, *Jazz City* (Englewood Cliffs, N.J.: Prentice-Hall, 1978), p. 146.

5. *Ibid.*, p. 143.

6. Nat Shapiro and Nat Hentoff, *Hear Me Talkin' to Ya* (New York: Dover Publications, Inc., 1966), p. 284.

7. Joachim Berendt, *The Jazz Book* (New York: Lawrence Hill & Company, 1975), p. 171. Originally published in 1953.

8. Martin Williams, *The Jazz Tradition* (New York: New American Library, 1971), p. 96. Original edition published by Grove Press in 1959.

9. Schuller, *op. cit.*, pp. 159–160.

10. Shapiro and Hentoff, *op. cit.*, p. 304.

11. Stearns, *op. cit.*, p. 200.

12. *Ibid.*, p. 184.

13. *Ibid.*, p. 182.

14. Foreword by Frank Sinatra, p. ix, in George T. Simon, *The Big Bands* (New York: Collier-Macmillan, 1974).

15. Shapiro and Hentoff, *op. cit.*, p. 238.

16. Ralph J. Gleason, *Celebrating the Duke . . . & Other Heroes* (Boston: Little Brown & Co., Inc., 1975), p. 168.

17. Ross Russell, *Jazz Styles in Kansas City and the Southwest* (Berkeley: University of California Press, 1971), p. 136.

18. Stanley Dance, "Earl Hines," in *Contemporary Keyboard*, November 1977, p. 14.

19. Richard Hadlock, *Jazz Masters of the Twenties* (New York: Macmillan, Inc., 1974), pp. 73–74.

20. Bill Simon, "Charlie Christian," in Nat Shapiro and Nat Hentoff, *The Jazz Makers* (New York: Grove Press, Inc., 1957), p. 322.

21. Francois Postif, "Lester Young: Paris, 1959," in *Jazz Panorama*, Martin Williams, ed. (New York: Crowell-Collier Press, 1962), p. 141.

22. Shapiro and Hentoff, *op. cit.*, p. 201.

23. According to Leonard Feather's liner notes to *Billie Holiday: The Golden Years, Volume II*, a three-record set. Many of the tracks on this double album appeared in the C3L-40 boxed set by Columbia Records. It is still available.

24. Glenn Coulter, "Billie Holiday," in Martin Williams, *The Art of Jazz* (New York: Oxford University Press, 1959), p. 162.

25. Shapiro and Hentoff, *The Jazz Makers*, p. 160.

General Discography of Available, Recommended Albums

COUNT BASIE AND ORCHESTRAS

Retrospective Sessions: Dedication Series, XI (1962 and 1969), IA-9351/2; *Count Basie and the Kansas City Seven*, AS-15; Impulse. *Good Morning Blues* (with Jimmy Rushing and Helen Humes, 1937–1939), MCA2-4102, MCA. *The Count Meets the Duke*, CS-8515; *Super Chief*, CG-31224; *One O'Clock Jump*, JCL-997; Columbia. *Basie Big Band*, 2310-756, Pablo. *At the Savoy* (with B. Holiday, L. Young, and J. Rushing, 1937), FS-318, Archives. *The Count Basie Years* (ca. 1960), RE-102; *Kansas City Suite*, RE-124; Roulette. *Count Basie Swings/Joe Williams Sings*, V-68488, Verve. Later albums on Pablo.

CHARLIE CHRISTIAN

Charlie Christian, FS-219, Archives (Everest). *Charlie Christian: Live!* (with Goodman), JA-23, Jazz Archives.

TOMMY DORSEY and JIMMY DORSEY

Beat of the Big Bands, C-32014, Columbia. *The Complete Tommy Dorsey, Vol. 1 (1935)*, AXM2-5521, Bluebird (RCA). *The Best of Tommy Dorsey*, MCA2-4074; *The Best of Jimmy Dorsey*, MCA2-4073; MCA.

ROY ELDRIDGE

Dizzy and Roy, VE2-2524; *Dale's Wail* (with Oscar Peterson), VE2-2531; *Jazz Giants* (with Lester Young, 1956), VE1-2527; Verve. *Oscar Peterson and Roy Eldridge*, 2310-739; *Happy Time*, 2310-746; *What It's All About*, 2310-766; *Roy Eldridge 4* (Oscar Peterson), 2308-203; *Jousts* (2 tracks), 2310-817; Pablo. *Roy Eldridge*, GNP9009, GNP Crescendo.

DUKE ELLINGTON

Duke Ellington—1938, R-003; *Duke Ellington—1939*, R-010; Smithsonian Collection (mail). *Duke Ellington Carnegie Hall Concerts, 1944*, P-24073; *1946*, P-24074; *1947*, P-24075; Prestige. *Duke Ellington at Fargo, 1940: Live!* (3 discs), 30-5622, Book-of-the-Month Club Records (mail order). *Duke Ellington's Greatest Hits*, CS-9629; *Ellington Indigos*, CS-8053; Columbia. *Duke Ellington—The Pianist* (1966), F-9462; *Afro-Eurasian Eclipse*, F-9498; Fantasy. *Ellington at Newport* (1956), CS-8648, Columbia. *Duke Ellington/John Coltrane* (quartet, 1962), AS-30; *Duke Ellington/Coleman Hawkins* (small combos, 1962), AS-26; Impulse. Reissues combined on *Dedication Series, Vol. X*, IA-9350/2, Impulse. *Such Sweet Thunder*, JCL-1033; *Ellington Jazz Party* (with Gillespie, Hodges, Rushing), JCS-8127; *Music of Duke Ellington*, JCL-558; *Masterpieces by Ellington*, JCL-825; *Ellington Uptown*, JCL-830; *A Drum Is a Woman*, JCL-951; *Black, Brown and Beige*, JCS-8015; Columbia Special Products. *The World of Duke*

Ellington (1947), CG-32564, Columbia. *Suite Thursday/Controversial Suite/Harlem Suite*, P-14359, Encore. *Giants of Jazz: Ellington* (1926–1956, 3 discs, liner booklet), J-02, Time-Life Records (mail).

BENNY GOODMAN

A Jazz Holiday (1927–1929), MCA2-4018, MCA. *The King of Swing* (orchestra, trio, quartet), *1937–1938, Jazz Concert No. 2*, OSL-9283E, Columbia. *The Complete Benny Goodman, Vol. I* (1935), *Vol. II* (1935–1936), *Vol. III* (1936), *Vol. IV* (1936–1937), SXM2-5505; SXM2-5515; SXM2-5532; SXM2-5537; Bluebird (RCA).

LIONEL HAMPTON

The Best of Lionel Hampton (orchestra), MCA2-4075, MCA. *Hamp's Big Band*, 5913, Audiofidelity.

COLEMAN HAWKINS

Coleman Hawkins (with Roy Eldridge and Benny Carter, 1940–1943), XFL-14936, Commodore. *Meets Duke Ellington*, A-26, Impulse. *The Great Tenor Encounters: Dedication Series, Vol. X* (with Ellington and Coltrane), IA-9350/2, Impulse. *With Ben Webster* (with Oscar Peterson and Roy Eldridge, 1947, 1959), VE-2-2520, Verve. *The Hawk Flies* (various groups—Monk, Kenny Clarke, J. J. Johnson, Fats Navarro, 1944–1946), M-47015, Milestone. *Jam Session in Swingville with Pee Wee Russell*, P-24051; *Hawk Eyes*, P07857; *Bean and the Boys*, P07824; *Blues Groove*, P07753; *Night Hawk*, P-7671; *The Real Thing*, P-24083; Prestige. *Meets the Big Sax Section* (Basie's, 1958), SJL-1123, Savoy. Famous "Body and Soul" (1939), on *Smithsonian Collection of Classic Jazz* (mail order). *Fletcher Henderson's Orchestra* (1923–1927), with Hawkins, BLP-12039, Biograph. *Coleman Hawkins*, FS-252, Archives.

FLETCHER HENDERSON

The Complete Fletcher Henderson, 1927–1936, AXM2-5507, Bluebird (RCA). *Fletcher Henderson Orchestra, 1923–1927*, BLP-12039; *Fletcher Henderson's Orchestra, 1924–1941* (only 3 cuts after 1925), BLP-C-12; Biograph. (The albums include Louis Armstrong, Coleman Hawkins, Don Redman, and Rex Stewart, but with the typically poor fidelity of acoustic recording.)

WOODY HERMAN

The Beat of the Big Bands (vintage repertoire, updated), C-32020; *Greatest Hits*, CS-9291; Columbia. Of historical interest: *The Best of Woody Herman* (1939–1941), MCA2-4077, MCA. Later albums: *40th Anniversary Carnegie Hall Concert* (Getz, Phillips, Condoli, 1976), BGL2-2203, RCA. *Giant Steps*, F-9432; *Children of Lima* (composer Broadbent; Houston Symphony), F-9477, Fantasy.

EARL HINES

The Father Jumps (big band), AXM2-5508, Bluebird. *A Monday Date/ 1928*, M-2012, Milestone. *The Incomparable*, F-8381, Fantasy. *Solo Walk in Tokyo*, BLP-12055, Biograph. *The Legendary Little Theater Concert, Vol. 1*, DE-602, Muse. *Earl Hines at Home* (1970's), DS-212, Delmark. *Earl Fatha Hines, Vols. I* (1954) and *II* (1964), FS-246, FS-322, Archive. *The New Earl Hines Trio* (1964), JCS-9120, CSP. *Earl Hines* (1949), GNP-9010, GNP Crescendo. *Hines and His All Stars, Vols. I* and *II* (with Muggsy Spanier, mid-1950's), GNPS-9042, GNPS-9043, GNP Crescendo.

Live at the New School (1960's), CR-157; *Quintessential*, CR-101; Chiaroscuro.

BILLIE HOLIDAY

The Billie Holiday Story, Vols. I and *III*, PG-32121, PG-32127; *God Bless the Child*, CG-30782; *The Golden Years, Vols. 1* and *2*, C3L-21, C3L-40 (3-disc sets) reissued on *Billie Holiday Story, Vols. I–III: Billie's Blues* (1937–1958), 32080; Columbia. *Strange Fruit* (1939–1948), SD-1614, Atlantic. *Fine and Mellow* (1939–1944), XFL-14428, Commodore (duplication of tracks on previous Atlantic). *Swing Brother Swing* (1935–1938), P-14388, Encore. *The Billie Holiday Story* (1944–1950), MCA2-4006, MCA. *Giants of Jazz*, STL-J03, Time-Life Records (mail order). Of historical interest: *First Verve Sessions* (1952–1954), VE2-25-3; *All or Nothing at All* (1955–1956), VE2-2529; *Stormy Blues* (1954–1955), VE2-2515; Verve.

GLENN MILLER

The Complete Glenn Miller, Vols. I–III, AXM2-5512; (1939) SXM2-5514; (1939–1940) SXM2-5534; Bluebird (RCA).

DJANGO REINHARDT (with Stephane Grappelli)

Vols. I–IV, FS-212, FS-230, FS-255, FS-307, Archive. *The Quintet of the Hot Club of France, Vols. I* and *II* (1935–1939), GNP-9001, GNP-9019, GNP Crescendo.

ART TATUM

Art Tatum: Masterpieces (solo, trio, Joe Turner, vocals), MCA2-4019, MCA. *Piano Starts Here*, CS-9655, Columbia. *The Tatum Solo Masterpieces, Vols. 1, 2, 4–8*; 723; 729; 789–793; *Solo* (13-disc set), 2625.703; *Group Masterpieces*, 731; *Vols. 1* and *2* (Benny Carter), 732, 733; (Roy Eldridge), 734; (Red Callender and Jo Jones), 735; (Buddy DeFranco), 736; (Ben Webster), 737; *Group* (8-disc set), 2625-706; Pablo. *Art Tatum Trio* (Slam Stewart and Tiny Grimes), FJ-2893, Folkways. *At the Crescendo*, Vols. I and II, GNP-9025, 9026; GNP Crescendo.

JOE TURNER

(See Count Basie Selected Discography; *Art Tatum: Masterpieces*.)

BEN WEBSTER

Ballads (with strings), VE2-2530; *Tenor Giants: Ben Webster/Coleman Hawkins* (1957–1959, Peterson and Eldridge), VE2-2520; Verve. *Ben Webster Quartet*, IC-2007, Inner City. *At Work in Europe*, P-24031, Prestige.

TEDDY WILSON (see Benny Goodman)

Statements and Improvisations (1934–1942), R-005, Smithsonian Collection (mail). *Three Little Words*, CJ-101; *Live at Santa Tecla*, CJ-32; Classic Jazz (Inner City). *Teddy Wilson*, GNP-9014, GNP Crescendo. *And Then They Wrote*, JCS-8238, CSP.

LESTER YOUNG (see also Count Basie and Billie Holiday)

Lester Young Story, Vols. II–IV, *A Musical Romance*, JG-34837; *Enter the Count*, JE-34840; *Lester Leaps In*, JG-34843; Columbia. *Lester Young: Kansas City Six and Five* (1938), XFL-14937, Commodore. *Lester Young: The Aladdin Sessions* (1945–1948), LA456-H2, Blue Note. *Pres/Complete Savoy Recording* (1944 and 1949), SJL-2202, Savoy. *Lester Swings* (with Nat "King" Cole, Hank Jones, John Lewis, 1945, 1950–1951), VE2-2516; *Bird and Pres* (with Gillespie): *At the Philharmonic* (1946), VE2-2518;

Pres and Teddy and Oscar (with Wilson and Peterson), VE2-2502; *The Jazz Giants: '56* (with Roy Eldridge), VE1-2527; Verve.

MISCELLANEOUS

Smithsonian Collection of Classic Jazz (6-disc set, 25 tracks, liner book), P6-11891, Smithsonian Collection (mail order). *Volume 8: The Big Bands* (Henderson, Ellington, Moten, Lunceford), FS-2808, Folkways. *The Changing Face of Harlem* (1944–1945), SJL-2208; *Savoy Jam Party: Don Byas*, SJL-2213; Savoy. *The Walter "Foots" Thomas All Stars, 1944–1945* (Hawkins, Webster, Shavers, et al.), P-7584, Prestige. *Cat Anderson* (quintet, 1977), CJ-142, Classic Jazz. *Anita O'Day—The Big Band Sessions* (1959–1961), VE2-2534, Verve. *Chu* (Chu Berry with Teddy Wilson's Orchestra, 1936–1941), JEE-22007, CSP. *The Duke's Man* (Hodges, Bigard, Stewart, Williams, 1936–1939), JCE-22005, CSP. *Sax Greats* (Hawkins, Byas, Webster), FS-331, Archive. *Red Norvo & His All Stars* (1933–1938), JEE-22009; *Gene Krupa* (with Anita O'Day and Gerry Mulligan), JCL-753; *Jazz Spectacular* (Frankie Laine/Buck Clayton, 1955), JCL-808; *The Sound of Jazz* (TV sound track: Billie Holiday, Lester Young, Coleman Hawkins, Red Allen), JCS-8040; *Swing Street* (4-disc set, bands of the 1940's and 1950's), JSN-6042; CSP. *All Star Swing Groups* (Pete Johnson and Cozy Cole), SJL-2218, Savoy. *The Complete Artie Shaw, Vols. I* and *II* (1938–1939), AXM2-5517; AZM2-5533; *The Complete Charlie Barnet, Vol. 1* (1935–1937), SXM2-5526; *The Smoothies: Easy Does It* (1939–1940), SXM2-5524; *The Cats & the Fiddle: I Miss You So* (1939–1941), SXM2-5531; Bluebird (RCA).

Above left, Scott Joplin, the greatest composer of classic ragtime, ca. 1911. (*Duncan Schiedt Archives*) Above right, Eubie Blake, nearing 100 and still a vibrant performer, ca. 1970. (*Courtesy CBS Records*) Below left, James P. Johnson, teacher of Fats Waller and an influence on Duke Ellington and Thelonious Monk. (*Duncan Schiedt Archives*) Below right, Fats Waller (a still from the film *Stormy Weather*, 1943. *Courtesy RCA Records*).

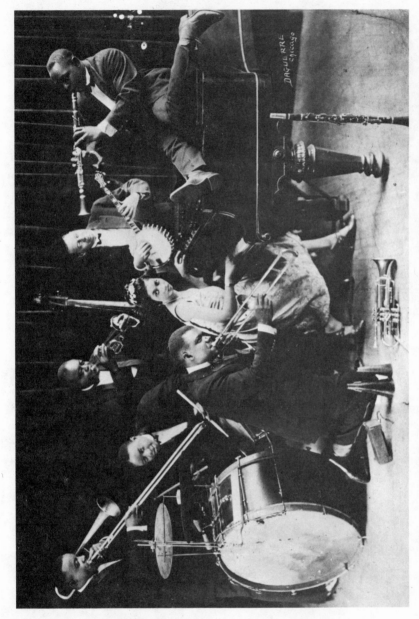

King Oliver's Creole Jazz Band (1923). From left to right: Honoré Dutrey, Baby Dodds, Joe "King" Oliver in the background, Lil Hardin at the piano, Bill Johnson, and Johnny Dodds. Louis Armstrong kneels in front with a slide trumpet he rarely played. (*Courtesy Hogan Jazz Archives, Tulane University Library*)

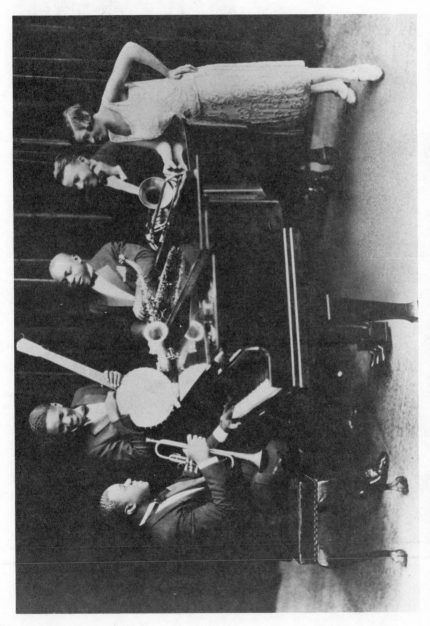

Louis Armstrong (seated) and His Hot Five (1925). Johnny St. Cyr, banjo; Johnny Dodds, reeds; Kid Ory, trombone; and pianist Lil Hardin, soon to be Louis's wife. (*Courtesy CBS Records*)

Above, Ferd (Jelly Roll) Morton, an innovative composer and bandleader (of the Red Hot Peppers) and a controversial pianist, ca. 1920. (*Courtesy Orrin Keepnews*) Left, Earl "Fatha" Hines, the father of modern jazz piano, posing in 1926 prior to his historic association with Armstrong. (*From the Stanley Dance Collection*)

Bessie Smith (a famous Carl Van Vechten portrait of the tragic Empress of the Blues, ca. 1925). (*Courtesy CBS Records*)

Above, Bix Beiderbecke and His Rhythm Jugglers in 1925, at a recording session in the Gennett Studios, Richmond, Indiana. Bix, one of the few white cult heroes in the history of jazz, is leaning back against Tommy Dorsey to his left, Don Murray to his immediate right. (*Courtesy Orrin Keepnews*) Below, the first Fletcher Henderson Orchestra (1924). With the arrangements of Don Redman (on the far left), Henderson (seated behind the drums) pioneered the swing style. The two men seated on the right are Louis Armstrong (above), who had just left King Oliver's band, and saxophonist Coleman Hawkins. (*Duncan Schiedt Archives*)

Above, Duke Ellington at work. (*From the Stanley Dance Collection*) Below, Duke Ellington and His Orchestra. This 1940 group was probably his greatest. From left to right, back row: Rex Stewart, Cootie Williams, Wallace Jones, Joe Nanton, Lawrence Brown, Fred Guy, Billy Strayhorn; front row: Sonny Greer, Duke, Johnny Hodges, Barney Bigard, Ben Webster, Toby Hardwicke, Harry Carney, and Jimmy Blanton. (*From the Stanley Dance Collection*)

Above, Bill "Count" Basie and His Orchestra, the greatest exponent of Kansas City-style swing. This 1940 publicity photo shows the unexcelled original rhythm section intact: Basie, the leader and pianist, standing; Walter Page, bass; Jo Jones, drums; Freddie Green (partly hidden), guitar. The innovative Lester Young ("Prez"), seated on the right, holds his tenor sax in his typically eccentric fashion. (*Courtesy Orrin Keepnews*)

Facing page, bottom, a historic shot of Lady Day and Prez filming a mid-1950's TV show. Billie Holiday is seated in front of the mike. In the background are Lester Young and Coleman Hawkins on tenor saxes and Gerry Mulligan on baritone sax. (*Courtesy CBS Records*)   Right, Billie Holiday performing (probably early 1940's). (*Courtesy CBS Records*)   Below, Art Tatum, solo pianist *par excellence,* ca. 1945. (*Courtesy Orrin Keepnews*)

Above, the Benny Goodman Quartet, a band within a band. From left to right: Lionel Hampton, Teddy Wilson, Benny, and Gene Krupa, ca. 1938 (Goodman's prime). (*Duncan Schiedt Archives*) Below, Woody Herman (clarinet) recording with the First Herd for Columbia Records, 1946. (*Courtesy CBS Records*)

part two
MODERN JAZZ

5

BEBOP AND MODERN JAZZ (the Early Styles)

The Golden Age

THE CREATION OF bebop was a more consciously cooperative venture than any of the earlier jazz styles. The bop sound began to emerge from 1940 to 1944 in the nearly ceaseless jam sessions at Minton's Playhouse on 118th Street in Harlem. The club was managed by Teddy Hill, an ex-bandleader, who gave the musicians unlimited freedom to experiment, an opportunity they welcomed eagerly. America's increasing involvement in World War II put the fate of the big bands in jeopardy. Their ranks were gradually being depleted by the draft, and eventually a dance tax, levied to raise public revenues, put many of the large dance halls out of business. The four even beats for dancers which Count Basie had insisted upon were no longer as important or as appealing to listeners on a heightened artistic level, a task that was more easily accomplished with a small, flexible, extremely improvisational unit.

Historical considerations aside, the seeds of change had been sown in the previous decade and were beginning to take root. Many of these changes were identified in the preceding chapter: Lester Young's light, vibrato-less tone and relaxed sense of swing on tenor sax; Charlie Christian's smooth, elongated phrases on guitar; the fluid drumming of Jo Jones and Sid Catlett; and Jimmy Blanton's aggressive, melodic bass playing. Each of these transitional players participated in the Minton sessions, sometimes side by side with the seminal musicians of the new style—Dizzy Gillespie, Thelonious Monk, and Kenny Clarke—who were part of the house band hired by Teddy Hill—and Charlie "Bird" Parker, Oscar Pettiford, Max Roach, Bud Powell, and others too numerous to list. As the pianist Mary Lou Williams recalled, "you couldn't get in Minton's for musicians and instruments."

Of course, the new ideas were spread by musicians on the road who dropped by to jam after hours, or were even introduced elsewhere. Charlie Parker, the most celebrated improviser of the era, did not visit Minton's bandstand until 1943, although most of the Minton group had heard him at Monroe's Uptown House twenty blocks away. Nevertheless, Minton's on 118th Street (like Sedalia, Missouri, and the Harlem rent parties of the ragtime years) deserves to be remembered as a crucial site for the testing and developing of a radically different kind of music.

The Minton sessions were intensified by an undercurrent of competition in which the young soloists would often try to outblow their idols. The cutting that went on between Dizzy Gillespie and Roy Eldridge was closely watched by many of the regulars. Supposedly, once Gillespie emerged the clear winner, Eldridge never returned to the club. In any case it took a virtuoso player to keep up with the difficult chord changes and lightning-like tempos, which were often introduced intentionally to keep amateurs off the stand. "So on afternoons before a session," Gillespie explained, "Thelonious Monk and I began to work out some complex variations on chords and the like, and we used them at night to scare away the no-talent guys. After a while we got more and more interested in what we were doing as music, and . . . our music evolved." [1] Jazz was in fact rebuilt from the ground floor up.

As is often the case, a rhythmic innovation served as the new style's foundation: the subdivision of the four-beat measure into an eighth-note pulse. Martin Williams has noted that similar increases of pace have characterized jazz's evolution:

> . . . the whole-note rhythmic basis of the cakewalk (was) subdivided into halves ($\frac{2}{4}$ time, or two beats per measure) by ragtime, subdivided with syncopated quarters in New Orleans, subdivided fully into quarters by Louis Armstrong, made into even fours by Basie, subdivided into eighths . . . by a bop style which, partly because of a wartime tax on dancing in clubs, could play for the listener. [2]

The eight pulsations per measure meant that a great deal more would be happening—and intensely so—within the same span of time. Thus within this music, the tempo of life itself has suddenly doubled—a true sign of its modernity.

Kenny Clarke was the first drummer to depart from the clear four-beat swing rhythm. Clarke maintained a continuous pulse on the ride (top) cymbal. Instead of keeping time with the bass drum, snare, and sock cymbal (high-hat cymbal), he used them for establishing cross-rhythms and for accenting (or, as it was called, "dropping bombs"), which could fall anywhere in the measure. The term "bebop" itself is thought to have been an onomatopoeic imitation of a common accent pattern, expressed melodically as two staccato eighth notes at the end of the line. (The word "bop" is also commonly used.) Max Roach and Art Blakey are Kenny Clarke's immediate descendants, but by the mid-1950's his polyrhythmic style had spread to the majority of jazz drummers.

In general the rhythm section became more agile, expressive, and sensitive to the nuances of the soloists. The string bass, as developed by Jimmy Blanton and Oscar Pettiford, became its workhorse, establishing a continuous momentum with, at best, contrapuntal melodic lines. Thus the pianist's left hand was liberated from the timekeeping task it had assumed in ragtime and stride, and, like the drummer's left hand and bass-drum foot, the left hand provided a source of accents and "feed" chords for the soloist, adding another level of polyrhythms to those of the drummer. Like drumming, piano accompaniment was streamlined in one aspect so that it could become more complex in another. (Even the name for piano accompaniment was abbreviated to " 'comping.") Finally, the pianist's right hand grew more exploratory and articulate, as if challenged by the pyrotechnics of horn players like Parker and Gillespie. Bud Powell was the bebop pianist par excellence for his hornlike fluidity in the right hand and his sharp accents in the left.

Unlike the predictable riffs of swing, bebop melodies were complex and convoluted. Bebop characteristically employed the higher intervals of the scale (beyond the eight notes of the octave) and unusual intervals like the flatted fifth tone of the scale. New chords were invented to accompany this melodic innovation. Charlie Parker was probably the first to grasp the significance of these scale tones. His enlightenment took place in a Harlem chili house on Seventh Avenue in December 1939:

> Well, that night, I was working over "Cherokee" and, as I did, I found that by using the higher intervals of a chord as a melody line and backing them with appropriately related changes (chords), I could play the thing I'd been hearing. I came alive.[3]

Bebop compositions were quite different from everything that had preceded them. In fact, there had been very little original jazz composition before the modern era save for the music of Jelly Roll Morton and Duke Ellington. Certainly the big bands and the singers who sang with them were woefully committed to the commercial output of Tin Pan Alley. But modern jazz was instrumental by nature. Even the vocalists resorted to "bop singing," or scatting nonsense syllables (and sometimes words) in direct imitation of the horns. Thelonious Monk wrote the most impressive compositions of the period, presenting abstract ideas to be expanded upon thematically in the improvisation. Many bebop tunes are based upon the blues, but a blues which has evolved into art music, thick with substitution chords and passing tones, remote from its folk and rural roots. Other melodies are based upon the chord changes of standard melodies, again transformed beyond recognition. One would hardly guess that Parker's "Chasin' the Bird," "Ornithology," and "Donna Lee" are based upon the harmonic structure of "I Got Rhythm," "How High the Moon," and "Back Home Again in Indiana," respectively. The number of tunes derived (unrecognizably) from "I Got Rhythm" and "Cherokee" alone is staggering. And many of the tunes evolved with complete spontaneity. The leader would mount the stand and call out " 'Rhythm' changes," and presto (which was very likely the tempo as well) a new song was born.

By the time these diverse elements began to fuse, the musicians who had frequented Minton's were working downtown in the numerous clubs on Fifty-second Street, a locale so alive with jazz it was known simply as The Street. The war had ended, the soldiers had come home, and the nation's economy was swinging. Bebop's best jazz musicians seemed to absorb the city's abundant energy, jamming from dusk till dawn at the Onyx, the Famous Door, the Spotlite, and the Three Deuces; or, on Broadway, at the Royal Roost and Bop City. Racially mixed performing groups, a rarity during the 1930's, became quite common, permitting white musicians to acquire a deeper facility with the jazz language. It was a golden age, comparable to the swing explosion in Kansas City during the Depression years. But by 1948, heroin addiction, which had become rampant among jazz musicians, began to take its toll. Pushers, prostitutes, and strip joints became The Street's main attraction. Modern jazz would have to seek its fame, fortune, and creative development on records.

The Boppers Versus the Figs

Bebop had no easy time overcoming the resistance of traditionalists, many of whom maintained that good jazz had not been played since the closing of Storyville. Their views earned them the epithet "moldy figs," a label many of them wore with great pride despite the spirit in which the boppers had applied it. The majority of the figs took pains to denounce the swing musicians too for departing from "real" (i.e., New Orleans) jazz. Such were the circumstances in which (as noted in Chapter 3) sixty-year-old Bunk Johnson was rescued from picking vegetables in Louisiana, outfitted with a new trumpet and a new pair of teeth, and propped up as a figurehead of the dubious New Orleans revival.

The bebop musicians' attitude toward performing did little to mollify their opponents. The big bands of the 1930's, and the Dixieland and New Orleans players were eager to please their audiences, but the younger black musicians of the 1940's recoiled from the minstrelsy legacy which they believed lurked behind the euphemism "entertainer." Dizzy Gillespie, ironically the best entertainer of the bebop era, went so far as to brand Louis Armstrong "a plantation character" in a *Down Beat* magazine interview (July 1, 1949). Black jazz musicians were no longer willing to accept their role as "crowd pleasers." Their new attitude toward performance was, in so many words, "if you don't like it, don't listen." This stance, adopted in varying degrees, remained the dominant one until the 1970's.

Another source of hostility was the clear lack of economic justice suffered by black musicians. In short, their music had long been imitated by white bands, who proceeded to reap the lion's share of profit from the ballrooms and record companies. It is not too surprising, therefore, that Thelonious Monk once tried to assemble a band of young boppers with the promise "We're going to create something that they can't steal because they can't play it." [4]

Naturally the figs and their allies had plenty of objections to bop on musical grounds. Mistaking its intensity for anger, Louis Armstrong called the music "modern malice." He and Dizzy Gillespie seemed to have a running feud over their mutual accusations, but there is much evidence that this was carried on for the benefit of the press. For many years they were neighbors on Long Island and rather good friends. In 1941, however, Dizzy, who was experimenting with some Minton-style chord progressions, was ordered by Cab Calloway to stop playing "that Chinese music" in his band. Rudi Blesh, the brilliant chronicler of ragtime, boldly asserted that "bebop is not jazz at all, but an ultimately degenerated form of swing, exploiting the most fantastic rhythms and unrelated harmonies that it would seem possible to conceive." [5] One record reviewer in an April 1946 issue of *Down Beat* magazine denounced Charlie Parker's breakthrough recordings of "Billie's Bounce" and "Now's the Time" as a mixture of "bad taste and ill-advised fanaticism."

Curiously some of the moldiest figs of the 1940's became the most enthusiastic producers of modern jazz records during the next decade. Early on, the great John Hammond declared: "Bop is a collection of nauseating clichés, repeated *ad infinitum*"; Norman Granz, whose multimillion-dollar "Jazz at the Philharmonic" concerts used an impressive roster of beboppers, stated: "Jazz in New York stinks! Even the drummers sound like Dizzy Gillespie . . . Charlie Parker's combo is rigid and repetitive." [6]

The major record companies were, of course, reluctant to become involved with a music of such ill repute. Thus the best early bop was originally recorded for offbeat, *ad hoc* labels which specialized in the new music, companies such as: Savoy, Dial, Roost, Guild, Musicraft, Black & White, Three Deuces, and Blue Note, many of whose names came from the popular Fifty-second Street clubs. Gradually the outlook began to change with the success of Woody Herman's band, a transitional group between swing and modern jazz, on the Columbia label. The Gillespie big band, profiting equally from stunning musicianship and Dizzy's showmanship, also turned a lot of heads in the new direction. RCA even had a minor hit with a record called "New 52nd Street Jazz" (now out of print) produced by one of the music's early advocates, critic Leonard Feather.

Bebop's popularity began to spread, acquiring a cult-like following in some circles in which the boppers' affectations were adopted along with their music. Dizzy's beret and goatee, Monk's dark glasses, and even Parker's drug addiction were seen as keys to the kingdom of the hip (or the "hep," for it was then hip to be hep). Fortunately there were a few critics—Feather,

Martin Williams, and Ross Russell (also the owner of Dial Records) among them—who understood modern jazz in musical terms well enough to disseminate helpful information. Before long there were some surprising turnabouts among bebop's earlier foes: John Hammond and George Avakian (at Columbia); Norman Granz (founder of Clef, Verve, and Pablo Records); Nesuhi Ertegun (president of Atlantic); and Orrin Keepnews (cofounder of Riverside and, until 1980, vice-president of Fantasy-Prestige-Milestone Records). These ex-figs have produced some of the best available modern jazz on records, yet each of them scorned the music publicly upon first hearing it. Moreover, many of the 1940 recordings of those tiny, often short-lived independent labels listed above were by 1976 being distributed in respectably packaged two-disc sets by the major companies.

There is a particularly unfortunate gap in the discography of bebop's developmental years. In August 1942, James Petrillo, president of the American Federation of Musicians, invoked a recording ban in response to the threat of unemployment posed by the increased use of recorded music on the radio and in juke boxes. The ban was not lifted until 1944, when Columbia, RCA, and Decca agreed to contribute to a royalty fund for the hiring of A. F. of M. members. Gone forever are the sounds of the Earl Hines and Billy Eckstine big bands, each of which contained for a time the budding genius of Charlie Parker, Dizzy Gillespie, and Sarah Vaughan. However, there is ample compensation in the many riches which have been reissued, starting with the first wholly successful modern jazz on record, the 1945 Parker and Gillespie sessions for Guild and Musicraft (see *In the Beginning*, Selected Discography).

East Coast/West Coast

Once jazz had become modernized, it began to become diversified into styles known as "cool," "West Coast," "third stream," "progressive," and "hard bop." Afro-Cuban (or "Latin") jazz set out on its own path after Gillespie hired the Cuban drummer Chano Pozo to play in his big band at a Town Hall concert in 1947. (See Gillespie Selected Discography, and *Afro-Cuban Jazz*, General Discography.) Of course, these critical categories are not mutually exclusive, and many players excelled in several of them. But one fundamental dividing principle is clear in this post-bebop era: hard bop continues the thrust of early bebop, while the other substyles reveal jazz's flirtation with the European tradition.

There were two apparent motivations for "Europeanizing" modern jazz. First, jazz after World War II had become concert music played not for dancing but listening. Thus a greater sophistication of its elements (such as tone, harmony, and instrumental arrangement) seemed desirable. Second, growth toward polyphony was prompted by the homophonic nature of early bebop in which the two horns usually played the melody in unison. Jazz could not be expected to drop completely its ability to use countermelody, which had been present since the earliest collective improvisations of New Orleans musicians. Thus using "secondary horns" or other instruments in contrapuntal roles was designed to move jazz toward a European concert model. Unfortunately, the results usually sounded as intellectualized and contrived as they, in fact, had been.

Cool jazz was characterized by a clean, vibrato-less, and studied tone placed within a meticulously articulated musical environment. If bebop had been an intuitive outpouring of energy, cool jazz seemed to say, "We are now *artistes*; we think, therefore we play." A precursor to the cool instrument tone, one which was light and calm compared with the piercing cry of Charlie Parker's alto sax, was found in the playing of Lester Young (Chapter 4) or Bix Beiderbecke (Chapter 3). Lennie Tristano's ingenious chord progressions and superimposed time signatures were another example of the intellectual interpretation of bebop. Tristano's playing, though, is not nearly so "cerebral" as it is often made out to be (see Tristano, General Discography). Claude Thornhill's band, with music arranged by Gil Evans, introduced French horns, woodwinds, and the tuba to create textures derived from modern classical music. This band was also the model for the Miles Davis nonet, whose *Birth of the Cool* (1949) was the first album in this style. Miles's understated, muted trumpet tone on this album and on later collaborations with Gil Evans set an influential precedent for the cool tonal posture. Alto saxophonist Lee Konitz, a student of Lennie Tristano's, and baritone saxophonist Gerry Mulligan, who wrote many of the *Birth of the Cool* arrangements, were crucial to the Davis band's sound.

A new phase in the development of cool music took place on the West Coast; it was a style even further removed from the fury and intensity of early bebop. Its first home was in a Los Angeles club called The Lighthouse, owned by a sympathetic bassist, Howard Rumsey. A number of musicians were attracted to the area by Hollywood and the new TV studios, an expanding source of employment. Life was less frantic than in New York, and the music reflected it.

West Coast jazz accepted the more pensive and relaxed emotional attitude of cool jazz, and then thinned out the harmonic component. The effect was an airy interweaving of melodic voices stretched over a moderately taut rhythmic pulse. Gerry Mulligan's quartet (with Chet Baker on trumpet, Red Mitchell on bass, and Chico Hamilton on drums) dispensed with the piano entirely in order to open up the musical texture. Their unique instrumentation was discovered by accident in 1952, when pianist Jimmy Rowles failed to show up for a private recording session being taped by Richard Bock. These first pianoless recordings were so successful that Bock started the Pacific Jazz label to distribute them. Dave Brubeck's quartet moved a step closer to the European style in its "chamber jazz," with Brubeck making frequent forays into classical composition and studying with Darius Milhaud and Arnold Schoenberg. Paul Desmond, the quartet's alto saxophonist, is an inheritor of the Lee Konitz style. The fuguelike interplay of sax and piano found its most receptive audiences on the college campuses, and "white, cool, and intellectual" described the typical college student's taste in jazz for the next decade. (Colleges became exceedingly universalistic in their appreciation of jazz after 1970.) Other players who contributed to the West Coast sound are Shorty Rogers, Stan Getz, Bob Brookmeyer, Jimmy Guiffre, Shelly Manne, Barney Kessel, Zoot Sims, and Art Pepper.

Jazz's preoccupation with European classical music reached its peak in the third stream and progressive styles. The term "third stream" was coined in 1959 by Gunther Schuller to denote the confluence of the first stream (the European classical tradition) and the second stream (the Afro-American jazz tradition). Strictly speaking, the third stream was neither classical nor jazz but a perfectly balanced hybrid. "Progressive," a misnomer which predated the term third stream, was quite similar in principle. In fact, many progressive arrangers were self-consciously imitative of the modern European composers Igor Stravinsky and Béla Bartók. Stan Kenton's band epitomized the progressive style, summarized in Kenton's credo: "the integrated composition is the thing, not the solo." But if one listens to the Bob Graettinger compositions on Kenton's *City of Glass/This Modern World*, it will be clear that jazz feeling has been sacrificed at every turn for a modern classical effect. The word "progressive" came to be used loosely for any jazz that sounded weird or unfamiliar, but the music was actually a *regression* from spontaneity and the blues, basic elements of jazz feeling.

The Modern Jazz Quartet (Selected Discography) was the only recording group to succeed in integrating classical devices into jazz without a loss of jazz feeling. Pianist John Lewis, vibraphonist Milt Jackson, bassist Percy Heath, and drummer Kenny Clarke (replaced in 1955 by Connie Kay) had met in Gillespie's big band of the 1940's. Lewis, classically trained and disciplined by nature, had been the pianist on Miles Davis's *Birth of the Cool* album, but on the hot side, as a favorite accompanist of Parker and Gillespie, his credentials were equally impressive. The swinging lyricism of Jackson also helped rescue the group from its potentially stultifying classicism. But the Modern Jazz Quartet (MJQ), which remained vital for twenty-three years, turned out to be a one-of-a-kind band, spawning nothing in its likeness. (As we shall see in Chapter 8, modern classical music was absorbed into jazz differently and more successfully by free jazz musicians.)

Since the dissolution of the MJQ, the center of third stream activity has been Boston's New England Conservatory of Music, where Schuller served for a decade as director. At the Conservatory the Third Stream Department, under the guidance of pianist Ran Blake (General Discography), has broadened the original concept by synthesizing jazz with other ethnic musics. However, there are not many albums available that are representative of such attempts.

The funky, high-spirited hard-bop combos of the mid-1950's are usually credited with having rescued jazz from the seemingly sterile intellectualism of the cool and West Coast styles. What this really means is not that there was a battle of styles in progress, but that the music that was recorded in the mid-1950's, especially in New York and other eastern cities, redirected the listeners' focus back to the hot, emotional core of classic bebop. Hard bop, however, moved away from the contortions and complexities of the late 1940's style. Hard bop was a music of toe-tapping, finger-snapping energy and optimism, which was best represented by Art Blakey and Horace Silver (Selected Discography). Rejecting Europe as the direction of the future, hard bop became the rightful heir to bebop.

The hard-bop style combines the fluidity and raw emotionalism of bebop improvisation with a bluesy earthiness derived in part from the gospel music of the modern black church. Art Blakey, Horace Silver, Sonny Rollins, Clifford Brown, and others turned away from the goals implied by Gil Evans, Stan Kenton, Dave Brubeck, Gerry Mulligan, and Chet Baker. They worked with a blues-based sonority—which at its best was dubbed "soulful"—strongly chiseled melodic features, and a driving rhythmic vitality. In fact, the hard-hitting accents of drummers like Blakey, Max Roach, and Philly Joe Jones may have given *hard* bop its name.

There is an abundance of good early modern jazz on record and more worthy musicians than can be discussed in this book. Thus the following list contains some of the important instrumentalists of the bop styles:

Trumpet: Dizzy Gillespie, Miles Davis, Clifford Brown, Fats Navarro, Freddie Hubbard, Thad Jones, Kenny Dorham, Blue Mitchell, Lee Morgan, Clark Terry, Nat Adderley.

Alto Sax: Charlie Parker, Sonny Stitt, Lou Donaldson, Charlie Rouse, Cannonball Adderley, Jackie McLean, Phil Woods.

Tenor Sax: Lucky Thompson, Sonny Rollins, John Coltrane, Jimmy Heath, Yusef Lateef, Rahsaan Roland Kirk, Joe Henderson, Wayne Shorter, George Coleman, Johnny Griffin, Dexter Gordon.

Piano: Bud Powell, Thelonious Monk, Hampton Hawes, Horace Silver, Oscar Peterson, Red Garland, Tommy Flanagan, Cedar Walton, Bobby Timmons.

Bass: Oscar Pettiford, Curly Russell, Paul Chambers, Sam Jones, Percy Heath, Ron Carter.

Drums: Art Blakey, Max Roach, Philly Joe Jones, Roy Haynes, Art Taylor, Elvin Jones, Kenny Clarke.

Guitar: Wes Montgomery, Herb Ellis, Joe Pass, Kenny Burrell.

Despite the fertile period from 1945 to 1959, the early modern jazz musicians suffered greatly during the 1960's due to the disastrously poor jazz record sales, a slump that will be discussed in some detail in the introduction to Chapter 7. Thus many players fled to Europe and took up residence there. But during the 1970's, hard bop enjoyed a healthy and heartening renaissance, stimulated at least in part by the tremendous commercial impact upon jazz of the fusion style (Chapter 7). Dexter Gordon, an important influence upon John Coltrane and Sonny Rollins, symbolized bop's regeneration in his live album, *Homecoming* (1976), the title alluding to his return from Copenhagen to an informed and deeply enthusiastic new audience at the Village Vanguard in New York (see also General Discography). Johnny Griffin's return from Holland for regular recording (General Discography) and touring was another indication of—and stimulant to—the bop revival. The extensive reissuing from 1976 to 1979 of classic bop music has put listeners in touch once again with the intricate and passionate foundations of modern jazz.

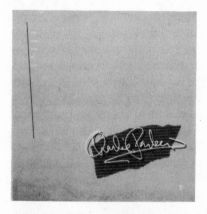

CHARLIE PARKER

The Very Best of Bird (The "Dial Sessions")

Warner Brothers, 2WB 3198
two discs, liner notes
1946–1947

Musicians: Charlie Parker, alto sax; Miles Davis, trumpet; Max Roach, drums; Tommy Potter, bass; Duke Jordan, piano. Also with Erroll Garner, piano; Red Callendar, bass; Doc West, drums. Also with Lucky Thompson, tenor sax; Dodo Marmarosa, piano, and band. Also with Howard McGhee, trumpet; Wardell Gray, tenor sax; Barney Kessel, guitar; Red Callendar, bass; and Don Lamond, drums.
Compositions: Side one: Bird of Paradise; Embraceable You; How Deep Is the Ocean?; Out of Nowhere; Don't Blame Me; My Old Flame. *Side two:* Moose the Mooche; Yardbird Suite; Ornithology; Famous Alto Break; A Night in Tunisia; Max Is Making Wax; Bird's Nest. *Side three:* Cool Blues (Hot Blues); Relaxin' at Camarillo; Cheers; Carvin' the Bird; Stupendous; Dexterity; Bongo Bop. *Side four:* Dewey Square; The Hymn; Bird Feathers; Klactoveedsedsteen; Scrapple from the Apple; Drifting on a Reed; Charlie's Wig.

CHARLIE PARKER

Bird/The Savoy Recordings (Master Takes)

Savoy, SJL 2201
two discs, liner notes
1944–1948

Musicians: Charlie Parker, alto and tenor saxes (four tracks); with Miles Davis, trumpet; Max Roach, drums; Tommy Potter, bass; and Duke Jordan, piano. Also with Miles Davis, Max Roach, and Bud Powell, piano. Also with Curly Russell, bass; John Lewis, piano. Also with Dizzy Gillespie, piano and trumpet ("Ko Ko" only). Also (in 1944) with Clyde Hart, piano; Tiny Grimes, guitar; Jimmy Butts, bass; and Doc West, drums.

Compositions: Side one: Tiny's Tempo; I'll Always Love You Just the Same; Romance Without Finance; Red Cross; Warming up a Riff; Billie's Bounce; Now's the Time. *Side two:* Thriving on a Riff; Meandering; Ko Ko; Donna Lee; Chasin' the Bird; Cheryl; Buzzy. *Side three:* Milestones; Little Willie Leaps; Half Nelson; Sippin' at Bells; Another Hair-Do; Blue Bird; Klaunstance; Bird Gets the Worm. *Side four:* Barbados; Ah-Leu-Cha; Constellation; Parker's Mood; Perhaps; Marmaduke; Steeplechase; Merry-Go-Round.

IF YOU HAVE NEVER heard Charlie Parker, the experience could permanently change the way you think about music. That is precisely what it did for a generation of jazz musicians. No more than two other instrumentalists—Louis Armstrong and John Coltrane—have had that powerful an impact. Parker, or "Bird," a nickname for which a half-dozen different origins have been claimed, influenced players on every instrument. He taught them unique phrasing and a rhythmic pattern (which became standard) based upon a hesitation before the unleashing of a melodic stream and on an abrupt ending consisting of two eighth notes. He unveiled a seemingly endless flow of melodic ideas, using the higher intervals of the scale and "passing" chords which enriched commonplace harmonic structures. He also broke down a major psychological barrier, proving it was possible to improvise lyrically and swing furiously at tempos his predecessors had never even attempted. Parker's innovations were adopted so pervasively that, after his death in 1955, the pianist Lennie Tristano could joke with some plausibility that "if Charlie could have invoked the plagiarism laws, he could have sued every jazz musician who made a record in the last ten years."

Bird's recording formats varied greatly: from quintets, in which his fire burned most brightly, to fully orchestrated, "with strings" sessions, the first of their kind in jazz. He was recorded at his artistic peak by two independent companies, Dial and Savoy, for whom bebop was a primary musical commitment. Somehow, it seems insufficient merely to say that these reissues are two of the best, most important albums in all jazz. Bird at his finest provokes that flimsy critical exclamation when one's powers of description have failed: "Incredible!"

There are two circumstantial reasons for the superiority of the Dial and Savoy sessions. One is that the vast majority of cuts come from a healthy, relatively well-adjusted period in Bird's short life; one immediately following his seven-month recuperation at Camarillo State Hospital in California. He had been remanded to the hospital after a drug-induced physical and emotional breakdown precipitated while recording for Dial in Hollywood.

Second, Parker was supported on these sessions by musicians who bore a natural kinship to his own style. Max Roach was wholly comfortable with Parker's rhythmic gymnastics, one of the few drummers at the time who was. He was also capable of dropping propulsive "bombs" behind the soloists and some adroit soloing on his own, as in "Klactoveedsedsteen" (Dial) and "Ko Ko" (Savoy). The young Miles Davis, while often criticized for a lack of technical dexterity, provides a beautifully subdued tonal trumpet complement to Bird's alto sax. He also improved markedly as the sessions progressed, becoming an imaginative melodic player by late 1947. Duke Jordan was Bird's most reliable piano accompanist, but the solos turned in by John Lewis and Bud Powell (Savoy) are fascinating examples of their earliest work. On Dial the two tracks with Erroll Garner contain the most exciting keyboard surprises. Garner, a highly idiosyncratic pianist (see Selected Discography ahead), had been working with Bird in Los Angeles, and his buoyant humor proved an ideal foil for Parker's intensity.

Nothing in Charlie Parker's background seemed to prepare him for the godlike role he assumed. His youth was filled with failures and one error of lifelong consequence. Born in 1920, an only child, he grew up in Pendergast's corrupt Kansas City where music became the focus of his life. As he once told Leonard Feather, he "spent three years in high school and wound up a freshman." His major interest was hanging out behind the city's nightclubs to hear the blues-based swing bands. Although he frequently practiced his alto sax, given to him by his mother when he was eleven, and his baritone sax, which he played in the school band, his first jams with professional musicians were disastrous and humiliating. Parker later recalled one session: "I knew a little of 'Lazy River' and 'Honeysuckle Rose,' and played what I could. I was doing all right until I tried doing double tempo on 'Body and Soul'! Everyone fell out laughing. I went home and cried and didn't play again for three months." [7] At seventeen, he jammed with members of the Basie band and made an equally poor impression.

That summer was spent profitably, however, working with a band in the Ozark Mountains and listening to Count Basie records, from which he learned Lester Young's solos note for note. When he returned, Parker worked for Buster Smith, a blues-oriented alto sax player who is credited with being an early influence on Bird. The ultimately fatal disaster of his youth was his involvement with drugs, which began at the age of fifteen when "friends" of the family introduced him to heroin. Parker was an addict by the time he was seventeen, when he joined Jay McShann's Texas-based big band, with whom he recorded some popular (but no longer available) blues pieces for Decca. At this point Parker's style was fundamentally an alto sax version of Lester Young's, and it did not evolve significantly until his move to New York in 1939.

Parker played sporadically in New York, working part time as a dishwasher, but he engaged in two jam sessions of momentous consequence. One was with the pianist and composer Tadd Dameron, whose harmonic ideas, which probably included "passing" chords, so delighted Bird that (as Dameron said) "he kissed me on the cheek." Although it is not certain exactly when Parker was enlightened by Dameron's chord changes, his melodic revelation occurred in 1939 in a Harlem chili house. While jamming with guitarist Biddy Fleet on the chord changes to "Cherokee," Parker realized that scale tones from the ninth to the thirteenth, along with corresponding "substitution" chords, created the unique melodic sound he had been hearing but thus far had been unable to play. After returning briefly to McShann's band, Parker began to work regularly at Monroe's Uptown House on Fifty-second Street. His unique phrasing and awesome technique were applied to the new harmonic and melodic ideas, and musicians took notice. His development was so far independent of but parallel to Dizzy Gillespie's and Thelonious Monk's.

In 1943 Parker joined the Earl Hines band as a tenor sax player, but his personal habits made him somewhat of a liability. According to Hines's vocalist, Billy Eckstine, Parker wore dark glasses so Hines would not know he was asleep on the job. "He was the only man I knew who could fall asleep with his jaws poked out to look like he was playing." [8] Bird was always being fined for showing up late, and on one occasion promised Earl to stay in Detroit's Paradise Theater overnight so he could not fail to be on time for the next day's concert. No one was surprised when he did not appear at all; but after the curtain fell and the band started to break up, a rumbling was heard from underneath the platform. Parker emerged in a daze. He had slept under the bandstand through the entire performance.

Dizzy Gillespie's presence in this band (which was unrecorded due to the union ban) was of long-term significance for Parker. They left Hines together to join a new Eckstine big band (1944), joining forces at the Three Deuces (1945) in a quintet which changed the course of jazz. (The 1945 recordings by Bird and Dizzy of "Groovin' High," "Dizzy Atmosphere," "Hot House," and "Shaw 'Nuff" were the first signals that a new jazz era had arrived. They are available on *In the Beginning*, to be discussed ahead.)

The Dial and Savoy sessions are a magnificent testimony to Parker's spontaneous, fertile imagination and unrelenting intensity. The Savoy recordings contain his first date as the featured performer, for which he had prepared less than a day. According to his roommate, pianist Sadik Hakim,

Bird composed two classic blues, "Now's the Time" (later pirated into a blues hit, "The Hucklebuck") and "Billie's Bounce" (actually it should be "Billy's Bounce"—named for his agent Billy Shaw), within hours after receiving Savoy's telegrammed invitation. Parker brought his nineteen-year-old apprentice, Miles Davis, into the studio with him, and also Dizzy Gillespie, with whom Bird was working at the Three Deuces. Dizzy plays piano except on "Ko Ko," where he takes over on trumpet since the melody was too difficult for Miles. Max Roach was nearly omnipresent in Parker's groups for the next three years. While every note Parker blew during these recording years is precious, the most noteworthy gems are "Warming up a Riff" (literally a warm-up) and "Ko Ko," an improvisational masterpiece. Both tunes are based on the chord changes to "Cherokee," revealing the vast differences between Bird's successive explorations of the same material. (While he could be totally spontaneous, Parker was also hard to please, as during the "Night in Tunisia" date (Dial), which required three hours of takes before he was satisfied.)

The virtues of "Ko Ko" are what make all of Parker's work compelling. His tone on alto sax is a cutting, searing one that penetrates to the listener's core. Like it or not, Bird commands attention, communicating with inner urgency. The swing, fury, and agility of his technique are too obvious for comment. His phrasing, splintered into jigsaw-like patterns, fits together miraculously as an integrated whole by the end of the piece—exemplified perhaps a bit more conspicuously in "Ah-Leu-Cha" (Savoy) and "Klacto-veedsedsteen" (Dial). The music's overall "*hot*ness"—comparable to Armstrong's trumpet style—is due to Parker's delivery: his lines can be likened to a shower of sparks.

A comparison of the "Ko Ko" session with the four tracks on Savoy made with the Clyde Hart-Tiny Grimes band in 1944 reveals the quantum leap in Parker's style within that year. The lacuna during 1946 on Savoy is partly picked up by Dial, recorded by Bird during his year in Hollywood. Parker had gone there to work with Dizzy at Billy Berg's club. The band was in sorry shape because of Parker's increasing drug abuse and the hostility of local critics and musicians. Dizzy returned to New York, but Parker sent for Miles Davis and recorded a wonderful session on Dial, including "Moose the Mooche," "Yardbird Suite," and "Ornithology." As an example of his fertile improvisations, an eight-bar phrase from "Yardbird" shows up later on the Dial recordings as the melody to "Cool Blues (Hot Blues)." Parker's compositions are like snowflakes—similar in structure outwardly but intricately unique within. The great majority of them grew out of improvisations upon the blues or of familiar sets of chord changes from popular songs like "How High the Moon," "Cherokee," and "I Got Rhythm."

The next session three months later was catastrophic for Parker, who had swallowed six benzedrine tablets to fight off the need for heroin. "Max Is Making Wax" shows some disorganization, but the following "Lover Man" track (now unavailable in keeping with Bird's wishes) was allegedly frenzied, agonized, and out of control. After the recording Bird was driven back to his hotel, where he set fire to his room, possibly by dropping a cigarette, and then ran down to the lobby without his pants on, demanding to make a phone call. His arrest led to the recuperative stay at Camarillo State Hospital alluded to earlier. Seven months later he was in peak form.

Every session from 1947 to 1948 produced masterpieces which make up the bulk of the Savoy and Dial sessions. Miles's technique had improved, and—except for the pianists—the group's personnel remained relatively constant. Eloquent improvisations gush forth on the blues "Cheryl" and "Buzzy" on Savoy and on "Dexterity" on Dial. The first improvised line on "Dexterity'" is a full eight-bars long, drawn out like a magician's interminable silk scarf. No matter how complex his phrasing, Parker instinctively knew where he was in a song, although his tricks frequently confused his colleagues. Miles has said he often felt ready to quit the band whenever Parker came in on the eleventh measure or some other odd place, threw everyone else off, and magically ended his phrase precisely on time.

Parker is no less passionate on ballads, such as "Embraceable You" and "Don't Blame Me" (Dial), which serve primarily as springboards for his soaring imagination. The blues on Savoy's "Parker's Mood" is an equally gorgeous performance taken at a sane tempo. Although the Savoy recordings contain no ballads as such, "Meandering," which is actually a reworking of "Embraceable You," comes quite close. (The Savoy sessions are available in a five-disc boxed set containing every take Parker made for them and a scholarly liner booklet—perfect for aficionados.)

By 1948 Bird was the acknowledged master of bebop, an inspiration and a challenge to every musician he worked with. Within two years the greatest of the modern jazz clubs, Birdland, would be named for him. But his personal life was heading downhill quickly. Another of his four marriages had fallen apart, and he returned to heroin. In this period of transition, he left the small Dial and Savoy labels for Mercury Records, where Norman Granz recorded him with the Machito and Chico O'Farrill bands (*Afro-Cuban Jazz*); these sessions reveal his marvelous adaptability. Subsequent sessions with strings (1949) were more controversial, resulting in accusations that Granz was attempting to commercialize Parker. In fact, Bird had asked to be included in some previously scored music, for he had long desired to record in such a context.

There are three Verve two-disc sets that chronicle the years with Granz (1948–1954), the best of which is *The Verve Years, 1948–1950*. This set contains seven tracks of a spirited reunion with Dizzy Gillespie and Thelonious Monk on piano. The string arrangements on this reissue, although original in concept, are not the most favorable milieu for Parker. Nevertheless, his "Just Friends" improvisation has long been considered one of his most lyrical and well developed. The remaining two Verve sets, including various groups and more "with strings" dates, are of less interest.

Two Columbia albums from 1950 and 1953 (General Discography), which catch Bird at Birdland with Dizzy, Bud Powell, and Fats Navarro, are more fitting conclusions to his recording career. The grand finale, however, occurred at Massey Hall in Toronto, Canada in an all-star quintet with Dizzy Gillespie, Bud Powell, Charles Mingus, and Max Roach (available on *The Greatest Jazz Concert Ever*, to be discussed ahead).

Parker never lost competence on his alto sax, but rapidly lost major life battles. Neither rural living in Pennsylvania nor psychotherapy at Bellevue could undo the harm he had done himself, abuse which continued in the form of excessive eating and drinking. To offset the potential "glamour" of his addiction, he once told *Down Beat* magazine: "Any musician who says he is playing better either on tea, the needle, or when he is juiced is a plain straight liar. When I get too much to drink, I can't even finger well, let alone play decent ideas." [9] But Bird's behavior had been so erratic that since 1951, Birdland itself had not allowed him to play there. An exception was made for a March 1955 appearance that ended abruptly when Bird and Bud Powell began feuding on stage, prompting Parker to walk out. Charles Mingus grabbed the mike, telling the audience, "These men are killing jazz." More accurately, jazz—or the life-style which then prevailed around it—was killing them. A week later at the age of thirty-four, Charlie Parker died of a heart attack while watching the Dorsey brothers on television in a friend's apartment.

Ross Russell, owner and producer of the Dial sessions, has written an intimate biography of Parker, *Bird Lives!*, the title taken from graffiti which appeared all over New York following his death. Despite Parker's short life, he has achieved as much as any jazz musician a kind of immortality through his music.

DIZZY GILLESPIE

In the Beginning

Prestige, P-24030
two discs, liner notes
1945–1950

Musicians: Dizzy Gillespie, trumpet; with Charlie Parker, alto sax; Clyde Hart, piano; Remo Palmieri, guitar; Slam Stewart, bass; Cozy Cole, drums. Also with Charlie Parker, Al Haig, piano; Curly Russell, bass; Sid Catelett, drums. Also with Sonny Stitt, alto sax; Milt Jackson, vibes; Al Haig, Ray Brown, bass; Kenny Clarke, drums. Also with Gillespie's big band on four tracks, and Sarah Vaughan on "Lover Man" only with Gillespie and Parker.

Compositions: Side one: Blue 'n Boogie; Groovin' High; Dizzy Atmosphere; All the Things You Are; Salt Peanuts; Shaw 'Nuff. *Side two:* Lover Man; Hot House; One Bass Hit, Part I; Oop Bop Sh' Bam; A Hand Fulla Gimme; That's Earl, Brother. *Side three:* Our Delight; Good Dues Blues; One Bass Hit, Part II; Ray's Idea; Things to Come. *Side four:* Emanon; He Beeped when He Shoulda Bopped; I Waited for You; Nice Work If You Can Get It; She's Gone Again; Thinking of You.

The Original Dizzy Gillespie Big Band in Concert (with Chano Pozo)

GNP-23, GNP Crescendo
one disc, no liner notes
1948

Musicians (probable personnel): Dizzy Gillespie, trumpet; Ernie Henry, Howard Johnson, alto saxes; Cecil Payne, baritone sax; James Moody, Joe Gayles, tenor saxes; Taswell Baird, William Shepherd, trombones; Chano Pozo, bongos; Dave Burns, Elman Wright, Raymond Orr, Matthew McKay, trumpets; Nelson Boyd, bass; pianist unknown; Kenny Clarke or Joe Harris, drums; Kenny Hagood, scatting vocal with Gillespie on "Ool-Ya-Koo." (Milt Jackson, normally on vibes, is absent.)

Compositions: Side one: Emanon; Ool-Ya-Koo; 'Round Midnight; Stay on It. *Side two:* Good Bait; One Bass Hit; I Can't Get Started; Manteca.

The Greatest Jazz Concert Ever

Prestige, PR-24024
two discs, liner notes
1953

Musicians: Dizzy Gillespie, trumpet; Charlie Parker, alto sax; Bud Powell, piano; Charles Mingus, bass; Max Roach, drums. (Powell, Mingus, Roach only on sides three and four.)
Compositions: Side one: Perdido; Salt Peanuts; All the Things You Are. *Side two:* Wee; Hot House; A Night in Tunisia. *Side three:* Embraceable You; Sure Thing; My Devotion; Polka Dots and Moonbeams; Cherokee. *Side four:* Jubilee; I've Got You Under My Skin; My Heart Stood Still; I Want to Be Happy; Lullaby of Birdland.

ALTHOUGH BEBOP WAS developed cooperatively, Dizzy Gillespie—through technical brilliance, harmonic adventurousness, and sheer showmanship— was the greatest single force for its acceptance by the public. He expanded the trumpet's range markedly, maneuvering in the highest register with more facility than his own idol, Roy Eldridge, or Eldridge's model, Louis Armstrong. At Minton's Playhouse, Dizzy and Thelonious Monk worked out new chord progressions and "substitution" chords, based upon the higher intervals of the scale. Their discoveries spread among the musicians who jammed there, and became the foundation for more sophisticated melodic ideas.

Gillespie also led the first fully modernized big band, projecting the flexibility of the new music onto a larger canvas. Although Dizzy's flair for clowning, scat singing, and pranks drew fire from some quarters, his ability to communicate with his audiences—at a time when most musicians snubbed them—became bebop's sole public relations asset. It should be noted that the albums selected focus upon Gillespie's historically significant period, represented by the most awesome single performance of his big band and by the continually challenging small groups in which he played with Charlie Parker. These choices, however, are not intended to diminish the value of the recordings he made from 1954 to 1979, a quarter century of music which can only be highlighted in the present discussion.

John Birks Gillespie was born in South Carolina in 1917, the last of nine children. His father, who died when he was ten, was a bricklayer and an amateur musician who kept numerous instruments around the house. John began to learn the trombone at age fourteen but stopped when he realized his arms were too short to reach the seventh position. At fifteen he borrowed a trumpet from a friend and for a full year played only in the key of

B♭, not realizing there were any other keys. But his talent was obvious and soon earned him a scholarship to the Laurinburg Institute, an industrial school for blacks which offered courses in music theory.

In 1935 the Gillespies moved to Philadelphia, where John began working in local groups and listening intently to Roy Eldridge, who frequently performed on the radio with Teddy Hill's band. Two years later Gillespie auditioned for Hill's band as a replacement for Eldridge, who had joined Fletcher Henderson's Orchestra. He showed up at the audition with his trumpet in a paper bag—the way he usually carried it—and mounted the stage to play with his overcoat and gloves on. Although he soon became an excellent reader and arranger, Gillespie at that time was unable to follow the band's chart. These initial encounters, according to some sources, led Hill to dub his new trumpeter "Dizzy." (Other accounts claim he acquired the nickname in Philadelphia for his free-wheeling, unorthodox approach to life.) Gillespie's pranks in Hill's band—playing with his back to the audience, wearing his mute like a hat, and clowning while others took solos—did not stand in the way of his becoming first trumpet by 1939. He recorded often with Hill, but the first available Gillespie on record is found on the Lionel Hampton anthology (Chapter 4), a side cut in September 1939 with Coleman Hawkins, Ben Webster, Benny Carter, and others. Not surprisingly, Dizzy took a back seat.

After the Hill band broke up, Dizzy joined Cab Calloway in whose band he began to evolve a more personal style, partly motivated by a need to stop sounding like Eldridge. The 1940 sides with Cab's band—"Pickin' the Cabbage," composed and arranged by Gillespie, "Boo-Wah Boo-Wah," and "Bye Bye Blues"—reveal Dizzy's new tone, longer soloing potential, and sense of logical development. These cuts are available on the Smithsonian two-disc albums, *The Development of an American Artist,* which also traces Gillespie's progress through the bands of Coleman Hawkins (1942), Billy Eckstine (1944), Oscar Pettiford and Boyd Raeburn (1945), and Gillespie's own combos (1946) with partners Dexter Gordon and Lucky Thompson. Gillespie's progress during the years with Calloway was supplemented with after-hours work at Minton's with Thelonious Monk and Kenny Clarke.

The job with Cab, however, ended abruptly in 1941, after a concert in Hartford, Connecticut. Gillespie had been accused of throwing a spitball during a bass solo, a charge he denied (though he admitted guilt on other counts). Dizzy and Cab got into a fight backstage, and a knife came into play. Calloway had to have ten stitches taken, and could not sit down comfortably for some time. But Gillespie made news and soon joined Earl Hines's band.

In the Earl Hines band from 1942 to 1943, Gillespie and Charlie Parker were brought together in a meaningful way for the first time. Although they had jammed on the same bandstand before, Gillespie had not really savored Parker's originality. In truth, most musicians were dropping into Monroe's Uptown House to hear Bird during these years because they thought he sounded like Lester Young. After several months in the same band—and after hearing trumpeter Benny Harris play some Parker solos, Dizzy began to pay closer attention. It was Parker's phrasing, involving a prominent hesitation before each string of melody notes, which influenced him and, for that matter, the entire bebop style. When Billy Eckstine, Hines's vocalist and star performer, left the group to pursue his own career, Dizzy and Bird followed him, helping to make Eckstine's big band the most popular black group of the 1940's. As noted earlier, these two groups went unrecorded due to the union ban.

In 1945 Gillespie's career hit a new plateau. He was on the air frequently with the Eckstine band. His remake of Bunny Berigan's 1937 hit "I Can't Get Started," available on the Smithsonian album, enjoyed wide circulation. Its improvised ending was later adopted as the classic introduction to " 'Round Midnight." Most important, Dizzy was leading a quintet, with Parker on alto sax, which was stunning the musician-filled audiences nightly at the Three Deuces. Thus a new company, Guild (soon to be bought out by Musicraft), signed Dizzy at a most favorable moment and recorded him for the first time as a group leader.

In the Beginning collects those Guild-Musicraft sessions, documenting the first phase of Gillespie's vital contribution. Moreover, the five Gillespie-Parker collaborations of 1945 are the real beginnings of bebop on record. Gillespie has clearly blossomed as a soloist, descending from the stratospheric regions of his horn on "Salt Peanuts," his classic bebop version of "I Got Rhythm" changes, and double-timing with ease on "Dizzy Atmosphere." Although Charlie Parker has not reached the consistency of his Savoy and Dial recordings, his solos on "Salt Peanuts" and Tadd Dameron's "Hot House" (based on "What Is This Thing Called Love?") are in the blistering and melodic style of his best improvising. Most of all, Dizzy and Bird breathe together in unison on "Hot House," the bridge to "Salt Peanuts," and the tortuous "Shaw 'Nuff," creating the kind of music that made Fifty-second Street jump all night long.

By the following year, Gillespie had enough technique to begin flaunting it, as he comes near to doing on "One Bass Hit." His lines are alive with new tension, deriving from his capacity to jump instantly to any area of his range. Side two is also noteworthy for the presence of Milt Jackson, whose vibes would play an important role in the big band, and of Sarah Vaughan, whose "Lover Man" here is the only available side with Bird and Dizzy, two of her most ardent fans. The big-band tracks on side three are a bright promise of things to come. The arrangement of "Things to Come" by Walter "Gil" Fuller makes bold use of bebop riffs in the sax section, and puts the trumpet section through Gillespie-like paces. Woody Herman's band was the only other group to achieve such flexibility, but Gillespie's unit, powered by Kenny Clarke on drums, severed the ties to swing more profoundly. Nevertheless, the band's adventurous performance on *In the Beginning* was primarily a prelude to greater achievements. (The order of song titles on side three is listed incorrectly on the album; it has been corrected above.)

Gillespie's big band, which was more or less a flickering entity from 1946 to 1950, was too frequently at the mercy of economic obstacles to be sufficiently recorded. Musically the organization had much in its favor, beginning with the impressive soloing potential of its players. (The album liner notes do not identify the personnel, making the above listing a highly probable reconstruction.) The Cuban drummer Chano Pozo, hired by Dizzy to perform George Russell's "Cubano Be, Cubano Bop" at Town Hall in 1947 (available in a studio recording on a Verve set of the same title), deserves special mention. Jazz had always been amenable—in the words of Jelly Roll Morton—to "a Spanish tinge," but it was not until Pozo's fiery Afro-Cuban rhythms merged with the Gillespie band that "Latin jazz" became a distinct genre. (See *Afro-Cuban Jazz,* including performances by Parker and Gillespie with the bands of Machito and Chico O'Farrill, General Discography.) This young drummer's influence far exceeded his recording legacy, for Pozo was shot and killed in a Harlem bar, reportedly over an unpaid debt, months after the 1948 Los Angeles concert discussed here. Milt Jackson on vibes and John Lewis on piano formed another seminal element of the Gillespie band, although they did not make the Los Angeles date. Supplemented by Ray Brown and Kenny Clarke, Jackson and Lewis performed as a quartet to give the trumpet section a respite, evolving, after the big band broke up, into the Modern Jazz Quartet.

The Original Dizzy Gillespie Big Band in Concert captures the group's overflowing spirit and enthusiasm. They may have been, as Gillespie himself once observed, "a little rough around the edges," but the joyful, at times ecstatic feeling they transmit is of more lasting value than technically "perfect" musicianship. Pozo's passionate conga performance on the famous "Manteca" (known later as "I'll Never Go Back to Georgia") must have been the concert's main event. But there are rousing solos all the way through —by James Moody on the blues, "Emanon," and by Gillespie on "Good Bait," the awesome opening of "Emanon," and "One Bass Hit." Tender moments are achieved by Ernie Henry's alto on " 'Round Midnight," probably arranged by John Lewis, and on Dizzy's crowd pleaser, "I Can't Get Started." (Tadd Dameron and Gil Fuller were also contributing to the Gillespie book.) "Ool-Ya-Koo" exemplifies the lighthearted, exceptionally fluent scatting of Dizzy and Kenny Hagood, whose phrasing faithfully reflects the new instrumental concepts. Even if the section-playing did not have the precision of Woody Herman's band, individual performances never failed to ignite the atmosphere. The band's size seemed in no way to limit its spontaneity and unpredictability. (A concert at the Salle Pleyel in Paris performed six months earlier is available on a somewhat hard-to-find Prestige album, *Dizzy Gillespie in Paris.*)

Later in 1948 Gillespie became a public symbol of bebop by virtue of a *Life* magazine article that had little to do with his musical contribution. It emphasized Dizzy's goatee, beret, horn-rimmed glasses, and alleged conversion to Mohammedanism. (Gillespie was never a Moslem, but did join the Bahai faith many years later.) Despite Dizzy's popularity, the closing of the large dance halls forced him to disband his group permanently in 1950. Gillespie worked numerous jam-session concerts staged by Norman Granz during these years. But his most exciting and fascinating performance on record, with an all-star quintet including Bird, Bud Powell, Charles Mingus (Chapter 6), and Max Roach, was taped at a weird, poorly attended event organized by The New Jazz Society of Toronto, Canada.

Considering the adversity of circumstances, it is a wonder that any music at all took place in Toronto's Massey Hall that night in May 1953. Parker was irate over receiving what he thought was second billing under Gillespie. His reference to Dizzy as "my worthy constituent," one of the few samples of Bird's voice on record, is as sarcastic as it sounds. Dizzy himself was more interested in the Marciano-Walcott heavyweight title bout, which was probably responsible for the poor turnout at the concert, than he was in remaining on stage. Bud Powell had recently recovered from one of many nervous breakdowns and reportedly was drunk. Charles Mingus, who taped the concert with surprisingly good fidelity for his own Debut label, was characteristically irked by everyone else's behavior. The evening might have turned into a bizarre parody of everything that could go wrong in a single concert.

Miraculously, *The Greatest Jazz Concert Ever* comes somewhat near to justifying its boastful title. Bird—listed as "Charlie Chan" on the original issue due to contractual obligations—and Dizzy seem intent on blowing each other off the stand. Bird's borrowed white plastic alto sax seems only a minor inconvenience on the first few bars of "Perdido." He cuts loose on "Salt Peanuts" and continues to breathe fire for the remainder of the set. Dizzy's horn is as precise as a scalpel, packing the power of a full trumpet section as he trades accents with the unflappable Max Roach on "Perdido," uncoils serpentine melodies on "Wee," and scales some mountainous peaks on his own classic of the era, "A Night in Tunisia," dating from his days in the Earl Hines band. ("Tunisia" was a Gillespie composition derived from tracing chromatic thirteenth chords on Benny Carter's piano, not, as Art Blakey once claimed, from something scribbled on the bottom of a garbage can in a flash of inspiration.) On sides three and four, devoted to the rhythm section, Bud vacillates between brilliance ("Cherokee," "Jubilee," and "I Want to Be Happy") and some agonized Tatum-style ballads, "Polka Dots" being the richest harmonically. Mingus and Roach compensate somewhat for Powell's lack of consistency. Jazz listeners are fortunate to have this album between legitimate covers and receiving adequate distribution. The competitive spirit and disruptive problems suffered by the band members has done the music no harm.

Gillespie's recording formats during the 1950's were varied. A few sessions made in 1952 for his own label are available on Savoy's *Dee Gee Days*. GNP's *Paris Concert* (1953) is a fine display of Gillespie's charisma on stage and of some spirited playing with a young band he had gathered for the

European tour. In 1953 he began several small-group studio sessions under the guidance of Norman Granz's matchmaking. The Verve sets of these dates find Dizzy paired in the front line with Sonny Stitt, Sonny Rollins, and Stan Getz. While lacking the fire of the live dates, there are some gems throughout these sessions, notably "The Eternal Triangle" with Rollins and Stitt. (See General Discography for these Verve recordings.)

Dizzy accidentally acquired a horn with an upswept bell in 1954 when a comedy dance team knocked his trumpet off the stage. After his anger subsided, Gillespie noticed that he could hear himself better, and he adopted the misshapen trumpet as a trademark. While not yet forty, an elder statesman's role began creeping up on Dizzy in 1956, when he led a band in the first U.S. State Department tour abroad. Performances of the later big band, which included many soloists of the earlier vintage, were recorded from 1962 to 1964 for Mercury, available on *Composers Concepts. The Giant* (1973), with tenor virtuoso Johnny Griffin, is one of the best small-group albums of later years.

Since 1974 Gillespie has been reunited with Granz on the Pablo label, where he has fronted various small combos and a strikingly effective Afro-Cuban big band (General Discography). While he has encountered much criticism for a failure to evolve stylistically—and a few perennial complaints about his playful stage manner—his virtuosity remains undiminished. The Pablo albums, however, lack the fire of his earlier work, but several of the more interesting sessions are listed in the General Discography.

THELONIOUS MONK

The Complete Genius

Blue Note, BN-LA579-H2
two discs, good liner notes
1947–1952

Musicians: Thelonious Monk, piano; with various small combos, including Art Blakey or Max Roach, drums; Milt Jackson, vibes; Sahib Shihab or Lou Donaldson, alto sax; Lucky Thompson or Ike Quebec, tenor sax; Kenny Dorham, trumpet; Gene Ramey, Al McKibbon, Robert Paige, or John Simmons, bass.
Compositions (all by Monk unless indicated): *Side one:* 'Round Midnight; In Walked Bud; Monk's Mood; Who Knows?; Thelonious; Humph; Suburban Eyes (Quebec);

Evonce (Quebec). *Side two:* Off Minor; Ruby, My Dear; April in Paris (V. Duke); Well, You Needn't; Introspection; Nice Work If You Can Get It (Gershwin); Evidence; I Mean You; Epistrophy. *Side three:* I Should Care (Cahn/Stordhal/ Weston); All the Things You Are (J. Kern); Misterioso (two takes); Carolina Moon (Davis); Hornin' In; Skippy; Let's Cool One. *Side four:* Ask Me Now; Straight, No Chaser; Four in One (two takes); Criss Cross; Eronel; Willow Weep for Me (Ronell).

Brilliance

Milestone, M-47023
two discs, good liner notes
1956, 1959

Musicians: Thelonious Monk, piano (and celeste on "Pannonica"); Sonny Rollins, tenor sax; Ernie Henry, alto sax; Oscar Pettiford, bass; Max Roach, drums. Also Clark Terry, trumpet, and Paul Chambers, bass, replacing Henry and Pettiford. Also Monk with Thad Jones, cornet; Charlie Rouse, tenor sax; Sam Jones, bass; Art Taylor, drums.
Compositions (all by Monk): *Side one:* Brilliant Corners; Ba-lue Bolivar Ba-lues-are. *Side two:* Pannonica; Bemsha Swing; Jackie-ing. *Side three:* Straight, No Chaser; Played Twice (two takes). *Side four:* I Mean You; Ask Me Now.

Pure Monk

Milestone, 47004
two discs, good liner notes
1956–1957

Musicians: Thelonious Monk, piano.
Compositions (On sides two and four by Monk): *Side one:* Solitude; Memories of You;
  I Surrender, Dear; April in Paris; I Don't Stand a Ghost of a Chance with You;
  I'm Getting Sentimental over You. *Side two:* Functional (take one); Functional
  (take two); 'Round Midnight. *Side three:* I Should Care; All Alone; Everything
  Happens to Me; You Took the Words Right out of My Heart; Remember; There's
  Danger in Your Eyes, Cherie. *Side four:* Blue Monk; Ruby, My Dear; Round
  Lights; Pannonica; Bluehawk; Reflections.

THELONIOUS MONK WAS the most misunderstood musician of the early
modern period, suffering the first decade of his artistic maturity (from 1946
to 1956) in neglect. Monk's harmonic experimentation—his use of the
flatted-fifth tone of the scale (tritone), unusual intervals, dissonance—and
his unique rhythmic displacement of notes were major contributions to bebop,
strongly influencing the styles of Dizzy Gillespie, Bud Powell, and countless
others of the era. Monk's music was confusing because it was unlike the
music of those to whom he was historically linked. While most pianists,
like Powell, imitated the flowing, sensuous lines of horn players, Monk
plunked out spare, seemingly choppy ideas. In the geometry of the style,
the boppers specialized in curves; Monk, in angles. On piano he was a descendant of Ellington and, when soloing, of James P. Johnson's stride style.

Soon after Monk emerged from obscurity by virtue of the music reissued
on *Brilliance* (and subsequent bands at the Five Spot Café in New York),
he was acknowledged as the most original composer in jazz since Jelly Roll
Morton and Duke Ellington. Although he used the common thirty-two-bar
ballad and twelve-bar blues forms, he was able to create within them—to use
Gunther Schuller's distinction—not "songs" or "tunes" but *pieces*. The
sanctity of each nuance in Monk's music prompted Coltrane to remark,
"When you learn one of Monk's pieces, you can't learn just the melody and
chord symbols. You have to learn the inner voicings and rhythms exactly.
Everything is so carefully related; his works are jazz compositions in the
sense that relatively few jazz 'originals' are." Monk worked only with basic
elements, peeling his music down to the core. Public testimony to his status
as a modern "master" reached its peak in February 1964, when he made

the cover of *Time* magazine, perhaps with as much attention drawn to his dark glasses, funny hats, and eccentric stage mannerisms as to his music.

Thelonious Sphere Monk was born in North Carolina in 1917. He acquired his middle name later on, allegedly to indicate that he was not "square." Within a year his family moved to New York, where he has made his home ever since. Monk had a few years of private piano lessons, although he is primarily a self-taught, idiosyncratic pianist. During his teens, he played the organ at a nearby church and toured briefly as part of a blues-oriented band which accompanied an evangelist. His crucial formative period began in late 1940 at Minton's Playhouse, where he was invited by the new owner, Teddy Hill, to play in the house band, which was rounded out by trumpeter Joe Guy, bassist Nick Fenton, and drummer Kenny Clarke. Minton's became a center for jam sessions that included Charlie Christian (until 1941), Dizzy Gillespie, Tadd Dameron, Fats Navarro, Don Byas, Lester Young—in short, a meeting place for the major jazz talents of the day.

Monk's impact upon jazz in these years far exceeded the recorded evidence. He was engaged in composing several masterpieces which were to become classics, the foremost being, " 'Round Midnight," a haunting and harmonically adventurous ballad of eternal beauty. Monk was collaborating with Kenny Clarke and Gillespie on difficult progressions and "substitution" chords, designed both to expand the improviser's options and to scare the "no-talent" guys off the bandstand. Charlie Parker and his twenty-year-old apprentice, Miles Davis, attended many of these sessions, paying close attention to Monk's harmonic discoveries. (Monk and Parker eventually recorded together; this is available on *Charlie Parker: The Verve Years 1948–1950*, [General Discography].) Monk's piano playing, especially his sporadic left-hand punctuations, was being absorbed by the teenage Bud Powell, for whom Monk was an early mentor.

Nevertheless, Monk's recording debut, available on Everest's *Charlie Christian* (a player with whom Monk had great affinity) is brief and unimpressive. After an unrecorded stint with Lucky Millender's band, Monk was hired by Coleman Hawkins, one of the few established leaders who did not disparage his "strange" ideas. Their two tracks together on *The Hawk Flies* (Chapter 4) offer another glimpse of a formative period. However, Monk's flowering did not begin until 1947, when Alfred Lion of Blue Note signed him as a leader, billing him as "The High Priest of Bebop," a phrase which may well have alienated more listeners than it attracted.

Commercial response notwithstanding, Blue Note's *Thelonious Monk: The Complete Genius* (1947–1952) is an essential collection of Monk's most important compositions. Various levels of his achievements can be discerned: from the beautiful (" 'Round Midnight," "Ruby, My Dear"); to the swinging —by means of constantly shifting accents—("In Walked Bud," written for Bud Powell; "Straight, No Chaser," an ingenious blues destined to become a standard; "Off Minor"; "Well, You Needn't"; "I Mean You"; and "Epistrophy," an early collaboration with Kenny Clarke); to the abstract compositions, presenting ideas and themes to be expanded upon by improvisation ("Evidence"; "Misterioso," a simple yet fascinating series of "walking" sixths; "Criss Cross"; and "Four in One"). In the last category, Monk challenges the improviser to make thematic use of his melodies rather than simply stating them at the beginning and the end of the piece. To bring Monk's originality into sharp focus, compare any of his melodies with Ike Quebec's "Evonce," a passable bebop line which beside Monk's writing comes off as pure cliché. Monk's "Eronel" is probably the closest he comes to a genre piece, and it is a superb one at that.

The soloing honors, too, belong to Monk. He alone constructs the motivic improvisations (as on "Evidence," "Four in One," and "Misterioso") that his music calls for. The opinion of Monk as a pianist *manqué* which then prevailed appears a bit laughable in retrospect. Monk's articulation of phrases is exacting. Moreover, his omnipresent sense of humor, heard in long silences, gapped intervals, and unpredictable bursts of dissonance, cynically thumbs its nose at our musical expectations. Art Blakey and Max Roach, who are both precise and explosive, are ideal drummers for Monk, as they proved later in the 1950's, too. Milt Jackson on vibes (see also Modern Jazz Quartet) has a sure grasp of Monk's harmony but is prone to flourishes, typified by the "I Mean You" solo, which undermines some of Monk's strength. Ultimately it was the saxophonists—Sonny Rollins, John Coltrane, Johnny Griffin, and Charlie Rouse—who provided the ideal tonal color to accompany Monk's stark keyboard sound. While the soloing is not always adequate, *The Complete Genius* is a Monk *tour de force* on the compositional level.

Monk suffered a setback in 1951 when the police department revoked his cabaret card, a work permit for the New York City nightclubs. Without performing, he had little hope of drawing attention to his records. Monk and his wife, Nellie, endured several lean years, during which Thelonious was contracted to Prestige, where he recorded as a sideman once in a great while. His prospects remained abysmal until 1955 when Riverside Records—a company formed by Orrin Keepnews and Bill Grauer in 1953—initiated a relationship that would make Monk and Riverside prominent forces in modern jazz. Although Keepnews and Grauer had specialized in reissues of traditional jazz by Louis Armstrong, Bix Beiderbecke, and Jelly Roll Morton, they were seeking a way to modernize the label. Through critic Nat Hentoff, they learned that Monk and Prestige had little use for one another; Riverside then purchased Monk's contract from Prestige for the price of a royalty overpayment of $108.27.

The Riverside Trios (1955–1956) is essentially the reissue of a false start, one album devoted to Ellington tunes and another to various standards. Despite Monk's debt to Ellington the pianist, these are the least Monk-ish Monk sides ever recorded save for the early 1940's tracks with Christian and Hawkins. Riverside had vainly attempted to ease their "High Priest of Bebop" into acceptance with a recognizable repertoire. Fortunately, they swung drastically in the other direction on their next effort, a 1956 album—originally entitled *Brilliant Corners*, a hard-core, hard-driving set of Monk-arranged originals. The compositions possessed Monk's characteristic touch of genius, and the soloing made it immediately accessible if not irresistible.

Brilliance, which contains the breakthrough album and a similar session from 1959, is uniformly gripping. "Brilliant Corners" itself is a theme of darkness and intensity with a double-timed chorus built into its structure that gives the listener two distinct perspectives on the same idea. The incisive logic of Sonny Rollins, who is a thematic player, and Ernie Henry's blues-based linear approach on alto sax create an exciting contrast. "Bolivar Ba-lues-are" is alive with rhythmic shifting; it launches Ernie Henry's opening "growl" on a solo as earthy as the country-blues tradition this track evokes. It is astonishing to note how closely Monk can adhere to the blues form and tonality while creating a distinctly original statement within these contexts. "Pannonica" is one of Monk's marvelous ballads, a subtle combination of delicacy and strength. The melody is tender, aching, and even a bit agonized. Monk combines sonorities exquisitely, making use of a celeste that happened to be in the studio at the time. His simultaneous playing of both keyboards quickly becomes an integral part of "Pannonica" rather than simply an effect. "Bemsha Swing," another blues, takes its distinctiveness from the rhythmic pattern, with Monk and Max Roach communicating intimately throughout. Monk's piano is nowhere more aggressive than on these cuts, trumpeting dissonances, for example, behind Rollins on "Jackie-ing." In other tracks on these sides, Clark Terry on trumpet and Thad Jones on cornet are integrated by Monk with equal integrity. *Brilliance* is the essential Monk band album, illustrating the completeness and self-sufficiency of his music.

The next year Monk went to the Five Spot with a band consisting of John Coltrane on tenor sax ("Trane" had been temporarily dropped from the Miles Davis band), Wilbur Ware on bass, and Shadow Wilson on drums. Monk quickly became as fascinating as his music. He would often arrive at the club two hours late. On the bandstand, armed with a drink, he would dance, trance-like, around the piano or even leave the stage five minutes at a time while Trane soloed. The club's new grand piano, which Monk had picked out himself, wore the scars of his fierce outbursts: "There were hundreds of scratches, even gashes on the wood just above the keyboard, where Monk, slashing at the keys, bangs the wood with his big ring or tears it with his nails." [12] Monk's groups were the main attraction, drawing full houses regularly over the next two years.

Two important albums came out of the Five Spot dates. *Monk/Trane,* recorded the year after the group performed there, includes three beautiful collaborations on "Ruby, My Dear," "Trinkle, Trinkle," and "Nutty." The remaining sides were made with Gigi Gryce and Coleman Hawkins, neither of whom interpret Monk with great depth or sensitivity. After Trane returned to Miles's band, Monk worked with the remarkably fluent tenor saxophonist Johnny Griffin, Roy Haynes on drums, and Ahmed Abdul-Malik on bass.

At the Five Spot reissues two live dates, one of which was the famous *Misterioso* album in its first incarnation. These sessions are nothing short of sensational because of the consistently intense level of the soloing. Griffin's unaccompanied choruses on "Let's Cool One" and "In Walked Bud" are hair-raising, and Monk's solos are no less electrifying. *At the Five Spot* is second only to *Brilliance* in collecting Monk's best group recordings. (One sour note, however: "Misterioso" was mysteriously abbreviated by seven minutes, an error which will be rectified on the next pressing, according to the album's producer.)

Monk's importance as an inimitable pianist is as certain as his status as a composer. But during the early 1950's, his apparently "faltering" technique —relative to the flowing, *legato* lines of Bud Powell, Oscar Peterson, Teddy Wilson, and of course Art Tatum—was frequently disparaged. But Monk's technique, with its rocky runs and splattered tonal clusters, is clearly ideal for the percussive, oddball blues message he communicates. While his ideas burst forth in the context of the band, they are appropriately more measured and contemplatively expressed in his solos.

Pure Monk (1956–1959), containing all the Riverside studio sessions, is the definitive solo album. In this recording Monk is relaxed, confident, child-like, and even whimsical as he explores his material for its inherent themes and humor. " 'Round Midnight," "Ruby, My Dear," and "Pannonica" receive unsentimental but tender treatment. "Functional" and "Blue Monk" tran-scend their strict blues forms by virtue of subtle interior design. Two sides of these discs are pop standards, many of which—like "I Should Care" and "I Surrender, Dear"—emerge transformed into genuine piano *pieces*. Monk's left-hand stride echoes that of James P. Johnson; his right hand, playing whole-tone scale runs which plunge swiftly into a stark bass note or chord, is Ellingtonian, as confirmed by a comparison with side three of *The Golden Duke* (Chapter 4). Monk's momentum was aptly described by critic Paul Bacon in an issue of the now-defunct *Record Changer*: "And Monk has a beat like the ocean waves—no matter how sudden, spasmodic, or obscure his little inventions, he rocks irresistibly on." Monk has the composer's facility for carrying melody, harmony, and rhythm in just the right balance. Recalling his numerous detractors, it is ironic to note that during these years following the death of Art Tatum, Monk was the *only* pianist, except for the semiretired Earl Hines, who dared to record without bass and drum accompaniment. (A good solo LP of uncertain vintage is available on GNP Crescendo's *Thelonious Monk*.)

Monk's final working band, begun in 1959, was built around Charlie Rouse, and is heard on two sides of *Brilliance*. After 1960, they recorded for Columbia. (The last Riverside album was a big-band date of Monk's music arranged by Hal Overton, reissued as *In Person*). Monk's performances had by then become a bit more polished and consequently less provocative. *It's Monk's Time* warrants special mention for its sense of humor. For example, it includes a hard-driving version of cute tunes like "Lulu's Back in Town,"

and a lovable Monk-ied stride solo on "Nice Work If You Can Get It."
Underground Monk contains the best soloing by the blues-oriented Rouse,
and *Greatest Hits* offers a good sample of the composer's repertoire (General
Discography).

Monk's performances have been severely curtailed in the 1970's due to
illness, although his quartet's appearance at the Newport Jazz Festival in
1975 was one of its high points. His recording has been limited to two albums
released by the Italian label Black Lion. Whether or not he returns to the
studio, it is certain that Monk's unique music will continue to play a vital
role in jazz repertoire.

ART BLAKEY

A Night at Birdland, Volume 1

Blue Note, BLP-1521/BST-81521
one disc, brief liner notes
1954

Musicians: Art Blakey, drums; Horace Silver, piano; Clifford Brown, trumpet; Lou
   Donaldson, alto sax; Curly Russell, bass.
Compositions: Side one: Split Kick; Once in a While; Quicksilver. *Side two:* A Night in
   Tunisia; Mayreh.

HORACE SILVER QUINTET

Doin' the Thing: At the Village Gate

Blue Note, BLP-4076/BST-84076
one disc, brief liner notes
1961

Musicians: Horace Silver, piano; Junior Cook, tenor sax; Blue Mitchell, trumpet; Gene Taylor, bass; Roy Brooks, drums.
Compositions (all by Silver): *Side one:* Filthy McNasty; Doin' the Thing. *Side two:* Kiss Me Right; The Gringo; The Theme.

ART BLAKEY AND HORACE SILVER are founding fathers of funky hard bop, a style crucial to jazz's development in the mid 1950's. They were among the first to offer an alternative to the light, cool West Coast sound of the day. Their hard-driving, blues-based music communicates viscerally with the listener. Blakey and Silver first worked together at Birdland and became co-leaders of the original Jazz Messengers group in 1956. They are still recording with their respective quintets nearly a quarter century later in much the same style.

Art Blakey was born in Pittsburgh, Pennsylvania, in 1919. He learned to play the piano at school but switched to drums when Erroll Garner took over the piano in a band he played with. He worked for Fletcher Henderson in 1939, then in a trio with Mary Lou Williams, and, most significantly, from 1944 to 1947 he played in the Billy Eckstine big band (General Discography), where he attracted the attention of Alfred Lion, the owner of Blue Note. Thus Blakey began his long-term association with Blue Note records, beginning with the historic Thelonious Monk sessions which are available on *The Complete Genius* (Monk, Selected Discography). Blakey organized an unrecorded big band in 1949, naming them The Messengers in his belief that the jazz musician has a spiritual role comparable to that of the gospel singer or minister.

In the late 1940's Blakey traveled to Africa and remained long enough to study philosophy and religion and to become a Moslem. He returned home with the name Buhaina. Blakey has downplayed the idea that his African sojourn increased his understanding of the drums. Certainly Kenny Clarke and Max Roach were more prominent influences. Blakey also argues that jazz is a purely American phenomenon, much less dependent upon African inheritances than musicologists believe.

Jamming at Birdland in the early 1950's, Blakey and Silver drenched the hard-bop quintet form in the blues, which they powered with a driving, emotional style. Although the group was not yet called the Jazz Messengers, the Birdland sessions, which were recorded unrehearsed, capture the band's explosive beginnings. (See also *Volume 2* of the selected title and side four of *Live Messengers* for more tracks, General Discography.) "Quicksilver" exemplifies Blakey's major innovation as a drummer—his readiness to interact with the other soloists, closing the traditional gap between the "front line" (horns) and the rhythm section. The music's pulse in hard bop is picked up by the bassist, who establishes the momentum through his countermelodies. Thus the drummer is free to provide a running commentary on the soloists' lines. Bringing the drums into the front line was a prophetic transition. During the next two decades, drummers like Elvin Jones (Chapter 6) and Tony Williams (Chapters 6 and 7) would make the percussionist's sound nearly equal to that of the melodic instruments.

Blakey is also a master of the "press roll," which serves as a giant springboard for the soloists' melodic leaps. At least a half-dozen examples can be heard during "A Night in Tunisia," the most stunning of which launches the wild alto break with which Lou Donaldson begins his improvisation. Blakey often follows the press roll with a splashing ride cymbal, as he does when lifting Clifford Brown into his solo on "Quicksilver," and later in the middle of the solo. Blakey's sound is always explosive; it indicates the significance of, and confidence behind, every rhythmic move he makes. As saxophonist Ike Quebec once put it, "Other drummers say *thump*, Blakey says POW!"

Blakey alumni include the teams of Hank Mobley and Kenny Dorham; Lee Morgan and Benny Golson and Bobby Timmons; and Freddie Hubbard and Wayne Shorter. Blakey was successfully reunited with Monk in 1958 on *The Jazz Messengers with Thelonious Monk.* Hubbard and Shorter turn in impassioned performances on Blakey's best 1960's albums *Free for All* and *Mosaic,* and they are also represented on the reissue *Live Messengers.* Blakey has continued to lead groups with such consistency that not even the General Discography can list all his worthwhile albums.

Silver, born in 1928 (nine years after Blakey) and raised in Norwalk, Connecticut, was far less experienced at the time the *Birdland* album was cut. Records were his primary source of instruction:

> I used to take those Charlie Parker, Bud Powell, and Dexter Gordon records on Savoy and put them on an old wind-up machine and slow the speed down. I'd hear the chords that way and pick them out note by note. . . . The very first tune I learned was "What Is This Thing Called Love?" I'll never forget it because it took me about five minutes to find C^7 in the root position. Later on, from Teddy Wilson records, I learned how to play 10ths and open the voicings up. I used to play a lot of Bud Powell solos off the record, and when I played tenor, I practiced with Lester Young records every day. In fact I'd go

out on gigs and play parts of his solos. In a sense I'm self-taught, but my teachers were all these great guys on records.[10]

Silver's first records (not available) were made in 1951 with Stan Getz, who had heard him playing at the Sundown Club in Hartford. It is unfortunate that these sessions are out of print because Getz was at a melodic peak on them. These early sessions were Horace's first opportunity to hear himself with some objectivity, and he became aware of a personal element in his playing which he committed himself to developing. "I took my record player and records, packed them in the closet, and played no records for a long time. I just practiced. I didn't want to be influenced by anybody." [11] After traveling with Getz for a year, Silver moved to New York and began to work with Blakey at Birdland.

Silver's playing is derivative of Bud Powell's single-note right-hand figures. Silver simplifies them, emphasizing the blue areas of the scale. While Powell's lines are long and tortuous, Silver works with short, finely chiseled phrases that build upon one another. Many of these phrases, like the brilliant procession that makes up the "Filthy McNasty" solo, sound like clichés. Far from it: They are catchy and compositionally sound, thus *appearing* familiar even when they are new. (The name "Filthy McNasty" comes from a character in W. C. Fields's *The Bank Dick*; Silver composed it at the piano after seeing the movie on late-night television.) However, Silver is fond of interpolating other song fragments into the harmonic structure of his solo. His excellent bebop composition "Quicksilver" lifts an entire phrase from "Oh, You Beautiful Doll," while the solo incorporates a reference to Bud Powell's "Reets and I" (*The Amazing Bud Powell, Volume 2*).

Silver's left hand is used percussively and with even greater impact and complexity than Powell's punched-out chords. He can almost make the lower register of the keyboard growl or bark, as in his piano solo on "Doin' the Thing," in which his left hand loses all sense of harmonic definition and becomes drumlike. In 'comping for other soloists, Silver's rhythmic figures are designed to in his words "goose" the horns into more explosive blowing. The propulsive momentum of "Filthy McNasty," the album's best track, is due in great part to the two powerfully accented chords which Silver slips in between the third and fourth beats of each measure in the chorus. Drummer Roy Brooks also gives Blue Mitchell and Junior Cook a boost by using some Blakey specialties, such as the building "press" rolls following Silver's solo in "McNasty," in the first eight bars of "Doin' the Thing," and just prior to the rhythmic break from "Latin" to swing in "The Gringo."

Silver's greatest talent, and the one he cares most deeply about, is for composition and arrangement in the quintet form. One can easily hear his debt to bebop in "Mayreh" (*Birdland*) or in "Cool Eyes" (*Village Gate*), and to what he refers to as "Latin" (Afro-Cuban) music in "The Gringo" (*Village Gate*). To experience the full range of Silver's lovely songwriting, it is necessary to hear several more of the albums on Blue Note, for whom Silver has recorded since 1954. These include *Blowin' the Blues Away* (with "Blowin'," "Sister Sadie"); *The Best of Horace Silver* ("The Preacher," "Senor Blues," "Doodlin' "); and the two-disc *Horace Silver* with cuts from 1953 to 1969 ("Cookin' at the Continental," "Song for My Father," "Strollin'," "Cape Verdean Blues," "Nica's Dream," and "Opus de Funk"). These are classics of the genre. On later albums (*Silver 'n Brass, Silver 'n Voices*) Horace works with larger ensembles, but not with the success he enjoyed on the finely cut quintet gems. Silver's use of trumpet and sax, generally in close harmony, falls somewhere between bebop's riffing in unison and the big band's brass-and-reed concept. His groups always hit with a powerful punch far beyond their size. Finally, *The Trio Sides* is an excellent study of Silver the pianist from 1952 through 1968.

Both Blakey's Jazz Messengers and Silver's quintets have evolved into traveling finishing schools of jazz, playing clubs and festivals around the world. Good soloists emerge far better having absorbed the energy and craftsmanship of these perennial leaders.

BUD POWELL (with FATS NAVARRO)

The Amazing Bud Powell, Volume 1

Blue Note, BLP-1503/BST-81503
one disc, liner notes
1949, 1951

Musicians: Bud Powell, piano; Curley Russell, bass; Max Roach, drums. *On four tracks:* Tommy Potter, bass; Roy Haynes, drums; Fats Navarro, trumpet; Sonny Rollins, tenor sax.
Compositions: Side one: Un Poco Loco (three takes); Dance of the Infidels; 52nd Street Theme; It Could Happen to You. *Side two:* A Night in Tunisia (two takes); Wail; Ornithology; Bouncing with Bud; Parisian Thoroughfare.

EARL "BUD" POWELL WAS for a time the bebop pianist par excellence. If Earl Hines played "trumpet-style" piano, etching the power of a Louis Armstrong into his melodies, Powell's right-hand lines suggested the alto

sax, seemingly a magical transfer of Charlie Parker's searing, tortuous melodic concepts onto the keyboard. Although Powell inherited Art Tatum's heavily harmonic, two-handed approach on ballads, illustrated here by "It Could Happen to You," his most original music was up-tempo, establishing a wholly revised use of the left hand: sharp, jabbing chords which irregularly punctuated his elastic melodic lines.

Bud Powell was perhaps the most innovative pianist in the period between Earl Hines and Cecil Taylor. His use of the instrument influenced nearly every modern pianist who came after him—Horace Silver, Red Garland, John Lewis, Hampton Hawes, Oscar Peterson, and Bill Evans, to name a few—but none matched Bud's desperate intensity, a reflection of his tortured psyche. Powell's reign at the keyboard was thus painfully brief, overthrown not so much by other players as by inner demons.

Powell was born in 1924 into a musical family in New York. His father, grandfather, and two brothers were musicians. His brother Richie, who was seven years younger, played piano and arranged for the Clifford Brown-Max Roach band (see Brown-Roach discussion ahead). Bud began studying piano when he was six, quickly developing a fine technique for European classical music. At fifteen, however, he was working with his older brother's band around Coney Island and studying the newest ideas in bebop by frequenting Minton's Playhouse, where he came under the influence of Thelonious Monk. Bud learned all of Monk's music, which he would later record in abundance, and possibly took Monk's spare, discordant left hand as a model in developing his own style. Monk also recognized Bud's talent immediately and acted as his patron at Minton's, later writing "In Walked Bud" for him, an ingeniously accented melody based upon Irving Berlin's "Blue Skies."

At nineteen Powell joined the Cootie Williams band, with whom he recorded for the first time in 1944. Early signs of emotional instability were creating difficulties for him. Occasionally if Bud did not like the tune Cootie called on the bandstand, he folded his arms above the keyboard like a mischievous child and adamantly refused to play it. Later incidents were less amusing. In 1946 Bud was arrested for disorderly conduct and while in jail, was beaten severely about the head. Afterward he was hospitalized and transferred to Bellevue Hospital, where he received the first of many electroshock treatments.

His first available recordings were made later in 1946 with Dexter Gordon (on Savoy's *Long Tall Dexter*) and the following year (1947) with Charlie Parker on "Cheryl" and "Buzzy," two stellar Bird performances from the *Savoy Sessions* discussed previously. Bud, though not yet at the peak of his powers, was very much in demand as an accompanist, despite bouts of irrationality. However, he was hospitalized again for electroshock therapy for most of 1948.

When Bud returned to Fifty-second Street, he found that his passionate creativity and stunning technique had been acknowledged. Blue Note offered him his own date as Bud Powell and His Modernists, the original title of the selected album here. It marked the beginning of four brilliant years of flawless, inspired playing that he would never recapture with the same consistency.

The Modernists on *The Amazing Bud Powell, Volume I* include the young Sonny Rollins, then a stylistic hybrid of Coleman Hawkins and Charlie Parker, and the great Fats Navarro, one of the most influential and least acknowledged of modern trumpeters. Musically Fats and Bud were perfect partners, seeming on these cuts to be lyrical extensions of one another. They had played together before, sometimes sitting in with Parker at Birdland in 1949. Fats, a twenty-six-year-old from Florida, had replaced Dizzy Gillespie in Billy Eckstine's early-bop big band, and was seemingly Gillespie's equal in technique (see *Mr. B. and the Band*, General Discography). After eighteen months he worked with pianist Tadd Dameron's quintet, where his fluency achieved its height. That band's fast-paced, intricate music can be heard on Blue Note's two-disc set, *Prime Source*, seven tracks of which are takes from the Powell-Navarro (without Dameron) session here. (*Prime Source* is highly recommended but was not selected here due to the duplication of tracks.) Another good sample of Navarro can be heard on Savoy's *Fat Girl*, which was Navarro's derisive nickname, given him because of his weight, high-pitched voice, and genteel manner. (See also Milestone's *Fats Navarro*, General Discography.)

Fats's music was of a romantic cast, a good contrast to Powell's more agonized emotional tone. He had a warm, rich tone and, like Bud on piano, a fluid delivery, creating an important alternative to the jagged peaks of Gillespie's lines. Fats had a definite melodic influence upon Clifford Brown (to be discussed ahead) and consequently upon the great trumpeter of the 1960's, Freddie Hubbard. His goal was to "sing" on his instrument, which was achieved to a remarkable degree in his improvisation on Powell's "Wail." Although his health was soon to deteriorate due to heroin, he was still able, as on Monk's "52nd Street Theme," to maintain Bud's blistering pace, his melodic line voraciously devouring passing chords in the process.

For all their artistic compatibility, these men were frequently feuding. Once Bud antagonized Fats mercilessly on the bandstand, and Fats retaliated by bringing his horn crashing down onto the keyboard, just missing Bud's hands. At any rate this band had a short life, as did Navarro who died in 1950 at twenty-seven, a victim of tuberculosis and his own bad habits.

Bud's performance on Blue Note's *Volume 1* is uniformly brilliant in content and technique. His compositions—"Wail," "Dance of the Infidels," and "Bouncing with Bud"—are compelling examples of the bebop genre, full of delightful twisting, pausing, turning, and rhythmic shifting. (Bud's "Un Poco Loco," developed over three takes, and "Parisian Thoroughfare" are atypical—emphasizing rhythmic variety and ambience, respectively.) Bud's improvising gushes forth at breakneck, nonstop pace, overflowing with ideas. A first-hand account of Powell in action at Birdland during these years attests to the intensity he radiated:

> For twenty or twenty-five choruses he hung the audience by its nerve ends, playing music of demonically driven beauty . . . right leg digging into the floor at an odd angle, pants leg up to almost the top of the shin, shoulders hunched, upper lip tight against his teeth, mouth emitting an accompanying guttural song to what the steel fingers were playing, vein in temple throbbing violently as perspiration popped out all over his scalp and ran down his face and neck.[12]

This is the image of Bud readily conveyed by his improvisation on Gillespie's "A Night in Tunisia," a bebop standard. His speed on the long break which opens the solo (on take one) melts these notes into a liquid, hornlike line. The take of Charlie Parker's "Ornithology" is yet another classic bebop performance of perpetual invention. Finally, the ballad "It Could Happen to You" reveals the harmonic sophistication left implicit in Powell's playing at faster tempos and, unmistakably, Powell's debt to Art Tatum.

The Amazing Bud Powell, Volumes 2–5, recorded over the next several years, are also available, but the most satisfying is *Volume 2*, with the superb linear improvisation on "Reets and I" and the harmonically bizarre "Glass Enclosure," Bud's powerful comment upon his many months in the asylum. Blue Note has been promising for some time to reissue these volumes in a two-disc set—an idea whose time is long overdue.

There are two more important albums from Powell's healthy, technically sharp period. The first is the set with Charlie Parker, Dizzy Gillespie, Charles Mingus, and Max Roach on *The World's Greatest Jazz Concert*, a 1953 album (discussed previously) on which Bud's performances are somewhat inconsistent. The second is Verve's two-disc *The Genius of Bud Powell* (1949–1951), which includes the fine compositions "Tempus Fugue-it"; "Celia," written for his daughter; and "Hallucinations," frequently recorded by Miles Davis as "Budo." A second Verve set from later years (General Discography) is less impressive.

Although Powell was able to keep himself out of institutions after 1955, his health improved but little, even after he moved to a more salubrious environment in Paris. Bud had begun drinking, and his reputation as a sad man of borderline sanity had settled in to stay. Nevertheless, he produced some occasional masterpieces, like Delmark's *Bouncing with Bud*, recorded in Copenhagen in 1962 with the fifteen-year-old prodigy bassist Niels-Hennings Orsted Pedersen (Oscar Peterson's favorite bassist during the 1970's). Bud's improvisations on the title track "Rifftide" by Coleman Hawkins and on several Monk tunes are singable, nearly begging for lyrics. Bud's technique may have been blunted but not his imagination. Xanadu's *Bud in Paris* contains another example of his resurgent powers during the early 1960's.

In 1964 Powell returned to the United States, accompanied by his second wife and a mystical twenty-year-old artist, François Paudras, who claimed to be supervising Bud's affairs and (some say) "curing" him. Paudras, however, returned to Paris alone. In 1966 Bud Powell died in New York, a victim of tuberculosis and alcoholism.

**CLIFFORD BROWN (with
MAX ROACH)**

The Quintet, Volume 1

EmArcy/Mercury, EMS-2-403
two discs, liner notes
1954–1955

Musicians: Clifford Brown, trumpet; Max Roach, drums; Harold Land, tenor sax; Richie Powell, piano; George Morrow, bass.
Compositions: Side one: Delilah; Parisian Thoroughfare; Jordu. *Side two:* Sweet Clifford; Ghost of a Chance; Stompin' at the Savoy. *Side three:* I Get a Kick Out of You; Joy Spring; Mildama. *Side four:* Daahoud; Gerkin for Perkin; Take the 'A' Train; Lands End. Swingin'.

CLIFFORD BROWN, an inheritor of Fats Navarro's trumpet style, played with a full-toned, linear lyricism which proved to be the only vital alternative during the 1950's to Miles Davis's understated melodic style. Brown's lengthy improvisations, which juxtaposed smoothly flowing phrases with staccato notes, displayed a fertile imagination and an impeccable sense of form. Some of his solos were so well developed and ordered that they seemed preplanned, an illusory notion, as shown by comparing various takes of the same piece. He was never more vibrant than after 1954, when Max Roach invited him to colead a quintet. Roach was able to boost Clifford to greater heights, powerfully accenting his lines, smoothing out the rhythmic flow by his use of the top (ride) cymbal, and enhancing Brown's lyricism with melodic, well-tuned drumming. Unfortunately, the ultimate Brown-Roach performance, *At Basin Street* (with Sonny Rollins), went out of print in 1979, when Trip Records went out of business. The album will no doubt return some day, along with the other riches on the Trip label. Nevertheless, Brown was recorded frequently from 1952 to 1956, when his life was cut tragically short at the peak of his powers.

Born in Wilmington, Delaware, in 1930, Brown had little interest in music as a child, although his father played trumpet, piano, and violin non-professionally. He was fascinated by the trumpet itself, however, and received one from his father at the age of thirteen. In high school he began studying piano and arranging, as well as playing trumpet in the band. Brown attended the University of Delaware, majoring in mathematics, for which he had considerable talent. Filling in one night for an ill trumpet player in Gillespie's big band, Clifford impressed Dizzy who encouraged him to pursue a career in music.

By 1948 Brown had moved to Philadelphia, where he sat in regularly with accomplished musicians and built a reputation among the upper echelons of the beboppers. Fats Navarro, Clifford's idol, coached him in a few private sessions. Charlie Parker hired him, again to fill in for an ill sideman, and was astounded by Brownie's facility for invention, reportedly telling him, "I hear what you're saying, but I don't believe it." Brownie's career was interrupted in 1950 by an automobile accident, which hospitalized him for most of the year.

Brownie's earliest recordings convey his round, sweet sound, virtuosity, and lyricism, although he was seldom heard in the most favorable contexts. Columbia's *The Beginning and the End* captures him in 1952 with Chris Powell's Blue Flames, an R & B group, as well as a lengthy blowing session from 1956. After working briefly with Tadd Dameron's band, Clifford traveled to Europe in 1953 with Lionel Hampton's organization, recording there with French musicians and members of the Hampton band (available on Prestige's two-disc *Clifford Brown in Paris*). After returning from Europe, Clifford was hired by Art Blakey—acting upon Charlie Parker's recommendation—for the early Jazz Messengers, heard on *A Night at Birdland, Volume 1* (1954) (see Blakey, Selected Discography), the first adequate vehicle for Brownie's articulate, imaginative solo flights.

It was the Blakey recordings which particularly impressed Max Roach, who was then leading an assortment of bands at The Lighthouse, a club in Hermosa Beach, California. Roach, five years Brown's senior, had been the favored drummer of Parker and Gillespie, and had received his training by listening to Kenny Clarke at Minton's during the early 1940's. Roach had been approached for a tour by the promoter Gene Norman, and sent for Clifford, who was flattered by Roach's invitation to become coleader. Alto saxophonist Sonny Stitt was the first reed player; he was soon replaced by Harold Land, an exponent of the big "Texas tenor" sound.

The Quintet is a strong mixture of lyricism and fire, featuring Brown's beatific tone and flawless execution of imaginative, complex phrasing, A talented composer, Brownie's most enduring compositions, "Joy Spring" and "Daahoud," which are characterized by a smooth succession of key changes, receive their definitive treatments here. The flowing, song-like improvisations on "Daahoud" and (Bud Powell's) "Parisian Thoroughfare" compare favorably (despite the date of their recording) to most of his solos during 1956 after Sonny Rollins had joined. Brown's virtuosity comes near to being flaunted on "Mildama," also a showcase for Roach's ability to develop a lengthy, intense drum solo. Brown and Roach communicate most intimately on "I Get a Kick Out of You," trading accents and phrasings in a fast-paced, witty conversation. On this solo Brown's technique is put to its highest melodic use, deftly drawing continuous, intricate, logical lines with no extraneous flourishes anywhere. The song opens with metric variations from ¾ to 4/4, a trick used by the band on other standards like "Love Is a Many-Splendored Thing" on the out-of-print Trip LP. Brown's performance on "Stompin' at the Savoy" is a close second to "Kick."

Other high points include a classic version of "Jordu," soon to become a standard but receiving its debut here. Land is at his fleet best on "Gerkin for Perkins," a clever blues-based tune by Brown, and in the strongly evocative arrangement of Strayhorn's "Take the 'A' Train." The arrangement, like that of "Parisian Thoroughfare," is probably due to Richie Powell, Bud's younger brother, also a fine pianist. Due to Bud's reputation, Richie first lacked the confidence his abilities warranted, but his self-esteem grew considerably within this band He soon became its most prolific writer until his death along with Brown's in 1956.

There are two good single-disc albums of the group during its tenure from 1954 to 1955: *The Best of Max Roach and Clifford Brown: In Concert*, one of the live dates the band played for Gene Norman; and Mercury's *Remember Clifford* (General Discography). In November 1955, however, the band was in Chicago, and Land was called back to the West Coast on family matters. This led to a fortuitous change of personnel. Sonny Rollins, recently cured of drug addiction, was living at the Chicago Y.M.C.A. where he was engaged in a physical fitness program. Roach persuaded him to brave a return to the jazz scene. No one could have been a better influence upon Rollins than Clifford, who had become nearly legendary for his clean living, reliability, and cheerful disposition. Later on Rollins credited Brownie with proving to him that it was possible to live decently and still play good jazz. *Live at the Bee Hive*, a low-quality tape of a pickup session in Chicago with Rollins on tenor sax, has been released by Columbia, but it is virtually unlistenable and superfluous, considering the sessions available from the following six months.

The best of the Brown-Roach-Rollins albums is the out-of-print *At Basin Street*, followed by Prestige's single-disc *Three Giants*, which demonstrates why Rollins's incisive logic made him the perfect match for Brownie in the front line. *Three Giants* has not been selected because it lacks Brown's all-important compositions and because the same band is represented on side four of Rollins's *Saxophone Colossus*, to be discussed.

The band, which then seemed to have the brightest future in jazz, came to a catastrophic end on June 27, 1956. Clifford, Richie Powell, and his wife, Nancy, were in Philadelphia, planning to meet Roach in Chicago for an engagement. They set out at 3:00 A.M. on a rainy morning. Presumably

Nancy, an inexperienced driver, was behind the wheel while Richie and Clifford slept. The car went over a guard rail and down an eighteen-foot embankment, killing them all.

Roach, who for years afterward could not play Brown's music, continued to work with Sonny Rollins and George Morrow, using Kenny Dorham on trumpet and Wade Legge on piano. Rollins, however, soon went to work with Monk and then became a leader. Roach went on to record abundantly with others and since 1972 has been a professor of music at the University of Massachusetts.

SONNY ROLLINS

Saxophone Colossus and More

Prestige, P-24050
two discs, good liner notes
1956

Musicians: Sonny Rollins, tenor sax. *On sides one and two,* selections marked *: Tommy Flanagan, piano; Doug Watkins, bass; Max Roach, drums. *On side two,* selections marked ** and *on side three:* Kenny Dorham, trumpet; Wade Legge, piano; George Morrow, bass; Max Roach, drums. *On side four:* Clifford Brown, trumpet; Richie Powell, piano; George Morrow, bass; Max Roach, drums.

Compositions: Side one: Moritat (Mack the Knife)*; Blue Seven*; Strode Rode. *Side two:* St. Thomas*; You Don't Know What Love Is*; Kids Know.** *Side three:* The House I Live In**; I've Grown Accustomed to Her Face**; Star Eyes.** *Side four:* I Feel a Song Comin' On; Pent-Up House; Kiss and Run.

More from the Vanguard

Blue Note, BN-LA475-H2
two discs, good liner notes
1957

Musicians: Sonny Rollins, tenor sax; Wilbur Ware, bass; Elvin Jones, drums. Donald
   Bailey, bass, and Pete LaRoca, drums on selections marked *.
Compositions: Side one: I've Got You Under My Skin*; A Night in Tunisia. *Side two:*
   What Is This Thing Called Love?; Softly, as in a Morning Sunrise. *Side three:*
   Four; Woodyn' You; All the Things You Are. *Side four:* Get Happy; I'll Remember
   April; Get Happy (alternate master).

SONNY ROLLINS'S INSTINCTIVE GRASP of thematic improvising made him the
most influential soloist during the late 1950's. As noted in Chapter 1, most
improvisation consists of the extemporaneous creation of melody within a
given harmonic structure. That was clearly the approach of the beboppers
and hard boppers. It often produced works of great beauty; but at its worst,
it amounted to a pointless exercise known as "running chords," or playing
a banal sequence of the chords' scale tones. The linear melodic approach,
however, does not exhaust the dimensions of extemporaneous playing. Why,
as Thelonious Monk reportedly asked,[13] should jazz musicians throw away
the melody after the first chorus and just use the chord changes afterward?
Jelly Roll Morton, Duke Ellington, Monk himself, and the Modern Jazz
Quartet (under the guidance of John Lewis) were all aware of the advantages
of restating and developing themes and motifs. But they planned for such
melodic "cross-referencing" as arrangers and composers. Then Sonny Rollins,
with his historic "Blue Seven" (*Saxophone Colossus and More*), demonstrated the potential for thematic development in improvisation. Suddenly
new goals appeared attainable within the jazz solo.
    Sonny, born Theodore Rollins in New York in 1930, grew up in a
neighborhood distinguished by the presence of both Bud Powell, at whose
home he frequently attended jam sessions, and Coleman Hawkins, his first
idol on tenor sax. Rollins made his first recording session with Powell in
1949 on *The Amazing Bud Powell*, which was discussed previously. Rollins
imitated Hawkins's hard, virile sound, but without the vibrato. He also absorbed Lester Young's easy sense of swing and breathy tone, as demonstrated
in the varied dynamics of "Blue Seven." Charlie Parker, however, was the
strongest influence upon Rollins, who was briefly known as the "Bird of the

tenor sax." "Now's the Time" and "Billie's Bounce" were both quite popular in Harlem, although the fifteen-year-old Rollins first heard Bird on the awesome "Ko Ko." Unfortunately, Rollins also followed Parker in cultivating a heroin addiction, which led to a voluntary hospitalization from 1954 to 1955. Before this hiatus, one of several sabbaticals Rollins took from the music business, he made two significant recordings with Miles Davis. The first, available on *Dig* (see Davis, Selected Discography), occurred shortly after Miles heard Rollins playing at a small Harlem club. At the more impressive session in June 1954, on *Tallest Trees*, Rollins's best bebop compositions, "Oleo," "Doxy," and "Airegin," are included. Rollins the improviser was beginning to find himself on these dates.

After his rehabilitation in 1955, Rollins assumed a crucial role in the Clifford Brown-Max Roach group with whom he had first jammed while living at the Chicago Y.M.C.A. Brown set a salubrious example for Rollins, proving that it was possible to live a good clean life and still play jazz. It was Brown who dubbed him "Sonny" when Rollins tired of his former nickname, Newk—for his resemblance to Brooklyn Dodger pitcher Don Newcombe. Rollins lost a beloved mentor when Clifford Brown died just four days after *Saxophone Colossus* was recorded. (Rollins with the Brown-Roach band is heard on side four of *Colossus*.)

But the years from 1956 to 1959 proved to be the most fertile, yielding several albums of Rollins's incisive, hard-edged improvisations. His thematic compatibility with Monk was obvious on *Brilliance*, and was repeated in "Misterioso," "Reflections," and "Why Don't I?" with Monk and Art Blakey on the Blue Note dates (1956–1957), reissued on the two-disc *Sonny Rollins*. His drive and inventiveness were at their peak when trading lines with Gillespie and Sonny Stitt on "Sumpin'" and "The Eternal Triangle," reissued on *The Sonny Rollins/Sonny Stitt Sessions* (see Gillespie, General Discography). For Prestige, Rollins recorded with the Miles Davis band of 1956. He played with John Coltrane on the famous tenor battle "Tenor Madness" on *Taking Care of Business*; with Thelonious Monk, Art Blakey, Clifford Brown, and others on "Valse Hot," the first modern jazz waltz, and "St. Thomas," Rollins's famous Calypso piece, on *Sonny Rollins*; and with Oscar Pettiford and Max Roach on the politically motivated, four-part "Freedom Suite," a twenty-minute side of *Freedom Suite Plus*. Nevertheless, the key to Rollins's innovations is laid out most clearly in the *Saxophone Colossus* session, specifically on "Blue Seven."

The unity of Rollins's three improvisational segments on "Blue Seven" is achieved by a consistent reference to material set forth in the composition itself. The solo's development is outlined meticulously by Gunther Schuller in an excellent analytical study, which concludes with the following observation:

> . . . the crowning achievement of Rollins' solo is his eleventh, twelfth, and thirteenth choruses in which out of twenty-eight measures

all but six are directly derived from the opening and (additionally) two further measures (which) are related to the four-bar section introducing Max's drum solo. Such structural cohesiveness—without sacrificing expressiveness and rhythmic drive or swing—one has come to expect from the composer who spends days or weeks writing a given passage. It is another matter to achieve this in an on-the-spur-of-the-moment improvisation.[14]

Schuller's analysis, penetrating and thorough as it is, fails to mention a crucial aspect of Rollins's method. A hint of the omission is couched in an amusing comment attributed to Rollins in the *Colossus* liner notes: "I really didn't understand what I was doing until I read Gunther Schuller. . . . This thing about the thematic approach, I guess it's true, but I had never thought about it; I was just playing it." But once he did begin to think about it, as he told writer Joe Goldberg in the early 1960's, the process became inhibited: "People said I did a certain thing, and I began to believe them, and by the time I figured out how I did it, I was unable to achieve the effect any more." [15] The reason for the interference, one may suspect, is that Rollins began to *plan* for motivic development, while his style of improvising demanded that it come about more naturally, in the course of blowing his horn.

For Rollins, playing the saxophone is a process of discovery, a probing of the melody for the themes essential to it; this is the point that is absent from Schuller's analysis. Rollins then is an incisive logician of musical structure who thinks with his horn, not with pen and paper beforehand (like a composer) or after the fact (like a critic). One can hear him turning phrases one way and another, upside down, and inside out, examining them from inner core to nuances. If thematic depth is reached and adhered to, as in "Blue Seven," the type of development Schuller observes will take place organically; if not, as in the first improvised chorus to Miles Davis's "Four" (on *More from the Vanguard*), the result is a certain amount of roaming and searching until Rollins finds what he is looking for, which he does in the second chorus. There are, of course, gradations in between, in so far as achievement is concerned: "Moritat" and "You Don't Know What Love Is" (*Colossus*), or "I've Got You Under My Skin" and "What Is This Thing Called Love?" (*Vanguard*) are all successful, though not the paragon that "Blue Seven" is. In Rollins's case, it must be added, the search itself is a pleasure to hear, for his ideas, even those he passes over and rejects, possess integrity and originality.

Sonny's well-known talent for transforming a potentially corny repertoire into intriguing jazz pieces reflects his ability to think deeply about commonplace harmonic and melodic content. Kurt Weill's "Moritat (Mack the Knife)" is a perfect example. However, on *Way Out West* he subjects "I'm an Old Cowhand" and "Wagon Wheels" to equally impressive transformations; and similarly to "How Are Things in Glocca Mora?" and "Surrey with the Fringe on Top" from Blue Note's important *Sonny Rollins* (1956–1957) reissue.

The relatively "straight" treatments of pieces like "Moritat" or "I've Got You Under My Skin" (*Colossus*) acquire their jazz character in part from Rollins's creative reorganization of rhythmic elements. His patterns display simplicity, strength, and assertiveness. When he fails to establish this definiteness, a rarity exemplified by "Softly, As in a Morning Sunrise," his interpretation is seriously weakened. (The same song is conceived much more forcefully on the earlier *A Night at the Village Vanguard*.) Rollins is masterful with Calypso feeling. His boyhood in New York was filled with these rhythms through the influence of his mother, who grew up in the Virgin Islands.

Colossus reveals that Rollins, unlike many of the hard-bop players, is as exciting on ballads as he is on up-tempo tunes. The momentum on "You Don't Know What Love Is" comes not only from the beat but from the tension he creates by anticipating or lagging behind the underlying harmonies. While this is true of the faster pieces as well, it is more evident at a slower tempo. The track also reveals the warmth and sensuality which characterize Rollins's intonation in its romantic moments.

More from the Vanguard is innovative on still another front. Its pianoless format anticipates the freer sytle of blowing heard in saxophonists like John Coltrane (Chapter 6) and Ornette Coleman (Chapter 8). Rollins is flying high on these tracks, searching out, discovering, and inventing lines of ingenious tensions and resolutions. The sense of freedom is exhilarating, and although the harmonic field is wide open, Rollins is rarely at a loss for direction.

Rollins is superb on three more albums with only bass and drums as accompaniment: Contemporary's *Way Out West*, which received wide critical acclaim at the time of its issue; Prestige's *Freedom Suite*, already described; and the first session from the Vanguard date, *A Night at the Village Vanguard*. While the first two albums were pianoless by design, the story behind the Vanguard sessions is simply that Rollins could not find a pianist he liked. "They all played too much," he complained. This assessment leads one to believe that the stark, open, and driving quality of the music was a primary goal. (Years later Rollins claimed the "busy-ness" of pianists was not a factor, that he simply desired to work with bass and drums alone.)

In 1959 at a new peak in his career, Rollins appeared headed for a showdown with the blossoming John Coltrane for the role of "King of the Tenors," a title they might well have shared to everyone's advantage. But it was not to be. Rollins dropped out of sight, disconnected his phone, and was rumored to be practicing late at night on the walkway of the Williamsburg Bridge in Brooklyn. Rollins had invoked another sabbatical, intending to rebuild his health with nutritional foods and exercise, and to study harmony, composition, and piano. He was indeed practicing on the bridge to avoid bothering his neighbors. His return to public playing in 1961 led to disappointment among some critics, who expected him to foray into the controversial, pianoless free jazz being explored by Ornette Coleman (Chapter 8), especially since Rollins had pioneered the territory years earlier. But Rollins was very much the same man, as demonstrated by his first album, aptly entitled *The Bridge*, which was recently reissued by RCA. A less satisfying album with several "Latin" tracks was cut shortly afterward (originally entitled *What's New*). It has been reissued as *Sonny Rollins: Pure Gold*. His most commercial format during these years was playing on the sound track to the movie *Alfie*.

By 1969 Rollins was gone again, this time to live on an *ashram* in India, where he hoped to find "a lot of esoteric secrets about life." He had returned by 1972, much the wiser for having concluded such secrets are not matters of geography. He has recorded for Milestone since that time, most frequently with electronic bass, keyboards, and guitar because "there is a lot of energy among the people who are now playing electric instruments." [16] *The Milestone Jazzstars*, an excellent collection from a 1978 live concert tour (with McCoy Tyner, Ron Carter, and Al Foster), is the noteworthy exception to the amplified bands. Although several of the later albums make good listening (General Discography), they do not compare to the perfect settings and inspired performances of the golden years from 1956 to 1959. Rollins sounds best, in fact, with minimal accompaniment. One can easily imagine him in glorious duos with bass or drums or piano. The high points of his nightclub performances in the 1970's have often been lengthy, unaccompanied tenor sax solos, a tactic he first employed in the 1960's to enliven club appearances. One must hope for at least an occasional return on record to simpler, more revealing formats of this sort.

THE DAVE BRUBECK QUARTET

Dave Brubeck's All-Time Greatest Hits

Columbia, PG-32761
two discs, good liner notes
1956–1965

Musicians: Dave Brubeck, piano; Paul Desmond, alto sax; Eugene Wright, bass; Joe Morello, drums. *On some tracks:* Norman Bates, bass, Joe Dodge, drums, or Joe Benjamin, bass.

Compositions: Side one: Take Five; Night and Day; I'm in a Dancing Mood; Castillian Drums; Camptown Races. *Side two:* St. Louis Blues; Unsquare Dance; Two Part

Contention. *Side three:* Trolley Song; It's a Raggy Waltz; My Favorite Things; Let's Get Away from It All; The Duke. *Side four:* Coracao Sensivel; Someday My Prince Will Come; Blue Rondo à la Turk.

FOR MANY YEARS the Dave Brubeck Quartet symbolized jazz to the crew-cut, V-neck-sweatered generation on American college campuses. Stylistically the group was exploring a cool, West Coast terrain of short-lived fertility. Yet its success within that genre was stunning, drawing the spotlight toward other musicians of more long-range consequence to the music's development. Brubeck's sound, and perhaps his appeal to the college audience, was based on a blend of European "classical" harmony and counterpoint with jazz rhythmic feeling and improvisation. In some cases this meant the rather obvious introduction of fugal elements, as on "Two-Part Contention," a wordplay on Bach's two-part *inventions*; while at other times, the classical strain consisted of a more subtle interplay between Brubeck's throaty, percussive piano and Desmond's lyrical, airy alto sax, as on the first improvised chorus of "Let's Get Away from It All." Brubeck was not the first to conceive of a classical/jazz hybrid; Claude Thornhill and Stan Kenton had experimented in the genre in their bands of the late 1940's. However, the quartet was the first small group to do so with phenomenal commercial success, a status that was confirmed when Brubeck made the cover of *Time* magazine in November 1954.

Dave Brubeck was born in 1920 in Concord, California. His mother and two brothers were musicians. (Later, his older brother Howard would compose "Dialogues for Jazz Combo and Symphony Orchestra," which the Brubeck quartet performed with the New York Philharmonic.) At four years old Brubeck began piano lessons with his mother, and by his early teens was playing with local Dixieland groups. In college he began more serious studies in composition (to be discussed ahead) and worked with talented local musicians like Cal Tjader, a drummer who later found his identity on vibes (with George Shearing in 1953), and the alto saxophonist Paul Desmond, then a literature student at San Francisco State College.

Paul Desmond's light, clear tone became the quartet's trademark. It is derivative of Lester Young's sound on tenor sax and the alto work of Lennie Tristano's early 1950's disciple Lee Konitz. Konitz is a more artful player than Desmond, and his albums (General Discography) demonstrate a cool alto sax with a sound closer to the roots of jazz. At his best ("Let's Get Away from It All"), Desmond weaves a thread of relaxed, confident lyricism around the more hard-edged sounds of Brubeck and Joe Morello.

The Brubeck quartet began recording for Berkeley's Fantasy Records in 1949, remaining there until 1954, when their growing popularity brought them to the attention of Columbia. Brubeck's early success was due at least in part to a creative booking policy which reached an untapped college audience. Although colleges became quite sophisticated in their tastes during the mid-1970's, they had experienced little beyond the Dixieland revival and a few swing (dance) bands during the early 1950's. The majority of America's white, middle-class collegians were hardly prepared for Minton's, Fifty-second Street, or the meaning of bebop. Thus Brubeck signified modernity in jazz to them. *Jazz Goes to College* (with drummer Joe Dodge) became their first success. (This album and other college dates are reissued on *Brubeck on Campus*, which includes the best of these performances from 1954 to 1957, and on *The Art of Dave Brubeck* and *The Fantasy Years*.)

The quartet's highest achievements were reached after 1956, when the nearly blind, brilliant drummer Joe Morello, who had previously been working with Stan Kenton and pianist Marian McPartland, was hired by Brubeck. The best of their studio sessions have been collected on *All-Time Greatest Hits*, Brubeck's essential album.

The group's achievements are often based upon excursions into odd time signatures, such as Desmond's "Take Five" ($\frac{5}{4}$), "Blue Rondo à la Turk" ($\frac{9}{8}$), and "Unsquare Dance" ($\frac{7}{4}$). (An edited single of "Take Five"/ "Blue Rondo à la Turk," the brainchild of CBS Records president Goddard Lieberson, was the first jazz instrumental to sell a million copies.) Many of the tracks on this collection come from the earlier *Time In, Time Out*, and *Time Further Out* albums. *Adventures in Time* reissues most of the odd-time tracks. These pieces succeed because of an inner tension between the unusual rigid rhythms juxtaposed with the loosely swinging solos. There is no denying that the alternation of $\frac{4}{4}$ improvisations on "Blue Rondo" with the neatly arranged sections in $\frac{9}{8}$ offers a pleasurable sense of release.

Joe Morello elevates "Take Five" above the gimmick-and-novelty genre by spreading an ingeniously accented solo across bar lines, which generates an intriguing cross-rhythm against Brubeck's steady 'comping. "Night and Day" demonstrates the engaging dialogue he could maintain with the piano while remaining properly in the background. Morello is a muscular drummer, neither melodic nor fiery like Roach or Blakey but thrillingly precise. He and Gene Wright, a dependable bassist, provide the drive which Brubeck and Desmond frequently need.

Brubeck's piano playing has received frequent criticism for its heavy-handedness. His style does rely on "block" chords, thick with color tones played in the middle-to-lower register. At best, they are used to exciting rhythmic effect, as on "I'm in a Dancing Mood" or "Let's Get Away from It All." Much of Brubeck's harmonic influence came from the modern European classics, a tradition he studied sporadically between 1946 and 1951 with Darius Milhaud. (Milhaud, however, encouraged Brubeck's interest in jazz.)

Brubeck also had two rather revealing lessons with the composer Arnold Schoenberg, who proved none too amicable toward the practical approach of jazz. "At the second one (lesson) I brought him a piece of music I'd written," Brubeck reported,

> He said, "That's very good. Now go home and don't write any-thing like that again until you know why everything is there. Do you know now?" he asked. I said, "Isn't it reason enough if it sounds good?"

He said, "No, you have to know why." That was my last lesson with Schoenberg.[17]

Brubeck seems the most at ease with his own piece "The Duke," written for Ellington and performed at the Newport Jazz Festival (originally on *Newport Festival, 1958*). His solo is crisply executed and melodically interesting; there is also a satisfying balance between single-note melody and chording, plus a sense of building force. Such complete solos did not occur often.

During the early 1960's, the quartet began to travel extensively, subsequently releasing a series of "local color" albums, such as *Brandenburg Gate Revisited, Jazz Impressions of Japan*, and *Jazz Impressions of New York*. Unfortunately, the best of the series, *Jazz Impressions of Eurasia* (CL 1251), has been deleted from Columbia's catalog.

Brubeck seemed to know precisely what he was after from the outset of his recording career. Even before the quartet days, he organized an octet which recorded its only album (no longer available) for Fantasy in 1950. The group consisted of Desmond, Cal Tjader, and five musicians who were then students of Milhaud. According to Desmond, quoted on the liner notes, the music aspired to "the vigor and force of simple jazz, the harmonic complexities of Bartók and Milhaud, the form (and much of the dignity) of Bach, and at times the lyrical romanticism of Rachmaninoff." Not surprisingly this grandiose synthesis was far from realized, but Brubeck never gave up his attempts to achieve it. (See General Discography for albums by Brubeck and his children, and in a duo with Paul Desmond. The Fantasy octet music is scheduled for reissue as *Early Fantasies* by Book-of-the-Month Club Records.)

THE MODERN JAZZ QUARTET   Atlantic, SD 2-603
                                      two discs, liner notes
European Concert   1960

Musicians: John Lewis, piano; Milt Jackson, vibes; Percy Heath, bass; Connie Kay,
    drums.
Compositions: Side one: Django; Bluesology; I Should Care; La Ronde. *Side two:* I Re-
    member Clifford; Festival Sketch; Vendome; Odds Against Tomorrow. *Side three:*
    Pyramid; It Don't Mean a Thing (If It Ain't Got That Swing); Skating in Central
    Park. *Side four:* The Cylinder; 'Round Midnight; Bags' Groove; I'll Remember April.

THE MODERN JAZZ QUARTET was virtually a style unto itself. When it disbanded in 1974, after twenty-four years together, *Down Beat* magazine aptly
likened the group's demise to "the abrupt disintegration of Mt. Rushmore."
The MJQ exemplified a synthesis of the European classical approach with
jazz feeling and improvisation. Although the West Coast and "progressive"
bands of Brubeck and Kenton aspired to a similar goal, the MJQ was much
stronger in blues feeling and, consequently, closer to the heart of jazz.

The MJQ evolved out of Dizzy Gillespie's big band of the late 1940's.
John Lewis, who also served as Gillespie's arranger, and Milt Jackson,
backed by Ray Brown on bass and Kenny Clarke on drums, formed a small
performing unit, or mini-band, which was designed to give periodic respites
to the tired members of Dizzy's brass section. Later, with Percy Heath on
bass the group recorded as the Milt Jackson Quartet for Dizzy's label, Dee
Gee (now on Savoy's *The First Q*). John Lewis began to apply the classical
tradition he had mastered at New York's Manhattan School of Music to
bebop, a musical synthesis for which Lewis's background uniquely qualified
him. Subsequent to his classical training and arranging for Gillespie, he recorded with Charlie Parker on the famous take of "Parker's Mood" (Selected
Discography) and with Miles Davis on the influential *Birth of the Cool*
sessions. In short, he had been immersed deeply in every movement of consequence to modern jazz.

Within a few years the group had found its personnel and its niche. Kenny

Clarke, unhappy with Lewis's restrictions on his style of drumming, dropped out in 1955 and moved to Paris. Lewis hired and coached the young Connie Kay, who had been working for Lester Young, and the MJQ assumed its permanent form. Then Bob Weinstock, owner of Prestige, preferring the hard-bop swinging of Milt Jackson, decided to withdraw his support for Lewis's jazz/classicism. Weinstock, in fact, recorded the MJQ, with the earthier Horace Silver replacing Lewis, on a session reissued as *Opus de Funk.* But the band was not without a home for long. They were offered a trial contract by Atlantic Records, where, with the exception of a few albums, they remained for two decades.

European Concert, recorded live in Stockholm, Sweden, in 1960, has long been considered the band's "perfect" album for its ideal balance between structure and self-expression, its consistently creative soloing, and its fine versions of the best MJQ originals. The quartet's members demonstrate an uncanny ability to fuse their individuality into a single voice. Writing for *The New Yorker* magazine, Whitney Balliett provided an evocative description of their unmistakable sound: "The Quartet . . . is tintinnabulous. It shimmers, it sings, it hums. It is airy and clean. Like any great mechanism, its parts are as notable as their sum."

John Lewis inaugurated uniform dress by insisting on tuxedos and an orderly presentation on stage, giving the MJQ the dignity (and, some say, the pomp) of classical masters. The group would arrange itself in a semicircle, bow in unison, and bend over their instruments, as Balliett put it, "like jewelers intently at their work." The group's demeanor projected the seriousness which Lewis felt the music warranted. However, Miles Davis was a bit skeptical of the formality and aloofness: "I don't go with this bringing 'dignity' to jazz. . . . The way they bring 'dignity' to jazz in their formal clothes and the way they bow is like Ray Robinson bringing dignity to boxing by fighting in a tuxedo." [18] Ultimately audiences did accept the MJQ's music in the spirit of its presentation, and it became rare for the group to perform other than in a large concert hall.

Lewis's basic idea was to strengthen his music by planning its structure. Thus he introduced contrapuntal melodies into the band's arrangements. Noting that improvisation was not unique to jazz, he told Nat Hentoff:

> What makes jazz unique is that it is *collective* improvisation that swings . . . except for the best Dixieland people and a few others, there is often a rhythmic dullness beneath the improvisation. Yet the bass, drums, and piano should, and can, do more than simply supply chords and a basic pulsation.[19]

Consequently, the MJQ developed a sound of strong fiber in which not only the sonorities but the melodic lines of piano and vibes were frequently interwoven. This can be heard in sublime form on "Django," a dirge for gypsy guitarist Django Reinhardt and possibly Lewis's best composition.

Counterpoint is also essential to "Bags' Groove," "Vendome," "The Cylinder," "Odds Against Tomorrow," and "Festival Sketch." "Bags' Groove" contains an equivalence of the piano and vibraharp voices in the opening chorus which achieves an effect similar to the collective sound of a New Orleans group.

If John Lewis was the quartet's chief designer, Milt Jackson was certainly its showpiece. In fact, most criticisms of the group's stilted early years amounted to the suggestion "Let Milt blow." His sense of swing is unflagging at any tempo. He proved as much in the late 1940's on piano with Navarro (*Prime Source*) and on vibes with Monk (*The Complete Genius*). On vibes he has lyricism, boundless energy, and a warm, glowing sound, which is achieved by slowing down the instrument's motorized fans and, hence, deepening its tremolo. Although he does not achieve great tonal variety, the sheer momentum of his lines keeps the listener involved in the development of every phrase.

Milt Jackson, a spontaneous player and personality, is "emotionally contrapuntal" to the austere, restrained Lewis. Their complementary natures contributed to the wide range of moods the MJQ could achieve. Jackson ultimately precipitated the group's disbanding in a dramatic protest against the economics of jazz. He believed the MJQ's income should equal that of the popular rock groups and entertainers, an unrealistic point of view not shared by his colleagues. Insisting that he could earn more without the group, Jackson began to record for CTI and Pablo, and to tour on his own. He did *not* quit the MJQ after all those years, as some critics speculated, because of Lewis's disciplined musical approach.

Despite Lewis's conservative image, his discipline seldom inhibited his ability to swing. His crisply articulated, single-note lines achieve a subtle profundity, as in the exciting treatment of " 'Round Midnight." He takes powerfully emotional solos on "I Should Care" and "I Remember Clifford." At times, Lewis's left hand is barely audible, leaving the impression that his music lacks "bottom." Thus when he does plunge into the piano's register, as at the end of the improvisation on "Festival Sketch," the shock waves are felt keenly. Finally, Lewis's blues frequently match Milt's for soul, even surpassing it on "Bags' Groove."

The contributions of Connie Kay and Percy Heath, though less conspicuous, can hardly be ignored. Kay's sensitive drumming, which emphasizes subtle shading and a gentle sense of swing, is ideal for the MJQ's fragile crystalline sound. Yet he can be more forceful when necessary, eliciting a vibrant, shimmering splash from the ride (top) cymbal, as in "The Cylinder." Heath is the quartet's strong man, for he must provide a continual pulse and the harmonic bottom that Lewis generally avoids. His contribution to the band's drive is readily apparent on "Bags' Groove." "I'll Remember April," with its customary Afro-Cuban choruses, features both Kay and Heath in prominent roles.

While the overall quality of the MJQ's recorded work is dependable, there are relatively few superior albums. *The Art of the Modern Jazz Quartet* offers an excellent sampler of the years from 1957 through 1966, including three cuts from *European Concert*. *Pyramid* and *Fontessa* are albums of enduring beauty and the closest in feeling to *European Concert*, although they were recorded several years earlier. Prestige's *Modern Jazz Quartet* is the best collection of the group's formative years, an album for the listener with a historical interest in the band. *Third Stream Music* is also available; however, *European Windows*, recorded with the Stuttgart Orchestra, has been deleted from RCA's catalog.

Lewis has frankly admitted that the MJQ's earliest recordings of fugues like "Vendome" felt unnatural, for it took the band some years to feel at home in the genre they created. However, the degree of freedom they achieved continually increased, reaching a peak in *Last Concert* (1975), taped in performance in New York a year after the group disbanded. The performance is a "blowing session" compared with their previous degree of planning. Superb fidelity conveys the quartet's "shimmering tintinnabulations" especially well and provides an appropriately gorgeous final documentation of the MJQ's unique sound.

MILES DAVIS

'Round About Midnight

Columbia, CL 949/PC 8649
one disc, brief liner notes
1956

Musicians: Miles Davis, trumpet; John Coltrane, tenor sax; Red Garland, piano; Paul Chambers, bass; Philly Joe Jones, drums.
Compositions: Side one: 'Round Midnight; Ah-Leu-Cha; All of You. *Side two:* Bye Bye Blackbird; Tadd's Delight; Dear Old Stockholm.

Porgy and Bess

Columbia, KCS 8085
one disc, liner notes
1958

Musicians: Miles Davis, trumpet, flugelhorn; Louis Mucci, Ernie Royal, John Coles, Bernie Glow, trumpets; Jimmy Cleveland, Joseph Bennett, Dick Hixon, Frank Rehak, trombones; Cannonball Adderley, Danny Banks, saxes; Willie Ruff, Julius Watkins, Gunther Schuller, French horns; Phil Bodner, Romeo Penque, flutes; John Barber, tuba; Paul Chambers, bass; Philly Joe Jones, drums.
Compositions (compositions by George Gershwin; arrangements by Gil Evans): *Side one:* The Buzzard Song; Bess, You Is My Woman Now; Gone, Gone, Gone, Gone; Summertime; Bess, Oh Where's My Bess? *Side two:* Prayer (Oh Doctor Jesus); Fisherman, Strawberry and Devil Crab; My Man's Gone Now; It Ain't Necessarily So; Here Come de Honey Man; I Loves You, Porgy; There's a Boat That's Leaving Soon for New York.

Milestones

Columbia, CL 1193/PC 9428
one disc, brief liner notes
1958

Musicians: Miles Davis, trumpet; John Coltrane, tenor sax; Cannonball Adderley, alto sax; Red Garland, piano; Paul Chambers, bass; Philly Joe Jones, drums.
Compositions: Side one: Dr. Jekyll; Sid's Ahead; Two Bass Hit. *Side two:* Milestones; Billy Boy; Straight, No Chaser.

MILES DAVIS IS ONE of the great stylists. More than any other improviser, he has dominated jazz not with blowing power or prodigious technique but with style alone. His best playing is lyrical, lean, intense, and sometimes mystical. The fact that Miles plays almost exclusively in the middle register of his horn and cannot by his own admission hear well in the higher register has not diminished his range of expression. Miles's magnetism derives from his unique emotional stance, a detached sensitivity which elicits from his audience a fascination with the man as much as with his music. Davis emerged from the highest echelons of classic bebop, defined the standards of "cool" jazz, influenced the development of modal improvising (Chapter 6), and inaugurated the "fusion" style of the 1970's (Chapter 7).

The influential music Miles recorded from 1947 to 1958, the period covered by this discussion, proved it was unnecessary to emulate the technical acrobatics of a Dizzy Gillespie to play the trumpet effectively. As writer Joe Goldberg 'put it, "Miles made virtuosity irrelevant." During this period Davis led the most distinguished modern jazz soloists in a historic group that achieved its highest expression on side two of *Milestones*. At the same time, he and arranger Gil Evans created a genre of richly textured "orchestral" jazz—exemplified by *Porgy and Bess*—which communicated with the directness of a small group.

Miles Dewey Davis III was born in 1926 and grew up in St. Louis, where his father was a successful dentist and well-to-do property owner. After the family moved to a predominantly white neighborhood, Miles endured numerous incidents of racism, which helps to explain the bitterness towards white society he has often expressed. He received a trumpet from his father at the age of thirteen, joined the school band, and studied privately. Clark Terry, who was an important local trumpeter in those days, was his first influence. Miles was playing in a band called the Blue Devils when he was noticed by alto saxophonist Sonny Stitt, who recommended him to Tiny Bradshaw, a traveling bandleader. Miles received his first job offer from Bradshaw, but had to turn it down because his mother insisted that he finish high school.

Davis graduated in 1944, shortly before Billy Eckstine's great prebop band came to town featuring both Dizzy Gillespie and Charlie Parker. Knowing some of their music, Miles came down to the hall early, trumpet in hand, hoping for a chance to show what he could do. He was allowed to sit in, but impressed no one, being clearly deficient in technique and harmonic knowledge. Allegedly Gillespie advised him to learn the piano to improve his understanding of chords. As it turned out, Miles worked with Eckstine's band briefly two years later when one of the trumpeters fell ill.

In 1945 Miles's father sent him to the Juilliard School of Music in New York. This was a crucial year in Miles's development for reasons having nothing to do with his course of study at Juilliard, in which he lost interest very quickly. First, he met the soulful trumpeter Freddie Webster, who profoundly influenced Miles's tone before he died in 1947 at the age of thirty. Even more important, Miles abandoned his studies to track down Charlie Parker, soon sharing his apartment and shadowing him from one club to the next, writing down Bird's chord changes "on the covers of matchbooks." In the midst of this musical revelation, Miles also witnessed Parker's self-destructive habits. Davis recalls having to rescue him from "panics" and having to "put him to bed sometimes with the needle still in his arm and him bleeding all over the place." [20]

Parker chaperoned Miles's first trip to the recording studio in November 1945 for the well-known "Billie's Bounce," "Now's the Time," and Parker's *tour de force* "Ko Ko." For Miles these tunes served primarily to document his limitations, so severe on "Ko Ko" that he could not play the melody, forcing Gillespie to double on piano and trumpet. (See *Savoy Sessions*, Parker Selected Discography.) On "Yardbird Suite," "Ornithology," and "Moose the Mooche," which were recorded with Parker (*The Very Best of Bird*) the following March in Hollywood, Miles is more sure of himself, providing in his restraint an effective foil for Bird's searing tone. In 1947 Parker played tenor sax on Miles's first date as a leader and on subsequent 1947 sessions (contained in both albums mentioned above), in which his contribution as a melodic improviser became substantial.

Miles had learned to negotiate within his limited range. More important, his tone was acquiring its own identity, one of very fine, fragile beauty. Bob Weinstock, who produced many of Miles's Prestige albums in the early 1950's, analyzed his developing sound as a reaction to Parker's piercing alto: "Bird's savageness and deep fire and emotion . . . was overpowering Miles everytime (they) would play on the same stand; here was an outlet for Miles Davis to let out the sensitivity he had as a musician." [21]

Davis's sensitive, poignant tone became a rallying point for "cool jazz" in 1949, when Parker deserted the quintet format temporarily to record with strings for Norman Granz. Miles had been discussing with several musicians, the arranger Gil Evans among them, creating a tonally rich, well-ordered ensemble sound modeled after that of the Claude Thornhill band, which had experimented during the 1940's with arrangements for French horns and tuba. Some of the other musicians in this clique were Gerry Mulligan, Lee Konitz, Stan Getz, pianist John Lewis, and the arranger Johnny Carisi. Gil Evans's one-room apartment in New York was the site of these meetings. The result was a nonet, a band of nine players, which recorded the legendary "Birth of the Cool" sessions for Capitol, now available on *The Complete Birth of the Cool*.

The influence of the *Cool* sessions far exceeded their musical quality. Miles's vibrato-less, deliberate tone was their focal point, and the music's complex texture, when contrasted with the simple, near-unison horn playing of the quintets of the 1940's, was the source of their uniqueness. There was little soloing of consequence, and only a few pieces, like "Boplicity" and "Israel," are of lasting merit. In addition to giving impetus to the cool and West Coast styles of jazz which blossomed during the 1950's, the Miles Davis-Gil Evans association was important because it led to future collaborations in meticulously planned large-ensemble settings like *Miles Ahead* (1957), with a nineteen-piece band; *Porgy and Bess* (1958), a taut, sensitive, and elegant collage of arrangements (to be discussed ahead); and *Sketches of Spain* (1959), a coolly romantic excursion into Spanish music, which became Miles's most popular album of the 1960's.

Miles played the Paris jazz festival in 1949 shortly after the *Cool* sessions, recording—in poor fidelity—wtih Tadd Dameron (on Columbia's *The Miles Davis/Tadd Dameron Quintet*). More significantly, he acquired a heroin habit shortly afterward, a vice so common among jazz musicians during the 1940's that it was almost to be expected. By 1953 Miles had kicked the habit by going "cold turkey," but there had been little important playing or recording in the interim.

During the next five years, Miles made his first major contribution to jazz with a series of small groups which, along with Art Blakey's Jazz Messengers and Horace Silver's quintet, defined the hard-bop style. There were two striking innovations in Miles's style, which had become distinguishable almost from the playing of the first note. One was his ability to create tension by understatement, a quality he had particularly liked in the piano playing of Ahmad Jamal (General Discography), a quiet but powerful stylist. As noted earlier, this tact was essential because Miles was in no position to compete in the technical arena with men like Dizzy Gillespie, Fats Navarro, and Clifford Brown. Second, Miles became a marvelously effective ballad player, capable of transforming ditties like "Bye Bye Blackbird" (on *'Round Midnight*) into a bed of hot, glowing embers.

Prior to the Columbia recordings, however, Miles began to develop his combo in some memorable recordings for Prestige. The "Walkin' "/"Blue 'n Boogie" session of 1954 has been credited by critic Ralph J. Gleason with "calling all the children home" from the cool West Coast to toe-tappin', finger-poppin' New York. These sessions, reissued on *Tune Up*, show that Miles was digging in rhythmically, lagging a split second behind the beat to increase the band's swing and even double-timing with confidence. The "walkin' " bass set the music's pulse.

Tune Up is an important reissue historically; it matches Miles with various impressive players, like pianists Horace Silver (on "Walkin' "), John Lewis, and Thelonious Monk. The Lewis session includes the earliest recording of one of Miles's best compositions, "Four." Davis's colleagues, however, were not the ones he needed, and the music shows it. In the case of Monk, as a matter of fact, the result was a distinct animosity. Miles felt Monk was not supporting him sufficiently and told him not to play during the trumpet solos, a request Monk obliged by leaving the studio while Miles played. Their collaboration ended with that session.

By the end of 1955, Miles had formed a quintet of musicians who were among the finest soloists of the 1950's and who were, at the same time, so complementary in approach that they could record nothing short of superb jazz. John Coltrane's torrential outpouring of sixteenth notes balanced Miles's quiet, spare strength. Philly Joe Jones was exquisite in his placement of accents and excitingly aggressive; the twenty-year-old Paul Chambers played with astounding maturity in his plucked and bowed solos; Red Garland excelled in his percussive 'comping and lyrical, Bud Powell-style right-hand lines. Interestingly, Miles spent the early months defending Coltrane and Jones, who were frequently criticized for being "too loud."

A stunning performance by this group at the Newport Jazz Festival led to an offer from Columbia Records, with which Miles has remained ever since. Before leaving Prestige, however, contractual obligations had to be fulfilled and four quick albums were recorded without a single retake: *Cookin'*, *Workin'*, *Steamin'*, and *Relaxin'*. "Cookin' " and "relaxin' " are words that describe these sessions perfectly. Miles reaches an artistic peak in his classic treatments of "My Funny Valentine," "If I Were a Bell," and "When I Fall in Love." The albums are available on two reissue sets: *Miles Davis* and *Workin' and Steamin'*, representing the earliest examples of much beautiful music by Davis, Coltrane, Garland, Chambers, and Jones.

The spontaneity with which the final Prestige sides were cut was typical of Miles's approach with the quintet and, later, the sextet—quite the opposite of his well-considered planning with Gil Evans for the orchestral *Miles Ahead*, *Porgy and Bess*, and *Sketches of Spain*. Philly Joe Jones recalled that when he once asked Miles to run over the tunes, Davis replied: *"Rehearse? I can hear you play at the gig!"* Jones said, "We rehearsed on the stand. If he liked what someone played, he'd say 'Play that way tomorrow night.' Miles called it arrangements while you wait." [22] The young alto sax player from Florida, Cannonball Adderley, who joined for some of the Columbia sessions from 1957 to 1959, estimates there were no more than five rehearsals in the two years he was affiliated with the band.

> And the rehearsals were quite direct, like "Coltrane, show Cannonball how you do this. All right. Now, let's do it." Occasionally Miles would tell us something on the stand. "Cannonball, you don't have to play *all* those notes. Just stay close to the sound of the melody. Those substitute chords sound funny." [23]

The special quality of *'Round About Midnight*, which was recorded before Miles invited Adderley into the group, is its intense treatment of ballads like "Bye Bye Blackbird" and Monk's haunting " 'Round Midnight." The first thing to notice is Miles's delicate, yet electrifying sound, achieved by using a Harmon mute with the bell of the trumpet held inches from the microphone. The same effect predominates on the ballads in *Porgy and Bess*: a great volume of emotion condensed within a still, small voice. Miles's way with a ballad calls to mind James Baldwin's description of him as a "miraculously tough and tender man." His sound is strong and unyielding but warm and human.

Miles's ballads also depend upon a terseness and an economy of notes. Superfluous frills and flourishes could only diminish the intensity. One can almost feel his deliberateness as each sound his horn emits receives full consideration. Thus an element of *un*played emotion is smoldering beneath the surface calm of his lines. Miles's lyricism asserts itself equally on ballads and up-tempo tracks. Like Louis Armstrong and Billie Holiday, he effortlessly recomposes melodies, occasionally elevating popular songs to artistic creations as on "Blackbird" or "Summertime" from *Porgy and Bess*.

For all the quiet beauty of *Midnight*, the playing on *Milestones* reaches an unparalleled level of spirit and inspiration. First, Miles's virtuosity, judging by the fleet phrases of "Dr. Jekyll," has never been more adequate—not that it is impeccable, as illustrated by the fractured tone one hears in the twenty-eighth measure of his solo. His lyricism borders on the abstract in his composition "Sid's Ahead," essentially a blues, and in the magnetically attractive solo on his "Milestones." "Milestones" is also this band's first venture into the innovative concept of "modal" playing—basically, improvising on scale patterns instead of chord changes (Chapter 6). Miles's solo on this piece is framed by Adderley's high melodicism on alto sax, revealing the fluidity of expression inspired by Charlie Parker and Cannonball's potential to transcend the "funkiness" characteristic of his later work, and by Coltrane's incantatory tone on tenor sax, taking on the first stage of its spiritual intensity. The rhythm section drives like a lightweight piston beneath it all, uniting this succession of solos into an unforgettable piece of improvised music.

Miles's rhythm section is, in fact, a band unto itself, as is demonstrated by "Billy Boy," featuring the quintessence of Red Garland's power-block chords matched by his equally commanding lyricism in the right hand. Brilliant solos are turned in by Paul Chambers (playing arco, or bowed bass) and by Philly Joe Jones. It is a tribute to Davis's egoless good judgment that he allowed this lengthy trio track on *his* date.

Four months after the *Milestones* session, Miles went into the studio with a seventeen-piece ensemble to breathe new life into the Gershwin chestnut *Porgy and Bess*. The advances over the *Birth of the Cool* session, which had initiated these endeavors, and even *Miles Ahead*, which was essentially a big-band record, were notable. The integration of the orchestra and soloist was completely successful, and the emotional tone of tenderness is maintained throughout. The horn sections have an Ellingtonian vocal quality to them, especially on "Prayer," answering Miles's trumpet directly, as on "Bess, You Is My Woman Now." Miles's use of the mute once again is electrifying, and he also experiments with the deeper-toned flugelhorn, pitched to the lower trumpet range where he hears so well.

It is the rhythmic achievement of *Porgy and Bess* which qualifies it as the foremost Davis-Evans collaboration, preferable even to the more popular *Sketches of Spain*, an admittedly beautiful tapestry dominated by the "Concierto de Aranjuez." *Spain*'s beauty is rhythmically static, while *Porgy* maintains the sauntering hard-bop "walk"—as on "The Buzzard Song," "Gone," "It Ain't Necessarily So," and the brilliant "Summertime"—which is crucial to the jazz of the period. The presence of Chambers and Philly Joe Jones are very much felt in this music. (These observations, of course, are not criticisms of *Sketches of Spain,* which succeeds remarkably on its own terms, but rather reasons for highlighting *Porgy and Bess.*)

Miles Davis's contributions to jazz did not end in 1958, although the music he had recorded by that year was sufficient to secure him a prominent role in its development. The modal (scalar) thinking inherent in "Mile- stones" would soon lead to another major innovative album, *Kind of Blue* (Chapter 6). Then the maturation of John Coltrane, who would leave to form his own quartet in 1959, forced Miles to tap a younger generation of musi- cians, forming a second quintet no less brilliant than the first. The albums of Davis's second great quintet will also be discussed in the next chapter.

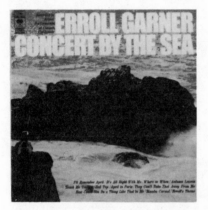

ERROLL GARNER

Concert by the Sea

Columbia, CS 9821
one disc, brief liner notes
1956

Musicians: Erroll Garner, piano; Eddie Calhoun, bass; Denzil Best, drums.
Compositions: Side one: I'll Remember April; Teach Me Tonight; Mambo Carmel;
   Autumn Leaves; It's All Right with Me. *Side two:* Red Top; April in Paris; They
   Can't Take That Away from Me; How Could You Do a Thing Like That to Me?;
   Where or When; Erroll's Theme.

Concert by the Sea may well be the steadiest selling jazz album in history. It has never been out of print, nor even reissued as part of a larger set in nearly twenty-five years. This is not due to any commercial gimmickery. Commercial intent in jazz (that is, recording designed for AM radio airplay) may lead to large-volume, quick killings, but never to steady sales over the years. This album endures because it captures in peak form Garner's effervescent nature and his whimsical imagination, which was in top form on this night in Carmel, California. Garner's imagination rarely failed him, though; he was a virtual cornucopia of melodic variation. In a typical studio session he would tape a dozen first takes, hardly pausing between songs—a facility which enlarged his discography perhaps beyond its due. Critic Whitney Balliett made the startling claim that Garner's solo records alone numbered (by 1959) "between five hundred and a thousand for well over seventy labels, some of which, it is said, stay in existence by simply pirating his records back and forth." [24] In any case, of the two dozen or so available LP's, none attain the consistently creative level of *Concert by the Sea*.

Garner has two basic modes of playing which he can vary with startling rapidity. One is a lush romanticism ("Autumn Leaves," "April in Paris") in which tremolo chords which sometimes seem to be "trembling with emotion" dissolve into runs and arpeggios which cascade over the keyboard like waterfalls. These will suddenly give way, as they do in the above songs, to a delicately "strummed" left-hand chord, occurring regularly on every beat, and a tinkling right-hand improvisation, played between the beats.

The heart and soul of his style, however, lies with the uniquely syncopated jump, or bounce, which characterizes the other tracks. On "Where or When," the album's *tour de force*, and "It's All Right with Me" there seem to be two pianists at work, so disjointed are the left and right hands. A powerful cross-rhythm results from the right hand playing the song a half to a full beat behind the left. Clearly ragtime, especially of the Harlem variety, is in Garner's past. It is as if he were playing a "stride" left hand but without hitting the customary single note in the bass register. Instead, a regular pattern of strummed chords is heard in the middle register. Yet there is a hint of the march-like left hand of classic ragtime in the introduction to "It's All Right with Me" and "How Could You Do a Thing Like That to Me?" It is not surprising to learn that Garner sat by the hour listening to Luckey Roberts (Chapter 2) in Roberts's Rendezvous Club. Garner worked there, too, after moving to New York in 1944.

Garner was born in Pittsburgh in 1921, the son of a pianist. He never studied music but learned from schoolmates like Dodo Marmarosa, also a pianist, and early colleagues like Billy Strayhorn. He admired Art Tatum and Teddy Wilson but his style was derivative of bebop, especially in the right hand with its multiplicity of notes, presupposing numerous substitution chords and spilling across bar lines. In 1946 Garner served Charlie Parker admirably as an accompanist on the Dial sessions discussed earlier in this chapter. Yet Garner departs from the bop image in a crucial respect: He would never let go of a song's original melody. As he put it quite cogently, "I like to play certain tunes because of their melody. Why should I disguise that melody?" [25]

Garner's idiosyncratic sound does not mean he should be placed on the periphery of the Afro-American heritage. On the contrary, he exemplifies this heritage profoundly in numerous ways. He is a self-taught musician and uses the piano solely for personal expression, never for the interpretive playing of fully notated music. His playing is a caldron of polyrhythms, blue notes, blued chords, and call-and-response dynamics. His "Where or When" illustrates many of these strengths to a high degree, and the thirty-two-bar passage preceding "Where or When" is a composition unto itself, the type of spon-

taneous introductory passage Garner was known for. The melody is played
in a rocking jump which gathers terrific momentum from Garner's polyrhythmic sharpness.

Garner's thirty-year recording career ended with his death in 1977. Surprisingly he had never learned to read music, a fact verified by several colleagues. His beautiful ballad "Misty" (1958), which became one of the
most popular songs of the 1960's, had to be transcribed from his piano playing by others.

**THE CANNONBALL ADDERLEY
QUINTET**

Coast to Coast

Milestone, M-4703
two discs, liner notes
1959, 1962

Musicians: Julian "Cannonball" Adderley, alto sax; Nat Adderley, cornet; Bobby Tim-
   mons, piano; Sam Jones, bass; Louis Hayes, drums. On sides three and four: Josef
   Zawinul, piano; Yusef Lateef, tenor sax and oboe.
Compositions: Side one: This Here; Spontaneous Combustion. *Side two:* Hi-Fly; Straight,
   No Chaser; You Got It. *Side three:* (Introduction by Cannonball) Gemini; Planet
   Earth. *Side four:* Dizzy's Business; Syn-Anthesia; Scotch and Water; Cannon's
   Theme.

THE CANNONBALL ADDERLEY QUINTET, which recorded between 1959 and
Julian's death in 1975, epitomizes the earthy, bluesy, and soulful nature of
the hard bop genre. Cannonball on alto sax and his brother Nat on cornet
attack a melody in unison with the precision of expert swordsmen. The fire
of the rhythm section on these live dates galvanizes the group into producing
a powerful sound greater than their size. Ensemble passages, as on the
"Spontaneous Combustion" and "Gemini" tracks, never fail to raise the
music's level of excitement, but Adderley's band also allows the individual
soloist ample freedom of expression.

The original issue of sides one and two, recorded at the Jazz Workshop in
San Francisco, was one of the earliest successful live albums. Cannonball persuaded the struggling Riverside label to come out from New York to record
on the West Coast, where Timmons's blues waltz "This Here" was eliciting
a wild response night after night. (The year before, Timmons had an equally

big hit for Art Blakey's Jazz Messengers with "Moanin'," a blues which also reveals the heavy influence of black church music. See *Moanin'*, Blakey, General Discography.) The live session, however, was a last resort for producer Orrin Keepnews who, having promised to record Adderley on request, discovered that there were no acceptable sound studios in San Francisco. Although recordings of club dates were by no means innovative in those years, neither were they of predictable quality. This one exceeded all expectations. The original *Quintet in San Francisco* LP sold ten thousand copies on word-of-mouth enthusiasm within a month of its issue, and it made the band's reputation.

Cannonball's showmanship is clearly a great asset to the live format. His introduction to "This Here" is historically informative, while the monologue on "hipness" which precedes "Gemini," if sarcastic, is also charming. In a decade when most jazz musicians assumed an aloof posture, Adderley, the relaxed and unaffected *bon vivant*, was a refreshing change. He had also been a music teacher in Tallahassee, Florida, for six years prior to his arrival in New York, and was an able spokesman for jazz. In short, his outgoing manner kept the audience in tow even between pieces.

Adderley's alto style is clearly derivative of Charlie Parker's, although Cannonball often expressed his indebtedness to Benny Carter. Born in 1928 into a musical family, he studied most of the brass and reed instruments. He had his own band from 1948 to 1950, played in an army band from 1950 to 1952, and studied at the U.S. Naval School of Music during 1953. After moving to New York and sitting in with Oscar Pettiford's band at the Bohemia in 1955, he was proclaimed "the new Bird" for his similarity to Parker, a reputation which led to his earliest sessions for EmArcy, available on *The Beginnings*.

While Adderley does not have Bird's speed, he does possess the same fluidity and vocalized style, as demonstrated on the "Hi-Fly" solo in which he nearly talks and sings through the horn. Yet his tone is warmer than Bird's and certainly less piercing and agonized; by contrast, he is joyful and optimistic. Adderley's deepest commitment is to the blues, but in a more down-home and earthy form than in the classic bebop discography. There are times during "Hi-Fly" when his sax takes on the soulful intonation of a blues harmonica.

Adderley's solos on "This Here" and "Spontaneous Combustion" are good examples of his strengths and limitations. He communicates the blues with direct phrasing, as if telling a story on his horn. Yet the harmonic underpinnings do not challenge him to reach beyond the blues tonality. For this reason it is often held that his best playing is heard in the Miles Davis sextet that included John Coltrane (*Milestones* and *Kind of Blue*, Chapters 5 and 6). Adderley was invited to join the Davis group while he was playing opposite Miles at the Bohemia during 1957. He had been prepared to join Gillespie's band when Miles casually asked, "Why not join my band?" "You never asked me," Cannonball reportedly replied. Adderley later admitted that from 1957 to 1959 his playing in that band was affected by Trane's brilliant use of chord progressions. Nevertheless, the tracks on *Coast to Coast* cannot be found wanting unless the listener seeks harmonic adventures. As a matter of fact, Cannonball indulges his capacity for complexity on the solo on "I Got It," in which the opening two-bar break is reminiscent of Bird's most convoluted phrasing.

Nat Adderley, an eclectic on cornet, usually solos in a clever vein. In some cases he lacks emotional force, but his contribution here is enormous, especially in rhythmic drive. Drummer Louis Hayes, who had been working with Horace Silver before he joined the quintet, comes alive most conspicuously in his fills behind Nat, crowning the solo on "Combustion" with beautiful press rolls and bombs.

Nat's stylistic predecessors are Miles Davis, Clark Terry, and Dizzy Gillespie, whose high-register approach can be heard on "Dizzy's Business." Generally, however, like Miles, Nat favors the middle or lower register but with an extroverted tone. He is also adept at using the mouthpiece to create whines, howls, and slurs, as he does on "Gemini." An even better example can be heard on the fabulous "74 Miles Away," an exotic 7/4-meter composition (by Josef Zawinul) issued on a Capitol album of the same name; unfortunately, this wonderful album has been deleted, but the title track is reissued on *The Best of Cannonball Adderley*. Nat's elastic sound often contrasts favorably with Cannonball's uniformity of tone.

Yusef Lateef, a virtuoso multireed player who is intimately familiar with indigenous African forms, adds to the rich tonal coloring of "Gemini," his own "Planet Earth," and "Syn-Anthesia," a piece which departs significantly from the blues mode.

Bobby Timmons is an especially effective soloist with the Adderley band because of his gospel-flavored blues piano. Phineas Newborn, Jr., a technically flashy pianist, had been Adderley's first choice, but Phineas demanded the featured status reserved for Nat. In terms of playing and composing, Adderley was ultimately better off with the soulful Timmons. Timmons's best performance can be heard on "Combustion" and Thelonious Monk's "Straight, No Chaser." His right-hand lines are derived from Bud Powell, though they are simplified in the same sense that Cannonball refined Bird's style. One of his models may well have been Red Garland's treatment of "Billie Boy" on Davis's *Milestones*. In both "Combustion" and "Straight, No Chaser" he uses two-handed block chords expertly to build an explosive climax.

The quintet began recording for Capitol in 1964 when the Riverside label went out of business. Their recording of Zawinul's soulful "Mercy, Mercy, Mercy" (on a Capitol album of the same name) made Billboard's Top 100, though it does not compare with the ecstatic heights attained by "74 Miles Away." The second best Adderley reissue is Milestone's *The Japanese Concerts* with the "Gemini" personnel. The liner notes contain a remembrance of Julian Adderley by his friend and producer, Orrin Keepnews. Keepnews recalls that Cannon, as he was known to his intimates, served as an astute talent scout for the Riverside label, bringing Wes Montgomery and Chuck Mangione (Chapter 7) into the fold well before these major talents had made a name for themselves. It is hoped that Fantasy Records, which owns the Riverside masters, will reissue the quintet's excellent *At the Lighthouse*, also recorded live during the group's peak years. After 1973 the Adderleys recorded several albums on the Fantasy label; the most interesting contains new versions of the repertoire on *Coast to Coast*. Appropriately the album is called *Phenix*. Sam Jones, the Adderleys' comrade since their Tallahassee days, still plays bass.

Julian's nickname comes from an earlier epithet, "Cannibal," which he earned in his high school days for his voracious appetite. As Keepnews remarks, it was indicative of a lust for living and playing which was never tempered. However, diabetes and high blood pressure made his life-style a dangerous one as he knew; and the combined force of these illnesses caused his death at the age of forty-six. By then the Adderley quintet had become a virtual institution. Only the Art Blakey and Horace Silver groups were left to carry on the tradition of which Cannonball had been an acknowledged master.

WES MONTGOMERY

While We're Young

Milestone, M-47003
two discs, good liner notes
1960–1961

Musicians: Wes Montgomery, guitar. On sides one and two: Tommy Flanagan, piano; Percy Heath, bass; Albert Heath, drums. On sides three and four: Hank Jones, piano; Ron Carter, bass; Les Humphries, drums; Ray Baretto, conga drums on selections marked *.

Compositions: Side one: Airegin; D-Natural Blues; Polkadots and Moonbeams: Four on Six. *Side two:* West Coast Blues; In Your Own Sweet Way; Mister Walker; Gone with the Wind. *Side three:* Twisted Blues; Cottontail*; I Wish I Knew*; I'm Just a Lucky So and So. *Side four:* Repetition*; Somethin' Like Bags*; While We're Young; One for My Baby.

WES MONTGOMERY WAS the first new voice in jazz guitar since Charlie Christian. It was Christian's "Solo Flight" (Chapter 4) that inspired the teenage Wes to take the instrument seriously, and his formal training on the instrument amounted to learning all of Christian's solos from records. Montgomery's originality is often described in terms of his advances in guitar technique.

Certainly innovative improvisers usually do something on their instruments which their predecessors never thought of doing. Yet once Montgomery broke through these barriers, others who followed *still* did not sound like Wes. Clearly the real source of his importance is in the way he used his technique.

Montgomery fashions orderly, progressively building, and warmly communicative solos. This is the Wes of *While We're Young* and *Movin'*, cut for Riverside from 1959 to 1964 (see also the Milestone reissues, General Discography). The albums on Verve, recorded from 1965 to 1968, enjoyed a much wider commercial success. "Goin' out of My Head" (on *The Best of Wes Montgomery*) became one of the biggest AM radio hits of 1966, at least within the so-called "easy listening" genre. But the heavy background orchestrations left no room for improvising at all. Wes was simply "playing pretty," motivated in part by financial considerations. Thus these Verve recordings leave us with Wes's special techniques minus the personal spark which made his dexterity significant.

The suddenness of Wes's discovery by Riverside in 1959 made him an imposing figure in the jazz community. He had only been on the road once, from 1948 to 1950, with Lionel Hampton's band. He had also had a brief and unremarkable recording session with his two brothers, Monk (bass) and Buddy (piano), as the Mastersounds (reissued on Blue Note's *The Beginnings*). But most of his adult life had been spent in Indianapolis, supporting his burgeoning family (he had seven children) with an exhausting routine: a nonmusical day job, then a five-hour gig at the Turf Bar followed by after-hours sessions at the Missile Room. Cannonball Adderley happened upon Wes at an early morning session and returned to New York praising Wes to the skies to Riverside's co-owner, Orrin Keepnews, who flew to Indianapolis days later. Keepnews signed Wes to Riverside before they left the Missile Room the next morning. Montgomery was already thirty-four years old in 1959, and it is fortunate that his playing was then at its peak, for neither life nor the record business allowed him much time to develop.

One reason for the superior quality of *While We're Young*, aside from the consistently high level of Wes's solos, is the piano of Tommy Flanagan (sides one and two), whose playing unfailingly continues Wes's line of improvisation and reflects much of his sonority and feeling as well. On "Four on Six," a Montgomery original and one of the album's best tracks, Flanagan actually starts his own solo on Wes's last note. The next best Milestone, *Movin'*, includes an excellent live date (originally issued as *Full House*) with Miles Davis's rhythm section (Wynton Kelly, Paul Chambers, and Jimmy Cobb) and Johnny Griffin on tenor sax. The best of the later Verves was also recorded live, again with Kelly, Chambers, and Cobb. Creed Taylor, the mastermind behind Wes's popularity on Verve, issued the original recording with overdubbed orchestration. But the reissue, ironically entitled *The Small Group Recordings*, returns the tracks to their unadorned and uncluttered state. Wes's most unusual playing invitation occurred in 1962, when he was asked to join the John Coltrane Quartet with Eric Dolphy at the Jazz Workshop in San Francisco. The group also performed at the Monterey Jazz Festival, but the results of this unique collaboration were never recorded.

"West Coast Blues" is perhaps the best example of Wes's guitar playing on *While We're Young*. The tune is a simple riff and virtually a pretext for the improvisation which follows. The first chorus is not well organized, but immediately afterward Wes moves toward strength, depth, and simplicity. The single-note lines possess a symmetry which makes them seem like mini-compositions. Wes uses his thumb, rather than a pick, to give each note a round, soft quality. Montgomery often criticized himself for not using a pick, which would have enabled him to play faster; however, the delicate control that is possible with the thumb, as opposed to a mechanical plectrum, accounts for much of his unique touch. Wes favors the lower regions of the guitar, obtaining on ballads here such as "Polka Dots and Moonbeams" and "One for My Baby," an amber, mellow tone. Of course, this makes his effectiveness in contrived, romantic contexts quite understandable. The inventive lines on Dave Brubeck's "In Your Own Sweet Way" and the guitar solo on "While We're Young" are also excellent examples of his sensitive touch.

After a subdued press roll by drummer Jimmy Cobb, Wes shifts into the second stage of his "West Coast Blues" solo, in which the lines are formed solely out of doubling the melody note in the next octave. These octave runs, which were considered "impossible" to play before Wes demonstrated otherwise, became the most famous mark of his style. They enrich the melody note with the sound of a second register, giving his lines an added dimension. Necessarily, soloing in octaves is simpler in movement, although stronger for being pared down to the bare essentials. The Gypsy guitarist Django Reinhardt had learned to play in parallel octaves before Wes had, but his records demonstrate more dexterity than depth in creating jazz lines. Wes had tremendous difficulty with playing octaves at first, explaining in an interview with Ralph J. Gleason that until he grew accustomed to it, he had headaches from the effort and concentration required. (The interview with Gleason is reprinted in the liner notes to *Wes and Friends*.) Interestingly a guitar attachment was invented later to enable less skilled players to imitate Wes's octaves.

Montgomery's solo finishes with two choruses of thick block chords voiced in such a way that their top notes create a new melody. If soloing in octaves was considered impossible, soloing in chords was—in the words of Gunther Schuller—"even 'impossibler.'" Barney Kessel, whose chords Wes admired, had also played this way, though not nearly to the same extent. These broad structures, again requiring a simplification of the melody, bring the improvisation to a conclusion that has bold texture and the essential melodic ingredients. One should not, of course, overlook the beauty of the chords themselves. Their rich structure is easiest to hear on "In Your Own Sweet Way."

Wes's solo on "Gone with the Wind," taken at a swinging medium tempo, is structured just like "West Coast Blues." But even when he does not progress to soloing in block chords, the double-octave lines, as well as his extremely clear melodic sense, give each improvisation a sense of development. "Somethin' Like Bags" communicates an inner balance and a calm confidence about where he is headed. Those who knew Wes recall that his personal manner was of the same high quality as his finest music. In his liner notes to *While We're Young*, Keepnews says, "The warmth and directness and spontaneity and love you seem to hear in his music was really there."

After Riverside went out of business in 1964, Montgomery's career changed dramatically. Although Keepnews had also tried to launch him in a 1963 session with strings (reissued on *Pretty Blue*), a lack of promotion and bad timing probably doomed the effort from the start. With Creed Taylor everything changed, including Wes's attitude toward his music. Montgomery stated quite frankly that he was now playing pop music, and that it should be regarded as such. Both Keepnews and Wes's brother Monk offer evidence that Wes really did not like what he played during those years, though it is not hard to understand why he played it. After a long time working three jobs merely to feed his family, he was at last making big money. The real tragedy is that he did not live to enjoy it for long. Wes Montgomery died of a heart attack at forty-three at the peak of his popularity, having made music far richer than it made him.

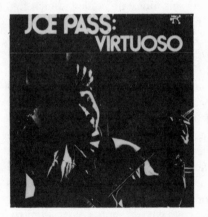

JOE PASS

Virtuoso

Pablo, 2310 708
one disc, brief liner notes
1974

Musicians: Joe Pass, guitar.
Compositions: Side one: Night and Day; Stella by Starlight; Here's That Rainy Day; My Old Flame; How High the Moon; Cherokee. *Side two:* Sweet Lorraine; Have You Met Miss Jones?; 'Round Midnight; All the Things You Are; Blues for Alican; The Song Is You.

JOE PASS WAS an unknown forty-four-year-old guitar player until the recording of *Virtuoso*, which catapulted him within one year to the top of *Down Beat* magazine's Readers' and Critics' Polls. As a player he is exceptionally accomplished. He has a prodigious dexterity, an encyclopedic harmonic knowledge, and a driving sense of swing. All of these attributes are necessary to sustain a solo guitar LP, but are not sufficient in themselves; if they are flaunted for their own sake, as occurs in the work of too many flashy guitarists, these resources become mere distractions. Pass understands this instinctively and he never applies his skills self-consciously. He knows intuitively where to embellish a melody, where to display a panache of chord changes, where to swing, and how to vary and balance everything effortlessly.

The music of *Virtuoso* is warm, human, and spontaneous. Pass went into the studio with no particular repertoire in mind, nor even any prior decisions about the keys in which songs would be played. Members of the studio crew suggested tunes to him, which he began to play in most cases out of tempo, gradually improvising a concept for the track. There were twenty takes in all. "I found myself getting into traps and then having to get out of them," he recalled. "Here and there you'll find places where I hesitated or doubted a bit." [26] One can only admire the compositional sense that brought forth masterful renditions of "How High the Moon," "Have You Met Miss Jones?" and "All the Things You Are" out of such spontaneous beginnings. His arrangements possess completeness, variety, and intensity. "Have You Met Miss Jones?" has Pass "walking" a bass line all over the lower strings, while fingering the melody in the upper register. Fluent single-note runs on "Moon" create harmonic changes without chords. Then come highly rhythmic chord configurations breaking up the runs. The music's flow, its momentum, and its melodic sense are never interrupted.

Born in 1929, Pass was the son of Mariano Passalaqua, a Pennsylvania steel worker. He received his first instrument, a seventeen-dollar Harmony guitar, at the age of nine. He learned to play from exercise books, encouraged by his father's enthusiasm. Pass considers himself to be in the Charlie Christian-Wes Montgomery tradition. Although he plays with a similar round, warm tone, he does not seem to have their hornlike melodic sense. Pass's guitar playing is more akin, despite the difference in instruments, to Oscar Peterson's piano style, paying allegiance melodically to hard bop and harmonically to Art Tatum. An especially Tatumesque harmonic treatment is heard in the stop-time chord modulations in the last choruses of "Sweet Lorraine" and "The Song Is You." Like Peterson, Pass unleashes double-timed blizzards of notes, as on "Cherokee," in which every note maintains clarity and individuality. These passages are played with a pick; the slower and medium tempos, requiring subtler touch, are played finger-style.

Joe Pass's story is that of a man conquering his past. After the music of Charlie Parker and Dizzy Gillespie drew him to New York in 1948, he succumbed to an addiction that had him living, as he expressed it, "in the cracks of society" for a decade. When he entered the Synanon Foundation for rehabilitation in 1960, he had not owned a guitar for years. He began to play once more, and even cut a record (*Sounds of Synanon*) with a neophyte drummer and bassist for World Pacific Records, whose owner, Richard Boch, was then a Synanon sponsor. Pass found work with Gerald Wilson's big band and with pianist Les McCann. Because of his increasing mastery of the instrument, he was hired by the lucrative, if uninspiring, TV studio bands of *The Donald O'Connor Show* and *Good Morning*. After Pass had toured for two years with George Shearing, Norman Granz signed him to Pablo, and Pass was at last ready to bring a healthy body, mind, and spirit to the task of improvisation. *Virtuoso*, for all the ease with which the music spills from its source, is also a victorious conclusion to a long, hard battle. Pass's guitar playing is dependably excellent, and several albums—some with colleagues like Oscar Peterson and Ella Fitzgerald—are recommended in the General Discography.

OSCAR PETERSON

In Concert

Verve (England), 2683 063
two discs, brief liner notes
1950–1956

Musicians: Oscar Peterson, piano; Herb Ellis, guitar; Ray Brown, bass. Barney Kessel, guitar on selections marked *. No guitar on selections marked **.

Compositions: Side one: Gai**; Sweet Georgia Brown*; Tenderly*; C-Jam Blues*; Seven Come Eleven*; Love for Sale (take one). *Side two:* Lollobrigida; Pompton Turnpike; Swingin' Til The Girls Come Home; Love for Sale (take two); Nuages; Avalon. *Side three:* Come to the Mardi Gras; Baby, Baby All the Time; Easy Does It; Sunday; Falling in Love with Love. *Side four:* Noreen's Nocturne; Gypsy in My Soul; Flamingo; Love You Madly; 52nd Street Theme.

OSCAR PETERSON'S CONSISTENT virtuosity has made him one of the most recorded pianists in jazz. His dexterity, unabated by chronic arthritis in his hands, overwhelms the listener with its flawless accuracy. The forcefulness of Oscar's beat and swing exceeds even that of his eminent models. From Teddy Wilson he learned the value of the long, interconnected melodic lines; from Nat "King" Cole's early trios, a lightness of touch; and from Art Tatum, a harmonic fluency and sweeping, graceful runs and arpeggios. Tatum, most of all, was the precursor of Peterson's orchestral solo approach, best represented on Pablo's *Oscar Peterson in Russia*. But Peterson's most personal milieu is the trio which, in addition to his stints as a studio accompanist for Lester Young, Ben Webster, Stan Getz, Ella Fitzgerald, and others, became his principal recording format from 1950 to 1967. It is possible that the precedent for this English Verve recording of *In Concert* was set by Tatum's mid-1940's trio with Slam Stewart on bass and Tiny Grimes on guitar (see Tatum's *Masterpieces*, General Discography, Chapter 4). As a trio pianist, Peterson was able to step out of Art's shadow in a way he could not as a soloist.

Good Peterson albums are abundant, but great ones are rare. One reason is that his technique is often more prominently displayed than his creativity. The problem is neatly summed up by Max Harrison in a *Jazz Review* critique (January 1960) of one such album: "(Peterson) appears to be concerned mainly with playing the piano and only incidentally with making music." Other albums, like the steady-selling *We Get Requests*, exhibit an innocuous "bounce" rhythm and trite melodic embellishments that have led to a general —and unfair—condemnation of Peterson as a "cocktail pianist" with a jazz player's "chops." *In Concert*, which curiously has never been reissued by American Verve, suffers from neither pointless virtuosity nor commercialism. Rather, its driving, highly original lyricism conveys a wholesome *joie de vivre*, which accurately reflects the pianist's private personality. While the album is more expensive than American issues (and may require a special order), it is worth any three of the other Petersons available, and reveals Peterson as an improviser of the first rank.

Except from 1967 to 1972, when he recorded for the German MPS/BASF label (not currently available), Peterson's thirty-year recording career has been supervised by Norman Granz, who discovered him by coincidence in 1948. Granz had been in Montreal, Canada, to promote a "Jazz at the Philharmonic" tour and, while riding back to the airport in a cab, heard the twenty-three-year-old Peterson on the radio. The driver knew that the performance was a live broadcast still in progress at the Alberta Lounge, so Granz had him turn the cab around and take him directly to the club. A year later Peterson was the sensation of Granz's "Jazz at the Philharmonic" Carnegie Hall concert in New York.

Peterson's smooth, rhythmic, and flawless delivery was the earliest cornerstone of his style. Born in Montreal in 1925, he was trained thoroughly in the classics and practiced tirelessly for years, often putting in twelve hours a day. His goal, which he says he accomplished by the end of high school, was to be capable of executing every musical idea he could imagine. The rest of his technique came from listening and from on-the-job experience, which consisted in part of recording boogie-woogie singles for a small Canadian recording company. His brother and two sisters also played piano, but it seems unlikely that they had easy access to the instrument while Oscar was at home.

Art Tatum was the sole pianist to intimidate Peterson, and the only one who surpassed him in total command of the instrument. Peterson recalls listening to Tatum's "Tiger Rag" (on MCA's *Masterpieces*) while he was still in high school, and refusing to believe there were not two pianists at work. His father had bought him the record to combat the boy's swelled head. In the early 1950's when he was playing with Ray Brown, Ray would tease Oscar by whispering to him that Art was in the audience. Once Tatum really was listening at the bar; and Peterson ended the set abruptly, unable to play while he was in the room. Although the two became close, Peterson's phobia persisted until Tatum took him aside and told him, "You can't afford this. You have too much going for you. I don't care if you have to hate me when I walk into the room, I want you to play." [27] The spell was broken at the Old Tiffany in Los Angeles, when Tatum came into the club and called out, "Lighten up, Oscar Peterson." "I knew it was Art, but it didn't bother me. I got deeper into the music instead, and I knew I was over it. Both Art and my father died within a week of each other, and I realized that in one week I lost two of the best friends I had." [28]

The ultimate Peterson trio performance is heard on the final six tracks of *In Concert*, recorded in 1956 at the Stratford Shakespearean Festival in Ontario, Canada. The originality of Peterson's phrasing, the frenzy of the beat, and the uncanny rapport among the trio elevate every song to an invaluable musical experience. Peterson's blistering speed is the servant of his imagination. He comfortably articulates phrases on "Falling in Love with Love" and "Gypsy in My Soul" which become increasingly complex and builds each solo to a dramatic conclusion. During the climactic three chords of Ellington's "Love You Madly," the audience, which had been asked not to applaud during the solos, bursts helplessly into ecstatic cheering.

The opening to "Noreen's Nocturne" displays the independence of the three voices. Their potential for collective improvisation emerges fully in the frantic tempo of Thelonious Monk's "52nd Street Theme," played as a roundelay with each instrument continuing the melodic line of the previous one. Both Ray Brown, who remained with Peterson until 1967, and Herb Ellis are consistently exciting soloists in their own rights, notwithstanding their fundamentally supportive roles here.

Although the 1956 concert is indisputably the album's high point, two more performances, "Tenderly" and "C-Jam Blues," have justly acquired a reputation as classic Peterson. "Tenderly," converted from its waltz meter into a romping $\frac{4}{4}$ beat, is improvised entirely out of thick block chords, which demonstrate Peterson's rhythmic prowess in naked glory; while Ellington's "C-Jam" overflows with the ornate, bluesy cascades that have always typified Peterson's melodic concept.

The Oscar Peterson trio, in which drummer Ed Thigpen replaced guitarist Herb Ellis after 1959, remained one of jazz's most popular recording groups until 1967. *Return Engagement* is the best reissue set of their work. After five years with MPS/BASF, which produced the excellent solo album *My Favorite Instrument* (now out of print), Peterson returned to the Granz roster with the founding of Pablo Records in 1973. At Pablo he assumed the dubiously privileged status of "house pianist," a role which quickly diminished the selectivity of his work. Nevertheless, the solo, duo, and trio formats of both *Peterson in Russia* and *History of an Artist* reveal his ageless touch, awesome technique, and impeccable taste.

JOHN COLTRANE

Giant Steps

Atlantic, AT-1311
one disc, good liner notes
1959

Musicians: John Coltrane, tenor sax; Tommy Flanagan, piano; Paul Chambers, bass; Art Taylor, drums. Wynton Kelly, piano, and Jimmy Cobb, drums on "Naima."
Compositions: Side one: Giant Steps; Cousin Mary; Countdown; Spiral. *Side two:* Syeeda's Flute Song; Naima; Mr. P. C.

IN HIS DOZEN YEARS of recording, John Coltrane challenged himself artistically to a greater extent than any saxophonist in jazz's history. *Giant Steps*, especially in the title track and in "Countdown," is the culmination of his passionate love for chord progressions, a subject which preoccupied him through the 1950's. Yet his own favorite piece, "Naima," as well as "Syeeda" and "Spiral," reveal his growing interest in exploring a modal approach to improvising—in which lies his major historical significance (Chapter 6). Thus the album is pivotal in Coltrane's career. It is also a monumental achievement in tenor sax playing, and the first album to rely solely on Trane's compositions.

John Coltrane, despite his immense talent, was a late bloomer. His early years reveal only one trait that would contribute to his greatness—the capacity for ceaseless hard work. He was born in 1926 and grew up in a small town near Greensboro, North Carolina. John was an only child and very close to his cousin Mary, for whom the blues on *Giant Steps* was written. John's father, a tailor, taught himself the violin and the ukelele, and liked to sing country music; his mother played the piano and had been trained as a singer. Religion, not music, was the focus of the household, for both of

John's grandfathers were ministers. One of them, the Reverend William Blair, was especially active in black politics and a pillar of the community. John's father and grandfather died within a year of each other. After John had graduated from high school, he and his mother moved to Philadelphia, hoping to find more lucrative employment there.

John's major instrument in his early teens had been the clarinet, although he took up the alto sax, too. He was known to practice for hours in the backyard of the family's North Carolina house. In Philadelphia he attended the Granoff School of Music, where he distinguished himself as a hard worker and a good student. He continued to study composition at the school years after he had graduated. He was still playing alto in the U.S. Navy band during the 1940's, but once he had returned to the United States and experienced the overwhelming influence of Charlie Parker, he felt it was necessary to switch horns.

> On alto, Bird had been my whole influence, but on tenor I found there was no one man whose ideas were so dominant as Charlie's were on alto. Therefore, I drew from all the men I heard during this period on tenor, especially Lester Young and his melodic phrasing. I found out about Coleman Hawkins later and became fascinated by his arpeggios . . . I got a copy of "Body and Soul" and listened real hard. Even though I dug Pres, as I grew musically, I appreciated Hawk more and more.[29]

The influence of Coleman Hawkins is especially apparent on "Giant Steps" in the way Trane breaks up chords into arpeggios. His hard-edged tone, like Sonny Rollins's, also leans toward Hawkins's. Dexter Gordon was another powerful influence, inspiring a driving momentum in his playing.

Before he was hired by Miles Davis, Coltrane worked as a tenor sax player in the bands of Dizzy Gillespie (1949–1951, on *Dee Gee Days*), Earl Bostic (1952–1953), and Johnny Hodges (1953–1954). Since his apprenticeship with Davis was discussed elsewhere (see previous Davis discussion and *Kind of Blue*, Chapter 6), it remains only to take note of the impact that Thelonious Monk had upon his development. Coltrane had gone to work for Monk at the Five Spot in New York because Miles, without warning or explanation, decided not to rehire him during 1957. Monk gave Coltrane his postgraduate course in harmony. Trane would later tell of going to Monk's house early in the morning to ask him how to solve certain voicing and chord-progression problems. Monk would get out of bed, go straight to the piano, and play the solutions. During a performance, Monk often left the stage for up to ten minutes, allowing Coltrane to experiment with the sustained, involved soloing which would become his trademark. Monk also kept him on his toes to a greater extent than Miles had, because he was so unpredictable. Trane once commented that any lapse in attention made him feel as if he had stepped into an empty elevator shaft. Only four tracks of their sessions at the Five Spot are available—on *Thelonious Monk and John Coltrane*—but they justify the entire two-disc reissue, for these men brought out the best in each other. Trane carries off some of his best soloing prior to *Giant Steps* within Monk's ingenious frameworks.

In 1959 Coltrane was a bubbling volcano of ideas ready to erupt. Having spent four years with Miles Davis and after a brief tenure with Thelonious Monk (see also Davis and Monk discussions), he made a serious commitment to find a group of his own. He was already thirty-three, quite old to be establishing his reputation, but determined to leave his mark on jazz. He hired Harold Lovett, Miles's manager and lawyer, to negotiate his new contract with Atlantic. He plunged into preparing his music with more ardor than ever. As we noted in the Miles Davis Selected Discography, Coltrane was already playing with a dark, penetrating tone that came through with equal strength at the high and low ends of the horn. His rhythm was driving; his mood, urgent, with no room for flippancy or even humor. He burned with dedication, practicing long hours daily, running scales and arpeggios, holding long tones, listening to other musicians, and studying theory. Naima, his wife, would occasionally find him asleep in a chair late at night with the horn still strapped around his neck.

Giant Steps is the earliest album to reveal the full extent of Coltrane's harmonic originality. Yet one notices his virtuosity first, especially on "Giant Steps" and "Countdown," for he slices through stacks of harmonic changes with surgical accuracy and, in the case of "Countdown," at a scorching tempo. Chords are packed into these songs in awesome density, and successive chords have few notes in common, making the transitions between them traversable only by abrupt leaps. As Trane explains in the liner notes, "Giant Steps" gets its name from the fact that the bass line is "a loping one," and does not progress according to the more ordinary, comfortable skips. Interestingly "Countdown," a harmonic extension of Davis's "Tune Up," is structured inside out in that the musicians improvise separately at the beginning of the piece and do not play ensemble until the very end. The opening duet with Art Taylor foreshadows Coltrane's free-style sax/drum tracks with Elvin Jones and Rashied Ali (on *Interstellar Space*, Chapter 8).

The phrase "sheets of sound" was coined by critic Ira Gitler to describe the waterfall of notes that pours out of Coltrane's horn. The image aptly conveys the density of his playing as well as its "vertical" nature. Coltrane was thinking in *groups* of notes, and the incessant stream of these groups gave his music a surging momentum, a force of larger scope than the finger-snapping rhythm common to hard bop. Unlike Hawkins, whose arpeggios were grouped in four- or three-note phrases, Coltrane would arrange them in groups of five or seven, or whatever was required to fit them all in.

Naturally the other musicians were at pains to keep up with him; and, as one can hear on Flanagan's "Giant Steps" and on the "Countdown" solos, they did not always succeed. Coltrane had done his best to prepare the band, rehearsing them on his own time. Nesuhi Ertegun, the album's producer, recalled there were no more than two takes of each piece:

> John and the musicians walked in without any sheet music . . . I noticed there was less back-and-forth conversation than with any other group I ever recorded. John rarely talked at all. He simply signaled to the musicians what he wanted, and he seemed to know exactly what he wanted at all times. After they had finished recording, the musicians just put on their coats, packed up their instruments, and left.[30]

"Naima" illustrates a tender side of Coltrane that is often overlooked. The song has a simple and elegant melody which is neither altered nor embellished. Trane sings through his horn in a plaintive yearning tone. One has the feeling he had predetermined precisely how much breath he wished to use on every note. Naima, his wife, who was a devout Moslem, represented to Coltrane the purity and discipline he displays on this track. Its harmonies hover over only two tonal centers, E♭ in the chorus and B♭ in the bridge. Paul Chambers's bass strums its note repetitively, acting as the drone, or *tamboura*, in classic Indian music, to which Coltrane had begun listening in the late 1950's. "Naima's" modal orientation may explain the presence of Wynton Kelly, a pianist familiar with the modal approach from his work with Miles Davis (Chapter 6).

Coltrane's unadorned treatment of "Naima" brings to mind the lovely *Ballads* album which, despite its 1962 recording date, belongs in this discussion. On *Ballads* Coltrane's historic quartet (Chapter 6) interprets unrehearsed popular songs with virtually no improvising. Coltrane is tranquil and romantic, not intense, and his tone is disturbingly thin, due to difficulties he was having at the time with his mouthpiece. Yet in its simplicity the total effect is more beautiful than the individual parts. A similar session later on produced *John Coltrane and Duke Ellington*, with Duke on piano. Coltrane is in top form on Duke's "In a Sentimental Mood," surpassing the mellower tracks of *Ballads*. Although motivated by ABC's desire to launch a more commercial Coltrane image, this pair of LP's is highly recommended.

Within a year of recording *Giant Steps*, Coltrane made several exceptional albums for Atlantic. The first, *Coltrane Jazz*, contains the famous "Harmonique," during which Coltrane plays two and three notes simultaneously on his horn. This was a trick he learned from two sources—Monk and a Philadelphia saxophonist, John Glenn. He experimented with it liberally in his freer playing later on. The next album, *Coltrane Plays the Blues*, reinterprets the blues form in the exotic manner he presents on "Cousin Mary," making use of nontraditional harmony and pedal point. *The Art of John Coltrane*, a two-disc Atlantic set, collects several tracks from the LP's mentioned above, including *Giant Steps*, and provides a wonderful documentation of the transitional yars 1959–1960. *My Favorite Things*, Coltrane's most popular album, was also recorded in 1960, but it is more appropriately discussed in Chapter 6 due to its modally based improvisation.

The earliest display of Coltrane's originality—apart from his performances with Miles Davis—is found on the title track of Blue Note's *Blue Train* (1957), in which his solo builds intensity with increasingly large groups of notes. Zita Carno, a musician and critic who befriended Coltrane, transcribed this solo as an example of the new boundaries he seemed to be crossing. She brought the transcription to his apartment, asking to hear it played from the music. Trane attempted to oblige her but soon gave up, explaining that it was too difficult. This anecdote strongly suggests that improvisation brings not only spontaneity to jazz but a level of accomplishment that forethought could never produce.

Coltrane's historic recordings from 1960 to 1965 will be discussed in the next chapter.

Modern Jazz Singers

ELLA FITZGERALD

Mack the Knife: Ella in Berlin

Verve, VS-64041
one disc, no liner notes
1960

Musicians: Ella Fitzgerald, vocals; Paul Smith, piano; Jim Hall, guitar; Wilfred Middle-brooks, bass; Gus Johnson, drums.
Compositions: Side one: Gone with the Wind; Misty; The Lady Is a Tramp; The Man I Love; Summertime. *Side two:* Too Darn Hot; Lorelei; Mack the Knife; How High the Moon.

SARAH VAUGHAN

Sarah Vaughan & Count Basie

Roulette, SR-42018
one disc, no liner notes
ca. 1960

Musicians: Sarah Vaughan, vocals; The Count Basie Orchestra (pianist not identified): Freddie Green, guitar; Sonny Payne, drums; Edward Jones, bass; Frank Wess, Billy Mitchell, Charles Fowlkes, Marshall Royal, saxes; Thad Jones, Joe Newman, George Cotten, Eugene Young, trumpets; Albert Grey, Henry Coker, Benjamin Powell, trombones.

Compositions: Side one: Perdido; Lover Man; I Cried for You; Alone; There Are Such Things; Mean to Me. *Side two:* The Gentleman Is a Dope; You Go to My Head; Until I Met You; You Turned the Tables on Me; Little Man.

CARMEN McRAE

The Greatest of Carmen McRae

MCA, MCA2-4111
two discs, liner notes
1955–1959

Musicians: Carmen McRae, vocals, also piano on selections marked *. On other tracks the orchestras of Ralph Burns, Tadd Dameron, Ernie Wilkins, and more. Accompanists include Billy Strayhorn, piano; Ray Bryant, piano; Mundell Lowe, guitar.
Compositions: Side one: Love Is a Simple Thing; Yesterdays; Good Morning, Heartache; I'm Putting All My Eggs in One Basket; I Remember Clifford; Lush Life; Something to Live For; Yardbird Suite. *Side two:* All the Things You Are; Dream of Life; You Took Advantage of Me; Isn't It Romantic?; I Was Doing All Right; Last Night, When We Were Young; If You'd Stay the Way I Dream About You; His Eye Is on the Sparrow. *Side three:* Falling in Love with Love; The Night We Called It a Day; Guess Who I Saw Today?; Summertime; Suppertime; The Little Things That Mean So Much; Exactly Like You; Perdido. *Side four:* Nice Work If You Can Get It; Bob White; Baltimore Oriole; Skylark; Love Is Here to Stay*; He Was Too Good to Me*; All This Could Lead to Love*; Nowhere.*

ELLA FITZGERALD, SARAH VAUGHAN, AND CARMEN McRAE communicate very different emotions through a song; yet they share a common heritage in the style of jazz singing established by Bessie Smith (Chapter 3) and Billie Holiday (Chapter 4). Their rhythmic feeling, instrument-like voice quality, and preference for improvising within bebop's boundaries place them in the mainstream of the music. They have also accepted the big band's singers' repertoire of popular ballads, occasionally varied by jazz compositions. Their major departure from Bessie and Billie has been twofold: They are less tied to the blues (in Billie's case, blues feeling—in Bessie's, the blues form) and more inclined to use their voices flexibly, interacting freely with other instruments in the band.

Ella Fitzgerald was born in 1918 and began her career in Chick Webb's band of the 1930's. One can still hear in the full-blown dynamic style and the rhythmic punch of *Mack the Knife* that she has not left the swing era too far behind. Her first hit record with Webb in 1938, "A-Tisket, A-Tasket," is available on MCA's two-disc set *The Best of Ella Fitzgerald*, but it by no means represents her mature work, which began when she signed with Norman Granz's Verve label in 1955. The first products of this union were the famous "songbooks" of George Gershwin, Cole Porter, and Rodgers and Hart, all available on two-disc sets (General Discography). While these orchestral sides are pretty and sensitive, they are quite short on jazz content. (The best album of that series, which is devoted to Ellington's music and arranged by Duke for Ella and his 1956 orchestra, was reissued by Verve in February 1980; it is highly recommended.) The feeling is much looser on a series of sessions with Louis Armstrong, collected on Verve's *Ella & Louis*. Ella and Louis are backed here by the Oscar Peterson trio plus Herb Ellis on guitar, a group that unleashes Fitzgerald's rhythmic verve and imagination. She and Louis Armstrong communicate with genuine affection and spontaneity, making this one of three essential Fitzgerald collections. The second, *Ella & Duke at the Côte D'Azur*, documents an exciting 1966 live performance by both Fitzgerald and Ellington's orchestra. The band's drive becomes a reservoir of energy for Ella, who sings on fewer than half the tracks.

Mack the Knife is unsurpassed for energy and consistency. Ella is obviously at home with the band, a copy of the earlier Peterson combo. "How High the Moon" is a *tour de force*. Its six improvised choruses end on a note it is hard to imagine her hitting after her marathon scatting performance. Ella's infallible pitch and the clarity of her voice allow for an instrumentalist's degree of flexibility, as one hears on the up-tempo improvisations like "Gone with the Wind" and "The Lady Is a Tramp." Ella makes masterful use of melodic embellishments. Although she lacks the sense of tragedy that wells up so frequently in the work of Bessie Smith and Billie Holiday, she replaces it with imagination, warmth, and an uplifting rhythmic feeling. These qualities emerge equally on ballads like the gracefully improvised "The Man I Love," and on swinging romps like "Mack the Knife," for which she found herself improvising words as well as music. The spontaneity of this concert album, along with her bold and flawless performance, reveal Ella's major asset—the ability to communicate joy and exhilaration.

Sarah Vaughan has revived the dramatic potential of Bessie and Billie without sounding like either. She has a weighty, original voice that communicates seriousness and the impression that each of her interpretations is definitive. Sarah was born in 1924 in Newark, New Jersey, where she studied piano and organ and sang in a church choir. Billy Eckstine heard her perform at one of the Apollo Theater talent shows in Harlem, and he sponsored her first job at nineteen with the Earl Hines band of 1943. In the following year, Sarah sang in Eckstine's bebop band, in which she was the favorite vocalist of Charlie Parker and Dizzy Gillespie with whom she recorded a classic "Lover Man" in 1945 (see Gillespie's *In the Beginning*). She has recorded more frequently with bebop stars like Eckstine, Charlie Parker, Bud Powell, and Tadd

Dameron than currently available reissues indicate. However, her finest singing was recorded in small groups after 1954: with Clifford Brown (*Sarah Vaughan*—her own favorite album); with an ensemble from the Count Basie band (*No Count Sarah*); and a collection called *Great Songs from Hit Shows*. Sadly none of these are available. When Trip Records went out of business, these albums dropped out of print, though one day they will no doubt return to circulation. An Encore album, *Sarah Vaughan in Hi-Fi*, is the only record available from the early 1950's. It was cut with a small studio group including Miles Davis, and its high points are the wordless vocal "Pinky," "Mean to Me," and "Ain't Misbehavin'." The remaining ballads convey the power of her voice along with an inclination toward melodrama and—on "It Might As Well Be Spring"—a fascinating recomposition of the melody.

Roulette's *Sarah Vaughan and Count Basie* captures Sarah's energy and enthusiasm, which are elevated by the *sock!* and *pow!* of the Basie band—(without the Count, however, for contractual reasons). In a rare burst of scatting, Sarah brings "Perdido" to life in a commanding performance. Sarah is neither as flashy nor as facile in her improvising as Ella, but her substantial recasting of the melody on "Mean to Me" illustrates the harmonic understanding which has always characterized her work. Sarah's greatest asset has been her voice. This is not always the case with jazz singers, as Billie Holiday's example teaches us. Vaughan's exquisite control, powerful vibrato, and rather stunning range, especially in the bass register, emerge in the Holiday classic "You Go to My Head." "You Turned the Tables on Me" hits with the driving swing of her bebop heritage, quite different from the relaxed, Lester Young-inspired momentum established by Billie and, in many cases, by Ella. Overall, Sarah's ability to build each song into a dramatic entity, exemplified here by the remake of "Lover Man," is unmatched in jazz. (Roulette's two-disc *The Sarah Vaughan Years* reissues "Perdido," but is otherwise a more commercial set, occasionally enhanced by the sensitive string arrangements of Benny Carter, Quincy Jones, and Lalo Schifrin.)

Vaughan's albums have become increasingly commercial since her 1960's hit "Brokenhearted Melody." The trend peaked with a 1977 album of Beatles songs. However, a promising turnabout on Pablo's *How Long Has This Been Going On?*, with swinging support from Oscar Peterson and Joe Pass, gives one hope for the future. Additional albums are recommended in the General Discography.

No singer has represented herself less adequately on records than Carmen McRae. *The Greatest of Carmen McRae*, which pairs her with orchestras and small bands, reveals the extent of her potential. Born in 1922 of West Indian descent, Carmen grew up in Brooklyn and began auspiciously as the vocalist in Benny Carter's band from 1946 to 1947. She absorbed more lasting musical influences shortly afterward as an intermission pianist and singer at Minton's and as the wife of the innovative bebop drummer Kenny Clarke. It was the feel for scatting heard on "Yardbird Suite" and the flashes of improvisational brilliance on "You Took Advantage of Me" that earned her *Down-beat* magazine's Top New Singer award in 1954. McRae's reputation as a jazz singer, which is considerable in view of her "cabaret"-style inclinations, derives almost wholly from these sessions of the 1950's. Her recent albums lack the seriousness of intent or the sense of building tension evident on the tracks of this reissue. The exception may be *Alone*, for which she returns to self-accompaniment on piano; but so far this record is available only in Japan.

The field of modern jazz singers cannot be represented comprehensively in a book which surveys all of jazz. Dinah Washington, however, deserves special mention, even if her discography cannot be discussed in detail. Her clear, clean delivery, heavily steeped in black church music and occasionally closer to blues than jazz, was universally admired by musicians. But her premature death in 1962 left us with only one superb collection, EmArcy's *The Jazz Sides* (see General Discography).

BETTY CARTER

Betty Carter

Bet-Car, MK 1002
one disc, no liner notes
ca. 1966

Musicians: Betty Carter, vocals; Daniel A. Mixon, piano; Onaje Alan Gumbs, piano; Buster Williams, bass; Louis Hayes, drums; Chip Lyles, drums.
Compositions: Side one: You're a Sweetheart; I Can't Help It; What Is It?; On Our Way Up (Sister Candy); We Tried. *Side two:* Happy; Sunday, Monday, or Always; Tight; Children Learn What They Live; Sounds.

BETTY CARTER, born in Newark, New Jersey, in 1930, is the last of the modern jazz singers and in many ways the most exciting. Her independence is uncompromising. Two years after this album was released on her own label, she was offered an advance of six figures to record for Warner's, an enticement she rejected adamantly for fear a large company would ultimately exert some control over her work.

Betty Carter must be set apart from Fitzgerald, Vaughan, and McRae. In them one can hear to varying extents the influence of Bessie Smith and Billie Holiday. But Carter is more strongly influenced by the sound, inflection, and phrasing of instruments themselves. As indicated by the three albums discussed previously, jazz singers usually limit themselves to interpreting the standards and a few jazz classics, leaving the challenges of creating new material to the instrumentalists. But more than half the songs on this album are Carter originals, revealing an effort to distinguish herself in repertoire. Carter also captures instrumental timbres in her voice, and even thinks like an instumentalist about her music.

Betty Carter's independent streak was obvious at the outset of her career when she worked with Lionel Hampton's band in 1948. She made no secret of preferring the bebop Parker, Gillespie, and Roach were playing. She claims to have survived numerous "firings" by Hamp for telling him frankly that she would rather be working with Dizzy's band. Not surprisingly, this relationship did not last long. Her first (available) record date cut shortly after leaving Hamp is "Red Top," on singer King Pleasure's album *The Source*.

Later, through a recommendation from Miles Davis, she began to tour opposite Ray Charles, who was enchanted by her voice. Despite his R & B image, he persuaded ABC Paramount to let him record an album of ballads with her in 1960. *Ray Charles and Betty Carter* turned out to be a gorgeous collection of sensitive duets, but, despite its initial popularity, ABC deleted the album a few years later. Under Charles's aegis she cut her own session on the company's Impulse label, but *What a Little Moonlight Can Do* does not measure up to her potential. *'Round Midnight* on Roulette, a smaller company where she enjoys more artistic freedom, is a better example of her style. Motivated by increasing pressure from the major companies to come up with hit records, Carter established her own label in 1969, originally calling it Bush. The name was changed to Bet-Car in 1971 when its first album, *Betty Carter Live*, was released. This album and the selected one here, although stocked in jazz-oriented record stores, must normally be ordered by mail (see the Appendix for the address). The music is well worth this slight inconvenience.

Betty's music on *Betty Carter* is exciting and unpredictable because she is so flexible in technique and concept. The phrasing on the up-tempo tracks like "On Our Way Up" and "Tight" is strikingly original, dividing time in uncommon but well-balanced patterns as an incisive horn player (say, Sonny Rollins) might treat it. She is not unconcerned with the words, for in none of these songs are the lyrics incidental; the clearly autobiographical "I Can't Help It" should be taken as her credo. But the music comes first. Her instrumental conception emerges clearly on the brilliant interplay of string bass and voice on "I Can't Help It" and "Sunday, Monday, or Always." She sounds best with the deep, resonant bass lines which run all through this album, giving the band a strong sense of countermelody and an aura of collective improvisation. Carter is right in there among the instruments; they are not "behind" her. If one wanted to compare the sound of her voice to a particular instrument, a flute would come to mind but one played with guts rather than concert-style "purity." "You're a Sweetheart" contains a chilling example of her ability to plunge into a musky, resonant lower register. (Compare her voice with Eric Dolphy's flute on "Glad to Be Unhappy" in his Selected Discography, Chapter 6.) Ascending into the airy, upper regions of her range, as on "Happy," her voice remains weighty but becomes clearer and brighter. "Sounds" is a *tour de force* of scatting and is even more thrilling in live performance.

Carter's second line of attack is steeped in drama and tension. By slowing down the tempo almost to the point of free-form expressiveness, she allows the dark, mysterious qualities of her voice to evoke a hair-raising effect on "You're a Sweetheart" and "We Tried." Her didactic "Children Learn What They Live" is virtually a dramatic reading in which rhythms vary from rubato to rock with swing in between. One never knows—or quite remembers in a familiar track—what to expect of her except power. Comparable to Sarah Vaughan in this respect, her best work has a seriousness which contributes to its depth.

It is a shock to hear "two" Carters singing on "Sweetheart" and "Sunday" in countermelody and close harmony. Accomplished tastefully, the overdubbed parts are not disruptive, although neither do they seem necessary. What is more significant is that she departs from the modern jazz singer's conception of a record as solely a documentation of a performance. A record can be much more, as will be made abundantly evident in Chapter 7; but singers with their roots in swing and bebop are generally not open to such alterations. In this case, however, Carter's overdubbing must acquire more artistic purpose to justify itself.

Betty Carter's following is small compared with Sarah Vaughan's and Ella Fitzgerald's, but it is devoted and discriminating. Decades from now when modern jazz singing is looked back upon with even greater perspective, her recordings will rank among the greatest examples of the style.

LAMBERT, HENDRICKS,
AND ROSS
The Best of Lambert, Hendricks & Ross 1960

Columbia, C-32911 or JCS-8198
one disc, no liner notes (on C-32911)

Musicians: Dave Lambert, Jon Hendricks, Annie Ross, vocals. The Ike Isaacs Trio (no further identification) with Harry Edison, trumpet.
Compositions: Side one: Charleston Alley; Moanin'; Twisted; Bijou; Cloudburst. *Side two:* Centerpiece; Gimme That Wine; Sermonette; Summertime; Everybody's Boppin'.

THE VOCAL TRIO of Lambert, Hendricks, and Ross (L., H. & R.), whose wittiest songs appear on this album, excelled at "vocalese," the setting of lyrics to improvised instrumental solos. Vocalese is distinguished from scat singing by the fact that words are used instead of nonsense syllables, and that the melodies are usually not improvised. The idea was first explored in the 1940's by Eddie Jefferson, whose initial attempts were applied to Coleman Hawkins's 1939 "Body and Soul" solo. His efforts stirred little excitement until he tailored the lyrics to James Moody's tenor sax solo on "I'm in the Mood for Love," which he called "Moody's Mood for Love." When King Pleasure sang Jefferson's piece at the Apollo Theater Amateur Hour in Harlem, the strength of his performance won a contract with Prestige Records. "Moody's Mood" became a minor hit record (available on *The Source*). Jon Hendricks's fogged, hornlike intonation is clearly derived from Pleasure's style, and his interest in vocalese was inspired by the recording of "Moody's Mood for Love."

The Lambert, Hendricks, and Ross trio began in the late 1950's when Dave Lambert, a singer and vocal arranger from Boston, collaborated with Jon Hendricks, a frustrated singer/songwriter who had been working as a record-company shipping clerk. Jon Hendricks had been singing professionally since his teens in Toledo, Ohio, where on several occasions he had enjoyed the accompaniment of the great Art Tatum (Chapter 4). Then Annie

Ross, the niece of the British singer Ella Logan, joined them to provide the essential "brass" sonority.

Despite obvious allusions to bebop, the group's close harmony and ensemble approach owe much to the swing era's use of reed and brass sections. This is especially apparent on "Charleston Alley," "Centerpiece," and Ralph Burns's "Bijou" as performed by the Woody Herman band. The influence of modern jazz instrumentals is elsewhere: the gospel-blues flavor of Bobby Timmons's "Moanin' " and Cannonball Adderley's "Sermonette"; the scatted "Boppin' "; and the beautiful re-creation of "Summertime" from Miles Davis's *Porgy and Bess* (Selected Discography).

There are several classic performances on this album. Ross's lyric "Twisted," ingeniously contoured to Wardell Gray's sax solo, depicts the zany mental geography of a psychoanalyst's patient. The way Ross lags behind the beat and accents her syllables swings powerfully. A less convincing version appears on folk-rock singer Joni Mitchell's *Court and Spark* album, but one must hear the original to appreciate its lasting beauty, for Annie Ross draws from an ample reservoir of real jazz feeling.

Hendrick's "Cloudburst" is his best vehicle. On it, he demonstrates impeccable articulation at a tempo in which it is a challenge merely to get the words out. "Gimme That Wine," a comfortable, medium-tempo blues, depends heavily on his imaginative storytelling and ironic humor. Hendricks has said he wrote the words while observing winos in Washington Square Park in New York. "Everybody's Boppin' " is set at an outrageous tempo. Wisely the group scats rather than attempting to articulate words at this pace. Nevertheless, the fours and ensemble breaks near the end are superb, as the trio's timing and timbre allow them to simulate the punch and drive of a full band.

The trio remained intact from 1958 to 1963, when Yolande Bavan replaced Annie Ross until 1965, after which Lambert left to lead his own group. By 1960 Hendricks had already laid the groundwork for a second career with his dramatic revue "Evolution of the Blues," commissioned by the Monterey Jazz Festival. The show, starring Hendricks, played through most of the 1960's at the On Broadway Theater in San Francisco, but it is not available on record.

The trio's next best album was their earliest (1958), *Sing a Song of Basie*, which re-creates through multitaping the entire Basie big band including the individual solos in vocalese. The critical response to the first album led to *Sing Along with Basie*, for which Joe Williams was added as a fourth voice and the Basie band as accompaniment. Unfortunately, the album has been deleted from the Roulette catalogue. *L. H. & R. Sing Ellington* suffers from several bad performances by Lambert and Hendricks. *The Best of L. H. & R.* selected here, however, proves the trio had more to offer than the resurrection of musical history. (It is unfortunate that Columbia decided to replace the album's original cover, which included the lyrics to the up-tempo tunes and a good photo of the group in action. A "used" first issue in good condition will make a more satisfying purchase than the later dressed-down package.)

MOSE ALLISON

Seventh Son

Prestige, 10052
one disc, no liner notes
1963

Musicians: Mose Allison, piano and vocals; Addison Farmer, bass; Ronnie Free, drums. Nick Stabula, drums on selections marked *. Taylor LaFargue, bass, and Frank Isola, drums on selections marked **.

Compositions: Side one: The Seventh Son; Eyesight to the Blind; Do Nothin' Til You Hear From Me; Lost Mind*; I Got a Right to Cry; Baby, Let Me Hold Your Hand*. *Side two:* Parchman Farm*; If You Live; Don't Get Around Much Anymore*; One-Room Country Shacks**; I Hadn't Anyone Til You*; A Young Man**; That's All Right.

MOSE ALLISON IS A rough-hewn pianist and singer who achieves an authentic merger of country blues and modern jazz. In the late 1950's he had been a fairly good accompanist for Stan Getz, Gerry Mulligan, and the Al Cohn-Zoot Sims band, but he remained virtually unnoticed until he began to sing material inspired by the rural setting of his youth in Tippo, Mississippi. With *Seventh Son* (originally issued as *Mose Allison Sings*), he established himself as a wandering urban minstrel, recording songs of an increasingly philosophical nature during the next two decades. But it is the down-home Mose, pungent as mustard greens, whose flavor has not diminished over the years.

"Parchman Farm" and "If You Live," written in the standard twelve-bar form, are the trenchant originals here, but Mose adheres to the country blues tradition throughout with a repertoire that draws on Sonny Boy Williamson, Willie Dixon, and Percy Mayfield. Mayfield was an important influence on Allison's vocal style, which is delivered in an unadorned, slightly nasal Southern drawl. Somehow even the Ellington ballads "Do Nothing Til You Hear from Me" and "Don't Get Around Much Anymore," which are far from the blues in harmonic structure, take on the aura of blues tonality in Mose's treatment.

"Seventh Son," a hypnotic track, displays the directness of his style. He rejects what he calls the "wrought-up" sound of a professionally trained voice, aspiring to simplicity, naturalness, and a feeling of conviction. He is uncanny in creating blue notes which somehow sink into the microtonal cracks between a major and a minor third. The words "I'm the one" at the end of the first chorus of "Seventh Son" provide an excellent example. Allison is adept at bending notes. On the first "man" of "A Young Man," one is tempted to hear his note as slightly "off," until closer listening reveals the circuitous route the pitch takes toward its final resting place.

Allison's piano playing is also earthy and unpretentious, qualities it did not retain after the late 1960's when he became infatuated with the sophistication of Béla Bartók, Aleksandr Scriabin, and Charles Ives. He is genuinely expressive on solos like "Eyesight to the Blind," a clear filtering of blues piano through the modern jazz tradition. But he is also effective on "Parchman Farm," which shows an affinity for the barrelhouse style of his earliest influences—boogie pianists Pete Johnson and Albert Ammons, and Mose's father, a self-taught ragtime player. Mose establishes a call-and-response relationship between voice and piano that is evident on every track.

Allison's best lyrics focus on psychological ambivalence. The first line inflates a pretty balloon, and the next line pops it: "I Don't Worry About a Thing ('cause nothing's going to be all right)"; "I Feel So Good (it must be wrong)"; and "Everybody's Cryin' Mercy (and they don't know the meaning of the word)." He has also devised a clever and effective weapon for silencing unruly patrons in the audience with "Your Mind Is on Vacation (and your mouth is working overtime)." A particularly good collection of these can be heard on Atlantic's *The Best of Mose Allison*. Unfortunately, the newer versions of "Seventh Son" and "Parchman Farm" on this set are taken too fast, and "Parchman" also lacks the effectiveness of the original lyric. Several other Atlantics include good tracks of his later work: *Western Man, Your Mind Is on Vacation,* and *I Don't Worry About a Thing.*

About a decade after jazz listeners responded to Allison's unique style, several folk and rock stars "discovered" him and began to record his material. From *Seventh Son*, The Who recorded "A Young Man"; John Mayall, "Parchman Farm"; Bonnie Raitt, "Everyone's Cryin' Mercy"; and Leon Russell, "Smashed." If Allison became a prime source for the pop heroes of the 1970's, it is largely due to *Seventh Son*'s initial impact and its subtle mix of rustic charm and artistic urbanity.

Notes

1. Nat Shapiro and Nat Hentoff, *Hear Me Talkin' to Ya* (New York: Dover Publications, Inc., 1966), p. 337.

2. Martin Williams, "Bebop and After: A Report" in Nat Hentoff and Albert J. McCarthy, *Jazz: New Perspectives in the History of Jazz* (New York: Holt,

Rinehart & Winston, Inc., Da Capo Press ed., 1959), p. 293.

3. Shapiro and Hentoff, *op. cit.*, p. 354.

4. *Ibid.*, p. 341; the statement is attributed to Monk by pianist Mary Lou Williams.

5. LeRoi Jones, *Blues People* (New York: William Morrow & Company, Inc., 1963), p. 190.

6. Leonard Feather, "John 'Dizzy' Gillespie" in Nat Shapiro and Nat Hentoff, *The Jazz Makers* (New York: Grove Press, Inc., 1957), p. 340.

7. Ira Gitler, *Jazz Masters of the Forties* (New York: Collier-Macmillan, 1966), p. 18.

8. Nat Shapiro and Nat Hentoff, *Hear Me Talkin' to Ya*, p. 357.

9. *Ibid.*, p. 379.

10. Len Lyons, "Horace Silver," in *Contemporary Keyboard*, January-February 1976, p. 19.

11. *Ibid.*

12. Gitler, *op. cit.*, p. 110.

13. Martin Williams, *The Jazz Tradition* (New York: New American Library, 1971), p. 144. Williams attributes this phrasing of the question to Monk, but with no source for the direct quotation

14. Gunther Schuller, "Sonny Rollins and Thematic Improvising," in *Jazz Panorama*, Martin Williams, ed. (New York: Crowell-Collier Press, 1962), pp. 245–247. In this excerpt the parenthetical words were added by the author to clarify Schuller's meaning, which is ambiguous as originally phrased. The essay first appeared in a 1958 issue of *The Jazz Review*, an excellent journal which folded a few years later.

15. Joe Goldberg, *Jazz Masters of the Fifties* (New York: Collier-Macmillan, 1968), p. 102.

16. Chuck Berg, "The Way Newk Feels," *Down Beat*, April 7, 1977, p. 39.

17. Shapiro and Hentoff, *op. cit.*, p. 393.

18. Joe Goldberg, "Who Are Those Guys?" in *Wax Paper*, Vol. 4, Warner Brothers Records, Inc., February 12, 1979, p. 16.

19. Goldberg, *Jazz Masters of the Fifties*, p. 121.

20. Goldberg, "Who Are Those Guys?" p. 13.

21. Goldberg, *Jazz Masters of the Fifties*, p. 70.

22. Goldberg, "Who Are Those Guys?" p. 16.

23. *Ibid.*

24. Whitney Balliett, *The Sound of Surprise* (New York: E. P. Dutton & Co., Inc., 1959), p. 206.

25. Mimi Klar, "Erroll Garner," in *The Jazz Review*, Spring, 1980, p. 8.

26. *Down Beat*, March 13, 1975, p. 14.

27. Len Lyons, "Oscar Peterson," in *Contemporary Keyboard*, March 1978, p. 33.

28. *Ibid.*

29. *Down Beat*, September 29, 1960, p. 17.

30. J. C. Thomas, *Chasin' the Trane* (New York: Doubleday & Co., Inc., 1975), p. 115.

General Discography of Available, Recommended Albums

CANNONBALL ADDERLEY (Quintet)
   The Japanese Concerts, M-47029, Milestone. *74 Miles Away*, ST-2822; *The Best of Cannonball Adderley*, SKOA-2939; *Mercy, Mercy, Mercy*, SM-2663; Capitol. *Phenix*, F-79004, Fantasy. See also, Miles Davis (1957–1959): *Milestones, Kind of Blue* (Chapter 6). *Beginnings* (1955–1959), EMS-2-404, EmArcy. *Cannonball and Eight Giants* (1958), M-47001, Milestone. *Big Man* (with Joe Williams, vocals—a score, 1975), F-79006, Fantasy. *Cannonball with Nancy Wilson* (1961), SM-1657, Capitol. *Something Else* (Miles Davis, 1956), LA-169F, Blue Note.

AFRO-CUBAN
   Afro-Cuban Jazz (Machito, Chico O'Farrill, Dizzy Gillespie and "Manteca Suite"), VE2-2522, Verve.

MOSE ALLISON
   I Don't Worry About a Thing, 1389; *The Best of Mose Allison*, SD-1542; *Western Man*, SD-1584; *Your Mind Is on Vacation*, SD-1691; Atlantic. *Mose Allison*, P-24002, Prestige. *Mose in Your Ear*, SD-1627; *Hello There, Universe*, SD-1550; Atlantic.

RAN BLAKE
   Breakthru, IAI-373842, Improvising Artists. *The Blue Potato*, M-9021, Milestone. *Rapport*, AN-3006, Arista Novus.

ART BLAKEY
   A Night at Birdland, Vol. II (with Clifford Brown and Lou Donaldson), BST-81522; *Live Messengers* (1954–1962), LA473-J2; *Mosaic* (with Wayne Shorter and Freddie Hubbard), BST-84090; *Free for All* (with Hubbard and Shorter, 1964), BST-84170; Blue Note. *Art Blakey and The Jazz Messengers with Thelonious Monk* (1958), AT-1278, Atlantic. *Hard Drive* (1957, with Johnny Griffin), BCP-6037, Bethlehem. *Thermo* (with Hubbard and Shorter), M-47008, Milestone. See also Billy Eckstine, *Mr. B. and the Band*, and Thelonious Monk. Numerous Blakey-Jazz Messenger albums are listed in commercial catalogs.

CLIFFORD BROWN
   Three Giants! (with Rollins and Max Roach), P-7821, Prestige. *Jazz Immortal* (with Zoot Sims, 1954), ST-20139, World Pacific Jazz. *Art Blakey: Live Messengers* (sides 3 and 4, at Birdland 1954), LA473-J2, Blue Note. *The Best of Clifford Brown and Max Roach*, GNPS-18, GNP Crescendo. *Art Blakey: Live at Birdland, Vols. 1* and *2*, BLP-1521; BLP-1522; Blue Note. *Sonny Rollins: Saxophone Colossus and More* (1956, one side only), P-24050, Prestige. *Remember Clifford*, 60827, Mercury.

DAVE BRUBECK
    (A historical overview) *Brubeck on Campus* (1954–1957); CG-31298; *Gone with the Wind/Time Out*, CG-33666; *Newport Festival*, 1958, JCS-8082; *Greatest Hits*, CS-9284; *Adventures in Time*, CG-30625; Columbia. (With Gerry Mulligan, see Mulligan discography.) *Brandenburg Gate Revisited*, JCS-8763, CSP. *Jazz Impressions of Japan* (1964), CS-9012; *Jazz Impressions of New York* (1965), CS-9075, Columbia. *Two Generations of Brubeck* (1973), SD-1645; *All the Things We Are* (1973–1974, with Anthony Braxton, Roy Haynes, Lee Konitz), SD-1684; Atlantic. *Brubeck and Desmond: Duets* (1975), 703, Horizon.

KENNY BURRELL
    Kenny Burrell/John Coltrane (1958), PR-24059, Prestige. *When Lights Are Low*, CJ-83, Concord Jazz.

JAKI BYARD
    Solo Piano, PR-7686; *Freedom Together*, PR-7463; Prestige.

BETTY CARTER
    The Betty Carter Album, MK-1001, Bet-Car. *Finally Betty Carter*, RE-5000; *After Midnight*, RE-5001; *Now It's My Turn*, RE-5005; Roulette.

JOHN COLTRANE (also see Chapter 6 and Chapter 8)
    See Miles Davis and Thelonious Monk Selected Discographies. *Ballads*, A-32; *Duke Ellington and John Coltrane*, A-30; *John Coltrane with Johnny Hartmann*, A-40; Impulse. *Coltrane Plays the Blues*, SD-1382; *Coltrane Jazz*, SD-1354; Atlantic. *The Best of John Coltrane*, SD-1541; *The Art of John Coltrane—The Atlantic Years*, SD-2-313; Atlantic. *Blue Train* (1957), BST-81577, Blue Note.

MILES DAVIS (see also Chapters 6 and 7)
    Workin' and Steamin', P-24034; *Tallest Trees*, PR-24012; *Miles Davis*, PR-24001; *Tune-up*, P-24077; Prestige. *Sketches of Spain*, PC-8271; *Miles Ahead*, PC-8633; Columbia. (See also Charlie Parker Discography.) Of historical interest: *Green Haze*, P-24064; *Dig* (with Sonny Rollins), P-24054; Prestige. *Basic Miles*, PC-32025; *Some Day My Prince Will Come*, PC-8456; *The Miles Davis/Tadd Dameron Quintet*, 34804; *Quiet Nights* (Gil Evans and Orchestra), PC-8906; Columbia. *Facets*, JP-13811, CSP.

BILLY ECKSTINE
    Mr. B. and the Band (with Fats Navarro and Art Blakey), SJL-2214; *Billy Eckstine Sings*, SJL-1127; Savoy.

GIL EVANS (see also Miles Davis)
    Out of the Cool, A-4; *Into the Hot*, A-9; Impulse. *Pacific Standard Time*, LA-461-H2, Blue Note. *Svengali*, SD-1643, Atlantic. *Evans/Dameron: The Arrangers' Touch*, P-24049, Prestige. *There Comes a Time*, APL1-1057, RCA.

TAL FARLOW
    Guitar Player (1955, 1969), P-24042, Prestige.

ELLA FITZGERALD
    The Duke Ellington Songbook (with Ellington, 1957), VE2-2535; *Ella & Duke at the Côte D'Azur*, V6-4072-2; *Ella & Louis*, 2V6S-8811; Verve. Of historical interest: *Ella Fitzgerald: The George & Ira Gershwin Songbook*, VE2-2525; *The Cole Porter Songbook*, VE-2-2511; *The Rodgers and Hart Songbook*, VE2-2519; Verve. *The Best of Ella Fitzgerald* (1940's–1950's),

MCA2-4047; *Vol. II*, MCA-2-4016; MCA. *Ella and Oscar* (with Oscar Peterson, 1975), 2310-759; *Take Love Easy* (with Joe Pass, 1974), 2310-702; *Fitzgerald & Pass . . . Again* (1976), 2310-772; *Montreux '77* (with Tommy Flanagan Trio), 2308-206; Pablo.

STAN GETZ

Getz/Gilberto (with Astrud Gilberto), V-68545; *Diz and Getz* (1953), VE2-2521; *Stan Getz: The Chick Corea and Bill Evans Sessions*, VE2-2510; *Getz Au Go Go*, VE6-8600; Verve. *Stan Getz/Sonny Stitt*, RE-123; *The Best of Stan Getz*, RE-119; Roulette. *Focus* (with strings arranged by Eddie Saunter, 1961), VE1-2528, Verve. Of historical interest: *Stan Getz & Friends* (1949–1953); *Stan Getz*, P-24019; Prestige.

DIZZY GILLESPIE

Dee Gee Days (1951–1952), SDL-2209, Savoy. *The Development of an American Artist*, R-004, Smithsonian Collection (mail). *Sonny Rollins/ Sonny Stitt Sessions*, VE2-2505; *Afro-Cuban Jazz*, VE2-2522; *Jazz at the Philharmonic* (1946, with Charlie Parker and Lester Young), VE2-2518; *Dizzie Gillespie/Stan Getz*, VE2-2521; *Diz and Roy* (with Eldridge), VE2-2524; Verve. *The Giant*, P-24047; *At Salle Pleyel* (1948), P-7818; Prestige. *Echos of an Era* (with Charlie Parker), RE-105; Roulette. *Paris Concert*, GNP-9006, GNP Crescendo. *Composer's Concepts*, EM52-410, EmArcy. *Big 4* (with Ray Brown and Joe Pass), 719; *Oscar Peterson and Dizzy Gillespie*, 740; *Big 7 at Montreux* (with Milt Jackson and Johnny Griffin), 749; *Afro-Cuban Jazz Moods* (with Machito), 771; Pablo. Many more Pablo sessions available.

DEXTER GORDON

The Hunt: Dexter Gordon & Wardell Gray (1947), SJL-2222; *Long Tall Dexter* (with Bud Powell and Tadd Dameron 1947), SJL-2211; Savoy. *Dexter Gordon* (1957–1964), BN-LA393-H2, Blue Note. *Power* (with James Moody, late 1960's), P-24087, Prestige. *Homecoming* (with Woody Shaw, 1976), PG-34650; *Sophisticated Giant* (with Woody Shaw, 1977), JC-34989; *Manhattan Symphonie* (1978), JC-35608; Columbia.

JOHNNY GRIFFIN

Blowin' Sessions (with John Coltrane and Mobley, 1957), LA521-H2, Blue Note. *Little Giant* (1958–1962), M-47054, Milestone. See also Monk's *At the Five Spot* (1957). *Return of the Griffin* (1978), SN-5117, Galaxy.

HAMPTON HAWES

Live at the Montmartre, AL-1020; *A Little Copenhagen Night Music*, AF-1043; Arista. *The Challenge*, JPL1-1508, RCA. *All Night Sessions, Vol. 3*, S-7547, Contemporary. *As Long As There's Music* (with Charlie Haden and duo), AH4, Artists House (mail).

AHMAD JAMAL

Genetic Walk, T-600; *Jamal Plays Jamal*, T-459; 20th Century. *Tranquility* (1973), SF-9238, Impulse.

LEE KONITZ

Tenorlee (on tenor, with Jimmy Rowles, piano), CRS-1019, Choice. *Satori*, M-9060; *Spirits*, M-9038, Milestone.

EDDIE JEFFERSON

The Jazz Singer (1959–1961), IC-1016, Inner City.

LAMBERT, HENDRICKS & ROSS
Sing a Song of Basie, AS-83, Impulse.

YUSEF LATEEF
The Savoy Sessions (1957), SJL-2205, Savoy. *Blues for the Orient* (1957–1961), P-24035, Prestige. Also see Cannonball Adderley Selected Discography. Later, mode-based: *The Live Sessions: Dedication Series, Vol. III* (1964), IA-9353/2, Impulse. *Autophysiopsychic* (1977), 7082, CTI.

MARIAN McPARTLAND
Solo Concert at Haverford (1974), Hal-111, Halcyon. *At the Hickory House* (2 discs, 1952), SJL-2248, Savoy.

THE MODERN JAZZ QUARTET
The Art of the Modern Jazz Quartet (1957–1966), SD2-301; *Fontessa*, 1231; *Pyramid*, 1325; *Third Stream Music*, 1345; *Last Concert*, SD2-909; Atlantic. Of historical interest: *Blues at Carnegie Hall*, 1468; *The Legendary Profile*, SD-1623; *The Modern Jazz Quartet*, 1265; *Blues on Bach*, QD-1652; Atlantic. *In Memoriam*, LD-3001, Little David. *The First Q*, SJL-1106; *Second Nature* (Jackson), SJL-2204; *Opus de Jazz*, SJL-1116; Savoy. *Opus de Funk* (Jackson), P-24048, Prestige. (Milt Jackson recorded prolifically during the mid-1970's for Pablo.)

THELONIOUS MONK
At the Five Spot (1957, with Johnny Griffin), M-47043; *Monk/Trane*, M-47011; *In Person*, M-47033; Milestone. *Thelonious Monk*, P-24006, Prestige. *It's Monk's Time*, CS-8984; *Monk*, CS-8984; *Straight No Chaser*, CS-9451; *Underground*, CS-9632; *Solo Monk*, CS-9149; *Who's Afraid of the Big Band Monk*, PG-32892; *Misterioso* (1966), CS-9216; Columbia. *Monk's Dream*, JCS-8765; *Criss Cross*, JCS-8839; CSP. *Monk's Blues* (1969), CS-8906; *Greatest Hits*, CS-9775; *Miles and Monk at Newport*, PC-8978; Columbia. *Art Blakey and Thelonious Monk* (1958), AT-1278, Atlantic.

WES MONTGOMERY
Movin' (Kelly-Chambers-Cobb-Griffin, 1962), M-47040; *Wes and Friends*, M-47013; Milestone. *The Small Group Recordings*, VE2-2513, Verve. Of historical interest: *Beginnings*, LA531-H2, Blue Note. *Pretty Blue*, M-47030, Milestone. *Wes's Best* (with Buddy and Monk, 1967), 8376, Fantasy. *Bumpin'*, V6-8625; *Best of Wes Montgomery*, V6-8714; *Return Engagement*, V3HB-8839; Verve. *A Day in the Life*, SP-3001, A&M.

LEE MORGAN
The Sidewinder, BST 81451, Blue Note.

GERRY MULLIGAN
Mulligan and Getz and Desmond (1957, 2 discs), VE2-2537, Verve. *The Gerry Mulligan Quartet*, JCS-8732; *What Is There to Say?* (with Art Farmer), JCS-8116; CSP. *Arranger* (1946–1957), JC-34803, Columbia. *Complete Birth of the Cool* (with Miles Davis), M-11026, Capitol. *Mulligan and Paul Desmond: Quartet/Quintet*, F-8082, Fantasy. *At Berlin Philharmonic* (with Dave Brubeck), C-32143; *Blues Roots*, CS-9749; Columbia.

FATS NAVARRO
See Eckstine. *Prime Source*, LA507-H2, Blue Note. *Fats Navarro* (with Tadd Dameron), M-47041, Milestone. *Fat Girl*, SJL-2216, Savoy. (See also Bud Powell Selected Discography; Charlie Parker's *One Night in Birdland*.)

HERBIE NICHOLS

The Bethlehem Years, BCP-6028, Bethlehem. *The Third World*, LA-485-H2, Blue Note.

CHARLIE PARKER

One Night in Birdland (1950, with Bud Powell and Fats Navarro), J6-34808; *Summit Meeting* (1951–1953), JC-34831; Columbia. *Charlie Parker* (Miles Davis, Max Roach, et al.), P-24001; Prestige. *The Verve Years, Vols. 1–3*, 1948–1950, V2-2501; 1950–1951 (with strings), V2-2512; 1952–1954, V2-2523; Verve. *Echos of an Era* (with Dizzy Gillespie), RE-105, Roulette. *Bird at the Roost*, SJL-1108; *Encore* (1944–1948), SJL-1107; Savoy.

JOE PASS

Virtuoso #2, 2310-788; *#3*, 2310-805; *The Trio* (with Oscar Peterson and Niels Pedersen), 2310-701; *Chops* (duo with Pedersen), 2310-830; *The Paris Concert* (with Peterson and Pedersen), 2620-112; Pablo.

OSCAR PETERSON

NHØP, 2308-213, Pablo. *Return Engagement*, V3HB-8842, Verve. *Trio in Transition* (1965–1966), EMS2-405, EmArcy. *In Russia*, 2625-711; *The Trio* (with Joe Pass and Pedersen, 1974), 2310-701; *The History of an Artist* (Brown, Ellis, Kessel, Mraz, Hayes, Jones, 1974), 2625-702; *Paris Concert: Salle Pleyel* (Pass and Pedersen, 1978), 2620-112; Pablo. As accompanist: *Oscar Peterson and Clark Terry*, 2310-742; *Ella and Oscar*, 2310-759; Pablo. *Lester Young: Pres and Teddy and Oscar* (1956), VE2-2501; *Ella & Louis*, 2V6S-8811; Verve.

OSCAR PETTIFORD

(See Rollins, Monk, Ellington's *Golden Duke*, Chapter 4.) *Big Band: The Finest of Oscar Pettiford*, BCP-6007, Bethlehem.

KING PLEASURE

The Source, P-24017, Prestige.

BUD POWELL

The Amazing Bud Powell, Vol. 2 (Curly Russell and Max Roach), BLP-1504; *Bud! Vol. 3* (Paul Chambers, Art Taylor, Curtis Fuller), BLP-1571; *Time Waits, Vol. 4* (Sam Jones and Philly Joe Jones), BLP-1598; *The Scene Changes, Vol. 5* (Chambers and Taylor), BLP-4009; Blue Note. *The Genius of Bud Powell, Vol. 1*, VE2-2526, Verve. *Bud in Paris* (with Johnny Griffin), 102, Xanadu. *Bouncing with Bud*, DL-406, Delmark.

SONNY ROLLINS (See also Clifford Brown)

Sonny Rollins, P-24004, Prestige. *The Freedom Suite Plus*, M-47007, Milestone. *Taking Care of Business* (with Coltrane on "Tenor Madness"), P-24082, Prestige. *Way out West*, S-7530, Contemporary. *A Night at the Village Vanguard*, BLP-1581; *Sonny Rollins* (with Monk, Roach, Blakey, 1956–1957), LA-401-H2; Blue Note. *The Bridge*, AFL-1-0859; *Pure Gold Jazz*, ANL1-2809, RCA. Later albums: *The Milestone Jazzstars* (with Tyner, Carter, Foster, 1978), M55066, Milestone. Later albums of historical interest: *There Will Never Be Another You* (1965), IA-9349, Impulse. *Horn Culture* (1973), M-9051; *The Cutting Edge* (1974), M-9049; *The Way I Feel* (1976), M-9074; *Nucleus* (1977), M-9064; *Don't Stop the Carnival* (1978), M-5505; *Easy Living* (1975), M-9080; Milestone.

GEORGE SHEARING
The Best of George Shearing (1964), SM-2104; *Black Satin*, SM-11800; *The Shearing Touch*, SM-1472; Capitol.

HORACE SILVER
Horace Silver (1953–1968), LA402-42; *The Best of Horace Silver* (1954–1962), BST-84325; *Blowin' the Blues Away* (with Blue Mitchell and Junior Cook), BST-84017; *Sterling Silver* (1956–1963), LA495-H1; *The Trio Sides* (1952–1968), LA474-H2; Blue Note. *A Night at Birdland, Vol. 2* (see "Art Blakey"); *Song for My Father* (1964), BST-84185; *Cape Verdean Blues* (J. J. Johnson, 1966), BST-84220; Blue Note. Later albums of historical interest: *Silver 'n Wood*, LA581-6; *Silver 'n Brass*, LA406-6; *Silver 'n Percussion*, LA853-H; *Silver in Voices*, LA708; Blue Note.

LENNIE TRISTANO
Descent into the Maelstrom, IC-6002, Inner City. (Tristano's out-of-print Atlantics are preferable.) One track on *Piano Giants, Vol. 1*, P-24052, Prestige.

SARAH VAUGHAN
Sarah Vaughan in Hi-Fi, P-13084, Encore (CSP). *How Long Has This Been Going On?* (with Peterson, Pass, Brown, Bellson, 1978), 2310-821, Pablo. *The Sarah Vaughan Years*, RE-103, Roulette. *Live in Japan*, MRL-2401; *More from Japan Live*, MRL-419; Mainstream. *Golden Hits*, SR-60645; *After Hours at the London House*, MG-20383; Mercury. *Sarah Vaughan* (1946–1948, 1 cut with Bud Powell), FS-250, Everest. Of historical interest: *After Hours with Sarah Vaughan*, JCL660, Columbia. *I Love Brazil* (Latin rhythm, 1977), 2312-101, Pablo.

DINAH WASHINGTON
The Jazz Sides (1954–1958), EMS-2-401; *What a Difference a Day Makes* (1959), SR-60158; *Golden Hits, Vols. 1* and *2*, SR-60788/89; Mercury. *Echoes of an Era*, RE2-104, Roulette.

PHIL WOODS
The Phil Woods Six: Live from the Showboat, BGL2-2202; *Song for Sisyphus*, 782-0798; Gryphon.

6

MODERN JAZZ IN TRANSITION (the Later Styles)

Jazz for Jazz's Sake

DURING THE 1960's, jazz record sales were proportionately lower relative to other popular genres than in any other decade of the music's history. Yet the diversity and creativity of jazz had never been more apparent. More liberties were taken with improvisation. Such fundamental concepts as chord progressions and a song's "key" were being challenged by modes, bitonality, and pan-tonality. (The infrequent cases of atonality, which are more relevant to free jazz, will be discussed in Chapter 8.) The familiar "My Funny Valentine," "A Night in Tunisia," and other bebop and hard bop chestnuts were conspicuously absent from the 1960's repertoire, replaced either by more sophisticated, expansive compositions or by a mere wisp of a line intended primarily as a springboard for lengthy improvisations. The audience for this music, however, was dwindling to a virtual handful of *aficionados.* Jazz was being called intellectual and esoteric, accusations that many of the younger players, like Chick Corea and Herbie Hancock, took to heart, as will be noted in more detail in Chapter 7. Elitism, though, was only part of the story, for jazz was being eclipsed by more commercial music forms—rock, soul, and folk music—which were able to reflect and interact with the alienation of the general public.

During the 1960's, America desperately needed a music which responded, either through escapism or through a social commentary, to the profound political turmoil of the decade. The nation was in the throes of protest against governmental authority, the sexual mores of the 1950's, and, most deeply, the war in Vietnam. Although the effects of these issues will be examined more closely in Chapter 7, it must be noted that jazz did not speak to these problems in the bold, overt terms of its competitors. Rock, soul, and folk music simply crowded jazz out of the airwaves and record bins, thus resulting in diminished record-company support and the temporary demise of notable jazz nightclubs. As an art-for-art's-sake movement in a time of great social upheaval, it is no wonder that jazz withered commercially. It was literally marching to the beat of a different drummer, and the other drummer was getting all the work.

The black community in particular was preoccupied with growing nationalist movements, especially the Black Muslim sect, and a much-debated militancy on civil rights. Jazz musicians were as caught up in these social crises as other black Americans, perhaps more so because their art form was intimately related to their African heritage. One can find numerous examples of heightened black consciousness that went beyond the mere naming of compositions, like Sonny Rollins's "Airegin" (Nigeria spelled backward) or Duke Ellington's "Black, Brown and Beige," which had been the extent of national identification in the 1940's and 1950's.

An increasing number of musicians began to investigate African music for inspiration and resources. A well-known case in point is John Coltrane's use of two drummers in his post-1965 bands, simulating the heavily polyrhythmic nature of African music. Coltrane sent regular contributions to the Center of African Culture in Harlem, founded by the Nigerian drummer Olatungi. The influence of the singing of pygmy tribes on the improvising of Eric Dolphy is also documented. African personal names became more common. At the end of the 1960's (to select only two of many possible examples), liner-note credits read Mwandishi and Sulieman Saud, rather than Herbie Hancock and McCoy Tyner.

Allusions to the oppression of American blacks were abundant. Charles Mingus's *Passions of a Man* (Selected Discography) is bursting with fierce diatribes against racism. As John Coltrane wrote in a letter to a *Downbeat* magazine editor, "We all know that this word which so many seem to fear today, 'Freedom,' has a hell of a lot to do with this music." [1] The music seemed to seek freedom itself in the loosening of improvisational and chordal bonds. And of course, free jazz (Chapter 8), as the name suggests, went even farther in this direction.

Yet jazz served America politically by continuing to develop itself as an art form, for the music gave even the political leaders reason for hope. Malcolm X, in a June 1964 address before the Organization of Afro-American Unity, drew an optimistic analogy between the techniques of jazz and the task of the black citizen:

> . . . But that black musician, he picks up his horn and starts blowing some sounds that he never thought of before. He improvises, he creates, it comes from within. It's his soul; it's that soul music. It's the only area on the American scene where the black man has been free to create. And he has mastered it. . . . He can come up with a philosophy that nobody has heard of yet. He can invent a society, a social

system, an economic system, a political system that is different from anything that exists or has ever existed anywhere on this earth. He will improvise; he'll bring it from within himself.[2]

Black consciousness and an awareness of African music, while they account for emotional overtones in the playing, do not explain jazz's strikingly new sound. In fact, Indian classical music, for reasons which will become clear in the album discussions, had a more direct effect on Coltrane's and Dolphy's playing—and on the stylistic evolution—than did the indigenous African forms. Severing the intimate connection between the black's social existence and the meaning of his music is impossible; an entire volume, along the lines of LeRoi Jones's *Blues People*, could and should be devoted to the subject.[3] But a concern for jazz as an art form demands focusing on other considerations, too. While no artist creates in a social vacuum, neither can the elements of music be explained satisfactorily by the political climate of the day.

Jazz à la Mode

An accurate image of jazz in the 1960's is that of a structure being stretched elastically in all directions simultaneously. Thus the albums described in this chapter are a *potpourri* of challenges to the basic premises of modern jazz. While even more revolutionary breaks with the music of the past will be discussed in Chapter 8, the music ahead constitutes the first indication that jazz can transcend the blues and ballads of its first half-century without losing its spontaneity, earthiness, and swing.

The "modal" or "scalar" approach to improvising is central to the new developments. Modality offers musicians the unprecedented possibility of improvising upon a series of tones, similar to a scale, rather than upon chord progressions. Simply defined, a mode is a sequence of notes in a given whole-step, half-step pattern that establishes a tonality (that is, a keynote to which the others eventually gravitate). Far from being a jazz invention, the modal sequences are found in modern European music, in European music of the 1600's, in church music of the Middle Ages, and in the ancient Greek music system. In fact, the names for the common modes—Ionian, Dorian, Phrygian, Lydian, Mixolydian, Aeolian, Locrian—are taken from the Greeks, who had named them after their conquered territories and islands.[4] For jazz musicians, however, these sequences became the vehicles of increased freedom and self-expression.

Miles Davis's *Kind of Blue* (1959) was the first album to demonstrate the fertility of the modal approach, although other musicians—notably Charles Mingus, George Russell, and Bill Evans—had experimented with it earlier in individual pieces. Davis adopted the modes because he felt jazz compositions were becoming "thick with chords" and consequently restrictive: "I think a movement in jazz is beginning away from the conventional strings of chords, and a return to emphasis on a melodic, rather than a harmonic, variation. There will be fewer chords but infinite possibilities as to what to do with them." [5]

The modal approach lifts the burden of constantly changing harmonies, thereby increasing the burden of inventiveness upon the improvisers. While a sense of variety was often built into bebop and hard bop by using dozens of chord changes in a thirty-two-bar piece, modal jazz employed a single sequence of notes as its "raw material" for as long as sixteen bars (for example "So What," *Kind of Blue*, Selected Discography). Thus the melodic freedom that was gained had to be matched by the players' melodic imagination.

John Coltrane was the most influential of the modal improvisers. His profound understanding of chord progressions, as demonstrated on *Giant Steps* (Chapter 5), allowed him to take even greater advantage of the relative harmonic emptiness of modal music. As Coltrane explained to Don DeMichael in a *Down Beat* magazine interview (September 29, 1960):

> This approach allowed the soloist the choice of playing chordally (vertically) or melodically (horizontally). I found it easier to apply the harmonic ideas that I had. I could stack up chords—say, on a C^7, I sometimes superimposed an Eb^7, up to an $F\#^7$, down to an F. That way I could play three chords on one. But on the other hand, if I wanted to I could play melodically. Miles's music gave me plenty of freedom.

Since the modes required so few specific harmonies, the players were free to improvise whatever harmonic movement they desired—or to build with hypnotic intensity upon a single tonal center. In discussing Coltrane's albums, it will become clear that he frequently increased the tension within his music by playing chords made up of notes *outside* of the given mode. Ornette Coleman (Chapter 8), a daring improviser who did not feel bound by chord changes at all, influenced Coltrane strongly in this direction. Eric Dolphy (Selected Discography) also explored the idea of soloing beyond the boundaries of established harmonic structure under the influence of Coleman and Coltrane.

Chords were no longer the well-defined entities they had been, once the superimposition of chords upon chords had begun. The innovative sound of *Speak Like a Child* (Selected Discography) is explained in these terms by Herbie Hancock, one of the great young pianists and arrangers of the 1960's:

> For the most part, the harmonies in these numbers are freer in the sense that they're not so easily identifiable chordally in the conventional way. I'm more concerned with sounds than chords, and so I voice the harmonies to provide a wider spectrum of colors than can be contained within the traditional chord progressions. In much of the album, there

are places where you could call the harmonies by any one of four desig-
nations, but no one designation would really include everything that's
involved.[6]

Charles Mingus, perhaps more than any other musician, personified the
transition from bebop to a freer jazz style. From behind a powerful, articulate
string bass, Mingus led his ensembles across the boundaries of blues and
ballad structures. As early as 1956 he juggled modes, polytonality, atonality,
and rhythmic freedom with consummate skill in the mature "extended form"
composition "Pithecanthropus Erectus" (on *Passions of a Man*). "Extended
form" allowed the player to improvise at length on any chord by making use
of a mode built upon its tonal center. Mingus did not limit his bands to one
tempo. He realized that as long as the beat could be felt, it did not have to be
stated explicitly or adhered to rigidly.

The evolution of jazz styles generally occurs through trial and error; practice precedes theory. In the case of the transitional modern styles, however,
an impressive theoretical work by the composer George Russell facilitated the
thinking and the progress of the musicians who studied it. Russell's views are
documented in his *Lydian Chromatic Concept of Tonal Organization* (1953),
a far-reaching manifesto of jazz's inevitable movement toward polytonality.
His research on the theory had been worked out during the mid-1940's on the
piano at a New York sanitarium, where he was recuperating from tuberculosis.
His premise was that the Lydian mode and the scales obtainable from it are
the actual sequence of tones upon which most improvisers rely. Russell
argued that the Lydian scale superimposed upon a song's original harmony
conveys its true tonal center. In effect, each chord (vertical arrangement of
notes) is to be expanded into the Lydian scale (horizontal arrangement) that
best expresses the sound of the chord. Numerous tonal centers coexist, expanding the harmonic and melodic breadth of the music to the breaking point.
The breaking point beyond which Russell would not go was atonality, since
Russell believed that jazz is rooted in a tonal folk music, specifically, the blues.

Russell did not believe in the absence of tonal centers but in a multiplicity
of them, or pan-tonality. He believed that any one of the twelve tones within
the octave was eligible as the tonal center. The purpose of the Lydian modal
patterns in his book is to provide the improviser with "the full spectrum of
tonal colors available." The success with which he put his theory into practice
can be heard on *Outer Thoughts* (Selected Discography).

Not surprisingly, the radically evolving styles met with skeptical and even
angry denouncements from some critics. The most notorious of these criticisms appeared in *Down Beat* magazine (November 23, 1969), and one can
be sure the sentiments it expressed were shared by many: "Go ahead, call me
reactionary. I happen to object to the musical nonsense currently being
peddled in the name of jazz by John Coltrane and his acolyte, Eric Dolphy
. . . They seem bent on pursuing an anarchistic course in their music that
can but be termed anti-jazz." Another reviewer concluded that in the final

analysis Coltrane's "Chasin' the Trane" (on *"Live" at the Village Vanguard*, Selected Discography) amounted to "sputtering inconclusiveness." [7]

The new and more diffuse idea of tonality, one that is difficult for some listeners to adjust to, was at the root of such discontent, a point recognized by Eric Dolphy in his rebuttal of this criticism: "I think of my playing as tonal . . . I play notes that would not ordinarily be said to be in a given key, but I hear them as proper. I don't think I 'leave the changes,' as the expression goes; every note I play has some reference to the chords of the piece." [8] In a way, Coltrane's more philosophical response to the accusation points directly to the heart of the misunderstanding: "People have so many definitions of jazz, how can antijazz be defined?" [9] It was simply a case of the musicians being able to hear beyond their critics.

Ultimately time has proved what argumentation could not—two decades later this music has lost none of its beauty and freshness while it has gained considerable acceptance and recognition. The albums which follow are rooted in bebop and yet reach out for new horizons, striking an exciting balance between accessibility and adventure.

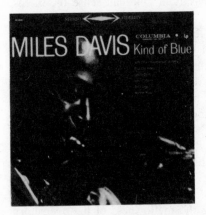

MILES DAVIS

Kind of Blue

Columbia, PC 8163
one disc, brief liner notes
1959

Musicians: Miles Davis, trumpet; John Coltrane, tenor sax; Cannonball Adderley, alto sax; Bill Evans, Wynton Kelly (where marked *), piano; Paul Chambers, bass; Jimmy Cobb, drums.
Compositions: Side one: So What; Freddie Freeloader*; Blue in Green. *Side two:* All Blues; Flamenco Sketches.

Kind of Blue, a collection of first takes recorded without a single rehearsal, is one of the most influential albums of the modern period, and is loved equally by musicians and listeners. It is the first album to demonstrate the haunting beauty soloists could achieve by improvising upon modes and around tonal centers. With the musicians liberated from the constant flow of chord changes, their melodic lines develop more freely, building tension by straying from and returning to the tonal centers; the album maintains an exquisite balance of relaxation and tension throughout. *Kind of Blue* is one of a kind in the Miles Davis discography. While the modal concept played a role in his future recordings, Miles never pursued it again—as John Coltrane and others did—with complete commitment.

The contribution of pianist Bill Evans to this album's style should not be overlooked. Miles had worked with him in 1958 after Red Garland left to form his own trio. The new musical approach dictated his rehiring. Evans, a student of George Russell's Lydian scale concept, had one of the most original and thoroughly analyzed harmonic conceptions of the late 1950's, along with a lyricism which complemented Davis's own. He had impressed Miles with his solo playing between sets at the Village Vanguard and—most relevantly— with his own modal composition "Peace Piece," actually an improvisation recorded shortly before the present session. The beginning of "Peace Piece," in fact, serves as the opening to "Flamenco Sketches" here. Miles went to Evans's home the morning of the session, where they roughed out the music's form together. Although the album credits do not indicate it, Evans composed "Blue in Green" and collaborated on the other compositions except for Miles's "Freddie Freeloader."

The playing on these tracks, like that of the early New Orleans bands, is virtually a spontaneous collective improvisation. One can sense the intense concentration and seriousness of purpose of the individual soloists in the care they lavish on every phrase. "So What," with its mysterious "kind of blue" tonality, revolves around two tonal centers: one for the first sixteen bars and the final eight bars; the other center, a half-step higher, for the third eight-bar segment. Theoretically the piece does not rely on chords at all, but on a tonal sequence known as the Dorian mode. The bass and horns engage in a call-and-response pattern that adds momentum and dynamic variety to the piece.

The open structure allows Davis's rhythmic genius to emerge fully. He need not concern himself with getting to the next harmonic change. Thus his phrasing becomes even more fascinating and compelling. He remains an artist of the short line, allowing long silences between his flowing sequences and punched-out notes. Never abandoning the mellowness of his open horn, Miles stacks these lines one on top of another, building to a natural climax, then he descends slowly, allowing Coltrane to pick up the line.

As noted in the discussion of *Giant Steps* in Chapter 5, Coltrane greeted the modal approach to improvising as if it had been invented for him. The absence of prescribed changes freed him to superimpose "chord" patterns (in a modal context one should really say "scale" patterns) in fresh combinations of his own choosing. He is, however, more conservative in that regard on this album than on the "Milestones" cut (see *Milestones*, Chapter 5) of five months earlier. Perhaps the cautious mood of the session moved him in that direction. His power comes less from the flurries of notes one usually associates with Trane than from his chant-like intonation on tenor sax and his ability to keep the tonal center droning throughout his solo. "So What" and "Freddie Freeloader" both have this quality, while "Flamenco Sketches" profits from Trane's strong sense of dynamics. Notice how the solo ends in the breathy tones of a·Prez or Stan Getz, a significant departure for a horn player who is given to the hard-edged attack of Coleman Hawkins.

Cannonball Adderley (Chapter 5) is an elegant lyric player on "So What" and "All Blues," a twelve-bar blues conceived in a swaying ⁶⁄₈ meter. On "So What" he indulges in a heavy, romantic vibrato, but avoids a corny "ballroom" sound with his rhythmic drive and melodic originality. It is astonishing how much more music Adderley could play than the hard bop for which his quintet become known.

Bill Evans's role as a pianist here is every bit as crucial as his collaboration with Miles prior to the session. One need only compare his performance with Wynton Kelly's. Kelly sat in for the "Freddie Freeloader" track, playing a linear solo in a style similar to that of Bud Powell. It is not that Kelly's solo does not swing; it does, but it swings too much at the expense of the music's texture. As we shall see in the Evans discussion later, Evans introduced new textures to the keyboard, many of which became a standard vocabulary for the next generation of pianists; and these textures were perfectly suited to the impressionistic lyricism Miles had in mind for *Kind of Blue*. His chords are especially prominent on "Blue in Green." However, "Flamenco Sketches" provides a better illustration, if one listens carefully to Evans's lush and spreading chords in the background. In a sense the Evans touch recalls Bix Beiderbecke's famous piano solo "In a Mist" (Chapter 3). Evans and Bix (in his later years) had in common a love of Ravel and Debussy, both of whom made use of similar modes in their compositions for piano.

"Flamenco Sketches" is the earliest manifestation of Miles's interest in Spanish music, which found full expression six months later in *Sketches of Spain* (Chapter 5). This track offers the improviser more freedom than any other on the album, for it adopts Mingus's "extended form" technique; each soloist runs through a series of five scales, playing as long as he wishes on each one until the series is complete.

Jimmy Cobb, who joined Miles a year earlier for *Porgy and Bess* (Chapter 5), is less aggressive in his fills than Philly Joe Jones, enhancing the quiet lyricism of *Kind of Blue*. Chambers as usual commands the central rhythmic pulse throughout. Miles maintained the Chambers-Cobb-Kelly rhythm section (Evans left to establish himself as a trio pianist) until 1963, when he once again returned to a harder-hitting accompaniment in Ron Carter, Tony Williams, and Herbie Hancock, whose dynamic albums with Miles will be discussed next.

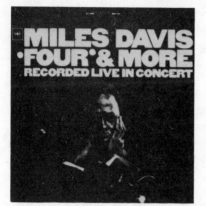

MILES DAVIS

'Four' & More

Columbia, PC 9253
one disc, brief liner notes
1964

Musicians: Miles Davis, trumpet; Herbie Hancock, piano; George Coleman, tenor sax; Ron Carter, bass; Tony Williams, drums.
Compositions: Side one: So What; Walkin', Joshua/Go Go (Theme). *Side two:* Four; Seven Steps to Heaven; There Is No Greater Love/Go Go.

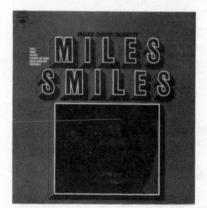

Miles Smiles

Columbia, CS 9401
one disc, brief liner notes
1966

Musicians: Same as above, except Wayne Shorter, tenor sax.
Compositions: Side one: Orbits; Circle; Footprints. *Side two:* Dolores; Freedom Jazz Dance; Ginger Bread Boy.

In 1964 Miles Davis's music went through a transition from the hard bop style (Chapter 5) to a rhythmically and harmonically freer format, exemplified by several excellent albums: *E.S.P.*; *Miles Smiles*; *Sorcerer*; *Nefertiti*; and *Filles de Killimanjaro*. In these recordings Miles departs from the ballads and bebop repertoire for which he was known in favor of band originals. The new pieces are more instrumental in concept, and Davis's own musical statements are bolder and more outgoing. His band, made up of young, uncompromising musicians, burns with energy and sparkles with virtuosity.

Herbie Hancock (discussed ahead) was an important source of information about this band, for Miles had grown more remote and tight-lipped with every passing year. His leadership was oblique and aloof. He maintained a master-apprentice relationship with the younger players rather than treating them as the colleagues Coltrane and Garland had been. His directions were often cryptic. According to Hancock, Miles provoked drummer Tony Williams's whipcrack sound on snare drum when he told the teenager to "play that *Rat Patrol* stuff." No one knew what he had in mind, nor did he explain. *Rat Patrol*, it was discovered, was a television series about a tank battalion, implying that Miles was requesting a more martial drum sound. "He got Tony off the cymbals-with-brushes behind the horns, the way everybody else played, and onto the snare-with-sticks," Hancock said. "It gave us a whole new sound." [10]

Hancock's own hiring was a fact that he had to infer from Davis's elliptical conversation. He had been invited to jam with the rest of the group in the basement of Miles's home, but Davis himself appeared only briefly to play a few notes and mutter an expletive, after which he disappeared upstairs. Hancock had no reason to believe anything had come of the session until several days later when Miles called, telling him to show up at the Columbia studios the next afternoon. Herbie finally had to ask outright, "Does that mean I'm in the band?" "You're making the record date, ain't you?" Miles responded.[11] Herbie learned later that Miles had been listening to his "audition" upstairs on an intercom.

Davis gave lessons in creativity primarily by example. He put to artistic purpose nearly every sound and idea which crossed his path, a virtue recalled in a *Down Beat* magazine interview with Hancock in 1973. The incident occurred at a concert of the *Miles Smiles* band in Germany—Herbie was 'comping for Miles's solo:

> I played the chord too soon, way to soon. It clashed with everything that was going on. Miles played . . . something on top of my chord to make it sound right. He made it fit. . . . He didn't hear it as a clash, he heard it as 'this is what's happening right now, so I'll make the most of it,' and he did.

'Four' & More, recorded at a benefit performance for the Congress on Racial Equality (CORE), catches this band virtually at the point of Miles's transformation. While much of the old repertoire is performed, it is rejuvenated by the new style of playing. From the bite of Miles's opening solo on "So What," it is clear he means to dig in. Many of the Davis bands exhibit a contemplative strain in their music, as if they were stepping backward, bemused by their own creations; but on this occasion their virtuosity is clearly on its toes, pitched forward. The rhythm section, powered by Tony Williams's exuberant fills, crackles beneath Miles on every track. As Davis's biographer Bill Cole recalls the concert, "The total energy level between the performers and the spectators set sparks flying."

Miles is a new man on trumpet. He boasts a bold, sometimes harsh, slashing tone. His new technical mastery allows for lines requiring greatly increased agility. The "So What" solo remains aloft in the upper register, a thrillingly expressive area for Miles, where he would not (and could not) have ventured a few years earlier. He seems at last to use his technique with complete confidence, prompting more abstract, faster-moving interpretations of material that had become second nature. "Stella by Starlight" and "My Funny Valentine," on *My Funny Valentine*, the second album to come out of the CORE concert, provide a stunning example of his progress in this direction, especially when compared with his 1956 version of "Valentine" on Milestone's "twofer," *Miles Davis*.

Herbie Hancock, who a decade later would become the first of the gold-album artists of the fusion style (Chapter 7), is crisply articulate and harmonically astute. The highly inventive scalar solos on "Walkin'," "Joshua," and "There Is No Greater Love" are influenced by Bill Evans's style more than any other single source; but Hancock's timing and keyboard attack are entirely personal. Hancock's forte has always been accompaniment, which emerges here most vividly on "Four," in which his intuitive rapport with Williams and his crashing chords supply powerfully timed accents beneath Miles's solo.

On *Miles Smiles* the new Davis band has completed its metamorphosis. While Davis never approved of the iconoclastic freedom claimed by Ornette Coleman, Eric Dolphy, or John Coltrane, there is no mistaking the increased loosening of structure on the albums from 1965 to 1968. The compositions seem now to be mere melodic gestures, as are Wayne Shorter's piece "Orbits" and Davis's "Circle"; they are lines which can be moved away from quickly, or, like "Footprints," have virtually no harmonic movement, thus offering the soloists an unrestricted environment for exploration.

Miles Davis and Wayne Shorter solo on four tracks without piano accompaniment, liberating them entirely from harmonic demands. When Hancock 'comps on the other two tracks, he carefully stays out of Miles's way and no longer "feeds" him with the frequency he did on *'Four' & More*. It is Ron Carter and Tony Williams who become the catalytic agents, boosting Miles to jagged melodic heights and spurring him into aggressive rhythmic patterns. Williams has an extraordinary facility, most evident on "Dolores" and on "Ginger Bread Boy," for sustaining a polyrhythmic feeling while adding fills and accents with stimulating sharpness and originality. However, Williams feels free to project himself into dialogue with the horn soloist because of Ron Carter's unshakeable rhythmic sense. Carter plays with a rich, resonant tone and stalwartly defends the music's pulse, anticipating the soloists' every move with the right harmonic choice—not an easy task on a track like "Freedom Jazz Dance." Before Miles hired him in 1963, Ron Carter (who holds an M.A. from the Eastman School of Music) had been playing with Eric Dolphy (on Prestige's *Magic*), an experience which must certainly have improved his ability to listen and respond. Note the ease with which he holds the rhythm together on the classic Shorter composition "Footprints," a swinging $\%$ waltz with periodic spurts of $\frac{4}{4}$ meter. His ability to glide into the correct pitch allows him to insinuate himself sensuously into the pockets of silence, as on the slow-paced, muted Davis original "Circle."

Wayne Shorter (General Discography), a brilliant improviser whom Davis finally succeeded in luring away from Art Blakey's Jazz Messengers in 1964, became an ideal foil for Miles's challenging originality. [Sam Rivers (Chapter 8) had a brief tenure with the band first, but he was reportedly too "free" improvisationally for Miles.] Shorter, who has a composer's sense of order and balance, tends to adhere more closely to the composition's theme. His tenor sax playing was first influenced by John Coltrane, whom he befriended in the late 1950's. However, a solo like that on "Orbit" shows that the brief phrases and care for thematic development, so typical of Sonny Rollins, are also present. Wayne Shorter turned out to be this band's most prolific composer, whose compositions are best represented here by the engaging "Dolores." Shorter is also capable of sensuous, slowly developing themes such as those found on *Nefertiti*. (His performance on *V.S.O.P./The Quintet*, discussed ahead, should not be missed.)

The *Miles Smiles* band is a clean, precise instrument that set its sights on a goal beyond the music of the day. Thus its abstract versions of pieces like "Freedom Jazz Dance" and "Gingerbread" evoke a futuristic, even ethereal image which is appropriate to the music's historical role. In addition to Davis's consistently creative soloing, the unanimity of spirit elevates this album above the others of the same period.

Of the remaining albums, *Nefertiti* (1967) is fully realized compositionally, achieving a broad range of moods. While Davis does not solo with the brilliance of *Smiles*, the sessions yield one of Hancock's best unaccompanied piano solos on "Madness." One year later *Filles de Killimanjaro*, with Chick Corea replacing Herbie Hancock on most cuts, offered the dazzling jewel "Petits Machins," a piece that contains a bursting, high-register solo of compressed ideas which rates as one of Miles's best.

Early in 1969 Miles Davis began a new transition toward a jazz/rock fusion with *In a Silent Way*, an experimental album which will be discussed along with the controversial *Bitches Brew* in Chapter 7. In this final innovative period, Miles would more than triple his audience and, at the same time, stun and alienate many of his oldest fans.

BILL EVANS

The Village Vanguard Sessions

Milestone, 47002
two discs, good liner notes
1961

Musicians: Bill Evans, piano; Scott LaFaro, bass; Paul Motian, drums.
Compositions: Side one: My Foolish Heart; My Romance; Some Other Time. *Side two:* Solar; Gloria's Step; My Man's Gone Now. *Side three:* All of You; Alice in Wonderland; Porgy. *Side four:* Milestones; Detour Ahead; Waltz for Debby; Jade Visions.

Intuition

Fantasy, F-9475
one disc, no liner notes
1974

Musicians: Bill Evans, piano and electric piano; Eddie Gomez, bass.
Compositions: Side one: Invitation; Blue Serge; Show-Type Tune; The Nature of Things. *Side two:* Are You All the Things?; A Face Without a Name; Falling Grace; Hi Lili, Hi Lo.

BILL EVANS WAS the most innovative and influential pianist between Bud Powell and Cecil Taylor, and the albums selected above document his performances at two major peaks in his twenty-five-year recording career. As a pianist Evans moved beyond the sharply etched, blues-based melodies and sporadic chordal 'comping of hard bop as typified by Horace Silver and Oscar Peterson toward a romantic, sensitive, and introspective style using lush harmonies and lengthy, scale-based improvisations. Thus he became an important model for many of the pianists who developed during the 1960's, including Herbie Hancock, Paul Bley, Keith Jarrett, and Chick Corea. The precedents set by Evans's trio with Scott LaFaro and Paul Motian were equally historic. Their telepathic, spontaneous interplay led to a feeling of collective improvisation, setting new standards for the trio form.

Born in 1929 Bill Evans grew up in Plainfield, New Jersey, and began studying piano, flute, and violin at the age of 6. As a teenager he had his own band, which included his brother and vibist Don Elliott. He received a music scholarship to Southeastern Louisiana College, where he played his first jazz dates during the summer with bassist Red Mitchell and guitarist Mundell Lowe. It was Lowe who first brought Evans to the attention of Riverside Records later on (in 1956) by playing a taped performance over the telephone for Orrin Keepnews. But Evans would broaden his experience considerably between graduation from college and the Riverside dates reissued here.

In 1950 Bill Evans went on the road with the dance band of Herbie Fields, until he was drafted in 1951 and assigned to play flute in the Fifth Army band. While serving at Fort Sheridan until 1954, he was able to work nights in nearby Chicago, where he began playing with the clarinetist Tony Scott and, more important, composer George Russell. Russell, who had already formulated his *Lydian Chromatic Concept of Tonal Organization* (see the introduction to this chapter and Russell, Selected Discography ahead) introduced Evans to the idea of modality, which has permeated his playing ever since. Evans was the pianist on Russell's celebrated early composition "All About Rosie" (unavailable).

After his stint in the Army, Evans enrolled in the Mannes College of Music in New York for graduate studies, augmenting his academic training with a personal analysis of the jazz and classical styles which had impressed him. These included those of Bach, Ravel, Charlie Parker, Stan Getz, Bud Powell, Horace Silver, and the harmonically complex thinker Lennie Tristano. Evans did not settle for imitating the sounds that appealed to him, but painstakingly reconstructed these styles on the piano like—in his own words—"an architect or a draftsman." [12] His playing increased in depth and complexity, although these very qualities drew criticism throughout the 1960's as being overly intellectual and self-absorbed.

In 1958 Evans was hired by Miles Davis for the historic sextet which included John Coltrane and Cannonball Adderley. Miles's first pianist, Red Garland, had left to lead his own trio. Later that year Evans followed in Red's footsteps, recording the atypically hard-driving sessions for Riverside reissued on Milestone's *Peace Piece and Other Pieces*, the first essential album in an Evans collection. With drummer Philly Joe Jones from the Miles band, Bill plays aggressive versions of the bebop classics "Oleo" and "Minority" in his most spirited pre-LaFaro performance. The ballads "Tenderly" and "What Is There to Say?" reveal his blossoming harmonic conception. Of course, the album's historic track is the modal construction "Peace Piece," which evolved as an in-studio improvisation for the opening to a Broadway show tune ("Some Other Time" from *On the Town*). "Peace Piece" was an important inducement for Miles to rehire Evans for the *Kind of Blue* session discussed previously.

Evans's pianistic identity was not fully established until his meeting with Scott LaFaro and Paul Motian, who joined him at Basin Street in New York, where Evans had been hired (shortly after leaving Miles) as a warm-up act for Benny Goodman. LaFaro was a teenage extrovert with plenty of guts to make up for his lack of experience. His rapport with Evans and Motian allowed the trio to realize its goal of playing as a single unified "instrument." Their first studio sessions, recorded in 1959 and in February 1961 and reissued on *Spring Leaves*, are a very good two-disc set, but markedly more tame than their full-blown, legendary triumph taped live at the Village Vanguard in June 1961.

The Village Vanguard Sessions contains the peak performances of this historic band just ten days before its tragic end with Scott LaFaro's death in an early morning automobile accident in upstate New York. LaFaro is heard playing melody almost continually in the bass's upper register, an area to which his counterparts on the instrument only strayed occasionally for effect. (The year before, LaFaro had had the distinction of playing opposite Charlie Haden on Ornette Coleman's *Free Jazz* session, Chapter 8.) LaFaro deserves equal credit with Evans for the success of their interlocking improvised lines. Evans is in top form, displaying the sensitive, lyrical touch which distinguished him from his more bluesy, earthy, hard bop contemporaries. His calm, introspective harmonic building transforms such commonplace ballads as "My Romance" into rich, impressionistic studies. The collectively improvised choruses on "Gloria's Step," "Solar," and "Milestones" show the genuinely (not superficially) pretty results of Bill Evans's scale-based melodic thinking. Although his own composing is rarely celebrated, Evans's "Waltz For Debby" here, written years earlier for a niece, possesses a fragile, swaying beauty that has made it a standard of his repertoire into the late 1970's.

The shock of LaFaro's death caused the reflective, rather introverted Evans to retreat into a kind of retirement for a year until the bassist Chuck Israels motivated him to return to the studio, again with Motian on drums. *The Second Trio* reissues several sessions from 1962, one of which was conceived of as an all-ballads album by Riverside. The major attraction of these sides, the music of which is not up to the standards of the Vanguard cuts, is the presence of five originals by Evans, including the excellent "Show-Type Tune."

Most of Evans's playing from 1963 to 1969 was recorded for Verve, which has kept little of it available, including the 1963 Grammy winner *Conversations with Myself*, in which he foreshadowed the multitracking of the 1970's by playing duo with his own prerecorded tracks. The available albums are the two-disc *Trio*, an uneventful set with Paul Motian and Gary

Peacock (guitarist Jim Hall was added on two sides), and Evans's first straight solo LP *Alone*—a studied, too contemplative work which marked the beginning of the pianist's continuing association with producer Helen Keane. *Alone (Again)* recorded for Fantasy in 1975 is a far superior solo performance and one of Evans's very best records, for reasons which will be explained presently.

In the 1970's Evans emerged as a new man without the cerebral, brooding quality which had plagued his less successful early albums. He once attributed the change to his refreshed personal outlook, brightened by a happy marriage and the birth of his first child.[13] His playing began to show more vitality in 1971 with his new trio, including Eddie Gomez (bass) and Marty Morell (drums), on Columbia's two-disc *The Bill Evans Album*. However, the definitive breakthrough was on the live *Tokyo Concert* (1973), the first of many excellent Fantasy releases. This album, which reexamines two tunes played on the Vanguard sessions of 1961, has all the virtues of *Intuition*, and the choice between the two is strictly a matter of taste.

Intuition is one of the few of his own records which the self-critical Evans plays at home. There is no doubt that "Show-Type Tune" and "Are You All the Things?" possess a rhythmic drive and snap not present in Evans's earlier work, even the best of it. On every track his melodic lines are longer and more definite, revealing a new clarity to his ideas and the ability to develop them at length. The unfailing momentum makes the duo format quite satisfying, especially since Gomez, an elegant, articulate bassist in the improvisational LaFaro tradition, can swing as hard as necessary without losing contact with the melody. Although it may come as a shock to admirers of Evans's beautiful touch at the keyboard, *Intuition* is also a high-water mark in the use of the electric piano in modern jazz. Using a phase shifter, Evans gets a swirling, singing sound out of the Rhodes on which he improvises with forceful lyricism. No one but Chick Corea has done as well with this controversial instrument in a swinging, straight-ahead approach.

Montreux III, recorded live the next summer (1975) at the Montreux (Switzerland) Jazz Festival, repeats the duo format and succeeds equally on all counts except for the electric piano tracks, which are undermined by faulty sound. *Alone (Again)*, which was mentioned earlier, shows the benefits of his more energetic, outgoing style being applied to a solo concept that exchanges the pastel shadings of the 1960's for more vibrant, primary tonal colors. In 1977 Evans moved to the Warner Brothers label, where he picked up another theme from the Verve years with *New Conversations*, miraculously overdubbing up to three piano parts without getting in his own way. Evans's move to Warner's was motivated in part by the possibility of experimenting with an orchestral format which would be arranged by a longtime admirer, Michel Legrand. While the collaboration has not occurred to date, it is worth watching for. In the meantime a few more sessions from the 1970's are listed in the General Discography. Far from wearing his talent thin, Evans is one of the few players to have enjoyed more than one prime.

CHARLES MINGUS and ERIC DOLPHY

The Charlie Mingus Jazz Workshop/
Stormy Weather (includes *Charles Mingus*
Presents Charles Mingus)

2-6015, Barnaby (GRT Canada)
two discs, brief liner notes
1960

Musicians: Sides three and four: Charles Mingus, bass; Eric Dolphy, alto sax and bass
   clarinet; Ted Curson, trumpet; Dannie Richmond, drums. *Sides one and two,* add
   Jimmy Knepper, Britt Woodman, trombones; Lonnie Hillyer, trumpet; Booker
   Ervin, tenor sax; Nico Bunick or Paul Bley, piano.
Compositions (all by Mingus except as indicated): *Sides one and two:* MDM; Vas-
   salean. Stormy Weather (Gershwin); Lock 'em Up. *Sides three and four:* Folk
   Forms, No. 1; Original Faubus Fables. What Love; All the Things You Could Be
   by Now If Sigmund Freud's Wife Was Your Mother.

CHARLES MINGUS

Passions of a Man (An Anthology)

Atlantic, SD-3-600
three discs, liner notes
1956–1961, 1973–1977

Musicians: Charles Mingus, bass, piano, and voice; Jackie McLean, alto sax; Mal
   Waldron, piano; J. R. Monterose, tenor sax; Willie Jones, drums. Also Shafi Hadi,
   alto sax; Jimmie Knepper, trombone; Wade Legge, piano; Dannie Richmond, drums.
   Also John Handy, alto sax; Booker Erwin, tenor sax; Pepper Adams, baritone sax;

Horace Parlan, piano. Also Rahsaan Roland Kirk, tenor sax, flute, siren, manzello, stritch. Also George Adams, tenor sax; Don Pullen, piano; Jack Walrath, trumpet. Also Ricky Ford, tenor sax; Philip Catherine and Larry Coryell, guitars; George Mraz, bass; Bob Neloms, piano.

Compositions (all by Mingus): *Side one:* Pithecanthropus Erectus; Profile of Jackie; Reincarnation of a Lovebird. *Side two:* Haitian Fight Song; Wednesday Night Prayer Meeting; Cryin' Blues. *Side three:* Devil Woman; Wham Bam, Thank You Ma'am; Passions of a Man; Tonight at Noon. *Side four:* Passion of a Woman Loved; Duke Ellington's Sound of Love. *Side five:* Better Git It in Your Soul; Sue's Changes. *Side six:* Canon; Free Cell Block F; 'Tis Nazi U.S.A.; Goodbye; Pork Pie Hat; Mingus on Mingus (monologue).

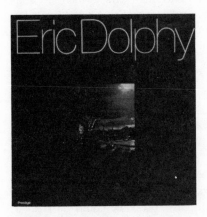

ERIC DOLPHY

Copenhagen Concert

Prestige, PR-24027
two discs, brief liner notes
1961

Musicians: Eric Dolphy, flute, alto sax, and bass clarinet; Chuck Israels, bass. *Also on sides three and four:* Bent Axen, piano; Eric Moseholm, bass; Jorn Elniff, drums.

Compositions: Side one: Hi-Fly; Glad to Be Unhappy. *Side two:* God Bless the Child; Oleo. *Side three:* Woody'n You; When Lights Are Low. *Side four:* In the Blues (3 takes).

CHARLES MINGUS AND ERIC DOLPHY were crucial transitional figures between modern jazz and the free style to be discussed in Chapter 8. Mingus's writing was ahead of its time in allowing musical content to determine form, which meant making room for spontaneous departures from twelve-bar blues, thirty-two-bar ballads, or other predetermined structures. Thus his "extended" form enabled bold, expressive improvisers, Dolphy foremost among them, to follow their imaginations and emotions to the limit. Dolphy was a masterful, fluent improviser on three instruments, introducing jazz to the starkly sensuous bass clarinet and setting standards on flute which have yet to be matched. His tone on alto sax was even more highly vocalized than Charlie Parker's. Interestingly Mingus—an impulsive, tempestuous man—and Dolphy—studious and self-effacing—were mirror opposites in temperament; yet musically they were perfectly complementary, never recording together with less than electrifying results.

Mingus was born in 1922 in Nogales, Arizona, but grew up in the Watts section of Los Angeles. His first instrument was the trombone, on which he was coached by a teenage friend, Britt Woodman, who later played with the Duke Ellington Orchestra. During his childhood, Mingus absorbed the first of his two lasting influences as a worshipper in the call-and-response prayers of the Pentecostal and Holiness Churches. Woodman exposed him to the second shaping force of his career by taking him to a Duke Ellington concert. "When I first heard Duke Ellington," Mingus wrote in his stream-of-consciousness autobiography (*Beneath the Underdog*), "one piece excited me so much that I screamed. I nearly jumped out of the bleachers." In fact, Mingus never abandoned the highly vocalized use of horns and multithematic composing which characterized Ellington's music.

On Woodman's advice, Mingus switched to the cello, which he soon played in the high school band's classical concerts. Realizing there were virtually no symphony jobs for black cellists, he took up the string bass and worked in local dance bands, studying the instrument when he could with Louis Armstrong's young bassist, Red Callendar. Over a five-year period, Mingus also took frequent lessons from H. Rheinschagen, an ex-New York Philharmonic bass player. Of course, he was also impressed (after 1940) by two Ellington bassists, Jimmy Blanton and Oscar Pettiford, who influenced him toward a melodic, aggressive style of accompaniment.

Beginning in 1941, Mingus experienced a history of jazz styles in a succession of bands. His first major assignment was with Armstrong, who fired him in 1943 prior to a tour of the South. Mingus had proved himself to be a firebrand with outspoken, if not militant, views on racism. Louis, whose attitude was quite the opposite, feared that Mingus's presence could be fatal to the tour if not to Mingus himself. After leaving Armstrong, Charles joined the New Orleans-style group led by Kid Ory, where he was content until the bebop trumpeter Fats Navarro (Chapter 5) set out to modernize him. Fats persuaded Mingus to join him in Lionel Hampton's band from 1946 to 1948, where swing and what Hamp used to call "rebop" were in vogue. Mingus's first recording was made with vibist Red Norvo and guitarist Tal Farlow in a closely knit, swinging session that is available on Savoy's *The Red Norvo Trio*.

Shortly after the Norvo date, Mingus angrily dropped out of music, feeling that he was both taken advantage of economically and artistically unappreciated. He began working as a postal clerk until several musicians, Parker among them, prevailed upon him to return. Mingus formed Debut Records, a short-lived attempt to circumvent the companies. Debut will be remembered primarily for having captured the historic Massey Hall concert of 1953 with Charles Mingus, Charlie Parker, Dizzy Gillespie, Bud Powell, and Max Roach on *The Greatest Jazz Concert Ever* discussed in Chapter 5. In the trio performances on sides three and four, it is clear that Mingus has entered the modern era as a commanding bassist. Within a few short years, he would broaden his horizons considerably.

In 1954 Mingus founded the Jazz Composers' Workshop, the earliest cooperative, self-help group of the modern era. Its first album, Savoy's *Jazz*

Workshop, does not yet incorporate the innovative practices he would implement—varying tempos and nonwritten scores. Mingus soon realized that if classical and folk music did not need to keep a steady beat, neither did jazz; rhythmic unity could be expressed and felt without being stated explicitly. He began teaching players their parts by singing or by playing the "framework" on the piano, a radical departure from Ellington who would even write out solos at times. "In this way," Mingus said, "I find it possible to keep my own compositional flavor in the pieces and yet to allow the musicians more individual freedom in the creation of their group lines and solos." [14] In short, Mingus left ample room for spontaneous, emotive interpretation, a superabundant element in his best recorded music.

Prestige's *Charles Mingus* (1955) reveals the fruits of the Workshop's looser approach in such swinging original structures as "Jump Monk" and an outright free-jazz colloquy with Max Roach entitled "Percussion Discussion." But the Mingus pieces which were to affect jazz permanently were recorded the next year for Atlantic by a band that was noticeably improved by the presence of altoist Jackie McLean and pianist Mal Waldron.

Passions of a Man anthologizes the Atlantic sessions from two periods of Mingus's work, the first of which (1956–1961), taking up two of the three discs, will be discussed here. "Pithecanthropus Erectus," intended with Mingus-like grandiosity to depict no less than the rise and fall of man, epitomizes his creativity on several counts: varying tempos; extended form; virtually atonal collective improvising; and use of pedal-point tonality instead of chord changes. Mingus integrates these elements—which were less artfully employed in the previous year's "Jump Monk"—into a continuous, flowing whole of infectious spirit. It was his first major successful piece.

The power of Mingus's music is partly due to his mastery of a wide range of emotions, the most violent and aggressive of which are expressed in "Haitian Fight Song" and the furious sound collage "Passions of a Man," two of his most potent political statements. By this time his band had been enhanced by Dannie Richmond, an ex-tenor saxophonist who Mingus himself trained on drums, having found no established percussionist sufficiently flexible for his needs. Mingus was then able to organize his music irrespective of meter and bar lines, using simple cues from his bass—when he did not resort to the screaming exhortations often heard on these tracks. Two radically different moods are communicated in the famous gospel blues, "Wednesday Night Prayer Meeting," and the sensuously romantic (also Ellingtonian) "Passions of a Woman Loved." His lyrical side—with occasional free-form instrumental conversations—asserts itself on "Profile of Jackie" and "Reincarnation of a Lovebird" (written for Charlie Parker), both of which owe much to the graceful melodicism of Jackie McLean's interpretations.

In 1960 a briefly working Mingus band, which surpassed all others improvisationally, was formed with the addition of Eric Dolphy, a native of Los Angeles with whom Mingus had once played at a high school dance. Dolphy, born in 1928, began to play the clarinet at age seven. In high school he became interested in the alto sax, when a classmate, pianist Hampton Hawes, played him the records of Charlie Parker. Dolphy's talent and unceasing practice in the family's garage earned him a music scholarship to Los Angeles City College, from which he graduated in 1948.

Dolphy played in the Roy Porter big band, attended the Naval School of Music during his hitch from 1950 to 1953, and then jammed or worked sporadically with the Los Angeles-based band of Gerald Wilson, with Buddy Collette, and with soloists like Harold Land and Clifford Brown. At the age of thirty, Dolphy had his first steady job with Chico Hamilton's West Coast-style quintet, which played in a highly arranged manner entirely too restrictive for Eric's strengths. When the group disbanded in 1959, Eric moved to New York, where Ornette Coleman (Chapter 8) had recently stunned the entire jazz community with a free style of blowing which Dolphy found exciting and validating.

Almost immediately Dolphy was in demand for recording with the most advanced musicians of the decade on albums discussed further on in this book: Ornette Coleman (*Free Jazz*); George Russell (*Outer Thoughts*); Oliver Nelson (*Abstract Truth*); and John Coltrane (*Live at the Village Vanguard*), with whom he shared a strong interest in the modes of classical Indian music. Eric and Trane also admired Coleman's bypassing of chord changes. But they continued to relate their "outside" notes, however tenuously, to a chordal base. It was Mingus with whom Eric worked regularly (at the Showplace in Greenwich Village), because he was attracted by the liberty to express everything he needed to in Mingus's permissive structures. Dolphy's assets were an astonishing facility with his instruments, a poetic imagination capable of jumps and leaps to any part of the horn, and an intonation which seemingly "talks" to the listener. Dolphy's solos come alive like no other improvisers'. Although he had only four short years of recording ahead of him, there is ample documentation of the burning urgency and lyric ecstasy with which he always played.

The Mingus-Dolphy band did not last long, due to the leader's volcanic personality and to Eric's readiness to lead a group on his own, an event long overdue as he was already thirty-two. Fortunately, critic Nat Hentoff induced them into two historic recording sessions, finally reissued together by Barnaby in the selected album: *Stormy Weather*. Sides three and four (originally entitled *Charles Mingus Presents Charles Mingus*) have long been famous for the "argument" over the band's demise by a steadfast Dolphy on bass clarinet and a cursing Mingus on bass in what may be the most powerfully vocal use of instruments in recorded jazz. The dialogue occurs in "What Love," an "extended form" based on the changes to "What Is This Thing Called Love?" Their pianoless quartet, including Dannie Richmond on drums and the young trumpeter Ted Curson, allowed Dolphy plenty of freedom to roam. Despite the phony nightclub atmosphere invoked on all tracks—prompting Mingus's gratuitous announcements requesting that "the audience" not applaud—the performances are genuine, eliciting intensely personal statements from everyone.

"Folk Form, No. 1" spans the historical spectrum from early black music to the shifting rhythms, melodic drumming, and spontaneous shaping of content by Dolphy and Ted Curson. Mingus leads them with his bass into a furious collective climax. "Original Faubus Fables," another of Mingus's political diatribes, reasserts the connections to bebop, at the same time raking the segregationist governor Orval Faubus over the coals with lyrics which were censored by another label when Mingus tried to record the piece again. "Freud's Mother," based on "All the Things You Are," reveals Dolphy in his glory, showing the way toward free blowing without leaving the blues behind.

Sides one and two (originally entitled *Stormy Weather*) augment the ensemble with horns—up to eight players in all—setting the studio stage for Mingus's flexible, Ellingtonian arrangements. "MDM," which stands for Monk, Duke, and Mingus, opens with a gut-level version of "Straight, No Chaser," and evolves into the alternating ensemble-solo style that Duke and Mingus use so artfully. Dolphy, of course, is still sailing out of everyone else's reach, although Booker Ervin on tenor sax and Britt Woodman, Charles's old high school mentor, on trombone, also provide emotional high points.

(The Mingus-Dolphy quartet was also recorded in Europe earlier that year (1960). In 1980, prompted by Mingus's death, Atlantic released the concert as a two-disc set called *Mingus at Antibes*. Bud Powell, in uneven form during 1960, is on some tracks, which enhances the set's historical value. The album, which was issued too late to be included here, is probably excellent.)

After leaving Mingus, Eric Dolphy led a quintet at the Five Spot with the brilliant, ill-fated trumpeter Booker Little. Dolphy's recordings with Little and other bands including that of Freddie Hubbard, who was then Eric's roommate; with Mal Waldron or Jaki Byard on piano, Roy Haynes or Ed Blackwell on drums, and Ron Carter, George Duvivier, or Richard Davis on bass, were all made (except for one side) in 1961. The one three-disc and four two-disc sets are all listed in the General Discography, for absolutely everything Dolphy played is worth hearing. *Copenhagen Concert* was selected here for the odd reason that the accompaniment is of no consequence, leaving the lion's share of soloing to Dolphy, who liberally exercises his three instruments.

The unaccompanied "God Bless the Child" is a masterpiece of self-sufficiency, compressing pulse, harmony, melody, and shadings into every phrase. The effect of Dolphy's never-ending practice on his horn is apparent on every track. (Like his friend John Coltrane, Eric Dolphy's practice sessions seemed to increase every year. Mingus recalled a party in Europe which Dolphy also attended: "When I got there the room was full of people, talking and drinking. In a corner, listening to a Charlie Parker record, there was Eric practicing along with the record. He had music on his mind all the time." [15]) On the "Hi-Fly" duet with bassist Chuck Israels, the only accompanist who makes a real contribution here, Dolphy shows off his lyrical fluency on the flute, which he often practiced in the early morning with the birds "to get the notes in between notes." Again on "Glad to Be Unhappy," his naturalistic, vocal style escapes the hollow "prettiness" which has generally plagued the flute in jazz. Dolphy takes up the alto sax on Gillespie's classic "Woody'n You," invoking a harmonic boldness that threatens to render bebop antiquated. While any of the Prestige LP's may justifiably be selected for their more noteworthy bands, Dolphy's extensive soloing between the covers of *Copenhagen Concert* is thrilling to experience. (Inner City's two-disc *Berlin Concerts*, recorded just one month earlier with another undistinguished European rhythm section, is similar in format, repertoire, and quality to *Copenhagen Concert.*)

In late 1961 Dolphy returned to New York where he began working frequently with John Coltrane, who also became his closest companion. (The albums they recorded together are noted in the Coltrane discussion ahead.) He also recorded two albums with bassist Richard Davis and trumpeters Woody Shaw and Freddie Hubbard, respectively: *Jitterbug Waltz* on the Douglas label is out of print; but Blue Note's *Out to Lunch* contains Eric's most consciously "outside" blowing and several atypical experiments with odd-time signatures.

In the early 1960's Mingus was recording prolifically for Columbia and Impulse. The most memorable Columbia LP is *Mingus-Ah-Um*, with the touching memorial to Lester Young "Goodbye, Pork Pie Hat," and the soulful ⅝-meter blues "Better Git It in Your Soul."*Better Git It in Your Soul* reissues both these classics and is highly recommended, despite *Nostalgia in Times Square*, which restores ten of the tracks to their original unedited form (to the surprise of many who never imagined Mingus would submit to editing in the first place). "Soul" and "Pork Pie" were omitted from the *Nostalgia* reissue. *Charles Mingus—The Impulse Years* is also first-rate Mingus from the 1960's, including new versions of the songs mentioned above plus "The Black Saint and the Sinner Lady," Mingus's longest composition.

Mingus persuaded Dolphy to return with him to Europe in 1964 for what turned out to be their most awesome banquet of improvisation. Prestige's three-disc *The Great Concert of Charles Mingus* contains only five tracks, many of which are thirty minutes long. Tenor saxophonist Clifford Jordan and Jaki Byard, a multistylistic pianist, are on and off as soloists, while Richmond is more consistent. Mingus and Dolphy are titans, embarking upon some magnificent, virtuoso excursions. Yet the alternation of arrangement with solos, one of Mingus's specialties, is absent, leaving us with a one-dimensional, if brilliantly so, expanse. This set is a gourmet's delight for those with a taste for strings of solos, but it is taxing if one longs for the big, colorful sound Mingus can get when he chooses from a combo this size.

After the Mingus concert, Dolphy decided to remain in Europe where he felt more appreciated. Several critics were still assailing him (and Coltrane) as perpetrators of "antijazz," and even Miles Davis had cast aspersions upon Eric's music in some comments for *Down Beat* magazine.Dolphy's answer to his detractors is cited in the introduction to this chapter. But the man had a more powerful enemy than his critics—diabetes, a condition he had been fighting with years of clean living and nutrition-conscious eating habits. After a club date in Germany on June 29, 1964, Eric Dolphy collapsed and died of a heart attack, presumably a consequence of his illness. Perhaps no other improviser had left so much beautiful music on record in so short a time.

By the next year, Mingus also was ill, although not seriously yet. He went into temporary retirement to work on *Beneath the Underdog,* a piece of writing as voluptuously emotive as his music. In 1972 he recorded *Reincarnation of a Lovebird* which, by Mingus standards, is uneventful. The next year he began a series of albums for Atlantic with large ensembles, sparked by the talent of the faithful Dannie Richmond on drums, George Adams on tenor sax, and Don Pullen on piano. Mingus was again a vital, creative leader, often drawing more out of his musicians than they could from themselves. *Changes One, Changes Two, Mingus Moves, Three or Four Shades of Blue* are a cut below the great Mingus of the 1950's and 1960's, but there is still much excellent music, six tracks of which are reissued on the selected *Passions of a Man* anthology. The best piece, "Sue's Changes" (for his wife), is a seventeen-minute-long catalog of the many moods Mingus had mastered. The only disappointment among the 1970's tracks here is "Goodbye Pork Pie Hat," which lacks the sensitivity of the earlier Columbia and Impulse versions.

Mingus was not an easy man to know or work for. Stopping a substandard performance on stage and giving the culprit a tongue-lashing was not uncommon for him. One night during the 1960's at the Village Vanguard, according to owner Max Gordon,[16] Mingus was so enraged that he leaned his bass against the piano and punched his longtime trombonist, Jimmy Knepper, in the stomach, knocking him down. Mingus himself was felled by an awesome adversary known as "Lou Gehrig's disease," which confined him to a wheelchair, unable to speak or write for the last year of his life. Still, he communicated new musical ideas to his wife and to the singer Joni Mitchell, who was collaborating with him on a new album. But Mingus died on January 5, 1979, before Asylum's *Mingus* was completed. This album and *Mingus Dynasty* by former colleagues are well-done tributes, but they do not compare with the work of Mingus himself, whose albums document an essential chapter in modern jazz's transition toward greater freedom of expression.

JOHN COLTRANE

My Favorite Things

Atlantic, 1361
one disc, brief liner notes
1960

Musicians: John Coltrane, tenor and soprano saxes; McCoy Tyner, piano; Steve Davis, bass; Elvin Jones, drums.
Compositions: Side one: My Favorite Things; Everytime We Say Goodbye. *Side two:* Summertime; But Not for Me.

Coltrane Live at the Village Vanguard

Impulse, A-10
one disc, liner notes
1961

Musicians: John Coltrane, tenor and soprano saxes; Eric Dolphy, bass clarinet (where marked *); McCoy Tyner, piano; Reggie Workman, bass; Elvin Jones, drums.
Compositions: Side one: Spiritual*; Softly As in a Morning Sunrise. *Side two:* Chasin' the Trane.

A Love Supreme

Impulse, A-77
one disc, liner poem (Coltrane)
1964

Musicians: John Coltrane, tenor sax; McCoy Tyner, piano; Jimmy Garrison, bass; Elvin
   Jones, drums.
Compositions: A Love Supreme (Acknowledgement, Resolution, Pursuance, Psalm).

JOHN COLTRANE HAS HAD a greater impact upon jazz since 1960 than any
other musician, including Miles Davis. His quartet from 1960 to 1965 has
probably been the most influential small combo since the Parker-Gillespie
quintet of 1945. Coltrane's music defies a summary description. Coltrane's
enormous influence is based on (1) his tone and technique on the soprano
and tenor saxes; (2) his lengthy, developmental modal, or scalar, improvising; and (3) his wholehearted dedication to music as a moral and spiritual
force.

There are many first-rate albums from 1960 to 1965, and those selected
here are simply the peaks among the mountains. For example, albums such
as *Impressions, Coltrane Live at Birdland,* and *First Meditations (for quartet)*
are filled with great moments and should not be missed. The three selected
albums are broadly representative in mood and compositional style. (Other
albums from 1965 to 1967, such as *Meditations* and *Ascension,* make use
of "sound-surfaces" and "sound-fields," to be discussed in Chapter 8.)

By 1959 Coltrane had reached a plateau of sorts (see Chapter 5). He
had played successfully with Miles Davis and Thelonious Monk, and on his
own *Giant Steps,* but he was not well known to the public. Sonny Rollins was
the most revered tenor saxophonist that year, and Ornette Coleman, the most
controversial. Coltrane needed his own band to further his career and, more
important, to advance his music's evolution.

His first job after leaving Miles's band was at the Jazz Gallery in New
York, where he used Steve Kuhn on piano, Steve Davis on bass, and Pete
LaRoca on drums, but he made an important change quickly. Coltrane had
planned on hiring pianist McCoy Tyner with whom he often played in
Philadelphia between stints with Miles. But McCoy was already working
for Benny Golson's Jazztet, and Trane was reluctant to interfere until his
wife, Naima, and a friend, trumpeter Calvin Massey, persuaded him that a
change of pianists was necessary. Tyner's rich harmonies, sense of form,

and acute sensitivity to Coltrane's needs were an immense asset. Tyner was also a religious Moslem, further stimulating Trane's spiritual interests. While he was on a cross-country tour, Coltrane also came to realize that LaRoca's drumming was not expansive enough, so he tried Billy Higgins, who was also not right. Eventually Coltrane flew back to New York and hired Elvin Jones, a more mature, muscular, and polyrhythmic drummer with whom he had jammed frequently. Jones remained with Coltrane longer than anyone else in the historic quartet.

During 1960 two fortuitous events combined to launch Coltrane's career commercially. One was his introduction to the Rodgers and Hammerstein show tune "My Favorite Things," which a customer had brought into the Jazz Gallery in sheet-music form, thinking John might like it. Second, by fluke he discovered the soprano sax, an instrument Coltrane would soon make extremely popular. It came into his life on a drive home from a job in Washington, D.C., with two passengers, one of whom, an unnamed saxophonist, sat in the back seat. "He was being very quiet," Coltrane recalled,

> At Baltimore we made a rest stop, then got back in the car, and 30 minutes later realized that the guy in the back wasn't there. We hoped he had some money and drove on. I took his horn and suitcase to my apartment in New York. I opened the case and found a soprano sax. I started fooling around with it and was fascinated. That's how I discovered the instrument.[17]

Sidney Bechet and Johnny Hodges, for whom Coltrane had worked in the early 1950's, were his first models on the small horn. Its range was a natural one for him. He loved to play his most expressive, vocal utterances in the upper range of the tenor sax, and now he had a reed devoted to this register.

My Favorite Things, the new band's first album, was a remarkable success for both Trane and the soprano sax. The title track is transformed into an intense chant by extensions of the opening E minor scale and the closing E major scale to several choruses each. The modal, or scalar, approach to improvising (see the introduction to this chapter) allowed Coltrane to pack in his own chord changes if he chose, or to pursue a thematic melodic idea, thus providing both vertical and linear internal development. The swaying waltz rhythm is hypnotic, and the exotic sound of the soprano sax, haunting. "Giant Steps" was a great individual achievement for Trane, but "My Favorite Things" was the first track on which his band found a distinctive sound of its own.

"Summertime" also uses the modal extension of chords impressively, and Coltrane sweeps us into his solo with a blizzard of notes in the opening tenor break. "But Not for Me," though tied to chord changes, is even more exciting. Trane recomposes the melody by stressing notes in the scales that had been ignored by Gershwin's original composition. The piece has a compelling momentum driven by the constantly shifting rhythmic patterns of Coltrane's phrases. Both these tracks show that Tyner and Jones, who had not yet played together a year, could already anticipate each other's accents.

My Favorite Things did more than give Coltrane the exposure he needed; the title tune became his theme for the next two years. He would often improvise on it up to twenty minutes in concert, bringing the audience to its feet. Within a year Coltrane was voted the best tenor sax player in *Downbeat* magazine's Readers' and Critics' Polls. The soprano sax became the most popular alternative horn in jazz, a status it still maintains.

At this point in his career, Coltrane was immersed in a whirlwind of ideas and influences. Ornette Coleman's free soloing without regard to chords encouraged him to take more chances. Eric Dolphy's great intervallic leaps between registers had a similar effect. Coltrane was also listening earnestly to the nearly atonal solos of John Gilmore in Sun Ra's Arkestra. Indian music was central to his development at this time. He devised his own scales on which to improvise which were, in effect, hybrids of Indian and western modes. The *sitar* player Ravi Shankar, whom the Beatles would later help popularize in America, came to hear Coltrane in 1961, and the two discussed making an album together. (The project never materialized; but their mutual admiration continued, and in 1966 Coltrane named his second son Ravi.) With his close friend Eric Dolphy, John also listened to the music of the African pygmies. Books about theory and scales piled up on his living room floor.

In 1961 Coltrane's recording prospects took a fortunate turn when he was selected as the first artist to be signed by ABC's new Impulse label. Except for the couple of commercial ploys noted in Chapter 5, Impulse and producer Bob Thiele allowed Trane to follow his muse anywhere. The first effort was *Africa/Brass*, an atypically large ensemble arranged by Dolphy. The next sessions were recorded live in a period of a week and were later released as *Live at the Village Vanguard* and *Impressions*.

Village Vanguard was selected here for Trane's sixteen-minute solo on "Chasin' the Trane," one of his best performances on record, perhaps revealing the liberating influences of Ornette Coleman, Eric Dolphy, and John Gilmore. Elvin Jones comes into his own on *Vanguard*, helping Coltrane to build intensity with a wide range of dynamics. In many ways "Chasin' " demonstrates the qualities which made Trane the most exciting horn player of the 1960's. The composition itself, which is very loosely a blues, was improvised on the spot. Its length and scalar style produce a hypnotic effect, drawing the listener into the solo with a potent magnetism. Its tone is searching and urgent. The climax erupts into vocal cries bubbling up over the horn's normal range in squeaks and partial harmonics. The endeavor is earnest, demanding, satisfying, and ultimately exhausting. Trane leaves nothing unsaid, recalling an answer he once gave to Miles who had asked him, "Why do you play so long, man?" Trane replied, "It took me that long to get it all in." Beyond its emotional catharsis, Coltrane's lengthy soloing showed improvisers that—with sufficient ideas and stamina—more than the obligatory one or two choruses was possible.

The album's remaining two tracks show the diversity of his interests. "Spiritual," another waltz on the order of "My Favorite Things," reveals Trane's solemn, incantatory strength on tenor (also soprano, as he uses both horns). The music is a modal piece based upon an actual spiritual John found in the book *200 Negro Spirituals*. Dolphy joins him on this track on bass clarinet. Dolphy's solo, not one of his best, is noticeably soft around the edges, suggesting the influence of Trane's less angular melodic style. "Softly, As in a Morning Sunrise," however, does reveal an increasing flexibility and a firmness of sound on soprano, on which Trane achieves a furious, chord-change-based climax. McCoy opens the track with one of his best solos of the early 1960's.

Impressions is equally solid and inspired, though it does not have a *tour de force* piece like "Chasin' the Trane." The high points are "India," with its unique modes and intense solos by Trane and Eric Dolphy, and the title track, a raging treatment on tenor sax of Trane's lasting composition. *Impressions* marks the beginning of Coltrane's six-year association with bassist Jimmy Garrison, who had dropped out of Ornette Coleman's quartet. Coltrane liked Garrison's ability to support him without being intrusive; it was from Elvin Jones that he wanted aggressive contributions. Coltrane and bassist Reggie Workman parted ways over a basic difference of styles, something John would never attempt to overcome by instructing his employees. In fact, when Reggie once made the mistake of asking him for advice on one of the band's pieces, Coltrane replied harshly, "I can just about play the saxophone. I'm busy working on that. I can't tell anybody how to play their instrument, so don't ask me." [18]

Live at Birdland (1963) was the Coltrane quartet's next formidable accomplishment. Side one consists of a lengthy "Afro-Blue" on soprano and a sensitive, balladic tenor improvisation on "I Want to Talk About You." It ranks with Coltrane's best playing. Trane's playing was impassioned on virtually every live recording after 1960.

His interests turned decidedly religious by 1963, reaching their first full musical expression in the album-length "humble offering to God" *A Love Supreme*. His religious awakening had begun in 1957 when Naima introduced him to the ideas of Islam. McCoy Tyner, also a Moslem, reinforced her influence. But Coltrane's spiritual quest quickly became self-motivated, perhaps surpassing in intensity that of any other jazz musician. He read often from Krishnamurti and the cabala, yet remained steadfastly a Christian in the tradition of his grandfathers, both well-known ministers (see Chapter 5, *Giant Steps*). Coltrane now spoke of his playing as meditation or prayer.

The events of the year prior to *A Love Supreme* must have been a severe test of Coltrane's faith. In 1963 the bombing of a black church in Alabama that killed three children deeply saddened him. His "Alabama," on *Live at*

Birdland, was written as a memorial; it was set to the speech rhythms of the Reverend Martin Luther King's eulogy for the youngsters. Closer to home, his marriage to Naima, which had been foundering for some time, finally broke up. Then in June 1964 Eric Dolphy, John's closest friend and musical confidant, died suddenly in Europe of diabetic complications. They had been so close that it was John to whom Eric's mother gave his flute and bass clarinet after his death, when she began to have nightmares that Eric was practicing on them in the family's garage.

In the light of this sad background, *A Love Supreme,* recorded in December, is a remarkably warm, hopeful, and energetic outpouring. Coltrane was explicit about the religious inspiration of the music in his poem which serves as the album's liner notes. John once told his mother that he had experienced visions of God while preparing this music, which was ominous to her because she felt that "when someone is seeing God, that means he is going to die." [19]

The music opens with the shimmering peal of a gong, indicating the seriousness of what is to follow. Coltrane's full, majestic tone during the rhythmically free prelude to "Acknowledgement" accentuates the mood. Then the four-note motif of the suite is taken up by the bass: a-LOVE-su-PREME a-LOVE-su-PREME, a perfect union of melody and speech rhythm. Throughout the album, Coltrane displays a dazzling variety of tonal color on his tenor, ranging from a newly adopted vibrato to climactic, harmonic "screams" and cries in the horn's highest register.

A Love Supreme takes as a premise the Indian notion that scales and sounds can be used to convey specific emotional meanings. The gong, for example, generally signifies an exalted presence, the "One" to whom Coltrane addresses this music. The free-time opening to "Acknowledgement" and the closing of "Psalm" symbolize the transition into and out of the devotional state. The instrument's "screams" are ecstatic releases. The clear, strong middle-register "call" is the energetic offering of the music itself. That Coltrane had these particular meanings in mind is, of course, conjecture. The point is that his musical "cues" achieve these effects throughout, evoking more predictable and deeper responses in the listener because of their consistency.

Although the four-part suite is admirably integrated, each part is independent and self-sustaining. Parts two and three swing with exuberance which typifies the band on *Vanguard;* yet the momentum is in no way inconsistent with Coltrane's solemn intentions. Tyner takes fleet, compelling solos on both "Pursuance" and "Resolution"; and Elvin guides his awesome power and all-encompassing rhythms with flawless control, contributing a brilliant and compact solo on "Pursuance." Coltrane's theme to "Resolution" exudes simplicity, elusive rhythmic strength, and completeness. It is perhaps his finest composed line, save for "Naima."

Trane's music evolved radically again in 1965, when he began to use his tenor horn to create emotionally expressive sounds which were no longer based entirely on notes related to modes. *Ascension,* a collective improvisation by eleven players, to be discussed in the introduction to Chapter 8, was the first major change. However, several months later an excellent sequel to *A Love Supreme* was recorded by the quartet, which was finally released in 1977 as *First Meditations (for quartet).* It contains the same suite-like composition and incantatory soloing of the highest integrity. The session was held back during the 1960's to emphasize the stunningly intense "screaming" of *Meditations,* which was recorded only two months later with the addition of the amelodic Pharaoh Sanders on tenor and frenzied Rashied Ali on drums, who became permanent sidemen. Coltrane felt compelled to go beyond the boundaries of his earlier music, recording several cogent, demanding albums (General Discography, Chapter 8). Tyner left the band after *Meditations,* and was replaced by John's second wife, Alice McLeod Coltrane (General Discography).

Coltrane was in no mood either to rest or repeat himself after *A Love Supreme,* although his income approached a quarter of a million dollars. He was practicing harder than ever, playing ninety-minute nightclub shows and then disappearing into the back room to practice until the next set. At home in the early morning hours, he would finger the keys without blowing the horn to avoid waking the household. John continued to seek out new influences, inviting young players to sit in with the band to hear their ideas. He searched incessantly for the perfect mouthpiece, a quest he had been engaged in since 1962.

In 1966 Coltrane began to suffer from a liver ailment, which may have resulted from a bout with drugs and drinking during the 1950's. His stringent health-food diet did not improve matters significantly, and working himself to exhaustion aggravated his condition. Nevertheless, his manner was marked by serenity. Coltrane's thoughts turned increasingly to religion, and he considered it a mission "to uplift people" through his music. Coltrane lived by his credo. When club patrons, shocked by the overblowing, split notes, and screeching in his music after 1965, criticized him abusively, an ordeal he endured with increasing frequency, he did not attempt to silence his detractors. He looked at them calmly with his large eyes, said nothing, and walked away. In the three biographies of his life (see Bibliography), there is only one account of Coltrane raising his voice in anger—when he was provoked by a club owner who did not pay the band as promised. His goals became simple and profound. In the summer of 1966, he told an interviewer: "I know that there are bad forces, forces put here that bring suffering to others and misery to the world, but I want to be the force which is truly for good." [20] One year later on July 17, 1967, Coltrane died in a New York hospital. Although his own life had been short, he left music of sufficient beauty and originality to inspire others for generations to come.

McCOY TYNER

Echoes of a Friend

Milestone, M-9055
one disc, no liner notes
1972

Musicians: McCoy Tyner, piano.
Compositions: Side one: Naima; Promise; My Favorite Things. *Side two:* The Discovery;
Folks.

Enlightenment

Milestone, M-55001
two discs, no liner notes
1973

Musicians: McCoy Tyner, piano, percussion; Azar Lawrence, tenor and soprano saxes;
Joony Booth, bass; Alphonse Mouzon, drums.
Compositions (all by Tyner): *Sides one and two:* Enlightenment Suite (Genesis, The
Offering, Inner Glimpse); Presence. *Sides three and four:* Nebula; Walk Spirit, Talk
Spirit.

McCOY TYNER IS a master of the piano on the order of a Hines, a Tatum,
or a Cecil Taylor, all of whom are self-sufficient soloists. As a member of
the previously discussed John Coltrane Quartet from 1960 to 1965, Tyner
established himself as a lyrical, richly modal player intimately connected with
the most influential jazz improviser since Charlie Parker. Yet as he struggled
financially through the late 1960's, he discovered an original harmonic conception and a percussive dimension of the piano which breathed new life
into the instrument during the 1970's. While there are numerous excellent

LP's from this decade, *Echoes of a Friend*, an awesome solo *tour de force*, and *Enlightenment*, his band's unedited triumphant concert at the Montreux Jazz Festival, is the perfect pair for hearing Tyner at his best in distinct contexts.

Tyner's musical education began in Philadelphia, where he was born in 1938. His interest in private piano lessons was encouraged by his mother, an amateur pianist, and in his teens he began studying at the West Philadelphia Music School and later at the Granoff Music School. At fifteen he was leading a seven-piece rhythm-and-blues band which held rehearsals in the Tyner living room, adjacent to his mother's home-style beauty parlor. McCoy enjoyed the rural blues stylists "Leadbelly" and Sonny Boy Williamson, whose albums remain among his favorites. However, he was also listening carefully to Bud Powell—then a neighbor in Philadelphia—Charlie Parker, and Miles Davis on borrowed records he could not afford to buy.

In 1955, McCoy began playing with trumpeter Calvin Massey at the Red Rooster, where he first met John Coltrane. McCoy worked on and off with Coltrane, who frequently returned home to Philadelphia between stints with the Miles Davis band. They agreed to work together as soon as John was able to form a group of his own. Also in 1955 Tyner married and adopted his wife's commitment to the Moslem religion, which he continues to practice. He could only get sporadic work as a musician, however, and supported himself as a warehouse shipping clerk until 1959, when the Art Farmer-Benny Golson Jazztet came through town in need of a pianist. He remained with them for a matter of months before the call from Coltrane finally came. After some deliberation and apologies to the Jazztet, Tyner went to take his place in the most influential combo since the Parker-Gillespie quintet of 1945.

Tyner was beginning to evolve his own style, one based upon Trane's modal harmonies and upon a synthesis of earlier influences like Bud Powell, Red Garland, Thelonious Monk, and Duke Ellington. But McCoy's role in the group was largely supportive. He looked up to Coltrane as his teacher and later recalled: "I submitted to leadership, although the submission didn't take the form of his telling me what to do." [21] As the music of the Coltrane quartet grew in importance, Impulse Records tried to cultivate a separate image for Tyner with albums of ballads in the standard trio style of the 1960's. The seven available LP's are pleasant but primarily of historical interest, for Tyner's true identity was being expressed in his music with Trane all along. *Reevaluation: The Impulse Years*, a two-disc set which includes four tracks with Coltrane, is a good summary of those attempts.

Nevertheless, Tyner's piano playing of the early 1960's is understood better through Coltrane's own assessment, which handily isolates important elements:

> First there is McCoy's melodic inventiveness . . . the clarity of his ideas . . . He also gets a very personal sound from his instrument; and because of the clusters he uses and the way he voices them, that

sound is brighter than what would normally be expected. . . . McCoy has an exceptionally well-developed sense of form . . . he will take a tune and build his own structure for it. . . . And finally, McCoy has taste. He can take anything, no matter how weird, and make it sound beautiful.[22]

In December 1965 Tyner decided it was time to find his own way when he could no longer hear himself play above Trane's two drummers, two saxes, and quasi-atonal "screaming." From 1965 to 1969 the lack of playing opportunities, partly due to the dominance of rock, prompted him to seek employment with the taxi cab company that had driven him to the airport during the years he had played with Coltrane. The company did not take his inquiry seriously. McCoy worked occasional, poorly paying sessions as a sideman for Blue Note, but he turned down other offers to play strictly commercial music.

Despite the adversity, these were productive years for Tyner due to the long hours he spent "woodshedding" at home. His growing interest in Igor Stravinsky and Claude Debussy began to be reflected in harmonic complexity on the keyboard, and his technique grew surer and sharper. He found a new voice in the piano when "the bass register became like a drum." Upper-register notes took on a similarly percussive quality comparable to bells or chimes. Tyner has frequently attributed his ability to work creatively amid the stress of these years to his religious commitment and his wife's supportive attitude. "This was a fulfilling period of my life," he once said, "because it was a test of my ability to survive personally and as an artist. I had a chance to compromise, and I didn't do it." [23]

The first evidence of McCoy's growth is documented on Blue Note from 1968 to 1971. *Expansion* and *Extensions* reveal the new density of his playing and a rhythmic, chant-like style of composing; the music is greatly enhanced by the impassioned soprano sax solos of Wayne Shorter (borrowed from Miles Davis's band) and Gary Bartz on alto sax. *Asante*, while less satisfying as a performance, marks McCoy's first incorporation of auxiliary percussion instruments to reflect his pianistic intent and some specifically African effects. Neither *Asante* nor *Cosmos*—a two-disc reissue of similar, less notable tracks—are recommended as highly as the first two albums.

Tyner's budding originality blossomed fully in 1972 when he moved to the Milestone label, on which there are a half-dozen LP's of great virtuosity and integrity. The first two released were *Sahara* (1972), which concludes with an evolving twenty-three-minute title track richly colored with auxiliary instruments, and *Song of the New World* (1973), an album of stunning bigband arrangements featuring McCoy's swirling piano solos. At the same time, however, he recorded a majestic pair of albums which best convey the qualities that make him (along with Cecil Taylor) the foremost pianist of the 1970's.

Echoes of a Friend, recorded with Coltrane in mind while on tour in

Japan, contains one side from the old quartet's book and one side of Tyner originals. Each piece is a work of shifting rhythms, dramatic contrasts, and gradual development. Tyner keeps chunks of sound in motion, dividing them rhythmically with a booming, tympani-like bass register. "The Promise," "My Favorite Things," and the sensitive "Naima" are excellent, but his own "Dedication" is the most personal, original, and impressive cut, introduced regally like "A Love Supreme" with the peal of a gong. Tyner has not abandoned the modalities Trane explored, though he has enriched them with series of chromatic chord progressions within them. These constantly "strummed" chords support sharply articulated flurries of notes in the upper register; this is a radical break with the linear right-hand style of the 1960's. Frequent bass register melodies show Tyner to be the kind of two-handed pianist one has to be in order to solo across such a broad canvas. Interestingly "Folks" (the nickname of Tyner's first employer, Calvin Massey) intermingles his newly thickened playing with the smoother diatonic progressions of the past. This emphasizes the continuity of piano tradition, which readily shows through Tyner's music in a way it does not, for example, in Cecil Taylor's. To a large extent, McCoy's uncommon popularity—for a musician who never once succumbed to popularizing his sound—is due to the straight-ahead swinging and comfortable stride passages that surface regularly in his performances.

Enlightenment captures Tyner's quartet on an evening of cathartic intensity. "Genesis" and "Walk Spirit, Talk Spirit" are based on earthy, simple chants similar to the earlier Blue Note material except that the rhythms have become nearly danceable and reminiscent of Tyner's youthful infatuation with R & B. The soloing, however, returns to the surging momentum that is typical of his playing with Trane. Tyner's "Enlightenment Suite" solo (Part II: "The Offering") ranks with—if it does not surpass—"Discovery" on *Echoes;* it fairly reels from his alternately thunderous and ringing touch. Even with the bass and drum accompaniment, Tyner remains an orchestral pianist, evoking the sounds of chimes, harp, and brass on "Presence" and "Nebula," the latter opening with a telling collage of percussion.

While the band is of secondary interest on *Enlightenment*, it provides crucial support with a most enjoyable consistency. Alphonse Mouzon's muscular drumming is a natural asset to the music's drive, while Joony Booth's sonorous bass keeps the tonal centers alive. Booth plays a delightful, singable solo on "Walk Spirit." Azar Lawrence's performance, his debut on a major album, is understandably in the shadow of Coltrane but satisfyingly so.

Atlantis (1975), another two-disc set which was recorded live at the Keystone Korner in San Francisco, adds color to the same type of music with the Brazilian percussionist Guilherme Franco. The compositions are less ambitious, though they still possess the hypnotic, swaying rhythmic feeling; and the improvising does not sustain the level of intensity present on *Enlightenment*. Tyner's piano playing does not come through with the necessary clarity either except on the wonderful unaccompanied solos "In a Sentimental Mood" and "My One and Only Love," two more hybrids of the old and the new on the order of "Folks." *Atlantis* is a worthy album, but not on the level of *Enlightenment*.

The next two Tyner albums one should acquire are *Trident* with Ron Carter and ex-Coltrane colleague Elvin Jones, and *Supertrios*, a two-disc set with Ron Carter and Tony Williams plus Eddie Gomez and Jack De-Johnette, the kind of mature accompaniment which allows McCoy to spread his wings. The repertoire in both albums is a fine assortment of Tyner, Monk, and Coltrane, all providing for serious, masterful improvisations. The only LP's to differ from Tyner's customary formats are *Fly with the Wind* (1976), which he arranged for brass and strings, and *Inner Voices* (1977), in which a small choral group is added. While these sides have the quality and integrity one has come to expect from McCoy, they do not contribute anything original or unforgettable.

Although there is no shortage of good Tyner on record, he must be heard on the eight albums recommended here, which trace his personal development from 1968 to the present. They reveal Tyner to be a principal source of the continuing vitality of modally based modern jazz.

HERBIE HANCOCK

Maiden Voyage

Blue Note, BLP-4195/84195
one disc, liner story ("Maiden Voyage")
1965

Musicians: Herbie Hancock, piano; Freddie Hubbard, trumpet; George Coleman, tenor sax; Ron Carter, bass; Tony Williams, drums.
Compositions (all by Hancock): *Side one:* Maiden Voyage; The Eye of the Hurricane; Little One. *Side two:* Survival of the Fittest; Dolphin Dance.

Speak Like a Child

Blue Note, BST-84279
one disc, no liner notes
1968

Musicians: Herbie Hancock, piano; Ron Carter, bass; Mickey Roker, drums; Thad Jones, flugelhorn; Peter Phillips, bass trombone; Jerry Dodgion, flute.
Compositions (by Hancock except where indicated; all arrangements by Hancock): *Side one:* Riot; Speak Like a Child; First Trip (Ron Carter). *Side two:* Toys; Goodbye to Childhood; The Sorcerer.

HERBIE HANCOCK is one of the most versatile musicians in jazz, the creator of modally based modern jazz, a funky brand of fusion (Chapter 7), and experimental, electronically garnished free jazz (Chapter 8). His talents as a composer and arranger led to three film scores (*Blow Up, Fat Albert Rotunda*, and *Death Wish*). However, the short, lyrical jazz compositions he recorded for Blue Note (1962–1969), which will be discussed here, are his most enduring contribution. As demonstrated by *V.S.O.P.: The Quintet* (see page 295), recorded in 1977, Herbie never lost the ability to return to this style with authenticity.

Born in 1940 in Chicago, Hancock studied the European classics with great success. At eleven he was selected by competition to perform Mozart's "Piano Concerto in D Major" with the Chicago Symphony. Hancock continued to study the classics until he was twenty, but shifted to jazz during high school, when he witnessed with astonishment a fellow student's ability to improvise. Herbie set out to learn jazz piano by listening to the records of George Shearing and Oscar Peterson, transcribing their solos note for note. Hancock was also fond of analyzing Clare Fischer's arrangements for the Hi-Lo's, a popular vocal group of the time, and Robert Farnon's harmonically sophisticated "mood-music" arrangements for his British-based orchestra. Hancock put his arduous ear training to use by writing for a seventeen-piece band at Grinnell College in Iowa, where he enrolled in 1956, initially as an engineering student. After four years of college, he returned to Chicago, where he was hired by trumpeter Donald Byrd.

Byrd became Herbie's mentor for the next several years, sponsoring his first date for Blue Note in 1962; *Takin' Off*, with Freddie Hubbard and Dexter Gordon, yielded his first hit song (in Mongo Santamaria's version), "Watermelon Man," a funky blues later resurrected on Herbie's gold album *Head Hunters* (Chapter 7). In 1963 Hancock was playing at the

Village Gate with Clark Terry's band when Miles Davis heard him. This led to an audition and the stunning series of Hancock-Davis albums discussed earlier. While the Davis band recorded for Columbia, Herbie led his own Blue Note group, usually with Davis colleagues Ron Carter and Tony Williams, and recorded several superb albums (General Discography) represented by the two selected here.

Maiden Voyage and *Speak Like a Child* contain his best compositions of this period, many of which were recorded contemporaneously by the Davis band. "Maiden Voyage," "Riot," "Dolphin Dance," and "Sorcerer" are ideal improvisational vehicles by virtue of their simple, open melodic lines which float above a soft, wide bed of quilted harmonies, allowing each soloist sufficient latitude for exploration. Hancock is also a master of shifting rhythmic patterns, such as those on "Eye of the Hurricane."

Maiden Voyage, despite its graceful compositions, is primarily a blowing session with plentiful soloing; chord changes have now clearly given way to the more permissive idea of tonal centers. "Survival of the Fittest," intended to convey the menace of the sea, has built-in sections for rubato playing and allows a free use of both harmony and time. Hancock's piano playing (on all the Blue Note sessions) shows the influence of Bill Evans's style in its concern for texture and shape, especially on the architectonic "Survival" solo, which is really a construction of sharply defined, well-integrated fragments. Ron Carter, Tony Williams, and George Coleman, with whom Herbie had worked on Miles's *'Four'* & More session, enjoy an intuitive rapport with the leader. In the soloing department, Freddie Hubbard, then with Art Blakey's Jazz Messengers, is the bonus treat. Aware at every moment of the need to swing, Freddie is in powerful form, expertly controlling the lyrical phrasing he extracted from the Fats Navarro-Clifford Brown tradition. "Survival," "Eye," and "Dolphin Dance" contains some wonderful samples of his intense, expressive style. (*Empyrean Isles*, similar to *Maiden* in its composition, wide-open soloing, and personnel, is another masterpiece well worth obtaining.)

The major achievement of *Speak Like a Child* is its fresh, warm ensemble sound. It is romantic without becoming sentimental. Hancock's writing for this album was strongly influenced by the work of Gil Evans (see *Porgy and Bess*, Chapter 5) and Oliver Nelson, to be discussed later in this chapter. In fact, "Toys" is derivative of Evans's "Blues for Pablo" (on *The Complete Birth of the Cool*) in its attempt to create "a tune with the colors of the blues but not the form." The music is also a testimony to the increased harmonic liberties musicians were enjoying in these years. Herbie explains that he is "more interested in sounds than in definite chordal patterns." Thus his technique—exemplified by the title tune—is to write the melodies first, making whatever harmonic adjustments are necessary to accommodate that melody. Similarly, the harmonies for piano and horns need not have a "legitimate" theoretical basis. The criteria for harmony are thus twofold: color and the right sound. On this album the sound Herbie wishes to capture is the sweetness of childhood; hence the title. He succeeds remarkably, for the music has not aged one whit over the years.

Herbie's soft touch on the keyboard, somewhat atypical for him during this period, is appropriate to the subdued mood of the setting. As a matter of fact, Herbie had been criticized for soloing too little on his previous albums. One intent of this session, on which Hancock is the only soloist, is to project him into the limelight. His playing makes use of long lines with soft edges. This is particularly easy to hear on "Goodbye to Childhood," in which the left and right hands are separated by several registers. The sound of his piano is more wistful than usual. Again there is a noticeable Bill Evans influence, especially in the lower-register clusters of notes that fall directly on top of the beat. The left hand seems to be giving the right hand a palette of tonal colors with which to construct melody. Hancock is both inventive (as on "Toys") and subtle (as on "Childhood") when the piano gently lifts the melody off of the horns' opening statement. A delicate touch is an essential characteristic of his piano here. Compare it with the crisper, more varied attack on "Survival of the Fittest" from *Maiden Voyage*. One can only marvel at the variety of effects he can elicit from the instrument.

Herbie's arrangements here qualify as some of the most original brass-band music in jazz—far from the blaring idiom one normally associates with the word "brass." The rich, contrasting timbres of the alto flute and bass trombone heard in unison on "Toys" gave impetus to much of the music's character. The middle register is anchored by Thad Jones's flugelhorn. The group was a forerunner of Hancock's subsequent sextet, which included Joe Henderson on tenor sax and Johnny Coles on flugelhorn. *The Prisoner*, like *Speak*, is an arrangement *tour de force* with much more solo space taken up by the horns, which may lead many listeners to prefer it.

(Blue Note's two-disc sampler *Herbie Hancock* contains a retrospective smattering of *Maiden, Empyrean, Speak*, and *Prisoner*, but not enough to get the full flavor of any one date.)

After Hancock left Blue Note in 1969, he took the name Mwandishi, Swahili for "composer," a role Hancock broadened in his group, a sextet, which recorded for Warner Brothers from 1969 to 1972. This group included reed player Bennie Maupin, Hancock's close associate throughout the 1970's, and two talented, underrecorded brass players, trombonist Julian Priester and trumpeter Eddie Henderson. Their boldly experimental albums, which depend increasingly upon electronic keyboards, will be discussed in Chapter 7.

**HERBIE HANCOCK, FREDDIE
HUBBARD, WAYNE SHORTER,
RON CARTER, TONY WILLIAMS**

V.S.O.P.: The Quintet

Columbia, CS-34976
two discs, brief liner notes
1977

Musicians: Herbie Hancock, piano; Freddie Hubbard, trumpet, flugelhorn; Wayne Shorter, tenor and soprano saxes; Ron Carter, bass; Tony Williams, drums.
Compositions: Side one: One of a Kind; Third Plane. *Side two:* Jessica; Lawra. *Side three:* Darts; Dolores. *Side four:* Little Waltz; Byrdlike.

THE RECORDING OF *V.S.O.P.: The Quintet*, whose original impetus was the protean career of Herbie Hancock, became a magical reunion of the most important young players to emerge in the mid-1960's. Far from having grown stale, the group captures the adventurousness of that time with precision and renewed energy. The compositions and solos are first-rate, and the level of intensity never drops. The album conveys a sense of fearsome power being unleashed under subtle control. As improvisers, these men partake of a freedom which, as exponents of the "fusion" style (Chapter 7), they had not enjoyed for years.

The album grew out of a Herbie Hancock retrospective at the 1976 Newport Jazz Festival in New York. The V.S.O.P. rubric—which generally refers to a gradually aged, mature brandy, a favorite of Hancock's—was intended to embrace all the Hancock bands from the Miles Davis years (1964–1968) through the free-jazz (1969–1973) and fusion (after 1973) periods. The 1976 album *Herbie Hancock: V.S.O.P.* was thus diffuse in its moods, suffering from a jam-session atmosphere which did justice to none of the styles. Hancock's frequent use of the Yamaha electric grand piano, an instrument of rather synthetic warmth and resonance, was also a disappointment. *The Quintet* has none of these problems, for it is single-minded in its commitment.

The band improvises as a flawlessly welded unit, even in the out-of-time passages of Hubbard's "One of a Kind" (dedicated to Miles Davis), Hancock's "Darts," and the collectively improvised "Lawra." The rhythm section, displaying an uncanny rapport, is the group's heartbeat; they are consistently sharp and aggressive. Hancock, who appeared to have deserted this style for jazz-funk years earlier, returns to it with markedly increased technique and confidence. His 'comping is brilliant in color, tone, and rhythmic definition. When the pace needs a boost, which is infrequent, drummer Williams snaps the listener to attention with a snare as sharp as a whip crack.

Freddie Hubbard's performance is a most welcome surprise, for available recordings of his best playing are very scarce (see *Breaking Point* ahead.) If Hubbard has a difficulty here, it is that he is laboring under Miles Davis's shadow. His acknowledged feelings of intimidation are understandable, to some extent, simply because the rest of the band *is* a former Davis group, while his melodicism comes out of the Clifford Brown (Chapter 5) tradition. Hubbard, however, is his own man and brilliantly so on "Darts." Miles seldom attempts such rapidly articulated phrases in the upper register. Hubbard also shines on "One of a Kind," his own "Byrdlike," and Ron Carter's bebop-style "Third Plane." He does give in to the Davis concept in the chromatic figures of "One of a Kind" and in the understated lyricism of "Jessica" or "Little Waltz," but he carries it off beautifully. If there were more Hubbard solos around like those on this album, his fans would be delighted. In fact, *The Quintet* did renew Hubbard's interest in serious playing and led to the recording of his best Columbia LP, *Super Blue*.

Wayne Shorter also had not played much horn in recent years, having taken a back seat to Josef Zawinul in *Weather Report* (Chapter 7). As noted earlier (see Miles Davis, Chapter 6), Shorter constructs intelligently designed and balanced solos, which are heard on the straight-ahead up-tempo blowing of "Darts" and "Third Plane." Yet his expressiveness on soprano sax, especially on "One of a Kind" and "Lawra," adds crucial tonal color. When the nasal soprano and the mellow flugelhorn work together, as on "Lawra," they evoke a feeling of speech and communication that makes this record come alive.

"Lawra," with its rapid-fire, martial opening, is an excellent vehicle for Tony Williams, though the entire album threatens to serve as a Williams *tour de force*. His dramatic, narrative drum solo is an excellent contrast to his heavily polyrhythmic ensemble style. A more traditional Williams solo occurs in "Byrdlike," preceded by explosive drum breaks. Only an intuitive drummer with an acute melodic sense could have supplied the fills heard alongside (to say "behind" would be misleading) Wayne Shorter's tenor solo on "Third Plane." Listening to Ron Carter's performance on this track reveals why Williams can afford to engage in front-line dialogue with the other soloists. Carter's bass has been described earlier as "resonant, stalwart, and sinewy," and the importance of his role as the band's deepest source of pulse cannot be overemphasized. That Carter's strength is graced by a glowing, exotic tone and sensitive melodicsm, especially evident on his showcase "Little Waltz," justifies his revered status as the premier bassist of the 1960's.

Generally it is rare that the kudos on record jackets accurately describe *all* the music inside, but critic Conrad Silvert's assessment on the back of *The Quintet* is an exception:

What the audience applauds on this album transcends mere form, technique, and instrumentation. They were thrilled by the charisma generated by five masters who listened to one another's inner ears, spoke to each other at multiple levels, and, no matter how dense the musical content, conveyed their messages to the audience with amazing clarity.

The music really does fulfill this promise.

GEORGE RUSSELL

Outer Thoughts

Milestone, M-47027
two discs, excellent liner notes
1960–1962

Musicians: George Russell, piano; Al Kiger, trumpet; Dave Baker, trombone; Dave Young, tenor sax; Chuck Israels, bass; Joe Hunt, drums. Also Don Ellis, trumpet; Eric Dolphy, bass clarinet, alto sax; Steven Swallow, bass. Also John Pierce, alto sax; Paul Plummer, tenor sax. Also Garnett Brown, trombone; Pete LaRoca, drums; Sheila Jordan, vocal.
Compositions (all arrangements by George Russell): *Side one:* Stratusphunk; Bent Eagle; Nardis, 'Round Midnight. *Side two:* Ezz-thetic; Thoughts; Honesty. *Side three:* Pan-Daddy; The Stratus Seekers; The Outer View. *Side four:* Au Privave; Zig-Zag; You Are My Sunshine.

CRITIC ROBERT PALMER aptly characterizes George Russell's music as alternately "pan-tonal dixieland, free-form bebop, and 21st century soul music." Russell's forte is filling traditional structures with futuristic (but accessible) content. This album, recorded just before Russell's extended residence in Scandinavia, is stunning and, if one cannot let go of certain preconceptions, a bit disorienting.

Russell's innovations are based upon his own *Lydian Chromatic Concept of Tonal Organization* (1953), a far-reaching manifesto of jazz's inevitable movement toward polytonality. While his point of view has already been discussed in the introduction to this chapter, it is worth recalling that the purpose of the concept is to make the entire spectrum of modal scales available to the improviser. Russell's pan-tonal philosophy permits a player to move freely among all twelve tones in the octave and to establish any one of them as the tonal center of an appropriate scale. The scales, superimposed upon the original composition, create a broad and diffuse tonal foundation for the improviser.

Russell's accomplishments seem even more awesome when one considers that he is primarily self-taught. Born in 1923, he was raised by foster parents near Cincinnati, Ohio. His first instrument was the drums, and his earliest influences were the legendary riverboat band of Fate Marable and the arrangements for Benny Goodman's Orchestra by Jimmy Mundy. Although Russell was a scholarship student at Wilberforce University, his college career was interrupted the first year by tuberculosis. While in the hospital, he learned the basics of arranging from a fellow patient.

Russell then played drums in Benny Carter's big band and wrote arrangements for Earl Hines, though it was not swing but bebop which drew him to the New York area. His most successful work of this period was "Cubano Be, Cubano Bop" for Dizzy Gillespie's big band (on Verve's reissue of the same title). Charlie Parker was going to hire Russell as a drummer, but tuberculosis hospitalized him once again, providing him with the opportunity to spend sixteen months of crucial research on the Lydian chromatic concept. Two important compositions followed his release: "All About Rosie" and "A Bird in Igor's Yard," which was a synthesis of Parker and Stravinsky. Neither is available on record.

The earliest available full-length Russell LP's are reissued on MCA's two-disc *New York, New York and Jazz in the Space Age* (1958–1960), which includes a medley of traditional pieces about New York and an original experimental (Lydian) suite. Most tracks involve eight- to twelve-piece ensembles featuring solos by John Coltrane, Bill Evans, Max Roach, and more of jazz's finest. Everything Russell writes is fascinating; these sides are no exception. But there is an aura of the "exercise" or *étude* that is somewhat less inviting than the freely swinging atmosphere of his subsequent sessions as a leader on Riverside—music which was reissued on the selected album.

Outer Thoughts is a uniformly excellent performance by Russell's regularly working small band, supplemented by Eric Dolphy. "Ezz-thetic," "Thoughts," "Stratus Seekers," and "The Outer View" are intriguing compositions that illustrate Russell's capacity for embracing the old and the new simultaneously. These are well-knit bebop forms which sound as if they may burst open at the seams. During Dolphy's solos, they often do. Dolphy is the ideal improviser to breathe life into this music because his occasionally outrageous leaps from one tonal center to another reflect the novel harmonic relationships of Russell's pan-tonalism. Of course, every track is earthy, in keeping with Russell's view that jazz's tonality is necessarily rooted in the blues. The rest of the players were Russell's students at the School of Jazz in Lenox, Massachusetts. Trumpeter Don Ellis, who would soon lead a progressive big band, and trombonist Dave Baker, who became one of the leading jazz educators of the 1970's, must be singled out for their consistently creative soloing.

The full power of Russell's thinking emerges on the standards " 'Round Midnight" and "You Are My Sunshine." To hear these tracks is to perceive the songs through a prism that threatens to change our image of them permanently. Dolphy is gloriously original on "Midnight," roaming all over the tremendous range of his bass clarinet and making it speak in nearly surrealistic poetry. Russell is no less astounding in his piano chording. Their version of this Thelonious Monk classic is among the most intensely moving on record.

"You Are My Sunshine" is a bit more disturbing to listen to because it is an eerie and ominous reexamination of a song which usually passes for innocuous Americana. Sheila Jordan's vocal, cooler than jazz singing in its customary sense, is frankly chilling. In one sense the track is a fitting conclusion to the album, for we sense in it the reality and importance of the past along with the urgent need to press onward, a summary of Russell's values. But the track's mood is atypical. This arrangement of "Sunshine" came about while Russell and Jordan were playing and singing for fun in a tavern near Jordan's hometown in a coal-mining region of Pennsylvania. According to the liner notes, "the resulting treatment mirrors his (Russell's) impression of the humanity of the people pitted against the cold, bleak, often brutal demands of the region." As borne out elsewhere, Russell's vision is generally brighter and lighter than "Sunshine" indicates.

Shortly after these recordings were made Russell moved to Norway, where he became a respected teacher, influencing important young European musicians like Palle Danielsson and Jan Gabarek (Chapter 8). His conviction that he had been unappreciated at home is sadly confirmed by the state of his discography. Nevertheless, he returned to the United States in 1972 to accept a teaching position at the New England Conservatory of Music in Boston. A composition featuring Bill Evans on piano was released by Columbia as *Living Time*, an LP that has since been deleted. A very good new piece entitled "Electronic Sonata for Souls Loved by Nature" is worth looking for on the poorly distributed Strata-East label.

Unfortunately Russell's recording future may be doomed by the fact that major labels favor touring musicians, because they can promote their LP's on the road, over those with academic inclinations. One can only hope, nevertheless, that the broader interest in jazz that developed during the late 1970's will yield new recording opportunities for this stimulating, adventurous composer.

FREDDIE HUBBARD

Breaking Point

Blue Note, BLP-4172/BST-84172
one disc, good liner notes
1964

Musicians: Freddie Hubbard, trumpet; James Spaulding, alto sax, flute; Ronnie Matthews, piano; Eddie Kahn, bass; Joe Chambers, drums.
Compositions (all by Freddie Hubbard except "Mirrors"): *Side one:* Breaking Point; Far Away. *Side two:* Blue Frenzy; D Minor Mint; Mirrors.

FREDDIE HUBBARD, the major trumpeter to emerge from the free and modal styles of the 1960's, has not yet realized his potential. He suffers somewhat from an inability to commit himself fully to a serious musical identity. Furthermore, several mature albums which he recorded from 1966 to 1972, after which he began to play a kind of jazz/pop, are either deleted (the Atlantics) or, in the case of the CTI recordings, are hard to find. CTI's justly famous album *Red Clay*—noticeably influenced by rock and probably Hubbard's best seller—and *First Light* can probably be found in well-stocked stores, but neither have been reissued on the 8000 series, leaving them difficult cases at least for the present. Thus of Hubbard's own music, we have only the Columbias, a depressing lot except for *Super Blue*, and the early, earnest Blue Notes, which reach their full realization on the *Breaking Point* session of 1964.

Breaking Point was recorded with Hubbard's first band several months after he terminated a two-and-a-half-year stint with Art Blakey's Jazz Messengers. Only twenty-six, his apprenticeship had been an impressive one. Hubbard, the youngest of six children, grew up in Indianapolis, in Wes Montgomery's old neighborhood. In high school he studied a variety of horns, including the trombone, tuba, and French horn, before he discovered the trumpet. After a brief and unsuccessful career as a music student at Jordan College, he began working with local musicians, Wes and Monk Montgomery among them. In fact, Hubbard's earliest recording (1957) is with Wes and Monk on "Bock to Bock" and "Billie's Bounce," available on Blue Note's Montgomery reissue, *Beginnings*.

While rooming with Eric Dolphy in New York, Hubbard was catapulted briefly into the avant-garde when they were both invited to join Ornette Coleman on the historic *Free Jazz* session of 1960. (In 1965 Hubbard also played on Coltrane's free-style *Ascension*.) Yet Hubbard's affinity for the lyrical Fats Navarro-Clifford Brown approach to improvising made him better suited for a harmonic framework. Thus he was more effective on such albums as Oliver Nelson's *Blues and the Abstract Truth*, to be discussed ahead. Hubbard can also be heard as a sideman on the early Blue Note albums of Herbie Hancock, Dexter Gordon, vibraharpist Bobby Hutcherson, and, of course, Art Blakey. With Blakey, and opposite Wayne Shorter on tenor sax, Hubbard found his most fruitful niche, though it was temporary. His impassioned soloing (which is matched by Shorter's) on *Free for All* and *Mosaic* help make these albums Blakey's best recordings since the Messengers' Birdland sessions with Horace Silver and Clifford Brown.

Breaking Point is a challenging synthesis of modal, free, and chord-change-based playing. Hubbard's confidence is high, his tone full, and his phrasing adventurous. His quasi-free, Calypso-inspired "Breaking Point" and partly modal "D Minor Mint" force the solo improvisers to reflect compositional variety. James Spaulding and Ronnie Matthews are consistently strong. Hubbard reveals his greatest asset, the ability to explore melody without compromising his deep sense of swing. On the ballad "Mirrors" he demonstrates warmth, sensitivity, and a flawless control of tone. On all the tracks Hubbard maintains a forceful presence through dramatic contrasts in his playing. The power of his presence is what prompted critics of the 1960's to think of Hubbard as the new Miles Davis, despite his allegiance to the smoother, more rounded style of Clifford Brown.

The tracks from *Breaking Point* and numerous earlier sessions in the same style have been collected on Blue Note's two-disc reissue, *Freddie Hubbard*. This set is an extremely important anthology of his early work, especially because of the unavailability of the Atlantics and CTIs. While more comprehensive than the original issue selected here, it does not share the uniformly high quality of improvising.

Columbia's *Super Blue*, a hard-swinging straight-ahead album inspired by Hubbard's feelings about the previously discussed *V.S.O.P.: The Quintet*, is the one bright spot of the 1970's among lackluster efforts at catering to popular taste. While *Super Blue*, a product of Hubbard's deeper instincts, is headed in the right direction, it has not yet arrived. However, "Take It to the Ozone" and "Theme for Kareem" alone make the album a worthwhile purchase. Disappointingly *Super Blue* was followed by the heavily orchestrated *A Love Connection*, questioning once again Hubbard's ability to perceive and develop his own identity. One hopes that a better focus for his energy is forthcoming. As a jazz nightclub owner once said of Hubbard's forays into the pop field, "Freddie Hubbard could be the best jazz trumpet player in the world. What's wrong with that for an identity?"

Note: In a discussion of modern jazz trumpet, another, younger contender for leadership deserves to be recognized: Woody (Herman) Shaw, Jr. Born in the South in 1944, he moved with his family to Newark, New Jersey, while he was still a boy, and began playing professionally with a rhythm-and-blues band at fourteen. After quitting high school, he worked with a variety of bands until Eric Dolphy heard him play and hired him away from Willie Bobo's group. Dolphy, who used his eighteen-year-old discovery when he recorded *Iron Man*, left a profound impact upon Shaw's melodic conception, which makes use of unusual intervallic skips. As a trumpeter (and on cornet and flugelhorn, too), Shaw's attack is in the tradition of Navarro, Brown, and Hubbard. After Dolphy's death in 1964, Shaw was schooled in the bands of Horace Silver, McCoy Tyner, and Art Blakey.

Unlike Freddie Hubbard, Shaw leaves no doubt about his commitment to an uncompromised style of jazz. His most fully realized album, *Woody III*, which juxtaposes a large ensemble with his working quintet, is a collection of probing, hard-swinging tracks which he composed and arranged himself. The album follows two earlier Columbias: *Stepping Stones*, a straight-ahead live date from the Village Vanguard, and *Rosewood*, voted 1978 Album-of-the-Year in *Downbeat* magazine's Readers' Poll. Shaw's earlier recordings, which are in no way inferior, can be heard on the Muse and Contemporary labels (see General Discography). Columbia's enthusiasm for Shaw was prompted in part by Miles Davis, who had spoken highly of him, and by Shaw's performance on the successful Dexter Gordon LP *Homecoming*. There are now powerful indications that Shaw is about to emerge with some more music of lasting significance. Along with Hubbard, he is a trumpeter to listen for.

OLIVER NELSON

*Three Dimensions: The Dedication
Series/Volume III*
(Previous titles): *The Blues and the
Abstract Truth* and *Sound Pieces*

Impulse, IA-9335/2
two discs, excellent liner notes
1961, 1966

Musicians: (Abstract Truth, sides one and two) Oliver Nelson, alto and tenor saxes;
Eric Dolphy, alto sax, flute; Freddie Hubbard, trumpet; George Barrow, baritone
sax; Paul Chambers, bass; Roy Haynes, drums. (*Sound Pieces,* sides three and four)
Oliver Nelson, soprano sax; Steve Kuhn, piano; Ron Carter, bass; Grady Tate,
drums.

Compositions (all by Oliver Nelson except those marked * and **): *Side one:* Stolen
Moments; Hoe-Down; Cascades. *Side two:* Yearnin'; Butch and Butch; Teenie's
Blues. *Side three:* Patterns; Elegy for a Duck; Example 78. *Side four:* Straight, No
Chaser*; The Shadow of Your Smile**.

OLIVER NELSON is a little-known tragic hero—little known by the public,
a hero to many jazz musicians, and tragically swallowed up by Hollywood's
film and television industry. This album, which receives nearly the same
adulation among musicians as Miles Davis's *Kind of Blue* to which it is
similar in style, established Nelson's reputation as a composer and arranger.
Indirectly it led to his personal downfall, for he grew increasingly in demand
as a studio arranger, a lucrative and stressful field. When he died suddenly
in 1975 at forty-three, it was shortly after taping a new episode of the TV
serial *The Six Million Dollar Man.* A heart attack was the apparent cause,
but those who knew him well suspected that overwork and long-standing
frustration over not expressing himself musically were underlying causes.

However, the future looked bright in 1961 when Creed Taylor invited
Nelson to assemble a band for ABC's fledgling Impulse label. Oliver had
arrived in New York two years earlier, a graduate in composition from
Washington University in St. Louis with several classical pieces to his credit.
As an alto sax player, he was influenced by Sonny Rollins and John Coltrane;

as a composer, by the arrangements of Gil Evans and George Russell. However, as he explains in the liner notes, he first achieved his own musical identity on *The Blues and the Abstract Truth* session.

Prior to his beautifully crafted arrangements for *The Blues and the Abstract Truth*, Nelson was known primarily for his alto work in the bands of Louis Bellson, Quincy Jones, Count Basie, and Duke Ellington. He came to New York from St. Louis, where he had been raised in a family of musicians. His brother had also played alto in Cootie Williams's band, and his younger sister, to whom "Teenie's Blues" is dedicated, worked as a singer and a pianist in the Midwest. Nelson's playing had an original "sailing" quality. Critic John S. Wilson, writing in *Down Beat* magazine during the late 1950's, praised his "rich purity of tone; direct uncluttered attack; and singing projection that mark him as one of the most impressive saxophonists playing these days . . . not just a blower, but a builder as well, with a strong sense of structure." [24] Thus the quartet tracks, two of which are available for the first time on the *Three Dimensions* reissue, are a valuable addition to Nelson's discography. Thelonious Monk's "Straight, No Chaser" is a caldron of dynamic interchanges between Nelson and Grady Tate. "The Shadow of Your Smile" illustrates the way modal playing can transform a somewhat soft-cored ballad into a piece of dramatic tension. Both "Pattern" and "Example 78" originated in Nelson's book of saxophone exercises, *Patterns for Improvisation.* "Cascades" on the *Abstract Truth* session had a similar origin, providing further testimony to Nelson's talent for fleshing out a melody on the bare bones of a line. Pianist Steve Kuhn plays well on sides three and four, which were recorded the year following his brief tenure as John Coltrane's accompanist.

Nelson's favorite musical form as a composer is the blues in a driving hard-bop style, such as "Butch and Butch" or "Teenie's Blues," in which his whimsical melodic imagination takes flight. Yet his less frequent expressions of lyricism, like the classic "Stolen Moments," surpass the blues pieces in depth. The warm, clean quality he elicits from the horns is a triumph of craftsmanship and artistry. Above all, Nelson had the composer's sense of a memorable phrase, a line which, despite its originality, seems immediately familiar. He achieves this most clearly in "Hoe-Down," in which disparate rhythmic patterns and call-and-response are employed artfully.

Nelson could make the most of a simple and even hackneyed format, a talent which must have abetted his TV writing career significantly. For example, every piece on sides one and two is based upon either the blues or the thirty-two-bar changes to "I Got Rhythm." Yet he varies the music's character, as Miles Davis did on *Kind of Blue,* by selectively extending the number of measures devoted to a chord ("Hoe-Down") or by using tonal centers instead of a traditional harmonic progression ("Teenie's Blues"). Eric Dolphy, Bill Evans, Paul Chambers, and Freddie Hubbard were well practiced in these maneuvers, for an open, modal style was the focus of all the young modern-jazz musicians of that time. Of course, Evans and Chambers were crucial to the *Kind of Blue* session, too. All the soloing is flawless, and this album soon became a model against which a generation of improvisers measured themselves.

Nelson's serious jazz maintains a remarkably consistent level of quality, considering the sporadic nature of his commitment to it. There are three good albums in the *Abstract Truth* vein: *More Blues and the Abstract Truth* (1965), a sequel of excellent compositions played by new personnel: *Images* (1960–1961), featuring the solos of Eric Dolphy; and *Stolen Moments* (1975), his final reinterpretation of several jazz classics, including his own music. Two more albums provide an impressive glimpse of his compositional scope in a more unified and solemn context: *The Kennedy Dream*, a passionate tribute to the assassinated President; and *A Dream Deferred*, a response to the assassination of Dr. Martin Luther King, Jr. His earliest extended work, *Afro-American Sketches*, successfully integrates ethnic elements with modern jazz in a seven-part suite for big band. Even though Hollywood limited Nelson's achievements, there is after all a great deal of recorded music to be thankful for (see General Discography).

TOSHIKO AKIYOSHI-LEW TABACKIN BIG BAND

Insights

RCA, AFL1-2678
one disc, liner notes
1976

Musicians: Toshiko Akiyoshi, piano; Lew Tabackin, tenor sax, flute; Don Baldwin, bass; Peter Donald, drums; Bobby Shew, Mike Price, Richard Cooper, Jerry Hey, trumpets; Bill Reichenbach, Charlie Loper, Britt Woodman, Phil Teele (bass), trombones; Dick Spencer, Gary Foster, alto sax; Tom Peterson, tenor sax; Bill Perkins, baritone sax; (on "Minimata") Hisao Kanze, *utai;* Tadeo Kamei, *ohtsuzumi;* Hayao Uzawa, *kotsuzumi;* Michiru Mariano, voice; (on "Sumie") Hiromitsu Katada, *kakko.*
Compositions (all compositions and arrangements by Akiyoshi): *Side one:* Studio J; Transience; Sumie. *Side two:* Minimata (Peaceful Village, Prosperity & Consequence, Epilogue).

IN AN AGE when the big band is an endangered species, a victim of rising travel expenses, the Akiyoshi-Tabackin band is perhaps the last great hope for its continuance. The group was formed in Los Angeles in 1973 and quickly acquired its identity through Toshiko's distinctive writing and her husband Lew Tabackin's soloing on flute and tenor sax. The sixteen-piece band survives with little financial incentive on a tremendous esprit de corps motivated by the players' belief in Akiyoshi's increasingly impressive work. Their first album, *Kogun*, introduced in America through RCA in 1978, was released four years earlier in Japan where, according to Leonard Feather, it became the country's best-selling jazz album of all time. Its title track marked Akiyoshi's first successful synthesis of traditional Japanese sounds and modern jazz, an endeavor which reaches its artistic peak on "Minimata." This twenty-one-minute suite on side two is her crowning achievement as a composer. While *Kogun, The Long Yellow Road, Tales of a Courtesan*, and *Road Time* (a two-disc set of live dates) contain individually excellent pieces, *Insights* displays the scope of Akiyoshi's writing at its best.

Akiyoshi's piano training began during her youth in Manchuria, where she was born in 1929. When her family returned to Japan after the war, she played in an American occupation dance hall and learned to improvise by analyzing records. Akiyoshi's piano playing led to her first recording session for Norman Granz, to whom she was recommended by Oscar Peterson who had heard her at the Jazz Club of Tokyo in 1953. The Granz sessions are not available, but Toshiko recorded two good trio albums during the 1970's for Inner City (*Dedications*) and Concord Jazz (*Toshiko Akiyoshi*). Toshiko's playing was strongly influenced by Bud Powell, and she never gravitated toward the heavily chorded "arranger's piano" typical of other composers and bandleaders. Moreover, as Leonard Feather pointed out in his *Encyclopedia of Jazz* (1960 edition), "There is nothing delicately feminine in her (piano) work, which is fiery, powerfully articulated, and exceptionally fluent."

Akiyoshi moved to the United States in 1956 and studied at the Berklee School of Music in Boston. During the 1960's, she worked primarily as a pianist for trios and small combos, gradually developing an interest in writing for larger groups. She was looking for tonal variety: "If you compare piano music to a black-and-white brush painting, the big band is a picture with color. . . . Like a painter needs a yellow or blue, I need a horn." [25] In 1972 Akiyoshi and Tabackin moved to Los Angeles, where they created the sixteen-piece band using local talent.

Insights reveals her to be a dramatic composer who uses shifts of color and texture to stimulate a continual sense of expectation. In "Minimata," for example, she presents a large canvas in four parts, depicting the Japanese fishing village whose inhabitants were tragically decimated by mercury poisoning. In "Peaceful Village" after a brief introduction sung by a thirteen-year-old youth, a droning chord is held by a system of alternate blowing in which one horn imperceptibly takes over the note of another. There is no rhythm section at work, and time becomes plastic, seeming to stretch out indefinitely. It is as if one experiences the hum of life within the village, a sound that is at once undisturbed and ominous. The tension increases, for it becomes clear that something must happen to break the spell.

The "Prosperity" theme then whips the air with excitement. While the melody is similar to bebop, the interplay of the band sections packs the punch of the swing style. Tabackin's tenor solo, an extension of the Hawkins-Rollins tradition, builds in intensity through structure. Tabackin is a master of design, and these solos often take the form of long, unaccompanied, temperature-raising cadenzas in live performance. His solo here is punctuated by crisp blasts of brass, a compelling device which Akiyoshi has written into numerous scores. In sharp contrast the following alto sax improvisation by Dick Spencer is modal in approach and highly vocal in articulation. An impassioned Mingus-like voicing of the horns precedes the solo, and introduces the vividly different "Consequences" section. Finally, in the "Epilogue" a voice, supplied by a well-known actor in Japan's Noh theater, and *tsuzumi* drums reflect a solemn, eerie, and ageless perspective on the village's unexpected fate.

On the album's other side Akiyoshi renews two of the traditions which contributed to her own style. "Studio J," the name of a classroom at the Berklee School of Music in Boston where Akiyoshi had studied upon her arrival in America, is, in Tabackin's words, "idealistic bebop," demonstrating an extraordinarily supple use of the horns. After experiencing the varied rhythmic (and *a*rhythmic) landscape of "Minimata," we are reminded that a swinging beat is the cornerstone of the band's style and of Akiyoshi's concept of jazz. Her debt to the driving hard bop style is apparent in her opening piano solo, which is reminiscent of Bud Powell.

"Transience," a beautiful romantic and nostalgic piece, pays tribute to her major orchestral influence, Duke Ellington. Bill Perkins, an alumnus of the Woody Herman and Stan Kenton bands, carries the melody on baritone superbly. Akiyoshi again maintains complete control over the mood, establishing her credibility in still another emotional context. Although Toshiko rarely strives for an Ellingtonian sound, she does emulate what may be his most awesome achievement—the building of an entire library of original music with parts individually tailored to all the players in the band.

"Sumie" is another wholly personal work in a vaguely Oriental modality. The piece gathers momentum with increasingly complex statements of the theme. Although it was intended as a framework for Tabackin's light, clean flute playing, it never really gives him the freedom he requires. (There is an Inner City album entitled *The Rites of Pan*, with Akiyoshi on piano, which displays Tabackin's flute style to better advantage. His previous

Inner City release, *Lew Tabackin*, is devoted to his tenor sax playing.) The brilliant touch on "Sumie" comes in the dense, close harmony in the upper register, where it is not unusual for Toshiko to set four or five voices in motion. The horns' simulation of the Japanese *gagaku* at the end of the piece is equally intriguing. To evoke the sounds of the Orient with western instruments is a significant enrichment of modern jazz, one that has been attempted by some foremost modern improvisers such as John Coltrane and Eric Dolphy.

The decline of the big band is a great loss to jazz because the combination of power and flexibility in such ensembles is unique. The only other band comparable to Akiyoshi's was the Thad Jones–Mel Lewis Orchestra. When Akiyoshi-Tabackin won *Downbeat*'s top big-band award in the 1978 Readers' Poll (*Insights* placed third in the Album-of-the-Year category), the Jones-Lewis band was a negligible number of votes behind them; and Jones-Lewis edged out Akiyoshi-Tabackin in the *Down Beat* Critics' Poll. This East Coast big band was formed in 1965. It drew from the ranks of New York City studio musicians who were looking for a creative performing outlet. The band found a temporary home on Monday nights at the Village Vanguard, where its repertoire grew rapidly through the prolific composing and arranging of its flugelhorn soloist, Thad Jones, brother of pianist Hank and drummer Elvin. Thad had been known previously as a soloist with the Count Basie band of 1954–1963.

The Jones-Lewis band's strongly voiced arrangements were enhanced by impressive soloing from Pepper Adams, Joe Farrell, Jerome Richardson, Roland Hanna, Billy Harper, Garnett Brown, and Richard Davis, to name only a few of the frequently shifting personnel. Mel Lewis, the drummer, who had worked previously with Stan Kenton and Gerry Mulligan, had a full sound, swinging the band hard by coming down on top of the beat. Some of the best tracks of the Jones-Lewis orchestras from 1966 to 1970 are available on the Blue Note two-disc reissue *Thad Jones/Mel Lewis*, and on the single LP *Consummation*.

In 1979 Jones quit the band to work on his own, which seriously threatened its continuation. Their 1970's albums are an impressive legacy (General Discography), but none are masterpieces or particularly innovative. While their work cannot be faulted, it must be distinguished from the Akiyoshi-Tabackin contribution on the basis of historical significance.

Notes

1. C. O. Simpkins, *Coltrane: A Biography* (New York: Herndon House Publishers, 1975), p. 160.

2. Frank Kofsky, *Black Nationalism and the Revolution in Music* (New York: Pathfinder Press, 1970), p. 66.

3. Jones's book about late modern and free jazz, entitled *Black Music*, is a collection of portraits, some containing good insights and others superficially journalistic. The book in no way presents the kind of systematic historical investigation which makes *Blues People* an enduring work.

4. For a readable discussion of modes, with musical illustrations, see Mark C. Gridley, *Jazz Styles* (Englewood Cliffs, New Jersey: Prentice-Hall, Inc., 1978), pp. 324–329.

5. Joe Goldberg, *Jazz Masters of the Fifties* (New York: Collier-Macmillan, 1968), p. 81.

6. From the liner notes to the original album cover.

7. A record review by Pete Welding in *Down Beat*, April 26, 1962.

8. Martin Williams, "Introducing Eric Dolphy," *Jazz Panorama* (New York: The Crowell-Collier Press, 1962), p. 283.

9. Simpkins, *op. cit.*, p. 169.

10. *Wax Paper*, Vol. 4, Warner Brothers Records, Inc., February 12, 1979, p. 17.

11. *Ibid.*

12. Len Lyons, "Bill Evans," *Down Beat*, March 11, 1976.

13. *Ibid.*

14. Liner notes to the original *Pithecanthropus Erectus* (out of print).

15. Liner notes to *The Great Concert of Charles Mingus.*

16. From the unpublished reminiscences of Max Gordon as related by Whitney Balliett, *The New Yorker*, June 18, 1979, p. 100.

17. Simpkins, *op. cit.*, p. 101.

18. *Ibid.*, p. 127.

19. J. C. Thomas, *Chasin' the Trane* (New York: Doubleday & Co., Inc., 1975), p. 187.

20. Kofsky, *op. cit.*, p. 241.

21. Len Lyons, "McCoy Tyner," *Contemporary Keyboard*, October 1976.

22. Liner notes to *Inception.*

23. Lyons, "McCoy Tyner," *op. cit.*

24. Liner notes to Oliver Nelson's *Images.*

25. Len Lyons, "Toshiko Akiyoshi," *Contemporary Keyboard*, February 1977.

General Discography of Available, Recommended Albums

TOSHIKO AKIYOSHI/LEW TABACKIN BIG BAND
    Kogun, AFL1-3019; *Long Yellow Road*, JPL1-1350; *Tales of a Courtesan*, JPL1-0723; *Road Time* (2 discs, live), CPL2-2242; RCA.

GARY BURTON
    Matchbook (with Towner), ECM-1056; *Crystal Silence* (with Corea), ECM-1024; *Duet* (with Corea), ECM-1-1140; *The New Quartet*, ECM-1030; *Times Square*, ECM-1-1111; ECM. *Burton & Keith Jarrett*, AT-1577, Atlantic.

ALICE COLTRANE
    Transfiguration (2 discs, organ), 2WB-3218, Warner Brothers.

JOHN COLTRANE (also Chapters 5 and 8)
    Africa/Brass (quartet plus brass, arranged by Eric Dolphy), A-6; *Impressions* (with Dolphy, 1 cut), A-42; *Live at Birdland*, A-50; *First Meditations* (for quartet) (1965), AS-9332; Impulse.

CHICK COREA
    (See Chapters 7 and 8, and Gary Burton, this chapter.)

MILES DAVIS (see Chapters 5 and 7)
    E.S.P., PC-9150; *My Funny Valentine*, PC-9106; *Nefertiti*, CS-9594; *Seven Steps to Heaven*, PC-8851; *Greatest Hits* (reissued collection, 1 disc), PC-9808; *Sorcerer*, PC-9532; *In Europe*, PC-8983; Columbia. *Circle in the Round* (previously unreleased—as of 1980—cuts from 1955 to 1970), KC2-36278, Columbia.

ERIC DOLPHY
    The Great Concert of Eric Dolphy (3 discs), P034002; *Status*, P-24070; *Eric Dolphy*, PR-24008; *Magic* (with Ron Carter), P-24053; Prestige. *Berlin Concert*, IC-3017-2, Inner City. See also Charles Mingus, Oliver Nelson, and John Coltrane. *Out to Lunch* (see Chapter 8). *Jitterbug Waltz* (not available), *Stormy Weather*, *Mingus Presents Mingus*, and *The Great Concert of Charles Mingus* (see Charles Mingus, Selected Discography).

BILL EVANS
    The Tokyo Concert, F-9457; *Montreux III* (duo with Gomez), F-9510; *Since We Met*, F-9457; *Quintessence*, F-9529; *Alone (Again)* (solo), F-9542; Fantasy. *Peace Piece and Other Pieces* (1959–1961), M-47024, Milestone. *New Conversations* (solo overdubbed, 1978), BSK-3177, Warner Brothers. Of historical interest: *Spring Leaves* (1959, Motian, LaFaro), M-47034, Milestone. *Alone*, V6-8792, Verve. *The Bill Evans Album*, C-30855, Columbia.

HERBIE HANCOCK (see Chapters 7 and 8 and Miles Davis Selected Discography, this chapter) *Herbie Hancock* (1962–1969), reissues some of *Maiden Voyage* and *Speak Like a Child*, BN-LA399-H2, Blue Note. With Tony Williams on *Spring*, BST-84216, Blue Note. *Herbie Hancock and Chick Corea: In Concert* (piano duets, 1978), PC2-35663, Columbia. Highly recommended: *Empyrean Isles* (with Hubbard, Coleman), BST-84175; *The Prisoner* (sextet with Joe Henderson, tenor sax), BST-84321; Blue Note.

JOHN HANDY
Live at the Monterey Jazz Festival (1965), CS-9262, Columbia. See also *Mingus at Monterey*, Charles Mingus.

FREDDIE HUBBARD
Freddie Hubbard (1960–1965), BN-LA356-H2, Blue Note. *Super Blue*, JC 35386, Columbia. (Several excellent Atlantics and CTI's are out of print.) *Ready for Freddie*, BST-84085, Blue Note. (See also Art Blakey, Chapter 5; Oliver Nelson, Selected Discography; *V.S.O.P.: The Quintet*, Selected Discography.)

BOBBY HUTCHERSON
Knucklebean (with Freddie Hubbard), LA-7894, Blue Note.

THAD JONES/MEL LEWIS BAND
Thad Jones/Mel Lewis (1966–1970), BN-LA392-A2; *Consummation*, BST-84346; Blue Note. *Suite for Pops*, SP-701, A&M Horizon.

RAHSAAN ROLAND KIRK
The Vibration Continues (1968–1976), SD-2-1003, Atlantic.

YUSEF LATEEF (see Chapter 5)

CHARLES MINGUS
The Great Concert of Charles Mingus (with Eric Dolphy, 1964), PR-34001; *Reincarnation of a Lovebird*, PR-24028; *Charles Mingus at Town Hall*, F-JWS-9; *Mingus at Monterey* (with John Handy), F-JWS-1/2; Fantasy. *Mingus-Ah-Um* (1959), CS-8171; *Better Git It in Your Soul* (reissues *Ah-Um* and *Dynasty*), CG-30628; *Nostalgia in Times Square* (includes some of *Mingus-Ah-Um*), JG-35717; Columbia. *Charles Mingus—The Impulse Years* (reissues *Black Saint* and *Mingus, Mingus*), AS-9234-2, Impulse. *Mingus at Antibes* (with Eric Dolphy, 1960), SD2-3001, Atlantic. *Mingus Plays Piano* (1963, beautiful, atypical solos), A-60, Impulse. The 1970's: *Changes One, Mingus Moves, Three or Four Shades of Blue* (partly reissued on *Passions*, Selected Discography).

OLIVER NELSON
More Blues and the Abstract Truth. A-75; *The Kennedy Dream*, AS-9144; Impulse. *Images* (with Eric Dolphy), P-24060; *Afro/American Sketches*, P-7725; Prestige. *A Dream Deferred*, CYL-2-1449, Flying Dutchman (RCA). *Stolen Moments* (1975, last session), IC 6008, Inner City.

GEORGE RUSSELL
New York, N.Y. and Jazz in the Space Age, MCA2-4017, MCA. For early work, see Dizzy Gillespie, *Cubano Be, Cubano Bop*, Verve (uncertain availability).

WOODY SHAW
Woody III, 35977; *Stepping Stones*, 35560; *Rosewood*, 35309; Columbia.

Love Dance (1975, with Billy Harper), 5074; *Moontrane* (with Azar Lawrence, 1974), 5058; Muse. *Blackstone Legacy*, 7627/8, Contemporary.

WAYNE SHORTER

(See also Miles Davis, Weather Report, Chapter 7; Blakey, Chapter 5.) *Speak No Evil*, BST-84194; *Schizophrenia*, BST-84297; Blue Note. *Nature Dancer*, PC-33418, Columbia.

McCOY TYNER (see also John Coltrane)

Expansions, BST-84388; *Extensions*, LA-0060F; Blue Note. *Sahara*, MSP-9039; *Song of the New World*, MSP-9049; *Trident*, M-9063; *Supertrios*, M-55003; Milestone. Many good Tyner albums are available on Milestone.

MAL WALDRON

Blues for Lady Day, AL-1013, Arista. *Mal Waldron Quintet with Steve Lacy: One-Upmanship*, IC 3010, Inner City.

CEDAR WALTON

Cedar (with K. Dorman, Billy Higgins, Junior Cook, Leroy Vinnegar), PR-7519, Prestige.

One of the great Charlie Parker bands, 52nd Street, ca. 1945. Bird, alto sax; Miles Davis, trumpet; Tommy Potter, bass; Thelonious Monk (back to the camera), piano. The drummer (hidden) is unknown. (*Duncan Schiedt Archives*)

The Greatest Jazz Concert Ever band at Massey Hall, 1953.

Left, Bud Powell, bebop pianist *par excellence*. (*Duncan Schiedt Archives*)

Below, Max Roach on drums; Charles Mingus, who recorded the concert, on bass; Dizzy Gillespie, soloing on trumpet. (*Duncan Schiedt Archives*)

Left, Thelonious Monk, innovative composer and pianist (early 1960's). (*Lee Tanner*) Center, Art Blakey, leader for more than a quarter-century of the Jazz Messengers. (*Courtesy Orrin Keepnews*) Right, Horace Silver, the first funky pianist (early 1960's). (*Courtesy Orrin Keepnews*) Below, Dizzy Gillespie (with Miles Davis) backstage in 1959. The tilted-bell trumpet became Gillespie's trademark. (*Duncan Schiedt Archives*)

Above, lyrical trumpeter Clifford Brown and tenor saxophonist Sonny Rollins, his most notable partner in the Clifford Brown-Max Roach Quintet, 1956. (*Charles Stewart*) Below, Sonny Rollins in the 1970's. (*Photo by Jerome Knill*)

Above, Cannonball Adderley, alto sax, and brother Nat, cornet, ca. 1962. (*Steve Schapiro*) Below left, Wes Montgomery, the most influential guitarist since Charlie Christian, in a recording studio (early 1960's). (*William Claxton*) Below right, Joe Pass, a virtuoso of the 1970's. (*Pablo publicity photo*)

Above, the Modern Jazz Quartet, together for 23 years: John Lewis, piano; Percy Heath, bass; Milt Jackson, vibes; and Connie Kay, drums. (*David Gahr*)   Below, the Dave Brubeck Quartet: Joe Morello, drums; Eugene Wright, bass; Paul Desmond, alto sax; and (seated) Dave Brubeck, piano. (*Courtesy Dave Brubeck*)

Above, Cannonball Adderley, alto sax, and brother Nat, cornet, ca. 1962. (*Steve Schapiro*)
Below left, Wes Montgomery, the most influential guitarist since Charlie Christian, in a recording studio (early 1960's). (*William Claxton*)   Below right, Joe Pass, a virtuoso of
the 1970's. (*Pablo publicity photo*)

Above, the Modern Jazz Quartet, together for 23 years: John Lewis, piano; Percy Heath, bass; Milt Jackson, vibes; and Connie Kay, drums. (*David Gahr*) Below, the Dave Brubeck Quartet: Joe Morello, drums; Eugene Wright, bass; Paul Desmond, alto sax; and (seated) Dave Brubeck, piano. (*Courtesy Dave Brubeck*)

The historic *Kind of Blue* session, 1959.

Above, from left to right: John Coltrane, Cannonball Adderley, Miles Davis, and Bill Evans (seated). (*Photo: Don Hunstein*) Below left, Evans demonstrating chords for Miles on the piano. (*Photo: Don Hunstein*) Below right, a pensive John Coltrane. (*Photo: Don Hunstein*)

Above, the Bill Evans trio downstairs at the Village Vanguard, 1961. From left to right: Scott LaFaro, bass; Evans; Paul Motian, drums. (*Steve Schapiro*) Below, the "new" Bill Evans at the Fantasy Records studio (late 1970's). (*Courtesy Fantasy Records/Photo by Phil Bray*)

Left, George Russell, pianist, composer, and theoretician. (*Steve Schapiro*)

Above, Charles Mingus, composer, bandleader, and bassist. (*Photographer unknown*)

Left, Eric Dolphy recording on alto sax; the difficult bass clarinet stands in the foreground. Dolphy also mastered the flute. Photo is from 1961 or 1962. (*Steve Schapiro*)

Above left, John Coltrane, a tenor and soprano saxophonist of grandeur, intensity, and enormous influence, April, 1962. (*Charles Stewart*) Above right, John Coltrane with McCoy Tyner, his pianist from 1960 to 1965 (ca. 1964). (*Charles Stewart*) Below, McCoy Tyner became a major innovator on piano during the 1970's. (*Lee Friedlander*)

Above, Toshiko Akiyoshi leading the big band, as husband Lew Tabackin solos on tenor sax. (*Miguel Tejada-Flores*) Below, the V.S.O.P. band, 1978. From left to right: Wayne Shorter, tenor sax; Herbie Hancock, piano; Freddie Hubbard, trumpet; Ron Carter, bass; Tony Williams, drums. (© *1980 Tom Copi/San Francisco*)

Left, Ella Fitzgerald, probably late 1950's. (*Courtesy Orrin Keepnews*)

Above, Sarah Vaughan in 1943, the year of her debut with the Earl Hines band. (*From the Stanley Dance Collection*)

Left, Betty Carter, a great contemporary be-bop singer. (*Photo © 1980 by Veryl Oakland*)

part three
CONTEMPORARY JAZZ

7

FUSION
(Jazz/Rock/Soul/Pop)

THE FUSION JAZZ STYLE, which began in 1969, is based upon a synthesis of modern jazz with elements of rock, soul, and pop music of the 1960's. It makes frequent use of electronic instruments and sophisticated studio techniques. Unlike its predecessors (including free jazz, to be discussed in the next chapter), fusion introduced nothing original in the handling of rhythm, melody, and harmony. To an extent, fusion was a reaction to the predominant image of jazz as an art-for-art's-sake music assumed to be incapable of, and disinterested in, communicating with the public at large. That image had meant unemployment, public neglect, and minimal record-company support for a decade. Thus by the 1970's, many musicians felt a new attitude was called for. They began to see themselves not just as artists but as entertainers, a role which the beboppers had stigmatized as "minstrelsy." By incorporating the more popular forms of music into jazz, they turned a pauper into a prince within a few years, achieving album sales figures and concert-hall attendance never thought possible since the demise of the big bands.

Commercial motivation, of course, was not the whole story. Historically speaking, jazz had always been a fusion music and, in a healthy sense, an impressionable one. In the early 1900's, the black and Creole musicians of New Orleans played a synthesis of blues, African-derived rhythms, European-derived marching-band music, and many lesser-known genres of the day. Tin Pan Alley tunes worked their way into the jazz repertoire during the 1930's, as did Broadway show tunes during the 1950's. The modern European composers played a role in the "cool" and "progressive" styles of the 1950's and, as will be discussed in Chapter 8, in the music of certain free jazz musicians of the 1960's and 1970's. Keeping this background in mind, it should be clear that the idea of "pure" jazz is a myth. Jazz musicians have always absorbed the sounds around them. Thus the aesthetic development of rock and soul, along with the increased availability of electric pianos, guitars, and synthesizers, made a certain amount of cross-fertilization inevitable.

The degree and consistency of the fusion synthesis is attributable in part to the unprecedented impact of rock and soul upon America's listening habits. The profiles of these two forms are well worth tracing before we examine how they dovetail with jazz.

That "Different Drummer"

Rock and roll—its name is derived from a sexual euphemism common to blues lyrics—was itself a fusion of country-and-western music and rhythm-and-blues. Its earliest definitive records were those of Bill Haley and His Comets and of Elvis Presley. Presley, whose fame began to spread after several appearances on "The Ed Sullivan Show," a TV variety hour, was the most popular individual singer ever. He had been a modest local success around his hometown, Memphis, Tennessee, on Sun Records until Steve Sholes of RCA decided to invest in the young ex-truckdriver. Presley's contract was bought from Sun for between thirty-five and forty thousand dollars in 1955. By 1960 Presley had recorded eighteen million-selling singles for RCA. His fans were inexplicably loyal. *Rolling Stone* magazine reported that twenty million Presley albums were sold within one day of his death in 1977, and it is estimated that hundreds of millions of Presley records have been sold worldwide.

Rock's stylistic domination of the music business increased when the Beatles' music was imported from England in 1964. If Elvis proved that rock had mass appeal, the Beatles demonstrated its aesthetic potential. Their first *Meet the Beatles* album on Capitol sold three million copies in its first few months, and they soon surpassed their debut in both sales and musical quality with *Rubber Soul. Sergeant Pepper's Lonely Hearts Club Band* (1967) introduced the album suite, in which songs are interrelated and not simply a random collection of potential "hits." To the astonishment of a few remaining skeptics, the quartet remained innovative and exciting to the very end—on *The Beatles* (1968), a two-disc set packaged in a white cover (popularly called "the white album"), and *Abbey Road* (1969), their last important project together.

Rock's appeal was at least partly due to its capacity to express, and respond to, the moral confusions of the decade. The country's values and life-styles faced a barrage of challenges: the war in Vietnam; the assassinations of President John F. Kennedy and Senator Robert Kennedy; protest marches and left-wing politics; the burning of draft cards and American flags; right-wing patriotism ("America: Love It or Leave It"); sexual freedom; drugs; Black Nationalism and civil rights; the assassinations of

Malcolm X, Medgar Evers, and Dr. Martin Luther King, Jr.

It was natural for rock to become the voice of disenchanted youth, for that was its original role in 1955 when Haley's "Rock Around the Clock" was adopted as the theme for *Blackboard Jungle*, a film about juvenile delinquency. However, folk singers, too, like Bob Dylan and Joan Baez, were offering a direct commentary upon the plight of the sensitive individual in a seemingly impersonal and rapacious nation. The impact of rock and folk was felt as a massive broadside against the establishment. The rhythms provided an intense, predictable release of nervous energy; the lyrics and, to an extent, the iconoclastic image of the performers offered an alternative view of reality and a variety of escapes from it. Youth in turn became the target of record companies, for by 1965 more than half the population was under twenty-five years of age.

Soul music, essentially a revival of rhythm-and-blues initiated in the mid-1950's by Ray Charles, played an analogous role in the black community. Although the lyrics of soul music did not present the same sort of explicit challenge to conventional values as those of rock, they frequently served as a rallying point and an expression of pride and unity. The rise of soul music roughly paralleled the movement which Stokely Carmichael later dubbed "Black Power." The word "soul" itself became a racial designation. The records were played on black-owned "soul" stations by "soul-brother" and "soul-sister" deejays. Some of the best groups were developed by the black-owned company from Detroit, the Motor City—Motown Records. With Diana Ross and the Supremes, Smokey Robinson and the Miracles, and the Temptations on its label, Motown—in the slang of the day—was "boss." However, there was an abundance of top-selling talent on other labels strongly identified as black: James Brown, Aretha Franklin, Wilson Pickett, and Otis Redding, to cite a few examples. Their music, like the blues from which it derived, was not overtly political but dealt in the universal concepts of love, sex, sadness, and joy. While it did not speak to the black community's need to organize politically, it did become a strong common bond. Perhaps its greatest appeal was simply that it offered a comfortable haven from an angry and troubled world.

A new concept in radio programming proved to be a great asset to the mass marketing of these popular musics. The idea was born in 1955 at a time when most large sponsors had been lured from radio by the growing television industry. Suddenly live radio broadcasts were prohibitively expensive, and the stations had to fill hours of open air time by playing records. Todd Storz, the owner of a chain of stations based in New Orleans, created a programming concept modeled on the juke box. By tuning in one of his stations, listeners could "play" (that is, listen to) their "favorite" songs (that is, those rating the highest in local sales activity). His "50,000-watt juke box on the air" soon evolved into "Top 40" radio, a most effective promotional formula.

Even more than that of soul, rock's reception surpassed the most grandiose dreams of its entrepreneurs. Mo Ostin, president of Warner Brothers Records, recalled the reaction of the business community:

> When we saw the numbers that those records could sell in, we said, "Wow, there's something here!" You'd struggle with a middle of the road artist to sell maybe 300,000 albums, when you could sell two million Jimi Hendrix albums. Frank Sinatra never sold two million albums. Dean Martin never sold two million albums. I don't think there were too many artists who ever sold two million albums until this wave of "involving" records.[1]

When John Lennon, the Beatles' most active spokesman on social issues, remarked in the late 1960's that the group had become "more popular than Jesus," he was chastised from all quarters for his poor taste. Nevertheless, this sort of exaggeration may have been the only way to express the enormous impact of rock 'n' roll.

Most surprising of all, jazz would also hit the magic numbers at which, in the alchemy of the record business, vinyl is turned into gold and platinum.

Jazz/Rock/Soul/Pop

The rhythm, melody, and harmony of fusion have already been encountered in modern jazz and in rock, soul, and popular music. But it is important to review here the variety of ways in which these elements have been fused. It will become clear that there are two unique characteristics of this music which may have an influence upon the future of jazz—the use of electronic instruments and the expanded role of the recording studio.

Fusion developed more purposefully than other jazz styles, making it possible to pinpoint its beginning (at least on records) with the recording in New York of the Miles Davis album *In a Silent Way* on February 18, 1969. There are, of course, earlier recordings which exemplify the principles of fusion: Charlie Parker's 1949 Verve sessions of popular songs with string accompaniment; Stan Getz's 1954 improvisations over Eddie Sauter's light classical orchestrations (*Focus*, Chapter 5); Ramsey Lewis's 1965 hit, "In with the 'In' Crowd," a synthesis of hard bop piano with a rhythmic background that is a cross between rock and revival-meeting music; and Wes Montgomery's 1967 "Goin' out of My Head." There are no doubt several more predecessors of fusion, but their lack of development and continuity with the style being discussed argues against including them as historically significant material.

Although *In a Silent Way* came first, Miles Davis's *Bitches Brew*, which was recorded six months later, was a fuller expression of the rock-influenced drumming, the ostinato (or "ground") bass lines, and the electronic ambience which typified the genre. Miles led the band and channeled its reservoir of ideas, but—it must be understood—he was not the sole creator of its music, which evolved within spontaneous jam sessions. Tony Williams, Jack De-Johnette, and Lenny White contributed their own rhythmic interpretation of rock. John McLaughlin, a jazz guitarist from England, had played with Graham Bond and Jack Bruce and was influenced by Jimi Hendrix. Josef Zawinul, who had been playing electric piano in Cannonball Adderley's band, interested Miles in the instrument, although Davis made the crucial decision to generate cross-rhythms by using three electric pianos simultaneously. The brew was further enriched by Herbie Hancock, Chick Corea, Bennie Maupin, Wayne Shorter, and Larry Young, all of whom became crucial to the new style over the next few years. In fact, the major fusion bands—Hancock's Headhunters, Corea's Return to Forever, Zawinul and Shorter's Weather Report, McLaughlin's Mahavishnu Orchestra—came from the ranks of Miles's group, another reason for isolating it as the starting point of fusion.

In 1968 Miles had announced his intention of forming "the best damn rock and roll band in the world," [2] and in so far as jazz/rock is concerned, he succeeded in gathering the most original and prolific one. To sweeten the pot, *Bitches Brew* sold a quick 400,000 copies, four times Miles's previous top figure for *Sketches of Spain*, another fusion of sorts. So-called "pure" jazz had never fared so well.

Much was happening elsewhere. In Rochester, New York, Chuck Mangione's self-financed album, *Friends and Love*, recorded with the Rochester Philharmonic Orchestra, for whom he had composed and arranged jazz-oriented pop and light classical material, earned this ex-Jazz Messengers flugelhorn player a Grammy nomination in 1971. Mangione had not had a recording contract since 1962. In Los Angeles at about the same time, The Jazz Crusaders—a struggling Blue Note hard bop band—returned from a year's leave, dropped the word "jazz" from their name and revived the R & B format of their Texas origins. Five years later The Crusaders had three gold albums to their credit. Then the Mahavishnu Orchestra began selling out concert halls which were previously the turf of rock stars. With Billy Cobham's drumming this band equalled rock's volume and rhythmic muscle, and John McLaughlin could, as an improviser, play circles around his rock counterparts.

In 1973 Herbie Hancock, who had recently disbanded his sextet for lack of funds, recorded jazz's first gold album by combining a modicum of jazz harmonic and melodic feeling with the funky, danceable rhythms he heard in the music of James Brown and Sly Stone. Fusion's commercial peak was reached in 1976 by George Benson, a superb improvising guitarist of the 1960's. He was transformed into a semipop vocalist by *Breezin'*, which has since sold four million LP's. Benson followed this "monster," as such top sellers are known in the trade, with two more platinum LP's, one of which includes some heartening returns to his jazz background (Selected Discography). While it is impossible to cover all the notable fusion bands in a brief survey, Weather Report, which has lasted through the decade, and Return to Forever (1971–1978) deserve mention for their particularly rich discographies.

Without exception, the above bands have made significant use of electronic instruments, overdubbing and editing of separately recorded tracks, or both—factors which had played a minimal role in jazz prior to 1969. Electronic instruments were not an unprecedented phenomenon. Eddie Durham, Freddie Green, and Charlie Christian had played amplified guitars in the 1930's; Sun Ra (Chapter 8) and Ahmad Jamal had used electric pianos in the mid-1960's; and Jimmy Smith, Count Basie, and others had played electric organ for years. In fusion, however, the overall sound of the music itself (in many cases) had become electronic, creating a new stylistic feature.

The advantages of electronic sound were multiple: It captured the tone, timbres, and energy of much rock and soul music; it became easier to play faster and louder, an asset in the oversized halls needed to accommodate the fusion audiences; it offered new tonal colors to work with, especially the synthesizers, which could be programmed to create unique sounds; and it was a convenience in the studio because it eliminated the risk of "leakage" through a remote microphone.

In some minds, however, abandoning the subtlety and nuances of the (acoustic) guitar and piano for plugs, wires, and gadgetry was tantamount to selling out. Electronic instruments, it was argued, could not communicate the personality of the player. Musicians insisted, however, that electronics were as appropriate to fusion as acoustic instruments had been to modern jazz. Moreover, the singing sound of Chick Corea's electric piano and Mini-Moog solos and the creative orchestral use by Josef Zawinul of the polyphonic (multivoiced) synthesizers refutes the idea that these instruments cannot be used expressively. Thus it does not seem wise to reject electronics in principle—evaluations must be saved for the particular pieces of music in which they occur.

Fusion musicians also discovered the power of modern recording equipment; they learned to improve upon what had been played in the studio and even to record music that was physically unplayable by a live performing band. The modern electronic console records up to thirty-two separate tracks on a two-inch-wide tape, leaving an enormous range of editing possibilities. The mistakes of individual players can be eliminated quite easily without sacrificing the whole take. Voices, violins, or other background can be added later on what are called "sweetening" tracks, which are intentionally left blank for such overdubbing. Before the final "mix" of tracks, the music can be doctored with everything from a face lift to major surgery. When Teddy Wilson, whose recording prime was in the late 1930's (see Benny Goodman and Billie Holiday, Chapter 4), was invited to play piano for pop singer Phoebe Snow, he was astonished to learn that he would play her "accompaniment" while listening through headphones to tracks she had recorded miles away and weeks earlier. The fusion musician is comfortable with these technological facts of life and makes use of them. Keyboardists especially, like Zawinul, Corea, and Hancock, use the studio as if it were an instrument, improvising over prerecorded tracks and creating dense music in successive layers of sound.

For obvious reasons the role of the producer was rapidly expanded and was often taken over by the musicians themselves. Musically knowledgeable producers, such as Creed Taylor, David Rubinson, Dave Grusin, and Tommy LiPuma, have become silent partners with an increasing influence on the sound of fusion LP's. Naturally the spontaneous interplay among musicians, a trademark of jazz in other styles, is often sacrificed. On the other hand, musicians have become aware of the fact that a record can be more than a "document" of a live performance, a potential that has not yet been fully explored.

Ten Years After

Fusion has been both lucrative and controversial in its short lifetime. According to the music's many critics, its popularity and profits far exceed its aesthetic values, durability, or contribution to jazz's development. There are usually two justifications for this point of view, the first being that fusion is an eclectic rather than an innovative jazz style. Except for the exploration of electronic instruments and advanced studio techniques, no major artistic advances have been made. Second, and even worse, the lure of fame and fortune has lured some promising serious musicians into wasting their talents in pursuing financial goals.

On the other hand, there is undeniably exciting music on the albums discussed here, many of which have prepared and stimulated their audiences to explore other jazz styles. In their solos on "Sly" (*Head Hunters*, Selected Discography), Herbie Hancock and Bennie Maupin play with a jazz "content" similar to their music of the 1960's, despite the rock/R & B underpinnings. The result was a much enlarged audience for Hancock's "pure" jazz playing, as shown by the success of his 1978 tour with trumpeter Freddie Hubbard and the former (1964–1968) Miles Davis band (*V.S.O.P: The Quintet*, Chapter 6, Selected Discography). Since nearly every fusion musician had significant playing experience in the 1960's, their modern jazz discographies were often discovered retroactively. The case of John McLaughlin, who was profoundly influenced by John Coltrane's modal improvisations, provides another sort of example. His friendship with rock superstar Carlos Santana led to their *Love/Devotion/Surrender* LP, one side of which is devoted to Coltrane's music. While it is not easy to trace the inevitable spin-off interests of listeners, Coltrane himself surely acquired a wider posthumous audience through this association.

Record company support did not linger far behind the increased visibility of jazz, and fusion can take great pride in having contributed to that development. Columbia, which had only ten jazz artists under active contract in 1970, boasted a roster of fifty by 1979, including such major nonfusion players as Dexter Gordon (Chapter 5), Woody Shaw (Chapter 6), and Arthur Blythe (Chapter 8). Given that companies work by acquiring an impressive line or catalog in specific areas, there is no doubt that CBS's success with Herbie Hancock, Weather Report, John McLaughlin, and Miles Davis's jazz/rock idiom opened the doors to its Columbia label for others. Warner Brothers Records, which had virtually no jazz division during the 1960's, signed nearly a dozen powerful fusion performers in the 1970's, like guitarist George Benson, singers Flora Purim and Al Jarreau, percussionist Airto Moreira, and even the modernist Bill Evans. In 1978 Warner's acquired the nonfusion ECM catalog for distribution (see Chapter 8). And in the same year the director of the jazz division, Ron Goldstein, spoke of a rosy future in an interview with *Rolling Stone* magazine (December 28, 1978): "The more jazz-oriented music people hear, the more they will open up to pure, mainstream jazz. In two years we may start a separate label devoted to mainstream music. There just wasn't that kind of interest a couple of years ago."

For all fusion's limitations, it has overcome the "elitist," "uncommunicative" image jazz had projected during the 1960's. And if anything is certain in the confusion over fusion, it is that this music has become a very important part of the history of jazz on records.

MILES DAVIS

Bitches Brew

Columbia, PG-26
two discs, brief liner notes
1969

Musicians: Miles Davis, trumpet; Chick Corea, Josef Zawinul, Larry Young, electric pianos; John McLaughlin, electric guitar; Wayne Shorter, soprano sax; Bennie Maupin, bass clarinet; Dave Holland, bass; Harvey Brooks, electric bass; Jack De-Johnette, Lenny White, Charles Alias, drums; Jim Riley, percussion.
Compositions (by Davis unless indicated): *Side one:* Pharaoh's Dance (Zawinul). *Side two:* Bitches Brew. *Side three:* Spanish Key; John McLaughlin. *Side four:* Miles Runs the Voodoo Down; Sanctuary (Shorter).

DESPITE HIS POSITION in the vanguard of cool jazz, hard bop, and 1960's modal playing, Miles Davis's creativity was not exhausted. In a radical break with tradition, he outdid himself on *Bitches Brew*, a collage of jam sessions characterized by impressionistic soloing upon shifting, rock-influenced rhythms and a continuous interplay of electronic keyboards, guitar, and percussion instruments. This album, along with a few others from 1969 to 1972, sired the fusion movement by generating several major bands that played in this style (see introduction to this chapter). While album sales of four hundred thousand speak for the enthusiasm of public response, the critical reaction varied from ecstatic kudos to outrage. Surprisingly the hostility to the music lingers, even among Davis scholars and *aficionados*. Bill Cole, writing about this album in *Miles Davis: A Musical Biography* (1974), says: "Miles is overtly using technology for its own sake," resulting in music "like the longest airplane ever made going down the longest runway ever built and never getting off the ground." Such a point of view is hard to reconcile with the vibrant tonal colors used and the escalating tension produced by Miles's icy-smooth trumpet against the electrifying rhythmic backdrop.

Davis's innovation shocked his fans, but there had been earlier signs of his new style on *Miles in the Sky* (1968), in which Tony Williams played an atypically predictable, simplistic rock dance rhythm—and Herbie Hancock, a percussive electric-piano accompaniment—on "Stuff." *In a Silent Way,* a more mature and beautiful album, marked the next stage of development with its multiple percussionists and electric-piano players (Hancock, Corea, and Zawinul) improvising interlocking backgrounds. Historically this single-disc LP marks the beginning of jazz/rock, and can be recommended highly (see introduction to this chapter).

Bitches Brew pulled out all the stops Miles had been toying with for a year. He superimposed upon rock's intensity the more flexible phrasing and the sophisticated, modally based harmonies of jazz. Furthermore, his combinations of sonorities, such as using the soprano sax over a bluesy electric piano and guitar with the rich bass clarinet droning underneath ("Spanish Key"), produced new, brilliantly colored sound-surfaces.

The working principles of this Davis band (like all the others) are spontaneity and Miles's uncanny ability to capitalize on every bit and scrap of an idea which crosses his path. As noted in the chapter introduction, Miles was as influenced by his sidemen as they were by him, but for Miles such "influence" means that he *uses creatively* everything he hears. As Keith Jarrett (Chapter 8), who joined Miles later in 1970, observed: "If a guy's only capable of playing two notes, Miles will not let him play more. But if he *likes* the way those two notes feel . . . Miles will hire him and write (improvise) music around those two notes. Until he's tired of them." [8]

There were virtually no rehearsals for this album. According to drummer Lenny White, he went to Miles's house the day before the *Brew* session, carrying snare and cymbal only, and found Chick Corea, John McLaughlin, Benny Maupin, and Jack DeJohnette already there. "We played the opening vamp to 'Bitches Brew' for an hour, and that was the rehearsal." [4] In the studio Miles positioned the band in a U-formation with himself in the approximate middle; in this way he unified and focused the diverse elements he had gathered. Chick Corea, who had taken over the piano chair from Herbie Hancock a year earlier, recalled the nonverbal nature of Miles's direction: "With Miles there was never any sitting down to discuss the music, like 'a little more of this or less of that.' There was no analysis, no instructions. There were grunts, glances, smiles, and no smiles." [5]

The music reflects the boldness and unpredictability of its methodology. "Miles Runs the Voodoo Down" is a tightly organized track, perhaps the most likely to appeal to the fan of Miles's earlier styles. His melodic trumpet rhythm dovetails perfectly with the rock-like beat underneath, a characteristic that is absent in the looser structure of the twenty-minute-long "Pharaoh's Dance." Miles's solo effectively varies long tones and quick, punched-out phrases, a recognizable element of his straight-ahead jazz playing. The track is heavily spiced with Jim Riley's African and South American percussives (Lenny White was also playing *shakere*—a gourd wrapped in a net of beads —instead of traps). Percussion blossomed throughout the 1970's in Afro-Brazilian-influenced percussionists like Airto Moreira (see Flora Purim), Guilherme Franco (with McCoy Tyner and Keith Jarrett), Bill Summers (with Herbie Hancock), and Kenneth Nash (with various groups). Miles builds his solo dramatically on "Voodoo" until the climactic collective improvising of the final moments.

"Bitches Brew," by contrast, is an expansive, impressionistic, twenty-seven minute vamp-plus-improvisation. During the rubato introduction, Miles's open sound reverberates through an Echoplex chamber amid great chord splashes from the electric pianos and guitar. On top of an ostinato bass, the background comes to life with Mingus-like instrumental conversations while Miles's trumpet pierces and unites the diverse elements. Wayne Shorter's beautiful "Sanctuary" is played with sustained energy and sensitivity, eliciting one of Miles's longest roles. "Spanish Key" is perhaps its complement. This track features straight-out rock rhythm with the numerous stop-time breaks that became a formula for the style years later. In musicians' parlance the term "bitch" is applied only to the finest improvisers. Given the assembled talent and the improvisational nature of this session, there could have been no better choice of title.

While *Bitches Brew* is the high point of Miles Davis's 1970's music, there are two close seconds in *Jack Johnson*, a score for an (as yet) unreleased film about Miles's favorite boxer, and in *Live/Evil* (1970), which gives expanded roles to guitarist McLaughlin and percussionist Airto Moreira, both of whom are brilliant on the track "Sivad." Herbie Hancock rejoined Miles for these sessions, which may well have influenced the direction he took in 1973. On two albums from the early 1970's, Davis began to take advantage of overdubbing over his own heavily chorded organ playing on *Get up with It* and in the trumpet dialogue he conducts with himself on *Big Fun,* which was cut with the *Bitches Brew* band plus electric *sitar.* These sessions will be enjoyed by those already fond of Davis's fusion style, but they are not strong enough track-by-track to win any converts. *Agharta,* taped live in Japan in 1975, was Miles's last recording; it suffers from aimless solos and rhythmic repetition.

At the age of fifty-four, Miles Davis is now in virtual retirement due, some say, to a painful hip ailment, the consequence of a serious automobile accident. Yet his longtime friend and producer Teo Macero insists he is in fine health and taking a well-deserved rest. Miles's fiercely guarded privacy has kept the truth a mystery. Whether he records again or not, Miles's twenty-eight years on record qualify him as one of the few without whom jazz would be a different and lesser music than it is.

THE MAHAVISHNU ORCHESTRA
and John McLaughlin

The Inner Mounting Flame

Columbia, KC 31067
one disc, no liner notes
1972

Musicians: John (Mahavishnu) McLaughlin, electric guitar; Billy Cobham, drums; Jerry Goodman, amplified violin; Jan Hammer, piano; Rick Laird, bass.
Compositions (all by McLaughlin): *Side one:* Meetings of the Spirit; Dawn; The Noonward Race; A Lotus on Irish Streams. *Side two:* Vital Transformation; The Dance of Maya; You Know You Know; Awakening.

THE MAHAVISHNU ORCHESTRA, led by the British guitar virtuoso John McLaughlin, proved that challenging improvisation and precise interplay among group members was entirely compatible with the high-energy, high-decibel sound of hard rock. The band had a strong impact upon jazz and rock musicians dating from their long engagement at New York's Gaslight Club in 1972. Their music was a self-conscious synthesis of various elements: the electronics and muscular drumming of rock, the impassioned guitar style of Jimi Hendrix, and the modes, or scale patterns, found in the music of John Coltrane and Miles Davis, and in classical Indian ragas. At its best, the band's sound achieved an intensely spiritual aura because of the modes used and the unison playing of guitar and amplified violin.

The Mahavishnu Orchestra was also the first band to prove that jazz/ rock could fill large concert halls, in which the volume of their speakers often threatened to raise the roof. While each player fits precisely into the band's overall design, the band's success and image revolved primarily around John (Mahavishnu) McLaughlin, a clean-shaven, boyish anomaly in the wild, long-haired days of "acid" consciousness. Mahavishnu, who received his name (meaning "creator") from his guru, Sri Chinmoy, began each concert with a request for prolonged silence while he stood tranquilly center stage, dressed in devotional "whites" but armed with the ominous-looking "Double Rainbow" guitar, a two-headed monster with six-stringed and twelve-stringed necks. Before long, the band's screaming double-timed riffs would have the audience on its feet.

Born in 1942 in England, McLaughlin had emigrated to this country in 1969. He had studied classical violin and piano under the influence of his mother, who was also a violinist. At eleven he took up the guitar after hearing the American country-blues singers Leadbelly, Big Bill Broonzy, Muddy Waters, and the Sonny Terry-Brownie McGhee team. At fourteen he heard Django Reinhardt, who interested him in a linear approach to the instrument. Two years later he was drawn into modern jazz through the sophisticated harmonic approach of Tal Farlow, whose recording of "Autumn in New York" he had heard in a record store.

Recordings played an increasingly important role in McLaughlin's development. Miles Davis's "Milestones" (Chapter 5) and John Coltrane's *A Love Supreme* (Chapter 6) introduced him to improvising upon modes, which has dominated his approach ever since. *Miles Davis at Carnegie Hall* (Chapter 6) inspired in him an admiration for the richly accented drumming of Tony Williams, at whose invitation he came to America.

Before leaving England, McLaughlin worked with the Graham Bond Organization of 1962, which included Ginger Baker and Jack Bruce, later of the group Cream. In this group he began to use electronic feedback in his music, a technical "impurity" jazz would not tolerate until years later. Bond also exposed McLaughlin to writings on the occult and to theosophy, which soon led him to Indian religion and music. Through his study of the *vina*, an ancestor of the *sitar*, McLaughlin came to understand the power of modes and the spiritual role of Indian music, and applied these ideas to jazz quite conspicuously. He recorded *Extrapolation* for the (defunct) Marmalade label in England. Tapes of that session were brought to the United States by McLaughlin's roommate, bassist Dave Holland, who had been invited to join Miles Davis's band. When Tony Williams heard the *Extrapolation* session, he invited McLaughlin to join his Lifetime group.

John arrived in New York several months later on February 18, 1969, and—as if in a fairy tale—found himself playing with Williams and Holland the very next day on Miles's *In a Silent Way*. He also played on the subsequent *Bitches Brew* and *Live/Evil* sessions, during which he met drummer Billy Cobham. In the next two years McLaughlin recorded some excellent pre-Mahavishnu albums, most of which are no longer available. One that still remains in the Vanguard catalog is a straight-ahead jazz session entitled *Spaces* with sensitive duo-guitar work by John and the leader of the date, Larry Coryell, backed by Billy Cobham, Chick Corea, and Miroslav Vitous. John can also be heard with Vitous, Hancock, and Wayne Shorter on *Mountain in the Clouds*. Two less successful albums—McLaughlin's *Devotion*, an attempt at jazz/rock with drummer Buddy Miles, and *My Goal's Beyond*, half jazz and half meditative acoustic guitar solo, both on Douglas —are no longer available. The greatest loss to McLaughlin's discography is the final recording of the Lifetime band, *Emergency*, with Williams and the impassioned electric-organ playing of Larry Young. This two-disc Polydor set, now deleted but obtainable with luck and persistent searching, is one of the unheralded treasures of jazz/rock. The Lifetime group meant so much to McLaughlin that he turned down an invitation to join Miles's band so that he could remain with it. British rock bassist Jack Bruce joined the Lifetime band later, but due to disputes with management and inappropriate bookings, Lifetime never recorded with Bruce and soon broke up. (Williams formed another Lifetime band later in the 1970's.)

Encouraged by both Davis and Sri Chinmoy to form his own band, McLaughlin gathered Billy Cobham and Jerry Goodman (from the *My Goal's Beyond* session) and Rick Laird, with whom he had jammed several years earlier in England. Jan Hammer, then playing piano for Sarah Vaughan, was recommended by Vitous, who had invited McLaughlin to join Weather Report. After two weeks of rehearsals, the band took McLaughlin's original music into the Gaslight Club, and one month later recorded *The Inner Mounting Flame*. Although *Flame* is quite rough compared with the polish of later jazz/rock, it has a compelling urgency and enthusiasm.

The Mahavishnu Orchestra's music is generally simpler than its tempos make it appear. Their best piece, "Dance of Maya," is like many others in its use of a repetitive melodic cycle which gradually ascends the modal ladder and then finally launches the soloists. "Dance" is distinctive for its shifting rhythmic patterns and tempo changes. "The Noonward Race" has the same virtues along with difficult stop-time breaks executed by McLaughlin and Cobham, who are capable of playing as if their souls were connected. Both "Maya" and "Race" contain allusions to McLaughlin's first love, the blues, and some frantic scalar riffing that occasionally uses feedback and distortion to intensify the continually upward-striving lines. "Meetings of the Spirit," which usually opened the band's concerts, and "Vital Transformation" epitomize their alternation of high-velocity ensemble figures with ethereal rubato passages. On "Meetings" one feels the uplifting quality of Jerry Goodman's violin sailing over the wash of sound beneath it, powered by Billy Cobham's apparently unlimited energy.

Birds of Fire (1973) was a disappointment in both composition and improvisation after the novelty of *Flame*. But *Between Nothingness and Eternity*, recorded live in New York's Central Park the same year, was another high point in the orchestra's career, though the group disbanded only a month later because of personality conflicts. In 1973 McLaughlin also recorded *Love/Devotion/Surrender* with his friend and fellow Chinmoy disciple Carlos Santana. Despite cuts of Coltrane's "A Love Supreme" and "Naima," and the presence of Larry Young on organ, the music seems a bit aimless and lacking in rhythmic vitality. McLaughlin's second and expanded edition of the group produced *Visions of the Emerald Beyond*, featuring the amplified violin of Jean-Luc Ponty (with an exceptional unaccompanied solo on "Pastoral") and an occasional complement of strings and horns. But without Billy Cobham and Jan Hammer (Gayle Moran replaces him on keyboards), the music loses its steam and focus. The same group recorded several McLaughlin pieces with the London Symphony Orchestra (with Michael Tilson Thomas conducting), and although "Vision Is a Naked Sword" bears a pleasing resemblance to "Dance of Maya," there will be little to interest the jazz listener on this disc. *Inner Worlds* (1975), which has new personnel and features expanded use of keyboard and guitar synthesizers, like *Visions* suffers a lack of fire and direction.

John McLaughlin experienced a personal crisis in 1975, resulting in the termination of the Mahavishnu Orchestra and John's allegiance to Sri Chinmoy. According to one report, the $5000 "Double Rainbow" guitar had been smashed on the dressing room floor after the band's last concert. At any rate, McLaughlin returned to the acoustic guitar and the simplicity of Indian music, which he attempted to fuse with jazz-tinged improvisations in his Shakti group. The quartet, which included violin, *tabla,* and *ghatam* (a stringed bass instrument), plays exclusively linear music with a pulsating rhythmic sameness. Thus *Shakti* and *Handful of Beauty*, a more lyrical and heterogeneous effort, lack the drive and speech-inflected tone quality which made McLaughlin's reputation in jazz. Apathetic public response was another indication of the music's minimal appeal to McLaughlin's erstwhile audience.

In 1978 he renewed hope for his jazz revival when he became reunited with crucial colleagues of the early 1970's on *Johnny McLaughlin, Electric Guitarist,* a phrase taken from a calling card of his teenage years. Tracks reminiscent of the Mahavishnu style, of Coltrane's influence, and of the Lifetime group, and a solo on "My Foolish Heart," that recalls Tal Farlow, make *Electric Guitarist* the most satisfying of the recent albums. Its promise is partly fulfilled by *Electric Dreams* (1979) performed by the new One Truth Band, including L. Shankar, the violinist from Shakti, and Stu Goldberg, the keyboardist from the *Visions* album. "Miles Davis" and another McLaughlin original, "The Dark Prince" (also Miles?), are exhilarating and compelling performances of swinging, cliché-free riffing. While other tracks possess less vitality (the worst of all is the Indian pulse piece, "Love and Understanding"), *Dreams* and *Guitarist* are the true legacy of the Mahavishnu Orchestra and offer good reason to expect more worthwhile music from McLaughlin during the 1980's.

THE CRUSADERS

Scratch

Blue Thumb, BTS-6010
one disc
1974

Musicians: Wayne Henderson, trombone; Wilton Felder, tenor sax; Joe Sample, keyboards; Stix Hooper, drums; Larry Carlton, bass; Max Bennett, bass.
Compositions: Side one: Scratch; Eleanor Rigby. *Side two:* Hard Times; So Far Away; Way Back Home.

THE CRUSADERS WERE the first group to attempt to synthesize jazz with rhythm-and-blues, a style the founders of the band had been playing since their formative years. Their *Crusaders 1* (1972) album pioneered the territory in which modern jazz and soulful dance rhythms overlap, an area soon to be explored by Herbie Hancock, Donald Byrd and the Blackbyrds, and many more to follow. Crusader music is wholly uncomplicated by melodic and harmonic sophistication, which makes it seem virtually pointless to those who like adventurous improvisational jazz. However, the band is powerful and authentic when in the right groove, and after numerous gold LP's, its influence upon the jazz/funk fusion idiom of the 1970's has been (while not altogether healthy) undeniably profound.

Stix Hooper, Wilton Felder, and Joe Sample met during the early 1950's as members of their high school marching band in Houston, Texas. They formed their own group, The Swingsters, and played a brand of R & B influenced by B. B. King, Bobby Blue Bland, and Lightnin' Hopkins. As Joe Sample explained in a *Down Beat* magazine interview (June 17, 1976), their basic feeling came from "learning the blues and getting all those old gospel influences, the old Baptist churches that had tambourines, piano and choirs."

A local disc jockey, Vernon Chambers, introduced the group to bebop on records, which resulted in a lengthy detour in its career. Adding horn players to the band and donning tuxedos in imitation of the Modern Jazz Quartet, they became the Modern Jazz Sextet, performing frequently around Texas

Southern University, where they were enrolled. In 1968, they dropped out of school and moved to Los Angeles on the promise of a recording contract which never materialized. Changing its name to the Nite Hawkes, the group resorted to a rhythm-and-blues show format in Los Angeles and Las Vegas, until Richard Bock, owner of World Pacific Jazz, gave it its first recording opportunity. Blue Note's *Talk Tough* (1961–1962), is a two-disc reissue of these debut sessions, for which the group was renamed The Jazz Crusaders. But another Blue Note double LP, *The Young Rabbits* (1962–1968) captures them at a more advanced stage of hard bop development. While Wilton Felder, Joe Sample, and Wayne Henderson are competent soloists, their music of the 1960's is of less merit than that of contemporaneous bands led by Miles Davis, Cannonball Adderley, Art Blakey, and Horace Silver.

Another turning point was reached in 1969. The Jazz Crusaders took a year's leave of the music business, frustrated by a lack of recognition and the suspicion that they were attempting to live up to externally imposed critical standards not in line with their own musical convictions. Thus they returned to the studio as simply The Crusaders without "the shackles" the word "jazz" represented to them. Suddenly their edited three-minute singles received coveted AM airplay, and throughout the 1970's their albums regularly made the pop, soul, and jazz charts. The Crusaders' story is often taken as a proof that the word "jazz" is a commercial albatross, a point of view that is self-validating if nothing else; but this band changed a good deal more than its name in order to stimulate wide exposure.

Crusaders 1 set the tone for the next few years with the hit "That's How I Feel," an interminably repetitive vamp-riff combination occasionally broken up by restrictive solos. *Second Crusade* and *Southern Comfort* hold to the same unpretentious formula, the most attractive feature of which is a bluesy, virile tonal color achieved by Wilton Felder's tenor sax and Wayne Henderson's trombone playing in unison.

Scratch was an exception, due perhaps to the influence of a Los Angeles audience that was acutely responsive to the players' personalities, which rarely emerge on their other records. The title track, with its earthy, relentless dance rhythm, is what The Crusaders are all about rhythmically. But "Hard Times" is the best track for its varying tempos, another rarity in their discography, and for its potential for individual expression. Joe Sample's gospel-influenced piano is gripping and authentic. Wilton Felder, with his big, rough "Texas-tenor" sound derivative of Lockjaw Davis, Harold Land, and the southwestern R & B style, reaches beyond his immediate grasp with exciting results. Felder also steals the show on "So Far Away" with a long tone held for a full minute, driving someone in the audience of the Roxy to scream "Stop!" Wayne Henderson, who introduces the band at some length on the last track, achieves intense moments on "Hard Times" and "Eleanor Rigby," a swinging arrangement of the memorable Beatles creation. *Scratch* is looser than the other Crusader LP's, leaving the most room for spontaneity within the naturally confining R & B context.

With *Chain Reaction* (1975), The Crusaders initiated a tighter, bigger group sound, enhanced on *Those Southern Knights* (1976) by the hiring of Robert "Pops" Popwell on electric bass, relieving Felder who had been overdubbing the bass parts on the earlier studio albums. *The Best of the Crusaders*, a two-disc reissue of selections from the 1972–1976 albums, including three tracks from *Scratch*, is a very good sampler of their work thus far. Its chief artistic failure is a consequence of The Crusaders' failure to tax their conservative formula in any meaningful way.

With *Free As the Wind* (1977), *Images* (1978), and *Street Life* (1979), Joe Sample's competent string and horn arrangements increased the music's dimensions but not its creativity. *Free As the Wind*, for example, defines the term "overproduced"; it suffers from too much planning rather than emotion. The soloing is pleasant and safe. Unfortunately, this is just the sound which The Crusaders have helped to sell to the music "industry," which is precisely the term its manufactured excitement calls to mind.

In so far as the jazz listener is concerned, The Crusaders are more of historical than artistic interest. Their albums were intended to appeal to a mass audience, and they have succeeded without sacrificing either musicianship or taste. However, it is doubtful that these LP's, including *Scratch*, will inspire much discussion or affection a decade after their issue dates—a short life-span by jazz standards.

HERBIE HANCOCK

Head Hunters

Columbia, KC 32731
one disc, no liner notes
1973

Musicians: Herbie Hancock, piano, clavinet, ARP Odyssey synthesizer, ARP Soloist synthesizer; Bennie Maupin, tenor and soprano saxes, saxello, bass clarinet, alto flute; Paul Jackson, electric bass and marimbula; Harvey Mason, drums; Bill Summers, percussion instruments.
Compositions: Side one: Chameleon; Watermelon Man. *Side two:* Sly; Vein Melter.

Head Hunters, jazz's first gold album, was the earliest demonstration of Herbie Hancock's talent for jazz/funk, a fusion style more maligned than most because of its repetitive, danceable bass and drum figures. Hancock integrates R & B-derived riffs with synthesizer effects and elements of jazz that are far more original than those found in the Crusader albums. His music succeeds or fails on the balance and quality of the synthesis in a given piece. A categorical condemnation of his fusion albums, common in some critical circles, is unfair and pointless, as is the casual comparison of these LP's with those he made in the 1960's.

As noted in Chapter 6, by the age of thirty Hancock had distinguished himself as a pianist and composer of modally based modern jazz in the Miles Davis band on Columbia (1964–1968) and in groups under his own leadership on Blue Note (1962–1969). An insight into his development from 1970 to the recording of *Head Hunters* in 1973 is essential to understanding his fusion style.

In 1970 Herbie Hancock formed an excellent touring sextet consisting of Bennie Maupin on reeds, Eddie Henderson on trumpet, Julian Priester on trombone, Buster Williams on bass, and Billy Hart on drums. For their first Warner Brothers album, *Mwandishi* (1971), Herbie returned to the electric piano, which he had first used with Miles Davis in 1968. Surprisingly "Ostinato," despite its $15/8$ meter, is not vastly different from "Bitches Brew"; they both open with a similar vamp played by Maupin on bass clarinet over an electric bass line. The parallels increase with the soloing of the Davis-influenced trumpeter Eddie Henderson, a superb and underrecorded musician (as well as a practicing psychiatrist).

Mwandishi and its two successors are expansive and loosely improvisational; they represent Hancock's brief auspicious flirtation with free jazz. They also reveal a growing familiarity with multiple electronic keyboards and studio overdubbing. Hancock's expertise was acquired with the help of Dr. Patrick Gleeson, an ex-college English teacher who was one of the first jazz-oriented musicians to fathom the electronic intricacies of synthesized music. Hancock's new Mellotron synthesizer and Gleeson's Moog synthesizer are overdubbed on *Crossings* (1972), the most improvisationally free of the three albums. (*Mwandishi* and *Crossings* are also available as a two-disc Warner Brothers reissue, *Treasure Chest.*) But it was on Hancock's first Columbia session, *Sextant* (1973), that the studio itself became one of Herbie's "instruments." "During one session," Hancock recalled,

> our equipment manager turned on a random resonator which picked up and filtered all the noises in the studio. We liked parts of the tape and stretched it across the desks, file cabinets (around the room). We spliced together what we wanted and used it as a rhythm track for "Rain Dance" on *Sextant*.[6]

Six electronic keyboards—overdubbed by Hancock and Gleeson—played an important role on *Sextant*, with cameo appearances by a fuzz-tone, wah-wah pedal, and Echoplex. Furthermore, Billy Hart's drumming in "Hidden

Shadows" establishes a "get-down" rhythm that is up to that of many later funk tracks. While these three albums are justifiably associated with free or "avant-garde" jazz, *Mwandishi* and *Sextant* may be more appealing to Hancock's fusion fans than is generally assumed. (See General Discography, Chapter 8.)

The Hancock sextet was ahead of its time. Five years later they might have done quite well on the ECM or Arista labels, but in 1973 they were forced to disband for lack of funds. With nowhere to go, Herbie looked inward and discovered in his love of rhythm-and-blues the signpost to a new direction. His discovery was facilitated by the chanting of *Namu-Myōhō-Renge-Kyō*, the mantra of the Nichiren Shoshu Buddhists, a sect Hancock joined under the influence of Buster Williams. "One day while I was chanting," Hancock explained in 1974, "I realized that I'd been a musical snob, specifically avoiding playing straight either rhythmically or harmonically. Even though I like Sly Stone—in fact, I have a secret desire to play on one of his records—I had never attempted that kind of thing on my own dates." [7] Herbie attributed his resistance to funk to "pure jazz snobbism," an attitude he quickly abandoned. The next step was hiring bassist Paul Jackson and drummer Harvey Mason because "jazz musicians, generally speaking, don't know how to play funky, even though we think we do." [8] With Maupin the only holdover from the sextet and the addition of percussionist Bill Summers, Hancock's new band and identity were ready to "get down and boogey," as many of his new admirers would put it.

Head Hunters made it to the Top Ten of the industry's pop charts, where it remained for over a year on the strength of the edited hit single of "Chameleon." The full-length version of "Chameleon," however, is really two pieces of music, illustrating the ambivalence which characterizes this and later Hancock fusion albums. Its opening minutes are devoted to a bass-synthesizer—bass clarinet vamp underneath a simple R & B lead line, an example of the "simplicity and directness" to which Hancock aspires. After Harvey Mason's drum break, an electric String Ensemble forms a framework for Herbie's electric piano solo, one whose phrasing is more akin to that of his Blue Note albums than to Sly Stone or James Brown. After a stop-time break, the band segues into another section of alternating textures. Thus "Chameleon" is true to its name, more a succession of guises than a genuine fusion of related styles.

"Sly" is more integrated and successful, boosted by Maupin's excursion across the full range of the soprano sax and some interesting synthesized "whistle" effects by Hancock. "Watermelon Man," a remake of Hancock's jazz/funk piece of ten years earlier, is built upon an interesting rhythmic idea and a fresh combination of sound colors especially in the vamp, which became the group's signature in concert. "Vein Melter" has the most diffused identity of all, which turns it into a nebulous failure.

Hancock's next three albums, none of which enjoyed the commercial success of *Head Hunters*, were marked by a similar basic duality: a danceable simplicity on the one hand, true fusion on the other. On *Thrust* (1974), "Spank-a-Lee," which begins as no more than a rhythm track, evolves dramatically with some split-tone screaming from Maupin's sax, revealing the kind of personal intensity that is possible within jazz/funk. Hancock's electric piano solo on "Actual Proof" is another creative response to the context. While the music achieves these highs only infrequently, it is clear that for Hancock's band the best of both worlds is obtainable. The nadir is "Palm Grease," which—except for Summers's too-brief percussion interlude—seems intent upon suppressing anything which might relieve the boredom of uninspired R & B imitations. Despite Herbie Hancock's professed admiration for Sly Stone and James Brown, his own strengths clearly lie elsewhere.

Man-Child (1975) is a more consistent, mature album all-around, containing freshly conceived keyboard ideas on "Sun Touch," "Bubbles," and "Heartbeat." "Steppin' In It," however, does just that, despite a lengthy, wailing harmonica solo by Stevie Wonder, whose presence here is a feather in Hancock's recently acquired cap. The high points of *Secrets* (1976) are "People Music" and "Sansho Shima," while "Doin' It," with four consecutive minutes of the lyric "just keep on doin' it," badly overdoes it. In *Sunlight* (1978) and *Feets Don't Fail Me Now* (1979) Herbie "sings" through a Vocoder, a device that transmits pitch and tonality to a human voice which itself was not meant for singing. These efforts are left to the discretion of the listener willing to follow Hancock anywhere. (*The Best of Herbie Hancock* is a sampler of mostly R & B-style tracks from several albums and thus is not recommended.)

Hancock was willing to trade in his artist's image for an entertainer's; that, in fact, was part of his plan. But again his versatility allowed him to have it both ways, as demonstrated by *V.S.O.P.: The Quintet* (Chapter 6, Selected Discography) and a series of duo (acoustic) piano concerts with Chick Corea (Chapters 6 and 8, General Discography). However, his jazz/funk fusion deserves mixed reviews until there is at least as much fusion as funk.

FLORA PURIM and AIRTO MOREIRA

500 Miles High/At Montreux

Milestone, M-9070
one disc, no liner notes
1974

Musicians: Flora Purim, vocals; Airto Moreira, drums and percussion instruments; Ron Carter, bass; Milton Nascimento, vocals and guitar ("Cravo e Canela" only); David Amaro, electric guitar; Wagner Tiso and Roberto Silva, electric piano and electric organ.
Compositions: Side one: O Cantador; Bridge; 500 Miles High; Cravo e Canela. *Side two:* Baia; Uri; Jive Talk.

BRAZILIAN SINGER FLORA PURIM and her husband, percussionist Airto Moreira, have created a unique synthesis of jazz, jazz/rock, and their Brazilian heritage. Although they arrived in the United States in 1968 without work or personal contacts, they were soon jamming with some of America's best jazz musicians and within a decade had recorded with many of them, winning consecutive annual *Down Beat* magazine polls (three for Flora, six for Airto) in their respective categories. Flora's wordless vocals, different in effect and intent from the scat singing of bebop, reveal an unusual knack for reflecting the intonation of the instruments which surround her. Her flexible voice, along with Airto's assortment of primitive percussives, can produce music of rhythmic vitality and highly colored texture.

While Airto's own albums are less popular than Flora's, his impact upon the sound of jazz in the 1970's has been greater, due in part to his popularity in Miles Davis's band of 1970–1971. Airto helped familiarize jazz audiences with the *cuica, berimbau, reco-reco*, and *caxixi*, thus opening the way for other players like Dom Um Ramoa, Guilherme Franco, Bill Summers, and Kenneth Nash. By the mid 1970's, liner note credits frequently listed the band's "percussionist," a nearly nonexistent role during the 1960's.

In 1975, Flora and Airto were attracted to the big-budget Warner Brothers label, leaving behind them the raw, spontaneous, and loose style of *500 Miles High*, their only live recording. Thus many of their albums are a frustrating mixture of the spirited music which made their reputations and a slickly produced studio sound, apparently aimed at a broader, less jazz-oriented audience.

Flora's interest in jazz began in Rio de Janeiro where she was born in 1942, the daughter of accomplished, amateur classical musicians. Flora's mother, a pianist, also liked jazz and exposed her daughter to the records of Erroll Garner. As a teenager Flora began listening to Ella Fitzgerald, Dinah Washington, whose improvisations she memorized, and Miles Davis. At the same time she experienced the rhythms of the local black population at the carnival and in clubs.

Flora began to learn guitar at fourteen, working her first professional job six years later at Bottles Bar, one of the first homes of the *bossa nova*. Flora was already singing in a jazz style, her repertoire interspersed with Brazilian songs by Jobim, Milton Nascimento, and Egberto Gismonti. When Flora met Airto, who was then playing trap drums and percussives gathered from all over Brazil, she became immersed in the black-influenced music of the economically deprived Bahia province, which remains a dominant element of her style. Although Flora had recorded and appeared on television in Brazil, she and Airto came to America because it was the home of jazz, ignoring warnings that the competition would force her to "sing Brazilian" like her predecessor Astrud Gilberto.

Homeless in New York, Flora and Airto stayed at bassist Walter Booker's house, where musicians came to jam after hours. One night Flora sang Jobim's "How Insensitive" with Stan Getz (Gilberto's former employer) and Chick Corea at the piano. This led to an invitation to tour with Getz's group, in which she sang Brazilian after all. Subsequently she recorded with pianist Duke Pearson (*It Could Only Happen to You*) and worked with the band of Gil Evans, where she developed a strong rapport with tenor saxophonist Joe Henderson, bassist Stanley Clarke, and pianist Chick Corea.

In 1971 Corea gave up his year-long stint as a solo pianist in order to "communicate" with a wider audience, and he invited Flora, Airto, and Clarke to join him in recording some fusion classics (to be discussed ahead). *Return to Forever* and *Light As a Feather* are the first records to reveal Flora's "instrumental" use of her voice which blends uncannily with Joe Farrell's flute. During the same period, Airto recorded in a more experimental context on *Free*, reissued on CTI's 8000 series. Surrounded by stars like Keith Jarrett, Chick Corea, Hubert Laws, and George Benson, Airto paints the entire sound in vibrant percussive colors. The "free" format is often unfocused, however, leaving this record less than an unqualified success. (CTI has not reissued *Fingers*, whose availability remains questionable.)

Flora was continuing to develop as a singer in two important ways. First, through her dramatic training in the Stanislavsky method, she learned to project sound from her diaphragm, throat, nose, and head, attaining a broad range of sound qualities. The next breakthrough came at the suggestion of her voice coach and mentor, Hermeto Pascoal the Brazilian composer and flautist. He encouraged her while she was recording "Moondreams" on Airto's *Seeds on the Ground*, to aim at the *sound*, not the note. Suddenly she found she could extend her range from three octaves to nearly six. "When I finished the second voice track," she said later, "Airto, Hermeto, and Ron Carter ran into the booth and began hugging and kissing me. I was shaking from the effort . . ." [9] Flora told *Down Beat* magazine: "I extended my voice when I was no longer afraid that I'd miss the notes, or, rather, not hit them with quality. Then I found out that people like it better if you put your real feelings into the music, not caring if the quality is perfect or not." [10]

Flora's first opportunity to spread her wings came with *Butterfly Dreams*, her debut album for Milestone in 1973. The first track, "Dr. Jive," explodes with the shrieks, growls, and sighs which became Flora's signature, but the excitement diminishes over the four consecutive ballads that follow. The highlight of side two is "Light As a Feather," preceded by "Dr. Jive (Part 2)," with Flora joining the band as another instrument. Despite *Butterfly's* popularity, her next three LP's are those that should form the core of a Flora Purim collection.

500 Miles High, recorded at the Montreux Jazz Festival in July 1974, captures her singing at its most open and uninhibited, striking the emotional, imaginative mood she thrives on. Side one is a fitting summation of what she has meant to jazz in the 1970's. "O Cantador," one of her favorite ballads, elicits a romantic, tempo-less performance in a breathy voice that is reminiscent of Getz's tenor sax. "Bridge" heats up the atmosphere with wordless instrumentalese and her "sounds of life" vocal effects, and prepares the audience for "500 Miles High." On "High" Flora's improvisation demonstrates her remarkable progress since her 1971 recording of the Corea classic with Return to Forever. "Cravo e Canela"—with composer Milton Nascimento on guitar and vocal harmony—is a rousing finale, opening with Airto's solo on the twangy *berimbau* and shifting into powerful Brazilian dance rhythms. Side two starts more slowly, the result of little contrast between "Baia" and "Uri." "Jive Talk" repays the listener's patience with a furious and colorful voice-percussion collage. Airto's solo recalls Chano Pozo's legendary ability to elicit audience response, which at Montreux means participatory handclapping. The ten-minute track climaxes with the entire band's vocal riff, one which typifies the energy Flora and Airto communicate in their best moments.

One month later Flora entered the Milestone studios to finish *Stories to Tell. Stories* is a good collection of songs in a natural setting that allows Flora's personality to emerge. "Search for Peace," on which she sings her own lyrics to a McCoy Tyner composition, is one of her best straight-jazz performances, enhanced by a good acoustic piano accompaniment by George Duke. Her wordless vocalizing on "Silver Sword," in which she is joined by Miroslav Vitous and Carlos Santana, is the high point of side two. Airto's function on this track is to provide the colorful framework for Flora. *Stories* is probably her second-best LP.

Open Your Eyes, You Can Fly, completed in December 1975, is an indication of the direction she would take in the late 1970's. With a coterie of excellent jazz players, which now included her teacher Pascoal on flute and electric piano, she would make full use of the studio's power and precision. The album is a mix of good moments ("San Francisco River," "White Wing/Black Wing") and some dull, predictable ones. The neat, compact studio sound seems more of a restriction than an asset. Two more Milestone releases, which completed her contractual obligations to the label, *Encounter* and *That's What She Said*, are similar potpourris that lack the overall spontaneity and unity of *500 Miles High* and *Stories to Tell*.

When Flora and Airto moved over to Warner Brothers, which had already transformed George Benson into a platinum pop idol, one feared the worst. However, the results were neither total successes nor failures, only a frustrating combination of both. There are good tracks on *Nothing Will Be As It Was . . . Tomorrow* ("Angels," "Corre Nina"), *Everyday, Every Night* ("Samba Michel"), and *Carry On* ("From the Lonely Afternoon"), but most of the material suffers from a too-predictable pop sound with little room for cutting loose. Flora and Airto can still generate an infectious enthusiasm on stage, where the setting demands spontaneity. Perhaps, then, another live album will restore to their recorded music the earthy excitement they are so capable of generating.

(*Note*: Urszula Dudziak and Al Jarreau, both of whom also make use of wordless vocals and instrument-like vocalizing, are listed in the General Discography. While Dudziak has had difficulty finding a suitable context for her voice, Jarreau, a former rehabilitation counselor with a degree in psychology, shows great promise for his many original songs and variety of presentations.)

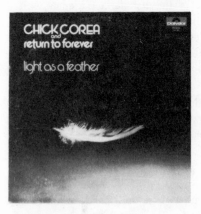

**CHICK COREA and
RETURN TO FOREVER**

Light As a Feather

Polydor, PD 5525
one disc, no liner notes
1972

Musicians: Chick Corea, electric piano; Stanley Clarke, bass; Flora Purim, vocals; Joe
    Farrell, tenor sax, flute; Airto Moreira, drums and percussion instruments.
Compositions: Side one: You're Everything (Corea); Light As a Feather (Clarke);
    Captain Marvel (Corea). *Side two:* 500 Miles High (Corea); Spain (Corea).

Where Have I Known You Before?

Polydor, PD 6509
one disc, no liner notes
1974

Musicians: Chick Corea, piano, electric piano, organ, clavinet, synthesizers; Stanley
   Clarke, electric bass, organ, chimes, bells; Lenny White, drums and percussion in-
   struments; Al DiMeola, electric guitar and twelve-string acoustic guitar.
Compositions (all by Corea unless indicated): *Side one:* Vulcan Worlds (Clarke); Where
   Have I Loved You Before?; The Shadow of Lo (White); Where Have I Danced
   with You Before?; Beyond the Seventh Galaxy. *Side two:* Earth Juice; Where Have
   I Known You Before?; Song to the Pharaoh Kings.

CHICK COREA

My Spanish Heart

Polydor, PD-2-9003
two discs, no liner notes
1976

Musicians: Chick Corea, piano, Mini-Moog, Moog 15, ARP Odyssey synthesizer, organ,
   Polymoog synthesizer, electric piano, handclapping, background vocals; Steve Gadd,
   drums; Stanley Clarke, acoustic bass (four tracks); Jean-Luc Ponty, violin (one
   track); Gayle Moran, vocals and background vocals; Don Alias, percussion. Narada
   Michael Walden, handclapping; plus two violins, viola, cello, three trumpets, and
   trombone.
Compositions (all compositions and arrangements by Corea): *Sides one and two:* Love
   Castle; The Gardens; Day Danse; My Spanish Heart; Night Streets; The Hilltop;
   The Sky (Children's Song, No. 8, and Portrait of Children's Song, No. 8); Wind
   Danse. *Sides three and four:* Armando's Rhumba; Prelude to El Bozo; El Bozo
   (Parts I, II, and III). Spanish Fantasy (Parts I, II, III, and IV).

No MUSICIAN HAS used the fusion concept with more variety, intelligence, and unimpeachable taste than Chick Corea. His work encompasses popular ballads, high-energy jazz/rock, and a light-orchestral approach, all represented by the albums selected here. Corea's music is characterized by a singing melodicism and on piano and synthesizers, by a clean articulation and driving sense of swing. His albums since 1972, even those which do not succeed musically, are marked by careful planning and forethought. He takes a sixteen-piece ensemble into the studio for an album of original music and supervises the final mix as soon as three weeks later, a process other bandleaders stretch out for six months.

Personally Corea is without pretense, straight-talking, and an extrovert. Like his music, his life seems clearly organized. Except for a playful side, which has become prominent in his music, his course is a deliberate one. As early as 1974 in an interview with *Rolling Stone* magazine he mapped out his career in terms which have been fulfilled to a remarkable extent: "My own personal ideal is combining all the most beautiful forms of music, classical, rock, and jazz, into a (form) that doesn't go over people's heads and doesn't go under them either. . . . the music isn't a radical departure. I guess you could call it a contemporary hybrid." [11] Corea's Return to Forever unit, retitled Chick Corea and Friends when partner Stanley Clarke left in 1978, has been the workshop in which much of the musical synthesis has taken place.

Corea has had an intense involvement with modern jazz and near-free jazz and compiled a high-quality discography in both these areas prior to his interest in the fusion idea. In fact, his lifelong relationship with music has been more varied than the records indicate. Chick was born in 1941 outside of Boston, the son of a society bandleader and trumpeter, Armando Corea, after whom he was named. Armando Sr., who is still an active musician, began his son on piano at the age of four, showing him how to play popular songs and familiarizing him with the language of music. Chick's only formal training came from a local teacher, Salvatore Suolo, with whom he studied the classics for five years.

In high school Chick played the trumpet in the marching band, and developed an intense feeling for jazz through his father's records of Charlie Parker, Dizzy Gillespie, and Bud Powell. He learned the hard bop style by transcribing the simple, logical, and swinging solos of Horace Silver from recordings of Silver's quintet with Junior Cook and Blue Mitchell. Corea was a good student, but he knew from an early age that music was his real interest. While still in high school, he played at weddings and *bar mitzvahs*, and with the Latin band of Phil Barbose, whose conga player, Bill Fitch, made Corea become aware of his deeply felt affinity for Spanish and Latin music.

Chick registered as a liberal arts student at Columbia University in New York in 1959, but dropped out one month later after hearing Miles Davis's band at Birdland. Realizing that music was his real calling, Corea returned

to Boston for eight months of intensive study with Suolo in preparation for an audition at the Juilliard School of Music. He practiced ten to fourteen hours daily and memorized a dozen major piano works. Juilliard accepted him as a piano major; but again Corea left after a month, this time to work with a variety of Latin and jazz groups around New York.

Corea's first recording was made in 1962 as Mongo Santamaria's pianist; several cuts are reissued on Milestone's two-disc *Santamaria: Skins*. Subsequently Corea worked for the Latin jazz bands of Willie Bobo and Herbie Mann. He played a more straight-ahead jazz with Blue Mitchell, John Gilmore, and Lee Morgan, and developed a crisp, melodic hard bop style.

In 1966 Corea recorded his first session as a leader on Atlantic's Vortex label, with a budding ensemble consisting of Joe Farrell, Woody Shaw, Steve Swallow, and Joe Chambers. The original title track, "Tones for Joan's Bones," and five more Corea pieces have been reissued on *Inner Space*, which gives one a good sample of Corea's piano playing in transition between the modally based style of early McCoy Tyner and the linear searching of Paul Bley. From 1966 to 1968 Chick was in the band of Stan Getz. Getz recorded two of the "Joan's Bones" pieces, "Litha" and "Windows," reissued on the excellent Verve set *Stan Getz: The Chick Corea/Bill Evans Sessions*. In 1968 Corea worked several months as Sarah Vaughan's accompanist, but shortly after an engagement at the Fairmont Hotel in San Francisco, he received a phone call from drummer Tony Williams, an old friend from the Boston area, which led to a turning point in his musical direction.

Miles Davis's regular pianist, Herbie Hancock, had become ill with food poisoning in Brazil, and was unable to return for a job in Baltimore. Chick was asked by Tony to replace Hancock in the Davis band, an invitation which, Chick said, "drove me through the ceiling." After finding a replacement accompanist for Vaughan, he called Miles to ask about rehearsing and was told, in Davis's terse style, "play what you hear." Chick knew the band's material from records, but he soon found out that they did not always play tunes the same way on stage. He vividly recalled the first piece Miles called at the Baltimore date:

> It was "Agitation,"—I'll never forget it. The band took off like a rocket ship. It was like the shock of suddenly traveling five hundred miles per hour. I just hung on. I knew they were playing tunes, but they had them so facile and abstracted that not even a musician's ear could tell what chord changes were going by. After the set I went up to the bar to buy myself a drink. Miles came up behind me and whispered in my ear, "Chick, you're a mutha." That was it! What more could I ask for? [12]

It was in Miles's band that Corea first used the electric piano. Miles insisted, over Chick's objections, that he play one at the Jazz Workshop in Boston. Corea gradually became accustomed to the Fender Rhodes electric piano, which he began to play with a singing melodicism and chordal "snap" (in the left hand), achieving a more personal sound than is generally thought possible on the Rhodes. Like his keyboard counterparts, Herbie Hancock and Josef Zawinul, Corea was initiated in the fusion concept on Davis's *In a Silent Way*. Chick remained with Miles, whom he came to regard as a fountain of creativity, through the 1970 *Bitches Brew* and *Live/Evil* albums (discussed earlier in this chapter). In 1971, however, Chick and bassist Dave Holland visited Miles at home and announced their intention of leaving the band to pursue a freer style of improvising with which they had been experimenting for the past several years.

From 1968 to 1971, at the same time he was involved with Davis, Corea was engaged in an auspicious flirtation with free jazz, which, unfortunately, was never consummated. His stimulating free-form trios and quartets are well documented on Blue Note and ECM albums, many of which are discussed briefly in the introduction to Chapter 8 (see also General Discography, Chapter 8). His group Circle contained Anthony Braxton (Chapter 8) and played primarily in Europe for small and musically sophisticated audiences. The listener is strongly urged to investigate this music, although it cannot appropriately be discussed here. (ECM's *Piano Improvisations, Volume 1*, a solo LP of first takes, is the crowning achievement of this period and should not be missed.)

Corea soon grew disenchanted with "experimenting on stage," playing on the piano's strings, and using rarified compositional approaches. He summed it up this way: "We took our way of thinking from Stockhausen, John Cage, and Cecil Taylor. But it got to the stage where we were sending our audiences up the river. The basic element, communication, was being left out." [13]

The term "communication" has played a major role in Corea's vocabulary and in his goals since 1971 when he became involved in the Scientology movement. Scientology, which Corea has called "the second great discovery of my life," prompted him to conceive of a group whose aim was not musical sophistication but reaching an audience. Therein, of course, lie the seeds of destructive artistic compromise, which Corea (like the group Weather Report) has managed to avoid to a greater extent than the other musicians represented in this chapter.

Return to Forever (that is, to "spiritual awareness") did not spring immediately out of these new commitments. When Corea left Europe, he was in debt and returned to Boston, where he borrowed his father's tuxedo and once again hired himself out for weddings and *bar mitzvahs*. However, a call to work with saxophonist Joe Henderson introduced him to bassist Stanley Clarke, who served as the catalyst Corea needed. The first edition of Return to Forever was completed by Joe Farrell on sax and flute; Flora Purim, with whom he had worked in Stan Getz's band; and Flora's husband, Airto Moreira, on traps and percussion—a preparation perhaps for Corea's Latin-jazz inclinations. *Return to Forever* (1972) was the band's first album, but its message was not communicated with great clarity because of lengthy improvisations. While the playing is fine and lucid and intensified by some amazing vocal gymnastics by Flora, *Return to Forever* lacks the focus, compositional identity, and happy rhythms of *Light As a Feather*.

Light As a Feather proved that Corea had something permanent and of high quality to offer a broad-based audience. While the title track "500 Miles High" (by Clarke) and "You're Everything" were presented as pop or standard jazz ballads, their melodies and melodic rhythms were original enough to make them the first fusion classics. Corea makes use of his Latin-jazz background to give "You're Everything" and "Spain" a folksy feeling. "Spain," which opens with a reference to the "Concierto de Aranjuez," evolves into an intensely rhythmic second theme and a joyous, handclapping celebration—Corea's most effective emotional mood. The dominant message Chick communicates, if it can be summarized succinctly, is that music—no longer the domain of *artistes*—is fun! *Light As a Feather* succeeds more than the earlier Return to Forever session because its joy is so infectious.

Moreover, there are signs within *Feather* of future developments of which Corea's continuing Latin-Spanish evolution is only one. Flora Purim's unique ability to join the band as another (vocal) instrument, absorbing—as in the title track and "Captain Marvel"—the qualities of the instruments around her (most conspicuously, Farrell's flute), became a mainstay of her own style. With Purim and, later, Gayle Moran, Corea became the only fusion composer to make use of the voice in its instrumental (and therefore jazzlike) dimension. The lighthearted unison of flute, voice, and electric piano would be recreated later by Corea with the Mini-Moog, his most personal synthesizer voice. The odd, whimsical piano piece "Children's Song," enhanced by Airto's percussion accents, showed the first emergence of a childlike strain in Corea's music, a strain heard later to good advantage on "Pixiland Rag" (*Leprechaun*). Finally, *Feather* previews the romantic idealism of Neville Potter's lyrics, which Corea called upon until 1977.

The first Return to Forever band broke up because Airto and Flora formed their own group (called Fingers), and also, as Corea put it diplomatically, because of a "difference of life-styles" among the members. The second incarnation of Return to Forever was based quite consciously on the defunct Mahavishnu Orchestra, and thus departed radically from the jazz-combo sound of the first band. With drummer Lenny White, with whom Corea had worked on *Bitches Brew*, and guitarist Bill Connors, Return to Forever breached the high-decibel walls of hard rock. They used up and outgrew the genre within four albums, but two of those LP's are of lasting merit.

It is difficult to choose between *Hymn to the Seventh Galaxy* (1973) and *Where Have I Known You Before?* (1974) because despite their identical commitment to heavily electronic, high-energy jazz/rock, they have very different virtues. *Hymn* is raw and primitive, a collection of fresh ideas played with the enthusiasm of a new discovery. The unison organ-drum riffs by Corea and White on "Hymn" and "Space Circus" show their intention to outdo Mahavishnu at his own game, though White lacks Cobham's muscle. The compositions are very good, with "Captain Señor Mouse" providing yet another sample of electric Latin ecstasy. For its rhythmic power and lack of pretense, this LP can be recommended without qualification.

Where Have I Known You Before? is more polished, featuring Chick's first outing with synthesizers. The Moog and acoustic-piano leitmotiv give this album more tonal variety than *Hymn,* which is the principal reason for its selection here. Guitarist Al DiMeola, whom Chick had heard on a private tape, joined the band by this time, proving to be a more interesting and a bolder soloist than Bill Connors, who dropped out to avoid spending ten months per year on the road. The compositions in *Where* are quite good, taking on some now familiar features. "Vulcan Worlds" by Clarke seems lifted from Mahavishnu's modal *misterioso* style, with DiMeola adopting John McLaughlin's ethereal sonorities for the melody; the synthesizer-drum riffs of "Beyond the Seventh Galaxy" contain some of Corea's archthematic writing, and yet they are invitingly singable. Ultimately, Chick's ability to solo meaningfully, now enhanced by pitch sliding and bending on the Mini-Moog, carries this set of varied, interrelated tracks to a satisfying finish.

Regarding the nearly impossible choice between *Hymn* and *Where,* a two-disc set reissuing both would resolve the dilemma wonderfully, representing the jazz/rock period of Return to Forever at its best. The group does have two more albums: *No Mystery* (1975), which relies too much on formula and too little on inspiration; and *Romantic Warrior* (1976), a more interesting album in which Corea is searching for the broader compositional range he found later that year on *Leprechaun,* the first album with the expanded Return to Forever orchestra.

In 1976 Corea's music underwent another metamorphosis. The Return to Forever quartet was dissolved because of what he called "a mushroom of uncontrollable sound,"[14] an admission that electronic effects were running away with the music. Corea dropped the electric guitar and expanded Return to Forever into a thirteen-piece group with a string quartet and a brass section, aiming for a big sound with his new collection of tonal colors rather than with boosted volume. Fortunately he retained the bank of synthesizers, which he would integrate subtly into the broader compositional framework.

On vocals Corea added Gayle Moran, who had previously been with the second edition of the Mahavishnu Orchestra. With less of a jazz background than Purim, Moran can be aligned more readily with the strings than the horns. Her pure-toned vibrato, suggestive of the formal voice training she received at the University of Washington, increases the "concertizing" image the third Return to Forever unit conveys. (A contractual change in 1976 resulted in a distinction between LP's using the name Return to Forever—requiring the presence of Stanley Clarke—which signed with Columbia, and others using the name Chick Corea, who remained with Polydor as an individual artist. Except for Clarke, the band is usually the same on both labels.)

Leprechaun (1976), the first product of Corea's new endeavors, failed to use the large band effectively, relying too heavily upon the soloing of the early Return to Forever reed player Joe Farrell. Corea had added instruments to the liner credits, but they were not yet playing an important role in the music itself. The strings, for example, are used only as an interlude within Moran's "Soft and Gentle." Nevertheless, there are two redeeming and delightful tracks. "Pixiland Rag" releases Corea's whimsical imagination in an intricate, tongue-in-cheek piano rag, which leads into the album's most impressive effort, "Leprechaun's Dream." On "Leprechaun's Dream" all of Corea's new instruments, including Moran's rather celestial voice, are integrated into a substantial composition. Overall the lack of interesting arrangements, a prerequisite for a thirteen-piece band, is the major flaw on the album, a problem that would be remedied with magnificent success on Corea's next album later that year.

My Spanish Heart, inspired by a trip to Spain and a reacquaintance with the flamenco style, explores to the limit Corea's long-brewing affinity for all Latin music and the concept of the *danse*. The infectious rhythmic vitality and romantic melodicism of the earlier "Spain" on *Feather* is carried to its conclusion, enhanced by a brass fanfare and a rich, bright string quartet. Sides one, three, and four are amazingly solid and varied, both in composition and arrangement. Side two comes near to sounding like a series of acoustic piano "exercises," not finished pieces with emotional content.

But there is more than enough music to rejoice in and plenty of thrills to be pointed out along the way. First, there is the use of Gayle's voice within the band on "Love Castle," which sets the album's spirited mood immediately. Corea's endearing Mini-Moog lines sail over the prancing background. Corea's solos are buoyant and lucid nearly everywhere, but the other Mini-Moog track, "El Bozo," must be singled out for its playful, whistling voice which, at the peak of each melodic phrase, somehow says, "Wheee!" "Day Danse" is a compelling synthesis of strings, handclapping, and acoustic piano, a match for the lively "Armando's Rhumba," which features a superb violin solo by Jean-Luc Ponty. "My Spanish Heart" itself is a brief but moving theme—just the type of sweeping line that could be used in the piano concerto Corea has been talking about writing since 1978. "Night People" is an especially successful arrangement, outdone only by the last track "Spanish Fantasy, Part IV," which integrates trumpet fanfare, string quartet, electric piano, and synthesizers in the grand finale.

Corea's next album in this style is the well-planned, studio-perfect *Mad Hatter* (1978), a piece of program music well suited to the composer's sense of fun. "The Woods" evokes a fantasyland in its opening collage of sound color and displays some of Corea's most sophisticated synthesized overdubs. Variety is the album's strongest virtue. "Tweedle-Dee" is an intentionally

Bartók-like use of string quartet with piano, while "Humpty Dumpty" elicits superb straight-ahead jazz soloing from Joe Farrell on tenor sax, Chick Corea on piano, and Eddie Gomez on double bass. "Falling Alice" and "Dear Alice" are excellent themes, but the track that is the richest in melody, "The Mad Hatter" enhanced by Herbie Hancock's wonderful guest solo, is saved for last. Side two accomplishes somewhat of a recording coup by packing in twenty-seven minutes of music with no significant loss of recording quality. The volume knob may need another quarter-turn, but it is heartening to note that LP's can occasionally offer more music rather than less. Although its good moments do not equal those of *Spanish Heart, Mad Hatter* is an exciting, unified piece of work well worth owning.

Corea has not always succeeded so handily. *Musicmagic*, recorded for Columbia in 1977, leans toward a pop vocal style designed to feature Moran. The integrity of the music is diminished, and the relentlessly didactic lyrics of Corea-Clarke-Moran do not help. One can only listen so often to such advice as "be free," "don't be afraid," "look on the bright side," and so on without tuning out. A few choice images (like Flora's "light as a feather") could say so much more. *Secret Agent* (1979) suffers from a lack of good material, which suggests a different sort of problem. One might hazard a guess that it was created out of contractual not artistic necessity. Columbia recorded the thirteen-piece band live in New York, issuing *Return to Forever: Live/The Complete Concert* in a four-disc set with an attractive photo-booklet and also in a one-disc version, *Return to Forever: Live*. This group always gives its audience a long, energetic show, but one LP's worth of what transpired on that particular evening is sufficient.

Corea is not one to close doors behind him. Since 1978 a duo acoustic-piano concert tour with Herbie Hancock yielded two LP sets; a renewed collaboration with vibraharpist Gary Burton resulted in a good duo on ECM; and a solo session on Corea's favorite piano, built by fellow Scientologist Mark Allen, has produced *Delphi 1*, with one side of free playing and one of stride revisited. These typically clean, intelligent, and tasteful albums are recommended in the General Discography of Chapter 8. Although Corea's light orchestral fusion style has not yet advanced past *My Spanish Heart* and *The Mad Hatter*, it is tempting to look ahead to that promised piano concerto, or perhaps to something entirely unexpected. However, foretelling the future of a musician like Corea is a risky business.

GEORGE BENSON

Weekend in L. A.

Warner Brothers, 2WB-3139
two discs, no liner notes
1977

Musicians: George Benson, guitar and vocals; Jorge Dalto, keyboards; Ronnie Foster, keyboards; Phil Upchurch, rhythm guitar; Stanley Banks, bass; Harvey Mason, drums; Ralph MacDonald, percussion.
Compositions: Side one: Weekend in L. A.; On Broadway. *Side two:* Down Here on the Ground; California P.M.; The Greatest Love of All. *Side three:* It's All in the Game; Windsong; Ode to a Kudu. *Side four:* Lady Blue; We All Remember Wes; We As Love.

GEORGE BENSON'S CAPABILITIES as an instrumentalist have been over-shadowed by his commercial success as a vocalist, a fate he shares with historical figures like Fats Waller and Nat "King" Cole. As a guitarist Benson has a warm, clean, melodic delivery along the lines of a notable mentor, Wes Montgomery (Chapter 5), whose career took a similar commercial turn in the late 1960's. Benson is not the innovator Wes was, but he is a master of playing pretty and, when he lets himself dig in, he is capable of churning up some excitement. *Weekend in L. A.* offers a synthesis of his singing and playing that is much closer to his jazz background than anything else he has recorded during the 1970's.

Contrary to a widespread notion, singing was not an afterthought in Benson's career, but a lifelong part of his musical background. Born in Pittsburgh in 1943, he won a singing contest at four years old, and a few years later he performed on the radio as "Little Georgie Benson." Benson's family lived in poverty, but when they finally moved into a house with electricity, George, at seven, began listening to his stepfather's records of Charlie Christian with the Benny Goodman sextet (Chapter 4). Benson's stepfather also bought him a fourteen-dollar guitar, on which he accompanied himself well enough to sing for money on street corners. An ambitious talent scout brought the ten-year-old "Little Georgie" to RCA, where he was recorded singing an R & B tune, "She Makes Me Mad." In his teens Benson also sang with the Altars, a choral group led by his cousin; but a year later he formed his own R & B band in which he first concentrated on guitar playing.

Benson's listening habits had expanded to include Charlie Parker, guitarist Grant Green, and a smooth country-picker, Hank Garland. But George had virtually no training and knew little about harmonic structure until at nineteen he began working with the soulful organist Brother Jack McDuff. McDuff had come to Pittsburgh without his guitarist, and Benson's audition for him resulted in a three-year tenure (documented on two funky Prestige discs, *George Benson/Jack McDuff*).

In 1965 Benson moved to New York, where he struggled to survive as a jazz player in a decade dominated by rock and soul. Columbia producer John Hammond, impressed with Benson's playing at a Harlem lounge, recorded him on two albums reissued as *Benson Burner*. Accompanied by organ, drums, and baritone sax, George riffs in the fast, hot style which earned him a formidable reputation among musicians. This album, which bears little resemblance to the jazz/pop on the Warner Brothers label, is highly recommended. Benson also befriended Wes Montgomery at about this time, absorbing some of his fluency and mellow tone.

On Montgomery's recommendation, Benson was signed by the A & M label, where he met the producer who turned him toward commercial goals, Creed Taylor. Taylor, who had transformed Wes into a top seller on Verve, took Benson into the fold when his own CTI label was formed in 1970. Benson recorded abundantly with the CTI stable of Airto Moreira, Herbie Hancock, Hubert Laws, Ron Carter, and Freddie Hubbard. He was featured on several LP's, only two of which have been reissued on the 8000 series (the 6000 series is not dependably available due to distribution difficulties): *White Rabbit* is a good-selling but quite dull set of uneventful noodling; but *Beyond the Blue Horizon* is an exciting, highly improvisational session with Clarence Palmer on organ and Ron Carter on bass, reminiscent of *Benson Burner*. (*In Concert*, CTI-6702, is worth looking for; George tears up Carnegie Hall with some impassioned playing.)

In 1976 Benson decided to accept an offer from Warner Brothers, motivated in part by Creed Taylor's policy of making all decisions at CTI regarding repertoire, personnel, and background overdubbing. *White Rabbit*, which had sold a healthy one hundred thousand copies or so, made him an attractive bet for Warner's, where he was paired with Tommy LiPuma, the first producer to encourage Benson to sing. *Breezin'*, their initial collaboration, became fusion's first platinum album and all-time best seller, approaching sales of four million copies. *Breezin'* sales were boosted by its hit-single version of Leon Russell's song, "This Masquerade," whose sole claim to originality lay in Benson's humming along with his guitar lines, something he claims to have done all along but without a voice mike to pick it up. Like *In Flight* (1977) and *Livin' Inside Your Love* (1979), *Breezin'* is essentially a slick, slightly improvisational "easy-listening" record of mechanical rhythms, repetitive vamps, and catchy melodies. Some lush Claus Ogerman string arrangements are added for sweetener. The results are lifeless and far short of what Benson could achieve in the jazz/pop context.

Weekend in L. A. is more like it, its success being attributable to a live format with minimal overdubbing added later on. It is more honest, personal, open, and varied than all the other Warner sessions put together. On tracks like "Windsong," "We All Remember Wes," and "We As Love," George returns to the fleet, flawless guitar riffing that made him the brightest star in the late 1960's. On "Ode to a Kudu" Benson turns his amp down and solos in a sensitive, natural tone suggestive of the African creature which is the song's subject. Of course, the pop "hooks" have not been retracted entirely. The remake of "On Broadway," which made it to the Top Ten, is enhanced in the LP version by some actual risk taking by Benson vocalizing with his solo. Benson's own hit, "The Greatest Love of All" from the Muhammad Ali film *The Greatest*, is treated in a sensitive, straight-from-the-heart style which surpasses the wrought-up emotion typical of the in-studio singing. The rhythm has loosened up somewhat, too, though not enough. Ralph MacDonald is a good percussionist who could be used to much greater advantage.

Significantly, the fact that Benson took more chances on *Weekend* by injecting some much-needed spontaneity into the music did not prevent the album from becoming platinum. It is to be hoped that this will influence Benson's attitude toward his work, which has become disturbingly commercial. Frequent press interviews reveal that his speech is sprinkled liberally with phrases like "universal appeal," "marketing trends," "AM airplay," and references to his own music as "product," more the jargon of company executives than that of an artist. Although Benson can hardly be blamed for sacrificing a bit of artistic adventure to become a millionaire, there is really little danger of his having to live without electricity ever again. He is a man of considerable talent and can afford to be an artist who plays to the limits of his imagination rather than to what he believes to be the limitations of his vast audience.

CHUCK MANGIONE

The Best of Chuck Mangione

Mercury, SRM-2-8601
two discs, no liner notes
1970–1973

Musicians: Chuck Mangione, flugelhorn, electric piano; Gerry Niewood, soprano and
tenor saxes, flute and alto flute; Al Johnson, electric bass; Joe LaBarbera, drums;
Esther Satterfield, vocals; Don Potter, guitar and vocals; Gap Mangione, electric
piano; Bat McGrath, guitarron, voice. Plus the Rochester Philharmonic Orchestra
(four tracks) and the Hamilton Philharmonic Orchestra.
Compositions (all compositions, lyrics, and arrangements by Mangione unless indicated):
Side one: Hill Where the Lord Hides; Lullaby for Nancy Carol; And in the
Beginning. *Side two:* Land of Make Believe; Sun Shower. *Side three:* Legend of the
One-Eyed Sailor; As Long As We're Together; Freddie's Walkin'. *Side four:* Friends
and Love (Mangione/McGrath/Potter/Watson).

CHUCK MANGIONE HAS come to represent the fusion of jazz with popular
song writing and arranging. His reputation has suffered as a result of some
undemanding, lackluster middle-of-the-road material. However, from 1970
to 1973 Mangione auspiciously combined his natural melodicism with a
talent for creating multistylistic orchestral backgrounds. *The Best of Chuck
Mangione* is an excellent collection of his important compositions from this
period, representing the best of his Mercury albums *Friends and Love,
Together*, and *Land of Make-Believe*.

Mangione had the advantages of extensive formal training and first-class
experience as a hard bop improviser. Born in Rochester, New York, in 1940,
he began piano lessons at eight, like his older brother Gap, but switched to
trumpet in high school after seeing *Young Man with a Horn*, a film based on
the life of Bix Beiderbecke (Chapter 2). Chuck's musical interests were
encouraged by his father, who ran a grocery store attached to the Mangiones'
home, where the boys hosted frequent jam sessions. The elder Mangione also
took Chuck and Gap to local clubs, introducing them to the stars who came
through town. Before long, Dizzy Gillespie, Cannonball Adderley, Art
Blakey, and others were stopping at the Mangiones' for a traditional Italian
meal. Gillespie was particularly impressed with Chuck and presented him
with a model of his upswept-bell trumpet, which Chuck used through the
early 1960's.

In 1958 Chuck and Gap formed The Jazz Brothers, which performed

locally and recorded for Riverside in 1961. The two-disc *Jazz Brothers* from this period swings with the energy of the Horace Silver quintet, which was in fact one of its models. Although two sides were made with a future Miles Davis rhythm section—Wynton Kelly, Sam Jones, and Louis Hayes—the better disc documents the regular band, whose hottest moments are due to Roy McCurdy on drums (later with Cannonball Adderley) and the fiery Sal Nistico on tenor sax. Gap is competent on piano; but Chuck, who tended toward Dizzy's approach, lacks the technique to execute many of his ideas. These sessions are enjoyable hard bop but not superlative.

At the same time, Chuck was a student at the prestigious Eastman School of Music, where he was soon attracted to the darker, more subdued sound of the flugelhorn, an instrument he adopted permanently. Although there was no jazz instruction at Eastman, one of Mangione's graduation exercises was a jazz-oriented orchestra piece (not recorded), "Feel of a Vision," his first conscious attempt at a fusion of the disparate styles he knew. After graduation Chuck moved to New York, where he worked briefly for Maynard Ferguson and Kai Winding. His coming-of-age began in 1965, when Art Blakey hired him as Freddie Hubbard's successor for a new edition of the Jazz Messengers. He remained with the Messengers for two years, during which several sessions of no great consequence were recorded for Limelight.

In 1968 Mangione returned to Rochester, where, as an Eastman School faculty member, he implemented a vigorous jazz curriculum. Eager to expose some of his own compositions, Chuck hired fifty musicians for a self-produced concert called "Kaleidoscope." Although the concert was a financial disaster, it represented the starting point of his career and his most productive three years in music. The concert's artistic success prompted Tom Iannaccone, manager of the Rochester Philharmonic Orchestra, to invite Mangione to be a guest conductor at the Eastman Theater. The televised performance of May 9, 1970, called "Friends and Love," was captured fortunately with decent sound quality on a four-track videotape unit. When Chuck heard the results, he borrowed money to package and distribute *Friends and Love*, which became a modest hit when Mercury picked it up the following year.

Of the three tracks from this concert on *The Best of Chuck Mangione*, the twenty-five-minute "Friends and Love" suite is actually the least interesting, though the pop-folk orientation of its major themes made it the concert's natural focus. The instrumental "Hill Where the Lord Hides," which combines a graceful melody with varied orchestral backgrounds, reveals the originality of his concept more clearly. "Hill" is also the piece that spread Mangione's name beyond the city limits of Rochester. But it is the rather pretentiously titled "And in the Beginning" which proved Mangione was a composer to be taken seriously. The opening segment is an intense, nearly abstract prelude to an electric piano solo by brother Gap. Unfortunately, the solo segment (including Chuck's arrangement) does not live up to the promise of its lengthy introduction, but valiant failures such as this one are far more exciting than some of Chuck's facile "successes" in later years.

The symphony orchestra became Mangione's canvas for the next two albums, whose reissued cuts here are original and powerful. Another outing with the Rochester Philharmonic (*Together*) yielded "Sun Shower"—an effective synthesis of light classical and big-band writing—and "Freddie's Walkin' "—a rousing gospel shout authentically sung by Don Potter. The most developed pieces on *The Best* anthology come from a 1973 performance with the Hamilton Philharmonic Orchestra, another upstate New York civic orchestra. The classic "Land of Make-Believe," sung by Esther Satterfield, is perhaps the most substantial jazz/pop track of the 1970's. Its melody is simple, memorable, and original in its use of larger-than-normal intervals. The twelve-minute arrangement has the continuity which "And in the Beginning" lacked, reaching its climax in Gerry Niewood's soprano sax solo, which is skillfully framed by strings and horns. (Niewood was a member of Mangione's late 1960's quartet, when they played in singles bars, and he remained their most fluent and exciting improviser until 1975.) Gerry Niewood also carries the heaviest load on "Legend of the One-Eyed Sailor," which reflects a Spanish influence and features a dramatic use of brass and tympani. "Lullaby for Nancy Carol," sung sensitively by Satterfield with a lush string background, must have produced a few moist eyes in the audience for its bare, yet controlled emotionality. Overall, Mangione's performance as song writer, arranger, and lyricist suggests a rare ability to incorporate jazz into varied and appealing pop contexts.

Mangione's quartet, however, is disappointing on *Alive* (1972), which was recorded at a benefit for flood relief held on the Nazareth College campus in Rochester. "One-Eyed Sailor" and Sonny Rollins's "St. Thomas" are the only compositions of interest, and Chuck is simply not daring or fluent enough on his horn to generate any sustained excitement. Switching to the A & M label in 1975, Mangione settled for a less integrated Hollywood studio orchestra on *Chase the Clouds Away*, a single unsatisfying LP, some of which is rescued by Satterfield.

Mangione joined the platinum elite of fusion with *Feels So Good* (1977), whose title track became an AM radio hit. "Feels So Good" is nothing more than a lively pop tune with two strong hooks, but it shows that a loosely structured quintet track without lyrics or artificial (that is, string) sweeteners could become a chart-buster, too. Mangione's new band, which is present on all the A & M releases, includes Chris Vadala on reeds and Charles Meeks on bass; it also has Grant Geissman on electric guitar, relieving Mangione of responsibility on the electric piano. Their albums are characterized by a lack of depth and serious intent, except for *Bellavia* (Chuck's mother's maiden name), which was composed in tribute to the loving, supportive household in which he grew up. *Live at the Hollywood Bowl* (1978) is an anthology of Mangione hits to date, but it is undermined by uninspired

performing, Satterfield's absence, and lack of rehearsal time with the seventy-piece orchestra.

Mangione's musical philosophy has retreated sharply from its early experimentalism, adopting instead a formulaic optimism. During interviews in 1979, he often expressed the view that music should be fun and make everyone "feel good." However, these goals could be realized in a deeper, more lasting manner if Mangione returned to the ambitious precedents he set when he first began to explore the synthesis of orchestral writing and jazz. And his contribution to jazz would surely be enhanced in the process.

WEATHER REPORT

8:30

Columbia, PC-2-36030
two discs, no liner notes
1979

Musicians: Josef Zawinul, electric piano and synthesizers; Wayne Shorter, tenor sax; Jaco Pastorius, electric bass, drums (two tracks); Peter Erskine, drums. Plus Erich Zawinul, percussion (one track); West Los Angeles Christian Academy Children's Choir (one track).
Compositions: Side one: Black Market; Scarlet Woman. *Side two:* Teen Town; A Remark You Made; Slang (bass solo); In a Silent Way. *Side three:* Birdland; Thanks for the Memory (tenor-sax solo); Badia/Boogie Woogie Waltz (medley). *Side four:* 8:30; Brown Street; The Orphan; Sightseeing.

WEATHER REPORT, led by Josef Zawinul and Wayne Shorter since 1971, is the most innovative and improvisational of the fusion bands. While their improvisations and harmonic sophistication come from the highest echelons of late 1960's jazz, the rhythmic electric-bass and drum patterns are more akin to R & B and occasionally to rock. Since 1976 their albums have acquired a nearly orchestral density, provided by Zawinul's masterful use of the polyphonic, or multivoiced, synthesizers. Their consistently excellent albums led *Down Beat* magazine readers to vote for five of their annual LP's as Albums of the Year, but *8:30* was selected here because of its live format. In addition to anthologizing Weather Report's best compositions, this album preserves the all-out blowing that makes their concerts memorable.

Zawinul (as he usually refers to himself) was born in Vienna in 1932, a descendant of Czechoslovakian and Hungarian-Gypsy families. He grew up as an only child after the death of his twin brother at the age of four. Zawinul endured much hardship during the war years, often stealing food for his family at the risk of being shot by occupying Russian troops. However, near the end of the war he began studying classical piano in a countryside hideaway for gifted youngsters. He received some of his lessons from a second-generation Franz Liszt protégé, Valerie Zschorney. A few years later Zawinul worked in U.S. Army clubs and local cabarets, playing the piano, organ, accordion, bass trumpet, vibes, and clarinet. Eventually he joined the bands of Hans Koller and Friederich Gulda, for whom he wrote arrangements taken from Woody Herman albums. He was then playing jazz piano "a lot like George Shearing" and, on the strength of a locally produced record, earned a scholarship to the Berklee School of Music in Boston, where he enrolled in 1959.

Zawinul, who had moved to the United States without a single personal contact, met Wayne Shorter days later at a breakfast café near Birdland in New York. They were soon working together in Maynard Ferguson's big band, to which Zawinul had defected after only three weeks at Berklee. But Wayne soon joined the Jazz Messengers and Zawinul, who had personal disagreements with Ferguson, joined the great singer Dinah Washington, whom he accompanied for nineteen months. He played on Washington's biggest hit, "What a Difference a Day Makes" (General Discography, Chapter 5), and first used an electric piano in her band, a Wurlitzer borrowed from Ray Charles.

In 1961 Zawinul joined Cannonball Adderley's quintet, with which he remained throughout the decade, recording over a dozen albums with the group and proving himself to be a soulful improviser and a prolific composer. He wrote some of the quintet's biggest hits, including "Mercy, Mercy, Mercy," "Country Preacher," and "Walk Tall," as well as more sophisticated blues-based gems like "74 Miles Away" (see *Coast to Coast,* Selected Discography, Chapter 5). Zawinul's use of the electric piano with Adderley contributed to Miles Davis's interest in the instrument.

From 1968 to 1970 Zawinul and Wayne Shorter crossed paths again under the long shadow of Davis's music. Zawinul was impressed again with Wayne's musical development on *Nefertiti* (Chapter 6). At Miles's invitation, Zawinul submitted a song to the band that he had written a few years earlier which became the title track of the innovative jazz-rock masterpiece *In a Silent Way.* He and Shorter also worked together on the sessions eventually released as *Bitches Brew* and *Live/Evil.*

In the meantime *Zawinul,* an album recorded for Atlantic in 1970, revealed the pianist's interest in multiple keyboards (Herbie Hancock joins him on electric piano) and auxiliary percussion instruments. This album also contains the first full treatment of "In a Silent Way," and Zawinul's new instrumental sounds in the special-effects piece "Arrival in New York." (*Concerto Retitled* offers other tracks from these sessions, including two repeats from

Zawinul and a delightful Tatumesque piano solo on "My One and Only Love.") Wayne's Blue Note record *Super Nova* (1969), using the *Bitches Brew* personnel, is a fine, highly improvisational testimony to his own interest in jazz/rock. Thus Weather Report had its beginning in Davis's late 1960's band.

Zawinul, Shorter, and Czech bassist Miroslav Vitous, who had played on the *Zawinul* session, brought their idea for a band to Columbia's Clive Davis, who reportedly signed them even before listening to the "demo" tape. Shorter dubbed the group Weather Report because, according to a popular account, their music changed from day to day. The first two releases— *Weather Report* (1971) and *I Sing the Body Electric* (1972)—are somewhat closer to the Miles Davis sound than they are to Weather Report's later music. *Body Electric* is, nevertheless, a superb collection of improvised, rock-influenced jazz, especially the live set from Japan on side two. Shorter solos passionately on soprano sax while Zawinul's biting electric piano stokes the fires continually. Eric Gravatt's all-encompassing drumming is more adequate to the group's polyrhythmic needs than was Alphonse Mouzon's on their first album, a studio-born project of various colors and textures. The high points of *Weather Report* are Zawinul's creative use of the electric piano, organ, and ring modulator on "Milky Way," the lyrical "Orange Way" (reminiscent of "Silent Way"), and the straight-ahead blowing on "Eurydice," which offers the record's only meaningful solos. Airto Moreira's kaleidoscopic percussion concept adds to the album's variety, but he left the band before their first tour and was replaced by Dom Um Ramoa; Ramoa plays on the preferable LP, *Body Electric*.

Weather Report's sound began to jell on *Sweetnighter* (1973), for which Zawinul wrote "Boogie Woogie Waltz" and "125th Street Congress" specifically to convey a more accessible, rock-oriented image. However, it was *Mysterious Traveler* (1974) which established the band's integrity and artistic identity. The title track, "Nubian Sundance," and "Scarlet Woman" typify the Weather Report originals in their simple yet entirely novel structure, while "Blackthorn Rose," a free-form Zawinul-Shorter duo, and "Cucumber Slumber" provide plenty of space for self-expression. The replacement of Vitous by the funkier Alphonso Johnson on Fender bass liberated Zawinul from supplying the music's "bottom," making possible a more expansive use of synthesizers. Weather Report proved it was capable not only of giving its audiences what they wanted but of demanding intelligent, active listening in return.

Talespinnin' (1975) marked an increased use of synthesizers such as the ARP 2600, the most powerful of the single-note models. These efforts, however, were surpassed by *Black Market* (1976), whose music was more orchestral due to the Oberheim polyphonic synthesizer on which Zawinul stacked up voices like horn sections of a big band. The technically proficient, dramatic bassist Jaco Pastorius is present on one track of *Black Market,* having introduced himself to Zawinul after a Miami concert and auditioned later via some tapes. Pastorius's influence, however, was not felt fully until *Heavy Weather* (1977), the best of the group's studio albums. Pastorius is simply the most exciting electric bass soloist in the field and his immediate contributions as a coproducer and composer show he understands Weather Report's needs. But it was the infectious gaiety of Zawinul's "Birdland" (which received substantial AM airplay) that made *Heavy Weather* the band's only gold album, a distinction it deserved on artistic grounds as well. The impeccable separation of voices brings the rich texture of this music to life, confirming Zawinul's superiority in the (as-yet-uninvented) category of Best Studio Technique.

Mr. Gone (1978) was a disappointment for its lack of substantial material. The bright spots were a light-hearted, bebop-style "Young and Fine" and Zawinul's new Prophet V (five-voice) synthesizer, which gave him a broader textural palette. There were four different drummers on this date, which revealed a lingering problem that was resolved by hiring Peter Erskine, also a Maynard Ferguson alumnus who had been Stan Kenton's drummer when he was only eighteen. The percussionist's role was also eliminated in the interest of clarifying the quartet's sound and giving everyone more space. *Mr. Gone,* however, is not nearly of the same caliber as *Mysterious Traveller* and *Heavy Weather,* the two essential LP's, after *8:30.*

Weather Report's only two-disc set *8:30* is an ideal summation of, or introduction to, the band's distinguished career. Its most obvious virtue is that it captures the intensity the band generates on stage. Culled from two California dates at the end of a 1979 tour, the first three sides contain highly charged versions of the essential originals composed by Zawinul: "Black Market," "Scarlet Woman," "Birdland," and "A Remark You Made." Although the studio LP's have increasingly deprived Shorter of the solo space he needs, the proper balance is restored here; there is ample soloing by everyone, including an unaccompanied *tour de force* by Shorter on "Thanks for the Memory." A simple comparison of "Black Market" as contained here, climaxed by Shorter's surging tenor sax solo, with the studio track from 1976 reveals the advantages of hearing the band live.

Weather Report's chief strength is its ability to play with the solidity of a big band and with the agility of an improvisational quartet. "Birdland" illustrates the former with Zawinul's synthesized orchestration serving as the brass and reed sections. The piece is a balanced fusion of a rock-influenced first theme and a second theme built upon a more swinging feeling, using the chromatic passing chords of modern jazz. The joy and exuberance of the principal riff has turned "Birdland" into a fusion classic, comparable to "King Porter Stomp" of the swing era.

The album's romantic, lyrical tracks, "A Remark You Made" and "In a Silent Way," are enhanced by Zawinul's preference for nonelectronic sounds on the synthesizers, a characteristic that was first noticed on the "wood-flute" lead voice of "Black Market" in 1976. On "A Remark," he has selected a clarinet-like lead, while "Silent Way" opens with a wash of more celestial tonal colors from the Prophet V synthesizer. Like Chick Corea, Zawinul has not settled for cheap effects or commonplace synthesizer "programs," but rather puts this circuitry to artistic use. "A Remark," incidentally, is one of Zawinul's most moving melodies, stated simply as it is by the electronic bass line.

Pastorius's "Teen Town" is another excellent fusion piece with a unique, almost frantic momentum that contrasts effectively with the relaxed blowing above it. However, his four-minute "Slang," a bombastic bass solo, transfers poorly to vinyl and probably succeeds in concert only because of Jaco's bold showmanship. Far more effective is Shorter's unaccompanied, impassioned interpretation of "Thanks for the Memory," one carried off in the elegant tradition of an Eric Dolphy or a Sonny Rollins. The ecstatic crowd response suggests that the fusion audience has far more receptive ears than record company marketing departments will admit.

Side four yields a potpourri of Zawinul's most recent composing, arranging, and studio technique. As usual, it is an unpredictable mixture of spontaneity and meticulousness. In the past Zawinul has improvised many of his synthesized orchestrations on his living room eight-track tape recorder, later writing out all the parts to improve the voice-leading and contrapuntal melodies. "Nubian Sundance" (from *Mysterious Traveller*), for example, turned into a twenty-two-page score before its final taping. "The Orphan" exemplifies this approach here: it is a taut, intense étude for synthesizers and overdubbed children's choir, not an everyday combination. With more development, it could have taken hold more strongly than it does.

The other pieces are more loosely conceived, beginning with "8:30," a virtual jam with Jaco on drums. The group was in fact passing time, with Peter Erskine absent and Wayne writing music nearby in the studio. The theme's simplicity is typical of Zawinul, who seems to be striving for a "French horn" voice to carry it off. "Brown Street" was taped at home; this time the group was waiting for Jaco to arrive. Thus Zawinul supplies all the bass lines with some percussion added by his son, Erich. After a slow start, the piece gathers momentum until it reaches the exuberance of a "Birdland." Finally, "Sightseeing," a straight-ahead Shorter composition whose style is reminiscent of the late 1960's, elicits some delightful straight-ahead soloing especially from Zawinul, who devours chord changes in an arpeggiated fashion remarkably similar to Coltrane's approach on "Giant Steps." "Sightseeing" was a first take, its title a pun on sight-reading. While this studio side is not marked by the tightness and perfectionistic tendencies of Weather Report's earlier albums, its vitality and variety compensates for this lack refreshingly.

Overall, *8:30* is an exciting and involving album. Yet the retrospective nature of sides one, two, and three raises the question of what Weather Report has in mind for the future. One would hate to think—as the retrospective theme suggests—that a band demonstrating such consistent progress and quality has reached the end of the road. As the fusion band of the greatest longevity, Weather Report certainly has much to build upon.

Notes

1. Roland Gelatt, *The Fabulous Phonograph, 1877–1977* (New York: Macmillan Publishing Co., 1977), p. 322.

2. Joe Goldberg, "Who Are Those Guys?" *Wax Paper*, Vol. 4, Warner Brothers Records, Inc., February 12, 1979.

3. Robert Palmer, "Keith Jarrett," *Down Beat*, October 24, 1974.

4. Conversation with Lenny White.

5. Len Lyons, "Chick Corea," *High Fidelity*, November 1978.

6. Len Lyons, "Herbie Hancock," *High Fidelity*, February 1979.

7. Robert Palmer, "Jazz/Rock '74," *Rolling Stone*, August 1, 1974.

8. *Ibid.*

9. Len Lyons, "Flora Purim," *Down Beat*, December 19, 1974.

10. *Ibid.*

11. Palmer, "Jazz/Rock, '74," *op. cit.*

12. Len Lyons, "Chick Corea," *High Fidelity*, February 1979.

13. Liner notes to Blue Note's *Chick Corea.*

14. Scott Yanow, "Chick Corea: The Definitive Interview," *Record Review*, February 1979. The author has found the biographical information contained in the Yanow interview very helpful.

General Discography of Available, Recommended Albums

GEORGE BENSON
> Pre-fusion: *Benson Burner* (1966–1967), CG-33569, Columbia. *Beyond the Blue Horizon* (1971, with Ron Carter and Jack DeJohnette), 8007, CTI. (See discussion for review of other available titles.)

ORNETTE COLEMAN
> *Dancing in Your Head* (see Selected Discography, Chapter 8)

CHICK COREA (see also Chapter 8)
> *Return to Forever* (with Purim, Farrell, Airto, 1971), ECM-1022, ECM. *Return to Forever: Hymn of the Seventh Galaxy* (jazz/rock, Bill Connors,

guitar, 1973), PD-5536; *The Leprechaun* (1975), PD-6062; *The Mad Hatter* (1978), PD1-6130; Polydor. Also available: *Return to Forever: Live 1977*), JC-35281; *Return to Forever: Live/The Complete Concert* (4 discs, liner booklet, unedited 1977 concert), C4X-35350, Columbia.

LARRY CORYELL
    Introducing the Eleventh House (1974), VSD-79342; Pre-fusion (superb improvising): *Spaces* (with McLaughlin), VSD-6558, Vanguard.

THE CRUSADERS (see Selected Discography)
    The Best of the Crusaders (1972–1976), BTSY-6027/2, Blue Thumb.

MILES DAVIS
    Miles in the Sky (1968), CS-9628; *In a Silent Way* (1969), CS-9875; *Live/Evil* (1970), CG-30954; *Jack Johnson* (1970), KC-30455; Columbia. Of historical interest: *Big Fun*, PG-32866; *Get up with It*, KG-33236; *Agharta* (live, 1975), PG-33967; Columbia.

AL DiMEOLA (see also Chick Corea)
    Land of the Midnight Sun (1976), PC-34074, Columbia.

URSZULA DUDZIAK
    Midnight Rain (1977), AL-4132, Arista.

JAN HAMMER
    Like Children, 430; *The First Seven Days*, 432; *Oh, Yeah?* 437; Nemperor (CBS).

HERBIE HANCOCK (see also Chapters 6 and 8)
    Thrust (1974), PC-32965; *Man-Child* (1975), PC-33812; *Secrets* (1976), PC-34280; Columbia. Of historical interest: *Sunlight* (1978), JC-34907; *Feets Don't Fail Me Now* (1979), JC-35764; *The Best of Herbie Hancock* (1979, R&B Sampler), JC-36309; Columbia.

AL JARREAU
    Look to the Rainbow (2 discs, live, 1977), 2BZ-3052; *All Fly Home* (1978), BSK-3229; Warner Brothers.

JOHN KLEMMER
    Prejazz-pop: *Intensity*, AS-9244; Impulse. Solo sax: *Cry*, AA-1106; MCA. Jazz/pop: *Barefoot Ballet*, AB-950; *Touch*, AB-922; MCA.

MAHAVISHNU ORCHESTRA/JOHN McLAUGHLIN
    Birds of Fire (1973), KC-31996; *Between Nothingness and Eternity*, C-32766; *Love/Devotion/Surrender* (with Santana), KC-32034; *Johnny McLaughlin, Electric Guitarist* (1978), JC-35326; *Electric Dreams* (1979), JC-35785; Columbia.

CHUCK MANGIONE
    (*Friends and Love, Together, Land of Make-Believe* reissued on selected album.) *Bellavia* (quartet and orchestra, 1975), SP-4557, A & M. Pre-fusion: *Jazz Brothers*, M-47042, Milestone.

JEAN-LUC PONTY
    Upon the Wings of Music, SD-18138; *Imaginary Voyage*, SD-19136; *Enigmatic Ocean*, SD-19110; *Cosmic Messenger*, SD-19189; Atlantic.

FLORA PURIM (with Airto Moreira; see also Chick Corea, Selected Discography)
    Butterfly Dreams, M-9052; *Stories to Tell*, M-9058; *Open Your Eyes You Can Fly*, M-9065; Milestone. See also Selected Discography for other Milestone and Warner Brothers albums.

WAYNE SHORTER (see also Chapter 6)
See Chapter 5 with Art Blakey; and Miles Davis, Chapter 6. *Super Nova* (1969, with McLaughlin, Airto, Corea, DeJohnette), BST-84332, Blue Note.

GROVER WASHINGTON
Live at the Bijou (1978), 36/37, Kudu.

WEATHER REPORT
Pre-Weather Report: *Zawinul*, SD-1579; *Concerto Retitled*, SD-1694; Atlantic. Also see Shorter's *Super Nova*. Presynthesizer: *Weather Report* (1971), C-30661; *I Sing the Body Electric* (1972), KC-31352; Columbia. Vintage: *Mysterious Traveller* (1974), PC-32494; *Black Market* (1976), PC-34099; *Heavy Weather* (1977), 34418; Columbia.

LENNY WHITE
Adventures of the Astral Pirates, 6E-121; *Streamline*, 164; Elektra. *Big City*, N-441; *Venusian Summer*, N-435; Nemperor.

TONY WILLIAMS (see Miles Davis, Chapters 6 and 7)
The Joy of Flying (1979, with Hancock, Benson, and various groups), JC-35705; *The Best of Tony Williams* (anthology of 1975–1979 Lifetime groups), JC-36397; Columbia.

FREE JAZZ

The Land of the Free: America or Europe?

FREE JAZZ made a more radical break than any other style with the music's past, yet it also readopted one of jazz's earliest practices, the collective improvisations first introduced by the New Orleans bands. The innovations associated with free playing evolved too gradually to fix a precise date for the birth of this style. As early as 1956 the collectively played, occasionally atonal passages in the music of Charles Mingus and of Sun Ra foreshadowed some aspects of what was to come; and the improvising without chords of pianist Cecil Taylor and alto saxophonist Ornette Coleman, recorded as early as 1957 to 1958, can be described fairly as near-free jazz. However, the music's artistically successful debut occurred in 1959 when Ornette Coleman brought his pianoless quartet into the Five Spot Café in New York.

Amid heated controversy, the band's music was dubbed "the new thing" or "avant-garde jazz," neither term being especially appropriate, now that this music has been around for a quarter of jazz's lifetime. The term "avant-garde" refers more properly to a large number of musicians who remain at the cutting edge of jazz. The term "free jazz," however, which takes its name from a collectively improvised Ornette Coleman album to be discussed ahead, correctly emphasizes the music's liberation from certain premises of traditional and modern styles.

An overview of free jazz characteristics and techniques serves two useful purposes: It conveys their great variety, and it reveals, when contrasted with the conventions of traditional and modern styles, their revolutionary nature. These are predominant elements of the albums to be discussed in this chapter:

(a) the liberation of melody from preset chord changes and fixed tempo;

(b) the creation of new song structures, some of which resemble modern classical music more than blues or ballads;

(c) the creation of sound-surfaces by the use of tonal coloration;

(d) the creation of sound-fields by the use of instrumental density and coloration;

(e) the use of new or uncommon instruments—and new uses of traditional instruments—to further (c) and (d); and

(f) group improvisation, composition, and overall interaction (collectivism), revising the previously dominant role of the soloist.

These pursuits, though separable for the purposes of discussion, are often interdependent, and as always are illustrated better by the music than by what can be written about it.

The hostile reception that free jazz received from some quarters provides an indication of its unprecedented nature. For example, one earnest *Down Beat* critic wrote (May 11, 1961):

I have listened long and hard to [Ornette] Coleman's music . . . I have tried desperately to find something valuable in it, something that could be construed valuable. I have been unsuccessful . . . Coleman's music, to me, has only two shades; a maudlin, pleading lyricism and a wild ferocity bordering on bedlam . . . "Beauty" from the Atlantic recording *This Is Our Music* descends into an orgy of squawks from Coleman, squeals from (trumpeter) Cherry, and above-the-bridge plinks from (bassist) Haden. The resulting chaos is an insult to the listening intelligence. It sounds like some horrible joke, and the question here is not whether it is jazz, but whether it is music.

Coleman was not the only one to suffer scathing, misguided criticism; nor were critics the only ones to offer it. Cecil Taylor, certainly the most innovative and influential pianist since Bud Powell, recalled the overt displeasure some jazz celebrities showed during a Monday off-night performance he gave at Birdland: "Miles just cursed and walked out. Dizzy wandered in and out and kept making all kinds of remarks to Sarah (Vaughan), who was in a pretty vicious mood. Miles later put me down in print." [1] Then playing at the Coronet, a black-owned club in Brooklyn, Taylor's trio was fired peremptorily after the first set. When the band continued to play they narrowly averted a fight with a few patrons.

Even the venerated John Coltrane, who along with Eric Dolphy was an ardent admirer of Coleman, became the target of angry attacks by former devotees once he launched into the split notes, overblowing, and "screaming" of *Meditations* (1965). Even less tolerance, of course, was granted less established reed players—Pharoah Sanders, Archie Shepp, Albert Ayler, Sam Rivers, and Marion Brown—who also searched for more expressive tonal dimensions.

Recording contracts were a rarity for free jazz players during the 1960's and early 1970's when rock was crowding out even more conventional styles of jazz from the studios. Ornette Coleman, for example, despite his prominence following the set of albums for Atlantic, recorded only once (except for private tapings) between March 1961 and August 1965. Moreover, he found himself virtually retired from live performance in 1962 at the tender age of thirty-two, though at least part of the blame for this misfortune rests with him. Coleman decided to charge a fee commensurate with his musical significance, a ploy which suggests a serious lack of realism.

Cecil Taylor attempted to make himself available but fared little better, playing approximately one concert a year throughout the 1960's interspersed with short nightclub or coffeehouse dates, many of which did not pay at all. Worse still, from 1962 to 1965 and from 1969 to 1973, Taylor—already acknowledged as a major innovator—did not record at all. He earned his living working as a cook and dishwasher. One can imagine how scant the opportunities were for unsung free jazz musicians. Archie Shepp, who was lucky enough to make several albums for Impulse under the aegis of John Coltrane, described his situation in 1965, a predicament especially common in free jazz: "I've been in this music for fifteen years, and I've never worked (as a musician) for a solid week in this country, I've never made my living playing jazz. I work now as a merchandiser for Abraham & Straus." [2] Although conditions would improve markedly by the late 1970's, when Shepp became a tenured professor of black music at the University of Massachusetts and had eight available albums in his discography, free jazz could find little sustenance for over fifteen years in the country of its birth.

Europe rescued free jazz from total starvation. There, where jazz enjoyed the respect of an art form, musicians were more likely to get a hearing even if wages were low. There were also more pervasive reasons for the musicians' alienation from the United States. As noted in some detail in the introductions to Chapters 6 and 7, the country was undergoing turbulence and disillusionment. Black nationalism and civil rights were key issues, and most free jazz players saw themselves as revolutionary not solely in a musical sense but politically, too. Never had a style of jazz been tied so closely to a social perspective. To Archie Shepp, a dependably articulate spokesman and moralist, the music itself had a political credo: "It is antiwar; it is opposed to (the war in) Vietnam; it is for (Castro's) Cuba; it is for the liberation of all people . . . Why is that so? Because jazz is itself a music born out of oppression, born out of the enslavement of my people." [3]

While blacks were certainly more disadvantaged and threatened by social conditions, discontent among musicians was not limited to them. Bassist Charlie Haden recalled his motivation for recording (along with composer/arranger Carla Bley) the since-deleted Impulse album *Liberation Music Orchestra* (1969), one of the most overtly political recordings in the history of jazz:

Che Guevara had just been murdered, and there was violence at the

Democratic (National) Convention, and Vietnam. There were demonstrations all over the country, people were getting arrested . . . Berkeley, Columbia, young people, everybody was dissatisfied about what the government was doing. The American people were very upset, and I wanted to say in music what was happening in the country.[4]

The musicians who either relocated or fled to Europe periodically for work are legion. The Art Ensemble of Chicago, the most accomplished of the collective groups, moved to Paris in 1969 for two years, recording eleven albums in that time. Anthony Braxton, a composer and multireed player, extended his stay from 1969 to 1974, teaming up briefly with Chick Corea, British bassist Dave Holland, and drummer Barry Altschul in the collective band Circle (General Discography). Their unique, airy, somewhat cerebral improvised structures gave free jazz a brief boost at home, but they disbanded in 1971 before reaching their prime. Don Cherry, whose playing with Ornette Coleman and Archie Shepp (in the New York Contemporary Five) was followed by an interest in Third World musics, became a permanent resident of Sweden, returning to America during the late 1970's for concert tours only.

Europe has remained the site of concerts, festivals, and recording for the best free jazz players, including many who cannot find comparable work at home. In the summer of 1979, according to a *Down Beat* news item (October, 1979), free jazz could be found simultaneously on club stages in Austria, Belgium, France, Germany, Holland, Italy, Norway, and Switzerland. In Montreux, Switzerland, the fourteen-year-old Montreux Jazz Festival, which has made recording an automatic byproduct of every performance, is responsible for about eighty LP's distributed in the United States, including some of the best available work of Sun Ra, Cecil Taylor, Anthony Braxton, the Art Ensemble, and the agile, young jazz collective Air (Selected Discography). Europe has also produced the only major musicological analysis of the free jazz style. Published in West Germany in 1974, *Free Jazz* by Ekkehard Jost is comparable in value to Gunther Schuller's *Early Jazz* and equally as technical. The numerous albums to be discussed ahead, are a telling indicator of the crucial role Europe had in documenting the music. Half of the ten best free jazz albums were taped there, a fact which speaks for itself.

Europe was not the sole saving grace of free jazz. The free jazz musicians themselves also took a hand in alleviating the neglect of their music at home, and their efforts began to take effect by the late 1970's. However, the new activism on the part of free jazz musicians will be examined after looking more closely at the characteristics of the music itself.

The Revolution in Music

Jazz always reflects the social condition of blacks in America. The very name free jazz suggests an issue that is central to black life in the United

States. An observation in John Coltrane's letter to *Down Beat* magazine, already quoted in Chapter 6, should be recalled here: "We all know that this word which so many seem to fear today, 'Freedom,' has a hell of a lot to do with this music." Further metaphors are readily available: the atonal clusters and dissonant harmonies of Cecil Taylor may well express for him the sound of a discordant society. The sometimes harsh or strident screeches heard from the reeds are often interpreted as anger and outrage, a kind of "tonal desperation." Collective improvising, too, in which no single voice is dominant, does aspire toward an egalitarianism that has never been a reality for blacks in America. Moreover, it may be argued, as Frank Kofsky asserts, that "collective improvisation symbolizes the recognition among musicians that their art is not an affair of individual 'geniuses,' but the musical expression of an entire people—the black people of America." [5]

In view of these correlations, the listener must be aware of jazz's historical and emotional bases. Yet the position taken in the introduction to Chapter 6 deserves to be reasserted here: political interpretation is not a substitute for musical analysis. There is more to free jazz than "protest," and the family of styles it encompasses can only be understood in terms of its revolutionary musical ideas.

The earliest innovation, ushered in by the Charlie Parker-inspired linear improvisations of Ornette Coleman, amounts to an affirmation of melodic supremacy. Coleman rejected the dominance of chord changes, which in 1959 (recall *Giant Steps*, Chapter 5) had assumed the proportions of a tyrant. In perspective, in previous chapters melody has been construed as a voice in the foreground, supported by harmony or chords (carried by rhythm) in the background. Coleman intentionally swept all this aside, enunciating his own point of view: "Let's play the music, not the background." [6] The music for Coleman, perhaps jazz's first "emotivist" improviser, is found in the *feeling* of the melody. He told his band to forget about the chord changes (or the mode, for Coleman himself was an essentially modal improviser), and instead to improvise upon the melodic feeling. Coleman knew that his lines must presuppose certain harmonies, but he insisted these harmonies be chosen spontaneously. The "right note" was not the one possible within theoretical limits, but rather the one which sounded right to the individual.

Coleman applied a similar approach to "measuring" a song in bar lines. In establishing, for example, a four-bar motif—and Coleman's music is frequently motivic—he saw no reason to limit what he did with that motif to four bars. Needless to say, the band had little idea of what a given performance of a piece would sound like until they played it. Consequently the structure of the music became as variable as its content.

Collectivism, as Coleman realized, was as old as the multivoiced "jams" of the first New Orleans bands. In free jazz, the freedom each individual player now had led directly to more participatory playing. Instruments which previously supported the soloist with the preset "background" had to invent their roles as the music progressed. Coleman wrote in his liner notes to *Change of the Century*: "Ours is at all times a group effort, and it is only because we have the rapport we do that our music takes on the shape it does. A strong personality with the star-complex would take away from the effectiveness of our group, no matter how brilliantly he played." As a matter of fact, this album is much more dominated by Coleman himself than the following year's *Free Jazz*, the classic example of collective improvisation.

A redefinition of the role of the piano, which had always been associated with chord changes and predetermined musical structure, was unavoidable in this context. Coleman's three earliest albums fail melodically due in part to the inhibiting presence of Paul Bley's piano. This is not to discredit Bley, a sensitive, sophisticated improviser who later became an important influence upon Keith Jarrett. Coleman's alto sax and the piano were simply a mismatch, one which Coleman has studiously avoided ever since. It took some time before pianists Bley, Jarrett, Sun Ra, Cecil Taylor, Muhal Richard Abrams, and Chick Corea developed a free-style pianistic conception. By the mid-1970's, there were new voices to be heard on records: Don Pullen, Anthony Davis, Richie Beirach, Art Lande, Denny Zeitlin, and Tete Montoliu (General Discography, Miscellaneous). The bass, too, was less tied to harmonic and rhythmic underpinnings, as we shall hear ahead in the work of Charlie Haden, Scott LaFaro, Jimmy Garrison, Malachi Favors, Fred Hopkins, and Dave Holland.

A fluid sense of time is also characteristic of free jazz. At the outset, Coleman distinguished between "diffuse, spread rhythm" and the feeling of conventional modern jazz, which he described as "netted" rhythm evenly divided into metric patterns and measures. His goal was to let rhythms be expressed spontaneously and flow as naturally as breathing or speech patterns. Thus because drummers Ed Blackwell and Billy Higgins were less tied to a demanding beat, they became liberated to pursue a variety of accent patterns.

Free jazz reveals a marked increase in the multidirectional quality of the drumming, the result of the number of cross-rhythms it encompasses. This is evident if one compares the work of Rashied Ali, Coltrane's post-1965 drummer, with the style of his earlier drummer, Elvin Jones (Chapter 6). Both Coltrane and Coleman experimented with two drummers, as did Archie Shepp in *The Magic of Juju* (with five drummers), thus suggesting a bold reexamination of the potential for polyrhythm on the grand African scale. Drummers were also able to devote themselves more fully to altering the tonal coloration and density of sound; this was the forte of the Art Ensemble's Don Moye and Air's Steve McCall. Naturally the traditional notion of swing applies less frequently, giving way to other types of polyrhythmic momentum or even an arhythmic rubato. Some of the other significant free-style drummers, most of whom will be heard in the albums ahead, are Sonny Murray, Andrew Cyrille, Milford Graves, Beaver Harris, Dennis Charles, Paul Motian, and Barry Altschul.

Free jazz does not lead inexorably to atonality, a characteristic that is often loosely ascribed to it. Strictly speaking, a piece of music is atonal when it has no keynote or tonal center, a rare occurrence in jazz. Atonal music was developed in Europe around the turn of the century by Arnold Schoenberg and his protégés, Anton Webern and Alban Berg. To organize an improvisation without a tonal center, or rather to avoid it purposely, is not easy, nor is it particularly encouraged by the blues-based (tonal) nature of the jazz tradition. Cecil Taylor's showers of thick chord clusters within which no keynote can be discerned is one case of atonality, but there are not many other ready examples. And even Taylor often vacillates between the tonal and atonal, as will be noted in the discussion of his music.

However, collective improvisations sometimes present what might be called an "atonal texture," even when the music itself is tonally based. This occurs when several tonal centers conflict or when highly altered instrumental sounds are used for coloration or emotional expression. Examples of atonal texture will be pointed out in the Taylor, Sun Ra, Anthony Braxton, and Art Ensemble of Chicago discussions.

Form: The Legacy of Free Jazz and Ascension

Freedom does not mean chaos, nor does it imply lack of discipline. Because notes cannot be called theoretically right or wrong does not mean one can play anything at all. As Ornette Coleman was fond of emphasizing, "It was when I found out I could make mistakes that I knew I was onto something." [7] The musician had to satisfy the music's internal logic, sometimes extemporizing that logic as a part of the improvisation, at other times following a minimal outline.

Free jazz gave improvisers and composers an opportunity to form music creatively, a giant step beyond simply playing creatively within a predetermined form. Gunther Schuller foreshadowed this conceptual advance in "The Future of Form in Jazz," which appeared in the *Saturday Review* (January 12, 1957).

It has become increasingly clear that "form" need not be a confining mold into which tonal materials are poured, but rather that the forming process can be directly related to the musical material employed in a specific instance. In other words, form evolves out of the material itself and is not imposed upon it. We must learn to think of form as a verb rather than a noun.

But in 1957 even the prophetic Schuller could not have imagined how boldly this new opportunity would be seized.

Free jazz, then, is not just freedom *from* traditional and modern ideas of harmony and time, it is also freedom *to* structure music in new ways. Cecil

Taylor identified this issue as central to the new style when he told *Down-Beat* magazine, "This is not a question of freedom as opposed to non-freedom, but rather a question of recognizing different ideas and expressions of order." Taylor himself, as will be clear from the discussion of *Unit Structures* (1967) in the Selected Discography, was a master "constructivist." His work, however, had two predecessors which have scarcely lost any of their power to shock, influence, and enlighten the uninitiated.

Coleman's *Free Jazz* and Coltrane's *Ascension* are the classic models of the innovative ordering of "sound" (deliberately a broader word than "music") that would come out of free jazz. Coleman's "double quartet" included drummers Billy Higgins and Ed Blackwell, bassists Charlie Haden and Scott LaFaro, trumpeters Don Cherry and Freddie Hubbard, Eric Dolphy on bass clarinet, and Coleman himself on alto sax. The music is built upon a given tonal center and upon the alternation of collective playing and solo improvisations. Its internal structure, which developed during the thirty-six-minute take, consists of motifs (none of which was preset) tossed back and forth among the players. As Coleman was quoted in the liner notes, "When the soloist played something that suggested a musical idea or direction to me, I played that behind him in my style. He continued his own way in his solo, of course." The same rapport is maintained in the brief ensemble preludes to each solo, another element of the music's plan. In effect, this marathon group improvisation is held together by a quite bare, subtle outline and a profound unanimity of feeling.

Ascension, which one critic was moved to describe as "the most powerful human sound ever recorded," is even more detailed in its organization, though it appears less so. The session, done in two takes, included Trane and ten other players, none of whom were acquainted with the music's form until they arrived at the studio. The lineup was as follows: tenor saxophonists John Coltrane, Pharoah Sanders, and Archie Shepp; trumpeters Freddie Hubbard and Dewey Johnson; alto saxophonists Marion Brown and John Tchicai; bassists Art Davis and Jimmy Garrison; and drummer Elvin Jones. As in *Free Jazz*, this music alternates soloing with group improvising; however, *Ascension* is also based upon four ascending modal scales which, along with Coltrane's spiritual aspirations, accounts for the album's title.

Ascension appears deceptively disorganized for a variety of reasons. First, it maintains such a uniformly high level of intensity that the listener has no respite during which to assimilate what is being heard, a feature which is perhaps the music's most serious flaw. Second, the ensemble passages, which are primarily amelodic, obscure the tonal center as often as not. Most significantly, *Ascension*'s goals are of a largely unprecedented type, quite distinct from those of *Free Jazz*. As Shepp expressed it in the liners, "(*Ascension*) creates various surfaces of color which push into each other, creates tensions and counter tensions, and various fields of energy." He might also have included the ponderous density of the sound.

Tonal color, density, and energy became as much a part of free jazz as the old triumvirate of melody, harmony, and rhythm had been of modern jazz. The paths pioneered by both *Free Jazz* and *Ascension* had been explored further by the Art Ensemble of Chicago, Air, the World Saxophone Quartet, the Revolutionary Ensemble, the Old and New Dreams Band, and other collective-style groups (see Selected and General Discographies).

Chamber Jazz

Another style of free jazz, one that is frequently referred to as "neo-classicism," derives its characteristics from neither *Free Jazz* nor *Ascension*, but from the aesthetic sensibilities of European chamber music. The style began to mature in 1972 with Keith Jarrett's first solo piano album (*Facing You*), and with the founding of the collective ensemble Oregon (Selected Discography). Most of the musicians who record in this style are white, although it is far from clear what conclusions, if any, can be drawn from such a generalization.

In any case, many white and European musicians have put the innovations of Ornette Coleman, Cecil Taylor, and John Coltrane to use with a new emotional orientation. Their music differs from the Afro-American free style in its intonation, which is more "pure" than vocalized, and in its rhythmic feeling, which is more regular and pulselike (four sixteenth notes to the quarter note) than the polyrhythmic momentum (based upon a three-against-four feeling) achieved by most black drummers. Generally (but *not* uniformly) the music is characterized by a self-conscious, pastoral romanticism. Overall, the order and decorum of chamber music replaces the intense drive of Coleman, Taylor, and Coltrane.

The large output of chamber jazz albums, whose importance to jazz is far less than its abundance implies, can be accounted for by a variety of factors. Part of the story is surely bound up with the flight of so many jazz musicians to Europe and, consequently, the increased involvement of European musicians in jazz. The European respect for jazz as a major art form has also encouraged university and government support to a degree equaled only recently in the United States. Another factor has been the higher level of education of contemporary jazz musicians, many of whom are thoroughly conversant with the work of modern European composers.

The chamber jazz style has been successfully promulgated by ECM Records, a company based in West Germany and directed by a classically trained bassist, Manfred Eicher. Eicher, formerly a producer for the classical Deutsche Grammophon label, applied his classical sensibilities to the recording of jazz. As he was quoted in *Down Beat* magazine (July, 1980): "I was raised on chamber music, and I want ECM to reflect this side of jazz, rather than the rough and bombastic side." So many chamber jazz groups were recording for ECM in the mid-1970's that some critics began to refer to "an ECM sound" to describe this type of jazz. (The label has since diversified its music.)

Keith Jarrett's brilliant *Köln Concert* (Selected Discography) boosted the label's reputation in the mid-1970's, and when Warner Brothers took over its distribution in 1979, there could be no doubt about the success of its "product," commercially speaking.

Artistically, the quality of chamber jazz ranges from the substantial achievements of Keith Jarrett and several exciting one-time-only combos; for example, *Batik*—guitarist Ralph Towner, drummer Jack DeJohnette, and bassist Eddie Gomez—to an aimless, indistinguishable lot of what could fairly be described as "musings" (formerly called "noodling"). There has been a tendency, too, for critics to damn chamber jazz by invidiously comparing it with the West Coast and progressive styles of the 1950's. For one example, Robert Palmer, in summing up the 1970's for *Rolling Stone* (July 26, 1979), claims that Jarrett and "neoclassicism" are "marginal if not wholly irrelevant to the evolution of jazz." Palmer correctly locates the heart of jazz's evolution in black-American rhythmic feeling and intonation, but he mistakenly construes chamber jazz as essentially "retrogressive," on the grounds that it is rooted (exclusively, he implies) in the jazz of the 1950's and in late nineteenth and early twentieth century romantic European music. He exhumes the ghosts of Charlie Ventura, Shorty Rodgers, and Stan Kenton to prove the point.

The contexts, however, are not parallel. First, the ECM groups, profiting from the innovations of free jazz, are more boldly improvisational. Second, jazz is more community-conscious than it ever was, which makes cross-fertilization more common. *Batik* is one example; *Codona*, an album by Collin Walcott, Oregon's percussionist, with Don Cherry (a Coleman alumnus) is another. There is no question that the Coleman-Taylor-Coltrane axis is central to free jazz, but condemning chamber jazz categorically as a dead end comparable to the cool and progressive styles of the 1950's is premature and very likely based on a faulty analogy.

United We Stand

Free jazz endured more than its share of rejection and neglect by both critics and record companies; yet by the end of the 1970's, the music radiated (relatively speaking) an aura of prosperity and even a bit of optimism about its future on records. Compared with other styles of jazz, of course, sales were minimal; but compared with its own past, the number of excellent albums with a reasonable distribution increased manifold.

The growth of free jazz's discography is due in great part to the musicians themselves. They initiated an era of cooperation which reflected their musical collectivism. Competition had been the prevalent attitude ever since Louis Armstrong ushered in the age of the soloist in the mid-1920's, an age typified by cutting contests, personality cults, and what Coleman referred to as the "star complex." Perhaps the era of the individual ended when John Coltrane died in 1967. In free jazz there was no Satchmo, Bird, Dizzy, or Trane to point the way and attract a crowd of followers. Gradually the group's inter-action replaced the individual's performance in significance. Free jazz musicians nurtured a crucial vision of themselves as a community.

The new social order found its first expression in Chicago, where the Association for the Advancement of Creative Musicians (AACM) was organized in 1965. Anthony Braxton, the members of the Art Ensemble of Chicago, and Air's personnel are only some of the major free jazz musicians to come from the ranks of the AACM, the most powerful self-help organization in jazz's history. The pianist Muhal Richard Abrams (General Discography) was its first president, and the AACM's character owes much to his mature guidance. In fact, Abrams's Experimental Band, which was primarily a large rehearsal band for the members' original music, was AACM's immediate predecessor. After two years the Experimental Band lost its rehearsal hall and disintegrated, leaving the realization that musicians were going to have to produce and promote their own music if they wanted it to reach the public. Abrams, Air's drummer Steve McCall, and Phil Cohran and Jody Christianson conceived of a grass roots organization to create these outlets. As McCall remembers it, "the AACM just came out of musicians getting together after the gig. All the South Side show people would meet at a restaurant at 53rd and Cottage and talk about conditions. A lot of the guys in the bands (felt) restricted in terms of creativeness." [8] The membership soon numbered a hundred, and Abrams was elected president, an office he held for over a decade, perhaps at the expense of his own recording career.

The AACM's influence was pervasive and profound, reaching deep into the life-styles of its members. The personal influence of Abrams himself was movingly expressed by Joseph Jarman, a multireed and percussion player in the Art Ensemble:

> Until I had the first meeting with Richard Abrams, I was like all the rest of the "hip" ghetto niggers; I was cool, I took dope, I smoked pot, etc. I did not care for the life I had been given. In having the chance to work in the Experimental Band with Richard and the other musicians there, I found the first something with meaning/reason for doing. That band and the people there was the most important thing that ever happened to me.[9]

Others gained a sense of acceptance and confidence, like Anthony Braxton who joined the AACM because it was "an organization I wouldn't feel weird in."

The AACM also developed the concept of "little" instruments—those rarely used colorful voices ranging in size from nose flute and police whistle to tympani—which greatly enriched the sound-fields and sound-surfaces of non–song-oriented playing. Dancers who had joined the Association added an element of theater, one which persists in the costumed performances of the Art Ensemble. (Sun Ra's Arkestra—which lived communally in Chicago from 1955 to 1961—also experimented with theatrical effects, and in several ways foreshadowed the achievements of the AACM.) The AACM demanded a great deal from its members beyond clean living: originality in composition and improvisational style; a thorough knowledge of the jazz tradition; and, in most cases, a desire to go beyond it. The association provided rehearsal space, produced concerts at nearby universities, and arranged to have the members' music documented in recording sessions, the first of which were Roscoe Mitchell's *Sound* (1966), Joseph Jarman's *Song For* (1967), and Abrams's own *Levels and Degrees of Light* (1967). In short, the AACM has been a model self-help society, one which came to jazz exactly when it was needed most. Interestingly, its precursors were the brotherhoods and "secret societies" of early New Orleans, which yielded the first era of musical collectivism.

Collectivism in New York, having to surmount a tradition of competitiveness and several sharply drawn personalities, evolved falteringly in stages. The first occurred in 1964 in the form of a concert politically dubbed "The October Revolution in Jazz," organized by trumpeter Bill Dixon with the help of Cecil Taylor and a few others. Over a four-day period in the Cellar Café near Broadway, "the new thing" was displayed by twenty different groups of musicians, ranging from the now famous to the long forgotten. The event confirmed two noteworthy facts: There was a large reservoir of talent working with the innovations of free jazz; and, what seemed more surprising, this music could get a hearing if the musicians took the initiative in producing it.

The more ambitious Jazz Composers' Guild was formed quickly on the heels of the October Revolution concert. Its charter members were Bill Dixon, Cecil Taylor, Sun Ra, Paul Bley, the composer Carla Bley, then Paul's wife, George Russell, and Archie Shepp. They had hoped, in effect, to replace the local chapter of the American Federation of Musicians (AFM), which they felt had failed them on several counts. The guild members did not recommend total severance from the AFM, but saw themselves as a special-interest group which the union was simply ill-prepared to serve. The guild, however, had its own problems in the strong, idiosyncratic personalities of its founders. Without a father figure like Richard Abrams to unify it, its life was short—but not in vain.

The Jazz Composers' Orchestra Association (JCOA) was created in 1966 by Carla Bley who with her partner, Austrian trumpeter Mike Mantler, transformed the advocacy idea into a quasi-commercial launching pad for new noncommercial music. The association's first *raison d'être* was to support composers who wrote extended works for large jazz orchestras. The JCOA established its own record label, which Bley described as "like the Wildlife Preserve, protecting all this possibly extinct music . . . that doesn't fit into (industry) categories." [10] As a nonprofit organization, the JCOA soon received funding from New York State for concerts and workshops, and from private sources for recordings. In 1972 the New Music Distribution Service (NMDS) was created as the JCOA's distribution arm, proving its product's viability by selling within two years over eighty thousand LP's on consignment from a variety of "new-thing" labels.

The JCOA label itself produced three classic albums of large orchestra works: Mantler's *The Jazz Composers' Orchestra* with soloists Cecil Taylor, Pharaoh Sanders, Gato Barbieri, Don Cherry, and Roswell Rudd; Bley's opera-like *Escalator over the Hill*; and Cherry's *Relativity Suite*. Ironically these albums are unavailable, perhaps only temporarily, because NMDS profits are being used to promote the new Bley-Mantler label Watt. That decision is questionable. While Watt's *13, 3/4, Dinner Music*, and *Music Mechanique* are amusing, even fascinating examples of the Bley-Mantler tongue-in-cheek style, they are not as worthy of attention as the JCOA trio of albums. (Sadly, Carla Bley's best music has had a difficult time remaining available. Her most moving album-length work, *A Genuine Tong Funeral*, played by the Gary Burton Quartet, has long been deleted from the Vanguard catalog; and the aforementioned *Liberation Music Orchestra*, a Bley-Haden collaboration, has been dropped by Impulse.)

Musician-owned record labels were another means by which musicians could take matters into their own hands. The earliest labels in free jazz were Sun Ra's Saturn label and Cecil Taylor's Unit Core (see Appendix), both of which have lapsed into uncertain distribution. The promising catalogs of the 1970's are Strata-East, founded by pianist Stanley Cowell and trumpeter Charles Tolliver; Paul Bley's well-recorded and distinctively designed LP's on Improvising Artists, Inc.; the cooperative label Artists House, whose original impetus came from Ornette Coleman; and the Art Ensemble's AECO. Independent labels have also made available a great deal of free jazz: the Arista Novus and Freedom labels, Delmark, Inner City, India Navigation, Nessa, Sackville (Canadian), Choice, Tomato, Passin' Thru, 1750 Arch, and Survival. As we have seen, ECM is the most heartening success story of the decade, diminished initially by its allegiance to chamber jazz. However, ECM's acquisition of the Art Ensemble and musicians like trumpeters Leo Smith and Don Cherry in 1979 makes a healthy diversity more likely.

The loft-jazz phenomenon of the 1970's has been a major asset in the development and exposure of younger or experimental musicians. (The five-disc set of loft sessions entitled *Wildflowers*, once available on Douglas, is no longer in print.) The term "loft jazz" does not refer to a style of playing, but to the small New York City apartments where it found a home. Musicians who play there either receive a small fee or pass the hat. There is no food or drink service, and seating is often on the floor. Sam Rivers's Studio Rivbea is one important concert and rehearsal space. The musicians who have played at Studio Rivbea and similar loft settings are the cutting edge of free jazz, and their albums (General Discography) are bound to affect the style's development. The most important players to listen for are the following: Arthur Blythe, alto sax; David Murray, tenor sax; James Newton, flute; Chico

Freeman, tenor sax; Julius Hemphill, tenor sax; Leo Smith, trumpet; and Leroy Jenkins, violin. (Those noted earlier or in the Selected Discography ahead have not been included here.) A most encouraging feature of the players listed above is that they are enthusiastic masters of traditional material, to which they frequently allude in their recorded work. Jazz's important innovations have always had their roots deep in the past.

Collective organizations, musician-owned labels, and lofts have by no means solved the problems of free jazz musicians, but they have demonstrated that these problems can be alleviated to some extent by activism and cooperation. The musicians' optimism is reflected by drummer Don Moye of the Art Ensemble of Chicago in an interview with *Down Beat* magazine (May 3, 1979):

> People are beginning to deal with this music more. All the major labels are checking out the music and making little ploys. Columbia signed Arthur Blythe; people like Braxton, Oliver Lake, Henry Threadgill all have contracts of one form or another with various companies. It's all part of the growing trend for the music to get wider acceptance by the business establishment. For us to be with ECM is just a reflection of that, and it's going to continue in the years to come."

Free jazz's struggles are not over, but, with the music in good health and the access to recording improved, there is much reason to be confident of the outcome.

ORNETTE COLEMAN

The Shape of Jazz to Come

Atlantic, SD-1317
one disc, liner notes
1959

Musicians: Ornette Coleman, alto sax; Don Cherry, cornet; Charlie Haden, bass; Billy Higgins, drums.
Compositions (all by Ornette Coleman): *Side one:* Lonely Woman; Eventually; Peace. *Side two:* Focus on Sanity; Congeniality; Chronology.

FREE JAZZ
A COLLECTIVE
IMPROVISATION
BY THE
ORNETTE
COLEMAN
DOUBLE
QUARTET

Free Jazz

Atlantic, SD-1364
one disc, liner notes
1960

Musicians: Ornette Coleman, alto sax; Eric Dolphy, bass clarinet; Don Cherry, pocket
trumpet; Freddie Hubbard, trumpet; Scott LaFaro, bass; Charlie Haden, bass; Billy
Higgins, drums; Ed Blackwell, drums.
Composition (a collective improvisation planned by Ornette Coleman): *Side one:* Free
Jazz—Part I. *Side two:* Free Jazz—Part II.

WHEN ORNETTE COLEMAN brought his quartet into New York's Five Spot
Café in 1959, he was the incarnation of "the new thing," the first free improviser, and the most revolutionary, controversial figure in jazz since Charlie
Parker. Coleman played his white plastic alto sax with a unique sense of pitch
and with a disregard for preset chord progressions, consistency of tempo and
meter, and phrasing in measures or bar lines. A self-taught composer and
instrumentalist, he could neither read nor write music in conventional notation. These irregularities were sufficient reason for some of his peers to
consider him a charlatan, at least initially. Miles Davis, never one to mince
words, declared that Coleman must be "screwed up inside" to play music
as he did. More than a few critics, as noted in the introduction to this chapter, questioned whether Coleman's jazz qualified as music at all.

At the same time, there were a discerning lot of admirers who perceived
a new freedom of self-expression in Coleman's apparent madness. John
Coltrane was profoundly moved by Ornette's abandon, though he was un-
willing to cut himself loose from harmonic and rhythmic restrictions to the
same degree. Eric Dolphy's alto sax style is remarkably similar to Coleman's
in its eerily vocal intonation and occasionally gigantic intervallic leaps. While
Coltrane, Eric Dolphy, and the composer George Russell (Chapter 6) expanded chords into scales (based upon modes), Coleman had the audacity
to bypass them altogether. Yet, at the same time, Coleman remarkably
maintained an internal variety, an overall logical structure, and the feeling
of the blues.

The Coleman quartet's brilliant series of albums recorded for Atlantic
represent a genuine breakthrough for modern jazz, establishing the primacy
of melody over chord changes. Despite Coleman's exaggerated reputation as
"weird and difficult," the albums from 1959 to 1962 are wonderfully accessible
and enjoyable: *The Shape of Jazz to Come, Change of the Century, The*

Art of the Improvisors, and *This Is Our Music.* (A few others, which would have fallen into this category, have been deleted from Atlantic's catalog.) *Free Jazz,* the first model for the collective jazz improvising of the 1970's, is more of an acquired taste and, consequently, will be discussed last of all.

Coleman was twenty-nine at the time of the Five Spot Café date, and his career thus far, except for two albums made for Contemporary Records in 1958, had been a series of disasters. He grew up in Fort Worth, Texas, the son of a seamstress and a semiprofessional baseball player, who died when Ornette was seven. Coleman took an early interest in the saxophone, probably because an older cousin played one, but he was fourteen before his mother could afford to buy him an instrument of his own. The family could not afford lessons either, so Ornette taught himself alto sax from a piano instruction book, which led to his mistaking the saxophone's C for the piano's A, and so on up the scale. The error was rectified two years later by a church bandleader. It is possible that Coleman's lack of conventional training, along with his innate genius, greatly enhanced his originality.

One of Ornette's major assets in those early days was the family living room, the site of frequent jam sessions which prepared him quickly for work in local rhythm-and-blues bands. He began to travel with these commercial groups throughout the South and Southwest, though he was entirely unprepared for the insensitive settings he encountered. The end came in Baton Rouge, Louisiana, after Ornette stopped the dancers cold with a wild, probably incomprehensible solo passage. During the intermission, a young woman invited Coleman outside, where three of the patrons jumped him, beat him up, and threw his horn off the side of a hill.[11]

Nevertheless, Ornette's background in these groups remains apparent, for the blues colors nearly everything he plays. Even the honk-and-growl style of the Texas tenor players emerges on the "Chronology" solo (*Shape*) and more clearly still on "Ramblin' " (*Change of the Century*), a blues with a country-and-western feeling to it.

When Coleman moved to Los Angeles in 1953, he supported himself as a stock boy and elevator operator, spending his nights getting kicked off every bandstand in town. The traveling bandleaders, like Dexter Gordon, Max Roach, and Clifford Brown with whom most of the local players were allowed to sit in, shunned Coleman openly. The only musicians receptive to his style at first were Ed Blackwell, a drummer from New Orleans who had been experimenting with shifting metric patterns, and Don Cherry, whom Coleman met through his wife, Jayne. Billy Higgins, a high school friend of Cherry's, was also brought into the fold.

Charlie Haden, whose acutely responsive bass was essential to the success of the Atlantic quartet, met Coleman on the stage of the Hillcrest Club in a band organized by pianist Paul Bley (on Inner City's *Live at the Hillcrest* and IAI's *Coleman Classics*). Haden had come to Los Angeles in 1956 from the Midwest to study at the Westlake Music School, though he soon deserted his studies to work with Les McCann, Art Pepper, and other local bands.

He had played bass from his earliest years and sang four-part harmony with his family, a professional singing group, and developed "a crystal ear." [12]

Coleman's instructions to Haden as the band was rehearsing in living rooms and garages during the late 1950's, reveal his expressionistic approach to improvising: "Here are the changes I was hearing when I wrote the melody, but you don't have to play them. Let's all listen to each other and remember the melody, the feeling of it, and play from that." [13] This was a difficult viewpoint to reconcile with the premise of the bebop and the hard bop years, which was that if the saxophonist is working off an F^7 chord, the other instruments must conform to it as well. Coleman's answer was: "But if he's allowed to use any note that he hears to express that F^7, then that note's going to be right because he hears it, not because he read it off the page." [14]

It is not surprising, then, that Coleman found it easier to eliminate the piano, which in those years was used primarily as a chord-oriented instrument. It has an inhibiting effect on the Hillcrest albums alluded to above and on the first Contemporary album, *Something Else* (1958), after which Coleman never worked again with a pianist.

Coleman managed to get his foot in the door to the recording business by virtue of his composing, which had impressed the respected bassist Red Mitchell, a mentor of Charlie Haden's. Mitchell set up a meeting between Coleman, Cherry, and Contemporary Records' owner Lester Koenig, who was eager to buy material for Contemporary's other bands. In these circumstances, songs are generally auditioned on the piano, but since Coleman could barely play the piano, he and Cherry demonstrated them on their horns. Koenig was astute enough not only to buy the songs but to have Coleman and Cherry record them themselves. The second Contemporary album (minus pianist Paul Bley), *Tomorrow Is the Question*, shows Coleman on the way to an abrupt break with bebop. *Tomorrow* contains two excellent cuts, the dirge "Lorraine" and the blues "Tears Inside." But overall the album lacks the certainty and grace of the Atlantic sessions. Neither Percy Heath nor drummer Shelly Manne, despite their enthusiasm for Coleman's free style, were able to give themselves to it as successfully as Charlie Haden, Ed Blackwell, or Billy Higgins.

Coleman's next benefactor was John Lewis, the pianist and leader of the Modern Jazz Quartet. Hearing the group in California, Lewis was quick to perceive their originality, describing Ornette and Don Cherry as playing "like twins." Lewis recommended them to Nesuhi Ertegun, the president of Atlantic Records, which paid for their trip in the summer of 1959 to the Lenox School of Jazz in Massachusetts run by Lewis and Gunther Schuller. Critic Martin Williams, who heard them there, preceded them to New York, and paved the way for the crucial Five Spot date, an event which marked the beginning of a new era in jazz history.

The Shape of Jazz to Come makes it clear that Coleman's starting point was the style of Charlie Parker, whom he could imitate quite accurately. While he was not Bird's equal in technique, he had the same fluid, linear urgency in his delivery. "Eventually" and "Chronology," perhaps more than any other tracks, attest to his indebtedness to classical bebop. "Bird Food" (on *Change of the Century*) and "Humpty Dumpty" (on *This Is Our Music*) reveal it equally well. As Coleman himself told the critics, "I'm beginning where Charlie Parker stopped. Parker's melodic lines were placed across ordinary chord progressions. My melodic approach is based on phrasing, and my phrasing is an extension of how I hear intervals and the pitch of the tunes I play." [15]

There are many ideas in this elliptical self-analysis that need to be explored, the first being Coleman's concept of phrasing. In short, he believes that "rhythmic patterns should be as natural as breathing patterns." While Charlie Parker divides the four beats of swing into eighths and Coltrane subdivides the eighth notes into sixteenths, Coleman swings free of mathematically divided measures altogether. As with his form and choice of notes, Coleman's phrasing comes from an inner necessity. Yet he is an extremely logical improviser, as on "Congeniality," in which ideas that are stated early in the improvisation are picked up later and examined from new angles.

Second, Parker's allegiance to predetermined chord progressions is discarded by Coleman on the grounds that these progressions limit his choice of notes and, consequently, his freedom and spontaneity. "If I'm going to follow a preset chord sequence," he said, "I may as well write out my solo." [16] Coleman, however, is not an atonalist, though his tonal centers occasionally conflict with Haden's and cause some "atonal texture" (see Introduction).

Coleman's pleading tone is even more vocalized than Parker's and deeply affecting. He thinks in terms of pitch rather than notes, which he identifies with the steps of the tempered scale corresponding to the keys of the piano. Since the saxophone can create tones, or "microtones," which fall between the piano's notes, Coleman reaches fearlessly beyond the boundaries of the tempered scale. As he cryptically expressed it, "you can play sharp in tune and flat in tune." Of course, this practice only fueled the fires of critics who accused him of playing out of tune. Coleman, however, insisted on "trying to express the warmth of the human voice," which for him could not be limited to scales on the piano. He also expressed its variety even in the playing of a single tone: "When I play an F in a song called 'Peace,' I think it should not sound exactly like the same note in a piece called 'Sadness.'" [17] Compare his haunting, plaintive sound on "Lonely Woman," a beautiful dirge, with the frenzy of "Focus on Sanity," in which numerous tonal centers fly by with rapidity.

During this period, Coleman wrote several tender, graceful melodies similar to "Lonely Woman": "Beauty Is a Rare Thing" (*This Is Our Music*) and "Just for You" (*Art of the Improvisors*), for example. "Focus" is representative of numerous tunes at the other end of the spectrum; it is a brief, functional line that serves as a springboard for the high-flying (in this case double-timed) soloing to follow.

The freedom inherent in Coleman's approach meant that the burden of organizing the music falls heavily upon the improvisers. Thus the rapport of the quartet—Higgins's shifting metric feeling, Haden's dovetailing melodic lines, and Cherry's bright melodicism (very much under Ornette's influence) —is crucial to its success. During their Los Angeles years, the band rehearsed daily at Cherry's home, not only to exercise its freedom but to learn not to fear it and, above all, to control it. As noted in the introduction, Coleman stressed that "it was when I found out I could make mistakes that I knew I was onto something."

Free Jazz, a thirty-six minute simultaneous improvisation by two quartets, is perhaps the boldest album in the history of jazz; certainly it is the first to depend primarily upon collective improvisation. That it does not always succeed is not so surprising as the fact that it succeeds at all. Aside from brief, prearranged themes which launch particular soloists, the piece is extemporized by the spontaneous interaction of the players. Its cohesiveness is astonishing when one considers that eight musicians were creating it on the spot more or less out of thin air. Coleman inspired and unified these musicians as no other leader could have primarily because he could navigate confidently in these uncharted waters. Not surprisingly, then, his solo is the longest and most satisfying. Meanwhile, the young Freddie Hubbard, bound to conventional playing, sounds a bit out of place. Eric Dolphy's and Don Cherry's playing falls somewhere in between these extremes. The expansive music is held together by the alternating ensemble and solo segments of constantly rebounding themes and fragments.

More than most albums, *Free Jazz* must be listened to as a complete, interwoven fabric. Rough, dense, and sprawling, it is teeming with color, rhythm, and sound. These qualities have made it a permanent and formidable model for group interaction. (See also the discussion in the introduction to this chapter.)

By 1962 Coleman was acknowledged as an innovator even by the skeptics of several years earlier. Yet he spent the next three years in virtual retirement, composing and learning the trumpet and violin. Coleman was irate over his income, which had somehow failed to increase significantly with his output and reputation. To prove a point, he began to charge what he thought he was worth, thereby precipitating his unemployment and the dispersion of his band. Unfortunately, he has never enjoyed an acceptance commensurate with the quality or even accessibility of his music.

Coleman began to record again in 1965 with an exciting live date from Sweden, *At the Golden Circle, Volume I*. This session introduces a new set of responsive, compatible colleagues: the classically trained bassist David Izenzon, and drummer Charles Moffett, a high school comrade of Ornette's in Texas. Blue Note's *New York Is Now* (1967) introduces the supple tenor sax of Dewey Redman capably "conversing" with Ornette and framed by the surging momentum of Jimmy Garrison and Elvin Jones. Redman— along with Charlie Haden—later played a major role in the Keith Jarrett quartet, which was strongly influenced by Coleman's free-flowing lyricism. Coleman also duoed with Charlie Haden on one track each of Haden's two A & M Horizon albums (General Discography) and on their superb Artists' House album *Soapsuds* (1980) which finds Ornette once again on tenor sax.

Two unusual albums are a testimony to Coleman's unceasing originality and continued influence. The first, *Dancing in Your Head* (1976), is one of the most excitingly danceable albums of the 1970's even compared with the countless fusion albums produced for that purpose. "The Symphony of A," an incantatory alto sax theme set against a furious background of African polyrhythms and rock, is electrified by the guitar dialogues of Bern Nix and Charles Ellerbee. Coleman's precisely phrased, blues-tinged improvising recalls the gutbucket style he must have used with the R & B bands in Texas, and after more than thirty minutes of driving intensity, "Symphony of A" is both exhausting and cathartic. Although emotionally more primitive than Coleman's earlier work, *Dancing* is highly recommended.

In 1979 Ornette was the subject of an ECM album on which he did not play at all. ECM's *Old and New Dreams* grew out of a cross-country tour which united Charlie Haden, Don Cherry, Dewey Redman, and Ed Blackwell, four men whose careers and thinking owe a great deal to Coleman. The music is sensitive, powerful, and fresh. Each of the players has grown considerably. One can only imagine the kind of music they might create led by Coleman himself. Coleman might well profit from such a reunion, as would his listeners, for there have been too few albums of significance from this still-vital original and historic figure.

CECIL TAYLOR

Unit Structures

Blue Note, BST-84237
one disc, liner notes by Taylor
1967

Musicians: Cecil Taylor, piano; Jimmy Lyons, alto sax; Eddie Gale Stevens, trumpet; Ken McIntyre, alto sax, oboe, and bass clarinet; Henry Grimes, bass; Alan Silva, bass; Andrew Cyrille, drums.
Compositions (all by Cecil Taylor): *Side one:* Steps; Enter, Evening (Soft Line Structure). *Side two:* Unit Structure/As of a Now/Section; Tales (8 Wisps).

Silent Tongues

Arista, AL 1005
one disc, no liner notes
1974

Musicians: Cecil Taylor, piano.
Compositions (all by Taylor): *Side one:* Abyss (First Movement), Petals and Filaments
(Second Movement), Jitney (Third Movement); Crossing (Fourth Movement).
Side two: Crossing (Fourth Movement) Part Two; After All (Fifth Movement);
Jitney, No. 2; After All, No. 2.

CECIL TAYLOR, who probably demands more of the listener than any other
musician in jazz, was the first of the avant-garde players to be recorded.
More single-minded than Ornette Coleman, he is still a vital force a quarter-
century later. Taylor's music is both dense and intense. In performance he
will often play uninterrupted and unaccompanied for an hour, pummeling
the piano mercilessly. The listener cannot presuppose conventional notions
of melody, harmony, and rhythm and expect this music to "make sense."
For the uninitiated Taylor's music requires emptying the mind of expectations
and welcoming a new experience. The music is not "jarring," though it may
sound that way if its terms are resisted. It is a powerful drama of continuous
tension and conflict, elements introduced with great control; its underlying
principles are order and structure.

This is nowhere more evident than on *Unit Structures* of 1966, a collective interpretation and improvisation along "constructivist" lines and is
defined by Taylor as "the conscious working-out of given material." [18] The
album also displays Taylor's explosive, virtually atonal piano style which
becomes self-sustaining on the unaccompanied Arista and Inner City LP's
of the 1970's. *Silent Tongues*, articulate in expression and acrobatic in technique, is nearly overwhelming. These two peak albums, along with a half-
dozen others to be examined ahead, provide a dramatic recorded history of
Taylor's development.

At the outset the thrust of his music must be distinguished from that of
Ornette Coleman who may appear because of his contemporaneous innovations to be a "cofounder" with Taylor of a particular style. While free jazz
in its historical sense here encompasses both musicians, their styles are
dissimilar from top to bottom. Coleman, untutored and rough-hewn, retained
the folksy roots of his blues experience in the ghetto of Fort Worth, Texas.
Cecil Taylor, born in 1933, was raised in a comfortable, primarily white

Long Island community. His formal training in the European classics was encouraged and, in fact, dominated his early experience. His father, a chef, played him records of Duke Ellington, who was to affect him deeply, but Cecil was not ready for them then. Taylor claimed to have been fairly oblivious to improvisation even through his high school years at the New York College of Music. Taylor and Coleman, who started out worlds apart, remained so even in maturity. A distinction made by Archie Shepp between melodic ("post-Coleman") playing and "energy-sound" playing (typified by Taylor) may be drawn clearly between them.

Taylor's awakening took place from 1951 to 1955 at the New England Conservatory of Music where he became involved with the atonalists (Schoenberg, Berg, and Webern) and the modern masters (Bartók and Stravinsky). At the same time he was drawn into the vital jazz society of Boston, which then included tenor saxophonist Sam Rivers, who would play in Taylor's band of the late 1960's; pianist Jaki Byard, soon to work for Charles Mingus; the West Coast-style composer Gigi Gryce and Parker disciple on alto sax, Charlie Mariano; trumpeter and bandleader Herb Pomeroy; and Serge Chaloff, the talented young baritone sax player who would spend the last years of his short life in Woody Herman's reed section. Taylor was being exposed to a vast assortment of points of view, but they did not yet counterbalance the classicism of his youth. His jazz influences at this time were the dense harmonies of Dave Brubeck and the challenging, intricate lines of Lennie Tristano, two players who often seem lacking in deep jazz feeling. On Taylor's first 1955 session (reissued on Blue Note's *In Transition*), he is therefore dominated by an intellectualism which almost totally eclipses his emotional side.

In *Looking Ahead!* in 1958, as a result of the gradual assimilation of influences like Bud Powell and Horace Silver, Taylor is still in his formative stages but has started moving in a more earthy direction. His own practice routine began to invigorate his music, as recalled by his first bassist (also a respected symphonic player), Buell Neidlinger, who was sharing an apartment with Taylor at the time:

> . . . His practicing revolves around *solfege* singing. He'll sing a phrase and then he'll harmonize it at the piano and then he'll sing it again, always striving to get the piano to sing, to try and match this feeling of the human production, the voice . . . Cecil's trying to get the vocal sound out of the piano, and I think he's achieved it on many occasions. You can almost hear the piano scream or cry.[19]

Taylor had also begun the limited use of clusters, groups of notes more dense than chords, which he introduces with a sharp, percussive attack. The clusters in "Of What," the most successful track on *Looking Ahead!*, do not permit individual pitches to be discerned, which consequently riddles his work with suggestions of atonality. Other tracks, which include Earl

Griffith's vibraharp, are less interesting. Elsewhere Taylor is held back by the rather stringent timekeeping and obvious patterns of drummer Dennis Charles. Although Charles was able to work with Cecil at a time when no one else could have, except Mingus's Dannie Richmond, he proved less adequate than either of the freer players who followed him—Sonny Murray from 1960 to 1964, and Andrew Cyrille after 1964.

Taylor has said his real education did not begin until he left the conservatory. At least, that is when his true spiritual ancestors—James P. Johnson, Thelonious Monk, and Duke Ellington—began to emerge in his music. As Cecil told Nat Hentoff, "I am not afraid of my European influences. The point is to use them—as Ellington did—as part of my life as an American Negro." [20] Ellington's music proved that one could construct jazz on orchestral principles without severing it from its roots, a realization which became the fundamental premise of Taylor's style.

The tracks "Bulbs," "Pots," and "Mixed" of 1961, released on one side of Impulse's two-disc *Dedication Series, Volume VIII: The New Breed*, are a significant advance for Taylor. Sonny Murray, who rejected the metronomic role of the drummer, joined him along with Henry Grimes, a more driving bassist than Buell Neidlinger. Taylor was able to write expansively for Archie Shepp, a tenor player who had recently been taken under John Coltrane's wing, and for Jimmy Lyons, an alto player who has remained with Taylor ever since. On "Mixed," the ensemble is augmented by Roswell Rudd on trombone and Ted Curson on trumpet, providing Taylor with his most expressive format yet. "Mixed," which borders on collective improvisation in its ad lib segments, adopts a unique rhythmic feeling that is no more akin to Ornette Coleman than to Duke Ellington. It does not swing but moves in "chains of impulses." [21] This composition is one of Taylor's richest and most vibrant in tone color. On "Pots" Taylor's note clusters fall with greater frequency. His two hands engage in continuous dialogue instead of conventionally using the left to accompany the right. He is beginning to make the bass register growl, enlarging the vocal and percussive capacity of the keyboard.

Along with *The New Breed*, Arista's *Nefertiti: The Beautiful One Has Come* contains, on four sides of Taylor, Lyons, and Murray as a trio, a full expression of Taylor's music in the early 1960's. It would be four years before Taylor recorded again.

Cecil Taylor's rapid maturation did nothing to enhance his earning power. His loose, seemingly erratic beat, bouts of atonality, and increasingly nonlinear right hand scared off most producers, who were having a difficult enough time stemming the tide of early rock with their already established talent. Club owners were not much more willing to take a chance. Buell Neidlinger realistically explained their reluctance: ". . . if there's anything they (club owners) hate to see, it's a bunch of people sitting around openmouthed with their brains absolutely paralyzed by the music, unable to call the waiter." [22] Taylor had fallen into hard times. No longer a student, he supported himself as a record salesman, cook, and dishwasher, though he triumphantly noted that at least he knew *why* he was washing dishes. Taylor was also undergoing Sullivan-style psychoanalysis, a process begun in the mid-1950's after the death of his father. The first glimmer of hope appeared in 1964 when Taylor with a new drummer, Andrew Cyrille, played a wonderfully successful, unrecorded concert at Town Hall in New York. After two years of work with this band, they would record the classic *Unit Structures*, a series of brilliant "sound-surfaces."

Unit Structures, a collection of diverse, carefully planned pieces of great expressive scope, contains some of Taylor's finest ensemble work. Again it is worth distinguishing its approach from Coleman's *Free Jazz*, which is a much more homogenous, minimally organized vehicle for improvisation. Both are collectively improvised, but the similarity ends there. Coleman had no interest in knowing what the music would sound like before it was played. But one must recall Taylor's dictum that freedom in jazz is primarily about "different ideas and expressions of order," and his constructivist goal is "the conscious working-out of given material."

"Enter, Evening (A Soft Line Structure)," for example, is a programmatic piece, uncannily evocative of nightfall. It opens with an essential ingredient of Taylor's best ensemble writing; a strikingly varied palette of timbres, each of which emerges individually. Taylor had told Nat Hentoff some years earlier that "one of the things I learned from Ellington is that you can make the group you play with sing if you realize that each instrument has a distinct personality, and (that) you can bring out the singing aspect of that personality if you use the right timbres for the instruments." [23] He accomplishes this beautifully in the free play of the oboe and alto sax, whose colors are heightened by contrast with the bowed bass and muted trumpet, and the dissonant chords from the piano. The music seems stretched out in space like a canvas, not marching methodically through time. So far as possible it is best not to single out one voice and relegate the others to the background, but rather to hear the music as a whole.

Another clearly Ellingtonian element in Taylor's music, one also used by Mingus, is the naturalistic intonation of the instruments. Eddie Stevens's muted trumpet and half-valve effects recall Cootie Williams or even Bubber Miley, the growling trumpeter from Ellington's "jungle music" days. In the flow of Taylor's "Evening," the trumpet at first suggests a baby crying in the distance, then the wailing of a cat in heat, and the still eerier half-valve squeals later on evoke a surreal jungle dream of the sort painted by Henri Rousseau. The other instruments, which continually pick up each other's themes, are conversational, stressing the collective nature of the improvisation.

In Taylor's music it is not easy to distinguish composed sections from improvised ones. Each is played with comparable spontaneity. Like Mingus, Taylor teaches his music aurally. For him it was a traditionally effective procedure: "I had found that you get more from the musicians if you teach them the tunes by ear, if they have to listen for changes instead of reading them off the page, which again has something to do with the whole jazz tradition, with how the cats in New Orleans at the turn of the century made their tunes." [24] (The reader is advised to reread Taylor's brief ode to traditional jazz quoted in Chapter 1 on page 26.) Sonny Murray recalls the days before *Unit Structures*, when Taylor was still passing out written music: ". . . when I could read his charts (Murray was not a competent reader when he began with Taylor), I still wouldn't play them exactly. I felt that it would be doing his music an injustice to play it exactly, because he could find anybody to do that." [25] While players may deviate from the given material—and in some cases are left intentionally on their own (for example, the piano–double-sax trilogue in the midst of "Enter, Evening")—they must not violate the seamless, self-contained unit. Taylor told Spellman: "The emphasis in each piece is on building a whole, totally integrated structure." [26]

"Tales (8 Wisps)" for piano, bass, and drums reveals the integral nature of the ensemble's sound quite clearly. Andrew Cyrille has now replaced Sonny Murray on drums, and seems more capable of shading Taylor's statements and engaging in a certain repartee with them. Taylor's piano aligns itself with the drums readily until the instruments seem to become extensions of one another. The track is translucent, its voices inextricably, even lovingly, woven together. "Tales" also illustrates Taylor's vacillating use of tonality, for near the end of the piece he alternates freely between a bluesy chord progression and outbursts of scattered clusters in which no tonal center can be discerned. Tonality, one may say generally of Taylor, has lost its function as a musical technique and has acquired a meaning as one type of sound, or raw material, among many.

The parity of voices evident on "Tales" is carried into a more ambitious context in "Unit Structures," a magnificent series of "sound-units" bonded tightly by Taylor's genius for structuring music. The piano is not heard in its typically supportive accompanist role, nor are the bass and drums evident. The players use the same elements, whether playing ensemble or "soloing" (i.e., emerging as the prominent voice). The themes are sometimes traded back and forth antiphonally, as when Cecil's piano and Jimmy Lyons's alto sax juggle the scalelike theme of the first segment. In Taylor's groups nothing is relegated to the background.

Again there are blurred boundaries between tonal and atonal segments, and between improvised and prearranged music. Taylor's interlocking units possess strong identities, each vibrant with distinct tonal colorings. The contrast between Lyons's mellifluous alto tone and Ken McIntyre's stark, dark, and cutting bass clarinet is especially effective. McIntyre, a former colleague of Taylor's at the New England Conservatory of Music, plays with abandon on "Steps," in which his alto frequently belches, shrieks, and screams. Jimmy Lyons, something of a foil for Taylor, is more tonally oriented; he is influenced by bebop in his phrasing and conservative in his range. On "Unit Structures," however, Lyons examines his melodic elements from every possible angle while working the music's pulsations into a feverish momentum.

Taylor makes use of intense, expectant silences to set the units apart from one another, a technique he employed later on the solo LP *Indent*. One critic observed that Taylor seems to be "indenting" each segment of his construction as if starting a new paragraph in a continuing story. The brilliance of Taylor, certainly so far as "Unit Structures" is concerned, is that his imaginative and colorful story is so coherently told.

The year following *Unit Structures*, Taylor recorded *Conquistador* with the same band except for Bill Dixon replacing Stevens on trumpet. It does not possess the internal variety of *Structures*, but is still among Taylor's first-rate performances. *The Great Concert of Cecil Taylor*, recorded live in Europe in 1969, is a three-disc set of Cecil Taylor, Andrew Cyrille, Jimmy Lyons, and Sam Rivers in the throes of Taylor's "Second Act of A," a piece accurately described in one review as "90 minutes of unrelieved intensity." Rivers, normally a great soloist (General Discography), contributes little meaningful improvisation here; but Lyons's performance is one of his most expansive. Inner City's *Dark to Themselves* (1976) with Raphe Malik on trumpet is a more measured, emotionally organic performance; unfortunately the fidelity of this recording, taped live at a concert in Yugoslavia, is less than desirable. (The "Spring of Two Blue J's," an important piece recorded for Taylor's own Unit Core label, is of uncertain availability. See Appendix for the mailing address.)

In the solo piano pieces the listener confronts Taylor's soul even more directly than in his bands; they are the undiluted, uninterrupted culmination of his art. In the clarity and precision of *Silent Tongues*, recorded live at the Montreux Jazz Festival, one has an unobstructed view of his passion and intellect hard at work. The other solo albums, Inner City's *Air Above Mountains* (recorded live in Austria, 1976) and Arista's *Indent* (recorded live at Antioch College in Ohio, 1973), are also mature works—articulate, impassioned, and intelligent—but they lack the exceptional lucidity of the six performances on *Silent Tongues*.

The awesome nature of the music can be conveyed by a brief description of the first track "Abyss." A dark voice scurries ominously back and forth in the bass register, quickly ascends the keyboard into a shriek, and then plunges back into the bass (abyss?). The crashing of tonal clusters alternates with taut silences; these atonal splashes are then connected by thorny scales and arpeggios whipping between them. Finally, the double-forte roar in the bass register brings the audience to spontaneous applause, after which a soft transitional, reassuringly modal phrase ushers in "Petals and Filaments," the second movement of the eighteen-minute-long composition.

Taylor's performance itself is an event of great physicality; it is very much influenced by modern interpretive dance, one of his passionate interests.

He once told A. B. Spellman, the critic and biographer, "I try to imitate on piano the leaps in space a dancer makes." He is strong and lithe, his hands leaping from one register to the other, pouncing on keys like graceful, rapacious cats. In the 1970's he began to use the heel of each hand as well as his fingers to hit clusters. Thus if one has the impression from certain recordings that there are four hands at work, there is some truth to that image.

In his percussive attack and orchestral use of piano, Taylor has only one predecessor—and a technically more limited one—Duke Ellington. But Taylor's keyboard constructions are models for a new style, elements of which can also be heard in McCoy Tyner (Chapter 6) and the under-recorded ex-Mingus pianist Don Pullen.

Taylor infuses his music with a tension and ferocity probably beyond that of any other pianist. The fury of "After All (Fifth Movement)" is quite difficult to accept save for its formal beauty and the precision of its execution. But there are emotional respites which, despite their rarity, the listener must not ignore. "After All, No. 2," which Taylor or the record's producer had the good sense to save for the last track, is an opportunity to be savored. The music's pulsations are slower, allowing Taylor's patterns to be examined more readily, as one might contemplate the design of a snowflake under a magnifying glass.

As the reader may have noticed, virtually all Taylor's music from 1967 to 1977 was recorded in Europe, for reasons described in the introduction to this chapter. However, that trend has recently been reversed with two double-disc sets of his performing band (Jimmy Lyons, sax; Raphe Malik, trumpet; Ameen, violin; Sirone, bass; and Ronald Shannon Jackson, drums), whose recording was supported with a Rockefeller Foundation grant. New World's *Cecil Taylor* and *3 Phasis*, both taped on four nights of studio playing in April 1978, rank with Taylor's most lucidly organized constructions and are highly recommended. Their domestic origins are also a hopeful sign that America may yet become a hospitable environment for his music.

SUN RA AND HIS ARKESTRA

Live at Montreux

Inner City, IC-1039
two discs, liner notes
1976

Musicians: Sun Ra, piano, solar organ, Moog synthesizer; John Gilmore, tenor sax; Marshall Allen, alto sax and flute; Pat Patrick, baritone sax and flute; Danny Davis, alto sax and flute; James Jackson, Ancient Egyptian Infinity drum, bassoon; Elo Omo, bass clarinet; Danny Thompson, baritone sax and flute; Reggie Hudgins, soprano sax; Ahmed Abdullah, Chris Capers, Al Evans, trumpets; Vincent Chaney, French horn; Craig Harris, trombone; Stanley Morgan, congas; Clifford Jarvis, Larry Bright, drums; Tony Bunn, electric bass; June Tyson, vocals. (Dancers: June Tyson, Judith Holten, Cheryl Banks.)

Compositions (all by Sun Ra except "Take The 'A' Train" by Billy Strayhorn, side three): *Side one:* For the Sunrise; Of the Other Tomorrow; From out Where Others Dwell; On Sound Infinity Spheres. *Side two:* The House of Eternal Being; Gods of the Thunder Realm; Lights on a Satellite. *Side three:* Take The "A" Train. *Side four:* Prelude; El Is the Sound of Joy; Encore 1; Encore 2; We Travel the Spaceways.

SUN RA'S ARKESTRA is a band of high contrast in which driving riffs, free soloing, sensuous orchestration, and atonal collective blowing spin like the vanes of a pinwheel. *Live at Montreux* captures Sun Ra's original music unfolding continuously in asymmetrical, unpredictable passages of vivid tonal coloration. Ellington's "Take the 'A' Train" consumes all of side three, suggesting Sun Ra's debt to the big band tradition from which he has evolved.

Sun Ra's background has been obscured somewhat by his "recollections" of having descended to earth from another planet and then beginning to read music flawlessly with no training whatsoever. Sun Ra is, in fact, Herman "Sonny" Blount who was born in Birmingham, Alabama, around 1915. He led his own band in high school and later at Alabama A & M College, where he enrolled as a music-education student. The first turning point of his career occurred when he moved to Chicago, where in 1946 he began to work for Fletcher Henderson at the Club de Lisa as a pianist and arranger. Sun Ra describes himself as an extension of Henderson and Don Redman, an assessment that is confirmed here in the powerful riffs of "Lights of a Satellite," "El," and " 'A' Train"; but it is a brilliant Ellingtonian style which shines through the revolving orchestral densities, bass register timbres, and seamless interweaving of solo and ensemble passages.

Sun Ra also wrote arrangements for choreographed shows at the Club de Lisa, and he has continued to use singers and dancers who parade through the audience in diaphanous, unearthly costumes, shaking and striking unique percussion instruments. The meaning of the pageantry—and of his cosmic song titles and nom de plume—is found in the thematic material they evoke. The space metaphor, while meant literally no doubt by Sun Ra, indicates an overriding transcendental awareness, the type expressed as God consciousness by John Coltrane, as Spirit by Albert Ayler, and as black consciousness by Cecil Taylor, Archie Shepp, and others. The idea that music has a meaning beyond itself is thus very common in free jazz, and receives its earliest expression in the Arkestra.

Sun Ra is often ranked with Charles Mingus, Ornette Coleman, and Cecil Taylor as an originator of the collective, free style. However, the Arkestra's early records are not entirely convincing in that respect. Delmark Records' *Sun Song* (1956) and Sound of Joy (1957) display varying tempos, one modal composition ("El Is the Sound of Joy"—but compare it with the version on *Montreux*), and a fascination with unusual sound combinations. But primarily the music is a hybrid of hard bop soloing, swing riffs, and Sun Ra's groping adventurousness. These early tracks do not merit comparison with the important cuts made by Mingus, Coleman, or Taylor.

On the other hand, Sun Ra's band served as a model for the development of Chicago Free Jazz and the Association for the Advancement of Creative Musicians (AACM). His musicians lived communally, experimented freely, and resolved not to cater to popular tastes. Their cooperative spirit and dedication to original music were also the founding principles of Muhal Richard Abrams's Experimental Band of 1964, the forerunner of the AACM. There were a few free jazz practices invoked in the band's Chicago days: at least some free collective blowing during rehearsal and performance; the use of unusual instruments, what the AACM would call "little" instruments; Sun Ra's use of the electric piano and organ; the multimedia theatrics, which emerged later in groups like the Art Ensemble of Chicago; and the high quality of soloing by players such as tenor saxophonist John Gilmore whose influence on John Coltrane was described in Chapter 6. Sun Ra left Chicago for New York in 1961, and his band went with him, but the Arkestra made a lasting impression on the young musicians who would pool their resources there a few years later.

The Arkestra quickly established itself in New York, which was a more fertile seedbed for free jazz than Chicago in the early 1960's. The band played in Bill Dixon and Cecil Taylor's "October Revolution in Jazz" concert, and briefly joined the Jazz Composers' Guild, from which Sun Ra's maverick ideology soon separated them. Albums of this period show they had reached a new level of achievement. Their most important albums are *The Heliocentric Worlds of Sun Ra, Volumes 1 and 2* (1965), which have disappeared along with the ESP-Disk catalog. Sun Ra also recorded dozens of Arkestra albums for his own Saturn label (see Appendix), which has never enjoyed any dependable distribution. A few Saturns were sold briefly on the ABC Impulse label but have since been deleted. Thus the only domestically available albums of the Arkestra since their debut on *Sun Song* and *Sound of Joy* are on the Inner City label.

Live at Montreux, while admittedly a choice made from slim pickings, is a superior performance, embracing the vastly different moods the band is able to explore. On the sensuous "Of the Other Tomorrow," the horns "heave and sigh," as critic Bob Blumenthal aptly describes it; "El" and " 'A' Train" are straight ahead and swinging; "Sound Infinity" and "Encore 2" and "Gods of the Thunder Realm" unleash bombastic barrages of Sun Ra's private language on organ and synthesizer. The band's intimate rapport allows them to move as one lithe body on the latter half of "House of Eternal Being," a passage which would deteriorate into chaos without the Arkestra's musical unanimity. The principal soloists—Marshall Allen, John Gilmore, and James Patrick—whose performances are identified by Blumenthal in the liner notes, are among the best in free jazz, yet they are thoroughly integrated with the leader's compositions, not surprisingly after their twenty-year tenure with the band.

Sun Ra's piano is a strong, unifying voice, excelling in accompaniment ("Of the Other Tomorrow," "House of Eternal Being") and in expansive soloing ("On Sound Infinity Spheres," " 'A' Train"). From the "atonal stride" which introduces " 'A' Train" to the wild pyrotechnics of "Prelude," in which notes fall like an asteroid shower upon the upper register, his use of color, texture, and dynamics is electrifying. Aside from occasionally bashing the keyboard with his fists or whipping across registers with the backs of his hands, Sun Ra is precise; he unleashes chord clusters with rhythmic and textural accuracy. In fact, the key to *Live at Montreux* as a fulfilling, big-band free jazz performance, is its intimate union of freedom and control, a goal to which Sun Ra has aspired since the band's first recording twenty years earlier.

Sun Ra's two solo piano albums, IAI's *Solo Piano* and *St. Louis Blues*, are recent addenda to his discography, and represent the first time he has ventured outside the Arkestra since Saturn's *Monorails and Satellites* (unavailable). The albums contain conservative performances more indicative of his past than his customary futuristic inclinations. Both are interesting studies of his piano style, unobscured by the magnificence of the band, but neither album presents the range and majesty of the solos on *Montreux*.

Sun Ra's deepest talents are revealed only with the Arkestra. Given the band's increasingly frequent live performances during the late 1970's, there is reason to hope that several buried treasures of the past will be unearthed and perhaps some new ones recorded.

ANTHONY BRAXTON

The Montreux/Berlin Concerts

Arista, AL 5002
two discs, brief liner notes
1975, 1976

Musicians: Anthony Braxton, soprano sax, alto sax, clarinet, bass clarinet; Kenny
   Wheeler, trumpet; Dave Holland, bass; Barry Altschul, drums. Also with George
   Lewis, trombone, replacing Wheeler. Also with Lewis and the Berlin New Music
   Group (side four).
Compositions (all by Anthony Braxton): *Side one:* cut one; cut two. *Side two:* cut one;
   cut two. *Side three:* cut one; cut two. *Side four:* cut one.

ANTHONY BRAXTON epitomizes the double role of the free jazz musician
as an individual improviser—in his case on several reed instruments—
and as a composer-designer of collectively played music. He has worked in
extremely varied settings ranging from *For Alto* (1968), *Saxophone Improvisations—Series F* (1973), and *Alto Saxophone Improvisations 1979*,
(all for unaccompanied alto sax), to the three-disc *Anthony Braxton*
(1978), containing what will doubtless remain the "definitive" version of
his two-hour-long "For Four Orchestras," rendered by 160 musicians. But
the most manageable, dependable vehicle for Braxton's adventurous spirit
is the quartet setting of *Montreux/Berlin.*
  Braxton wields an arsenal of reeds fluently, reintroducing the clarinet to
jazz (side three, cut two) in a more sensuous, vocalized guise than it has
yet been heard. His compositions, which he calls "controlled but open-
ended," manipulate materials as disparate as turn-of-the-century marches
(side two, cut two) and atonality (side two, cut one; side three, cut one).
Textural variation, dynamic balance, and a fascination with pure sound are
omnipresent. Braxton ventures successfully into the uncharted waters of
orchestral free jazz on side four.
  Penetrating Braxton's rewarding discography requires one to confront
(and conquer) the prevailing idea that he is a cold, cerebral, obscure,
European-style crusader for modernity. There are several reasons for this
badly overstated point of view, which is applicable primarily to the music
prior to his Arista album *New York, Fall, 1974.* The first of the "cool"
skeletons in Braxton's closet is Dave Brubeck's alto soloist Paul Desmond,
who influenced Braxton to switch from clarinet to alto sax while he was

still a high school student in the early 1960's. Braxton soon progressed to a more sublime prototype in Lee Konitz, and later to Charlie Parker and Ornette Coleman. The "too-white" stigma of his early inclinations still lingers in some minds.

After studying harmony and composition at the Chicago Musical College and serving a short stint in the Army from 1964 to 1966, Braxton developed an avid interest in the classical avant-garde composers, especially Charles Ives, John Cage, and Karlheinz Stockhausen. Their influence, detectable in his orchestral composing and even on *Montreux/Berlin* in the abstract "Kelvin" series (side two, cut one, and side three, cut one), contributed to the classicist image. Generally, Braxton's soloing during the late 1960's was in fact flat in rhythmic accentuation, confirming the subordinate nature of his jazz feeling in these years.

The early Braxton attempted to banish all feeling from his music, following the example of philosopher-musician Cage. He erected his compositions on a foundation of mathematical relationships: "I myself saw music from a mathematical perspective and worked with mathematical systems . . . mathematics concerning sound, relationships, density, structures, various forms. I call it conceptual transference, a mixture of the most different elements." [27] Thus Braxton's early pieces were usually titled with alpha-numerical equations, which gradually evolved into the diagrams of spatial coordinates that label the tracks on *Montreux/Berlin*.

Braxton's intellectualist image was heightened by his nonmusical activities such as his graduate studies in philosophy at Roosevelt University, and the fact that during the 1960's he earned more money playing chess than playing music. His penchant for philosophizing is occasionally evident in his copious liner notes, some of which are written in such multisyllabic jargon that one wishes he had let the music speak for itself. In any case, Braxton's academic strain, which initially overshadowed his more soulful side, is a genuine aspect of his nature.

But another side of his development began in earnest in 1966, when he was discharged from the Army and he returned to Chicago. Saxophonist Roscoe Mitchell, a friend from his college days, urged him to join the AACM, where his growing interest in the European avant-garde and the free jazz of Ornette Coleman and Cecil Taylor might find a home. As one can deduce from Braxton's interests, he could not run with an ordinary crowd. In a *Down Beat* magazine interview (February 14, 1974) he sadly recalled the mid-1960's as a time of isolation: ". . . I was beginning to feel like maybe something was wrong with me. Because the happier I got with my music, the more unhappy others got with me. At some point, if you don't have people who can reinforce your reality, it gets pretty lonely out there." Ultimately he was persuaded to join the AACM because "here was an organization that I wouldn't feel weird in."

The AACM group, as noted earlier, were staunch proponents of collectivism and the use of multiple and so-called "little" instruments to broaden the tonal palette, two practices which Braxton has adhered to ever since. The two "Kelvin" compositions alluded to earlier, as well as the free interplay of the quartet on side one, cut one, show that soloing is replaced by an exquisitely balanced parity of voices. These pieces also demonstrate a great variety of textures, one of the few predetermined elements in a Braxton composition. At the same time that Braxton vigorously (and justifiably) proclaimed his individuality within the AACM, he also required their sympathetic support for the first four years of his recording career. His debut album *Three Compositions*, using AACM-ers Richard Abrams, Leo Smith, and Leroy Jenkins, was an auspicious beginning. Side one is really a landscape of sounds that uses voices and "little" instruments (bells, harmonica, slide whistle, bottles, kazoo, and more); side two, cut one, is a piece of somber mood that is actually richer in jazz content, profiting from the emotional trumpet of Leo Smith. *Alone Together*, a duo with Joseph Jarman, is another available, though less successful, album of that period.

While the AACM contact offered a fertile milieu, it was hardly a conduit to financial security. During the bleak commercial climate of the late 1960's, Braxton was starving, and like many free jazz innovators, decided it was preferable to starve in Europe, where at least he could be nourished by artistic recognition. With fifty dollars in his pocket, he moved to Paris in 1969, accompanied by Leroy Jenkins, Leo Smith, and drummer Steve McCall.

During Braxton's five years in Europe, he became a more emotional player, influenced by several of his peers. The Art Ensemble of Chicago, for example, was maturing rapidly and recorded some of their most moving work at this time. Braxton occasionally worked with them, but there is no available album documenting their collaboration. Another important association *has* been documented—the short-lived, much-heralded group Circle, in which Braxton worked with an existing trio of pianist Chick Corea, bassist Dave Holland, and drummer Barry Altschul (see Circle, General Discography). When Corea left to devote his energies to Return to Forever (Chapter 7), Kenny Wheeler, a melodic, Canadian-born trumpeter living in England, joined them. Braxton profited greatly from the rhythmic drive of Altschul and Holland, though he took charge of the group musically by writing virtually all its music. Over several years the group developed into the cohesive, exciting unit heard on the first three tracks of *Montreux/Berlin*.

The Complete Braxton 1971 captures the transition from Circle to Braxton's *Montreux* quartet. It includes two fascinating, rather cerebral Braxton-Corea duets, three tracks of the quartet with trumpeter Kenny Wheeler, a Braxton solo on bass clarinet, an overdubbed soprano track, and a piece for five tubas. Braxton's emotional growth on this album is apparent, but the collection is of more historical than musical interest.

During the early 1970's, Braxton began to focus more on the content of his music and less on pure structure. This was the profound change which he outlined for *Down Beat* (February 14, 1974):

> I'm starting to accept feeling again. At one point I consciously wanted to eliminate feeling from my music—in the beginning when I was heavily into (John) Cage. To play music with feeling, the approach is different. You must deal more with the "is" than the "how" (structure). I've found that mathematics as a total basis for my music is interesting, but it's not what's happening.

The first thing to happen upon Braxton's return to the United States was a contract with Arista, yielding *New York, Fall, 1974,* an album of quartet tracks with AACM percussionist Jerome Cooper (later the drummer for the Revolutionary Ensemble) replacing Barry Altschul. One of the more influential tracks (side two, cut two) is a texture piece for four saxophones, which may have served as a model for its other participants: Julius Hemphill, Hamiett Bluiett, and Oliver Lake. They later joined with David Murray to form the World Saxophone Quartet (General Discography), one of the most exciting of the free jazz collectives. The sequel *Five Pieces, 1975* reintroduces Altschul and reveals the new fire in Braxton's alto soloing, especially on side one, cut three, and side two, cut two. Both LP's are highly recommended.

The Montreux Jazz Festival concert took place as the Braxton-Wheeler quartet was playing out the final weeks of its glory. The enthusiastic audience raises the music's temperature noticeably. Side one of *Montreux/Berlin* contains a well-balanced pair of compositions, the first of which is a free-collective interpretation of Braxton's composition. The piece appears to consist of predetermined density, texture, and balance, leaving the shading, at which Altschul excels, to the players' discretion. The more exciting second track is a reinterpretation of the bebop style, twisting and turning in an energetic, linear theme. Side three, cut two, which was recorded a year later in Berlin, is precisely the same sort of piece, although Braxton on clarinet and George Lewis on trombone give it a different sound. Both Braxton and Wheeler (on side one, cut two) launch into driving, melodic solos that hover vaguely around a tonal center; their screeches of excitement are well grounded by Dave Holland's masterful, emotionally reassuring bass interlude. Side three, cut two, is no less intense in momentum. George Lewis solos fluently and vocally on trombone and Braxton is simply astonishing on clarinet. Together they offer these traditional jazz instruments a new lease on life.

Side two, cut two, Braxton's first piece with George Lewis in the group, is quasi-improvisational parade music, a genre he explores with equal success in the big band of *Creative Orchestra Music* (side one, cut three). Even with its rather martial rhythm, this piece is clearly in the early black American music tradition and is therefore inviting to a scholarly pioneer like Braxton. The success of side two, cut two, derives from the use of "little" instruments (described earlier), the well-planned rhythmic scheme of the piece, the illusion of an entire band in motion, and the infectious joy of the players.

The dense, partly atonal "Kelvin" composition on side three, cut one, illustrates another contribution: exploring the deep bass register. John Coltrane, Ornette Coleman, Pharaoh Sanders, Albert Ayler, and Eric Dolphy explored squeals and squeaks above the sax's range, but except for occasional "blats," blasts, and honks, they did not attempt to elicit lyricism from the sub-bass register, which provides particularly rich, virile, and moving color. For one thing, these musicians did not play instruments which allowed for this type of tonal color save for Dolphy's bass clarinet. Braxton, however, saws back and forth at subterranean depth on that bullfrog of the brass, the contrabass saxophone; he never really achieves lyricism at that level, but opens our ears to a new world of possibilities. Other attempts at the same sonority on bass sax and bass clarinet are heard in the orchestral piece (*Montreux/Berlin*, side four) and on the superb *Duets with Muhal Richard Abrams, 1976*.

The *Duets* album with Abrams shows Braxton returning to the AACM context with a stronger, more soulful identity. These tracks with Abrams are models of clarity, substance, and variety, reworking and exploring the music's breadth from Scott Joplin's "Maple Leaf Rag" to an unpremeditated improvisation. Muhal Abrams's informed, eloquent piano style sparkles with colorful clusters and spare melodic twists. In 1978 Braxton played two versions of "For Trio" (on *For Trio*) using two pairs of AACM musicians. The piece is one of vast spaces, recurrent tension, and unique tonal coloration. Braxton's purpose was to show the diverse interpretations that were possible using the same set of compositional elements. *For Trio, Duets, Montreux/Berlin*, and *Creative Orchestra Music* make up an essential, thoroughly enjoyable Braxton collection.

Braxton has enjoyed a rare advantage in his relationship with Arista, whose Novus and Freedom labels document a great deal of free jazz. Producers Steve Backer and Michael Cuscuna deserve credit for their consistently informed and tasteful presentation of a great deal of that music. In Braxton's case, Arista's support of his unaccompanied alto album and the *For Four Orchestras* behemoth indicate a virtual permissiveness. An adventurer of Braxton's seriousness and capabilities deserves no less.

KEITH JARRETT

The Köln Concert

ECM, 1064/65
two discs, no liner notes
1975

Musicians: Keith Jarrett, piano.
Compositions (all by Keith Jarrett): Part I. Part IIa. Part IIb. Part IIc.

KEITH JARRETT is an uncompromising pianist and composer with a discography of solo, quartet, and chamber orchestra recordings that are varied enough to be the work of three individuals. During the 1970's he revived and reshaped the virtually dormant solo piano medium, and inspired other pianists to continue the tradition of Art Tatum, Earl Hines, Fats Waller, and James P. Johnson. However, Jarrett's five solo albums on ECM, the most influential of which has been *The Köln Concert*, break radically with the past masters. Jarrett's rhythmic feeling is pulselike not swinging, and his spontaneous improvisations which are up to twenty minutes long are wholly unplanned, free in both form and content. As a pianist, Jarrett's strength is in his right hand, which creates liquid streams of melody with an exquisitely sensitive touch that sometimes elevates his lyricism to the level of ecstasy.

Manfred Eicher, the owner of ECM Records, is Jarrett's silent partner in his solo career. Jarrett's songlike sensuous touch may well have been lost without Eicher's unique ability to give the piano a shimmering reality on vinyl. The two men met through Chick Corea, who suggested to Eicher the possibility of a duo album with Jarrett. Eicher contacted Jarrett, who declined the offer and proposed his own solo album instead. Thus *Facing You*, a studio date, was recorded in 1972. The more expansive three-disc set *Solo Concerts: Bremen/Lausanne* (1973) was more expressive, demonstrating Jarrett's ability to achieve greater passion in the presence of a live audience. But *The Köln Concert* album, the richest in ideas and the most cohesive, made the greatest impact of all, selling more than a quarter-million copies since its release. In a decade when heavily produced electronic funk threatened to define commercial viability in jazz, the power of Jarrett's acoustic simplicity was something of a revelation.

(Chick Corea, incidentally, preceded Jarrett as a soloist on ECM, although with less historical consequence, perhaps because he failed to continue these endeavors. Corea's *Piano Improvisations, Volume 1* [1971], a gorgeous collection of improvised first takes, is every bit as satisfying and durable as *The Köln Concert,* though space forbids a full discussion of it in this chapter [see General Discography].)

A review of Jarrett's career only increases admiration for his talents. Born in 1945, he began playing piano at the age of three, and was heralded by some teachers as a prodigy. He had a moderate appetite for practicing which, when necessary, was piqued by his mother's threat to sell the family piano. While Jarrett's father, a real estate salesman based in Allentown, Pennsylvania, did enough business to support five children (several of Keith's brothers are also musicians), family finances were never secure. Keith studied the European classics and gave a few local recitals, some of which included his own compositions. At seventeen, he allegedly turned down a scholarship to study in Paris with the celebrated pianist and teacher Nadia Boulanger. Instead he went on tour briefly with Fred Waring's Pennsylvanians, and then moved to Boston, where he enrolled in the Berklee School of Music to study jazz.

Jarrett listened to very little jazz in his youth, and he has never spoken of other jazz pianists as influences upon him. One can only surmise that he did his share of listening and, moreover, that elements of Bud Powell's linear right hand and Bill Evans's harmonic sense and lyricism have found their way into his style. According to Eicher, Jarrett also respected Paul Bley's music very much, especially the album *Footloose* with Steve Swallow on bass and Pete LaRoca on drums, available on the French BYG label.[28] In fact, listening to "Turns," "King Korn," and "Syndrome" on this very fine album leaves no doubt about the influence of Bley upon Jarrett.

Jarrett did not remain in Boston for long. The advances in improvisation during the early 1960's were taking place in New York, where Ornette Coleman was emerging. (Jarrett later used two ex-Coleman colleagues, Charlie Haden and Dewey Redman, in the quartet he organized in 1972.) Keith and his wife, Margot, a childhood sweetheart, lived in Spanish Harlem, desperately waiting for work while he learned drums and soprano saxophone, instruments he has continued to use on record. His first break came during a Village Vanguard jam session, when ten minutes in the limelight led to a four-month job with Art Blakey's Jazz Messengers. Jarrett left Blakey to work with tenor saxophonist Charles Lloyd, whom he had known from his Boston days. In the Lloyd quartet from 1966 to 1969 (available on Atlantic's *Forest Flower*), Jarrett often stole the show with his blistering lines which had a gospel-tinged blues feeling. In 1970 and 1971 he joined Miles Davis's fusion band along with drummer Jack DeJohnette, his colleague from the Lloyd group. He is heard on *Live/Evil* and *Live at Fillmore,* his only flirtations with the electric piano. In Miles's band Jarrett also experimented with organ, using a baroque pipe organ years later on *Hymns and Spheres* (1977), a two-disk, improvised performance recorded in the Benedictine Abbey of Ottobeuren, Germany. The music is as somber as its setting and sorely misses Jarrett's sublime pianistic touch.

The Jarrett quartet started as a trio of the late 1960's with bassist Charlie Haden, whom he had met in 1966 while jamming in a New York club called Dom's,[29] and drummer Paul Motian, a member of Bill Evans's first trio, whom Jarrett had heard in Boston. But it was not until Dewey Redman joined in 1972 that Keith found the tonal ingredient necessary to complete the group's sound. Redman, who can be heard playing tenor with Ornette Coleman on *New York Is Now*, is an imaginative, swinging improviser who balances Jarrett's clever melodic composing with a soulful voice. *Shades, Backhand, Bop-be,* and *Fort Yawuh* are among the best of their Impulse albums. The quartet has a hard bop feeling to it on most tracks. *Survivors' Suite*, however, is a lengthy free-form composition that reveals the group's intuitive rapport, their occasional emphasis of percussion and unusual tonal colors, and their ability to explore the outer fringes of tonality. *Survivors* is unique and highly recommended.

The second Jarrett quartet, which overlaps the first, consists of three Scandinavian musicians who were schooled abroad by George Russell (Chapter 6) in his Lydian chromatic concept: saxophonist Jan Garbarek, bassist Palle Danielsson, and drummer Jon Christensen. *My Song* is particularly interesting for the many sides of Jarrett it reveals. Side one contains some of his most lyrical, linear playing with the quartet. "Country" on side two is a folksy, gospel-like gem, an extreme example of the Americana that sometimes surfaces in his solo improvisations. "Mandala" is a free-form piece in which Jarrett skips agilely over the keyboard with atonal abandon.

Jarrett's audience knows him primarily through his solo concertizing, which consists of about twenty performances per year, many in prestigious halls like the Metropolitan Opera House in New York. (Quartet performances became a rarity in the late 1970's.) Jarrett's fee, probably the highest in the field, ranges from $10,000 to $15,000 a night. He frequently performs show-stopping antics, which have contributed to his controversial reputation as a self-indulgent performer. In one case he stopped playing abruptly in the midst of a piece, walked out to the footlights and instructed the audience to cough, which it did—en masse. Jarrett "conducted" these coughs for a while, naturally eliciting several more, and finally returned to the piano bench, asking aloud, "Now, where was I?" Often he delivers impromptu, quasi-philosophical pronouncements on such subjects as the meaning of music. He is consummately adept at focusing attention upon himself. For a writer in *New Times* (April 1, 1977), he brought to mind Franz Liszt, who used to slowly remove his white gloves and toss them to the swooning ladies before sitting down at the piano. At one nightclub concert in San Francisco, Jarrett complained to the audience at regular intervals about the quality of the sound system and the piano, until he was silenced by the club owner, who went up on stage and presented him with a baby bottle.

Whatever Jarrett's excesses, they are likely to be overlooked and probably forgiven when he sits down at the piano. Jarrett's format allows him nothing to hide behind, as he and his instrument make ninety or more minutes of music together on a bare stage. There is no mistaking the bold, lyrical expanse of *The Köln Concert* (and, equally, *Solo Concerts: Bremen/Lausanne*) for anything less than brilliantly creative improvised music.

Jarrett's greatest commitment as a soloist is to spontaneity. He has said in fact that what initially attracted him to the jazz tradition was its improvisational nature, not so much its differences in "content" from European music. This attitude partly justifies the neoclassicist label often applied to him. He does not simply refrain from deciding upon his program in advance but attempts to "forget" his past experience, even—he has said—his knowledge of how to play the piano. "At the beginning, I am completely empty of any musical thought. If I am not able to empty myself, I almost invariably have a concert that isn't as good." [30] Consequently Jarrett's thematic ideas are not laid out concisely at the outset of a piece as in the song form. They grow organically and with subtle drama. If an album of Art Tatum tracks can be likened to a collection of short stories, Jarrett's solo albums should be compared to novels.

The hypnotic "strumming" of his left hand, which contains the music's basic harmonic underpinning on *The Köln Concert*, is ideally suited to his needs. The regular pulsations allow for easy metric variations in the right hand, unhurried musings and exploring, and even long silences. This is a more forgiving left hand than is possible in the swinging cross-rhythms of stride or bop. Thus Jarrett frees himself to pursue the grand moment of pure lyricism (Part I at four minutes into the side and again at seventeen minutes) or the subtly varied harmonic progression (Part IIb, at eight minutes) or unusual tone effects (Part I, at twenty minutes) in which the piano evokes the sound of the *sitar*.

The clarity and deceptive simplicity of Jarrett's approach are evocative of the numerous folk musics. Gospel harmonies are heard in his left hand. Writer Neil Tesser in *Down Beat* magazine (February 12, 1976) associates side A of *The Köln Concert* with "English and Scottish-sounding folk melodies, bagpipe drone voicings in the left hand, ringing church chimes and organ-pipes in the right." Tesser's description of the sound also points to the degree of color Jarrett's touch and voicings elicit from his instrument.

His exquisitely sensitive touch infuses his melodies with passion. A single note from his hand seems to acquire the dimensions of a lush chord struck by other pianists. Some of these notes, as those who have seen Jarrett's keyboard ballet can confirm, are played with his whole body. He stands, hunches, or kneels at eye level with the keys, striking or caressing a note with acrobatic contortions. The enunciation of the melody on side A at four minutes gives a hint of what is to come at eleven minutes when it erupts in a fountain of molten, linear beauty. These are the ecstatic moments which redeem the unvarying pulsations of the left hand. Jarrett's two hands symbolize the romanticist and the orderly, intellectual composer; the tension between them creates a sense of anticipation which on *The Köln Concert* is always satisfied.

Jarrett's discography is also growing impressively in the compositional field, though these albums are of marginal interest to jazz. His writing is wholly separated from his spontaneous instrumental technique, which may well be the source of its greatest deficiency. In fact, he composes away from the piano in a sparsely furnished barn on his family's sequestered property in rural New Jersey. His first fully composed session *In the Light*, which includes competent arrangements for brass quintet, string quartet, and other chamber groups, lacks any real emotional charge.

Luminessence (1974) and *Arbour Zena* (1975), composed for string orchestra and tenor sax (played by Jan Garbarek) suffer from a similar deficiency. Thanks to Eicher's patronage, Jarrett has the opportunity to exercise his skills on such ensembles, and it would be fortunate and fruitful if this happened more regularly among jazz musicians. However, thus far it is only in "Mirrors" (side two of *Arbour Zena*) in which Jarrett employs sufficient variety of texture and sustained tension to hold the listeners' interest. Elsewhere the strings are used to mimic Jarrett's left hand on the piano, creating pulsation and smooth harmonic changes. But it is Jarrett's *playing* of the repetitive figures that makes them work; read from a written score by the string section, they are simply dull.

There is no denying Jarrett's magnificent talent. However, his latest solo release *Sun Bear Concerts*, a ten-disc unedited documentation of a five-concert tour of Japan in 1976, shows some evidence of the self-indulgence alluded to earlier. While Jarrett's soloing does evolve over protracted improvisational segments, the surfeit contained in *Sun Bear* borders on adding water to the soup to make it go farther. One must hope that Jarrett's future albums, whatever their format, will reflect the same good judgment and concern for proportion which has characterized his best work.

THE ART ENSEMBLE OF CHICAGO

Nice Guys

ECM, ECM 1-1126
one disc, no liner notes
1978

Musicians: Joseph Jarman, alto, tenor, soprano, and sopranino saxes, clarinet, flute, conch shell, vibes, gongs, congas, whistles, and vocal; Roscoe Mitchell, alto, tenor, and soprano saxes, flute, piccolo flute, oboe, clarinet, gongs; Malachi Favors Maghostus, bass, percussion, melodica; Famoudou Don Moye, Sun percussion: drums, bells, bike horn, congas, tympani, marimba, bongos, chimes, gongs, conch shell, whistles, wood blocks, cow bells; Lester Bowie, trumpet, celeste, bass drum.
Compositions: Side one: Ja (Bowie); Nice Guys (Mitchell); Folkus (Moye). *Side two:* 597-59 (Jarman); Cyp (Mitchell); Dreaming of the Master (Jarman).

THE ART ENSEMBLE of Chicago (AEC) is the most versatile and accomplished of the contemporary collective groups. They emerged in 1969 from the seminal Association for the Advancement of Creative Musicians (AACM), whose principles and practices (see introduction to this chapter) they helped establish. Their collectivism is deep and genuine. While the bands of Ornette Coleman, Cecil Taylor, and Sun Ra are stamped with the leaders' identities, each Art Ensemble member contributes equally to the group's repertoire, emotional direction, and overall sound. *Nice Guys*, which is a broad sample of their accomplishments, serves as an excellent introduction to the group, although several earlier albums must be discussed along with it to present the full scope and depth of their discography.

The AEC evolved gradually through the 1960's. It originally called itself the Roscoe Mitchell Art Ensemble, a quartet which included Malachi Favors, Lester Bowie, and drummer Phil Wilson, who soon defected to the popular Paul Butterfield Blues Band. Mitchell, born in Chicago in 1940, grew up surrounded by music of the black church and the records of Billie Holiday and Louis Armstrong. He played alto and baritone saxes in high school and then in the Army band, where he came under the influence of the sound-altering style of Albert Ayler. After his discharge in 1961, Mitchell returned to Chicago, working occasionally with Malachi Favors, a bassist influenced by the full-toned, swinging style of Wilbur Ware. Favors, whose father was a pastor, was well acquainted with the religious dimension of black music, but he had also worked in the driving post-bop bands of Dizzy Gillespie and Freddie Hubbard.

Mitchell and Favors joined the Abrams Experimental Band in 1965, the year that Lester Bowie began to play frequently in Chicago. Bowie, who came from Little Rock, Arkansas, had spent his teens in the South and Midwest as a trumpet player playing for R & B groups and taking brief excursions into jazz. But by 1966 Bowie was an active member of the AACM group, demonstrating a mastery of trumpet styles from Satchmo to Miles with a specialty in the growling vocalizations of Cootie Williams. Like other members of the AACM, the group recorded individually, collectively, and also infrequently, for the local Delmark and Nessa labels. Roscoe Mitchell's *Sound* (1966) on Delmark was probably the first recorded music to come from the ranks of the AACM.

Nessa's *Congliptious* (1968) is the Roscoe Mitchell Art Ensemble's only record. It consists of unaccompanied solo tracks by everyone and a twenty-minute free-collective improvisation. The results are promising and interesting for historical reasons, but unsuccessful by later standards.

In late 1968 Joseph Jarman, a multireed player, joined the group, enriching it on many levels. Jarman's interest in music was broad based, and, like Mitchell, he sought fluency on all the reeds. He also took up percussion instruments to fill the void left by drummer Phil Wilson. A more melodically inclined player than Mitchell, Jarman was influenced by John Coltrane and Eric Dolphy. Jarman's experience as the director of a drama troupe led the Art Ensemble to incorporate a theatrical element in their performances which was never really understood or accepted in the jazz context until the late 1970's.

The newly dubbed Art Ensemble of Chicago suffered the worst of the commercial slump in jazz. The members' free improvising, Third World costumes, and face paint (still a part of the program), and their attempts at concept art (such as giving members of the audience paper bags to wear over their heads) undoubtedly alienated rather than attracted listeners at first. They in turn were alienated by America's slow-moving progress on civil rights and its foreign policy in Southeast Asia. In 1969 they packed their considerable baggage, which—according to one source [31]—included 500 instruments, and moved to Paris.

The AEC matured rapidly overseas, enjoying a busy if not a lucrative schedule. In addition to radio, TV, and concert performances, they recorded eleven albums, a few of which are among the best available. The first was *People in Sorrow* (Boulogne, 1969), a forty-minute collective piece of drama, sensitivity, and compassion. Working with a varied sound-surface, the band builds tension gradually, culminating in an explosive climax. The music ranks with their best, although the format is not representative of everything they can do.

The ensemble reached full strength later in 1969 when it was joined by drummer Don Moye, who had been working in Europe with Steve Lacy and a quartet of young musicians known as Detroit Free Jazz. Although Moye had met Jarman during the mid-1960's at a workshop in the States, their paths crossed by chance at the American Center for Students and Artists in Paris. The unifying effect of Moye's precise, responsive drumming was felt immediately on *Les Stances à Sophie* (Boulogne, 1970), recorded originally as a film sound track. The music displays the band's stunning versatility, making this LP, like *Nice Guys*, a good introductory album. "Thème de Yoyo," sung by Bowie's wife, Fontella Bass, is an infectious rhythm-and-blues dance punctuated by bursts of atonal blowing; "Monteverdi (I)," a carefully crafted sound-surface of soft texture; and "Thème de Céline," a driving solo vehicle in a post-Coltrane style. Inner City's *Certain Blacks (Do What They Wanna!)* is another essential album. The band throws itself into the urban blues, complete with harmonica riff on "Bye Bye Baby," while devoting all of side one to the title piece, a politically inspired free improvisation.

Three superb albums remain available only as imports on the French BYG label: *Message to Our Folks*, *A Jackson in Your House*, and *Reese and the Smooth Ones*. The AEC's discography is a perfect illustration of the crucial role Europe played in the development of free jazz: eight out of the eleven albums available in America were recorded in Europe, including *Nice Guys*, which was made in Ludwigsburg, Germany.

When the Art Ensemble of Chicago returned from Paris in 1972, they boldly jeopardized their survival by beginning to demand wages commensurate with their abilities and critical status. Consequently, as Bowie put it, "We damn near died." [32] There were four recording sessions, two for Prestige (General Discography) and two for Atlantic (*Baptizum* and *Fanfare for the Warriors*, both since deleted from the catalog). Still available, however, is the exciting two-disc *Live at Mandel Hall* (Delmark, 1974), a triumphant return to the University of Chicago campus, three sides of which are devoted to a stirring, marathon performance of "Dautalty."

In the summer of 1974, the AEC returned to Europe for the Montreux Jazz Festival, where they played an excellent set accompanied by the incisive, virile piano of Muhal Richard Abrams. His chord clusters and spare lines add stimulating tonal color. *Kabalaba* may even be superior to *Nice Guys* from an improvisational standpoint, but it suffers from inferior recording quality, which is impossible to overlook. On side one especially, Abrams's piano occasionally sounds as if it were being played out in the wings. The album, which can be obtained by mail from the ensemble's own AECO Records (see Appendix), is a worthwhile purchase despite its poor fidelity. (AECO has also produced solo albums by Don Moye, Joseph Jarman, and Malachi Favors; all are of good sound quality but demanding of the listener due to their lack of variety.)

After *Kabalaba* the Art Ensemble did not record for five years, yet their reputation grew steadily through concerts and the gradual dissemination of their albums from Europe. Mitchell and Jarman were also elevated to the status of "sources," having been identified as influences upon important free-jazz players like Anthony Braxton and Henry Threadgill (see Air ahead), and upon numerous young multireed players. Thus the ensemble returned to active recording with the broad-based, two-disc *Nice Guys* for the powerful ECM label.

Nice Guys is a history of the band's principal involvements. Their modern jazz background is dominant on three tracks of increasing expressiveness: "Dreaming of the Master," a tribute to the Miles Davis groups of the late 1950's and (in the track's second half) the mid-1960's; "Nice Guys," a Mingus-like ensemble arrangement; and "579-59," a fiery free-form improvisation with a soaring alto sax solo by Jarman. Don Moye's speed and precision are evident in the double-timed segment of "Dreaming" and in his aggressive punctuation of "579-59." Bowie's re-creation of Miles's muted style on "Dreaming" is uncanny. He gives away his true identity only in the "talking" horn segment near the end of his solo. There is no question that this band has jazz tradition at its fingertips, and one of its most appealing virtues is the ability to revive it with freshness and originality.

But the AEC has genuinely innovative moments. On pieces like Moye's "Folkus" and Mitchell's "Cyp," the traditional New Orleans style of group exploration is transformed by free blowing. Everybody improvises, but nobody solos, since individuality is subordinated to the creation of a group sound. They control texture, tone color, density, and intensity as comfortably as a bebop soloist improvises melody over chord changes. While parts of "Folkus" seem to have been composed (much of the AEC's music is fully notated), "Cyp" (and "Nice Guys") is probably a head arrangement based upon aural "cues" which the players give one another. In general, the Art Ensemble's unanimity of mind, spontaneous delivery, and thorough rehearsing of every piece make it difficult to discern the composed from the improvised passages.

"Folkus" and "Cyp," apart from their collectivism, are quite different in intent. "Folkus" is a sound-surface, a rich tapestry laced with the AACM's so-called "little" instruments—from tinkling bells to the thunderous tympani. The unusual tonal colors are integrated with logic and symmetry, progressing from the ethereal chime of bells, vibes, marimbas, and celeste toward the earthy thump of a bass drum, played with marchlike regularity by Jarman. (The AEC's live performances often begin with a New Orleans-style march of the band through the audience.) Finally, the polyrhythmic essence of African music is evoked with the superimposition of congas and bongos. The touch of humor, never beyond the AEC's reach, should not be overlooked at the end of this track.

"Cyp," on the other hand, is a piece which builds through dramatic tension. There is high contrast between unorthodox instrumental sounds and between sound and silence themselves. Neither melody nor tonality (key) count for much here. Mitchell and Jarman, who have mastered the sax family from sopranino to contrabass, contribute firmly controlled smears, blats, and squeaks in their unsettling exploration of tonal color. Lester Bowie's half-valve effects and variations of embouchure are another source of "Cyp's" intensity.

The Jamaican Calypso "Ja," sung by Jarman, is a spirited and authentic embrace of a black folk music, a radical change of pace in the repertoire. Sincerity and enthusiasm are in no way compromised by the change of idiom, a precedent set almost a decade earlier on the R & B-oriented "Thème de Yoyo" and "Bye Bye Baby." Yet the sound color which surrounds the Calypso segment and Mitchell's hard-edged tenor solo reminds us that this is Art Ensemble music after all. The AEC style ultimately means a synthesis of fun, folk music, and fine art, a synthesis which emanates from the heart of the jazz tradition.

The Art Ensemble of Chicago owes much to its willingness to persevere without compromise through a lean, unrewarding decade. Now that they have recorded for a prominent label, there is reason to hope that their classic foreign discs will become available domestically, and that their vast repertoire, much of which has yet to be recorded, will be committed to vinyl on a regular basis.

OREGON

Out of the Woods

Elektra, GE 151
one disc, no liner notes
1978

Musicians: Ralph Towner, classical guitar, twelve-string guitar, piano, flugelhorn, percussion; Paul McCandless, oboe, English horn, bass clarinet; Glen Moore, bass; Collin Walcott, *tabla, sitar,* percussion, guitar.
Compositions: Side one: Yellow Bell; Fall 77; Reprise; Cane Fields; Dance to the Morning Star. *Side two:* Vision of a Dancer; Story Telling; Waterwheel; Witchi-Tai-To.

OREGON, LIKE THE Art Ensemble of Chicago, is a model of collective organization merging its distinct voices to explore new textures and tone colors. The group, however, is more influenced by modern European and Indian classical music than by the African tradition. Its inimitable sound is a direct consequence of the diverse backgrounds of the musicians, highly variable instrumentation (including over fifty different instruments), and an ability to weave these disparate elements into a close-knit, variegated fabric. *Out of the Woods* flows imperceptibly between fully composed segments and those that are primarily improvised. Each track has a well-defined, consistent character, achieving a goal expressed by Towner, who writes most of Oregon's material: "My notion of a song, including the improvisation on that song, is that from the first sound you establish a character, a sense of motion, and that you are committed to develop a history, a miniature lifetime that is a faithful development of the original atmosphere." [33] The key to Oregon's success, over and above its multi-instrumental capacity, is that the musicians are less soloists than improvisers. Their music is a genuine blend of personalities and sounds.

The quartet first worked together in 1967 as members of the Paul Winter Consort, a mini-orchestra which played an eclectic variety of ethnic musics and some jazz but with minimal improvising. The consort was crucial to the band's development for several reasons. As composers, they learned how to integrate uncommon combinations of instruments. They also became more familiar with Third World music, learning to improvise in the pulsating feel of four sixteenth notes to a quarter note, the meter that underlies most of their playing.

The backgrounds of Oregon's personnel seem almost too diverse to coexist. Paul McCandless, who has written big-band charts and has also performed with a classical woodwind ensemble, came out of the most conventional milieu. For Collin Walcott working with the Winter Consort was a continuation of the ethnomusicology studies he pursued at UCLA; shortly afterward, he worked as the road manager for Ravi Shankar, from whom he learned more about his principal instruments, the *tabla* and *sitar*. Bassist Glen Moore had worked with some jazz musicians and with singer Tim Hardin, but soon developed an interest in Eastern European folk music and in bluegrass. Ralph Towner, who became Oregon's most prominent member, took up the guitar when he was a student at the University of Oregon. To make up for lost time, Towner went to Vienna for two years of study with Karl Scheit, who turned him into a classical player. It was Paul Winter who insisted that Towner learn to play twelve-string guitar, which became a crucial voice in the unlikely Oregon synthesis.

The Winter Consort was not a comfortable home for long. The quartet committed itself in 1970 to developing original music in a more improvisational mode, traveling under the name Oregon because of Towner's and Moore's nostalgia for their home state. (A & M's *Earthdance* is a representative reissue of the Winter Consort's first three albums; it includes the Oregon players and several of Towner's best early compositions.)

All the band's albums on Vanguard, for whom it first recorded in 1973, are characterized by a light, acoustic sound and a loose, modal composition style. The quality is consistently high, but three LP's deserve special recommendation. *In Concert* (1975), taped before a by-invitation-only studio audience, is an excellent representation of the group's numerous hybrid forms, especially the modern classical fusion of "Tryton's Horn." *Together* (1976), with drummer Elvin Jones, offers a virility and a rhythmic aggressiveness often missing in the usual instrumentation; pieces like "Charango" and "Three Step Dance" are welcome anomalies in the repertoire. *Violin*, a later collaboration (1978) with Polish violinist Zbigniew Seifert, enhanced the band's use of minor modes and its occasional Eastern European flavor.

In late 1978 Oregon signed with Elektra in the hope of better distribution. Its first album, *Out of the Woods*, which can be thought of as a sequel to *In Concert*, reveals a new level of instrumental proficiency and collective interaction. The music can be profitably explored by examining the individual contributions. Towner is the group's best composer, his best efforts here being "Vision of a Dancer" and "Waterwheel," the latter a modal piece with a repetitive background pulse played on the twelve-string guitar in 11/4 time. (A more intense version with Eddie Gomez and Jack DeJohnette is contained on Towner's *Batik*, a bold and successful improvisational ECM album.) Towner writes simply, favoring tonal and textural shadings over harmonic movement. His sensitive guitar work is predominant throughout, assuming the lead on "Dance to the Morning," whose subtle tonal control is its great virtue. Using the classical fingerstyle instead of a pick, he plays each note with clarity and with the precise feeling called for by the context. Towner's unaccompanied *Diary*, in which a modern classical influence emerges clearly, is the most revealing album of his guitar work.

On *Out of the Woods*, Towner's piano playing shows a vast improvement over the Vanguard performances. In the mid-1960's, Towner spent a few years in New York working as a pianist very much influenced by Bill Evans, but for the most part, his piano was adequate only as background. Here, however, his unaccompanied passage on "Reprise" reveals progress toward a personal style of expression that is more akin to Jarrett than to Evans. His solo near the end of "Witchi-Tai-To" stands on its own merits as his best piano performance on record.

Collin Walcott is the motor which drives Oregon. There are no trap drums, and bassist Moore is conversational in his playing rather than pulse oriented. Walcott's most compelling percussive contribution here is the introduction to "Dance to the Morning" on *mbira*, an enlarged thumb-piano constructed out of plywood and gasoline cans. While Walcott's facility on Indian instruments is not great compared with the acknowledged masters, Walcott's *tabla* infuses Oregon with a gentle, omnipresent sense of energy. The *sitar*, which he uses less frequently, adds an exotic tonal color.

Oregon's most conspicuous lead voice is Paul McCandless's oboe, which more than any other instrument establishes the group's European leanings. McCandless demonstrates a fluid, logical style on his own "Cane Fields" and on "Witchi-Tai-To." Yet the instrument's stiff double reed does not permit the vocalization common to jazz articulation; it remains clean, pure, and sweet, even when McCandless blows so hard that the veins in his head stand out. His bass clarinet's occasional appearance, as on "Fall 77," is thus a vital contrast. The album's only deficiency is that it lacks the gutsy, extended bass clarinet solos with which McCandless ignites Oregon's live performances.

Bassist Glen Moore, who also plays piano, flute, and violin (by standing it up in his lap like a miniature cello), combines his deep, full sound with the other instruments to create rich colorations. He is a muscular, earthy player, though one seldom hears the typical jazz "lope" in his accompaniment. Moore has expanded the range of his instrument by tuning his bottom string lower and his top string higher than normal. With the altered fingerboard, new melodic patterns fall within easy reach, and Moore—like most free-style bassists—is quick to participate melodically.

The four voices merge on *Out of the Woods* to produce a variety of textures, tonal colors, and improvisational moods. Their performance on a second Elektra album, *Roots in the Sky* (1979), is also satisfying, leaving the choice between the two LP's a matter of taste. Towner's superlative piano and the compositions noted above are the reasons for the selection of *Woods* here.

Out of the Woods is a kind of "chamber jazz," a term applied in the introduction to Oregon's style and an accurate one insofar as it alludes to the group's European influences. However, the term may suggest a conservative approach to improvising which does not apply to this group, for Oregon is willing to take chances in the interest of spontaneity. As McCandless said in a *Down Beat* magazine interview (March 8, 1979), ". . . we allow ourselves to become amateurs in the sense of exploring and not knowing exactly how (the music is) going to come out." Oregon has thus ventured beyond the old Third Stream hybrid of jazz and European concert music with improvisational courage and a good collective imagination. While more removed from jazz's roots than the Art Ensemble of Chicago, Oregon is pioneering a terrain which has proved to be fruitful.

AIR

Air Lore

Arista, AN-3014
one disc, liner notes
1979

Musicians: Henry Threadgill, tenor and alto saxes, flute; Fred Hopkins, bass; Steve McCall, drums, percussion.
Compositions: Side one: The Ragtime Dance (Scott Joplin); Buddy Bolden's Blues (Jelly Roll Morton). *Side two:* King Porter Stomp (Jelly Roll Morton); Paille Street (Threadgill); Weeping Willow Rag (Scott Joplin).

THERE IS NO more accurate summation of the principles that guide Air than the group's own self-analysis which appeared in *Down Beat* magazine (March 25, 1976):

> Air is a cooperative effort on the part of three musicians who have been together since the latter part of 1972, and whose collective backgrounds encompass everything from polka to gospel, show tunes to classical, rhythm and blues to marching bands, spirituals, folk, dance music, traditional jazz, and what has variously been termed as New Music, New Jazz, or simply playing free. Such a varied preparation has created a broad musical experience which is historical, yet contemporary in nature.

After recording several albums for foreign labels and three American releases, Air has finally come up with an LP which confirms the above assessment. *Air Lore* is a spirited and varied work which uses contemporary instrumental concepts to breathe new life into traditional pieces by Scott Joplin and Jelly Roll Morton. Beyond its musical virtues, the album is a fitting one with which to end this volume because the group so convincingly unites jazz's past with its cutting edge.

Air, like the Art Ensemble of Chicago, is founded upon the equal and collective contributions of its members. Both bands grew out of the AACM, of which Steve McCall was a founding member. McCall learned to play drums in his teens by sitting in with various Chicago bands. He began to play more seriously after his discharge from the U.S. Air Force in 1954, traveling with some early modern horn players like Gene Ammons, Don Byas, and Lockjaw Davis. But by 1965 he had joined the Abrams Experimental Band, and later helped build the AACM upon its foundation.

In 1965 Henry Threadgill and Fred Hopkins were in their teens, working around Chicago with their contemporaries, the future AEC players Roscoe Mitchell, Joseph Jarman, and Malachi Favors. Jazz was one of many interests. Threadgill played tenor sax for gospel singer Jojo Morris and also worked with blues bands, a sideline he maintained until 1970. Hopkins, however, pursued his interest in European music as a part-time member of the Chicago Civic Orchestra.

Not surprisingly, Air and the AEC have several fundamental qualities in common: the equal interplay of instrumental voices; an interest in creating tone color and sound-surfaces; and the ability to draw upon all forms of black American music. The principal difference between them, and this is not meant to be merely cute, is Air's airiness. The band's sound is light, graceful, and agile, a consequence of its particular instrumental styles. Each voice—McCall's sensitive, understated drums, Hopkins's full, woody bass, and Threadgill's plaintive reeds (especially on *Air Lore*)—defines itself with clarity, receding and emerging inconspicuously like fine thread in a loosely woven fabric. By contrast, the Art Ensemble plays music of greater density.

In a way *Air Lore* represents a return to the band's debut repertoire, for it first worked together as the pit band for a stage play calling for Joplin's music. But they found few stages which welcomed their free-form originals, most of which were written by Threadgill. Their move to New York in 1975 increased their visibility and led to the recording of several LP's. Nessa Records' *Air Time* (1977) is their first domestically available album, and it contains two excellent tracks, "No. 2" and "G.v.E.," but the lengthy "Subtraction," despite McCall's subtle drumming, adds up to the aimless exploration that is Air's most frequent failing.

In 1978 Air signed with Arista, for whom they have recorded three very good, dissimilar albums. *Open Air Suit* (read "suite") is a series of four cohesive themes by Threadgill. The best features him on tenor sax in an aggressive, rhythmic mood that is reminiscent of his blues experience. *Montreux Suisse Air*, taped live six months later at the Montreux Jazz Festival, is less unified and rhythmic, though the tension and dramatic development in Threadgill's writing rescues the work from sounding overly experimental. These albums have been listed in the General Discography because there is so little of the band's music available in America, but their appeal is not nearly so strong as that of *Air Lore*, in which free, expressive improvising grows out of more manageable structure. The point of interest peculiar to the earlier albums is Threadgill's use of his patented Hubkaphone, a rack of automobile hubcaps with a percussive, quasi-melodic capacity.

Air Lore is more accessible than any of the group's previous LP's because throughout the players hold scrupulously to the thematic outlines—a legacy of marching-band music—set forth by Joplin and Morton. On Joplin's

"Ragtime Dance" (1906) and on "Weeping Willow Rag" (1903), Threadgill and Hopkins divide between them the right- and left-hand parts of the original piano score. Arrangements flow imperceptibly into improvisation by way of personalized interpretive touches like the blue note and smeared tones Threadgill plays (on alto sax) in the midst of the A theme of "Ragtime Dance." "Buddy Bolden's Blues," a composition not published by Morton until 1939 but possibly of turn-of-the-century origin, is delivered with poignant delicacy, capturing each sorrowful cadence and, simultaneously, the song's overall affirmation of beauty. Morton's "King Porter Stomp," jazz's acid-test tune during the 1930's, retains its original, essential cross-rhythm even in the spirited modal improvisation on tenor by Threadgill. Steve McCall continues to reflect the melody in his sharply accented drumming.

Threadgill's soul is surely found in the tone of his alto's upper register (on the two Joplin pieces). It is evocative of the New Orleans clarinet, perhaps intentionally, and is taut with control and restraint, reminders of the ragtime aesthetic. Nevertheless, it is a highly vocalized tone capable—as in the improvised segments—of a piercing, passionate edge recalling Charlie Parker and Ornette Coleman. Threadgill is also a linear, blues-based improviser here. On the earlier albums, which are predominantly free form, he shows a more abstract side and frequently employs a staccato attack. Threadgill also does most of the composing, exemplified here by the tranquil "Paille Street," played unimprovised on flute.

Steve McCall is a model of economy. There is not one superfluous cymbal crash, rim shot, or wire-brush stroke on this album. His tuning of the snare, tom-tom and bass drum also permits a melodic contribution most apparent in the extended unaccompanied introduction to "Weeping Willow Rag." McCall's time sense is fluid; it flows easily—as on the two Joplin pieces—from 2/4 meter (capturing the pristine march-like ragtime feeling), to 4/4 meter (or pulse-keeping), and accelerates into the momentum of modern jazz, into free time.

Fred Hopkins, whose warm, supportive style derives from two great Chicago bassists, Wilbur Ware and Malachi Favors, binds the horn and drum voices together with a deep, embracing tone. He alternates between contrapuntal accompaniment and more overtly melodic invention, maintaining the pulse when McCall concentrates on coloring the music or thickening its density. His solo on "Ragtime Dance" with its sliding double-stops typifies the fullness he extracts from the bass.

Air is not the only accomplished young collective to emerge from the AACM in the wake of the Art Ensemble of Chicago. The World Saxophone Quartet and the Revolutionary Ensemble (General Discography) are two promising bands which like Air are both rooted in tradition and contemporary in style. While these young free jazz musicians will never enjoy the popularity of the more faddish fusion style, they give jazz listeners every reason to greet the 1980's optimistically. It is only through this kind of uncompromised exploration grounded in the music's history that musical advances can be achieved.

Notes

1. A. B. Spellman, *Four Lives in the Bebop Business* (London: MacGibbon & Kee Ltd., 1967), p. 14.
2. Frank Kofsky, *Black Nationalism and the Revolution in Music* (New York: Pathfinder Press, 1970), pp. 142–143.
3. *Ibid.*, p. 141.
4. From a lengthy, unpublished interview with Charlie Haden, by the kind permission of Conrad Silvert.
5. Kofsky, *op. cit.*, p. 140.
6. Martin Williams, *The Jazz Tradition* (New York: New American Library, 1971), p. 172.
7. *Ibid.*, p. 176.
8. *Down Beat*, December 16, 1976, p. 5.
9. Liner notes to Joseph Jarman's *Song For*.
10. Bret Primack, "Carla Bley," in *Contemporary Keyboard*, February 1979.
11. Spellman, *op. cit.*, p. 101.
12. Biographical information from the Conrad Silvert interview (see footnote 4).
13. *Ibid.*
14. Spellman, *op. cit.*, p. 124.
15. Joe Goldberg, *Jazz Masters of the Fifties* (New York: Collier-Macmillan, 1968), p. 243.
16. Williams, *op cit.*, p. 173.
17. Ekkehard Jost, *Free Jazz* (Vienna, Austria: Universal/Graz, 1974), p. 53.
18. *Ibid.*, p. 75.
19. Spellman, *op. cit.*, p. 45.
20. Liner notes to Cecil Taylor's *Looking Ahead*.
21. Jost, *op. cit.*, p. 69.
22. Spellman, *op. cit.*, p. 8
23. Liner notes to *Looking Ahead*.
24. Spellman, *op. cit.*, pp. 70–71.
25. *Ibid.*, p. 45.
26. *Ibid.*, p. 38.
27. Jost, *op. cit.*, p. 174.
28. *Contemporary Keyboard*, September 1979, p. 52.
29. From the Conrad Silvert interview (see footnote 4).
30. Robert Palmer, "Keith Jarrett," *Down Beat*, October 24, 1974, p. 46.
31. Jost, *op. cit.*, p. 177.
32. *Down Beat*, May 3, 1979, p. 17.
33. Elektra/Asylum Records information sheet.

General Discography of Available, Recommended Albums

MUHAL RICHARD ABRAMS
  Duets (see Anthony Braxton). *Spiral* (solo piano at Montreux, 1978), AL-3007; *Lifea Bilenc* (with Jarman), AL-3000; Arista. *Things to Come from Those Gone Now*, DL-430; *Young at Heart, Wise in Time* (with AACM players), DL-423; *Levels and Degrees of Light* (1968), DL-413; Delmark.

AIR
  Air Time, N-12, Nessa. *Montreux: Suisse Air*, AL-3008; *Open Air Suite*, AL-3002; Arista.

ART ENSEMBLE OF CHICAGO
  Kabalaba, 004, AECO (mail). *People in Sorrow*, N3; *Les Stances à Sophie*, N4; Nessa. *Certain Blacks*, IC 1004, Inner City. *The Paris Session* (1960), AL-1903, Arista. *Live at Mandel Hall*, 432-33, Delmark. *Phase One*, 10064; *The Art Ensemble of Chicago with Fontella Bass*, 10049; Prestige.

ALBERT AYLER
  Albert Ayler in Greenwich Village, AS-9155; *Love Cry*, AS-9165; *New Wave in Jazz*, A-90; Impulse. *Vibrations* (with Cherry), AL-1000; *Witches and Devils* (with Sonny Murray), AL-1018; Arista/Freedom.

AZIMUTH (with Kenny Wheeler)
  Azimuth, ECM-1-1099; *Touchstone*, ECM-1-1130; ECM. Also Wheeler: *Deer Wan* (with Garbarek and Abercrombie), ECM-1-1102, ECM.

CARLA BLEY
  (JCOA label temporarily inactive.) *Musique Mecanique* (large, fun-loving band), Watt/9; *13¾* (Carla Bley and Michael Mantler, composers; piano and small orchestra), Watt/3; *Tropic Appetites* (with Gato Barbieri, Dave Holland, and others), Watt/1; Watt.

PAUL BLEY
  NHØP (duo with Pedersen, bass), IC-2005, Inner City. *Copenhagen and Haarlem* (quartet, 1965–1966), AL-1901, Arista. *Alone, Again* (solo piano, 1975), IAI-37.38.40; *Japan Suite* (with Peacock and Altschul, 1976), IAI-37.38.49; *Virtuosi* (with Peacock and Altschul, 1968), IAI-37.38.44; *Axis* (solo, 1977), IAI-37.38.53; Improvising Artists, Inc.

ARTHUR BLYTHE
  The Grip, IN-1029, India Navigation. *Lexington Avenue Breakdown*, JC-35638; *In the Tradition*, JC-36300, Columbia.

JOANNE BRACKEEN
  Tring-A-Ling, CRS-1016, Choice. *Keyed In* (1979), JC-36-75, Columbia.

ANTHONY BRAXTON (see also Chick Corea and Circle)
  Three Compositions, DS-415; *For Alto*, DS-420-421; Delmark. *Saxophone*

Improvisations—Series F, IC-1008, Inner City. *New York, Fall, 1974,* AL-4032; *Five Pieces, 1975,* AL-4064; *Creative Orchestra Music,* AL-4080; *Duets with Muhal Richard Abrams,* AL-4101; *For Trio* (with Threadgill, Jarman, Mitchell), AL-4181; Arista.

DON CHERRY
Where Is Brooklyn, BST-84311; *Complete Communion* (with Barbieri, 1965), BST-84226; Blue Note. *Don Cherry,* SP-717, A & M Horizon. *Old and New Dreams* (see Haden). *Codona* (with Walcott), 1-1132, ECM.

ORNETTE COLEMAN
Change of the Century, AT-1327; *This Is Our Music,* AT-1353; *Art of the Improvisors,* SD-1572; Atlantic. *The Best of Ornette Coleman* (selected from tracks of 1959–1960), SD-1558, Atlantic. *At the Golden Circle, Vol. 1,* BST-84224; *The Empty Foxhole,* BST-84246; *New York Is Now*; BST-24287; Blue Note. *Science Fiction* (1971), KC-31061, Columbia. *Dancing in Your Head,* SP-722, A & M Horizon. *Soapsuds* (duet with Haden), AH6, Artists' House.

JOHN COLTRANE (see also Chapters 5 and 6)
Ascension (see chapter Introduction), A-95; *Meditations* (quartet plus Sanders and Ali), A-9110; *Expression* (Alice Coltrane, Sanders, and Ali), A-9120; *Live in Seattle,* AS-9202-2; *Interstellar Space* (duo with Rashied Ali), ASD-9277; Impulse/ABC. Of historical interest: *Kulu Se Mama,* A-9106; *Om,* A-9140; Impulse.

CHICK COREA (and CIRCLE)
Piano Improvisations, Vols. 1 and 2 (solo, 1971), ECM-1014ST and ECM-1020ST, ECM. *Delphi 1* (solo, 1979), PD1-6208, Polydor. With Anthony Braxton and Circle: *Circling In* (1968–1970), BN-LA472-H2; *Chick Corea* (1968–1970), BN-LA395-H2; *Circulus* (1970), BN-LA882-J2; Blue Note. *Circle: Paris Concert* (1971), ECM 1018/19, ECM. (See also Gary Burton, Chapter 6, General Discography.)

CHARLIE HADEN (see Ornette Coleman and Keith Jarrett, Selected Discography)
With Coleman: *Closeness* (1976), SP-710; *The Golden Number* (1976), SP-727; A & M Horizon. *Old and New Dreams* (with Redman, Cherry, and Blackwell), 1-1154, ECM. *Liberation Music Orchestra* (deleted from Impulse catalog).

HERBIE HANCOCK (see also Chapters 6 and 7)
Treasure Chest (reissues *Mwandishi* and *Crossings*), WB2-2807, Warner Brothers.

KEITH JARRETT
Solo: *Facing You,* 1-1017; *Solo Concerts: Bremen/Lausanne,* 3-1035; *Staircase/Hourglass/Sundial/Sand,* 2-1090; *My Song,* 1-1115; *Ruta and Daitya* (duo with Jack DeJohnette), 1021; ECM. Quartet: *Fort Yawuh* (1973), AS-9240; *Death and the Flower* (1974), ASD-9301; *Backhand,* ASD-9305; *Mysteries,* AS-9315; *Shades,* AS-9322; *Bya Blue,* AS-9331; *Bop-Be* (1976), IA-9334; Impulse. *Survivors' Suite* (1976), 1-9084, ECM.

ART LANDE (and RUBISA PATROL)
Desert Marauders, ECM-1-1106; *Rubisa Patrol,* ECM-1-1081; ECM. *The*

Eccentricities of Earl Dant (solo piano standards), S-1769, 1750 Arch Street Records, *Red Lanta* (with Jan Garbarek), ECM-1-1038, ECM.

ROSCOE MITCHELL (see also Art Ensemble of Chicago)
Nonaah (Braxton, Jarman, et al., 1977), N-9/10; *L-R-G/The Maze/s II Examples* (same players, 1978), N-14/15; Nessa.

OREGON
Roots in the Sky, 224, Elektra. *Violin*, VSD-79397; *In Concert*, VSD-79358; *Together* (with Elvin Jones), VSD-79377; Of historical interest (debut): *Music of Another Present Era* (1973), VSD-79326; Vanguard.

THE REVOLUTIONARY ENSEMBLE
Manhattan Cycles (Jenkins, Cooper, Sirone), 1023, India Navigation.

SAM RIVERS
The Live Trios; Dedication Series, Vol. XII (1973), JA-9352-2; *Sam Rivers/ Dave Holland, Vols. 1* and *2* (1976), 34.38.43 and 37.38.48, IAI. *Crystals* (1974 big band), ASD-9286, ABC. *Involution* (1966–1967), BN-LA4530H2, Blue Note. Early work: *Fuchsia Swing Song*, BST-84184; *Contours*, BST-84206; Blue Note. See also Cecil Taylor, *The Great Concert of Cecil Taylor.*

ARCHIE SHEPP
Archie Shepp in Europe (with Cherry, 1964), DS-409, Delmark. *Mama Too Tight* (five drummers), AS-9134; *Fire Music*, A-86; *The Magic of Juju* (five drummers), AS-9154; *Four for Trane* (arranged by Shepp, Rudd), A-71; Impulse.

LEO SMITH
Divine Love (1978), ECM-1-1143, ECM. *Spirit Catcher* (with ensemble, 1979), N-19, Nessa.

SUN RA
Cosmos (with Arkestra, 1976), IC-1020, Inner City. *Solo Piano*, IAI-37.38. 58, Improvising Artists, Inc.

CECIL TAYLOR
In Transition (1955, 1959), BN-LA458-H2; *Conquistador* (1967), BST-84260; Blue Note. *Cecil Taylor*, NW-201; *3 Phasis*, NW-202; New World Records (mail). *The Great Concert of Cecil Taylor* (1969), PR-34003, Prestige. *The New Breed: Dedication Series, Vol. VIII* (one side, 1961), AS-9339, Impulse. *Dark to Themselves* (1976), IC-3001; *Air Above Mountains* (1976, solo), IC-3021; Inner City. *Indent* (1973, solo), AL-1038; *Nefertiti* (1962), AL-1905; Arista.

RALPH TOWNER (see also Oregon)
Solstice, 1-1060; *Solstice: Sound and Shadows*, 1-1095; *Batik*, 101121; *Diary* (solo), 1032: ECM. See also Gary Burton, *Matchbook*, Chapter 6.

WILDFLOWER "LOFT JAZZ" SERIES (no longer available)

WORLD SAXOPHONE QUARTET (only on imports)
Point of No Return, Moers Music, 01034. *Steppin'*, BSR-27, Black Saint. See Lake, Bluiett, Murray, Hemphill—Miscellaneous.

MISCELLANEOUS:
Richie Beirach: *Hubris* (solo piano), ECM-1-1104, ECM. Hamiett Bluiett: *SOS* (Pullen, Hopkins, Moye), IN-1039; *Birthright*, IN-1030; India Navigation. Julius Hemphill: *'Coon Bidness*, AL-1012; *DOGON, A.D.*, AL-1028;

Arista. *Jack DeJohnette: Special Editions* (with D. Murray), 1-1152, ECM. *Hidden Voices* (Anthony Davis/James Newton), IN-1041, India Navigation. *Old and New Dreams* (see Haden). *Pat Metheny: Bright Size Life*, 1-1073; *Watercolors*, 1-1097; ECM. *Henry Threadgill: X-75* (collective ensembles), AN-3013, Arista/Novus. *Oliver Lake: Heavy Spirits*, AL-1008, Arista/Freedom. *Dave Holland: Conference of the Birds* (with Braxton and Rivers), 1-1027, ECM. Denny Zeitlin: *Expansion*, 1758; *Syzgy*, 1759; 1750 Arch Street Records. Tete Montoliu: *Catalonian Folksongs* (solo piano, 1977), TI-304, Timeless Muse. Don Pullen (see also Charles Mingus, Chapter 6): *Montreux Concert* (piano, bass, drums, 1977), SD-8802; *Tomorrow's Promises* (large ensembles), SD-1699; Atlantic.

Miles Davis; the fusion styles of the 1970's were inaugurated under his leadership. (*Photo* © *1980 by Veryl Oakland*)

Above, John McLaughlin (post-Mahavishnu Orchestra), posing for an album cover. (*Courtesy CBS Records*) Below, Herbie Hancock, at home. (*Photo © 1980 by Veryl Oakland*)

Above, Chick Corea, coleader (with Stanley Clarke) of Return To Forever and an artful composer. (*Courtesy Chick Corea Productions*) Below, singer Flora Purim (left) and percussionist Airto Moreira, leaders of the Brazilian-influenced fusion style. (*Bruce Talamon*)

Above, Chuck Mangione. (*A & M Records/photo by J. Osaki*)   Below, George Benson.
(© *1980 Tom Copi/San Francisco*)

Right, Weather Report's Wayne Shorter, playing soprano sax, and Jaco Pastorius, electric bass. (*Photo © 1980 by Veryl Oakland*)

Below, Josef Zawinul, Weather Report's mastermind, in his living room. (*© 1980 Tom Copi/San Francisco*)

Left, Ornette Coleman, practicing (ca. 1962). (*Courtesy Atlantic Records*)

Below, the Old and New Dreams Band, consisting of Ornette Coleman alumni: Don Cherry, "pocket" trumpet; Charlie Haden, bass; Dewey Redman, tenor sax; and Ed Blackwell, drums, 1979. (*Photo © 1980 by Kathy Sloane*)

Above, bandleader and multi-keyboardist Sun Ra (foreground) with longtime Arkestra members. From left to right: Marshall Allan, John Gilmore, and vocalist June Tyson. (*Photo © Allan Tannenbaum*)

Right, Cecil Taylor, a pianist of awesome power. (*Photo © 1980 by Veryl Oakland*)

Above, Keith Jarrett, who did much to revive the interest in solo piano during the 1970's. (© *1980 Tom Copi/San Francisco*)   Below, Anthony Braxton, composer and multireed soloist. (© *1980 Tom Copi/San Francisco*)

Oregon, performing at the Great American Music Hall in San Francisco. From left to right: Ralph Towner, Collin Walcott, Paul McCandless (playing an alto recorder), and Glen Moore. (© *1980 Tom Copi/San Francisco*)

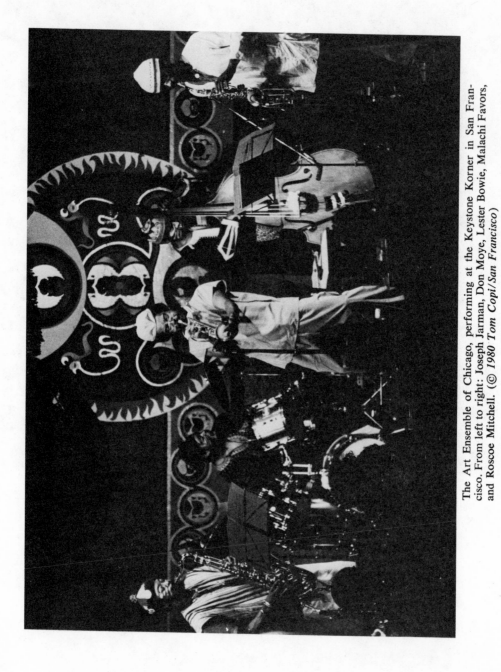

The Art Ensemble of Chicago, performing at the Keystone Korner in San Francisco. From left to right: Joseph Jarman, Don Moye, Lester Bowie, Malachi Favors, and Roscoe Mitchell. (© 1980 Tom Copi/San Francisco)

APPENDICES

THE 101 BEST JAZZ ALBUMS

1. Scott Joplin: *Scott Joplin—1916* (Biograph).
2. Max Morath: *The World of Scott Joplin* (Vanguard).
3. Eubie Blake: *The 86 Years of Eubie Blake* (Columbia).
4. Luckey Roberts/Willie "The Lion" Smith: *Luckey and the Lion/Harlem Piano* (Contemporary).
5. James P. Johnson: *The Original James P. Johnson* (Folkways).
6. Fats Waller: *Fats Waller Piano Solos, 1929–1941* (RCA).
7. King Oliver: *King Oliver's Jazz Band, 1923* (Smithsonian Collection).
8. Louis Armstrong and Earl Hines: *The Genius of Louis Armstrong, Vol. 1, 1923–1933* (Columbia).
9. *Louis Armstrong and Earl Hines, 1928* (Smithsonian Collection).
10. Bessie Smith: *Nobody's Blues But Mine* (Columbia).
11. Jelly Roll Morton: *Jelly Roll Morton and His Red Hot Peppers, 1926–1927, Vol. 3* (RCA France).
12. *Jelly Roll Morton, 1923–1924* (Milestone).
13. Bix Beiderbecke: *The Bix Beiderbecke Story: Bix and Tram, Vol. 2* (Columbia).
14. Fletcher Henderson and Don Redman: *Developing an American Orchestra, 1923–1927* (Smithsonian Collection).
15. Duke Ellington: *Rockin' in Rhythm, Duke Ellington and the Jungle Band, Vol. 3, 1929–1931* (MCA).
16. *Duke Ellington—1940* (Smithsonian Collection).
17. *The Duke Ellington Carnegie Hall Concerts: January 1943* (Prestige).
18. *The Golden Duke* (Prestige).
19. *Duke Ellington: Pure Gold* (RCA).
20. Count Basie and His Orchestra: *The Best of Count Basie* (MCA).
21. *Count Basie: 16 Men Swinging* (Verve).
22. Earl "Fatha" Hines: *Another Monday Date* (Prestige).
23. Benny Goodman: *Carnegie Hall Concert—1938* (Columbia).

24. Charlie Christian: *Solo Flight* (Columbia).
25. Lionel Hampton: *The Complete Lionel Hampton, 1937–1941* (RCA).
26. Lester Young: *The Lester Young Story, Vol. 1* (Columbia).
27. Billie Holiday: *The Billie Holiday Story, Vol. 2* (Columbia).
28. Art Tatum: *The Tatum Solo Masterpieces, Vol. 3* (Pablo).
29. The Woody Herman Orchestra: *The Three Herds* (Columbia Special Products).
30. Charlie Parker: *The Very Best of Bird* (The Dial Sessions) (Warner Brothers).
31. *Bird/The Savoy Recordings (Master Takes)* (Savoy).
32. Dizzy Gillespie: *In the Beginning* (Prestige).
33. *The Original Dizzy Gillespie Big Band: In Concert* (GNP Crescendo).
34. *Parker and Gillespie: The Greatest Jazz Concert Ever* (Prestige).
35. Thelonious Monk: *The Complete Genius* (Blue Note).
36. Monk: *Brilliance* (Milestone).
37. *Pure Monk* (Milestone).
38. Art Blakey: *A Night at Birdland, Vol. 1* (Blue Note).
39. Horace Silver: *Doin' the Thing* (Blue Note).
40. Bud Powell (and Fats Navarro): *The Amazing Bud Powell, Vol. 1* (Blue Note).
41. Clifford Brown (and Max Roach): *The Quintet, Vol. 1* (EmArcy).
42. Sonny Rollins: *Saxophone Colossus and More* (Prestige).
43. Rollins: *More from the Vanguard* (Blue Note).
44. The Dave Brubeck Quartet: *Dave Brubeck's All-Time Greatest Hits* (Columbia).
45. The Modern Jazz Quartet: *European Concert* (Atlantic).
46. Miles Davis: *'Round About Midnight* (Columbia).
47. Miles Davis and Gil Evans: *Porgy and Bess* (Columbia).
48. Davis: *Milestones* (Columbia).
49. Erroll Garner: *Concert by the Sea* (Columbia).
50. Cannonball Adderley: *Coast to Coast* (Milestone).
51. Wes Montgomery: *While We're Young* (Milestone).
52. Joe Pass: *Virtuoso* (Pablo).
53. Oscar Peterson: *In Concert* (Verve-England).
54. John Coltrane: *Giant Steps* (Atlantic).
55. Ella Fitzgerald: *Mack the Knife* (Verve).
56. Sarah Vaughan: *Sarah Vaughan and Count Basie* (Roulette).
57. Carmen McRae: *The Greatest of Carmen McRae* (MCA).
58. Betty Carter: *Betty Carter* (Bet-Car).
59. Lambert, Hendricks, and Ross: *The Best of Lambert, Hendricks and Ross* (Columbia).
60. Mose Allison: *Seventh Son* (Prestige).
61. Miles Davis: *Kind of Blue* (Columbia).
62. Davis: *Four & More* (Columbia).
63. Davis: *Miles Smiles* (Columbia).
64. Bill Evans: *The Village Vanguard Sessions* (Milestone).
65. Evans: *Intuition* (Fantasy).
66. Charles Mingus and Eric Dolphy: *The Charlie Mingus Jazz Workshop/ Stormy Weather* (Barnaby).

67. Mingus: *Passions of a Man (an Anthology)* (Atlantic).
68. Dolphy: *Copenhagen Concert* (Prestige).
69. John Coltrane: *My Favorite Things* (Atlantic).
70. *Coltrane Live at the Village Vanguard* (Impulse).
71. Coltrane: *A Love Supreme* (Impulse).
72. McCoy Tyner: *Echoes of a Friend* (Milestone).
73. Tyner: *Enlightenment* (Milestone).
74. Herbie Hancock: *Maiden Voyage* (Blue Note).
75. Hancock: *Speak Like a Child* (Blue Note).
76. Herbie Hancock, Freddie Hubbard, Wayne Shorter, Ron Carter, Tony Williams: *V.S.O.P./The Quintet* (Columbia).
77. George Russell: *Outer Thoughts* (Milestone).
78. Freddie Hubbard: *Breaking Point* (Blue Note).
79. Oliver Nelson: *Three Dimensions: The Dedication Series, Vol. 3* (Impulse).
80. Toshiko Akiyoshi-Lew Tabackin Big Band: *Insights* (RCA).
81. Miles Davis: *Bitches Brew* (Columbia).
82. The Mahavishnu Orchestra–John McLaughlin: *The Inner Mounting Flame* (Columbia).
83. The Crusaders: *Scratch* (Blue Thumb).
84. Herbie Hancock: *Head Hunters* (Columbia).
85. Flora Purim and Airto Moreira: *500 Miles High/At Montreux* (Milestone).
86. Chick Corea and Return to Forever: *Light As a Feather* (Polydor).
87. Corea and Return to Forever: *Where Have I Known You Before?* (Polydor).
88. Chick Corea: *My Spanish Heart* (Polydor).
89. George Benson: *Weekend in L. A.* (Warner Brothers).
90. Chuck Mangione: *The Best of Chuck Mangione* (Mercury).
91. Weather Report: *8:30* (Columbia).
92. Ornette Coleman: *The Shape of Jazz to Come* (Atlantic).
93. Coleman: *Free Jazz* (Atlantic).
94. Cecil Taylor: *Unit Structures* (Blue Note).
95. Taylor: *Silent Tongues* (Arista).
96. Sun Ra and His Arkestra: *Live at Montreux* (Inner City).
97. Anthony Braxton: *The Montreux/Berlin Concerts* (Arista).
98. Keith Jarrett: *The Köln Concert* (ECM).
99. The Art Ensemble of Chicago: *Nice Guys* (ECM).
100. Oregon: *Out of the Woods* (Elektra).
101. Air: *Air Lore* (Arista).

NAMES AND ADDRESSES OF RECORD LABELS AND COMPANIES

SOME SMALLER COMPANIES will send consumers up-to-date catalogs upon request. Information concerning forthcoming or newly deleted albums may also be available. Record buyers do not generally write companies to comment upon their "product," but the practice might well be beneficial to all concerned. Address correspondence to the Publicity Director/Jazz Division, except when purchasing an album from a mail-order catalog.

ABC Records (see MCA).
AECO (Art Ensemble of Chicago) (mail order). Box 49014, Chicago, Ill. 60649.
A & M Records. 1416 North LaBrea, Los Angeles, Ca. 90028.
Archives of Folk and Jazz Music (see Everest).
1750 Arch Street Records (mail order). Berkeley, Ca. 94709.
Arista. 6 West 57th St., New York, N.Y. 10019.
Artists' House (primarily mail order). 40 West 37th St., New York, N.Y. 10018.
Asylum (see Elektra).
Atlantic. 75 Rockefeller Plaza, New York, N.Y. 10019.
Audiofidelity. 221 West 57th St., New York, N.Y. 10019.
Barnaby Records. P.O. Box 1109, White Plains, N.Y. 10602.
Bet-Car (Betty Carter). 117 Felix St., Brooklyn, N.Y. 11217.
Biograph Records. 16 River St., Chatham, N.Y. 12037.
Eubie Blake Music Recording (mail order). 284-A Stuyvesant Ave., Brooklyn, N.Y. 11221.
Bluebird (see RCA).
Blue Note (see United Artists).
Book-of-the-Month Club Records (mail order). Camp Hill, Pa. 17012.
Cadet Records. 5810 South Normandie Ave., Los Angeles, Ca. 90044.
Capitol Records. 1750 North Vine St., Hollywood, Ca. 90028.
CBS Records. 51 West 52nd St., New York, N.Y. 10019.
Chiaroscuro (see Audiofidelity).

Choice Records. 245 Tilley Pl., Sea Cliff, N.Y. 11579.

Collectors' Series (see CBS).

Columbia (see CBS).

Commodore (see CBS).

Concord Jazz. P.O. Box 845, Concord, Ca. 94522.

Contemporary Records. 8481 Melrose Pl., Los Angeles, Ca. 90069.

CSP or Columbia Special Products (see CBS).

CTI Records. 1 Rockefeller Plaza, New York, N.Y. 10020.

Delmark. 4243 North Lincoln, Chicago, Ill. 60618.

Dial Records (see Warner Brothers).

Discovery. P.O. Box 48081, Los Angeles, Ca. 90048.

ECM (see Warner Brothers).

Elektra/Asylum/Nonesuch. 962 North LaCienega, Los Angeles, Ca. 90069.

EmArcy (see Mercury/Polygram).

Encore (see CBS).

Epic (see CBS).

Everest Records Group. 10920 Wilshire Blvd., Los Angeles, Ca. 90024.

Fantasy/Prestige/Milestone. 10th and Parker Sts., Berkeley, Ca. 94710.

Flying Dutchman Records (see RCA).

Folkways Records. 43 West 61st St., New York, N.Y. 10023.

Freedom (see Arista).

Galaxy Records (see Fantasy).

GHB (see Jazzology).

GNP Crescendo Records. 8560 Sunset Blvd., Suite 603, Los Angeles, Ca. 90069.

Good Time Jazz (see Contemporary).

GRT Records. 1226 16th Ave. South, Nashville, Tenn. 37212.

Gryphon Records. 157 West 57th St., New York, N.Y. 10019.

Halcyon Records (Marian McPartland). 302 Clinton St., Bellmore, N.Y. 11710.

Horizon (see A & M).

Impulse (see MCA).

India Navigation (see NMDS).

Inner City. 423 West 55th St., New York, N.Y. 10019.

Improvising Artists, Inc. 26 Jane St., New York, N.Y. 10014.

Jazz Archives (mail order). P.O. Box 194, Plainview, N.Y. 11803.

JCOA or Jazz Composers' Orchestra Association (see NMDS).

Jazzology-GHB Records. 3008 Wadsworth Mill Place, Decatur, Ga. 30032.

Kudu (see CTI).

MCA Records. 100 Universal City Plaza, Universal City, Ca. 91608.

MF/Distribution Company (mail order). 295 Madison Ave., New York, N.Y. 10017.

Mainstream Records. 1700 Broadway, New York, N.Y. 10019.

Mercury (see Polygram).

Milestone (see Fantasy).

Muse Records. 160 West 71st St., New York, N.Y. 10023.

Nemperor (see CBS).

Nessa (see also NMDS). 5404 North Kimball, Chicago, Ill. 60625.

New World Records. 231 East 51st St., New York, N.Y. 10022.

NMDS (New Music Distribution Service distributes numerous free jazz catalogs). 500 Broadway, New York, N.Y. 10012.

Novus (see Arista).

Pablo. 451 North Canon Dr., Beverly Hills, Ca. 90210.

Pacific Jazz (see United Artists).

Polydor. 810 Seventh Ave., New York, N.Y. 10019.

Polygram. 450 Park Ave., New York, N.Y. 10022.

Preservation Hall Records. 726 St. Peter Street, New Orleans, La. 70116.

Prestige (see Fantasy).

RCA Records. 1133 Avenue of the Americas, New York, N.Y. 10036.

Roulette. 1790 Broadway, New York, N.Y. 10019.

Saturn Research (Sun Ra; mail order, uncertain availability). P.O. Box 716, Radio City Station, N.Y. 10019.

Savoy (see also Arista). P.O. Box 279, Elizabeth, N.J. 07207.

Smithsonian Collection (mail order). Ordering: P.O. Box 10320, Des Moines, Iowa, 50336. Information: Jazz Division, 2100 L'Enfant Plaza, Smithsonian Institution, Washington, D.C. 20560.

Strata-East (see also NMDS, uncertain availability). 156 Fifth Ave., New York, N.Y. 10010.

Time-Life Records (mail order). Customer Service, Time & Life Building, 541 N. Fairbanks Court, Chicago, Ill. 60611.

Timeless Muse (see Muse).

Trend (see Discovery).

Unit Core (Cecil Taylor; mail order, uncertain availability). 96 Chambers St., New York, N.Y. 10007.

United Artists Records. 6920 Sunset Blvd., Los Angeles, Ca. 90028.

Vanguard Recording Society. 71 West 23rd St., New York, N.Y. 10010.

Verve (see Polydor and Polygram).

Warner Brothers Records. 3300 Warner Blvd., Burbank, Ca. 91510.

Watt (Carla Bley/Michael Mantler, see also NMDS). 6 West 95th St., New York, N.Y. 10025.

Xanadu. 3242 Irwin Ave., Kingsbridge, N.Y. 10463.

BIBLIOGRAPHY

Albertson, Chris. *Bessie: Empress of the Blues.* London: Abacus/Sphere Books, 1972.

Armstrong, Louis. *Satchmo.* New York: Signet/New American Library, 1955.

Asher, Don, and Hawes, Hampton. *Raise Up Off Me: A Portrait of Hampton Hawes.* New York: Coward, McCann & Geoghegan, 1972.

Balliett, Whitney. *The Sound of Surprise, 46 Pieces on Jazz.* New York: E. P. Dutton & Co., 1959.

Belz, Carl. *The Story of Rock.* New York: Oxford University Press, 1969.

Berendt, Joachim. *The Jazz Book: From New Orleans to Rock and Free Jazz.* New York: Lawrence Hill & Co., 1975 (1st publication, 1953).

Berton, Ralph. *Remembering Bix: A Memoir of the Jazz Age.* New York: Harper & Row, 1974.

Blesh, Rudi. *Shining Trumpets: A History of Jazz.* New York: Da Capo Press, 1976 (1st publication, 1946).

Blesh, Rudi, and Janis, Harriet. *They All Played Ragtime.* New York: Oak Publications (originally Alfred Knopf, 1950).

Boorstin, Daniel. *The Americans; The Democratic Experience.* New York: Random House, 1973.

Budds, Michael J. *Jazz in the Sixties.* Iowa City: University of Iowa Press, 1978.

Cole, Bill. *John Coltrane.* New York: Schirmer Books (Macmillan Publishing Co.), 1976.

Cole, Bill. *Miles Davis: A Musical Biography.* New York: William Morrow & Co., 1974.

Collier, Graham. *Jazz; A Student's and Teacher's Guide.* New York: Cambridge University Press, 1975.

Courlander, Harold. *Negro Folk Music: U.S.A.* New York: Columbia University Press, 1963.

Dance, Stanley. *The World of Duke Ellington.* New York: Charles Scribner's Sons, 1970.

Dance, Stanley. *The World of Earl Hines*. New York: Charles Scribner's Sons, 1977.

Dance, Stanley. *The World of Swing, Vol. 1*. New York: Charles Scribner's Sons, 1974.

Ellington, Edward Kennedy. *Music Is My Mistress*. New York: Doubleday & Co., 1973.

Ellison, Ralph. *Shadow and Act*. New York: Vintage Books/Random House, 1972 (1953).

Feather, Leonard. *The Book of Jazz from Then Till Now*. New York: Laurel Edition, Dell Publishing Co., 1976. (1957).

Feather, Leonard. *Inside Jazz*. New York: Da Capo Press, 1977 (originally published 1949).

Feather, Leonard. *The New Edition of the Encyclopedia of Jazz*. New York: Bonanza Books, 1960.

Feather, Leonard, and Gitler, Ira. *The Encyclopedia of Jazz in the Seventies*. New York: Horizon Press, 1976.

Finklestein, Sidney. *Jazz: A People's Music*. New York: The Citadel Press, 1948.

Gelatt, Roland. *The Fabulous Phonograph, 1877–1977*. New York: Macmillan Publishing Co., 1977.

Gitler, Ira. *Jazz Masters of the Forties*. New York: Collier-Macmillan, 1966.

Gleason, Ralph J. *Celebrating the Duke, and Louis, Bessie, Billie, Bird, Carmen, Miles, Dizzy, and Other Heroes*. Boston-Toronto: Atlantic Monthly Press Book, Little, Brown & Co., 1975.

Goldberg, Joe. *Jazz Masters of the Fifties*. New York: Collier-Macmillan, 1968.

Gridley, Mark C. *Jazz Styles*. Englewood Cliffs, N.J.: Prentice-Hall, 1978.

Hadlock, Richard. *Jazz Masters of the Twenties*. New York: Collier Books; London: Collier-Macmillan, 1965.

Harris, Rex. *Jazz*. England: Penguin Books, 1957 (1952).

Haskins, James, and Benson, Kathleen. *Scott Joplin: The Man Who Made Ragtime*. New York: Doubleday & Co., 1978.

Hentoff, Nat, and McCarthy, Albert J. (eds.). *Jazz: New Perspectives on the History of Jazz*. Da Capo Press, 1975.

Hodier, Andre. *Jazz: Its Evolution and Essence*. New York: Black Cat Book, Grove Press, 1961 (1956).

Holiday, Billie. *Lady Sings the Blues*. New York: Avon Books, 1976.

Jasen, D., and Tichenor, T. *Rags and Ragtime*. New York: Seabury Press, 1978.

Jones, A. M. *Studies in African Music*. New York: Oxford University Press, 1959.

Jones, Leroi. *Black Music*. New York, William Morrow & Co., 1967.

Jones, Leroi. *Blues People*. New York: William Morrow & Co., 1963.

Jost, Ekkehard. *Free Jazz*. Graz, West Germany: Universal Press, 1974.

Kofsky, Frank. *Black Nationalism and the Revolution in Music*. New York: Pathfinder Press, Inc., 1970.

Lomax, Alan. *Mister Jelly Roll*. Berkeley: University of California Press, 1973 (1950).

McCarthy, Albert; and Harrison, Max; Morgan, Alun; and Oliver, Paul. *Jazz on Record: 1917–1967*. New York: Oak Publications, 1968.

Ostransky, Leroy. *Jazz City*. Englewood Cliffs, N.J.: Prentice-Hall, 1978.

Ostransky, Leroy. *Understanding Jazz*. Englewood Cliffs, N.J.: Prentice-Hall, 1977.

Panassié, Hughes. *Louis Armstrong*. New York: Charles Scribner's Sons, 1971.

Ramsey, Frederick, Jr., and Smith, Charles Edward (eds.). *Jazzmen.* New York & London: Harcourt Brace Jovanovich, 1939.

Roberts, John Storm. *Black Music of Two Worlds.* New York: William Morrow & Co., 1974.

Russell, George. *The Lydian Chromatic Concept of Tonal Organization.* New York: Concept Publishing Co., 1959 (1953).

Russell, Ross. *Bird Lives! The High Life and Hard Times of Charlie (Yardbird) Parker.* New York: David McKay Co., 1973.

Russell, Ross. *Jazz Style in Kansas City and the Southwest.* Berkeley: University of California Press, 1971.

Sargeant, Winthrop. *Jazz, Hot and Hybrid.* New York: Da Capo Press, 1975 (1938).

Schaffer, William, and Riedel, Johannes. *The Art of Ragtime.* Baton Rouge: Louisiana State University Press, 1973.

Schuller, Gunther. *Early Jazz. Roots & Musical Development.* New York: Oxford University Press, 1968.

Shapiro, Nat, and Hentoff, Nat (eds.). *Hear Me Talkin' to Ya.* New York: Dover Publications, 1955.

Shapiro, Nat, and Hentoff, Nat (eds.). *The Jazz Makers.* New York: Grove Press, 1957.

Shaw, Arnold. *52nd St.: The Street of Jazz.* New York: Da Capo Press, 1977.

Simon, George T. *The Big Bands.* New York: Macmillan Publishing Co., 1974 (1967).

Simon, George T. *Glenn Miller and His Orchestra.* New York: Thomas Y. Crowell Co., 1974.

Simpkins, C. O., M.D. *Coltrane, A Biography.* New York: Herndon House Publishers, 1975.

Southern, Eileen. *The Music of Black Americans.* New York: W. W. Norton & Co., 1971.

Spaeth, Sigmund. *A History of Popular Music in America.* New York: Random House, 1948.

Spellman, A. B. *Four Lives in the Bebop Business.* London: MacGibbon & Kee Ltd., 1967.

Stearns, Marshall W. *The Story of Jazz.* New York & London: Oxford University Press, 1971 (1956).

Stewart, Rex. *Jazz Masters of the 30's.* New York: Macmillan Publishing Co., 1972.

Sudhalter, Richard M., and Evans, Philip R. with Dean-Myatt, William. *Bix: Man & Legend.* New York: Arlington House, 1974.

Thomas, J. C. *Chasin' the Trane.* New York: Doubleday & Co., 1975.

Waldo, Terry. *This Is Ragtime.* New York: Hawthorn Books, 1976.

Walton, Ortiz M. *Music: Black, White & Blue.* New York: William Morrow & Co., 1972.

Waterman, Guy. "Ragtime: Survey," from *The Art of Jazz,* Martin T. Williams, ed. New York: Oxford University Press, 1959.

Williams, Martin. *The Jazz Tradition.* New York, Toronto: New American Library, 1971. (1959, Grove Press.)

Williams, Martin T., ed. *The Art of Jazz.* New York: Oxford University Press, 1959.

ABOUT THE AUTHOR

LEN LYONS has published over one hundred articles on jazz for such publications as *Down Beat*, *Playboy*, *Rolling Stone*, *Crawdaddy*, *High Fidelity*, *Musician*, *Contemporary Keyboard*, *Guitar Player*, *Le Jazz Hot* (Paris), and *Swing Journal* and *Player* (Japan). Lyons, a Ph.D. in Philosophy from Brown University and a former professor at the University of Santa Clara (California), also studied piano improvisation and theory with the legendary bebop pianist Lennie Tristano. In 1976 he received the first annual Ralph J. Gleason Memorial Fund Award for Jazz Criticism, presented by the Monterey Jazz Festival awards committee. Len Lyons lives in Berkeley, California, with his wife, their daughter, and thousands of jazz albums.